# THE WAR AGAINST THE FAMILY

# THE WAR AGAINST THE FAMILY

*A Parent Speaks Out*

## WILLIAM D. GAIRDNER

First published in 1992 by
Stoddart Publishing Co. Limited
34 Lesmill Road
Toronto, Canada
M3B 2T6

Second printing February 1993

**Canadian Cataloguing in Publication Data**

Gairdner, William D. (William Douglas), 1940–
The war against the family: a parent speaks out

Includes bibliographical references.

ISBN 0-7737-2643-8

1. Family.   2. Family – Canada.   3. Quality of Life –
Canada.   I. Title

HQ734.G25 1992   306.85   C92-094966-5

Typesetting: Tony Gordon Ltd.

Printed and bound in Canada

*Stoddart Publishing gratefully acknowledges the support
of the Canada Council, Ontario Ministry of Culture and
Communications, Ontario Arts Council, and Ontario
Publishing Centre in the development of writing and
publishing in Canada.*

*For my family
and all who cherish
freedom and responsibility*


*Deepest gratitude is extended to those many
individuals: scholars, lawyers, physicians,
theologians, citizens, friends, editors — and of
course, mothers, fathers, and children — who have
contributed in ways too numerous to mention.
This is their book, too.*

# Contents

# Preface

My first book, *The Trouble with Canada*, was one man's view of this wonderful country. At first I felt alone in that view; I had told my wife before the book was released that if it was ignored by the public we would have to leave Canada because that would mean the citizens here were brain dead! But a lot of other Canadians — about 45,000 to judge by the number of buyers in the first two years — have made me feel more at home in my native land. So the Gairdners are staying put.

The most common remark I have heard from Heart's Content, Newfoundland, to Ucluelet, British Columbia, is: "Finally someone's put into words all the things I've been thinking and feeling." I'm now convinced there's a deep, unsatisfied hunger out there for values, principles, and honest debate on the central unresolved issues of human life — the ones we ought to be discussing forever, even if there is no ultimate answer. The people are starving for this dialogue. But our fragile belief system seems elaborately constructed to discourage honest inquiry. Keep them dumb and paying, is the thinking.

At any rate, that has meant finishing the whole sorry story, because it just wouldn't fit between the covers of one book. Some people criticized the first because it didn't deal with, say, education or homosexuality. I had to say — wait until the next one. And here it is. Of course, this is an independent book and stands on its own. But *The War Against the Family* shows how the political, economic, and social/moral troubles that play themselves out in the nation at large inevitably trickle down to alter our most private lives and dreams; how any democracy based on freedom and privacy will strangle itself if it drifts toward, or is manoeuvred into, a belief in collectivism of any kind. As we shall see, that's simply because in our Western civilization there is an inherent and deadly conflict between statism and the whole idea of the private family.

This conflict has in the past three decades erupted into a civil war of values that is being fought at every level of national life, though often in ways (and with a terminology) designed to disguise the struggle. That is so not because Canadian elites are conspirators. It is more a result of the fact that they are good people who share a lot of interlocking bad ideas or unexamined assumptions, which they are in a position to force upon the people. Most of these assumptions are very good for them and for their careers. They are also, directly or indirectly, antifamily.

My one hope is that this book will help readers understand the core values of our family-based civilization, and the subtle and not so subtle ways in which those values are now under attack, often right under our noses. For only when we recognize the bad ideas will we be able to reconstitute the good ones. Such recognition is especially difficult if we are personally benefiting from the bad notions. But reconstitute we must, for if there is any meaning to the concept of a civilized people, it is surely that individual citizens are able to rise above their own personal interests and choose instead what is good for the whole — and for the next generation.

A comment is necessary concerning the role of the reader. *The Trouble with Canada* was to many minds a controversial book on general subjects, calling for somewhat abstract policies and solutions that most readers felt ought to be applied vigorously to others. But *The War Against the Family* is a very personal book, and, on every subject in it, I have discovered, most people already consider themselves to be experts (that fierce, pro-family feeling!). And so, suspending judgment until the arguments are heard will be a more difficult, though no less essential, task. On every subject, however, I try to show how there is always a moral fork in the road, and I ask the reader to choose a direction for our society, one that in some cases may well conflict with personal advantage. This is not like asking individuals to plan society. Rather, it is asking them to acknowledge that what is moral often transcends the individual.

If my experience as a public speaker over the past two years is indicative of how the public *Zeitgeist*, or belief system, works, I would say Canadians are at present ill equipped to make such decisions at the fork. This lack may be in part due to the fact that the Canadian media — mostly self-acknowledged left-liberals — seem to shrink from a broad spectrum of opinion and debate. Their focus thus tends dangerously to narrow ordinary public discussion.

Troubling views or studies that offend the status quo are shunned. Writers like me have been shunned. For example, even though *The Trouble with Canada* had already sold 25,000 copies and had been seven months on the *Globe and Mail* national bestseller list (number one for a week), and despite the fact that 62 radio and television stations across Canada had already invited me to be a guest on their shows, it took over *10 months* for the CBC to offer an interview on a single national radio show — Peter Gzowski's "Morningside" — and that was only because I had been badgering his staff. With such an iron grip of collectivist stakeholders on the formation of public opinion, it is not surprising that the Canadian public does not relish debate on "sensitive" issues. As I said to CBC ombudsman Bill Morgan, to whom I complained about such treatment, the core issues of human life are off the table in Canada today. There is no debate. Subjects like the conflict between freedom and socialism, successful private vs. failed public education, capital punishment and parole, abortion as a contraceptive, the coming State control of euthanasia, the homosexual effort to restructure society — none of them has attracted active, slug-it-out intellectual debate. Morgan agreed with me and felt the media have a problem that we described as an overwhelming weight of assumption: most of the media come from the same schools and are taught by the same professors, who share the same left-liberal assumptions.

So as an alternative to genuine debate, we tend to rely on an adolescent technique that British philosopher Alasdair MacIntyre described as "emotivism," a sudden reaching for labels and slogans that have an established emotional charge. Instead of focusing with a hard clarity on the principles at hand, on logical inconsistency, on core values, or on the quality of the facts, we attempt to win by emotional intimidation. The winner becomes the one who is the most "extraordinarily offended" or "outraged"; or, if that tack doesn't work, he'll be the one who can most successfully label the opponent a "bigot" or a "racist" or a "sexist." But such labels are always the first sign of a lazy mind. My habit is to tell those who are offended that they could be no more so than I, and now that we have gotten our emotions out of the way — what is the point they wish to make?

My fear for Canada is that this intellectual burrowing behaviour, this national reluctance to grapple with argument and values, is the end of culture. It is the end that Alexis de Tocqueville imagined when he described how democracies in their later stages tend to cover the whole of society in an infinity of subtle regulations and restrictions requiring uniformity of thought and action. Thus they dull the minds of the people, readying them for such a narrow focus on merely material equality that they end up a nation of sheep. My hope for this book is that it will act like a fire cracker to jolt the sheep.

Part One of *The War Against the Family* sets out the conflict between the idea of community growing spontaneously on the bedrock of the family, and the idea of controlling community from above, via the State. It shows how these two ideas are incompatible from the start. It then describes the popular illusions, or beliefs, that commonly make the importance of the family difficult to understand and the dangers besetting it difficult to detect. From here, there follows a defence of the family, itself followed by an explanation of the antifamily tradition from Plato to modern radical feminism. A brief chapter on the Swedish antifamily example, included as a warning to increasingly socialist Canada, is followed by a set of charts showing what has happened to the family, here and elsewhere, over the past few generations.

Part Two traces the effects of antifamily political, economic, and social/moral policies through a variety of central issues. Four chapters devoted to the failure of public education in a free society show how no society based on the family unit can expect anything less than failure if it transfers its children to the State for education. Next, the antifamily ideology and arguments of radical feminism are examined, especially with respect to how they hamper the efficiency of the military and distort the truth about daycare and domestic violence.

The next antifamily topic examined is the radical homosexual movement, with its strident effort to destroy the concept of the traditional family and its widespread campaign of AIDS disinformation. Following that comes a look at the painful topics of abortion and euthanasia — two sides of the same coin — both of which have gone much further in Western democracies than the liberals who first championed them ever anticipated.

Part Two closes with a chapter on the liberalism of the mainstream churches, another on the antifamily role of the law, and a final "call to action" chapter. The first shows how the churches are mired in contradictory social gospel, in ancient Gnosticism resurgent, and in New Age cultism — all inherently antifamily. The second shows how from the personal, to the community, to the national and even the international level, the law has bent to the purposes of antifamily ideologues — to the detriment of freedom, the family, free enterprise, democracy, and the law itself.

The tone of this book is no-nonsense, tell-it-like-it-is. I have been reluctant to include some material, because it is frankly offensive. But my conclusion was that the public needs to know what is going on, and nothing but frank language would get the message across. Also, there has been an effort throughout to challenge not so much the research on any particular topic (all the experts are challenging each other, anyway), but the ideas, principles, and values. For it is my conviction that, since the dawn of science, one of the deleterious moral effects of technological society is the tendency of those under its sway to postpone moral judgment until someone does supporting research. But no society can thrive this way, simply because science can measure only what is measurable, and the most important things in human life are not. Science, for example, can never tell us what is right and wrong. That's why so many educated people have been involved in history's greatest evils. They use their science to justify their twisted values. So we must either push science aside, or else succumb to what I call "the conflict of expertise." This arises whenever the ordinary person, who is not the acknowledged "expert," is forced, too late in the day, to make the most important moral choice among alternatives offered by warring experts. In other words, science and technology tend to polarize basic moral choices and lend them a false sophistication — which is what produces intellectual intimidation and a numbing postponement of moral judgment among lay people.

But as I hope this book will show, moral action is required now, and it ought to arise from clear thinking of our own. I have written this book as a parent, and a father, both for my own five children and, I trust, for the reader's children. I am persuaded that the health of our entire civilization depends not on the autonomous individual, and certainly not on the State, but on the family, which lies between these two things and is our prime value-generating entity and source of freedom, privacy, and meaning. That meaning — and the importance and privileged status of the family — is being eroded before our very eyes. And it is happening not because the people do not care — they do, and passionately — but because they have lost touch with the arguments and values necessary for its defence.

They are here.

This triangle of truisms, of father, mother and child,
cannot be destroyed; it can only destroy those civilizations which disregard it.

G.K. CHESTERTON


No matter how many communes anybody invents, the
family always creeps back.

MARGARET MEAD


Knowledge of the constant is known as discernment.
Woe to him who wilfully innovates while ignorant of
the constant.

LAO TSU

# Part One

## The Conflict

# 1

# The State vs. the Family

*We are sliding down into the mire of a democracy, which pollutes the morals of the citizens before it swallows up their liberties.*

FISHER AMES. B.1758[1]

One of the few indisputable, universal facts about humanity is that we are all born of a mother, and begotten by a father. This is the basic procreative triangle of human history that survives within us all, regardless of how differently our lives are actually lived. For the lifelong values, meanings, conflicts, and loyalties of our personal existence spring generally from the intensely personal, private, and unduplicatable world of our own families. From the indelible impressions of that world, each of us charts, by action or reaction, a particular course through this hazardous life, the vast majority engendering a new family and, thus, a new world for our offspring. Much of the poignancy of aging arises from the simple loss of our personal irretrievable past, and so we spend much of our adult life attempting to re-create, through our children, a facsimile of that period when we were the fixed centre of the world. For when all is said and done, there is scarcely any love more fierce than the love of children, nor any death so mournful.

Although the basic *political* unit of modern society is the individual, the basic *social* unit throughout human history has been the family: that immemorial unit of a married man and woman and their dependent children living together in the same home. We shall see throughout this book that the modern confusion between the basic political and social units — explicit in totalitarian systems, implicit in democracies — brings grief to society in the name of high principle.

Another indisputable fact is that whether deliberate or unintentional, a sort of ongoing war has been waged from the start by small but powerful groups against our most cherished social institution. At first, it was difficult for me to believe there were ordinary people walking about who intensely dislike the family. Not their own families, necessarily; just the basic idea of the family — yours and mine, that is. Some of these people actively lobby against the family; or teach our students to disrespect it; or may even see the family as a symbol of Western oppression, or as incarnate evil, or as a kind of domestic jail. Generally, they would like to break it all up, and they imagine us all happier in a single homogenous tribe overseen by benevolent governors — among whom they expect to number.

For it does seem that one of the unavoidable consequences of the growth of the State in the modern period is the weakening — sometimes the total destruction — of families. We could even say, when this disintegration is the intended result, as it clearly is in all resolutely socialist nations, that proponents of the welfare State — in this respect they can all be called radicals — are committed to the *transformation* of the most important basic social unit (the interdependent family) into disparate political units (autonomous individuals, with as many of them as possible dependent on the State).

In Canada today, for example, an individual may qualify for welfare regardless of how wealthy his or her immediate family or relatives may be; increasingly, our courts grant the social and legal privileges of "spouse" to individuals who refuse to make a permanent commitment to each other, to their children, or in the case of homosexual "spouses," to society's procreational project. Married couples with children are generally taxed at a much higher rate than comparable unmarried couples. And Canada is awash with political radicals and interest groups, many of them subsidized by the State, for whom a cherished objective is the abolition of the traditional family. There, I said it.

## PRIVATE VALUES VS. PUBLIC POLICY

At heart, most public policy experts and social engineers are convinced that the "morality" of the State is higher than that of any lower entity; that the State knows better than individuals and their families how society must unfold; that the individual and the family must therefore yield to the political, economic, and moral direction of the State. Why? Because the private world of the family generates values that for the most part run counter to the public values of society. Families foster natural differences: some people end up weak, some strong; some well behaved, some poorly; some honest, some dishonest; some smart, some dull. Some people are extraordinarily successful at nurturing their own outstanding children; others are failures. Some are lazy, or stupid, or squander their wealth and forsake their children. But — and this is most galling to the statists of our time — others end up wealthy because they are from families that have learned to create and accumulate wealth.

Despite the fact that we are said to live in a free society, there are many who find such differences offensive and attempt to eradicate them by eradicating the family. They say they want to "rationalize" society by means of "policy instruments," and they know instinctively that autonomous individuals can be lured, seduced, or, if necessary, coerced into conformity and therefore dependency on the State — easily so if family roots and bonds have already been weakened.

What the enemies of the family understand far better than families themselves, who simply live naturally within the embrace of their expectations, is that the family as an institution is at the heart of an entire social order. It is no exaggeration to say that the family is the creative engine of all the crucial values of a free and private society. So it follows that for any other social order to dominate — say, any collectivist social order — the family must first be broken down. That is why Canadians — for that matter, all those living under welfare regimes — must realize that if they have any desire to preserve the cherished life of a free society for their children and grandchildren, they first will have to recognize, then take up moral arms against, all those who wish to destroy the family. In particular, they must challenge the welfare State itself. Every citizen will have to become a family activist; will have to learn why the family is the most important natural social institution; will have to fight to defend the family. This book is meant to help them.

For good reason, families are considered "reactionary" by modern liberals. The total political, economic, and moral focus of the family is inward to its own survival and ongoing regeneration, and to local friends and neighbours, not outward to the State, the machinations of which have always been and always will be seen by families as a potential threat. One of the main arguments of this book is that the welfare State has arisen from two connected philosophies — collectivism and egalitarianism — which are completely alien to our tradition and to the health of the family; thus, by the deadly unravelling of its own logic, it will inevitably create — must create — political, economic, and social policies that sap the family of its lifeblood. This sobering reality is a danger to the present generation and to all future generations of Canadians — for that matter, to the citizens of any modern society built upon the core beliefs, institutions, and values of the free world. For despite high-sounding aims and gossamer language, the overtures and blandishments of the welfare State are extremely dangerous seductions that strike at the very heart of our political, economic, and moral system. This is surely what the philosopher Robert Nisbet meant in his profound book, *The Quest for Community* (1953), when, sensing the coming dissolution of Western society, he wrote: "The real significance of the modern State is inseparable from its successive penetrations of man's economic, religious, kinship, and local allegiances, and its revolutionary dislocations of established centers of function and authority."[2]

In plainer words: the essence, logic, thrust, and consequence of the welfare State — *even when this is not the expressed intention* — is the invasion and eventual takeover of all private life by the State. In the totalitarian world, this invasion is purposeful and relatively efficient, even brutal. Millions who got in its way have suffered terribly and died. In the free world, however, because of the strength of the family in our history, the war against private life is usually carried out with a relentless sloppiness and confusion, but at enormous cost to social and economic harmony. The leaders of the invasion are the legions of well-intentioned but smug, educated elites who have agreed in advance to reject thousands of years of inherited wisdom, values, habit, custom, and insight and replace this heritage with their official utopian vision of the perfect society. They are the "progressives," and they can be found in every political party. Trained as scientific, or logical, rationalists, these social utopians haughtily treat all social or moral traditions and conventions as arbitrary, rather than as venerable repositories of indispensable social, family, and religious values. They despise natural authority, especially of a local or family variety, and they want to replace it with a sufficiently homogenous State power to bring about their coercive social dreamland. So with a government wage or grant in one hand and a policy whip in the other, they set about forcibly aligning individuals and customs with their dangerously narrow vision, then clamour after ever greater funding and ever more "progressive" legislation for the "education" or "socialization" of the people.

Even so-called social scientists who are not radical in this way become involved in such an intellectualized transformation of society because they adopt a specious "objective" posture. Such single-minded devotion to a task as if the participants played no part in its consequences is illustrated by the ancient seafaring story about an overcrowded lifeboat. When water started lapping at the ankles of the frightened passengers, there began a frantic search for the leak, and a passenger was discovered boring a hole in the bottom of the boat. When the astonished captain asked what in the name of heaven he was doing, the passenger replied that no one should be worried, for he was drilling the hole only under his own seat. Likewise, those so-called social scientists behave as if they have suddenly discovered a sinking ship, and they don't realize they're on it. They think the important thing is to make accurate notes and proposals. Instead, they ought to be rigging sail, or bailing water with all their might.

## COLLECTIVISM: THE "TOP-DOWN" STYLE

Collectivism is a political idea that argues for the central control of everything in human life. It is usually based on a simplistic set of interdependent and unfalsifiable ideas — an ideology — designed to steer society toward certain goals, and away from others. Of course, all governments in history do this to some degree. But citizens wary of the evils of excess government (those raised under the influence of English systems of governance seem wisest and most wary in this regard) have always tried to protect themselves against too much of this control by means of political rules or devices designed to restrain government power. Alas, those who govern merely work all the harder to overcome such restraints. What truly distinguishes the modern era is: the degree of social control exerted by so many political regimes; the diminished consent of the governed, most notably in the socialist/communist world*; and the human tragedy wrought in the name of egalitarian "fairness."

---

* For the purposes of this book, there is no need to distinguish the various forms of socialism. Whether so sweet-sounding they make the leader cry (Ontario), or so "progressive" they require secret police to maintain order (the former communist nations), all are based on the same elitist ideology of coercion and drastically reduce the sphere of human freedom. Even without machine guns, a government can drive its population to unprecedented depths of moral cynicism, can reduce freedom to a mockery of itself, and can paralyse productive activity through a heavy use of control, regulation, and supervision.

What is at stake may be State control of housing, schools, agriculture, medicine, energy markets, or even the languages the people do or do not want to use. Regardless, coercion and the concomitant loss of historical freedoms is the common denominator of this style, always accompanied by unprecedented taxation and other forms of control over private resources, initiatives, and rights. The answer to the question "What are you if the State takes one hundred percent of what you have?" is, "a slave." What, then, are you if the State takes half or more of what you have, as it does in Canada and most other welfare states? "Half a slave."

In 1950, Canadians turned over about 30 percent of gross national product (GNP) to government in taxes of all kinds, visible and invisible. But by 1991 that figure had climbed to just under 50 percent, and it's rising. Yet this massive transfer of wealth from the productive to the public sector was not sufficient for our greedy, power-hungry governments. By the early mid 1970s they proceeded to overspend and borrow heavily. Canada's total national debt as of 1991 remains twice as large, per capita, as the U.S. debt, and it hovers at about $100,000 for every family of four. The total federal portion of national debt as of 1991 was over $400 billion*; and when all three levels of government are combined, the total debt is well over $600 billion. Then, if we add the unfunded pension liabilities of the federal and provincial governments, the total comes to a staggering $1 trillion! If you divide that not by citizens, but by taxpayers (who shoulder the debt), it comes to over $55,000 each!

Because all deficits are just deferred taxes, this means that instead of investing in the future for our children, we are stealing from them. Thus — and this is often the first moral rupture of statism — we are breaking the moral bonds with defenceless future generations by forcing them to pay for our own current consumption. Tax Freedom Day, the day we stop working for the government and start working for ourselves, was around the end of April 30 years ago. It is now mid-July (August 4, if you include those unfunded government liabilities). In another 20 years, at the present rate, it could very well be October 1! High taxes are driving both spouses, willing or

---

* When Pierre Trudeau came to power in 1968, Canada's total federal debt since Confederation was about $20 billion. But by the time he left power, having overspent by fully 54 percent in his last year alone, it was about $200 billion. Simply the average rate of interest applied to that $200 billion pushed it to $400 billion by 1991. That was the fiscal legacy of Canada's most famous welfare statist.

not, into the work force, and consigning countless children to paid third-party care. Some people like it that way; but millions of less well-off people, by virtue of shrinking disposable income, see themselves as condemned to dispiriting, meaningless work and would rather be home raising their own children instead of imploring a relative, or paying a stranger to do this most valuable of jobs. Recommend Western "women's liberation" to a Russian woman in the former bastion of socialism, where most have been forced to work outside the home either by policy or by need, and she will spit with disgust and call you a fool. "A [communist] woman's dream is to not have to work — but work she must," says critic Tatyana Tolstaya.[3] High taxes, big government, and utopian social programs have been the enemy of Soviet women and their families, just as they have been the enemy of the family in the West. We shall see that that Russian mother was right to spit. The erosion in Canada of child-tax deductions over the past 40 years is just one damning indictment of the State's attitude toward the family — especially toward those who desperately want to raise their own children. Increased taxation triggered by inflationary "bracket creep" is a further nail in the family coffin. The story goes on, and on.

The usual alibi for all this taxation and erosion of our traditional way of life is that it is legitimate to take resources and freedom away from the people in exchange for more equality. But today, more than 70 percent of Canada's so-called "social spending" is in fact going to middle- and upper-income Canadians.[4] We are simply taxing each other to pay each other. It's a socialist boondoggle, and Canadians are tired of it. In fact it seems the whole world is tired of it! For the welfare State always ends up burdening the people with government and taxes, and eroding the well-springs of private and social life. How overgoverned are we? Today in Canada there is one government employee for every 5.5 citizens. At the current rate, we shall end up a three-part country, in which one-third work, one-third live off their work, and one-third administer the proceeds. In other words, two thirds take the majority of their income from the State. This is the stage Sweden has reached.

In *The Trouble with Canada*, I argued that this socialist, or "top-down" style (one initially perfected by French thinkers in the modern historical period, theoretically by Henri Saint-Simon, and emotionally by Jean-Jacques Rousseau),[5] is always inimical to true freedom, and in particular to all English-derived styles of government. It is concerned with power and control, not with liberty, and is an outgrowth of 18th century "rationalism," the idea that reason alone is sufficient to construct a perfect world. The result is what the French called a *dirigiste*, or directed style of government, and it is deeply rooted in the belief that ordinary people are incapable of knowing what is good for them, or for society, and that the way to keep anarchy at bay is to ensure that an elite political class is created, and maintained, with the instinct and the power to instruct the people in social virtue. In countries where this top-down phenomenon has occurred, these elites are called, variously, "the New Class" (Djilas, Lasch), or "the Knowledge Class" (Berger), or "the Educated Levellers" (Rieff). As a group, they inevitably create a "therapeutic" or a "client" State, which grows in the measure that the people surrender their traditional personal, family, and community obligations. This necessitates a managerial concept of government that rests on a utopian vision bent on social perfection — by force, if necessary — and such a notion is in deadly conflict with the whole idea of the individual, the family that produces the individual, and the democratic expressions of both.

The top-down concept operates like a State magnet that hovers over the people, who are seduced, induced, and coerced to align themselves with it like iron filings on a table. All truth flows from one source, creating an enormous pressure for conformity, the homogenization of social attitudes, and a consequent fear of differences. Legitimate public debate is overtly discouraged, gradually replaced with the emotionalism of those defending the utopian status quo. This signals the end of eccentricity, the beginning of Orwellian man, and widespread top-down pressure for "political correctness."

Political members of this new managerial class are expected to represent the government, not the people who put them into power. Hence the Canadian confusion over the meaning of democratic representation. (Should a member of Parliament obey the party or the people? How direct ought democracy to be?) Long ago, when the people were greatly illiterate, communication was ponderous, and national governments dealt mostly with remote national and international matters, delegation was a tolerable way to handle the boring job of government. But today the idea of delegation is manifestly inadequate because national governments all over the free world are intrusively attempting to control or direct local, family, and even sexual behaviour. This movement from the top into the heart of personal and family life — a natural thrust of the welfare State — was bound to cause a reaction, a clamour for more direct control. In short, the success of the one engenders the other. Alas, in Canada the people have no intermediate means to persuade their masters otherwise (unlike the Australians, the Americans, and the Swiss, who enjoy the referendum, an instrument described by the great constitutional scholar, A.V. Dicey, as "the people's veto"). This absence of a direct means begets elitism and the political disenfranchisement of the people. The response that, after all, we do have free elections and therefore adequate control, is no answer at all. For all practical purposes, the three parties we have to choose from are three ducks with different feathers but the same quack! For example, despite the presence of the crushing public debt mentioned above, not a single mainstream politician raised this as a subject of debate in the 1984 election, or attempted to campaign on the platform of less government and reduced spending. By 1990, Canadians continued to get more taxes *and* higher government spending (with politicians and bureaucrats granting themselves handsome wage increases). Ditto for the Americans. How did we, and they, get into such a pickle?

Although both Canada and the United States began as relatively decentralized, free societies, both have in varying degrees changed utterly in the past half century, moving from the concept of the classical liberal society to that of the social welfare State. Both nations were initially collections of more or less sovereign territories bound by treaties governing power-sharing and spending. That made them federal in the true (decentralized) sense of the term. But today, the provinces in Canada and the states in the United States have almost become administrative jurisdictions of their federal governments; and today the word "federal" means big central government. Canada transformed itself, basically, by contravening both the division and the spending-powers sections of the British North America Act of 1867, and the United States did the same through the Fourteenth Amendment to its Constitution, which granted Congress for the first time the constitutional right to overrule local state legislation.[6]

Of course, the extreme modern form of the top-down concept lies at the heart of all socialist nations and found its final form in the sclerotic and terrorizing communist states of the world, almost all of which we have seen crumble in the very recent past in what will surely qualify as one of the most astonishing historical events of the modern world. But the condition they got themselves into before their collapse should serve as a warning to all, and to Canadians in particular, who, despite the sobering pragmatism of this worldwide lesson on the eternal urgency of human freedom, have proceeded to vote into power outright socialist governments in a number of provinces, and could conceivably do so federally, whether by design or default. When a U.S. political observer first heard the news of Ontario's swing to the hard left, he opined that Canadians must be a rather strange people, for they seem to think that when the Berlin Wall was torn down, all the Germans ran to the East.

### Egalitarianism and the Handicap System: Making Everyone the Same

Egalitarianism, a first cousin and natural companion of collectivism, originally meant that all citizens, without regard to class, race, sex, or any other personal characteristic, should be treated equally by the law of the land. That is the meaning of the blindfold on Lady Justice. Today, however, egalitarianism has a vastly, and grievously different, meaning: not that all should be treated equally by the law, but that *all shall be made the same by the law*; that the law shall be used to modify the material and personal outcomes of their lives to make them equal to each other. Of course, this purpose does not require the law; rather, through social engineering, it requires the corruption of the law and the values of a free society. Thus has a noble idea concerning equality under the law succumbed to crass materialism. And thus was born the resentment-based society. (The ethics of envy arise whenever human beings descend to the level of comparing their possessions and believe that their lack of something is the fault of others.) Thus was opened the sluice-gates for the hordes of activists, professional lobbyists, paid politicians, greed-preachers, redistributionists, success-haters, social therapists, litigators, counsellors, media pundits, and the like, who basically make a living by feeding off the successful and the productive while excusing — as victims of society — the unproductive, the lazy, the criminal, and the unlucky.

In order to make the world right for these systemic "victims," egalitarianism now functions through an ideological imperative that grants the State *the right to abrogate or suspend the freedoms* of certain groups for the sake of other groups deemed unequal, be it now or in the past. As examples, Ontario's so-called pay-equity program is essentially a government wage discrimination scheme for low-paid women, based on sex (low-paid men may not apply); government employment quota systems discriminate against some ethnic groups in favour of others; and so-called regional disparity programs take resources from some who have earned them and transfer them to others who haven't. This process is obviously wrong and immoral, and in some cosmic court of law it would be clearly illegal, for it ends up rewarding those who haven't earned a reward and penalizing others who've done no wrong. Nevertheless, Canada's Charter grants the State such rights (clauses 1 and 15(2), in particular); as do all the human rights codes and the many quasi-governmental agencies and special organs of the State with their tribunals, commissioners, and supervisors, many with oppressive powers the average citizen ought to find extraordinary in a supposedly free country.

In short, the essence of this style lies in government's willingness to design different rules for different groups in the interests of achieving an equal outcome for all (and a lot of votes for itself). Again, the underlying assumption of the welfare State is that it is legitimate to sacrifice freedom for equality. This ideological imperative drives the State to attempt to *force* different groups to be the same, even if, left to their own devices, they would never, ever choose such an outcome. The result is a "handicap" system of government, whereby the successful are brought down and the failures rewarded: rent controls force successful landlords and builders out of the market; State medicine has the effect of penalizing those who keep themselves healthy, and subsidizing those who do not, State car insurance rewards bad drivers, penalizes good ones, and spreads costs over many who don't even drive; State daycare penalizes families that want to care for their own children by taxing them for the care of other's children; State welfare lures teenagers away from their parents, and rewards young girls for early illegitimate pregnancy by making this condition economically more viable; much of so-called unemployment insurance rewards people for not working, and so on. In the Atlantic provinces, unemployed workers ask, "Why do we need the 6/49 (lottery), when we've got the 10/42?" (42 weeks on welfare for 10 weeks of work). In the former Soviet disunion, they said, "They pretend to pay us, and we pretend to work."

Such a handicap system is totally contrary to our traditional way of life, to personal and family responsibility, and to any sense of honest values. A handy way to remember the values on which the West was built is to think of "the four Fs": Freedom, Family, Free enterprise, and Faith. The handicap system is built instead on the opposite of each, namely "the four Gs": Government, interest Groups, tax Grabs, and Godlessness. This latter system creates a great deal of resentment, envy, litigiousness, and cynicism, because the rules are quite rightly perceived as unfair. Effort doesn't count any more. When it comes to wealth creation and the pursuit of excellence, states that thoroughly promote the handicap system (like China, the former USSR and East Germany, and Cuba) are losers, as any economic atlas will show. And of course the spectacle of the old Soviet Union — formerly a supposed "superpower" and the world's pre-eminent handicap system — begging for loaves of bread, is a sobering lesson in the politics of resentment. The basic reason for this failure is that socialist societies have no economic theory or method of wealth creation. They have only economic theories of redistribution, based on handicapping excellence and subsidizing failure. We shall see that such systems always end up handicapping the entire society, simply because more equality requires more government, and absolute equality — a fool's pursuit — requires absolute government, the despot's delight.

When the State is minimal, people exercise their *inherent*, protected freedoms to create a myriad of different and hence *unequal* social groups such as the family, which they then strive to protect with legal and tax privileges. The most unfortunate consequence of the top-down State, now reaching deeply into the privacy of the families of the free world, springs from its reliance on the notion of individual egalitarian rights (to the exclusion of obligations) *conferred* by the State on all citizens equally. These rights are then used aggressively by individuals and interest groups, with the help of various charters, to destroy the traditional supra-individual privileges of all social groups. History will show that all democratic countries have more or less capitulated to the top-down idea of conferred individual egalitarian rights, the most notable example being Canada in 1982, one of the last democracies to create an entrenched charter of rights and freedoms.

This change in the definition of rights is part of a worldwide attempt to enshrine pure-seeming, noble-sounding abstract concepts in documents (handed down from above) to which formerly free people and their parliaments — and therefore democracy itself — then become subordinated. This subordination of democracy, of which we now have a dramatic example in Canada, is then overseen by unelected judges of the highest court, who themselves form a kind of political group — aptly described by University of Calgary professor F.L. Morton as "the Court Party."[7]

In addition to the Universal Declaration of Human Rights from the United Nations (a cornucopia of rights, with nary a mention of obligations), we now have "children's rights" and "women's rights," many of which have a direct and damaging effect on family privacy and parental authority (see Chapter Eighteen). Notice that no one has yet created a charter of "family" rights. And it's a safe bet they won't be drafting one either, for reasons to be explained in this book. These highly conceptual, abstract documents are in turn based on even more highly questionable assumptions about the goodness and perfectibility of man and the State, and about the efficacy of human reason. These assumptions (which we shall explore later) ultimately require, for their realization, a wholesale surrender of traditional family privilege and parental authority.

## MORAL AGENCY: THE BOTTOM-UP STYLE

Before it adopted its Charter, and thus subordinated its free parliament to the authority of the courts (that is, to unelected judges), Canada was one of the few countries left based on the notion of inherent, as opposed to conferred rights. This, above all, was the great legacy of the British tradition, and much of what is good in the world has flowed from this English, or "bottom-up," style of government.

Such governments are rooted in the ancient concept of "natural rights," which flourished in Britain as early as the 13th century, and were further developed in the 18th century by John Locke, among others, and by the enormous influence of Christianity, especially its Protestant variety.[8] Until very recently, the British have always had an antipathy to the State. The fully developed English style emphasized the idea that each man and woman in society shall behave as a kind of moral agent, adding to or subtracting from the moral fibre of society. Free will, individual responsibility for one's deeds, and political and economic freedom, with all the contractual rights and legal protections attached thereto, was the thing. The State? What could the State possibly know of morality, or virtue, or the good life? "Let the government run the government, and stay out of our private lives!" was the prescription for a healthy society. For the dominant feature of this sort of society is freedom, not power, and the role of government is to set "rules of just conduct"; to referee the game, but never to play it. Government should never attempt to manage or control the people's morality, or engineer their behaviour. Rather, it should create an environment in which each person, subject to the same rules, will control himself. This is a thriving, organic, natural, spontaneous, and inexpensive ideal that will always be stifled by planning from above. Its great formulation in Christian thinking is the doctrine of "subsidiarity," which is the idea that all human needs must first be answered at the lowest possible level, by parent, spouse, neighbour, and local community, before moving on to the highest — the clutches of the State.

## Freedom and the Bonus System:
## Letting Natural Differences Flourish

Such moral agents function best in a politically decentralized society in which the fullest expression can be given to personal freedom, family needs, free enterprise, faith, and local interests. Authority, under this method, is obtained through a sense of community in shared principles and values that spring naturally from the strength of family, church, town, and literally hundreds of voluntary, spontaneously created associations, organizations, and social and charitable groups, each with its own constraining traditions, each minding its own business yet cooperating with others in the larger whole.

Such a society is in every detail the opposite of the top-down State. It is non-egalitarian (natural differences are expected to flourish), non-managerial (for what could a distant bureaucrat possibly know of local or family matters? and what business is it of his anyway?), and promotes political and economic freedom under limited government. It assumes that human happiness is best achieved not through some predetermined forced equality, but through a wide range of differences, naturally expressed, in the context of the greatest range of human liberty. It assumes that ordinary human beings, provided they do no harm to each other and the very weakest are cared for, ought to be allowed to rise or fall according to their own efforts and moral lights. Most of all, such a society insists on the Rule of Law — a system of laws that applies to all, with no exceptions for the governors or the governed. It gives rise to a natural merit, or "bonus," system that not only recognizes but also rewards success at every stage of life, just as the handicap system rewards failure. Under the bonus system the referee gives a point to any team that scores a goal. Under the handicap system he runs onto the field and kicks the ball into the net of the winning team to help the losing side, since all must end up equal. This action obviously disorients the players and teaches them that doing less, gets more; that the game has changed from the pursuit of excellence to the pursuit of influence. Under the bonus system, the entire social order is oriented toward success. Not all may win, but all get to play, according to their skill. Such an order produces an infinitely detailed ranking of success, just as its counterpart produces an infinitely detailed ranking of failure.

Is it any wonder that these two different systems are in such deadly conflict? For they have utterly different goals, and wherever they are forced to coexist, unnatural political, economic, and moral/cultural results will always occur. These are normally manifested in irresolvable constitutional disputes of the sort Canada is now experiencing. And of course many other free — and not so free — countries go through the same struggles, usually as a result of their own conflict between these two visions. Certain lobby groups in the United States are currently embarked on a national campaign to trash the American Constitution and rewrite it to more forcefully legitimize the very sort of top-down State against which I argue.

But most importantly, the spontaneously evolving English, or bottom-up, style will always engender a sense of community that is based on freely derived and freely perpetuated (and, some would say, immutable) values, and a freely shared set of principles. Because many of these arise from cherished tradition and habit, they are most often felt deeply in the heart, if not always understood in the head. They are a result of thousands of inherited customs that as a whole form the ethos of our culture, passed on to us from past generations, those men and women whom Edmund Burke referred to with reverence as "the democracy of the dead," who wrestled with the same eternal dilemmas we do. It would be impossible to know how to perform the simplest social act or to behave with ordinary civility without this inherited complex of moral conventions, habits, and principles.

It so happens that there is only one social entity that has always nurtured the fundamental values and principles of freedom, the bottom-up system, and, crucially, the all-important idea of moral agency and the community that arises from it: the family. Nations have come and gone, but the family survives the barbarisms of every age. This is why, just as the free individual must always be set against unwarranted dependency or coercion, lest he lose his freedom and therefore his moral being, the family must always be set against the intrusive control of the State. The barbarism of late democracy arises from its persistent effort, in the name of egalitarian freedoms, to disintegrate the privileged status of the family, the better to secure for itself the allegiance and dependency of each individual.

This is the grand pattern of the subtle and pervasive conflict between the State and the family. Those who wish to resist its effect on their own family will soon see the difficulty, for in our country there is an ongoing civil war of values being waged, piecemeal, against the family. Skirmishes are fought and, mostly, won by antifamily forces filled with high-sounding, public-spirited intentions. Their motto is like Mao's: two steps forward, one step back. And they are careful to use the sweet-sounding phrases of egalitarian democracy to win their ground.

Anyone who wishes to protect his or her own family, and the institution of the family in general, along with all the ideas and values on which it is based, must first come to grips with a whole set of obscuring popular illusions that make such an understanding difficult. It is to these that we now turn.

# 2

# The Popular Illusions: Ten Unnecessary Obstacles

*Political "ideology" must be defined as a structure of interdependent ideas that results in the formation of distinctive political, economic, and social policies.*

Loosely speaking, all ideologies operate like belief systems. They are based not so much on fact as on theory or faith, and they are systematic, in the sense that all the ideas of which they are composed "fit" together. The crucial distinction between a bad political ideology and a good one is answered by the question: Has it been imposed on the people from the top down, or has it arisen freely among them from the bottom up? The first kind — all forms of collectivism fit here — are dangerous to humanity because they cannot tolerate internal contradiction. They thus require substantial coercion, and they appeal powerfully to idealists and fanatics who by definition are unable to bear the messiness of life. The second kind, like all religions and also like political-economic systems such as democratic capitalism, rely on voluntary commitment and free association for allegiance, and they shun coercion. Paradoxically, then, the key to any ideology of freedom is that it is rigidly opposed to all rigid idea systems; it sustains the all-important belief that human life is far too complex to be contained or directed by any single process or a formula.

The values that make up the core belief system, or the "founding myth," of a free society are communicated to all citizens in hundreds of ways: by families, teachers, priests, fellow workers, friends, wise neighbours, and so on. They are laid down in traditions, customs, books, poems, songs, habits, manners, sayings, the law, and ideally they are reflected in the many social and political institutions of the nation. Not surprisingly, these vehicles of community value are the first to be attacked by the rationalist planners of the new society (who are armed with the uniformitarian kind of bad ideology). They are eager to sweep away what they see as the faulty old, natural, private, spontaneous system, and impose their new, gleaming egalitarian political vision. What fires them up is the belief that human life can in fact be directed and improved by a single system.

So once in power they waste no time. First, there comes an explicit and implicit rejection of all symbols of past traditions, oaths, uniforms, flags, histories, religions, and beliefs. Propaganda, dressed in the language of democracy and fairness, replaces clear thought. Fear of incorrectness replaces love of learning. Citizens are allowed to say pleasant things about any group, but nothing critical is permitted. Committees are established to monitor "human rights" (there are apparently no human duties). All human groups are deemed equally good and worthy of esteem (no talk of earning goodness or esteem). Unnatural sexual practices are relabelled "orientations," to avoid "stigma." Sexual and racial quotas are used throughout society in a form of genteel apartheid. And so on.

In *The Trouble with Canada* I argued that Canadians have not equipped themselves to understand how such political and economic ideologies work, however inarticulate these might be. Until they do so, the nation will remain vulnerable to the processes of decline and will continue to be victimized by expediency-oriented politicians who, to further their aims, wilfully promote illusions such as those described in this chapter.

Each of these interlocking illusions may be understood as *a popular belief without foundation that conflicts with the core values of our society*. So let us keep in mind that no nation in history has survived for long without a basic consensus on values, and that for values to be socially binding they must originate and arise naturally from the bottom up. When imposed from the top, they survive for a time on a steady stream of State subsidies, ceremonies, force, and disinformation of one kind or another. Eventually, however, as community dissolves their falseness is exposed.

In a subtle way, all the popular illusions weave their way, like invisible threads, through the balance of this book. Most of them sustain what James Burnham in his *Suicide of the West* (1964) also called "liberalism."[1] Burnham, who showed how this once well-meaning but now thoroughly destructive idea has been transformed in the West beyond all recognition, argues that only two key assumptions underlie modern liberalism. The first is the idea that all people are basically good; the second is that if human life is problematic it is because people, although good, are ignorant, and therefore their social institutions are faulty. The liberal "solution," intended to provide heaven on earth, is to educate the ignorance out of the people and reform all social institutions. Its religious form is called "secular humanism" (see Chapter Seven). I shall argue throughout that despite the distinct successes of liberalism, the very nature of these two assumptions, combined with sufficient modernization and time, will lead to our decline.

In the heyday of Western freedom, we scoffed at totalitarian countries like "Red China" and other communist states for publicly scolding ordinary citizens and demanding renunciation of unpopular ideas. We could hardly believe how they punished "deviation" from the party line, and from our perch of freedom we pitied such people as brainwashed. Although we are still a long distance from such fanaticism, we are close enough to feel the hot official breath of it in Canada and many other Western nations. It is hoped that after completing this chapter readers will learn to spy all the illusions at work, and will spurn the liberalism they sustain for the unrealistic and unhelpful dogma it has become. Happily, there is no formulaic answer to the problems of human life. If there were, it would be inhuman life.

## THE INDIVIDUALISM ILLUSION

*How individualism is the foundation of moral choice — but is wrongly described as selfishness by its detractors.*

The concept of individualism springs from the dual notion of freedom and responsibility. It animates everything else in the tradition of a free society and pulses through it like a heart beating in a body. The enemies of freedom recognize its strength, and in the hopes of diluting our affection for this ideal seize every

opportunity to characterize the concept of individualism as something else, such as "selfishness" or "rampant individualism." Canada
has a lot of political scientists who like to claim that what differentiates
Canadians from Americans, for example, is that we are communally
minded, and they are "rampant individualists"; we, more English
traditionalists, and they, selfish Americans. Yet even a cursory
familiarity with history will show that England, above all, was the
birthplace of true individualism. Here it was fostered in practice and
protected in law centuries before Europeans got wind of it; and from
here it travelled to Canada, the United States, and all other countries
derived from Britain.[2] So let us arm ourselves against this illusion.
Individualism, rightly understood, is the farthest thing from selfishness. It must be defended by every proponent of the free society as our
most important social principle, for it constitutes a link in the *ethical
chain* that makes our type of society possible, as follows:

Free Individual  >  Choice  >  Moral Society  >  Community

Only freedom, manifest in individual choice leading to responsibility, can lead to the creation of a truly moral society. (For
many reasons, of course, it may not necessarily always lead there.
For example, we may decide to use our freedom to create an evil
society.) But if we wish to create a good society, we must insist
on the primacy of individualism in its fullest sense and not allow
this important concept to become diluted by the proponents of
collectivism. For at bottom, individualism and collectivism are
mortal enemies. The first charges the individual with responsibility; the second attempts to relieve the individual of responsibility
in exchange for votes.

Even the alert sociologist Reginald Bibby, in his recent book,
*Mosaic Madness*, which makes some valuable criticisms of the
"multiculturalism" mania sweeping modern democracies, says that
"individualism focuses on the individual to the detriment of the
group"[3] and refers to such individualism as "unbridled." What he is
really writing about is not individualism but selfishness, which is just
one of the bad uses we make of our freedom. True freedom and therefore
true individualism are always bridled. The question is, by what?

**Moral Agency**
Within the context of a clear set of rules, equal for all, the possibilities for excellence, goodness, or evil *reside in each individual* and
not in the programs of some overarching State. As a consequence, if
the warring concepts of moral agency and State control are forced

together, political, economic, and social conflicts will inevitably arise.

Of course, moral agency is utterly harmonious with our Judeo-Christian tradition (over 91 percent of Canadians reported Judeo-Christian as their religious affiliation on the last census), and it is not mere coincidence that as religious faith wanes, the State rises. For within this tradition, individualism leads to what philosopher Michael Novak calls "personhood" — a word applying to the distinctiveness of any individual who becomes "an originating agency of insight and choice."[4] The individual, rather than the State, becomes the *locus of morality*, you might say, and this is the most dangerous situation for any State craving control. In turn, this idea is nurtured and matured in the bosom of the family — itself a value-creating entity — and the producer of distinctive, free individuals. This entire interconnected process of private-value creation is inimical to any form of collectivism. That is why in his inspiring book, *Free Persons and the Common Good*, Novak reminds us that "no state and no society can legitimately frustrate the drive of each person for his true destination."[5] Karl Marx, the most totalitarian of the collectivist theorists, understood perfectly this clash between individualism and collectivism, which is why he so adamantly opposed Christianity and all forms of individualism. In this, he followed his intellectual mentor, Jean-Jacques Rousseau, father to so many top-downers, including our own Pierre Trudeau who frequently argued to the effect that *in order to be free, we need more government*. In 1964, in a statement either astonishingly naïve or chillingly tyrannical, Trudeau said that "the very purpose of a collectivist system is better to ensure personal freedom." This was an eerie echo of Rousseau, who in his *Social Contract* (1762) wrote that those who refused to follow the general will "will be forced to be free."[6] For such people, the State provides the highest form of freedom — as long as they are at the helm. When they use the word "freedom" they envisage the masses living happily under the authority of their utopian State, unhampered by any other authority (such as you might experience from family, or church). The simplest description of this clash comes from the great Soviet critic of socialism, Igor Schafarevich. In *The Socialist Phenomenon*, he wrote that "at least three components of the socialist ideal — the abolition of private property, the abolition of the family, and socialist equality — may be deduced from a single principle: *the suppression of individuality*."

What the "progressive" State really wants and requires, despite its avowed intentions, is not full-fledged individuals, each one upholding a web of voluntary interdependent familial relationships, but rather citizens *autonomous* from each other while obedient to, and preferably reliant upon, the State itself. Sweden today — which promotes "economic autonomy" as a matter of State policy designed to eliminate the influence of and dependency on the family — is the first country in the history of the free world in which the majority of citizens receive most of their income from the State. In Chapter Five we shall see what a disaster this policy has been for the Swedish family. For when the State falls, as all states eventually do, the people are bereft of their self-reliance and preserving traditions. As for the "group" that sociologists are concerned about? It is crucial to make a distinction between *community* and *communalism*.

## THE COMMUNALISM ILLUSION

*How those opposed to individual freedom always try to substitute communalism for true community.*

The ideal of all human societies is to achieve *community*. Faced with the unpredictability of the gods, the quixotic workings of nature, or the anguish of daily life, men and women historically have created spontaneous communities and dwelt within them. A community augments life for each of its members by supplying an ongoing feeling of solidarity of purpose and meaning larger than the solitary individual. It does this by affirming the value of each individual's choice to support community goals. Community thus validates existence. Human tensions are lowest and pride is highest in the presence of strong community. We can think of community as located at the apex of a triangle, with two radically different roads to reach it: the one successful, the other abortive.

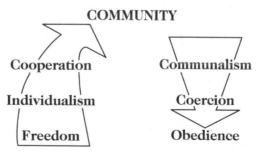

From this diagram, we can see that community, which is a bottom-up process, can never be reached from communalism, for the reason that communalism is a coercive and unitary top-down phenomenon. Communalism always produces the feeling of obedience (if we are sheepish) or rebellion (if we strain against it); but, because it is by definition imposed, it cannot produce the feeling of a freely sustained bonding with the values of others. All communalism, derived as it is from unitary ideas, is far too rigid and quickly loses the consent of the governed because it cannot tolerate natural differences, innate or acquired. Some forms, such as utopian communes, may indeed begin with enthusiastic consent, but they can't sustain it for long.

Coercive utopian states such as communist regimes (one-quarter of the earth's people still live under communism) have consent in the minds of their elites, but never in the minds of the people. They justify this absence of consent by the belief that it is temporary — that the ignorant masses will like their utopia once they are educated to understand it. But communalism survives only by the consent of the governors. When the governed rebel, the monolithic rationalism that gave the theory birth requires the police to enforce continued obedience. This process was displayed before the entire world in the Evil Empire of late, and in Tiananmen Square. It is visible also in a muted form in many North American jurisdictions where human rights police, pay police, employment police, language police, politically correct behaviour police, and all sorts of other people with police-type powers are forcing citizens to behave in ways they would never consider without the threat of coercion. Thus, here is the most crucial single truth of late democracy: *for the first time in our long history, the citizens of free nations are being punished not for what they are doing, but for what they are not doing.*

Community, in contrast, surges upward from the bottom, from individuals and the families that nurture them. It arises from the interaction of these two prior entities, and is not predicated on coercion, but on voluntary cooperation between free human beings within the context of prohibitive laws that forbid citizens to harm each other but otherwise leave them alone in their freedom. Community is always something greater than the sum of its parts, and thus yields an intangible, but palpable, *moral surplus*. Communalism, however, though sometimes successful at the start, always ends as a negative moral force: a subtraction from the whole; an intangible, but equally palpable *moral deficit* that shows in the behaviour of the people, in their faces, and in the widespread decay of society. That's why in all top-down states, not only the elites but also the entire populace ends up wallowing in systemic corruption as the last option for survival.

## THE FREEDOM ILLUSION

*How the idea of freedom is degraded into the idea of licence.*

### The "Paradox of Freedom," Obligation, and Licence

The popular notion of freedom holds that we should be free from the expectations of others, or not limited in our actions by rules. To do what we feel like doing. When people say they "yearn to be free," they usually mean to be unencumbered by obligations, life's stresses, the demands of a job, a spouse, or something else that is making them feel "hemmed in."

But in philosophical terms, the word freedom really pertains only to the notion of free will. And I have argued that even if scientists were able to prove that everything we are and do is predetermined — and that therefore we are not truly free — we would have to disregard this news and behave as if we are. Otherwise, human life would be impossible. So it's a useless argument. (Sadly, those who believe our lives to be determined cannot see that if everyone were to live as determined beings, then human existence would turn into one enormously chaotic, moral buck-passing game based on the psychology of excuse.)

### Freedom vs. Liberty

Of course, to say we have free will does not mean we can do or have whatever we want. Rather, it means we are free to try to do or to have something, or to behave or think in one way and not another. In this sense, it is important to distinguish between freedom and liberty. Freedom refers inwardly to our moral lives, and outwardly to choosing among alternatives that define our lives. Liberty, in contrast, refers to the physical aspects of freedom, like being in or out of jail, or under- or overtaxed. Strictly speaking, even a man in jail is "free" in this moral, spiritual, and philosophical sense, for although he has lost his physical liberty he is still free to sleep, eat, read, think, consider his actions, alter his own inner moral life, and decide on regret or anger, on penitence or revenge; and if he must meet the hangman, he is free even to decide, up until the last moment of his life, on the most important thing of all, which is the meaning of his entire existence. To sense the difference, imagine yourself in jail and in possession of a crucial piece of information that could result in another person's freedom or execution, depending on whether or not you tell the truth. It's up to you. In this situation you would have no physical liberty but almost a godlike moral freedom to control the destiny of someone else's life. So we may lose our physical liberty, our money, our friends — but, unless we are deranged, never our freedom to make moral choices.

The expression "the paradox of freedom" means that whenever we exercise our freedom we limit ourselves, simply by choosing one alternative over another. And this is the joy of moral freedom. As G.K. Chesterton put it, "the liberty for which one should chiefly care is the liberty to bind oneself." It is we who "hem ourselves in" by making choices that constrain us. Sometimes the constraint comes from the unforeseen consequences of our prior choices. Nevertheless, we did choose one alternative, and not another, and must live with the consequences or choose to escape them — and then accept the new consequences of our escape. The important point here is that *to use our freedom is to limit our freedom* in all sorts of ways. For example, we may want two different jobs, but can manage only one. Choosing one eliminates the other. It's the same in choosing between two equally attractive sports, or future spouses, or cars, or conflicting philosophies. Or choosing to have, or not to have, sex. The glory of our freedom is that by limiting it in one way, and not the other, we define ourselves by our actions. We live and feel our freedom by making positive decisions to say "no" to specific alternatives. At bottom, freedom is the ability to say "no." It is the only living thing that cannot be taken from you. Since we cannot have or do or be everything, our lives are defined, you could say, not by what we choose to have but by what we choose to refuse.

But as life is full of tough, and often very painful decisions, we conveniently confuse freedom with licence. And politicians feed this confusion, because it serves their purposes. Accordingly, we have many charters of "rights," from the United Nations on down, but no official charters of responsibilities or obligations. *Licence* basically means you can do what you like without fear of restraint, and it is the farthest thing from freedom because it means you have no immediate responsibilities or obligations (even though all our actions have eventual consequences, many unforeseen). It exists, perhaps, if you are alone in the forest or are an inmate in an asylum who doesn't know right from wrong, or if you are a very small child. Otherwise, it is an oft-peddled illusion, most likely to be found in travel brochures or in the State's assurances that we may enjoy everything we wish, if we simply agree to give up much of what we have.

## Freedom and Contract

So a necessary result of our use of freedom — the one aspect of it that creates a sense of community — is that *we are free to bind ourselves, legally and morally*. In short, we are able to give up some of our freedom voluntarily for some other person or purpose. Most of us make such *moral contracts* every day — or confirm those we have already made (to continue a marriage, to keep our word though personally inconvenienced, to get pregnant, to look after someone else, and so on). In this sense, it is useless to whine about not being "free" when it is we ourselves who have contracted voluntarily to limit our own freedom. A landlord restricts his freedom to use his own property whenever he signs a lease with a tenant. When we have children, we choose to restrict our freedom radically in order to raise them (and how!). And in the operation of our daily lives we place constant moral restraints on our own free behaviour, simply to maintain our personal integrity and community respect. Unfortunately, the Freedom Illusion has done the greatest harm to our society by substituting self-gratification and licence for the true meaning of moral freedom, which has to do with our freedom to make binding commitments. This has the undesirable effect of breaking the bonds of society by persuading individuals that their moral contracts can be voided at will simply if they don't feel like upholding them any longer. Or worse — that they have the right to enjoy life with no commitments at all. Anyone can see that this is a recipe for personal, family, and social dissolution.

One of the chief causes for the decay of Western democratic societies surely lies in the deadly compatibility between the Freedom Illusion, social welfare policies, and the growth of the State. In its unending search to invade the privacy of the family and convert familial interdependence to dependency on the State itself, its programs, and therapists, the State becomes a prime vendor of the Freedom Illusion. Of course, the free market relies on this confusion, too, but it has no coercive power. It has only the power of seduction, and although that can be considerable, the outcome of all seduction remains a matter of personal choices: we yield or we do not.[7] That is why the State is so eager to peddle the Freedom Illusion.

Regrettably for the history of democracy, it is politically expedient to undermine and degrade the concept of moral freedom and responsibility. In this sense, the very success of democracy and of democratic capitalism creates an atmosphere inimical to their own continuation.

## Sex as the Opiate of the People

The Swedish National Association for Sexual Education once declared: "Our aim is to encourage liberation through sex." This pronouncement proved indeed to be one of the cleverest, most successful methods ever used to create acceptance of the policies of the top-down State and lure the populace into a kind of civil docility. In his book *The New Totalitarians*, Roland Huntford details the insidious manner in which a populace can be duped by the exchange of countless personal, political, and moral freedoms for the illusory right to sexual freedom. He quotes this chilling statement made by Mr. Ingvar Carlson, Sweden's former minister of education: "The state is concerned with morality from a desire to change society."[8] (Watch out for teachers bearing condoms!)

The key to this formula is that if the welfare State can remove all traditional, sexual morality from the thinking of the people — especially through the education system, which intrudes right into the home — it can undermine all the less powerful moral precepts that otherwise make the work of the State too difficult. That's why, as Huntford reminds us, Aldous Huxley said in *Brave New World* that "as political and economic freedom diminishes, sexual freedom tends compensatingly to increase." The architects of statism know that if the sense of privacy, and the historically deep moral feelings associated with romantic love and sex, can be removed from the function of sex, then removing taboos and traditions from other areas of human life will be relatively easy. Once the State invades intimacy itself, converting the private into the public, the intimate into the banal, then what is public becomes paramount over what was private. The equation carried in the minds of those — especially the young — who have been through this "morals stripping" process goes like this: "If the State was right about something as powerful as sex, it must be right about everything else, too." And because planners are threatened by the private role of the family in all this, they especially enjoy by-passing parental authority and targeting sexual matters for "re-education." The tenor of instruction, Huntford writes, "is that morality is irrelevant, and that attitudes learned at home are to be discarded." Huntford shows how Sweden is one of the first examples in history of established authorities taking sides with the youth of the nation against their own elders. (They have a common enemy!) It's an ideological offensive, with sex education serving as the most damaging missile. This technique is used in Canada and the United States as well, with a scary intensity (see Chapter Eight).

The objective is to teach that sex is a mere physical need — like eating, or moving one's bowels, opines another Swedish education official. "[I]ts importance has to be reduced . . . What we want is that children talk it over, and come together *rationally*." (See the Rationalism Illusion, below.) Early sex is encouraged, if desired, as long as the partners are "protected." Masturbation is officially encouraged from 13 years onward, "with or without the reading of pornography"; marriage and divorce are now by simple contract and make no difference, legally or economically, to a family (Sweden has the lowest marriage and highest "couple dissolution" rate in the Western world);[9] condoms, abortion, and other forms of contraception are officially sanctioned and encouraged (even though sexually transmitted disease and teen pregnancy have risen there in inverse proportion to such programs, as in every other country where the so-called "sexual revolution" has been introduced).[10] In short, regardless of what some may think are good intentions, in their consequences such programs are not about sex or freedom. Rather, they serve as a key weapon in the effort of the progressive State to break down traditional morality, privacy, and the family. Once every citizen accepts the illusion of sexual freedom (always in conformity with official State policy and practice, of course), he or she can leave everything else up to the State. "Give me orgasm, or give me death" is the new rallying cry of the liberated citizen.

## THE RATIONALISM ILLUSION

*How rationalism is a limited tool for the understanding of human life.*

I do not want to attack the use of reason. I want to use reason to attack "rationalism," which is the unfortunate idea that only reason — or logical thought — and the proofs it requires can lead us to the truth of the world. Obviously, this notion leaves out a lot. Wisdom, instinct, feeling, intuition, tradition, customs, and values are just a few of the unwieldy things that rationalists have decided to deal with . . . by ignoring them. They have chosen to reject centuries of accumulated wisdom and habit, under the illusion that in one lifetime they can solve the problems and riddles of life with the rational faculty alone. But when we demote or ignore life's many other ways of knowing, and raise reason alone to the altar as our new god, we are asking for trouble.

## Secular Humanism

If there are any constants in human history, the spiritual longing for some sense of higher meaning must be the best candidate. Until roughly the 18th century, for most people the organized church in the Christian democracies satisfied this longing. But as the church went down, man went up, so to speak, as predicted. From a worship of the God-man (Jesus), the people turned to worship of the Man-god (ourselves). This transition has been achieved primarily through the promotion of rationalism as the highest human faculty, as well as through the ridicule of many other human faculties, values, and attributes and of spiritual, social, and family beliefs and customs that do not submit to rationalist analysis.

Many books have been written on the reasons for the decline of religion, and the potential villains include science, mass urbanization, the transition to materialism and a money economy, and the rise of literacy. And of course for many thinkers who lived during the so-called Enlightenment period of the 18th century, religion was the enemy. They saw the church as an oppressive force, keeping people illiterate, pregnant, poor, and subjected to lies about reality. The poor church. In Chapter Seventeen we shall see how it is contributing to its own decline by promoting the social policies of the rationalists themselves!

But spiritual hunger is a constant of human life, and either the church will satisfy it or into the breach will step some other reality, often a secular idea that gets elevated to a kind of theological status, complete with its guardians, ministers, censors, institutions, funding, and so on. That is precisely what happened with rationalism. But in becoming sacralized, so to speak, it also came into conflict with the human order. Thus it is that much of the political fallout of the 20th century is due to our ongoing struggle with the legacy of rationalism, to which many have clung in the measure of their spiritual hunger. Historian Gertrude Himmelfarb, speaking of the rationalists, aptly said: "[T]heir Religion of Humanity had only one dogma: that man was capable, by virtue of his distinctively human nature, of every higher impulse, every moral and spiritual quality, which had formerly been thought to require the inspiration and sanction of religion."[11]

## Rationalism and the Human Order

Without overstating the case, it is possible to say that the enormous optimism of the 18th century was due to the underlying idea that, at last, man himself was in possession of sufficient knowledge and reason not only to solve all human problems, but also to engineer a better society than the world had ever seen. In short, man was perfectible. Thus was born the idea of social "progress," the highest dream of the so-called "secular humanists." No less a figure than Herbert Spencer in 1892 wrote that "progress is not an accident, but a necessity. Surely must evil and immorality disappear; surely must men become perfect." Faced with a world they considered unjust, these secular humanists burned with a kind of monastic fervour to make everything right by means of rational methods. This they wanted to do by overthrowing the past, despite the obvious fact that no single generation could possibly reinvent the accumulated wisdom of so many prior ones. It was the ultimate in human pride to think they could.

But even then there was a choice between two radically irreconcilable methods for creating a human order. To our great sorrow, the intellectuals — the planners, the rationalists — won the day. And despite the fact that entire societies (even whole continents) that fell for this illusion are crumbling around us, the pride of the planners continues.

## The French vs. the Anglo-Scottish Enlightenment

Once the idea was accepted that rationalism was the highest human faculty, the die was cast. As it happened, the most resolute — and eventually damaging — statement of this position was the *cogito ergo sum* of René Descartes (1596-1650). This Latin phrase means "I think, therefore I am." The essence of this position was that the starting point of any philosophy should be that everything must and can be doubted. The one thing that could not be doubted was the existence of doubt itself and, therefore, of the doubter. This was Descartes' proof of his own existence, from which he could build rational demonstrations of the existence of other demonstrable truths, in a kind of rational chain. It so happens that this statement also formed the basis of his proof of the existence of God — but modern rationalists have conveniently ignored his religious proofs. At any rate, the idea of proofs based solely on a rational chain of arguments was a very attractive one for those who wanted to change human societies but had turned away from religious means. For Descartes this change amounted to a substitution, as Blaise Pascal put it, of the *geometrical*, for the *intuitive*, mind. Then, once rationalism became allied with technology and science, this style of problem-solving deteriorated into what is today called scientism: "that utterly superficial belief . . . that the empirico-quantitative method was the *only* reliable access to truth and reality."[12] The anthropologist Bronislaw Malinowski expressed this view precisely when he said of our cultural crisis: "I can see only one way out: the establishment of a . . . *scientific control of human affairs.*"[13]

Two other extremely influential thinkers followed in Descartes' footsteps: Jean-Jacques Rousseau (1712-78), who is still thought of as French although he was born in Switzerland, and Henri Saint-Simon (1760-1825). Saint-Simon believed that an utterly controllable human order could be brought about by applying rational planning to human societies, and he was an influential forerunner of modern socialism.[14]

The more influential of the two, however, was Rousseau. He believed that all human beings are by nature uncorrupted and complained that, despite this, "man is born free; and everywhere he is in chains." It is society, custom, property, and class that oppress, he argued, and therefore the way to free mankind is by constructing society properly, according to the general will — something those who govern are best suited to interpret and satisfy. This was a precise formula for the top-down State. One of his many inheritors was Canada's own former prime minister, Pierre Trudeau. He repeatedly used Rousseau's phrase to protest that Canada needed a will of its own, pleading for *"une volonté générale,* as Rousseau had called it."[15] And he advised us proudly, very early in his own career, that "the socialist mind is a planning one," and that federalism (he meant centralism) "must be welcomed as a valuable tool which permits dynamic parties to plant socialist governments in certain provinces, from which the seeds of radicalism can slowly spread."[16]

Even the casual reader of such authors will smell in most of their ideas the oppressive, elitist attitudes that support development of the top-down State. Such "constructivists," as Nobel laureate Friedrich Hayek called them, are completely intolerant of any organic society, naturally evolving from the bottom up. They regard the human will interpreted by themselves as the source of the highest good, and thus "society appears to them as a deliberate construction of men for an intended purpose."[17] This perception continues, even though the work of their hands always leads to coercion and, at the limit, to bloodshed. However, as Gertrude Himmelfarb reminds us in a delectable definition of utopianism, it is "a dangerous illusion which tempts us, in the name of the best, to reject the better and end up with the worse."[18]

It never occurs to people of such authoritarian mentalities that if simply left to their own devices amidst what Hayek calls "rules of just conduct," human beings will arrive at a *spontaneous human order*, designed by no single person or agency yet efficient and harmonious. An everyday example of this common fact of human life is the development of human languages. We all know that even totally illiterate people arrive at competence in a spoken language without understanding any of the rules of phonetics, morphology, or syntax. Simply as a result of millennia of speaking behaviour, an utterly spontaneous order of language arises that serves everyone in the community, without any one person or committee or planning agency needing to know how it works! The same spontaneity applies to economies and cultures. Left to themselves, within certain constraints (the need to speak, to trade, to enjoy life, not to harm others) complex, intricate orders evolve naturally, with *no central planning required*.

During the 18th century, certain Scottish philosophers, fascinated by this phenomenon, presented various defences of it as a rationale for the unplanned State. They argued that such natural human orders are *far too complex for any merely rational comprehension*; that the knowledge required for their formation is dispersed throughout millions of individuals, and any rational effort to understand, much less guide, these orders is doomed to failure. A concise summary of their arguments and views appears in a monograph by Ronald Hamowy, entitled *The Scottish Enlightenment and the Theory of Spontaneous Order* (1987). Hamowy shows how David Hume's *Treatise on Human Nature* (1740), Adam Smith's *Wealth of Nations* (1776), and Adam Ferguson's *Essay on the History of Civil Society* (1767) all focus on the theory "that the social arrangements under which we live are of such a high order of complexity that they invariably take their form, not from deliberate calculation, but as the unintended consequences of countless individual actions, many of which were the result of instinct and habit. The theory thus provides an explanation of the origin of complex social structures *without the need to posit the existence of a directing intelligence.*"[19]

This is a clear description of the order that arises naturally from what I have called the bottom-up, or English, system so crucial to our way of life outlined in Chapter One, and of the utter incompatibility between the two clashing methods for organizing human societies.

### Rationalism and the Family

Once the locus of morality officially shifts from the family to the State, all formerly private and family concerns are bound to become subjected to the rationalist tendency, because all planners see the family as a hotbed of value-creation inimical to their statist purposes. Better to get rid of it entirely. In short, the very existence of the family blocks the obsessive rationalist desire to extend the idea of the good social order, the notion of a "higher freedom," from top to bottom. As early as 1903, the American "progressive" Charlotte Gilman wrote that "there is no more brilliant hope on earth to-day than this new thought about . . . children as citizens with rights *to be guaranteed only by the state* . . . instead of our previous attitude toward them of absolute personal ownership — the unchecked tyranny, or as unchecked indulgence, of the private home."[20]

The prevalance of such intrusive utopian thinkers is worry enough. But an even more fundamental reason not to put our faith in reason has been forcefully articulated by the trenchant moral philosopher Irving Babbitt. Basically, his view, echoing the ancients somewhat, is that each of us is made up of three levels. The highest level is that of the spirit. In the middle is reason, and at the bottom lie our instincts and emotions. Babbitt argues that reason is simply a tool we may use to help raise ourselves to a more spiritual level or to sink us to a more instinctual level. In other words, reason is like a shovel. You can use it to dig a garden or to beat someone to death. In itself reason has no special purpose, but is used to assist in many good and bad purposes.

## THE RELATIVITY ILLUSION

*How the ideas of moral absolutes and moral hierarchy were replaced by feel-good ethics.*

### The Three Blows

In 1917, Sigmund Freud published an essay describing how man had been "three times severely wounded" by the researchers of science.[21] He was referring to the blows dealt to what he called "the self-love of humanity" by Copernicus, Darwin, and Freud himself. I would argue that their cumulative effect on human community has been disastrous, owing to the misleading assumptions they seem to perpetuate.

Before these "blows" were dealt, the general conception of man's place in the universe was that the earth, the heavens, and man himself were created by God, and that our main task on earth is to be good stewards of God's creation and lead a godly life according to the moral absolutes of Judeo-Christian teachings. But the blows described here quickly persuaded Western civilization that there were no longer any absolutes, and therefore no truth and no morality worth discussing, except of a utilitarian or self-interested sort.

## Moving Man from the Centre

**The Cosmological Blow.** Copernicus' blow — later verified by Galileo — was his proof that the earth orbited the sun, and not the reverse. We can scarcely imagine the distressing disorientation this revelation must have caused to the medieval worldview, which held that God had created the fixed universe and had given man his place in it — at the centre. The sun was created to light the day, and the moon the night. All proceeded in a predictable, preordained movement. Then we learned, contrary to all sense perception, that the earth was not fixed in place but orbited the senseless fiery sun along with other planets; and, worse yet, that there were other suns with possible planets and even possible life. Such physical relativity challenged and chilled the theological and moral order of the world, thus opening the door to a dangerous moral relativity that still plagues us.

## Making Man an Animal

**The Biological Blow.** One of the greatest intellectual and moral debates of the 19th century was occasioned by the publication in 1859 of Charles Darwin's book, *The Origin of Species*. Darwin's argument that man was created not by God but by natural processes, and had descended from earlier animal forms, insulted all theological explanations, then and now. His own theory insulted even the God-fearing Darwin, who delayed the publication of his thoughts for 20 years. To that point, man had always been considered superior to the animal kingdom, in particular by virtue of having a moral sense. The real shock of Darwinism was that "it did not so much displace God by man as displace man by nature, moral man by amoral nature."[22]

The unintended effect of Darwin's theory was to persuade generations of people that their lives were controlled by evolutionary forces adapted to the need for survival; that the conscious struggles of ordinary morality were incidental to these larger forces; and that, whereas previously man had been thought of as dominated by his human nature and a moral sense, he was now to be considered merely an animal (even if admittedly a bit more specialized than all other creatures).

### The Displacement of Character

**The Psychological Blow.**   The third blow, launched by Freud himself, was indeed a heavy one. Before Freud, psychology really dealt mostly with the art of living; of coping, that is, with the enormous task of developing what was called "character." The great struggle of civilized life was the effort to become a good person, to pursue virtue. By far the largest number of advice columns in popular magazines dealt with this universal subject. The inner workings of the human being were thought to be animated by a soul, or spirit. It was the responsibility of each person to learn, through good character, to control — or direct — the passions that constantly warred for dominion over the soul. To this end, religious wisdom, community standards, and the teachings of family and school were thought to be adequate.

The moral radicalism of Freud's work lay in his insistence that "what is in your mind is not identical with what you are conscious of." He had the effrontery to explain the working of our inner being according to a system he created that removed control over ourselves. Freud taught that the inner system of ego, id, and super-ego had a life of its own; that "the ego is not master in its own house."[23] This reasoning immediately caused people to see themselves not as moral beings operating within moral laws, but as instinct-driven animals coping with mysterious inner forces beyond their understanding. In fact, his system made a mockery of conscious moral deliberations. Enter thus the enormous loss of confidence in our ability to solve our own problems of living, and the therapeutic State, with its legions of highly paid "analysts" only too willing to decipher the mysteries of our inner depths for a hundred dollars an hour. Psychoanalysis thus helped to create what Philip Rieff called "psychological man," committed only to "his own careful economy of the inner life." This new therapeutic type, as one reviewer of Rieff put it, "was schooled against binding, permanent commitments; for him, *the bottom line of every social contract was the escape clause.*"[24] For the traditional outer moral hierarchy by which mankind had always guided itself, Freud substituted an inner democracy of warring dispositions of instinct and power.

There were two other blows dealt to Western man. One was rendered by Karl Marx in his *Das Kapital* (1869), a vitriolic polemical attack on democratic capitalism which persuasively, if erroneously, argued that history was unfolding according to predetermined, class-based laws. This work had the subliminal effect of persuading great masses of resentful people that individual choice was ineffectual; that man, as in Tolstoy's image of Napoleon, is merely riding inside the carriage of history, holding ribbons he thinks are the reins.

The other was delivered by Albert Einstein, whose theory of relativity unsettled whole generations by showing that all motion in the universe was relative. Those who enjoyed disparaging religion and morals were — to Einstein's great sorrow — quick to seize on his theories as proof that just as there was no absolute up or down, so there was no absolute right or wrong. Einstein's colleague Werner Heisenberg made matters worse by showing that at the level of quantum physics, the experimenter always influenced the outcome of his experiment — which meant that reality could never be precisely measured. This thinking in turn led to the "multiworld" theory, which states that there are as many worlds as there are observers. In moral matters, this became the "I'm O.K., you're O.K." type of reasoning, one of a thousand new forms of moral solipsism, or "situation ethics." The misapplication of the theory of relativity, in short, made it acceptable for people to walk about designing their own moral schemes and dismissing what others considered absolute moral transgressions as the opinion of fools.[25]

### What Are We Left with After Suffering These Blows?

Long after Copernicus, cosmologists still cannot tell us how the universe was created. In fact, as I write, the so-called big bang theory of creation, which has had the allegiance of most (not all) of the world's serious cosmologists for the past 30 years, is in serious disarray (*Nature*, August 1990). Whether the universe is "open" or "closed" — whether it is in a steady state, or expands forever, or perhaps expands and contracts forever — is unknown, and the many theories are irreconcilable. So at a dinner for famous astrophysicists in 1975, a New York *Times* reporter asked the scientists to vote! Humour for the gods. Commenting in *Nature* magazine on recent findings of an extraordinary complexity, U.S. astronomer Marc Davis said that if such findings were proven, then astronomers knew "less than zero" about the early universe. And one of the world's most famous astronomers, Allan Sandage, summed up his life's work by saying: "The main lesson of cosmology is that at the heart of existence is a mystery."[26]

Barely a hundred years after Darwin's blow, his theory, too, is being subjected to increasing doubt by serious scientists, as a number of recent books clearly show. The best of these is *Evolution: A Theory in Crisis*, by molecular biologist Michael Denton. No fundamentalist, Denton does not have an answer for how life developed on earth. And he clearly shows that evolutionary theory does not supply an answer either, for while the theory may seem sound, there is just no strong evidence to support it. Evolutionists are already back at the drawing board.[27]

And Freudian theory? Although fascinating, very few now take it seriously, and it has been frequently damaged by studies showing that treated psychiatric patients recover at about the same rate as those who are untreated. Even worse: that many of the patients Freud claimed to have treated and the results he claimed to have obtained were constructions of his own imagination.

What about Marx? Eastern Europe and China have recently given us a splendid lesson in the economic distortions, loss of human freedoms, and cruelty of Marxism in practice.

And what about Einstein and the theory of relativity? The great physicist himself said that "God does not play dice," by which he meant that our difficulty in measuring reality precisely is no proof that there is no causality.

**The Idea of Hierarchy**

For all these failed explanations of physical and human reality, we have gained mostly rampant moral relativism and, worst of all, the end of the idea of moral hierarchy. This should not surprise us, for in an egalitarian age we have declared that everything will be equal, including all moral values. This entire book is an argument against that view, and it champions the belief that some values are indeed higher, or better, than others; and more, that as long as such values are freely held, the idea of moral hierarchy is absolutely essential to the harmonious conduct of human societies. As Rieff put it, societies are soon gone if they fail to articulate and maintain their moral demands in some kind of shared vision that includes all that they forbid.

One of the surest signs of our moral, cultural, and therefore familial downfall is our loss of faith in the idea of moral hierarchy; in the idea that there is a good, better, best in all human affairs, and that all morally healthy human communities must sort themselves out and establish their rules according to this natural idea.

Not surprisingly, through the end of the 18th century the belief in hierarchy was widely upheld — until the rationalists got at it. In fact, a concept elaborated over the prior centuries, called "the great chain of being," deeply influenced the whole Western world. This idea was of course based on a belief in God as the highest good, downward from which all things flowed and upward to which all things ascended.[28]

It was an idea that argued for the existence of an unbroken chain of being from the lowest form of life to the highest, from amoebas to the supreme being. Man was thought to be the "middle link" in this chain, which fit well with the idea of moral hierarchy (and moral agency): the notion that by the wise or foolish exercise of will each of us could fall, to become more beastlike; or could rise to a higher moral plane and perhaps even reach a state of grace.

It would be difficult to overestimate the importance of this scheme of things in the daily life of the people, for it established a framework within which good, better, and best could be felt by all, spontaneously. In moral matters, we either must operate within the bounds of such a common hierarchical framework — one freely supported by all, not imposed — or must undermine this idea, thus allowing millions of personal hierarchies of value to vie for dominance. This latter route is, regrettably, what we have followed. Someone might wish to argue that personal values is what freedom is all about, so what's wrong with freely elected values? My answer is that in the absence of imposed values, free societies preserve themselves from such moral anarchy by the free creation of a positive community of hierarchical values, as a kind of moral framework. In strong societies, moral criticism is always directed at one's failure to align behaviour with those values, or "expectations." But in what Rieff calls a "negative community," moral criticism is directed not against individuals who fail to measure up, but against the system, or the hierarchy or values itself, which tells us a community is failing.

We are wallowing in a society that has lost its bearings because we have abandoned not only moral hierarchy, but also the notion of all moral gradations — despite the fact that ordinary people the world over naturally recognize the importance of moral demands (and moral transgressions), and maintain an intuitive moral hierarchy transmitted from the particularity of their own culture. But such consensus was surely doomed once the rationalist gurus of higher education promoted the notion that there was no scientific foundation for the truth of particular cultures, and likened moral feelings to primitive taboos. Accordingly, bereft of any shared defence, we have now subjected ourselves to the considerable power of innumerable interest and lobby groups — many of them state subsidized — that pursue their agenda with a vengeance, breathing moral fire into whatever purpose serves their interests. And let us not be fooled: *they* all have a very definite hierarchy of values, both in their ideological and moral persuasions, and it is in *their* strategic interest to make sure that the broader public, who might otherwise protest and from whom they hope to wrest their funds, does not!

So it is of crucial importance to us all to re-establish the idea that some forms of literature, art, moral systems, governance, marriage, sexual behaviour, teaching, courtship, table manners, civility, democracy, and so on are indeed better than others, and that much of what is important to human community flows simply from the ongoing effort to articulate such a hierarchical consensus, from the bottom up. Otherwise, teachers have no books to teach in common (we shall hear the argument that a comic book is as "good" as a play by Shakespeare); we cannot decide on the value of marriage (so let's confer benefits on all co-habiting individuals, without gender distinction); and tax dollars are used for purposes reprehensible to the morals of the community (such as for lesbian conferences, or for public "art" exhibits showing photographs of a man with a bull whip inserted in his anus).

Alas, the rejection of a freely established moral hierarchy means not that all will rise to the top, but that, without any common reference point, all will sink to the bottom.

## THE VICTIM ILLUSION

*How once we give up the idea of personal responsibility, everyone becomes a victim.*

Once a society loses its sense of community, it starts to crumble, breaking into innumerable groups with no common belief system. Thus begins a feeding frenzy in which each group attempts first to set itself up as distinct, and then to employ a special strategy to get everything it can from society, at the lowest cost to itself (the game is to get others to pay).

Normally, every weapon available will be used in this pursuit, such as the employment of professional agitators and negotiators, lawyers familiar with the use of "rights" legislation, and journalists either sympathetic to the cause or just hungry for a bit of "news." Everything seems to promote fractiousness according to the primitive law:

"If there is not going to be an orderly apportionment of goods, or rights, then let us get ours first."

This process becomes most prevalent in societies where the burgeoning state has driven out the traditional forms of self-reliance, private action, family values, striving for excellence, and charity. For into the vacuum rushes the State and the administrators of the therapeutic society. The best person to read on this wholesale surrender of our moral life — of our respect for personal and familial privacy — is, again, Philip Rieff. In his book *The Triumph of the Therapeutic* he details the process by which we ignore, at our peril, our inherent sense of moral hierarchy.

The modern turn to therapy to cure our ills began — with a vengeance — in the early part of this century, mostly inspired by the work of sociologists, who explained, and still explain, all "social pathology" as the outcome of sociological laws beyond the control of individuals. Educators proposed the public school as the institution that should replace what they saw as the failing family, whose "victims" were children. Social workers saw themselves serving society *in loco parentis* — in place of the parent. Criminologists and parole workers added to this mess because they were (and still are) dedicated to the idea that crime is basically the product of a sick family or social setting; the criminal, whom they say is merely a victim of circumstances, must therefore be cured, not punished.

These therapists hold three things in common. The first is an unshakeable elitist assumption as to the superiority of their professional cures and a corresponding disdain for the opinions of those outside their professional circle. They freely characterize the popular wisdom as "from the dark ages" and the work of dissenting scholars as "contentious." Secondly, they share an unquestioning faith in the correctness of their invasion of the private world of the family and of the transfer of family functions (they refuse to consider that their "help" may be causing more harm). Finally, they are financed primarily with tax dollars, and as a whole they too constitute tools used by the welfare State in its quest for a more dependent voting base. The inevitable result is the characterization of almost every citizen as a member of some oppressed, or victimized, group.

The techniques of "victimology" used by those who stand to gain from this corrosive process are well outlined by columnist Georgie Anne Geyer in *New Dimensions* magazine (December 1989). She refers to the cadres of victims who are "ruled by a professionally angry, theatrically self-righteous, highly entrenched, and handsomely rewarded class of organizers who have their jobs due to their anger — and their ambition." She quotes writer Joseph Epstein, who insightfully suggests that "the drama of daily life is greatly heightened if one feels that society is organized against one"; and also professor Shelby Steele from San Jose State University, who says, "We see student groups identifying one simple quality that makes them different [gender, race, colour] and, through that, pursuing power against one another," so much so "that vast areas of commonality are passed up."

Obviously, if we think all life's problems are the consequence of historical "laws," or "systemic discrimination," or "socialization," then there is no end to this cycle. Geyer thus outlines four key steps in the victimology game controlled by the radical lobbyists and their professionals, which I paraphrase here: (1) victimization must be never-ending, and there can be no compromises; (2) the oppressed (the clients) represented by these victim-professionals must never be allowed to integrate into the larger society; (3) all political action on behalf of victims must be solely self-directed (no communing with the larger society); and (4) society must be kept guilty, in a state of anxiety, constantly accused of oppressing some new group or other.

Regrettably, the presence in our world of so many charters of rights, from the U.N. on down, encourages this rights-seeking process, firing people up with indignation and provoking the State itself continuously to increase its sphere of influence in an effort to satisfy the demands it has engendered. Once stretched to its fiscal limit, the State then comes, hat in hand, to the very people upon whom it has conferred abstract "rights" it can never hope to satisfy, asking for more money, for more therapists, to help more victims, to build more ministries, and so on, in a cynical circle. Women are victims? Let's have a women's ministry. Children are victims? Let's have a children's ministry. That's the thinking.

## THE TOLERANCE ILLUSION

*How the idea of tolerance is turned into the idea of approval.*

There is a widespread "tolerance" scam in our society.

Properly speaking, to be tolerant of someone means to put up with him; to accept his legal right to do what he does — but not necessarily to like it, or him. A tolerant society used to be one in which differences were, well, tolerated. The idea that the rules of just conduct were equal for all held sway. If you said you were tolerant of something, the next question would be whether you were for it or against it. Even though you might not approve of many things others do, you tolerate them; otherwise, people may not tolerate what you do. Toleration in this historical sense has always been a self-serving, defensive, but wise measure. If you tolerate me, I'll tolerate you. Fair enough. The overriding assumption here was that everyone would operate within the same laws. What you do with your private life is your own business. But I am under no social or legal compunction to *like* what you do. Under such a system, the spontaneous likes and dislikes of everyone coalesce into the "values" of the society, establishing its tenor and its largely unwritten hierarchical code of right and wrong. This is the informal constitution of society. It is something that happens inside the context or structure of the laws, which may or may not reflect all those values.

But what is unique and unsettling about our present society is the degree to which the State has abandoned the administration of the laws and the extent of its effort to control the private world of spontaneously created social values. It's one thing for the State to rule that you cannot murder your neighbour. It's another for it to attempt to control what you think about your neighbour. At a U.S. university recently a student was charged with "lookism" and hauled before the university's human rights board. "Lookism" was defined as refusing to acknowledge the presence of someone of whom you disapproved. California has recently enacted "the most far-reaching 'anti-lookism' statute in the United States," one that "protects not only ugly people but fat people, skinny people, tall people, short people, toothless people and anyone else" ("Ugly People Now Protected in the Land of Beautiful People," Toronto *Star*, May 28, 1992). As I said earlier, for the first time in our history we are now liable to be punished for what we are *not* doing.

Little by little, the idea of tolerance has been forcibly altered to mean "approval," and it is used by the media and by activists, by human rights types, and by lobbyists of all sorts to promote their agenda against a soft-headed, gullible public. The quickest way to get a Canadian to back down on any issue, or maybe even to get him into his car, is to accuse him of being "intolerant." Instead of defending his opinion, he will be desperate to show that he is not intolerant. But by the time the word is out of their mouths, it's too late. He's had it. And if he protests, they will say, in effect, "Prove it"; or, "Aren't you reacting awfully strongly?" (meaning, "I told you so").

One of the best ways to control a political or moral agenda, or simply a debate over cocktails, is to put the opposition on the defensive by being the first to define their behaviour negatively. This is achieved most effectively by forcibly substituting a negative word for an ordinary one; the word *intolerant* for the word *disapprove*, for example. Soon, if repeated often enough, the negative word becomes a cover term for any of the ordinary words previously used. Rendered speechless by this negative contamination of their vocabulary, ordinary people react by backing down. They are then effectively silenced, terrorized, and neutralized by the group with the agenda. This verbal substitution phenomenon is utterly entrenched in North America today, so much so that most of us now walk around expressing only half our emotions. For example, it's acceptable to say something *nice* about a black, or a Jew, or a woman, but if you say something *critical* you're . . . intolerant. You can praise and clap when any of these people please you, but if they displease you, you have to keep quiet. Meanwhile, it's all right to exercise the full range of your feelings on WASPs. They're considered fair game. Even worse, you're probably nervous about praising a WASP publicly now; someone might interpret that as preferring WASP values — a definite no-no.

It's a turf war, and the territory being fought over is that of public opinion. The technique is first to change and then to control opinion by engineering a confusion between tolerance and approval. In this sense, there is no such thing as neutrality. You are definitely either for or against something, as far as the opposition is concerned. Here's just one example of how it works. If you say something *negative* about homosexuals, you will be labelled an intolerant "homophobic." But if you say something *positive* (like "I think they're fine. There's nothing wrong with them"), you are deemed neutral. Disapproval is intolerant, while approval is neutral? See what I mean? Approval ought to mean homomania, a promoter of homosexuality. But the reaction you get if you point this out? "Oh, I won't go that far!" In short, the fearful public, panicky at the mere idea that they may be seen as intolerant, has been effectively manipulated into *accepting the idea that approval is the politically neutral, correct posture.* Tolerance = approval. We are sheep, and the world is upside down. It's the same with the abortion issue. If you approve of abortion, you are "pro-choice" (tolerant). If you don't approve, you are "anti-abortion" (and to be "anti" anything in our culture is to be intolerant).

Just before writing this page I heard Ontario Premier Bob Rae announce on the radio that he wants "to redefine marriage" in our society so that any two (or more?) citizens, regardless of sex, will be considered legal spouses. And University of Toronto President Rob Prichard, desperately keen to please, announced he will encourage all university students to "wear jeans" and parade about on Gay Pride Day to show their support for these folks (the Levi Strauss company should sue; or is it behind the promotion?). What we have here are two people from the same mould using their public positions to engineer a change in public values. They are the vanguard of the turf war. And they're winning.

## THE RIGHTS ILLUSION*

*How rights to act freely become claims against the State for specific goods.*

There is rampant public confusion about "rights." What do we mean today when we say that someone has a "right" to something? I suggest we mean he has a claim against another person, an institution, or the State itself. He can throw a tantrum and "demand" his "rights."

But that is not our traditional concept of rights, which referred to *an envelope of general legal protections* surrounding each citizen equally. For example: the right to walk on a public beach means no one could throw us off (and no one could force us to take a walk on it, either). These traditional rights — the one that built Canada and the free world — are labelled "negative rights," because they protect our right *not* to be interfered with unless we break a law. Such negative rights are normally the same for all and protected by law. That's what equality used to mean.

Today, however, the term "rights" has been transformed into one with a very different — and dangerous — new meaning; as in, the "right" to demand *a bundle of specific goods, services, money, or privileges* from the State. Such rights are called "positive rights" because the person declaring them wants much more than to be left alone. He wants something specific, or positive, to be provided for him by the State. He has a shopping list of desires that he has been encouraged to claim as rights. I submit that this radical change — so common to welfare states — is a subtraction from the moral quality of our national life. Why should this be so? Simply because as a free person with the protected right to talk, think, speak out,

---

* These last three illusions appeared in *The Trouble with Canada*, attracted much comment, and are repeated here only slightly modified.

and so on, *you are undertaking these actions yourself*. No one else is being required or forced to *do* anything for you. Others are simply being *restrained* from preventing you from doing these things for yourself. That arrangement is a healthy situation for any society. But during the past 30 years this noble idea has deteriorated rapidly into the perverse notion that a right is a *claim* against others (represented by the State) for goods to be supplied by them (not by you). So now, instead of protecting our *freedom* with the law, the State is trying to enforce *fraternity* with the law. When in 1850 Monsieur de Lamartine said that Frederic Bastiat's idea of government was inferior because it stopped at *liberty*, while Lamartine's own system went on to *fraternity*, Bastiat replied: "The second half of your program will destroy the first!" Which is what is happening in Canada today. The law, as an instrument of justice, has been perverted into an instrument of injustice; an instrument not of protection, but of coercion.

This phenomenon has led to a wholesale "rights fever" in Canada, such that there's almost nothing left to which someone doesn't claim some right or other. I even heard a man argue that he had a "right" to marry! I pointed out, to his embarrassment, that this meant someone else had an *obligation* to marry him. A moment's reflection reveals that rights and obligations are reciprocal notions. So what it boils down to is that these modern positive rights, as claims against the State for goods and services, are really claims against other citizens, now or in the future. The government of the day just happens to be the broker, who takes a sizable commission for arranging all this feasting on each other. The real moral sin inherent in this process is that, through massive debt-financing of our welfare programs, it looks like we will be borrowing from future generations for a very long time. Somehow, as dependence on the State has increased, a terrible and immoral chain reaction has become established. It looks like this:

Wants > Needs > Rights > Claims

From *private* wants, to *public* needs, to *legal* rights, to moral *claims* against society. If you take one look at the Universal Declaration of Human Rights drafted by then U.N. employee John Humphrey, a Canadian who still teaches law at McGill University and was honoured December 10, 1988, on the 40th anniversary of the declaration, you will feel good all over. Who wouldn't? It reads like a cornucopia of the good life — especially articles 24 to 30, which virtually promise everyone on earth a right to the nicest, most secure, most enjoyable life possible. There is nothing imaginable in this declaration to which the individual does not have "rights" — many of them to be provided "free." And all the wonderful goods, services, and benefits are to flow from the simple *declaration* of these rights. In short, it is an inspired piece of misleading fantasy, which ought never to have confused the provision of equal *protections* by the State with the *provision* of actual goods and services by the State (other citizens). This illusion always leads to massive structural debt, which always eventually erupts like a cancer on the welfare State, a fiscal sign of the broken moral bonds of society. Yet Ontario's socialist Premier Bob Rae recently fired the imagination of our governing elites with his notion of a "social charter" for Ontario — and the nation. Surely any such declaration will entrench our moral and fiscal problems even further.

Future historians of Canada will say that we gobbled ourselves right up by means of this illusion. There is no need to look very far for a sharp example of it at work right now. On the cutting edge of welfare State policy is the national effort being exerted to convert the want of some for subsidized daycare into a "right" for all. In fact, the *specific* and purely ideologically based complaint of the proponents of free daycare is that it should not be a welfare good (only for the needy), but a "right" of all Canadians. Said Toronto councillor Roger Hollander: "Our objective is to move child care out of the welfare system and into a public service." Canada's federal government has nixed this money-gobbling idea for now — but the agitation for it continues. To the extent that such generalized claims for goods to be provided by others are successful, the private sphere of individual responsibility is reduced, liberty is defeated by enforced fraternity, and the wealth of the nation is redirected toward yet another transaction of decline.

## THE EQUALITY ILLUSION

*How the idea of equality is a logically impossible dream.*

As a child, it struck me as peculiar that whenever the whole school was required to run a foot race, the general result was always the same. The few fast and strong always finished up front, and then came a growing crowd of runners, which tapered off to a few stragglers at the end. When we went to watch a regional championship, the pattern was the same, at a higher level. And it held true even for the Olympic Games. In other words, no matter how narrowly defined the band of measurement, the spread of abilities always showed the same pattern.

It also seemed a truism that no two things are the same; that everything is in flux. As Heraclitus said, "You cannot step into the same stream twice." Little by little, the conflict between these two observations grew in my mind until resolved by the realization that it was possible to have every thing in the universe different from every other, and yet to have patterns formed by large numbers of these different things. People, seashells, intelligence, physical skills — no matter what, the patterns were quite predictable. Later in life, I discovered what statisticians call the "normal curve." This scientific vindication of my childhood perception seemed as miraculous and strange as my first reading of Old Testament stories. I had thought these were stories my grandmother had invented, and was stunned to discover someone had written them down. So it was with the normal curve, which looked like this:

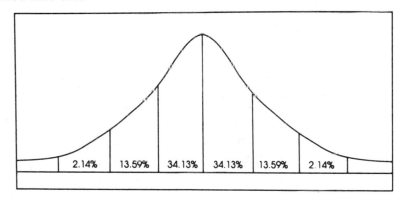

It was the pattern of the foot race, on paper. Some universal law must be at work! Further, It was even divided into precise percentages! I immediately drew several jarring conclusions:

1. If the law holds, then people can never be equal in anything; and
2. Equality, or sameness in things, is necessarily an illusion — an elusive quest.
3. Subdivisions of measurement, provided the sample group is large enough, will generally produce the same curve.
4. Therefore, regardless of how good or bad something may actually be, some people will always be at the bottom, or middle, or top, no matter what we are measuring.

Here's a simple example of this reality at work. You can apply it to poverty, education, intelligence, weight, money-earning ability, mathematical skill, heart-rates, blood pressure, strength — whatever you wish.

Let us imagine the pattern formed by a measurement of the height of *all Canadian males* (I am constructing the numbers). It would look something like this:

One foot difference:

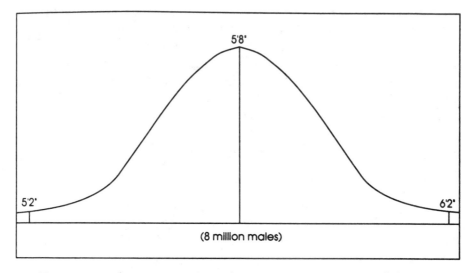

5'8'

5'2'                                                    6'2'

(8 million males)

However, when we narrow the measurement, it still looks the same. We again see a normal curve:

Six inches difference:

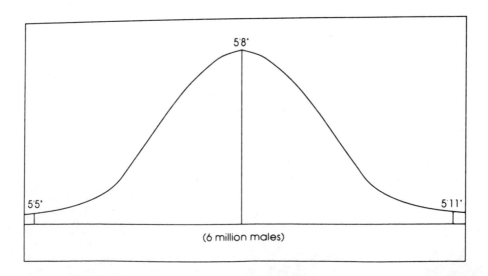

5'8'

5'5'                                                    5'11'

(6 million males)

This can be repeated once again for an even narrower band of heights — and it still looks the same, with the same percentage allocations from one end to the other:

Two inches difference:

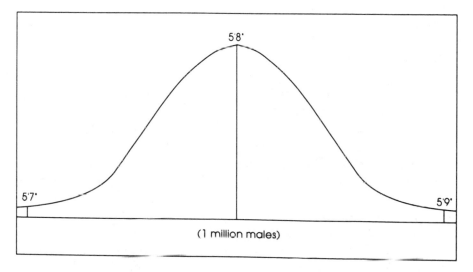

Theoretically, this could be repeated infinitely, provided we were willing to make infinitely fine measurements (as we have had to do for the 100-metre race, which was first measured in fifths of a second, then tenths, and now hundredths). We would always get our normal curve. The law of variation is at work, and therefore, to the extent that measurement is meaningful, *equality* is *impossible*. Now, how does this fact affect social policy?

Very simply, it strongly reinforces the idea that *liberty* and *equality* will always be mutually exclusive, if by equality we mean (this is what social engineers mean) striving for equal social results, or outcomes (incomes, material resources, intelligence, wages). It means that modern social policy, in striving for State-enforced equality, is striving for an unattainable illusion. And it explains why when we look at the human "happiness curve," we see that once subsistence level has been reached the peoples of the world do not differ in their levels of reported happiness. Within each nation, however, each vastly different in wealth, there is some unhappiness according to position on the wealth curve. In short, no matter how poor or wealthy a nation, happiness/unhappiness is a function of the curve, not of the real situation.

## THE DETERMINIST ILLUSION

*How we are encouraged to blame our environment for our troubles.*

Those unfamiliar with this debate might be surprised to learn that scholars, philosophers, and theologians have argued since the dawn of recorded history over the issue of *determinism* and *free will*. These are dry-sounding terms, but anyone used to the history of ideas will easily detect this debate overtly or covertly at work throughout history in all civilizations. Is man the result of causes he cannot alter (is he determined in his being?), or is he master of his own destiny (does he have free will?). Aristotle and Plato, all their students since, and all theologians have worried about this. You might even say it is the core issue of philosophy. After Heidegger, it made philosopher Jean-Paul Sartre famous, because he wrote a 700-page book on free will (*Being and Nothingness*) and then turned around and wrote an even longer one trying to negate the first (*Critique of Dialectical Reason*), after which he died.

It is crucial for any society to resolve the debate between determinism and free will because social policy is inevitably formed on the outcome of this debate. Therefore each society must decide — no, *declare* — whether or not we shall be treated as free agents, or as determined by our social circumstances, our personal history, and so on.

The moral reality is that all personal actions have consequences, and therefore *no society can be just if it cannot decide who is responsible for individual actions*; that is, to whom, to what party, to what institution, to what *cause* should consequences be allocated? Is the drunk a drunk because his father was? (How about his brother, who is *not* a drunk because his father was?) Is the criminal guilty, and to be fully punished? Or will the defence lawyer win the case by saying: "It was true, Your Honour, that he held the gun, but History pulled the trigger!"?

So the whole determinism/free-will debate turns on the matter of the just allocation of consequences. And it so happens that whole civilizations have risen and fallen according to how this matter was settled. One thesis of this book is that the welfare State mentality actively pushes public opinion in the direction of determinism, while democratic capitalism, because it fosters individualism and familism, does the opposite. The former seeks to allocate consequences to the social environment, the latter to the individual. Welfare states that attempt to blame the system for individual failings or bad luck are trying to hoist themselves by their own shoestrings. That's why you will usually hear determinists argue that the way to cure society's ills is to "socialize," or "educate" people (meaning, to instil others with their own biases and assumptions). For most societies, most of the time, this is an ongoing debate. Young, dominant cultures tend to be aggressive and achievement oriented, allocating consequences individually; but as cultures age, one of the weakening agents is the gradual shunting of this allocation to the environment (fate, etc.), or to other social groups (class warfare, envy, soak-the-rich), or to the factional warring of political interest groups.

My personal twist on the whole matter — to repeat a former point — is that this decline cannot be avoided unless the Determinist Illusion is settled by acknowledging that the debate is circular, cannot be solved with finality, and therefore must be set aside in favour of the following propositions:

### Proposition #1
Human affairs are hopelessly intertwined, and as good a logical (not moral) argument can be made for one side as for the other. It is as easy to argue that life is made up of infinite free possibilities as it is to argue that life is determined in its every minute aspect. For this reason, no scientist or philosopher will ever logically settle the debate to everyone's satisfaction. Therefore:

### Proposition #2
*Even if* science were to prove, logically, irrefutably, that we are determined beings, we would simply have to ignore this conclusion, *because no society can be moral unless its founding beliefs are grounded in the idea of free will.* This is an absolute requirement because human moral — and, therefore, social — life is not possible without clear support for the individual allocation of consequences. The demise of the "Evil Empire" was sufficient proof of this, if any more was needed.

There is a high correlation between the permitted freedom of a society and its insistence on free will and individual responsibility, just as there is a high correlation between the lack of freedom in a society and its insistence on determinism, or social causality.

My concern is that we have forgotten this bit of truth, to our great peril, and this lapse has loosed upon us what I call "the psychology of excuse." Through this, we will slowly become a dispirited people, blaming our history, our genes, our families, our social class, the rich, the bureaucrat, the privileged, illness, mental torment, some food we ate — and so on — for our condition. There is actually a now-famous murder case in which the lawyer won acquittal using the "Twinkie defence." He claimed his client had consumed a whole bag of Twinkies, was sugar-overloaded, and therefore was not responsible for the murder of his victims![29] When whole societies start falling for things like the Twinkie defence, or let murderers go free because they claim they were "sleepwalking" (he may have been, but for goodness' sake, lock him up before he kills someone else), or allow cases like a liability suit against a beer company because the plaintiff drank too much before his car accident; when such things occur without public outrage, the centre cannot hold much longer. Individual morality crumbles. Society itself crumbles. The fundamental problem here arises from our failure to distinguish between physical states, or feelings, and moral actions. After all, two individuals may be in exactly the same lifelong turmoil or pain, such that both may wish to kill someone. But the decision of one to go to a therapist or to a church to cope with this urge, and of the other to murder, is a moral, not a physical, choice. "The psychology of excuse" is just one outward manifestation of this transfer of responsibility — so common for the welfare State mentality — from the individual to society itself, in a self-consuming war of all against all.

The psychology of excuse is an obvious illusion simply because we are all part of the very society we are trying to blame. To the extent that we put in place methods — legal, cultural, or moral — allowing us to shuck off our responsibility to others, we create a circle. Others bear the weight of our actions, and we of theirs. After all, the total burden of social consequences to be faced does not diminish by this illusion; it merely gets inefficiently reallocated, or redistributed, in a grey moral whirlwind. The concept of fairness based on individual moral responsibility that has always lain at the root of our civilization may not be a perfect principle. It is, however, the most honest discovered so far, for it allocates consequences as accurately as possible to an identifiable perpetrator. It refuses to look beyond this to physical determinants precisely because to do so always destroys the general moral tenor of society. After all, it is not a great leap from blaming other individuals, to blaming our family life, to blaming society in general, to blaming our genes, to having no society left at all. Our system thus accords with basic and above all practical human justice. We must disabuse ourselves — and our legislators and judges — of the Determinist Illusion, in order to preserve our national moral health.

# 3

# The Traditional Family System

*Family autonomy is the only solid foundation for a free society, and the status of the family as a primary social institution was an established fact both of ancient law and of the major philosophical systems of antiquity and the Middle Ages.*

THOMAS FLEMING, *CHRONICLES MAGAZINE*, OCTOBER 1990

The primal and inescapable natural family triangle — mother, father, children — is the most basic universal fact of our existence. Everything else is a familial or social complexity arising from this singular reality. Whether a natural family is wandering forlorn in the desert, or living with parents, aunts, uncles, cousins, servants, and a few cows and goats under the same roof on a medieval farm, or with unrelated friends in a utopian commune, or in a single-family dwelling in a modern suburb, that does not alter the primal fact. Each of us is born of a mother and begotten by a father, and is therefore bound within the natural family like a pea in a pod, each stamped for life with the imprint of this reality, which is the same for all, yet different for each. The natural family is thus universal — a fact too seldom emphasized — and it never changes, for the good reason that this primal life reality doesn't change. In turn, the essential fact of and fundamental reason for the existence of the natural family in the first place is that *it is the only entity in human history that has ever been dedicated, with utter partiality, to the nurturing and protection of children.*

Sadly, very few influential people are speaking in defence of children, and the honeyed pronouncements of politicians about the importance of family are belied by the policies they institute that fracture it, even if unwittingly. Many of these people are well meaning, but we must learn to look at the *consequences* of their proposals, not at the *intent*. We must be especially alert to policies specifically designed for social revolution but presented in innocuous or even attractive language. At a time of cultural chaos such policies may lead parents to question their natural instincts. The alluring rhetoric of the Freedom Illusion, the economic seductions of the market, the tax policies of the State — any of these can be powerful inducements to evade family duties. And many a vote-seeking politician will tell overstressed people what they want to hear; will offer to take all personal problems off their hands. But children do not vote, and in the face of selfish political or parental ambitions, they are defenceless.

Part of the reason for this defencelessness is that the history of the family is usually written by sociologists with ideological axes to grind. They prefer to dwell on the differences between families, and societies, rather than on the harmonious and gratifying similarities. But differences in childrearing methods, for example, are far less important than the simple common fact that most parents are devoted to rearing their children. We should be studying and praising the devotion, rather than bickering over the method of rearing. The likely reason for this negative emphasis on differences (based on the proven strategy that any single problem can be divided into two smaller ones, ad infinitum) is that it creates reputations, jobs, and more "research"; agreement on similarities, in contrast, dries up the market for academic jobs, research papers, grants, social workers, therapists, and thousands of government employees *who have a vested interest in family breakdown*. Commenting on such vested-interest dangers, sociologist David Popenoe wrote that "there are few areas in the social sciences so fraught with ideology and subjectivity as family sociology," concluding that many sociologists actually *approve* of family decline because "most sociologists today are politically left-wing on most social questions." In short, they support "the decline of parental authority and the rise of female equality and women's liberation, economic egalitarianism, secularism, and sexual permissiveness."[1]

So don't look to these folks for support of the natural family. They are more likely to soak up tax dollars trying to bring it down. Canada, in particular, is rife with such scholars, most on the payroll of one level of government or another. They largely succeed in controlling the ideological tenor of scholarship through a large variety of censorship devices, such as the Social Sciences and Humanities Research Council, various governmental and academic "ethics" committees, and local government or university granting mechanisms which ensure that only "politically correct" research proposals will be approved and funded. Of course, such censorship devices exist in the United States as well. But at least Americans enjoy a wide diversity of opinion, thanks to the presence of so many private think-tanks that employ scholars and publish excellent material. Compared with that diversity, Canadians are intellectually landlocked by academic and media elites — one critic called them "the knowledge class" — determined to control what we know. The fact is, in Canada the probability of seeing a major academic paper funded or published criticizing abortion, or feminism, or egalitarianism, or economic redistributionism is equivalent to that of being shot by a terrorist at the North Pole.

To illustrate this point, I recently completed a thorough search of the top dozen academic, legal, sociological, and family-oriented journals in Canada for the years 1986-91, looking for any articles that opposed or even debated feminist or left-liberal views on the family.[2] Only one among hundreds of articles took issue with the liberal view. It was an article in the *Journal of Marriage and the Family* by U.S. scholars Rao and Trussell of Princeton University, refuting evidence by Canadian scholar James White of the University of British Columbia. White's study (1987) said that cohabitation has a positive effect on subsequent marital stability among Canadian women. The Americans say his methodology was faulty, and their analysis of *the very same data* shows that cohabitation in fact *increases* the risk of later marital breakdown by 50 percent. History will likely show which study was correct. What I am arguing here is that although we desperately need such free discussion and the protection from academic and political demagoguery it provides, we are utterly deprived of it by left-liberal members of the knowledge class, who seem to have cornered the academic market and refuse to air views that dispute their underlying philosophy. Canadians should be good and mad about this situation. What it boils down to is that we are financing our own brainwashing.

Those who dare to tackle such contentious subjects are not likely to get tenure at or even be lured by any university in Canada. Well, that's a deeply saddening comment. Legitimate and lively dissent ought to be encouraged in any free country. In short, there may be a positive traditional majority view of the family in Canada, but, like so many other politically incorrect views, it is being suppressed. We are kept uninformed by an elite and radical consensus of disinformation and silence.

The balance of this chapter has three purposes. The first is to familiarize readers with what has become the conventional history of the family. The second is to introduce recent scholarship that disputes that history and reaffirms the constancy of the natural family. And the third is to mount an impassioned defence of the natural family, which is the heart of the book.

What I want to show is that the natural family amounts to a dynamic, integrated, spontaneous system, or order, that serves to reproduce not only children but also our entire social order itself, and all its values; that there are political, economic, moral, and social ramifications to the way in which all human reproduction systems are set up. For in the general sense, all *social* systems are just *reproduction* systems or, if you like, mini-systems that support the larger reproductive whole. For example, the social system of the military has nothing directly to do with reproduction, but it defends reproduction. In the next chapter following, I will try to show how those who despise the natural family system are equally systematic in the way they argue for a totally different kind of social system, one based on a destructive utopian theory of the State. In short, we need to understand that calls for radical political or social change always become calls for radical change in the reproduction system, which is the family.

People the world over intuitively understand and support the natural family order. Once that order is invaded by inimical political, economic, or social policies, many of which the majority of us may not as yet see — or seeing, may not understand — we suffer an inner anguish. We watch our belief system and values suffer blow after blow, and a great and growing hunger for principles and arguments to defend what we hold dear begins to gnaw. But because of the general radicalization of society, most of us lack the means to respond and defend against those blows. In short, the progressivist, modern liberal consensus, largely engineered by the knowledge class and promoted by media elites, weakens us and successfully expunges primordial values. Divided, we fall.

## CONFLICTING VIEWS OF THE FAMILY

In what follows, it is important to distinguish between a marriage and a family. The former is childless, the latter is not. Marriage is obviously important in its own right, but this is a book about the family, and therefore mostly about the world we create for our children, even though we spend much of the day thinking we are creating it for ourselves. That's why my definition of the intact natural family is: *a married man and woman living together with their dependent children.* After the children are independent they are still part of the old family, but they in turn have renewed the natural process by creating their own basic unit. When young, we look upward for satisfaction and security; when adult, forming our own primal unit, we look around us; and when old, downward to our children and grandchildren. All other types of household organization, and the often ingenious attempts to define them positively, are something else. A single divorced mom or dad with a child is a broken family. Two gays or lesbians claiming common law status or marriage can never be a natural family. In fact, the extraordinary lengths to which some of these "alternative families" go to appear natural — such as when lesbians conceive through artificial insemination by a third party — belie their alternativeness. An unmarried couple with a child may be very nice people, but they have failed to make what anthropologist Margaret Mead called "a commitment of permanence" to the community. As Popenoe again points out, there are lots of books out there "that discuss under the heading 'alternatives to the family,' such 'alternative life-styles' as homosexuality and remaining single. These, of course, are alternatives, not to the family, but to marriage."[3]

Understandably, most of us have but a hazy idea of the history of the family. Has it always been the same? Does it change? Most of us are far too preoccupied with daily life to worry about such matters. And yet, if we do not know the truth we cannot defend it. If some ideologue or politician stands up to argue that marriage and family are on the way out, we are defenceless. It so happens that one way in which radicals soften the public up to accept their progressive agenda is by suppressing the good news on family permanence.

After reading a number of the experts on the history of the family, many of whom are at each other's throats, I have concluded that the *natural* family does not change in any important way — in fact, that the root natural family, parents and their children, has been the same for millions of years. It is true that the *social* family — all the extensions of the natural family, whether of blood relatives or just friends — does change. It responds to and itself generates all sorts of political, economic, and social forces that complicate the moral and legal meaning of marriage and childbirth. Anyone with a step-family is keenly aware of this. Regrettably, after observing changes in the social family, what the radicals do is wilfully confuse it with the natural family, then triumphantly announce that the natural family has changed forever, and will be no more. It is this confusion that then enables them to declare that because more change is likely, it ought to be engineered to meet their goals for society.

This leads to the inescapable conclusion that family sociologists have a vested interest in evolutionary, or "progressive," social theories of the family. They are process oriented, and they tend to link their theories of family change to grand historical forces — to which they say all families, past and present, are subjected. They take this approach because the whole idea of a constant human family, like the idea of a constant human nature, reduces their theories on historical forces and change to unimportance (there is no more ignominious end for an academic!). The concept of an enduring natural family is seen as an historical anachronism that must be argued out of existence because it stands in the way of "progress" and the social engineering that goes with it. If radicals and utopians can't demonstrate that the natural family is an unstable, evolving entity, *then they have little hope of forcing any future society into their utopian mould by restructuring the family*. As it happens, many of their progressive notions are either Marxist or influenced by some socialist school of thought. As sociologist Christopher Lasch (himself a former Marxist) put it, by the end of the 19th century, sociology "had already formulated its overriding assumption: that man is wholly the product of society and culture."[4] In short, most literature on the family labours under the Determinist Illusion (we are wholly shaped by outside forces), and also under the Rationalism Illusion of progress (by adjusting the forces, we can engineer society for the better).

Academic historians, in other words, tend to hold to the secular humanist idea that there is (and must be) social progress toward egalitarianism based on a rationalist ideal. That ideal says that humans are basically good, and evil is not within them but is a product of social institutions. Their answer is to educate ignorance out of the people and change the institutions. People must be turned away from the bondage of tradition and authoritarian values to enjoy new, openly contractual relationships. Humanity has no need for a concept of God, or of absolute moral standards. Science and reason can solve all human problems and create heaven on earth. Out of this persuasion has arisen the conventional, progressivist view of the social family.

## The Conventional View of the Social Family

The conventional view of the social family is derived mostly from the study of English society, which was the first to undergo "modernization," and there is an assumption that other societies undergoing modernization have shown or will show similar changes. The most widely recognized proponent is probably the historian Lawrence Stone, especially in his thorough book *The Family, Sex and Marriage in England 1500-1800*.[5] The thinking goes like this.

The premodern family of the medieval period was based on patterns of kinship and community, to which the individual was subordinated. All property was shared among the group; the household held many family members and non-members, and it was the basic unit of production and consumption. In the raw Marxist formulation — of which this view is a weak version — all production was for *use* by the kinship family only, and production for *exchange* (to sell on a market) was little known. Therefore, the theory goes, the evil idea of profits was unknown. There were no wage-labourers, no industries, no large towns, no desire to accumulate property. Fathers ruled the roost. Women and children were subservient, discipline was tough, and there was little love of children, who were thought to be at the bottom of the barrel and got lots of harsh treatment. There was little affection or love between spouses, and, some argue, prior to the 17th century there was no concept of childhood as a special stage of existence. The deaths of small children, we are told, went largely unmourned. Society was terribly mean and pinched.

With industrialization, however, and then with 18th century Enlightenment ideas, there came a transition and a change in mentality. People flocked to cities. Money became common as a means of exchange, and with it the idea of profits and the growth of a labouring class to supply them. The ordinary household changed radically as production increasingly took place in factories instead of the home. Private property became all important. So the household shrank in numbers, closed its doors to the community, and became a limited private space, mirroring the private property basis of capitalism. Social life became increasingly contractual, and children began to assume more rights against parents and exert more choice over marriage and future. In short, individuals were no longer subordinated to community. What Stone calls "Affective Individualism" began to replace both kinship and community. The family became a mirror of the capitalist society it nurtured, for which it turned out little producers. The family thus lost many of its functions — education, production, and health care — to paid teachers, factories, and professionals. Women increasingly stayed in the home to nurture children, men left to get wages and wealth. From the 18th century onward, the growing influence of romantic love and affection replaced those functions increasingly transferred outside the home, while the home was transformed into a centre for emotional nurture, of which children became the focus. From the middle to end of the 19th century and continuing into our own, this latter model of the bourgeois family was promoted everywhere as the ideal family, especially by women (and social workers), who were the acknowledged guardians of the new morality.[6]

In many ways, this last stage corresponds to the traditional family most of us carry about in our minds. The questions to be asked are, just how "new" is the whole model, and whether or not the family "evolves" at all. There are a number of recent "conservative" historians who maintain that in its essentials, the natural family doesn't change at all. That the family is a natural "organic" entity, not a process. That in this sense nothing progresses, or improves. How could it be otherwise? Truth, honesty, love of children, affection, loyalty — these are the cardinal virtues that have always been with us. A beguiling sparkle in a child's eye has always tugged the heart.

## The Natural Family
The statement that there are eternal verities, or that the family does not change, needs clarification, for the social family has always been buffeted. What alarms today, however, is the degree of penetration of the war against the family, through the outer social shell into the heart of the natural organism. We are at a point in history when the structure of the natural family is being menaced by a variety of inimical forces, in particular those emanating from the State. It doesn't really matter how many uncles, aunts, cousins, or friends live with you. That's like a social extension of the natural family. But it matters a lot if, say, the State has set up economic incentives to dissuade your mother from marrying your father, or to seduce young girls and boys into leaving their parents; or is helping arrange abortions for your daughters without your knowledge; or has taxed your family so heavily you have no money left over to look after your own children or your own parents. These are attacks on the natural family. The natural family can indeed be crushed by policy, or even ripped apart physically by it, as when in war time parents and their children are put into separate concentration camps. But

even then, although the family is no longer a physical unit, its biological, psychological, and moral significance in the lives of its members doesn't change. In fact, this significance may strengthen obsessively, precisely as a direct result of such physical separation.

Documentary scholarship since the mid-1970s has tended to support an intuitive belief in the permanence of the natural family, and of common human feeling and values. Perhaps the most frontal disagreement with the conventional view comes from British scholar Alan Macfarlane, particularly in his books *The Origins of English Individualism* and *Marriage and Love in England: Modes of Reproduction 1300-1840*,[7] as well as from Linda Pollock, whose fresh evidence has set all sorts of theorists on their ears.[8] Both scholars argue that the conventional (politically correct) view of the family was created largely from misleading secondary documents; from theories of economic determinism (a variation of the Determinist Illusion) which suggest that as society gets wealthier it becomes more feeling; and from theories of progressive evolution (the Rationalism Illusion) pushing the idea that society has "evolved" from medieval community, to individualism, to modern egalitarianism. But Macfarlane tells us that all these changes, at least for British-based societies (of which Canada is an offshoot), "did not occur at all; they are an optical illusion created largely by the survival of [certain kinds of] documents and the use of misleading analogies with other societies." In short, Macfarlane rejects the entire evolutionary model that sees human beings as the product of social forces, and says that "the idea of a massive transformation from a group-based, brutal, and unfeeling society to the highly individualized and loving modern one" is basically a myth. The medieval English (even before the 13th century) already enjoyed firm rights in private property, labouring classes were well established, money, markets, and profits thrived, the individual was the basic social and political entity with full legal and property rights (not subordinated to large family or kinship groups), and people were highly mobile.[9] So much for the conventional view!

As for spousal relations and feeling for children? In *Forgotten Children*, Pollock amasses support from the scrutiny of 500 diaries from a 400-year period to show that the conventional view of spousal love and the treatment of children was quite wrong. To begin with, much of the documentary evidence for family history is so problematic that we may never have a truly authoritative view of past families. What we do have from primary sources, Pollock says, tell us this: infanticide was a relatively rare occurrence; wet-nursing of children was also rare, and confined to the upper classes (under pressure from husbands who wanted to resume sex relations and thought such would curdle the mother's milk); and swaddling was for warmth and safety and was not a mark of neglect. Further, infant mortality has been greatly exaggerated, and was only about 150 per thousand in England and 200 in France. Even then, the historical, anthropological, and sociobiological evidence show, when child mortality is high, parents are more loving and attached to children, not less. Parents "maximize their offspring's chances of survival." Also, "while most authors insist that mothers and fathers in history were not distressed at the death of a child because so many died, this is quite untrue; parents were grief stricken at the loss of a child" (fathers as much as mothers). Children were not brutally disciplined, and newspaper records show that both the law and society abhorred child and wife abuse and punished offenders severely. Church documents dating back to the 11th century show that there was a well-defined concept of the child in the past, and "as far back as we have records, the simple family was the standard situation."[10] Pollock concludes that the vast material she studied "does not support the evolutionary theories on the history of childhood . . . there is no dramatic transformation in child-rearing practices in the 18th century"; and, in general, that much of the conventional view "is a myth brought about by over-hasty reading, a burning desire to find material to support the thesis and a wilful misinterpretation of evidence." She reminds us that historians, rather than looking for assumed changes, "would do well to ponder just why parental care is a variable so curiously resistant to change."[11]

In short, she chastises family scholars for ignoring the fixity and permanence of family values, affection, and child care. As I mentioned, accepting this view is a problem for them, because if the truth of family permanence were more widely known, they'd soon be out of work.

### More Historical Evidence
In the year 1308, the Inquisitor of Carcassonne, a beautiful walled city in the south of France, arrested the entire adult population of the nearby village of Montaillou and charged all 114 citizens with heresy. Ninety-eight were tried, many were punished with pilgrimages and the forced wearing of yellow crosses, and five were burned at the stake. This Inquisition was designed to sniff out a local Gnostic heresy called "Catharism" or, alternatively, "Albigensianism" because it centred on the nearby village of Albi. These people

believed the Church had become corrupt and worldly, straying from the teachings of the Bible, so they developed their own Protestant-type sect. A fanatical, meticulous bishop named Jacques Fournier acted as judge, and he so closely questioned everyone as to leave behind an extraordinary document called *Le Registre d'Inquisition de Jacques Fournier, evêque de Pamiers*, which records in painful detail the marital, religious, sexual, working, eating, child care, and just about every other imaginable aspect of their lives. French author Le Roy Ladurie analysed the Fournier Register and in 1978 published his analysis in a dry but fascinating book entitled *Montaillou*, which puts the lie to the conventional view of the family for France, as well. Here are a few snippets to illustrate.

On the subject of the family home — the domus, or *ostal* as it was called — "all the evidence we have emphasizes the mystical, religious and central significance of the domus for the people of Montaillou."[12] As for private property, the domus "was a moral entity and its goods were indivisible. It possessed a certain number of rights, rights which were expressed in ownership of the land and in the rights of usage in the forest and the common pastures of the mountains."[13]

As for those living in the home, regardless of how many from time to time: "One of the unwritten rules of the Montaillou *ostal* was that it might harbour all kinds of adults but, in the long term, it generally contained only one married couple [with children]."[14]

Spousal life was a mixed bag. Women were subjected to a lot of beatings and "feared their husbands even when they loved them." But the entirety of their lives was governed by an unwritten code of honour, which kept society smoothly running. Women, especially as they aged, were held in an exalted position. A woman, sometimes oppressed as a wife, was revered as a mother. Women were strongly held to have a quality of virtue called "virguenza," a kind of feminine honour of which all were conscious.[15]

As for childrearing and love of children? The record shows great grief from parents over the death of a child, and a great value placed on marriage, pregnancy, and birth. In their view, a baby was a cause for excitement, and "was bound to be good since it was immediately provided with an innocent soul. This was one more reason why it should be loved by its mother from the womb."[16] In short, "the spontaneous attitude of the villagers, [was] in favour of birth and friendly towards infants" and "despite what some writers have said about love of children being a comparatively recent phenomenon, this was undeniably an ambiance of affection, and the death or even illness of a young child, or separation from it, could be a source of sorrow and real suffering for parents."[17]

To end this section affirming the historical stability of natural family values, we go back a thousand years further to look briefly at *Daily Life in Ancient Rome* (1941) by Jerome Carcopino, detailing life at the end of the first century, A.D. For clearly, once past infancy, children even then had legal rights. In fact, Carcopino notes, husbands, wives, and children ended up with so many civil rights and so much freedom from traditional authority of any kind that the social structure of the Roman family eventually crumbled. The dissolution of the ancient Roman family can be seen as a prototype for the process of mutation of this social unit: from family to autonomous individual, via the invasion of the State and the transfer to the State of core family functions.

Carcopino emphasizes "the solemnity of the [marital] engagement and above all the depth of the reciprocal affection which contemporaries associated with it . . . The voluntary and public acknowledgment [of affection] was the essential element not only of the ceremony itself but of the legal reality of the Roman marriage."[18]

He goes on to cite numerous touching cases of the profoundest love between husband and wife, many of whom thought nothing of dying for each other or for their children, if necessary, especially during the height of Roman splendour. This period was followed, during the decline of Rome, by what he calls "feminism and demoralization," a period during which marriages occurred very late, few had children, and women showed "reluctance to perform their maternal functions," devoting themselves "with a zeal that smacked of defiance, to all sorts of pursuits which in the days of the republic men had jealously guarded for themselves." Among the defiant were women who would "join in men's hunting parties, and . . . with spear in hand and breasts exposed, take to pig-sticking," and "attend chariot races in men's clothes," and "devote themselves to fencing and wrestling."[19] As Robert Nisbet summed it up, the Roman Empire was characterized "by the successive invasions of the state bureaucracy into traditional kinship society . . . By the fourth century, Rome had become the first all-out totalitarian society in world history . . . its population now a vast aggregate of legally free, socially separated individuals . . . " Human social realities appear rather more cyclical than progressive.

# THE FAMILY VALUES

*The ancient trinity of father, mother, and child has survived more vicissitudes than any other human relationship. It is the bedrock underlying all other social structures . . . in the Götterdämmerung which overwise science and overfoolish statesmanship are preparing for us, the last man will spend his last hours searching for his wife and child.*

RALPH LINTON, *THE NATURAL HISTORY OF THE FAMILY,* 1951

## Political, Legal, and Economic

The conventional terms of debate in matters of political economy tend to focus on the individual and the State, not the family. This is unfortunate, for the family is the most important reality in our lives. It is far, far more than what sociologists call a "mediating structure" between individual and State. Rather, it is an *originating structure* in its own right. It is not the individual who creates the family, but rather the family that creates individuals. Arguably, all psychological, social, political, moral, and economic understandings and motives for the future flow from the power of the family's presence in our lives. It goes without saying that there are good and bad families. I do not pretend otherwise. But one of the reasons we have more bad families than we ought is that as a people we fail to celebrate the overwhelming importance of the family. We thus by-pass opportunities to defend it in our own homes, in our schools, and in our public life. In all my reading and searching, I have yet to find a thorough explanation and defence of family values, and so have attempted one myself.

### *The Home and Family as Protection*

*Between the omnipotent State and the naked individual looms the first line of resistance against totalitarianism: the economically and politically independent family, protecting the space within which free and independent individuals may receive the necessary years of nurture.*

MICHAEL NOVAK, *THE SPIRIT OF DEMOCRATIC CAPITALISM* [20]

Imagine your own daily life without a refuge or haven from the power of the State (or the corporation, or angry neighbours)! Without the family and all that we shall see it accomplishes for us, we would indeed be naked before the raw whim of anonymous and unyielding power. Thus has the family always served us, itself protected until very recently by powerful laws that recognized its sacred boundaries. From earliest recorded Indo-European times, the family served as protector of and provider for its members. Against enemies. Against hostile nature. Against malevolent spirits. But most of all against the concerted forces of other human beings operating under the aegis of the State. In a fine essay, writer Leonard Liggio points to *The Ancient City*, by Fustel de Coulanges, as an important book emphasizing how the ancient Indo-European family was rooted in the concept of the common law, private property, and religious belief; how religion "was first and foremost the prerogative of the family."[21] The Judeo-Christian tradition particularly, he reminds us, has strongly reinforced and further developed these notions so that "the sanctity of property and of the family permitted the emergence in the West of the greatest contributions of culture and the widest diffusion of wealth in the history of the world."[22]

Thomas Fleming, another writer on liberty, reminds us that several thousands of years later "settlers in the New World . . . did not achieve their liberties by fighting a revolution or by making a constitution. They wrested [liberty] from an unfamiliar land and under strange skies, minding their own affairs in their own households, cooperating freely with their neighbours, and settling their own problems, with little recourse to soldiery, constabulary, or judiciary."[23] In short, New World revolutions and constitutions were efforts to protect freedoms, not to create them. And although much of this family heritage and feeling remains with us, in modern times the change in European legal systems became part of a larger effort, Liggio tells us, "to enhance the power of the State against society and the institutions that comprise society: private property, the family, the church." Further, "to create the modern fiscal state, the Total State, *it has been necessary to fracture the institutions* that stood between the State and the property it coveted."[24] Only in England and America, Liggio writes, was resistance to this movement successful, particularly through the American Revolution, which was uniquely based on the idea of a natural law that is higher than the laws of the State.

Properly supported, and with a clear separation of powers, checks on government, and a Rule of Law, the institution called The Family — rich or poor — has at least some ability to protect itself from legal, political, therapeutic, physical, or commercial invasions. Thus, the family is supposed to protect its members, and the laws, the Family. Part of the civil war of values raging in our time has to do with opposing claims: on the one hand of those (like myself) who strive to defend and promote these historical family protections; on the other, of the statists who seek to invade the family realm and dissolve the traditional barriers to State action, thus exposing all family members to uniformitarian policy. What they seek is the forced substitution of a modern egalitarianism of outcomes for the traditional equality of status before the laws. To achieve their aim, they rely on what I have called "coercive humanitarianism," or sweet-sounding force. Such force, buttressed by permeation into every conceivable instrument of "socialization" — notably the schools and the media — is the key operating device of the social engineer (we shall see in Part Two how insidious this process can be). Without it, his opinions and values would be merely one set among many, like yours and mine. With it, the social engineer is poised to push us around and forcefully substitute his values for ours. The private family and the laws protecting it are the last bastion of protection against such ambition.

### The Home as Our Most Intimate Emotional Space
Part of the joy — and the sadness — of growing older is the experience and memory of the primal home. Almost regardless of its material comforts, the intimacy of the home and, for many, the memory of the land on which one first became aware of life lingers forever — often as a basic mood or condition we attempt ever afterward to retrieve, or to duplicate. When we return years later to this scene of intimate childhood life, we are likely to be shocked by the humdrum nature of a place or a mood that in our minds had assumed an almost transcendent quality of permanence. If by chance the primal dwelling is now gone, the wound of disbelief is palpable. The French writer Gaston Bachelard describes this sense of the intimate past as one of *retentissement*, a kind of reverberation of the experience in one's soul that lasts throughout life. *La poétique de l'espace* is his warm and insightful examination of the power of intimate spaces in our lives, particularly of the home and the spaces within the home. Memory and imagination, he argues, are far more than a passive record of reality. They are a major power of human nature, too much ignored. In this respect, our early life forms a kind of emotion-laden inner topography, replete with its special values that in turn create a kind of foundation for the way we live the present. On the first return visit to my own primal home after 30 years absence, I searched with excited apprehension for the spot where as a very young boy I retreated into the dense forest to a small, pine-needle-covered embankment beside a rivulet. There, amidst the odour of pine gum and the drone of cicadas in August heat, I was

transfixed by myriad shafts of light that pierced the delicate green tuber plants. The flowing clear water seemed mystically translucent as it rippled over sparkling pebbles. There, I would often daydream and laze away the hours. Or, restless, become a hunter, taking a favourite stick to stalk a rabbit and sometimes getting so close I could see the pink veins in its ears; just we two, rigid in the stillness. One with the world. He always got away.

Arriving again at this same spot, now pressed upon by subdivisions, I felt and still feel a crushing disappointment and betrayal. How is it that this little piece of earth, this insignificant twist in the creek that now looks so forlorn and dull, could have meant so much? It matters not, I have decided, for what I carry with me is the first experience, not the last.

In this latter sense, we relive our past home as what Bachelard calls "our first universe."[25] Once intimately inhabited, even the most humble abode is forever beautiful; it is a lived space, the not-me that protects the me. And any intimately lived space will be thus transformed into a home. A sheltered being will always sensitize the limits of the shelter, whether a mansion or a tent. Novelist George Eliot described it movingly in *The Mill on the Floss*, when she wrote: "There is no sense of ease like the ease we felt in those scenes where we were born, where objects became dear to us before we had known the labour of choice, and where the outer world seemed only an extension of our personality: we accepted and loved it as we accepted our own sense of existence and our own limbs."

The primal home thus constitutes an emotional, spiritual, and geographical centre of our universe, and a barrier to all outside. This is the birthplace of all our formative sensual experiences, the place where our ceaseless questioning of the world is first answered. When my children make a fort in the cupboard, or a tent over the furniture, they are making an even more intimate home within their home, one they invest with very powerful personal affections — teddy-bears and all. Writer Marcel Proust based the entire philosophy of experience in his huge novel *Remembrance of Things Past* on this very notion: that intimate early experiences form the core of our being and provide a continuity to our character throughout life.

Our primal home is also the stage on which is first acted out the most powerful authority play in a child's life: the mother and father in their relation to the child. Even a home with one parent missing is invested with the constant presence of that parent's absence. Here, the originating values of our young lives are transmitted. All other values learned in our lives will be amplifications or modifications, even sometimes rejections, of these values, to which we always will be intimately linked. The primal home is also the site of the all-important later desacralization of the parents, that crushing revelation that they are not really god and goddess, and, therefore, neither shall we ever be.

War reporters in Iraq described frightened soldiers curled up fetally in their rags, like little children. The most common last words of the dying, whether in battle or in institutions where the old and the sick languish, is "I want to go home one last time."

Can we really imagine a world in which the dying say, "I want to go to my daycare centre one last time?"

### Private Property and the Family

*Where there is no property there is no justice.*

NOBEL LAUREATE F.A. HAYEK[26]

It is impossible to defend the family and its rights without defending the notion of private property. Most of us might agree with this last statement, but we might be hard put to explain why it is so. Certainly, I have had to do some digging to find out. And here is my brief accounting of the reason why, without a right to private property — a right that Canadians will not find defended in their Charter of Rights and Freedoms — we may eventually bid the family farewell as a protected social institution.

Historically, there have been two important theories of government put forth, of which all others seem to be modifications. Both theories are predicated on the idea that man was first here on earth in a "state of nature," from which the idea of government somehow had to arise. What would be the best possible way to form a government?

Thomas Hobbes wrote *Leviathan* (1651) to argue that because in a state of nature there would be endless squabbling among men for things and rights, and none would be secure from danger, everyone ought to surrender all property and liberty to an absolute sovereign (Leviathan), who would retain a legitimate monopoly on force. This would be the convenant between the people and the sovereign: he gets power, the people get security. This is a close description of the socialist and in particular the communist states of the world. Under such regimes there is no right to private property (Soviet citizens were given the right to own their own homes, for the first time, in

July 1991), all values flow from the State, and the family is under constant socializing pressure from ideologues determined to raise the children of the State in its image. In such a world, families have no legal protection whatever against the sovereign power, since the intention is to remove all barriers to the top-down formation of citizens. In communist China today, families and children are encouraged to report "incorrect" behaviour of neighbours and parents to the civil authorities. Spying on neighbours has replaced sewing as the pastime of old ladies. This same spying-on-behaviour phenomenon can easily be seen, of all places, on our own university campuses, where politically incorrect attitudes toward racial, gender, colour, language, sexual, or other attitudinal matters are quickly reported to tribunals that have all sorts of unusual disciplinary powers. And of course in Canada there has been repressive national language legislation since the late 1960s, complete with a federal, provincial, and community spying network of language police and tribunal paraphernalia.

Unsatisfied with this statist attempt to solve the problem of unfettered freedom, John Locke wrote his *Second Treatise of Government* (1690). His basic objection to the Hobbesian view was that it left all power with the sovereign, whether Leviathan then or, later, Napoleon, Hitler, or Mao Tse-tung. So what he argued for was *a system that would leave most of the power with the people* and just enough with the government to accomplish its business. The building blocks of his argument were, first, that natural rights, including all property rights, do not flow from the sovereign but are the common gift of mankind. How, then, does what is common, become private? Locke argued that because the one thing we each indisputably own by natural right is our own effort, we can claim a right to private property whenever we "mix our labour" with something else, whether by cultivating a bit of raw land or fashioning a piece of wood to make a spoon. By our effort we change and improve what was common and without value, into something private and valuable. You can see how this notion fits with the bonus system. The reward for personal effort is ownership of the product, which, under the proper laws, we are then free to exchange voluntarily for a product someone else has created, and so on. Laws protecting such transformed property, especially against the power of the sovereign, provide social harmony and order. Ingeniously, the supreme economic power of the nation is thus dispersed among the people. The final physical form of this dispersed power is the institution of private property and the laws governing it. Once this condition is achieved, in Locke's view, the only legitimate function of government is to protect "lives, liberties, and estates."

In his *Takings: Private Property and the Power of Eminent Domain*, Harvard professor Richard Epstein writes that under this Lockean proposal "private property represents the sum of the goods that the individual gets to keep outside of the control of the state."[27] Thus, "the sovereign is demystified," becoming essentially like a private citizen who can get more property himself only by voluntary exchange or by giving just compensation for property taken for the public good, subject to the same laws as any other citizen. The beauty of this system, the one on which our own country was built, is that *it permits the individual to challenge the invading power of the State*. In this sense, our Western system is permanently revolutionary because it represents an ongoing rebellion against State power. For it disperses power, as represented by property, into the people's hands by legal right; and it permits families to generate wealth in the form of money, land, homes, and business assets, thus encouraging the intergenerational transfers of wealth that supply much of the motive for wealth creation in the first place. We shall see shortly that much of business is created and owned by families, and that national wealth in a free country depends utterly on the institutionalization of the concept of private property rights. These rights are being challenged daily in Canada and the United States by ideologues and leftist lawyers and judges who (correctly) see private property rights as a barrier to the creation of the egalitarian social-welfare utopia they crave. Whether we speak of laws that criminalize the private purchase and sale of basic medical care (Canada is the only advanced nation where this transaction is illegal); or rent control laws to prohibit the private negotiation of free-market rents; or laws that declare privately owned malls to be "public" spaces — it doesn't matter. These are all forms of interference with basic property rights, because property means anything you own or have created, whether an idea, a bicycle, a poem, your money, or your home. Excessive taxation at a level Locke could never have imagined now amounts to a legalized public plundering of private property, and it spreads this invasion over an entire nation — even over future generations, as the State is now doing in Canada. Such stealing from future generations by means of forced debt liability is usually the first sign of systemic moral corruption; that the State has lost all sense of principle, and is prepared to steal from the future to ensure its electoral success in the present. National debts, after all, are just deferred taxes. Those who want to defend the private family and private property rights would do well to understand the high and stirring principles on which they are based while there is still something of both left.

### The Bonus System

The family is part of a larger system I call the bonus system, upon which just about everything in our society has traditionally been predicated. It could have been called the merit system, but it implies much more than merit; namely, reward for merit. Hence, the term bonus system. It has as its underlying philosophy the idea of moral agency, as previously discussed, derived from the exercise of individual freedom and responsibility under rules of just conduct, equal for all. It is a system in which the State sets the rules at the bidding of the people, but never plays the game. The bonus system thus encourages the natural expression of differences, and because striving for excellence is a basic motive of human nature, it rewards success within the system. Everyone benefits from the system, but those who do best are rewarded the most. For the successful assumption of economic risk, there can be tremendous reward. And, of course, tremendous cost for failure. The bonus system lays no claim to perfection, nor does it pretend to moral superiority. In fact, as a system it is specifically amoral, on the grounds that whenever any political or wealth-creating system preaches morality it tends to convert a free bottom-up society to an unfree top-down State. Rather, the bonus system must be charged only with the creation of the *conditions* for the good society. The goodness itself must flow from the morals of the people. So the bonus system is not perfect, but it is the best system ever invented. It is a technique for wealth creation that is based, like the arches of a church, on a solid foundation — Western morality and law — and is supported by the underlying recognition that it is better to have a free society in which there is a wide range of natural differences, than an "equal" society with no wealth, no differences, and no freedom. Under the bonus system, the onus of morality, effort, and success lies squarely on the individual. Under the handicap systems used by egalitarian states, the onus lies on the State. One quick glance at the world quickly shows which of these two conflicting systems has been the most successful.

Such a system recognizes the plundering nature of all governments, and thus specifically separates the political, legal, economic, and social powers of the State and checks those powers wherever possible. It requires free democratic institutions, opposition parties, protections of property (as discussed above), free private banking, private rights to insure against losses, and accurate double-entry bookkeeping to allow the orderly transfer of private property and an accounting for increases or losses in value. It also permits the creation of private corporations, and joint stock companies.

All these things are instruments, or tools, of freedom and wealth creation, and they reflect the underlying bottom-up philosophy I have outlined in this book. They are locked in deadly battle with the "policy instruments" of the administrators of the welfare State, who nevertheless must be extremely careful to keep the bonus system healthy enough to feed their welfare State visions. Whenever the bonus system falters, as it does during recessions or under severe taxation (often the same), these visionaries backpedal faster than Charlie Chaplin.

Most important to the subject of this book, the bonus system encourages personhood, toward which all humans strive, and promotes and protects the family as its fundamental value-producing entity. Such free systems and nations are suspicious of human social and political systems that undermine their basic moral rules, and so they constitute themselves under God, without whom it is argued such a system must fail to locate its moral absolutes. Thus, the United States of America is constituted under the motto "In God We Trust." And Canada's Charter of Rights and Freedoms begins: "Whereas Canada is founded upon principles that recognize the supremacy of God and the rule of law." These are the only stirring words in the entire Charter, which then proceeds to contravene both these noble principles.

In free societies, the argument is that God gives us our freedom, *whereby we may choose to live by values higher than those of the State.* Better the rules of God, which leave us free and equal before His law, was the thinking, than the arbitrary, self-seeking laws of corruptible men who seek to bend our lives. To this combination of principles, values, and institutions has been added the enormous force of the Judeo-Christian ethic of striving for progress, not in any pure moral sense (since we cannot improve on the values of the major religions) but in the sense of personal self-betterment, both materially and in particular with respect to our personal pursuit of virtue, or good character. Capitalism, after all, was never intended to create the good society. It was intended to create the *conditions* for the good society, which depends on how the citizens use their freedom to become virtuous.

The private family is thus the origin of the bonus system, and wherever the family is left free, it will tend to generate all other aspects of the system, simply because these constitute what Adam Smith called "the natural system of liberty." Those who wish to defend the family must adamantly defend the bonus system that feeds it. Once this system is set up properly and protected, then out of it will flow, as from a cornucopia, astonishing amounts of freedom, responsibility, and wealth.

### Family Business Is the Engine of Wealth Creation

> The family firm is the predominant form of business organization in the Western world.
>
> FAMILY BUSINESS REVIEW, MARCH 1988

"Flabbergasted" would be a good word to describe my reaction to the utter absence of facts on family business in every standard sociological analysis of the family that I have read. The word "business" does not even appear in the indexes of these publications, all of them by academics steeped either in the public world of the university or in similar institutions primarily supported by the State. It crossed my mind that these people simply do not know or care much about wealth creation or business, or are inimical to it, despite the fact that it is business that pays their salaries by creating wealth and therefore taxes. They are willing victims, nay, perpetrators of the Free-Lunch Illusion — the idea that the government has money of its own that it has not first taken from you and me, or borrowed, to be later repaid through still higher taxes.

The astounding economic and social dynamics suggested by the figures below also suggest that the scholars are blinded by ideology. Their attitude is corroborated by a polling of the Canadian public in the spring of 1989, asking where the government should get money for new spending programs. Fully 75 percent of the people, including the well educated, answered: "The government should use its own money!" Is there really any hope for us? The chart below tells us in no uncertain terms where just about everyone, including government, gets their money from. The figures were located through The Canadian Association of Family Enterprise, a young and vigorous organization created to study and promote family involvement and success in our nation's business life.

**Families Own, or Control, or Produce, or Otherwise Represent the Following Percentages of National Wealth, 1991[28]**

|  | Canada (% of All) | U.S. (% of All) |
|---|---|---|
| All businesses (owned) | 80–85 | 90 |
| GNP | 40–50 | 60 |
| Public stock companies | 30 | 30–38 |
| Fortune 500 companies | — | 33 |
| Financial Post 500 companies | 30 | — |
| Labour force | 50 | 60 |
| New jobs | 70 | 60 |

How can we draw anything but the most stunning conclusion from such figures? Namely, that the engine of wealth creation in the West is the family unit, and that this fact has been all but ignored by governments, planners, and tax experts. If this country were truly backward economically, and if someone were to swoop down to announce the discovery of a foolproof family-based system that would create enormous wealth, I think all would drop whatever misguided policies they had theretofore followed and, between prayers of gratitude, would elevate the new system to the highest pinnacle of social respect and legal protection! Hard-working, risk-taking enterpreneurs — especially men and women prepared to create large families and teach them the same skills — would be especially admired. Personal parenting of children would be society's most honoured role. Instead, here's another amazing fact. Fully 70 percent of these family businesses do not survive into the second generation, and only 13 percent survive into the third! The combination of business risk and the difficulty in combining the necessary family dynamics are significant obstacles. As well, we seem to have made things as tough as possible for family enterprise. In the next chapter, we shall gain some insight into why a two thousand-year-old tradition of political and economic resistance to families and their wealth-creating powers is still making itself felt in our culture.

What these figures mean is that even though as much as 50 percent of GNP *each year* is being created by family enterprises, most do not survive beyond the life of the owner(s). Clearly, any enterprise is difficult to get started (the ratio of business deaths to new business startups each year is about 40 percent) and even more difficult to sustain. A recent study has discovered that two million Canadians work at home, and 23 percent of the working population does some work from the home (*Globe and Mail*, April 15, 1992). The

130,000 home-based workers in British Columbia alone generate
$1.2 billion in revenues annually (Toronto *Star*, February 24, 1992).
What these figures are telling us is that underneath the dollars
and percentages lies an extremely powerful motivational engine,
driven by the emotional, philosophical, and moral vision of the
family and its survival into the future — however difficult that may
be to sustain in practice. In the same way marriage provides young
men with a tremendous motive to create wealth (bachelors earn
about half as much as married men because they don't need the
money; and without children they aren't motivated to produce it for
the future), families provide the entire nation with a future motive
for the creation of a vast current wealth. Much of this wealth is
passed on to future generations in the form of active businesses,
wages, taxes, inheritance, or charity. (Not incidentally, the higher
the personal wealth, the higher the percentage of personal assets left
to charity. Most very wealthy family heads fear leaving too much to
their own children in the form of raw money, for the reason, as
megamillionaire William Vanderbilt said in 1885, that "inherited
wealth is as certain a death to ambition as cocaine is to morality."
And lawyer Alexander Sanger, of White and Case in New York, said
that of 20 wills he had drawn up for people with assets of more than
$20 million, 16 had left at least half their estates to charity [*Fortune*,
September 29, 1986].)
Far from being an outmoded form, family enterprise, we are
discovering, is the heart of the modern, unplanned, spontaneous
economy. Break up the sanctity of marriage, or the right of private
property, or the Rule of Law, or the right of inheritance, and you
will break up the family business and, therefore, the economy of the
free nation. The economies of unfree nations are not worth talking
about, except to demonstrate one stunning fact. In virtually every
unfree nation, by far the most vital sector of the economy is the
"informal" or black market, or private family sector. In the former
Soviet Union, just to consider the granddaddy of all "socialist
republics," private farm families produced 27 percent of that nation's
agricultural produce on only 3 percent of the arable land. And in his
book *The Other Path*, Peruvian economist Hernando de Soto
shocked Latin American experts when he proved that most of his
nation's economy was being run primarily by family-based "infor-
mals" who, discouraged by formal laws, create wealth for themselves
and their families outside those laws. If the one billion mainland
Chinese are ever freed to create family wealth, the world will see an
economic boom of major proportions. It's coming!

So just as marriage provides present-oriented young men with a motive to produce wealth for the future (young women, for biological reasons, are already far more future-oriented), the family unit provides whole societies with a motive for the future. Without this motive, whole societies can fester in self-interest and self-satisfaction. They can change from what Rieff calls a culture of control, to a culture of release. The latter is concerned with releasing everyone from cultural constraints; the former with teaching how adherence to the cultural norms enables us to contribute to the whole by relying on a cultural "design of motives." Release cultures are concerned with autonomous, inward-looking individuals eager to feel good. Control cultures are concerned with incorporation in those individuals of the culture's highest principles. Release cultures become obsessed with pleasure and spending, instead of with working, creating, building, and saving. That's our current economic and moral dilemma.

Faced with an increasing societal breakdown in values and likely inspired by the business culture the Japanese have created, top business experts are just now studying family enterprises and advocating many of the motives and values inherent in them. The company as a family culture is all the rage. For family enterprise is the very opposite of, say, publicly owned companies, which are oppressively concerned with earnings-per-share and are often ruined because they forsake long-term quality for short-term profits. Strong families are usually quite willing to see their enterprise through the roughest times, and unlikely to sacrifice name and quality for profits in the short term. Check the statistics on income levels by ethnic group in Canada and the United States, factoring for all normal differences such as age and education, and you will find a very high positive correlation between incomes and groups that cherish and promote family solidarity. These will also be the groups (and nations) with the least crime, least divorce, least drug and alcohol abuse, and least illegitimacy. So the solid, family-oriented groups that generate the most, cost us the least. When are we going to recognize this fact and cut our losses? The important message that arises from all this is that nations wanting long-term wealth and security had first better figure out how to promote and protect families.

### Marital Cooperation: The Division of Family Labour
In view of the fact that almost all men and women naturally desire children at some point and yet must also make a living, the domestic division of family labour has turned out to be one of the most fruitful

devices for wealth creation ever invented — as the numbers on family businesses show. This dual purpose: the co-production of children and wealth would be impossible without such a division. We shall see in the next chapter that this is precisely what the socialists and radical feminists object to, it being their view that women have been the only donkeys dragging home the hay. They see the higher wages of married men as exploitation of the family, instead of as a service to it (even though never-married men and women in Canada earn identical incomes).[29] Without marriage, men seem to be a confused and aimless, even dangerous, lot. With it, they stretch themselves to the limit.

The finest social accomplishment of the 19th century was its success in getting the women and children out of the factory, off the streets, and into the schools as well as the homes, which is where mothers wanted to be and where everyone wanted children to be. There were a few distinctive values underpinning the social prestige of the family: it was widely recognized as a social unit *higher* than the individual; the importance of children to the continuation of society was unquestioned; and finally, there was the accepted importance of *personal parenting* of children. It was then quite rightly assumed that to raise children with sufficient love and care, the earning of a wage sufficient to nourish the whole family would require *specialization* by both parties — a division of labour. Or, to put it in economic terms: marital efficiency requires a voluntary exchange of complementary functions. One of the reasons for current family decline may well be the loss of efficiency resulting from declining sex-role complementarity.

This division of responsibilities gave birth to the idea of a "family wage" sufficient to care for a family of five, and to the many laws designed to prevent unmarried men or women from unfairly competing with married workers for scarce jobs.[30] Men were thus driven deeper into the working market, and women deeper into the home. From the point of view of the production of wealth, this still is the most productive and specialized method of wealth creation the world over. What this system thereby created was not dependence, but familial *interdependence*. As anthropologist Margaret Mead long ago pointed out, the male role in every known human society is to provide for women and children. It is precisely this interdependence that radicals wish to eliminate in the name of "economic autonomy." In Sweden today, such autonomy is an official State policy for all citizens; alas, the Swedes don't yet see that the State seduces them with this idea by taking all their money first and then giving it back in the form of client services on which they become dependent — and which they cannot control. The Swedes have simply substituted dependence on the State for family interdependence. Conversely, the specific focus of divided family labour was and still is on children, although in our modern move from a child-centred to a more adult-centred world this tidy structure of motives is breaking down and the children, as we shall see, have grievously lost out. So have many parents, especially women, which is a shame; for a husband and wife bent on raising a family are like the pilot and navigator of the same airplane. Neither can get to the destination without the other, and neither can do both jobs. They have to work out, for themselves, who flies and who navigates.

What an irony it is that, after a century and a half spent consolidating these important gains for the family and the protection of children, radical groups are now assiduously lobbying to destroy the family ethic. Their ideal is that both parents should work outside the home, this made possible, inevitably, by *impersonal* daycare. Further, modern tax policy is now driving both spouses out of the home by eroding disposable income and child benefits while favouring "working" spouses. All this amounts to a kind of social entropy whereby every distinction will be lost as we settle into one indistinctive mass of State-dependent, tax-drained, autonomous citizens. In that earlier, family-centred time, society chose family and children over base material wealth. Now, degradingly, we are choosing material wealth over family and children. History will likely show that radical feminists in particular have become the new dupes of the consumer mentality. They have fallen for the money and played into the hands of a generation of men who do not object to the extra income earned at no cost to themselves, but often at great cost to their wives and children. There is even new evidence that as women increase their paid work outside the home — men decrease theirs! U.S. Census Bureau figures show that in 1975, 83 percent of married men worked in the labour force, but only 78.6 percent by 1988; meanwhile, figures for women in every category rose in the same period.[31]

At any rate, it is peculiar indeed to find yesterday's reformers striving to drive women and children into the home, only to see today's reformers striving just as hard to drive them out again. In many respects this trend can be viewed as the last stage of the Individualism Illusion. It is this stage that Alexis de Tocqueville warned us about long ago, where the highest motive for the people is "equality of condition," not responsible use of freedom. For equality, he said, "places men side by side, unconnected by any common tie." Such a social end-point leads to a shrill defence of "choice" *in* all things — but only *for* oneself. Through the defence of this selfish use of freedom, each autonomous unit strives to surround himself or herself with a bundle of "rights" (via the Rights Illusion), which are usually defended by charters or constitutions allowing claims against others for personal convenience, privilege, or material advancement.

Against this picture, the traditional family division of labour has always had as its purpose a simple efficiency in the consolidation of legal marriage, personal childrearing, and the nurturing and protection of family members. This is an arrangement that enables and has always enabled societies great and small to ensure their own continuation. Inevitably, because of strong laws and customs preventing any illegal consolidation of these motives, the traditional system made men dependent on women for marriage and children; and women on men for protection and support. The implicit social contract was that men would provide and protect, while women would process and nurture. Both sexes were seen to need each other equally, if differently. Women always knew they could bring men to heel by withholding what they wanted most: sex, the promise of marriage, children; in short, a culturally validated future for males. Men could retaliate by refusing support or protection. In order to prevent the wanton occurrence of the latter — especially during a woman's child-bearing years, when she was most vulnerable and most handicapped in terms of competitive wage-earning power — there were harsh laws to punish the wayward treatment of marriage, and legal, religious, and social sanctions upholding marital vows, responsibility, and child support. Incidentally, one of the ways in which the amazing century just past tried to prevent husbands from leaving wives was to saddle husbands, if they separated, with the care of the children.

The marital division of labour was far more than it appeared on the surface. It was the outer manifestation of a whole system of values — rather, of a hierarchy of values — that set the family's status well above that of the individual. What it also did was invoke a natural hierarchy of authority, which we like to call patriarchal and which all egalitarians dislike very much. Nevertheless, this seems to be the way of the world, since all social systems are inherently hierarchical. And anyway, what are the alternatives? A matriarchal order may be one, but there has never been one of these in all of human history. Even if there were, wouldn't a matriarchy also constitute a hierarchy of authority? And wouldn't it instil a variety of social devices, attitudes, and "expectations" to keep society in line, just as has our patriarchy? The only possible alternative to either of these family-based possibilities is some well-heeled organization outside the family. Unfortunately, the one usually proffered is the State, an unsavoury alternative to most.

The reasons for patriarchy are various, but the most brutal reason of all is that men are potentially frightening people. Even weaker men, let alone women, are afraid of strong men; and as long as this is so, strong men will continue to exert authority over both. In the home, when a married couple cannot agree on some pressing issue, the final decision must fall to someone. Historically, if it has to do with family survival it falls to the man. Hence the *paterfamilias* of ancient times, which is still very much with us. For reasons I have suggested, and as Thomas Fleming has noted, "Patriarchal power tends to be stronger in societies that emphasize personal liberty and self-government," and weaker in statist regimes. That is because society needs to be organized in some fashion, and the choice is between the "little platoons" (as Burke called them) of family, associations, church, local government, and so on, or the monolithic State. Someone has to do it, and the inverse relationship that Fleming presents is not surprising, "since the only alternative to patriarchal supremacy is government supremacy."[32] Organized social authority, in other words, must reside somewhere: either in the monolithic State or in millions of lesser hierarchies. As I said earlier, matriarchy could do the job of government, too, except that it doesn't do it, hasn't ever done it, and is therefore unlikely to do it. My view is that, whether under patriarchy or matriarchy, we will still end up with a chain of command or authority. Most couples confess this reality, even while they share the command post on less pressing matters or on those within agreed domains. In her refreshing and learned book *Sexual Personae* (1992), author Camille Paglia has really thrown the cat among the feminist pigeons by arguing with enormous flair that Western civilization owes everything to the ordering propensity of patriarchy. Left to women, she says, our civilization would "still be living in grass huts." At the least, in a free society men and women can sort this out for themselves within each family. The crucial point is not who rules the family roost, but that the family, instead of the State, rules the social roost. Much of today's grief has come from our woeful effort to replace this natural hierarchy.

### The Family and Community

A functioning community, as Charles Murray so convincingly points out in *In Pursuit of Happiness and Good Government*, is "one with functions to fulfill."[33] It is a natural result of the voluntary associations achieved through the nurturing of freedom and responsibility within the family. When the State takes away what are properly community functions, ostensibly for the purpose of creating communalism, it takes away the community itself — and it takes away freedom. Murray stresses that the spontaneous result of the family's presence-in-community is the opportunity for family members, especially young children, to see their parents practising virtuous behaviour with others. In this way, freedom creates a circle of value that can be transmitted from parents to the young through built-in social models. Murray says that the presence of community offers a "reality test" for everyone. He asks, for example, how one is to learn the "habit of helping others, of giving, of generosity, if this has not been a part of one's own life?" Once the State robs the community of this function, this crucial habit of the heart is never learned; after all, "watching parents support compassionate politicians just isn't the same."

The functions of a healthy community are, or ought to be, just an extension of its families and their values. When communities are healthy, strong values dominate and constitute a kind of moral substance that repels anticommunity values and actions. There is a flowing of motive from the family, through its children, into the community and back again, in an ongoing cycle that refurbishes and refines the concept of local virtue. But communities become dysfunctional whenever State policy, under the guise of helping, promotes the Determinist or the Relativity or the Victim Illusion in an effort to supplant community with State in exchange for taxes and votes. As Murray reminds us in relation to the most fundamental aspect of charity: "One of the important reasons for leaving the functions of a community *in* the community is that doing so increases the chances for the recipients of help to be givers of help as well." Throughout, Murray argues not for autonomy, but for *interconnectedness* and *interdependence* as the prime generators of community feeling. We shall see that these two familial social realities are precisely what the radicals wish to eliminate, and to substitute for them a social dependence on the State alone. Hence, the social welfare State. In attacking the family in any way, even, in many cases, by subsidizing it, the State quite clearly attacks the community. And in relieving the community of its human functions, the State deprives the family of its moral arena. Human beings, it turns out, do not form communities just to *be* together. They form communities to *do* things together — usually the most important and difficult human things, such as loving each other, nurturing each other, deciding on the important values, policing them, transmitting them, and looking after the needy. So when the State takes away the difficult things that communities do, ostensibly to relieve the community of the effort, it basically takes away the community.

### Love and Affection, Reproduction, Sexual Control

In his ground-breaking book, *Men and Marriage*, George Gilder remarks that "the crucial process of civilization is the subordination of male sexual impulse and biology to the long-term horizons of female sexuality."[34] He does not paint a pretty picture of men. And the high regard in which he holds women and their values has singled him out for special disdain from radical feminists. That's good. It means his argument has the sting of truth.

Men and women he argues, giving copious factual support from every conceivable field of study, are from birth very, very different from each other. But men become radically different from women around puberty, with the onset of male androgenic hormones, and from that point onward "a man's body is full only of undefined energies — and all these energies need the guidance of culture."[35] Women have no such biological confusion, since they are aware very early that they have the miraculous capacity to bear another living human being. A man of course makes this role possible for her, but a woman actually carries it out by devoting her physical being to the process. We could even say that the process itself commandeers her being. Nothing about a man's body tells us he is made for any such duty (and we could as well say he is made for hard labour, or fighting). But everything about a woman's is manifestly designed for this purpose.

Unless some social pressure is imposed to recruit men and their energies for a purpose higher than themselves and their appetites — in particular, if women are not present, or not willing, or lack confidence, or are afraid to tame errant male proclivities — then "over the whole range of human societies, men are overwhelmingly more prone to masturbation, homosexuality, voyeurism, gratuitous sexual aggression, and other shallow and indiscriminate erotic activity."[36] They are also overwhelmingly more prone to violent crime. Of the 12,500 federal prisoners in Canada's jails, barely 300 are women. Men are also far more interested than women are in hit-and-run sex, one-night stands, and multiple partners. Unless there is some barrier, immediate gratification is their choice (as it is the hallmark of the criminal in all he does). More than half of all homosexual men report having had hundreds, and some "thousands," of partners, while lesbians normally stick to one (see Chapter Thirteen). As for children? Until they have their own kids, men from childhood are far, far less interested in them than are women. From a sociobiological viewpoint, this all makes sense. A man's body, unlike a woman's, continuously creates a sexual product (sperm plus prostatic fluid, the latter being about 95 percent of the total) that accumulates in his body until released, rendering him capable of fertilizing many billions of human eggs. The buildup of this product creates in most men a very real physical, and thus emotional, tension until released. Ask any man with a prostate problem. He will identify with this release theory, and most sufferers are quite pleased when their urologists prescribe it as therapy for prostatic discomfort. This tension lends an urgency to the male's indiscriminate sexual interest, the primary aim of which, unless he is taught otherwise by reality, is sexual release, not reproduction. For all males in the biological and plant world, it seems, the natural order of fecundity is not one of efficiency but of enormous waste. Overproduction. For the female of our species, however, with but one microscopic egg at a time to protect and nurture, the entire procedure is reversed. Her tension is not driven by the need for release of a physical product, but for the emotional relaxation of security. She seeks the bonds of love and affection that orient and calm the indiscriminate male, and her best move biologically is to select the strongest one she can and at the same time prevent him from trying to fertilize someone else's egg and switching his protective allegiance.

Accordingly, what marriage and family have always provided for society is a means for taming male sexual and physical aggression, for drawing males into a long-term female pattern of procreation, and for protecting offspring. In exchange, both parties agree to refrain from sex with others. Hence, the sexual control function the family performs for society: Males give up their search for indiscriminate release, females give up their search for a stronger father. Both get access to legitimate and predictable love and affection.

Another control function that marriage and family serve is that of sexual apportionment. Without marriage and the laws that prescribe it, strong men end up with many wives, and weaker men with no wife at all. Monogamous marriage ensures that almost everyone gets only one partner. Younger males can seek their own mates without competition from older, stronger, wealthier, more experienced males. Multiple marriages — today's so-called "serial monogamy" — is a legalized form of polygyny (multiple wives), and should really be called serial polygyny. The result of it is that many more men tend to remarry, and sooner, than divorced women, and to younger females. The losers are the young men without wives yet, and the older single women with children.

Gilder rightly argues that the power of marriage and family in all societies arises not from women's physical *strength*, which is negligible compared with men's, but from their *control* — their ability to draw men into the female reproductive pattern and harness male energies for the future. It is this grand pattern that provides societies with their future orientation — but only if they are wise enough to recognize and protect it. So if we want a society that is not physically and morally truncated, we should stop talking about sexual orientation and start talking about family orientation. Societies that fail to so harness young men soon cease to reproduce themselves. (Our own Canadian society is now reproducing well below the replacement level of 2.1 children per woman, at a disastrous 1.65 level. The United States is about the same.) If they commit the folly — as we have — of embarking on a public philosophy that encourages all the illusions spelled out in Chapter Two, they will fracture the emotional and economic interdependence so crucial to families. Then they are investing not in reproduction for the future, but in polygyny, homosexuality, childlessness, abortion on demand, and single parenting. In 1908 there were only 108 divorces in Canada; by 1968 (the year of "liberalization" of divorce) there were 11,000; and by 1986, 78,000, even though we were only three times larger than in 1908. In 1970 there were perhaps 10,000 abortions, but by 1990, 95,000. As society loosens the sanctions that once kept the family together, men will tend, in the absence of strong legal and moral sanctions, to follow their biological proclivities and seek out younger, nubile women. Women and children, families, and even the younger men seeking a wife need protection against this trend. They are not getting it.

### Marital Love vs. Profane Sex
Without marriage and family to regulate sexual appetite, we would likely fall into a bacchanalia of sexual confusion, a sort of feeding frenzy of sexual satisfaction, with sex reduced to its lowest common

denominator much as is found with most male homosexuals (brace yourself for Chapter Thirteen). We would be rutting beasts, life-support systems for genitalia, for whom sensual stimulation is everything, and commitment nothing. The very conservatism of marital constraints and the family ethos is what forces humans to refine their base sensual emotions and drive them to a higher plane, exacting emotional commitment from marital partners. Of course, unmarried couples in love may feel emotional commitment, too; but what defines the quality of the relationship is the presence of future expectation. What any lover wants most is a continuation of love. And what the female, whose reproductive years are so limited, fears most is a male taking advantage of that hope, and "using up" her most fruitful years. The greatest formalization of this transformation of raw sensual excitement occurred in the Christian Platonism of the 16th century, which taught that human love was a stepping stone to the most blissful love of all, the love of God. Even those who do not believe in God tend to treat human love in this mystical way by seeking through it a feeling of oneness with the universe. Carl Jung described this as the "oceanic feeling" that comes over people in a state of profound peace, such as deep love engenders.

It is the formal presence in our lives of the publicly sanctified institution of marriage that directs human love upward from where it would otherwise fall. In the profoundest sense, it is the couple's swearing of an oath of marital loyalty — not before each other, but before the community — that constitutes the most meaningful moment in human marriage. By such an oath, every couple swears to rescue love from profanity and devote it to higher family, community, and spiritual purposes. When a union is considered this way, public policies describing a marriage as "any two people living together" appear as an unspeakable sham, a profanation of one of civilization's highest human forms. It is this sanctity of marital love that is destroyed first by invasions of family life.

### The Family as a Moral Entity
Something easily forgotten is that the family, unlike the egalitarian State, which declines to judge or to emphasize differences, is a highly judgmental institution. It may be the only judgmental institution. Where the State insists on sameness of everything, including moral systems, the family does the opposite. Where a teacher may say, "I don't want to tell people how to live their lives" or "right and wrong is whatever you decide," a parent will likely say the opposite, seeking to fulfil his or her duty of transmitting a hierarchy of values

from generation to generation. In this sense, the family transmits the very notion of duty itself.

Children see from a young age that parents have a duty to them, and learn that they in turn will have an increasing duty to their parents. Whereas the welfare State inevitably weakens these duties, or attempts to take them over entirely, the family strengthens them. When the family is weakened, this sense of duty dies. Michael Novak sums it up when he writes that "the family is the ordinary institution of self-transcendence."[37] (Religion is, for most, the extraordinary institution of transcendence, of course.) For if not a parent, who in the future will admonish a child to grasp the nettle, or to rise above? The role of the welfare State is just the opposite: it discourages any effort to transcend its own value system. In fact, it requires subordination (a poor substitute for transcendence) to its values and a transfer of many life functions to the State.

So the puzzle pieces begin to fit together: Where there are transcendent values and principles superior to all others, local associations, such as we find in families and religions, order their behaviour around these values and consider the State an instrument to protect them. But when the State insists on the pre-eminence of its own set of values, it drives all other free, value-producing entities underground, and makes a mockery of ordinary morality. But arguably the fatal flaw of all egalitarian democracies, as they slowly become despotic democracies by swallowing up the freedoms and resources of the people, is that their momentum is downward, via the handicap system described, to a nondescript sameness. In short, they lose the special overarching impulse that lies at the heart of all rising civilizations and tends to direct such societies toward higher planes of unquestioned virtue and excellence.

### The Family as a Humanitarian and Economic Social Force

If we think of humanity as a self-propagating species made up of an aggregate of individuals with certain specific daily needs, we must then ask ourselves, Who will satisfy those needs? By what organizational principle will human beings congregate to help each other? There are very few possibilities. Some intermediate paid group, such as servants? Some ultimate paid group, such as the professionals of the State? Or — and this has been the history of human help — a freely formed organization based on blood, or family reproduction, rendering voluntary services to all its members? What is clear is that the total requirements of daily work to satisfy individual needs, earn income, and tend to our young cannot be handled by one. Teamwork is needed. Interdependence is needed. And the family is, historically, the only social organization that has shown itself capable of fulfilling all these chores and duties. Children can seldom satisfy their own needs, nor can the feeble or the old. Even the young and healthy but overstressed husband or wife must rely on others.

The family is the finest humanitarian organization we know because it alone responds to the needs of its members on a voluntary unpaid basis throughout life. These contributions are a distinct form of social production, too long ignored. So when the ordinary husband goes off to earn far more than is required to care for himself, the difference between his own expenses and what he provides to the family is his voluntary cash contribution to its welfare. He makes many non-cash contributions, as well. His wife usually makes her own voluntary contribution in the form of labour, or labour and cash if she also works outside the home. Radicals who insist that government pay wives for their services not only ignore the horrible bureaucracy that snoopy domestic supervision would demand; they also forget that such pay could be provided only from tax dollars. We would only be taxing each other to pay each other, and government would be taking a sizable commission off the top, leaving all families much worse off financially. An unsound idea.

But consider just a few moves in the day of the average family. Father drops the kids off at school on the way to work, works all day for his boss, swings by the bicycle shop to pick up a new wheel for his son, takes out the garbage, walks the dog, spends an hour with irascible junior's math homework and perhaps another hour trying to raise funds for the new hospital. His wife has taken clothes to the cleaners, cleaned the house, bought necessities for the children, and spent an hour comforting her gravely ill mother. In addition, the parents provide each other with love, and sexual services. He provides security to all (she dislikes staying alone at night), and she an endless round of maternal contributions. Meanwhile, the whole family often works in the garden, or around the house. My point simply is that the sum of these voluntary services is far more than the State could ever afford to provide to such a typical family. What would it cost a single mom to hire a security guard each night, or a single dad to hire a mom? Or for the State to assume the voluntary duties that parents provide to children's schools, the boy-scout pack, the local hospital? And yet, the history of the welfare State in the West has been the gradual assumption of so many basic human duties that it threatens to destroy the motive for family formation and to dry up the well-springs of private giving.

At the end of the 20th century it is finally becoming clear that the total of all such voluntary intra- and extrafamilial services is so great that, if wholly undertaken by the State, they will financially bankrupt it. That is because the sum economic value of lifelong voluntary intrafamilial services far exceeds not only the total of government revenues, but even the total gross national product. This means that any State unwary of its willingness to encourage the transfer of such functions may irrevocably bind and burden itself or, at the least, set up a continuous and insatiable clamouring for more "free" services. At some point, caught in a maelstrom of inflation (in part a result of excess government support), intolerably increased taxation, and universal entitlements, the State begins to look for a way out. The history of the socialist states illustrates this pattern. They have progressively promised to assume the family's time-honoured and, yes, often difficult, functions in exchange for tax dollars and votes, and have buried themselves in the process. They rob families and communities of their productive essence. The will to succeed dies, taxes die, the State dies. On reflection, it seems evident that any State wishing to perpetuate itself, to preserve itself from social and economic self-immolation, could do no better than to invent an organization based on self-perpetuating internal bonds of family blood whose members are prepared to render each other a whole range of voluntary services far too expensive to purchase. A democratic State that wishes to succeed and survive must first recognize the importance of such natural community-forming associations as the family, and then resist its own tendency to erode them. Can we hope that any State will be clairvoyant and principled enough, sagacious enough, to limit its own short-term appetite for power in the interests of long-term health?

### The Family as a Force for Social Cohesion

One of the social miracles of family life is the task it performs stewarding the meek of the earth. Even strong family members are not always strong, and for unforeseeable reasons they can fall by the wayside. So it is that we must ask ourselves how in the world society would manage to look after the ungifted, the meek, the misfit, the awkward, the socially unskilled, the member who commits a crime or the one who makes a grievous moral error; in short, the many millions of temporary or permanent losers in the game of life who, without some buffering emotional or financial shelter, would be cast on the mercy of total strangers.

The family is the only social organization that treats its members with more love, patience, and care than they often deserve, or might receive from others. The very creation of a family normally produces a simultaneous *binding social force for caring that transcends the family itself*. We are prepared, for the sake of family cohesion, to put up with terrible heartache and inconvenience we wouldn't accept for a minute from other human beings. And long after emotional quitting time, we try and try again to mend seemingly hopeless disputes, or to implore family members to right their errant ways. In the pure financial sense, the family is the original and still unequalled charitable organization of the world. No State could possibly match its contribution to the education, health, or moral training of its members; nor could it supply the young of the world with the equivalent in financial assets transferred from generation to generation.

Perhaps most important of all, we stand ready in families to love and care for some, for the sake of all. We emotionally embrace even the undeserving for the sake of the whole, and invest that whole with a meaning and purpose greater than the sum of its parts. This simple human act of near-fanatical devotion is the envy of the State itself, of course, and is precisely what it aspires to create by eroding all the small associations of life in the hope of transferring our loyalty to the one big Association. All socialist nations strive for this result, which can indeed work for a time. Nazi Germany was very successful at breaking down the small voluntary associations and teaching the people to imagine the State as one large cohesive family. Hence, the power of the phrase "the fatherland." This sometimes fanatical devotion to the suprafamily-State concept can rivet entire nations . . . until the dynamics I have described begin to erode the State itself. Then individuals are bereft.

It is far from an exaggeration to say that the secret to the emotional power and success of the natural family is its inherent devotion to its own continuance and preservation, a devotion that requires a form of unconditional love to be found in no other type of social group. What can explain this unconditional love? Other groups may create strong emotional bonds, but they will not normally create unconditional ones. That is because for most groups, the objective is of higher value than the emotional bonds formed in its pursuit. For the family, however, these two purposes, the bonds and the objective, are the same. Only this fusing of purpose and emotion can explain the power of family love and forgiveness, the efficient manner in which families all over the world tolerate and protect their losers and misfits, ensuring them a status beyond what they may otherwise have earned, and instilling a confidence beyond their own reach. A State that ignores the enormous potential and social-binding power of such unconditional family love will, as it erodes the family's ability to perform, find itself saddled with these people. Many of the so-called "homeless" of the world are of this outcast tribe.

### The Family as Domain, Possession, and Purpose

We have a right to ask, What has happened to our world? Why is it that for almost a century now, our poets, artists, and critics have bemoaned the loss of community, focusing on alienation, meaning-lessness, and anxiety? Through what social structures is a human being to gain a sense of worth and fulfilment?

Consider the options. I see only four: the individual; the family; what Nisbet calls the "intermediate associations," such as commu-nity groups, clubs, recreational groups, and churches; and finally the State itself. The first three are social entities based on freedom. The last is based on coercion, and therefore it cannot be social at all. From the first three have flowed community and authority, in the sense of standards, controls, advice, assumptions, shalls, and shall-nots. From the State flows only power. Authority is based on freedom; but power is based on coercion. People voluntarily submit to authority; but they resist power in principle or obey it involun-tarily. The misery of this century is our unthinking replacement of one with the other. Hence the anxiety, neuroses, and aimless-ness of our age. We have surrendered the very things that once gave us local authority and, therefore, meaning; that gave us a sense that in some small way we were important to the definition of our *domain* — be it region, town, or home. The family is one of the last things still to give us *an arena of competence and authority all our own*. Woe to the State that deprives us of this last domain of personal competence. It is the ground on which each — some failing, most succeeding — can strive for personal success in an endeavour of indisputable value. If we were dictators of some totalitarian State composed only of autonomous individuals, we would — once spying the lassitude of the dispirited, aimless masses — cast desperately about for a way to provide them with profound meaning. We could do no better than to encourage the formation of millions of organizational and reproductive structures called the Family, each with a higher social, legal, and tax status than the autonomous individual, each within its own protected domain, and encourage the people to run them.

Which leads me to possession. When we say "my wife," or "my husband," or "my children," or "my parents," we are using more than a figure of speech. Something crucial to otherwise purposeless human beings is the manner in which marriage and family yield other humans to use as our possessions, providing us with a political, economic, and moral claim on one another, however transitory. The mutuality of this giving of ourselves must be the highest gift of which we are capable. It is fundamental to how we cope with the great initial chaos of life and death, each striving for a meaning recognized. The human satisfaction that we can gain only through meaning recognized, is a social thing. To write a book for no reader, to build a tower for no purpose, or to paint a picture for no viewers is an un-human action. The sense of reciprocal giving and possession that marriage and family make possible in the form of daily renewable commitment is available in no other social form. We cannot even imagine the idea of such a gift between ourselves and the impersonal State; it is a nonsensical idea.

So, too, for human purpose. Resistance to the invasion of the family by the State must arise from our deep awareness that perhaps our most primal purpose is slowly being stolen from us. Family provides most of the world with both short- and long-term purposes of the most compelling sort. Outside of war and, temporarily, politics, little other than family arouses human beings so intensely. As the war against the family continues, we will surely see a vast displacement of emotions — through broken homes, aimlessness, drug abuse, crime, and a general loss of discipline, civility, and authority. In short, at great social peril we are undermining the purposive, organizational behaviour occasioned by the existence of the natural family. For political power, which is coercive, cannot replace natural authority, which is freely accepted. Power in the absence of authority only produces the emptiness and anger that come from lack of purpose.

### Partiality, and the Victory over Mortality

> Parents have one great superiority over the government or the administrators . . . They have and feel the greatest interest in doing that which is for the real benefit of their children.
>
> SIR ROBERT LOWE, EDUCATOR, 1868 (IN *CHRONICLES*, OCTOBER 1990)

In addition to sexual control, the taming of males, and the reproductive and emotional functions of the family, there is another function, rarely mentioned and much undervalued. That is the function of partiality. I mean by this that the traditional family is so far the only social institution ever invented to provide the children of the world with a form of love that is unconditional. All other institutions designed to raise children, such as daycare facilities, government schools, or socialist-style utopias, are the opposite: they are intentionally *impartial*. They insist on treating each child the same. Such institutions are little islands of egalitarianism.

But that is not what children need. In order to differentiate themselves as individuals and grow secure, what they need is the partiality of their natural parents who, for the duration of their lives, will be the only ones to render them such love and concern. Within each family there may indeed be an egalitarian ethic of fairness toward offspring; but between families, this has never been so. Where their own offspring are concerned, parents have always been partial to the point of insanity. They commit heroic acts of endurance every day for their children (just putting up with them sometimes qualifies here) and would die for them if necessary. The message children receive, and only from their own parents, is that they are utterly special. No, impartiality, as Linda Pollock affirms, "is not enough: a developing personality needs to know that to someone it matters more than other children. That someone will go to *un*reasonable lengths, not just reasonable ones, for its sake."[38] But any daycare worker would be chastised for suggesting as much (see Chapter Twelve on the daycare disaster). It is arguable that without such partiality, especially in the early years, it would be impossible to raise healthy, emotionally secure children. In this sense, the natural family truly is, as Christopher Lasch described it, a haven in a heartless world.

What children provide their parents with in exchange for this partiality is something only they can give back. Faced with our mortality, and given the natural apprehension with which this knowledge colours our lives, parents commit the highest act of creation of which humans are capable by bearing children in their own likeness. Anyone on whom the miracle of this is lost has already departed our world. Many philosophers argue that we must keep our mortality steady before our eyes, lest we forget the meaning of life and make false choices. True enough. But children, in addition to the natural joys they can bring, enable us to slip loose our mortal coil for a fleeting moment and dare to imagine ourselves extended into a limitless future through them, and their children, forever. Through our own likeness, our very flesh and blood living after us, carrying forward our embodied essence, we snatch a brief human victory over death. In this small way the lives of our children still our anxious hearts.

Family is important. Very important. The vast majority of people, in poll after poll, repeatedly insist it is the most important reality in their lives. For this reason, each of us must decide, before it is too late for our civilization, what role we must play in the defence of the natural family. For there is a clear relationship between the human hunger for community and the manner in which even the most well-intentioned State erodes any possibility for community by eroding, in the name of liberal democracy(!), the very values and family duties that make human community possible in the first place. On such a downward-spiralling cycle are we now turning. And we must break that cycle, or lose our venture. We must recognize that there is no such thing as a mere passenger on the ship of life. Everyone is crew; each of us must decide whether we will help with the voyage or harm it, and in what way. When Edmund Burke (1790) said that the only thing necessary for the triumph of evil was for good people to do nothing, he meant it. Good people don't have to do bad things to create a bad society. They just have to stop doing good things — and the bad will quickly fill the vacuum.

# 4

# The Antifamily Tradition

*. . . Our men and women . . . should be forbidden by law to live together in separate households, and all the women should be common to all the men; similarly, children should be held in common, and no parent should know his child, or child its parent.*

PLATO, *THE REPUBLIC*, c. 375 B.C.

*In order to raise children with equality, we must take them away from families and communally raise them.*

DR. MARY JO BANE, ASSISTANT PROFESSOR OF EDUCATION, WELLESLEY COLLEGE (1990)

*Utopia must be our goal.*

ED BROADBENT, LEADER, THE (SOCIALIST) NEW DEMOCRATIC PARTY OF CANADA (*GLOBE AND MAIL*, SEPTEMBER 29, 1989)

Until we understand the long tradition of ideas from which the animosity of all antifamily activists springs, we cannot hope to defeat their efforts, whether in Canada or in any other country. To illuminate this sad tradition is the purpose of this chapter. It is a tradition born in violence and bathed in blood.

Consider this: we have recently witnessed the most significant event in modern history, which is the utter, irreversible, practical defeat of socialism around the world. The sight on television of crazed but happy citizens tearing and scratching at the Berlin Wall; the vision of physically and spiritually impoverished hordes streaming over European borders, desperately begging for clothing and crumbs of bread, many shot in the back by their own police; the anguished daily pleas for help from millions still crushed under the boot-heel of collectivism — these are all vivid demonstrations that socialism doesn't work, except, as someone has said, in Heaven where you don't need it, and in Hell where you already have it!

Yet despite this chilling evidence of the failure of a so-called political rationalism meant to replace the family with government services, we continue to produce and to harbour legions of faithful collectivists, many of them stridently antifamily, who bow and scrape ceaselessly before utopian ideals. That's why I used the phrase "practical defeat." For in theoretical terms, socialists the world over don't give up. They continue to exhibit a near patholog-ical preference for what Irving Babbitt called "dreamland." They fulminate as ever against the natural, spontaneous freedoms of men and women, the noblest expression of which is the family, and they seek ever more coercive means to arrange the conformity of others to their secret dreams. They are humanitarians of the whip, bent on driving a human galley of suffering souls toward that perfect harbour which shimmers in the distance like a mirage. But like all mirages, the harbour vanishes. So they change course, and push more feverishly toward a new mirage.

Few have described the process of democratic pacification that precedes the rise of this collectivism in free societies better than Alexis de Tocqueville. In his 1840 essay "Despotism in Democratic Nations," he wrote:

> After having thus successfully taken each member of the community in its powerful grasp and fashioned him at will, the supreme power then extends its arm over the whole community. It covers the surface of society with a network of small complicated rules, minute and uniform, through which the most original minds and the most energetic charac-ters cannot penetrate, to rise above the crowd. The will of man is not shattered, but softened, bent, and guided; men are seldom forced by it to act, but they are constantly restrained from acting. Such a power does not destroy, but it prevents existence; it does not tyrannize, but it compresses, enervates, extinguishes, and stupefies a people, till each nation is reduced to nothing better than a flock of timid and industrious animals, of which the government is the shepherd.[1]

The heart of this dynamic is absolutism. All collectivists have an absolute conviction that their social vision — the end, or goal, in mind: the perfect society — is correct and desirable for all. That is why it is proper to style them intellectual and moral terrorists. Their beliefs remain in force until their perfect vision crumbles from the brutality of the means used, engendering uprisings, revolutions, or fleeing. You could say theirs is a dynamic in which the cruel means eventually erodes, or consumes, the utopian ends. Thus must we heed the warning issued to all collectivists, whether conservative or liberal, by the marvellously sane British philosopher Michael Oakeshott: "the conjunction of dreaming and ruling generates tyranny."[2]

## Understanding the System: Simplicity, Unity, Interlock

What the citizens of free countries need desperately to understand is that from our earliest history, all collectivists have been dead set against the natural family; that their utopian thinking, even in its mildest forms, is utterly dangerous to the families and especially to the children of a free society. It is also crucial to see that what the collectivists propose is not simply a collection of random assumptions, but rather an *interlocked series of antifamily utopian ideas* that has its own systematic structure and erodes every important Western value. The family as the symbol of these values is the first target. The collectivists' ideas, in short, form a belief system as strong as that of any religious fundamentalist. Those of us who want to rehabilitate the natural family will never be able to do so until we understand the entire system of interlocking ideas from which the enemies of the family draw their strength.

For it is ideological simplicity that appeals as an explanatory model for a universe otherwise perplexing, and sometimes painful. From this simplicity springs the gratitude and relief of all worshippers of idea systems: the system spares the believer the pain of reconciling conflicting values and ideas — some of them forever irreconcilable. Religious fundamentalists succumb to the false comfort of this same dynamic. Such belief systems inevitably become an extension of the believer's consciousness, a kind of personal Strategic Defence Initiative that shoots down any invading ideas or beliefs before they upset internal equilibrium. It is an error to believe that such people can be dissuaded by the facts. To use facts against them — such as when we say that socialism has failed — only hardens their determination. The facts are the devil that must be conquered with the creed, and if the devil wins a round the effort must be redoubled. The only way to persuade such people, who are motivated not by factual evidence but by high principles, is to show them you are arguing from even higher principles. Then they may capitulate, because they feel safe in switching to a new belief system. That's why some of the very strongest conservative debaters are former socialists.

Let us now look at what utopian collectivists, from Plato through Rousseau to modern radicals, want to do to the family: how they propose to achieve their goals, and why, if unresisted, they may well ruin our society. Ponder the shocking vision planned for us.

# THE UTOPIAN COLLECTIVISTS: THE THEORETICAL ATTACK

### The Greeks Were at It

The most radically influential collectivist (and antifamily feminist) in Western history was the Greek philosopher Plato (427-347 B.C.). He was presented to me in university as a teacher of high morals and pre-Christian humanitarian sentiments, who argued strongly for the repression of selfishness in the interests of social harmony. Well, that sounded great. What do young students know, anyway? But many years later I began to see that Plato was quite the opposite.[3] In fact, virtually every key idea of modern totalitarianism can be found somewhere in Plato's work. In his *Republic* (c. 375 B.C.) he outlined his ideas both on the perfect State and on the family.[4] Here is what he believed.

For Plato, reality exists only in a transcendent world of ideas, or "universal forms," of which everything we experience in the real world is but a degraded instance. As an example, the only reason you are able to say that all the different cars in the street, none of which you have seen before, are indeed cars is because you have a universal, or general, idea of what a car is. That universal idea of the ideal car is, to Plato, the real car. All the actual, physical cars are merely imperfect examples of the ideal one. Since actual cars are all different, how could they otherwise be called the same, except in relation to the ideal car? There's no space here to examine fully this concept, but his is an interesting theory on how we know what we know, and it provides a clue to the way Plato's mind worked.

The essential notion is that for Plato the *actual* world is always subordinated to the *ideal* world that governs it — what Babbitt called "dreamland." Plato insisted on this hierarchical order of reality because he was horrified by the ideas of philosophers such as Heraclitus, who believed that change is the only constant. You cannot, as Heraclitus put it, step in the same stream twice. All is flux. So to defend against this menace of spontaneous change, Plato "derived his . . . fantastic philosophical doctrine that the changing visible world is only a decaying copy of an unchanging invisible world."[5] We will see that this structure of ideas favouring the ideal over the real is the intellectual template for all future utopian thinkers; hence, the rigidness and militarization of life that their ideas and policies always bring about. (Nations that adopt utopian collectivist policies are, for good reason, called "police States.") The ideal of an unchanging society is worshipped because such a world would supposedly spare human beings the pain of constantly assessing, choosing, and defending their values. It proposes to impose fixed, unchanging values, from which no deviation would be tolerated (or necessary). In essence, the Platonic world would do away with the need for individual moral agency — the foundation of our Judeo-Christian society.

This is the place to repeat, as simply as possible, that it was especially Plato who introduced rationalism to Western life because he taught that what makes man distinct from all other life forms is his detached, philosophical use of reason. Thus was Greek thought distinguished from the Hebrew, or Judeo-Christian, variety. The latter declared the soul, rather than reason, to be the centre of man, and saw the moral struggle between good and evil, not the struggle of reason to comprehend or master material reality, to be man's definitive quest. The Greek tradition, we could say, favoured the theoretical world, and the Judeo-Christian tradition the real, lived world. Greek thought has always appealed to abstract intellectuals. Judeo-Christian thought has appealed to real-world moralists and people who cling to a belief that the spiritual nature of man is not fully accessible to the analyses of human reason. The idealists got packaged away in the universities, where many of them live in "Greek" fraternity and sorority houses. The realists stuck to the living world.

This breakdown perhaps helps to explain why most intellectuals say they are secular humanists or atheists, while most ordinary people say they believe in God (82 percent of Canadians and 90 percent of Americans). The present split in Western nations, between educated levellers/elites and the masses, is really an extension of the ancient Greek vs. Judeo-Christian struggle for dominance in controlling the political, economic, and moral truth about reality. It is a split that is causing a civil war of values in our society. Again, where the Greek model saw reason as the centre of our being, the Judeo-Christian model saw the soul, and personal moral agency, as the nucleus. That is why ideas which attack our tradition of moral agency necessarily attack our society. Whether it be former Prime Minister Lester Pearson's (then Pierre Trudeau's) socialized medical system that removes personal health responsibility, or Trudeau's welfare state that destroys incentives, or Prime Minister Brian Mulroney's (temporarily halted) universal daycare dream, or the various "social charters" proposed everywhere in reaction to the growing dissolution of social bonds — all undermine moral agency. Moral agency is based on the idea of deriving a polity, or society, as the sum of the exercise of each individual's freedom and responsibility within limited rules equal for all, and the Greek/Platonic model of the polity is the opposite: it is based on *subordinating all individual freedoms to a single, rationalized ideal of the State* (just like each different actual car is subordinated to the one ideal car).

So Plato developed a model for the operation of the ideal State, the one in his mind, to arrest the inevitable change he felt would occur naturally through the "law of degeneration," which causes the cyclical fall of civilizations. Not a bad objective, if you don't have to destroy human freedom and moral agency to achieve it. Here are the basics of his model.

First, the subordination of all individual wills to the common will of the State, thus achieving social "harmony." To guarantee this condition, the State must *abolish private property and the family*, both of which, Plato argued, breed envy and differences between citizens. Next, all women must be forced to lead the same life as men, including mandatory battle duty.

Plato wanted to forbid marriage, to forbid childrearing by parents, and to allow the men to share all women in common. Finally, he wanted to police this whole scheme with a special class of citizens called "Guardians," to be selected by the philosopher kings of the State, and to impose a selective breeding operation on the people, allowing only the superior citizens to breed in special "mating festivals." All the children were to be raised in State nurseries and taught to respect their leaders. Plato argued that this eugenic program would get rid of the distracting loyalties, affections, and interests of the natural family system and recruit everyone for community service. For "it would be a sin either for mating or for anything else in a truly happy society to take place without regulation."[6] And what would society do with offspring? "Officers will take the children of the better Guardians to a nursery and put them in charge of nurses living in a separate part of the city [daycare — see Chapter Twelve]: the children of the inferior Guardians, and any

THE ANTIFAMILY TRADITION 103

defective offspring of the others, will be quietly and secretly disposed of [euthanasia — see Chapter Sixteen]."[7]

Well, this is not pretty stuff. And the plain fact to be drawn from it is that Plato was "the first to proffer a biological and racial theory of social dynamics, of political history."[8] History, for him, was nothing but the record of the breakdown of society according to his law of degeneration, and he would use any means to prevent such decay by *forcing* all citizens to live under his regime. Read what follows, and ask yourself why we hear modern professors applauding his philosophy instead of denouncing it:

> The greatest principle of all is that nobody, whether male or female, should ever be without a leader . . . he should get up, or move, or wash, or take his meals . . . only if he has been told to do so . . . he should teach his soul, by long habit, never to dream of acting independently, and to become utterly incapable of it . . . in this way the life of all will be spent in total community.[9]

There are many more examples like this. What stuns, however, is the realization that this man's thinking has been held up to generations of students as admirable. Ask people to volunteer their opinion of Plato's reputation, and I venture they all will say more or less what I used to say: "a moral philosopher of high repute, central to our tradition." Yet this is not completely true; he was also a maniacal planner of the top-down State. We are forced to conclude that his high reputation was and continues to be foisted upon generations of students by academics of the knowledge class who actually *approve* of his model! The philosopher Karl Popper mentions some of the more famous early scholars, who, although recognizing that Plato's work "is the most savage and profound attack upon liberal ideas which history can show,"[10] nevertheless believe it was good because he had good intentions: the creation of a "happy" State (something also desired by Hitler, Mussolini, Stalin, and Mao Tse-tung). In fact, many modern academics, including such sensitive critics of totalitarianism as Robert Nisbet, continue to hold out the hope of a "totalitarianism of virtue."[11] President Franklin Roosevelt in the United States and Prime Minister Trudeau in Canada proposed mild versions of the same ideal. But as Popper writes, "Plato's political program, far from being superior to totalitarianism, is fundamentally identical with it."[12] The fact is, Plato's thought formed a unified structure of collectivist ideas. Had he never written about the family, his prescriptions still would have been precisely deducible. Any defence of the family as a nonconforming institution would have eroded his logic in the balance of the *Republic*.

The shocker, however, is that Plato's views are diametrically opposed to those on which our own Western society is based. Plato was an enemy of individual human freedom as we know it. He constantly campaigned for a higher freedom — one dictated by the State — under which individuals would be "free" from the torments of social change and conflicting inherited authorities (but controlled by his unitary State). We soon shall see how all the modern ideas of the New Left and the radical feminists have their origin in Plato (with the proviso that he was smarter).

In a crucial essay, Popper explains how Plato suffered from the Individualism Illusion, and the Communalism Illusion. Basically he equated individualism with egoism, or selfishness, and thus set up a false opposition to further his argument. Because he despised individualism in all its forms, Plato also confused community with communalism (distinguished from each other in Chapter Two). In effect, he was forced by the nature of his ideology to detest true individualism, free choice, and moral agency and to favour communalism and the police State. But we have seen that individualism, rightly understood, is the foundation of any free society. It leads not to communalism, which is coercive, but to free community, which is inherently other-directed.

> This individualism, united with altruism, has become the basis of our Western civilization. It is the central doctrine of Christianity ('love your neighbour,' say the Scriptures, not 'love your tribe'); and it is the core of all the ethical doctrines which have grown from our civilization and stimulated it . . . there is no other thought which has been so powerful in the moral development of man.[13]

Plato was right, says Popper, "when he saw in this [essentially Judeo-Christian doctrine] the enemy of his caste state; and he hated it more than any other of the 'subversive' doctrines of his time." He insisted that everything possible be done "to eradicate from our life everywhere and in every way *all that is private and individual*."[14]

And to what kind of moral life does this lead? Straight to despotic leaders and a populace of moral imbeciles; to Tocqueville's timid sheep. Plato recognized, as have all collectivists since,

> only one ultimate standard, the interest of the state. Everything that furthers it is good and virtuous and just; everything that threatens it

is bad and wicked and unjust. Actions that serve it are moral; actions that endanger it, immoral. In other words, Plato's moral code is . . . collectivist or political utilitarianism. *The criterion of morality is the interest of the state*. Morality is nothing but political hygiene.[15]

It doesn't take much imagination to see a model here for the contemporary welfare State, such as we now endure (though not yet as thoroughly as Plato wished). Thus, it is helpful to keep Plato's ideas in mind in all that follows, for we shall see that history really does seem to be a record not of social decay caused by class strife, as Plato and Marx thought, but of decay caused by the war between proponents of the top-down State and the bottom-up society; between collectivism and freedom, in whatever garb.

To appreciate the uncanny persistence of Plato's ideas in modern totalitarian states some 2400 years later, it is sufficient to read Article Six of the Soviet Constitution:

> The Communist party, armed with Marxism-Leninism, determines the general perspectives of the development of society and the course of the home and foreign policy of the USSR, directs the great constructive work of the Soviet people and imparts a planned, systematic and theoretically substantiated character to their struggle for the victory of communism.

In short, all life shall be subordinated to the "theoretically substantiated" purposes of the State.

How, after all, does this credo differ, except in degree, from words in Canada's own Charter of Rights and Freedoms, sections 1, 6.4, 15.2, and 36.1? All these sections give the government of Canada the right to engineer the outcomes of society according to its public philosophy, even if doing so breaks the ordinary laws of the land applicable to all (except the government).

## The Later Utopians Were at It, Too

*The yearning for perfection that makes reality seem irredeemably flawed creates so large a discrepancy between the ideal and the reality that nothing less will suffice than a total transformation of reality — of society, the polity, the economy, above all, of human nature.*

GERTRUDE HIMMELFARB, *MARRIAGE AND MORALS AMONG THE VICTORIANS*, 1975

In addition to the common structure of their thought, as outlined above, the most obvious thread uniting all utopian collectivists, past and present, is their hatred of the natural family. They all recognize instinctively that blood loyalty and the instinctive natural love of children is the biggest obstacle to their political program. So they all plan, one way or another, to rid the world of the family. That's why the family is today the unlikely theatre for our current civil war of values. This is not a war of money, or property, or classes, as utopians are fond of suggesting. Those things are just outward expressions of any spontaneous social order. The real war, rather, is between those who are satisfied with that order because they see it as free and natural, and those who wish forcibly to change it from the top down; it is a war between the intellectual terrorists, and the living masses who have no designs on the lives or property of others. The intellectual terrorists constantly strive to seize the levers of political power, the media, and the education system ("political correctness" in the universities is their most recent hobby-horse), in order to impose their rigid views. Those who desire a spontaneous natural order and the individual freedom that arises from it meanwhile strive to establish rules of just conduct, precisely to protect themselves from such arbitrary power. These are the two camps into which the world has always been divided; this is the struggle still being waged all over the world today, regardless of the labels.

Let us examine briefly some of the more influential utopians in our tradition, until recently all of them men and most with deplorably irresponsible family situations — or childless.

First, the Swiss-Frenchman Jean-Jacques Rousseau (1712-78). Here was a man who forced his mistress (whom he kept for 33 years, refused to marry, and did not love) to give up their five children to an orphanage at birth. (It is certain they all died there.) Yet he postured as a man of deep feeling, and his writings sparked the whole Romantic movement by arguing that because the natural goodness of man is always corrupted by society, feeling and sentiment are the most important reality. In his recent book *Intellectuals*, the British historian Paul Johnson reveals the essence of his belief system. Briefly, it was a movement that flew in the face of moral hierarchy — in fact, of any established morality, religious or otherwise — on the grounds that man is naturally good and, if left alone, would be moral. The hippie movement of the 1960s was a modern resurgence of the same belief. Paradoxically, in Rousseau it led to a vicious theory of the State, which has had terrible repercussions for Canada (and most other developed nations). As I shall soon illustrate, there are unnerving parallels between the thinking of Plato and Rousseau, and the derivative ideas of our own former prime minister, Pierre Trudeau, and the current Ontario premier, Bob Rae.

Rousseau's contempt for family, property, the wealthy, indeed for all the spontaneous forces of authority in natural society, was so strong that he wanted to replace them with an *enforced egalitarianism*, after which further revolutionary disorder would not be permitted. Readers will not miss the irony in the logic of such intellectual despots, who argue for the removal of all forms of traditional authority and then constitute themselves and their theory as the single authority and tradition. When Rousseau heartlessly gave up his own children, he persuaded himself of the rightness of this despicable act by saying, "I thought I was performing the act of a citizen and a father *and I looked on myself as a member of Plato's Republic.*"[16] This new State was to embody what he called "the General Will" (la volonté générale), a phrase used often by Pierre Trudeau, both in his early book *Federalism and the French Canadians* and in his recent writings on our Constitution.[17] However, although Rousseau (like Trudeau) "saw the General Will in terms of liberty, *it is essentially an authoritarian instrument . . .*"[18] Here's why.

Rousseau assumed that through a process of democratic-centralism, the General Will would always express the will of the people. Unfortunately, it never works out that way. Typical of the top-down process described in Chapter One, the interpretation of the General Will *is always left to the leaders*, who believe that the General Will invariably favours the decision most conducive to the public interest. In short, it's a circular argument in favour of elite power. That's why Pierre Trudeau, like his mentors Plato and Rousseau, assumed that the way to make us free was to give us more and better government. Under his rule, Canada experienced "perhaps the most furtive expansion of central agencies the world has yet experienced," one that brought little Canada twice the per capita number of advisers used in the United States and five times the number in the United Kingdom.[19] In 1984, his government's last year, Trudeau's federal deficit was fully 54 percent of federal revenues — all to bring us more government programs!

Trudeau was an outright proponent of a French style of top-down government, derived from Rousseau and others, that is alien to the English style of bottom-up freedom and resistance to government. Just to give you the flavour of how demented this top-down illusion can become, here is what Rousseau wrote when asked to create a model constitution for the new nation of Corsica. Read, and shiver, for his was a political philosophy that demanded total submission to the State. He saw man as divided, and only the State could make him whole: "You must, therefore, treat citizens as children and control their upbringing and thoughts, planting the social law in the bottom of their hearts." Each Corsican citizen, he proposed, would take this pledge: "I join myself, body, goods, will and all my powers, to the Corsican nation, granting her ownership of me, of myself and all who depend on me." As Johnson points out, this is a recipe for fascism, whether of the Pol Pot variety or otherwise. Rousseau knew that "those who control a people's opinions control its actions." Johnson writes that this was an early rendition of Mussolini's doctrine: "Everything within the State, nothing outside the State, nothing against the State" (and, I might add, of Hitler's most famous slogan: "One People, One State, One Leader"). Thus the educational process, Johnson says, "was the key to the success of the cultural engineering needed to make the State acceptable and successful; the axis of Rousseau's ideas was the citizen as child and the State as parent." (We'll get to education in Part Two.) All forms of elitism thrive on this distinction. In essence, Rousseau wished to eliminate the natural biological family and absorb all families into a single social State "family." For him, virtue was the product not of individual moral struggle, but of good government. His hierarchy of values, like that of Plato, was based not on morals but on power. Thus was created a philosophy designed to legitimize top-down coercion and utterly opposed to the idea of moral agency and the free, bottom-up society bound only by common rules to which it naturally leads.

In conclusion, Johnson writes that Rousseau, through his influence on Hegel and Marx, "set in motion the great stream of ideas which produced the ruthless regimes of the twentieth century . . . since they all practiced the social and cultural engineering of which he was the ideologist."[20]

## The Burden of Morality
In a useful little book called *Utopia Against the Family*, Bryce Christensen quotes a telling line from T.S. Eliot's poetry that strikes at the heart of the utopian motive; to wit, we are "dreaming of systems so perfect that no one will need to be good."[21] This surely, in one powerful line, describes the lure of utopia. It gains its power from the promise that we will at last be able to escape from moral struggle, to escape the agony of choosing between good and evil. In

short, if we wish to escape the pain of our humanity, we have but to do the bidding of the State.

Christensen provides an analysis of a number of utopians after Rousseau who continue the antifamily tradition. Some of the more notable — all are just footnotes to Plato, really — were Edward Bellamy, William Morris, H.G. Wells, and B.F. Skinner.

Bellamy's 1888 book, *Looking Backward: 2000-1887*, urged the breaking of family economic interdependence, to be replaced by a new dependence on the State in which "the account of every person, man, woman, and child . . . is always with the nation directly."[22] Well, this plan resembles the economic "autonomy" idea Sweden has adopted today as official policy and is echoed in frequent recommendations in many Western nations for a guaranteed minimum income plan for all citizens. Hopeful they are, these people, who never stop to ask how the State, which cannot even manage its own fiscal affairs, could possibly manage the people's better; or what would happen to their economic program if the State founders (top-down States, as we have seen, inevitably do) or misinvests their life's earnings? And they never stop to recall that happiness really only comes from what Charles Murray aptly termed a "justified satisfaction" with one's existence, the basic condition for which is having earned one's own way in life.

Morris, Wells, and Skinner, following Bellamy, wished variously to end the "tyranny of the family," or recommended mutual free love, or, again, the end of familial economic interdependence. In Skinner's *Walden Two*, marriage is only by permission of a State "Manager of Marriages" (some sociologists in Canada and the United States are today proposing "parental licences"); children are to be raised by the State and the natural family is to be abolished, having lost all its traditional functions. In short, the State is to become the new *paterfamilias*.

As Christensen shows, there are also many who have warned against such scary utopias, notably Aldous Huxley in *Brave New World* and George Orwell in *1984*. They have not been heeded. Instead, we have witnessed a progressive dissolution of the natural family and the increasing transfer of its functions to the State (the next two chapters will show this in detail), all accelerated by lobby groups that push for no-fault divorce laws (Canada's divorce law was eased in 1968); by a blurring of the distinction between legitimate and illegitimate births (illegitimate parents is a more appropriate term); by the ongoing push for warehousing of children in national daycare facilities; by the eliminating of all traditional and legal

definitions and privileges of the family, even to including homosexuals as "married couples"; and by the bald facts that our tax
system penalizes married intact families, and our welfare system
rewards individuals and couples for not marrying (see Chapter
Eighteen).

More of these hare-brained utopian schemes are incisively
described in Gertrude Himmelfarb's engaging book *Marriage and
Morals Among the Victorians*,[23] this time as developed by two
notable English utopianists, Jeremy Bentham and William Godwin.
They are introduced here because the crucial difference between
the English and French styles, outlined both in Chapter One and in
*The Trouble with Canada*, was never meant to suggest that the
collectivists thrived only in French countries. Unfortunately, they
are everywhere. But for a lot of historical, religious, and cultural
reasons, the French embraced such ideas wholeheartedly — and
entrenched them in successive constitutions — whereas the English
just as wholeheartedly rejected them, as they have been doing for
the last millennium (until very recently). The English utopians who
agreed with their French counterparts found that this approach
merely earned them the status of eccentrics, rather than a job with
the government.

Bentham, the father of "utilitarianism," published a series of
essays in 1789 in which he proposed pauper houses for the poor,
and then for other classes of people as well. Soon called "industry
houses," these were to harbour all manner of people — at one time
up to one-tenth of the population of England![24] Bentham thought
them *so superior to a family environment* (where "every man is for
the first 16 or 18 years of his life a slave"), and the family itself such
an "absolute monarchy," that he imagined even those of the upper
classes would be eager to enrol their children as apprentices. The
man was a nut-case. His enumerated list of the comforts of these
houses reads like an early version of the U.N. Charter of Human
Rights: (1) extraordinary security in respect to health (better than
a private family); (2) long life; (3) security against want; (4) consciousness of security against want; (5) constant cleanliness and
tidiness; (6) employment favourable to health and recreation; and
so on. He even proposed that residents of these houses *would
eventually cease to feel want itself*.

There is a reason for this recurring theme of appetitive anesthesia
so often found in utopian writing. Much of human life, after all, is
swayed by appetite and emotion, and so it is inevitable for utopians,
who prefer control and stasis over spontaneity and change, reason

over emotion, and the ideal over the real, to imagine human beings in some perfect state, free from the living anguish of choice. Their solution is a commune of the living dead. Himmelfarb rightly remarks that "it is surprising," in view of the austere, rigorous, and oppressive regimen Bentham proposed, "to find so many reputable scholars taking so benign a view of him . . . "[25] Surprising? Not really. Most academics harbour the same utopian intellectual dreams, deeply rooted in ascetic monasticism.

William Godwin, another famous but equally delirious dreamer, "was perhaps the most ambitious utopian of all."[26] The basic premise of his writings was the perfectibility of mankind (the Rationalism Illusion again), expressed in his *Political Justice* (1793), a work, Himmelfarb reminds us, unimaginable without the French Enlightenment and Revolution. Unimaginable without Plato, too, I would add. Godwin planned a society without need of sexual passion (there's the anesthesia theme again), marriage, or contracts of any kind to restrict the development of rational, virtuous, free, and equal citizens. There would be no prejudice, no self-love, or self-interest, or competition, or acquisitiveness; or coercion or cooperation. More of the living dead. Notably, he argued that "*without family to divert them from their higher obligations*," all would be "at liberty to devote themselves to humanity at large."[27]

The result of this devotion to an abstract principle called "humanity" was a disaster in Godwin's personal life, for he became embroiled in a long series of marital, sexual, and incestuous complications almost impossible to untangle, involving himself, his daughter Mary, the poet Shelley, and many others. All of this was taken at the time to be a predictable consequence of his libertarianism as it rapidly transformed itself into libertinism — a natural end. Himmelfarb neatly puts her finger on the root of all such utopian thinking when she observes that "the desire to transcend the human condition is, in most religious traditions, an invitation to heresy. In politics, it is an invitation to tyranny, as we seek a perfection that inevitably eludes us and as we redouble our efforts to attain the unattainable."[28]

A soft-spoken truth, if there ever was one.

## THE ENVY EXPERTS: THE MARXIST DESTROYERS OF THE FAMILY

We should turn now to the most tyrannous manifestation of utopian thought the world has ever seen, as expressed in the antifamily

Marxism of Friedrich Engels. Marxism has been particularly dangerous for humanity because it links utopianism with an economic
conspiracy theory based on envy and resentment. In addition to its
damage to families, the coercive humanitarianism inherent in it led,
and is still leading, to unprecedented death and destruction in the
20th century, now totalling in the area of 70 to 100 million people,
almost all classifiable as the "internal enemy." These needless
deaths have not been caused by any war between nation states, but
by the calculated acts of tyrannical governments against their own
people! To get a sobering — correction, sickening — feel for the
tragedy wrought by utopian regimes of our own time, try Paul
Johnson's book *Modern Times*, a magisterial study of modern tyranny that will make any decent person detest collectivists forever.[29]

Neither Marx nor Engels was a scholar. Both were outright revolutionaries and polemicists, more interested in promoting their
ideas and overthrowing the social order than discovering the truth.
The work of both is full of well-documented errors, distortions,
deliberate untruths, and a constant and systematic misuse of
sources. Together, they compiled one of the most thoroughgoing
attacks ever attempted on human freedom, private property, and
the family.[30]

Marx was strongly influenced by Hegel, who was in turn influenced by Plato, and Marx's theories were extended and annotated
extensively by his friend Engels. The theory basically declared that
man's ancient past was idyllic; that society evolves according to
certain historical laws, from tribal communalism, to feudalism, to
capitalism, to socialism, and at the end will arrive at communalism
again, with the withering away of all classes and of the State itself.
Marx thought this wonderful utopian future would come about
through a revolution of the workers against their capitalist oppressors. His whole theory was based on the idea that the mode of
material production dictated social relations. (A simple formula for
his notion is "tell me what you have, and I'll tell you what you
think.") Owners of capital, as he saw it, got their profits by exploiting
workers, who would eventually rise up against them as fewer and
fewer got richer and richer, and the standard of living of workers
fell. Little did he know that capital and labour are wholly interdependent. Mired in his false view of how economics work, he could not
foresee that there would indeed be a revolution of the workers: not
against the capitalists and the free society, but against their Marxist
oppressors, because they couldn't provide the workers with enough

shoes, houses, bread, and the other plentiful goods of democratic capitalism. Even the well-off in the former USSR waited three years to buy a car, while in the West millions of labourers drive to work every day. Marxism, in short, has been an abysmal flop in theory, and unspeakably cruel in practice. Yet even after the liberation of Eastern Europe and the USSR, upward of 1.3 billion people, one-quarter of the earth's population, are still forced to exist under Marxist regimes, with little hope of escaping. (Tiananmen Square was a demonstration of this fact.)

One of the most successful methods Marxists use to enforce their tyranny is the destruction of the natural family, which they universally characterize as a tyrannous institution based on private property and — correctly — the main origin of individualism. In their 1848 *Manifesto*, Marx and Engels wrote that "the bourgeois family will vanish as a matter of course when its complement [private property] vanishes, and both will vanish with the vanishing of capitalism." (Instead, Marx vanished!)

What follows are a few selections from Engels' book *The Origin of the Family, Private Property, and the State* (1884), illustrating his hatred of the family. His ideas, one feminist writer tells us approvingly, were codified into "a blueprint for the emancipation of women . . . [and] exported not merely to the various countries that make up the Soviet socialist bloc, but to many third-world countries that have espoused Marxist or other socialist views."[31] Canada is one of those to espouse "other" socialist views, as we shall see. It is no accident that Judy Rebick, president of the publicly financed National Action Committee on the Status of Women (NAC) in Ottawa, is a confessed former Marxist (*Globe and Mail*, July 4, 1990).

Engels based his analysis on a belief, now discredited even by honest feminists, that human societies evolved from an ancient stage, in which they were controlled by women (the "mother right"), to the present, where they are controlled by men ("patriarchy"). Engels' reasoning was that as society passed from a hunter/gatherer stage to an agricultural, animal-husbandry stage, the men gradually took over the production of the livestock wealth. (Women could pick berries with the best, but the bulls frightened them. They frighten me, too.) Then, because men wanted to ensure their children inherited their property, they simply "decreed" that wealth should pass down through the men rather than the women. The institution that evolved and made this possible, he felt, was the patriarchal private family, which in fact once did hold near total power over women and children. (But then, many past political institutions, officers, princes, lords, courts, sheriffs, inquisitions, etc., held absolute power over everyone, regardless of gender.) Private property was the underlying evil, he argued, and so the way to eradicate the oppressive institution of the family was to outlaw private property, to get women into the labour market, and to turn the kids over to the state. Sound familiar? Here he is at his ranting and raving best: "The overthrow of mother right was the *world historical defeat of the female sex*. The man took command in the home also; the woman was degraded and reduced to servitude; she became the slave of his lust and a mere instrument for the production of children."[32]

Any self-respecting woman who reads this will likely find herself annoyed at Engels' patronizing attitude, for he assumes that men and women who marry are unconscious dupes, devoid of intimate and caring relationships; that women have no control over their domain or their sexual love, nor any natural desire for children; and that only men feel lust. Yet his words are fodder for the unthinking masses of head-nodding radical feminists who lack the courage to resist his — dare I say — male views. Sensible, confident women know better. As for the family unit? "The modern individual family is founded on the open or concealed domestic slavery of the wife, and modern society is a mass composed of these individual families as its molecules."[33]

Here again he has very little respect for the free intelligence of either men or women. Most women, in poll after poll the world over, continue to prefer family to work and express high satisfaction with traditional family life (see Chapter Eleven). But even then, if we argue that women are slaves of work in the home, we must surely argue that men are slaves of work outside it, subordinated to bosses all their lives, never truly free of the wishes of their superiors, condemned to a life of hard labour and the lust for children of their demanding wives. The truth is that very few men — or women — love their jobs. But most of us have the self-respect to consider our choices carefully, and simply don't believe we are automatons, or unwitting slaves of someone else, male or female. If you lack a lot of confidence, however, or feel a lot of free-floating hostility, Engels is the man to read. His answer to this "problem" is not too far from Plato's. In fact, he is close to plagiarism when he writes that ". . . the first condition for the liberation of the wife is to bring the whole female sex back into public industry, and that this in turn demands that the characteristic of *the monogamous family as the economic unit of society be abolished.*"[34]

So there you have it. His solution is that instead of being a slave of your own spouse and children you get to be a slave of the nearest State-owned company, or a slave of the government (as for most in Sweden, and for all in totalitarian nations). After the transfer of the means of production into common ownership (meaning after the State confiscates or taxes away all that you have), "the single family ceases to be the economic unit of society. Private housekeeping is transformed into a social industry. The care and education of the children becomes a public affair; society looks after all the children alike, whether they are legitimate or not."[35]

By now you can see this amounts to the same 2400-year-old story. He wants central economic planning, even though it's always been a lamentable failure. (If men and women are forbidden to produce for their families, they're certainly not going to produce for the State that takes their families away. As the enslaved Soviets said, "They pretend to pay us, and we pretend to work.") Note the way Engels writes "ceases to be," when he means at the nudging of a KGB-type rifle. And he talks of private housekeeping being "transformed" into "social industry." Are we to imagine a State fleet of Molly Maids (and butlers) roaring around the nation, cleaning and scrubbing our houses, fixing the drywall, clearing the snow, painting the garage, doing the dishes while the cheerful spouses bounce off to the National Widget factory and junior is coddled by State daycare workers who lose sleep over him at night? Give me a break, as they say. As for the "public education" he recommends? It's a national disgrace. Canada has a 30 percent high-school dropout rate, even though we spend more on education per student than any other country in the Organization for Economic Cooperation and Development (see Chapter Seven). Meanwhile, the nation's private schools, which are booming, graduate about 95 percent of their students and send most to universities of their choice!

Unfortunately, Marxist thinking has made a great deal of headway in our society, despite its fuzzy, angry, antifreedom agenda. Following are a few of the major points of the *Manifesto* as outlined by Marx and Engels in 1848, with a peek at where we stand today.

| The Communist Manifesto Insisted on: | Comments: |
|---|---|
| 1. The abolition of private property | The right to private property is not protected in Canada's Charter of Rights and Freedoms. It was excluded at the insistence of the NDP, Canada's socialist party. |
| 2. The abolition of the family | The social welfare State has this constant aim. |
| 3. A heavy progressive income tax | Canada's tax is very progressive and very high (the average Canadian family gives up 50% of income in taxes of all kinds; it was 32% in 1960). |
| 4. Free education for all children in public schools | The government has a monopoly. Those who want better must pay twice. Citizens have no choice. |

## WOMEN AGAINST THE FAMILY

The single most important point here is that modern radical feminism is a continuation of the utopian tradition established by Plato, combined both with Rousseau's belief that natural human goodness is corrupted by society, and with the male-hating theory of economic exploitation derived from Marx and Engels. The radical feminists' stock in trade is to lobby for radical changes in our legal, economic, and social/moral systems in order to implement an agenda designed to overturn every aspect of traditional life and substitute for it a communal, egalitarian society. This explains why so many of them are either outright or closet Marxists who hate democratic capitalism. If the people resist, they are quite prepared to rewrite the laws and customs of the people. That's why I say that inside every radical feminist is a little officer of the police State.

Such radicals rely upon coercive humanitarianism and the Rationalism Illusion of social progress, coupled with a theory of female exploitation by a male society. For them, everything culminates in the Determinist Illusion. Only they are the enlightened few to have escaped social conditioning; the rest of us are "socialized" to think the way we do and need "education" to make us think like them. Their movement is a revolutionary project to undo traditional society, and it is every bit as aggressive and dangerous to human freedom as any in the history of civilization. It is Platonism in drag. Here's just a taste of what I mean. (More to come in Chapter Eleven.)

From Simone de Beauvoir, author of *The Second Sex* (1952) — sold as "the Classic Manifesto of the Liberated Woman" — one of the books that initiated the modern feminist antimale movement: "No woman should be authorized to stay home to raise her children. Society should be totally different. *Women should not have that choice*, precisely because if there is such a choice, too many women will make that one . . ."[36]

There you have it. Like all socialists, she argues for freedom for women, but complains that if they don't use their freedom the way she thinks they should, the choice will be removed! Because these social engineers know that so much of what women and men do is perfectly voluntary, characteristically different, and typically biologically based, they want control over society so they can prevent any free expression of such natural differences. They want a forced substitution of politics for biology. In radical feminism we see the strident vanguard of a brigade fighting a civil war of values against Western civilization. It's Plato without a beard vs. the free society. De Beauvoir, a sometimes subtle and bright writer, imagines a perfect police society in which women are "authorized" by a central authority comprised of social engineers and therapists who think they know best how millions of others ought to live. That's "what the Soviet Union promised," she said longingly. Little did she know![37] Like her masters, she was a totalitarian thinker who wanted marriage to be a simple free agreement, breakable at will; children would be raised by the State, all pregnancy would be voluntary, everything to be paid for by the State, and so on. In short, she wanted a revolution: forced social change to suit the little plan in her head.

This urge was easily matched by Canadian Louise Dulude, a far less illustrious intellect and the former president of NAC, who in 1987 said: "You see, we want a whole transformation of society in the most revolutionary way . . ." Feminist Gloria Steinem said, "we're talking about a revolution, not just reform. It's the deepest possible change there is."[38] And Shulamith Firestone, in a flight of fancy that unexpectedly extended her vocabulary beyond her customary four-letter words, said: "If there were another word more all-embracing than *revolution*, I would use it."[39]

Now if you want a revolution, you have to force people to do things your way. That's why de Beauvoir and company say that *women should not have choice in the outcomes of their lives*. How does this stuff get into print, anyway, especially when feminists are always using "choice" as their philosophical excuse for whatever moves them? They are fighting for women's liberation, but they don't want women to be free? Hello? We shall see much later that such confused people always argue vociferously that women should have total free choice when it comes to their reproductive lives . . . but not when it comes to life itself. No, sir. That will be controlled by the feminist master-planners, thank you very much. Feminism is just the female version of the top-down State. The "choices" women are encouraged to make are designed to bring them all under control.

Here are a few more family-hating, man-hating, tradition-hating snippets from the most influential revolutionaries in this camp.

Betty Friedan, author of the best-selling *Feminine Mystique* (1963), often compared American society to Naziism (this ought to have outraged Jews, who know the difference between a concentration camp and suburban boredom). She characterized the traditional home as "a comfortable concentration camp," whose prisoners are housewives, brainwashed by "femininity," who are not "fully human."[40] Buyers of her book should ask for a refund.

In her *Sexual Politics* (1970), Kate Millet, a radical lesbian feminist, continued the utopian drive for perfection by arguing that the universality of patriarchy — a result of cultural, not biological, forces, she insists — must be ended by a "revolution" to install a new sexual order (an egalitarian one). In her eyes, the family is an oppressive institution, women are chattels of men — mere slaves — and the family itself a feudal organization designed to socialize the young into the order of the larger society. (Don't all social orders do this?) At one point, Millet's anger grows so irrational, she accuses patriarchal society of issuing a "death penalty" against women — because many who have illegal abortions die from them. (There is no mention of her compassion for the lives of the unborn; or any reference to a "death penalty" issued on those who die from self-administered illegal drugs, or from alcoholism, obesity, or smoking.) But her solution to the problem of what she sees as an oppressive society is . . . simply a far more oppressive one. She is no more original than Plato, Rousseau, or Engels, for she wants a cultural, economic, and political revolution that will transform a free

society into a model communist society. The family is to be abolished. The care of children "is infinitely better left to the best-
trained practitioners of both sexes," rather than to "harried and all
too frequently unhappy persons" (meaning natural parents).[41] She
agrees with her mentor: "The radical outcome of Engels' analysis is
that the family . . . must go."[42] Anyway, where does a professed
lesbian get off telling parents what to do? And what sort of character
models were, and are, these people?

Well, it turns out that de Beauvoir was the sycophantic, subservient mistress of Jean-Paul Sartre for most of her life. She never
married, remained childless, was slavishly obedient and catered to
his every whim, and accepted his double standard in sex. He kept a
bevy of underaged mistresses, while she had lesbian affairs with
some of them and violent relationships with others. Both coyly
described these women as their "children." From her dishevelled
quarters — "she could live in filth, surrounded by garbage," her
daughter said — she faked authorship of many of his articles and
invented ways to pry into his furtive life. A close friend interviewed
by her biographer declared that one can play at marriage, but having
children means having to grow up, "and none of us ever wanted
that." About her own life, she declared, "I was swindled."[43] So were
we. She was a fake, and a derivative one at that.

As for Millet, if this antimale, antimarriage, antifamily academic
weren't so serious, I'd say she was silly. In her utopia, what we used
to call fornication is everywhere, and all the important human
functions of the family have been turned over to the heady, glorious
ministrations of the therapeutic State. "The collective professionalization (and consequent improvement) of the care of the young," she
wrote, "would further undermine family structure while contributing to the freedom of women. Marriage might generally be replaced
by voluntary association . . ."[44] She's got the part right about collective professionalization undermining the family, but in every
other way she's terribly insensitive to the true desires of free men
and women.

Since when was marriage in the West involuntary?

Clearly, the unoriginal solution all such radical writers imagine
is a Pollyanna world of free and equal workers; a dial-a-baby world
tended by unharried, rational, professional educators and therapists, all paid by the State. An army of professionals is to assist them
in creating and maintaining that world (all at the expense, one must
assume, of the working people, whose taxes will be extracted for this
purpose). Which leads to the next wave of attack.

# THERAPEUTICS AGAINST THE FAMILY

*The death of a culture begins when its normative institutions fail to communicate ideals in ways that remain inwardly compelling, first of all to the cultural elites themselves.*

PHILIP RIEFF, *THE TRIUMPH OF THE THERAPEUTIC*

In a fascinating series of books, Philip Rieff has provided a deep analysis of the modern moral struggle, one that offers insight into why we have so easily surrendered control over the conduct and meaning of our lives to therapists of all kinds.[45] To discover his work — in the midst of writing this book — was a special pleasure that fortified me greatly.

Western civilization, he believes, has been dominated by three character ideals prior to modern times.[46] The first, derived from Plato, was the ideal of *political* man. As we have seen, Plato had a distinct political hierarchy of values that sorted both society and the individual into higher and lower levels. Each person would reach the highest potential by participating in the common good (as defined by Plato). It is sufficient to recall that for Plato, just as an educated man was better (or higher) in his system than an ignorant one, so were the higher educated classes better than the lower. The highest class of all was composed of his philosopher kings. Plato's hierarchy was based on political and elite power and not on individual moral agency, which became the key distinction of Western civilization. His was a distinct social hierarchy based on biological elitism.

Political man was then succeeded by *religious* man. Rieff says that Christianity grafted the ancient classical notion of hierarchy onto what was formerly a naïve faith, after which the church became a saving, and teaching, institution. Just as Plato's *Republic* was a system for the training of capable citizens, so the Gospels became a system for the training of faith. Salvation leads to a higher life. The medieval concept of the great chain of being (discussed in Chapter Two) was a manifestation of this extremely powerful hierarchical moral and social order.

After religious man came *economic* man, who in many complicated ways was also hierarchical. Max Weber, in his influential book of 1904, *The Protestant Ethic and the Spirit of Capitalism*, attributed the stunning economic success of capitalism largely to the idea of man seeking salvation — a higher state of grace — through material success. This was a case of making what by orthodox

Christian doctrine was formerly thought to be low, high. Much of what constitutes social ranking in our society now derives from material success.

Now, in our own time, has emerged *psychological* man. The distinguishing feature of this type is that he "repudiates the hierarchical master-idea of 'higher' and 'lower' to which all the predecessors of psychological man have been addicted."[47]

This creation was the linchpin of the crucial change from a hierarchical to an egalitarian order. Morally speaking, such a change can rest only on the idea that there is no good, better, best. None at all. No moral hierarchy within which to arrange one's life, no right or wrong, no good or evil. One's life is merely a psychological matter, and human nature a matter of reconciling within oneself a "democracy of opposing dispositions." Once such moral relativity arose as a belief system, psychology became a substitute for ethics. As the overarching authority of the ancient moral order, descending from God to the powerful in society to parents and moral teachers, began to weaken, man, having neglected to repair his moral house, suddenly found himself shivering under broken boards. With but fragments for protection, he now stares upon a landscape of huddled, frightened individuals.

There are two crucial results of this moral fragmentation. First, the abandoning of ethics for psychology has not ended the need for ministers of faith. On the contrary, there has been an explosion in their numbers. In the past they lived on charity and the knowledge of their good works. Today, they charge high fees, are called therapists of one kind or another, and sell a mind-boggling array of cures — from psychotherapy to massage, oriental mysticism, crystal cures, sex therapy, quack religion, group therapy, firewalking, fasting, vision-training, neurolinguistic training, and self-esteem counselling. Multitudes of these therapists have a financial interest not in healing the culture, but in perpetuating the idea of negative community — in order to generate more customers. In the past, our volunteer charity workers sought to return the unfortunate to society, newly prepared to uphold its values. Today's therapists keep as many files open as possible, and they seek to open more. Long-term care is the thing. Since negative communities always generate fragmentation and then look to government for help, therapists now have a powerful interest in the ideals of the welfare State. Indeed, it is indirectly their best customer and paymaster as they minister to its multitudes of the homeless, the unemployed, the single mothers, the abandoned and abused or latchkey children, the drug users and alcoholics, and so on. What a market! Only a saint could resist such a lure. The modern "recovery" and "co-dependency" movements for "adult children" present a current example of the modern therapeutic hysteria designed to fill the "hole in the soul." One enthusiast, Herbert Gravitz, estimates that 230 million Americans are co-dependents — only 25 million less than the entire U.S. population (*The American Spectator*, June 1990).

Secondly, following in the footsteps of Freud the new therapists attack the role of the father (i.e., the family) "as the main maker of the rules of the moral game as Western children must learn to play it." For the father "is the very personification of all those heights of repressive command that Freud leveled."[48] So, once the moral house tumbled, therapists set about destroying any lingering need based on a yearning for common authority and feverishly began to substitute the competing varieties of separate authority that sprang from their new therapies.

The deep crisis brought about by this therapy invasion has arisen because "the psychological man of our therapeutic doctrine is not reconcilable with the moral man of preceding doctrines."[49] Psychological man is neither interested in nor counselled to lead a *good* life, but simply a more *enjoyable* one. And with no transcendent standard of values, how could it be otherwise? All forms of ego therapy thus operate on the notion that the individual can arrive not at the truth of self or of life, but at some sort of *compromise* with the warring instincts within. Ego therapy actively teaches a subtle rejection of all external moral standards. Modern "values clarification," now taught in many of our schools, is a recent reflection of this view (see Chapter Eight). Such teaching is the primary-school version of the pursuit of the Man-god: the self as originator of all values, as the new soul. Tolerance of internal ambiguities is promoted as the new key to better living and a stable character. This attitude feeds the widespread notion of moral relativity, which is the basis of our current flight from values.

It is unfortunate. Even pathetic. We live in a culture dying of overweening but false pride in self. As Rieff so forcefully puts it, we have broken the outward forms and therefore the authority of the social order that has always helped men control "the infinite variety of panic and emptiness to which they are disposed."[50] For all healthy, strong cultures have what he calls a "design of motives" that directs the self outward to purposes that alone can satisfy it. And the therapists (priests, teachers, shamans, etc.) of all previous cultures "were predominantly supportive rather than critical of culture as a moral demand system."[51] This attitude is what distinguishes our own therapists, or healers, from all those previous. Ours reject any external design of motives, or moral control. Freud rejected them too. Schizophrenic patients were held by him and many other modern therapists to be the product of a repressive family structure.

But the crucial function of all cultures is precisely control, not release; for "every culture must establish itself as a system of moralizing demands, images that mark the trail of each man's memory; thus to distinguish right actions from wrong the inner ordinances are set, by which men are guided in their conduct so as to assure a mutual security of contact."[52]

"Inner ordinances." It's a great phrase. And it echoes Irving Babbitt's phrase "inner check," about which more in Part Two. When a culture becomes persuaded to refuse such ordinances or checks — refuses, that is, to internalize what the culture held sacred in moral hierarchy — it lies exposed to the ordinances of raw instinct, of biology, and of the mind run mad. Or worse: of no longer even knowing what mad is; or of defining as mad everything that does not arise from our own inner life. In the end and as we shall see, such egocentrism defines society itself as mad.

The great peace to be found in earlier cultures was the peace of release from appetite, longing, and unconstrained desires. The secret of the Greek ideal, Rieff reminds us, was to have as few runaway desires as possible. Certainly this was the Christian ascetic ideal as well. But "our culture has shifted toward a predicate of impulse release, projecting controls unsteadily based on an infinite variety of wants raised to the status of needs."[53]

This perception effectively underlines our damaging national embrace of the Rights Illusion, described in Chapter Two. We live in a new anticulture, in which we seek release from inherited controls (Rousseau was the master philosopher of this trend). "Religious man was born to be saved; psychological man is born to be pleased."[54] "Believing" has given way to "feeling." Whole nations such as our own clamour for charter-supported rights to satisfy these feelings through privilege, or material gain; politicians are quite prepared to cannibalize the nation to guarantee such satisfactions.

Once such a uniformity of objection to traditional values is achieved, the strategic outcome desired by socialists is the transfer of basic functions to the State: religious morals will be replaced by State utopian ideals; home parenting by national daycare; family values by therapeutic, egalitarian values; political and economic freedom by central planning and control.

By now, the reader should see that it is wrong to assume that the collectivists want to destroy values. Rather, they want to *replace* natural, spontaneous, hierarchical, family-based values with their own simplistic, utopian, egalitarian values, the enforcement of which requires a new hierarchy of both values and power, of which they hope to be the philosopher kings and queens.

The resulting decomposition of natural moral hierarchy and its replacement by hierarchies of power in Western society has opened the way for accusations by therapists that the typical Western family is sick, or violent, or evil, and thus for the transfer of the family's traditional functions to State-supported programs and therapists. Shelters for this, and shelters for that. We will examine their motives more thoroughly in Part Two. For now, what follows will give the flavour of this particularly virulent attack on the family.

## PSYCHIATRISTS AGAINST THE FAMILY

In ancient times we got the first relentless utopian attack on moral agency and the free individual, urging abolition of the family and transfer of its functions to the State (Plato and his followers). In the modern period we got Rousseau and other Romantic thinkers, who attacked all traditional social institutions and beliefs as agencies that enslave the free spirit ("Man is born free; and everywhere he is in chains" [he meant the chains of law, custom, family, and tradition]). Then came a coupling of this utopianism with a failed anticapitalist economic conspiracy theory (Marx and his followers: "working men of all countries, unite!" [against capitalist hierarchy, property hierarchy, and family hierarchy]). Next, a tiresome flood of radical, man-hating, family-bashing, anticapitalist tracts from modern feminists. And finally, from the therapists themselves, a radical, anticapitalist theory that the natural family is oppressive, twisted, and insane.

This last chapter in the story, a clever effort to degrade the family by declaring it officially incompetent, was brought to us by — you guessed it — all those State-tax supported state employees, certified "experts," or "tenured radicals" as author Roger Kimball called them, paid by you and me to produce more negative community.

Here's what they did with our dollars.

It began with the generation of the 1960s, from which arose the counter-culture movement searching, with the help of drugs, for some higher inner truth (having spurned the higher outer truths). It was a movement profoundly antitechnological, antibusiness, and antirational. "Credit-card hippies," I called them, in my classes at Stanford: their social criticism and search for inner truth were subsidized by the wealth of the very society — and families — that paid for their extremely expensive schooling. In their rejection of middle-class life and standard religious values, the flower children embraced moral relativity and the unrealities of LSD. They rejected what they saw as the repressive culture of their parents and the acquisitive society (that is, until they had to make a living of their own). But you can see where this is leading. In rejecting their parents' culture, these superannuated adolescents — perhaps the largest, wealthiest, best-"educated" mass of spoiled youngsters in the history of the world — also rejected their parents' values, chief among them the value of the middle-class family itself. They were into authority-bashing through free love; drugs; communes; I'm O.K., you're O.K.; share the wealth, the kids, love, peace, the world. Oh, it was so lovely and unrealistic. Try to imagine an extended prepaid bacchanalia with a university degree at the end for your troubles, and you'll get the flavour of it!

At any rate, this massive effort to create alternative realities was fertile ground for an attack on what became targeted as the primal repressive, authoritarian, old-value, spanked-me-once-and-made-me-do-my-homework structure called the family. For sure, most of those in the counter-culture just wanted a turn-on and a good time. But in their midst were a lot of determined utopian theorists and hard-core revolutionaries who gleefully rode this wave of cultural rejection in order to attack society and the family as the source of all social ills.[55] The counter-culture was their Trojan horse.

Even standard middle-class psychiatry came under attack as an ideology meant to assist in the suppression of political or moral dissidence. But most of the therapists attacking standard values and standard psychiatry were also anticapitalist ideologues of one sort or another, who chose to foment revolution by demolishing and discrediting our deepest relationships and freedoms. Like Marx and Engels, many of them saw that capitalism was based on "the four Fs": Freedom, Family, Free enterprise, and Faith. You can't get rid of any one of these without also getting rid of the others. Chief among these ideologues were R.D. Laing, David Cooper, and Thomas Szasz.

Although standard Freudian psychiatry already saw family dynamics (rather than a physical cause) as generative of mental illnesses like schizophrenia, Laing took this view further when he theorized that such mental illness was a *rational reaction to an unbearable family situation*. The family had no meaning but was simply a network, or structure, of power relationships — and therefore political. Of course, there is some truth in what he claimed. Anyone who has tried to share kids in a broken marriage will recognize how they can easily become ammunition in an ugly spousal power war. (For Laing, this sort of thing would be an obvious illustration of every family's more subtle workings.) Having considered this, he then succumbed to the Determinist Illusion, seeing all mental illness as a result of such family dynamics and the patient as a helpless sufferer. At the extreme, Laing even argued that the violence of cutting the umbilical cord at birth could shape a person's whole life, and that the implantation of a sperm cell in an unwilling mother could be the beginning of psychosis in the child! Just as he denied the place of free will in the formation of character (this is the logical end result of so much determinist thinking), he followed the determinist chain of logic right down to the fertilized egg. Next would be atoms and electrons. This reductionist process of thought is typical of all determinist-causation theories. They always end by disappearing into things. Eventually, the theorist disappears, too, and good riddance. At any rate, the insane, Laing told us, were really just sane people reacting to insane family dynamics — the losers in the family power games people play. In the sense that the family is symbolic of the organized society itself, Laing was condemning the entire social order of the West. Insanity was really sanity in an insane world. This conclusion suited political radicals, especially Marxists, just fine. So, by 1967, Laing was counted as "one of the main contributors to the theoretical and rhetorical armoury of the contemporary left."[56] The radical May Day Manifesto which he signed that year was a militantly anticapitalist document — the radicals had succeeded in recruiting a key therapist to their cause of overturning society in the name of the Marxist utopia. By this time, David Cooper, one of Laing's followers, had become so radical himself that, like many others of this camp, he argued that there really was no such thing as mental illness; that society itself was sick; that, as Laing had written, "psychiatry is concerned with politics, with who makes the law."[57] In short, the normal was sick.

When you read these next few lines from Laing, you may well wonder about the pot calling the kettle black. In discussing the way in which humans disguise the truth (such as when we call dead cattle "beef"), he wrote: "Our own cities are our own animal factories; families, schools, churches are the slaughter-houses of our children;

colleges and other places are the kitchens. As adults in marriages and business, we eat the product."[58]

If that's not sufficient, try Cooper, who wrote that "the initial act of brutality against the average child is the mother's first kiss,"[59] because that kiss is the child's induction and seduction into our whole system of Western values. Well, now . . .

Once such thinkers fall into creating angry conspiracy theories against all of society, the game is up. As Rieff warned, they have taken up the cudgel against the culture, instead of for it. These folks were now claiming that mental illness was in fact a higher form of sanity, and that the entire psychiatric establishment was just a reflection of Western imperialism. It's complicated stuff, but what it boils down to is that a small number of articulate radical therapists/ideologues succeeded in changing the course of modern psychiatry and, far worse, radically undermined public confidence in the traditional family. By the way, I don't mean to suggest that there are no sick or dysfunctional families out there. There are far too many. My complaint is that instead of rehabilitating the family — which is what most of us have always thought therapists were paid to do — these radical ideologues dealt it a definitional death. The best they could do by way of healing it was to allow hordes of sick people to walk the streets in a kind of delirious indictment of Western life and Western families. Could it be they were sending out messengers of their own anger? The asylums were emptied, the streets filled, and *the family was defined by them as the principal pathological agent of social despair.*

Thomas Szasz, an extremely powerful force in antipsychiatry for the past 30 years, as a libertarian theorist, also contributed mightily to this notion.[60] It is easy to sympathize with much libertarian thought simply because it holds the individual to be more important than the State; but Szasz, and most other libertarians, go too far. They also hold the individual and his freedom to be more important than culture, society, tradition, custom, transcendent values, duty, and many other supra-individual realities that lie *between* the individual and the State. In this sense, these theorists have provided a forceful philosophical tool now frequently used to destroy all the social and legal privileges of traditional society. Ironically, libertarian philosophy, initially and properly a weapon used to protect the individual against the State, has too often become a charter-supported philosophical weapon used by radicals against the family and society. Thus has Szasz forcefully argued that all versions of reality are equally viable (the counter-culture loved this). There is no such thing therefore as madness, and asylums and psychiatrists are the modern equivalent of the Inquisition: merely social devices for punishing harmless abnormals and keeping the inconvenient out of the way. There is, he insists, no physical determinant of mental illness. The mentally ill are simply an oppressed group, and the family is an agency of their illness. In a capitalist society, those with deviant views simply get packaged off and ordered to consume capitalist services and treatments. It's good for the economy. The mad are just an expression of a dysfunctional family — they are the ones each family has decided should assume the external scapegoat role, almost like a sluice for the whole family's illness.

In Szasz's partial defence, by the mid 1960s psychiatry in the West had embarked on what seems now to have been a crusade to define almost every human activity as unhealthy and in need of treatment. In 1962, the Midtown Manhattan study declared that 80 percent of the population was impaired, 23 percent severely enough to require treatment. (This kind of finding fits my thesis that the welfare State promotes the transfer of family functions to the therapists of the State: the therapists themselves are not above a little aggressive marketing and redefinition of human life, the better to balance their accounts.) At any rate, Szasz wears two hats. One, as the hero who exposed the overmedicalization of social life through what is called "psychiatric imperialism," and another as the villain who helped drive the spike further through the heart of the family by arguing for moral relativism, that there is no difference between the sane and the insane, and for the family-causation theory of mental illness.

Like so many of their followers, however, none of these men developed an effective cure for sick people, or found a method to help the families they blamed. In effect, they were not so much psychiatrists as they were political ideologues using their medical credentials to peddle their theories. I have dealt with them here simply to show the broad outline of family-bashing as it developed from Plato, who exalted the State, to Rousseau, who exalted the innocence of nature, to the Marxists, who created a vast materialist conspiracy theory, to modern radical feminists — who try it all, combined with what one critic called "spray-on indignation." The final expression of this antifamily offensive is by the radical medical professionals of our modern therapeutic State, most of whom share all the angry sentiments of their predecessors and attack the family by redefining it as a disease.

# DEFENDING THE FAMILY TRADITION

Although battered and reeling from the accumulation of such attacks, the family nevertheless continues to survive, and quite vigorously. It will always survive, simply because the theories and practice of its enemies are terribly flawed. But mere family survival is not enough to maintain a vibrant society. Those who care to defend the family must know the enemy inside out, must understand the dynamics of the social welfare State, and must passionately support strong family values. In short, you cannot solve a problem unless you first know what the problem is. From this review we are reminded that the antifamily forces of our society arise mostly from power-hungry collectivists whose reworked utopian theories and hopelessly sloppy solutions can lead only to social disintegration. Fine. That's bad enough. But even worse is the fact that the average person can produce only a feeble argument against them. And thus the world runs badly. That's why I now want to contrast vividly the two main political, economic, and social visions as they struggle for dominance in the world today. Clearly, *the traditional family can be defended only by arguing from a bottom-up position on all these matters.* Each of these ways, or visions, amounts to a political, economic, and moral system that is irreconcilable with its opposite.

### The Family and

### The Bottom-up Model    vs.    The Top-down Model

*Individualism*          vs.          *Collectivism*

Spontaneous freedom under a rule of law always gives rise to individualism, just as coercion (forcing a single way on others) inevitably gives rise to collectivism and egalitarianism. The natural family is the protector of human freedom and individualism, and thus the key institutional defence against collectivism.

*Personal Morality*      vs.      *State Morality*

We thus arrive at personal "moral agency" in the free society and its families (the key to Western civilization) vs. State control of morality. State morality is always political, not really moral at all. The subjects have no choice, and it leads to the "identitarian" State, or a kind of genteel totalitarianism compelling uniformity.

*Liberty*          vs.          *Power*

Liberty requires the creation of simple rules that are the same for all, without exception, and these constitute the legal structure of the bottom-up society. But top-down states never discuss liberty. They focus all their resources on the power required to implement their unitary vision of society, with which all personal liberty merely interferes. Family values of self-reliance and independence interfere mightily with this power.

*Cooperation, Community*   vs.      *Communalism*

Cooperation and community flow from everything prior. Free individuals exercising moral agency voluntarily form free communities and enterprises, and they share moral values; conversely, top-down states impose a single set of values, precisely in order to extinguish free community values in the name of communalism.

*Spontaneity*          vs.          *Planning*

Crucial to the bottom-up society is the natural, spontaneous growth of social institutions and free enterprise. But just as crucial, to the top-down State, is central planning of every detail of political, economic, and social life, and the need, therefore, to eliminate all spontaneous natural associations and motives.

*Pro-family*          vs.          *Antifamily*

Families are the core value-creating entity of the free society, and they usually create values according to high principles *that transcend those of the State*. The State recognizes this, and thus tends — be it openly or insidiously or by consequence of its drive for efficiency, and to create clients for its services — to transfer natural family functions to itself.

*Merit and Achievement*   vs.   *Envy and Redistribution*

Families want the very best for their children, and thus they emphasize merit and achievement. Economic differences are a natural outgrowth. But the welfare society must stress sameness for all, and thus it emphasizes not merit and wealth creation, but envy and economic redistribution. The bonus system is the operational method of the bottom-up society; the handicap system, of the top-down State.

*Private Property* vs. *Public Control*

The concept of private property is the legal and economic mainstay of the free individual and the family. It is the last bastion of protection for the common man against the invasive powers of the law and the State. Accordingly, the top-down State always attempts to erode this protection through the law, and through taxation. Canadians have common-law property rights — increasingly weakened — but no protection of these in their Charter.

*Limited Government* vs. *Unlimited Government*

Free people and free families recognize that the least possible government, kept that way by checks and balances on power, is the best way to protect the concept of moral agency and economic freedom. But the top-down State recognizes no limit on power. Total tax levels are a good indicator of such power. The average Canadian family now pays about 50 percent of income to governments (all three levels) in taxes of all kinds.

*"Dollar Democracy"* vs. *Economic Planning*

The right to make, save, and use money freely has, for the past few centuries, been the salvation of the common man and the family in Western society. The daily economic choices of individuals and their families amount to a spontaneous shaping of the national economy. But top-downers prefer the State to control the economy, in order to direct resources to objectives they think are best. Hence, their preference for taking the money out of the hands of families (through high taxes), for directing the economy through nationalized companies (by means of so-called "industrial strategies"), and for social programs that increase the people's dependence on the State.

*Common Law* vs. *Charter Law*

Bottom-up societies are based on the idea that human beings are inherently free, and need only laws that tell them what they cannot do. For this, the common law suffices. But top-down States seek to do more than simply *prohibit* bad behaviour. They want to *direct* all social behaviour. So they create charters that confer "rights and freedoms" on the people, the abstract meanings of which become controlled by the State, and impose egalitarian prescriptions (from which the State itself is often exempted). The people forget that, once granted a right to confer rights and freedoms, the State can as easily take them away.

*Parliamentary Sovereignty* vs. *Judicial Sovereignty*

Everything flows from the bottom up in a free society: from free individuals to freely created laws in a free parliament. The democratic ideal is that the people and their families are sovereign. But in states that create charters, unelected judges become the highest lawmakers, and we end up with Plato's philosopher kings. Once on the bench, they can easily pervert the laws to serve the unitary purposes of the State; and because the egalitarian welfare State is inherently antifamily, the Supreme Court of any nation can become the single most powerful instrument for social engineering and the destruction of the family. Imagine an unelected radical leftist, or rightist, judge with the power to strike down the laws of parliament, and you have a recipe for judicial activism — and despotism.

## THE WEAPONS

### National and Local Weapons

The first and most prevalent weapon of all antifamily radicals is always some kind of handicap system. The highest social goal then becomes not merely the virtue of sameness, but the limitless force required to bring it about. State affirmative action programs, so-called pay-equity and employment-equity programs, nationalized health and insurance schemes, unfunded pension plans, and a host of so-called regional disparity programs have the effect of destroying the work ethic while undermining families. Many of them end up establishing an intergenerational dependency on the State that removes all family pride and personal sense of commitment to higher purposes. Seeking loyalty from all voters in this way, and in an effort to remove the stain of immorality from its handouts and to escape the painful task of dividing the deserving from the undeserving, the State eventually declares such programs as "universal" or "sacred rights." In this way, the State generates instead universal moral and economic laziness. It is only a matter of time before moral and fiscal bankruptcy strike the states that choose this path of unconscionable spending and borrowing from the families of the future. Little wonder that widespread public cynicism inevitably follows.

Another insidious weapon used in the current war against the family is the effort to redefine the meaning of the word "family." Earlier radicals met resistance to their attempts to attack the family openly. Now they are more clever. *They attack it by redefining it.* Today, many radicals say they are "pro-family" and that they seek a "national family policy," [61] or seek to teach "family studies." But beware, for "they find it politically useful to cloak their utopian agenda in pro-family rhetoric."[62] Although most people think of the natural "family" as I have described it ("a married man and woman living together with their dependent children"), you will not find this definition in the literature. Sociologist David Allen argues that he and his colleagues must set about "opening up a plurality of definitions,"[63] which suggests the simplest ploy of the antifamily forces: to change the word from singular to plural. They now speak not of family, but of "families," and the most delirious of them suggest that we simply define any circle of friends — or those who share the same work, economic needs, political views, or sexual preferences — as a "consciously chosen family," or an "intentional family."[64] The antifamily forces have so broadened the definition of family that it now has hardly anything to do with marriage, blood, legal ties, or adoption. The Ontario Ministry of Education's definition for its "family studies" course (1987) is "a social unit of interacting persons who make commitments, assume responsibilities, nurture each other, become socialized, transmit cultural and religious values, and share resources over time."[65]

This is an official definition that filters down to our children in the schools. It contains no mention of marriage; or of the requirement for the presence of a male and female. There is no mention of children; nor does it specify what sort of "commitment" is required to constitute a legal marriage. In fact the word "legal" is also absent. Nor is there any mention of marital fidelity. This is a definition of the family loose enough to include a group of satanic Hell's Angels living together for a weekend orgy.

Another essential weapon in the antifamily armoury is the promotion of the notion that work outside the home is more important than work inside the home, which subordinates the human life of the family to the material and economic life of the workplace. And it's all wrong, simply because all moms are working moms, and no work could be more important for society than raising a child to adulthood properly. Plato insisted that the social ideal was something higher than the individual and the family. (I agree, but it must arise freely from them, and not be imposed by the State.) Modern radicals have simply substituted the notion of career, or "work," for this (the economic ideal), and voilà, we have a new hierarchy based on income and work for third parties (the capitalist State). Modern mothers who give such external work precedence over their children are the new dupes of the State. They turn out labour and services for third-party bosses, to the detriment of their own needy children. It's really a new version of the old factory system that lured women out of the home for bucks: it subsidizes escape from the unpleasantness of duty. For many, it disguises the tired emptiness of life with fur coats and fax machines. Those of the least means who, like their men, are condemned for life to work outside the home at dreary jobs (sewing, cleaning, or handling idiot work in unpleasant factories, as distinct from cushy law offices and boutique operations), are far less certain these tasks are more noble than the job of raising their own children.

Now to the State daycare lobby. There may indeed be some possible reason to provide daycare to some individuals in society who are truly needy. We'll get to that in Chapter Twelve. But the key weapon in the radical agenda for social change is not daycare for the truly needy. It's daycare as a universal right for all women, in order to reorganize social priorities and "free" women from parenthood. The policy makers don't want daycare as welfare, they want it as a Charter "right," regardless of economic or social condition. This arises straight from the handicap-system thinking of the top-down State, as it strives, against the forces of individualism and the family, to equalize everyone. The belief seems to be that once daycare is provided "free" for all, the natural family will have no reason to exist, women will compete equally with men, patriarchy will cease, and all will be on equal terms. This seems to be a very male view of the world (flight from children, competition, career-climbing, etc.), courtesy of utopian, tax-funded daycare, and it will be explored fully later. For now, we need only sensitize ourselves to the fact that all national daycare schemes are not really plans to help certain unfortunate mothers, who often are victims of uncaring partners and of lax marriage and divorce laws. And certainly not to help their children. Rather, they are plans for the radical reorganization of Western society along collectivist lines.

There's more. Antifamily radicals also lobby hard to modify the tax system to further their purposes. It is not an exaggeration to say that the family haven has been invaded more by the long arm of tax policy than by any other factor in our time. One simple example is the basic child deduction available to families in most Western countries. In Canada, if we had the same basic deduction today as was available to parents in 1950, we could deduct fully one-third (33 percent). But in 1991, we can deduct only 9 percent. Tax policy can have a dramatic effect indeed. For example, in Quebec in 1990, the number of births was radically increased by a whopping 18 percent in comparison to 1987, through the provision of cash bonuses to parents ($500 for the first child, $2500 for the second, $7500 for each succeeding child). Radicals say this is paying cows to give birth (half of all Canadian births in 1991 were from Quebec, which contains only one-quarter of the population). I argue it is giving back to families what should never have been taken in the first place; that, left with sufficient of their own income, parents would enjoy many more children. But the welfare State promotes not family economic interdependence, but economic autonomy. Sweden in 1970 instituted a radical taxation policy that disallowed the submission of joint family tax returns, "in pursuit of an egalitarian goal"; namely, to free women from "economic dependence" on the family. In doing so, Sweden unexpectedly created an "independence effect" that accelerated marital dissolution.[66] The point of this is clear. If you want to strengthen the family, you create tax policies that reward family formation; if you see the family — as Swedish and many Canadian radicals do — as a kind of undemocratic tyranny, then you create tax policies that turn family formation into a losing economic game. The irony of this latter tactic, of course, is that in so doing, birth rates fall below replacement level (2.11 per woman — termed the GRR, or gross reproduction rate), and thus the number of taxpayers declines (Canada's GRR is now 1.6). At that point, the welfare State suffers a severe lack of income. This amounts to a new "revenge of the cradle" against the State itself. Such a "birth dearth" is now afflicting all Western welfare states in the same way (see Chapter Fifteen) and is a predictable result of the life-denying policies described here. One hopes this negative effect will produce a purely pragmatic and political reaction by the turn of the century, resulting in stronger pro-family tax policies.

Needless to say, radical proponents of the welfare State also aggressively seek to change the laws to favour their utopian aims. These range from forbidding landlords to insist on married couples, to enacting legislation such as Ontario's Family Law Reform Act and no-fault divorce laws, which are similar to those of other jurisdictions and have the effect of removing any fault for marital breakup. Such laws simplify marital dissolution and often reward the provocative party, and many spouses who uphold the sanctity of marriage are therefore increasingly vulnerable, and may face marital breakdown at the hands of partners who decide divorce would be emotionally and financially profitable. In short — again a predictable result of any handicap system — the wrongdoers are rewarded by the system, instead of being punished by it. The quick and dirty way to wealth in our society is now the insincere marriage followed by a no-fault divorce. No wonder people are shy of marriage. Other legal strategems to eliminate the status of the natural family are examined more fully in Chapter Eighteen.

## The International Weapons

In a typically lucid and informative essay entitled "Is Totalitarianism Dead?" (*Crisis*, February 1989), British historian Paul Johnson answered his own question in the negative. The majority of the intellectual class, he writes, do not accept any religious or moral interpretation of the world, or of a world to come, "and therefore will continue to feel the itch to utopianize the earth"; and, as the drive to secular perfection is a continuing force, "we can be certain . . . that State compulsion will play a part in the new forms, and . . . that the forcing of human individuals into idealized State molds will be a salient characteristic." Typical are the moulds of pansexualism and sex-ed, meant to engineer social attitudes of the young and erode the Judeo-Christian sexual ethic, deemed too repressive. Homosexual politics, as we shall see, are also vitriolically antifamily. The international abortion/population movement is out of control, and with what Johnson calls a "breathtaking contempt for logic" it mounts simultaneous programs for "children's rights," most of them designed to help the State interfere with the family. The euthanasia movement, as we shall see, is an extension of the abortion/infanticide movement (see Chapter Sixteen).

Oh, and then there are arts politics, in which "the public culture sectors are used by radical artists of all kinds — who could not get their messages across in the market culture sector — to challenge the traditional assumptions of society and Judeo-Christian morality."

Complementing this is the worldwide "multicultural" movement, which aims to "dismember the elements of existing societies" and substitute for these a one-world culture based on racial social engineering. This too is an outgrowth, as Johnson says, of

Rousseau's belief that the State can improve human life. But such policies, ostensibly pluralistic, really aim to destroy traditional cultural affiliations, which tend to be toward one's particular roots, past, and history. And these policies, through various "positive discrimination" measures, force public allegiance to a one-world idea labelled multicultural, or globalist. This is despite the fact that no one has yet demonstrated how we are to get unity from diversity, and despite the reality that the whole world, fatigued with collectivism, is breaking up into smaller ethnic and culture-based units.

The last area, one Johnson does not mention, is the area of international rights. This will be delved into in Chapter Eighteen. It is sufficient to say here that all such movements, whether for the rights of women or the rights of the child, *are really about the rights of government*. What they seek is the wholesale transfer of traditional family rights to government, exercisable against the family. The new articles of the U.N. Convention on the Rights of the Child, for example, much of it created and influenced by Canadians, gives children all sorts of rights against family authority (especially in articles 13, 14, 15, 17, 18, and 24), which are going to shock once they are well known.

In short, the new collectivism, or democratic totalitarianism, is just as invasive as, if more subtle than, the old and will take many new forms to assert the hegemony of the State and its social engineers. What these forms have in common is the same old core idea found in both Plato and Rousseau: "that State power can be used to produce the New Man." If they succeed, we will no longer be married to each other. We will all be married to the State.

# 5

# The Swedish Lesson

*Sweden's famous economic model — the envy of the world for more than half a century — is dead. It passed away last Friday afternoon.*

THE FINANCIAL POST, OCTOBER 30, 1990

Sweden is certainly the clearest example we have of a non-communist country that was purposely changed by its governing elite from a strongly traditional, family-based society (what the people wanted) into an egalitarian, antifamily welfare State (what the radical elite wanted), in less than half a century. Prescient writers like Bastiat and Tocqueville in the last century and Nobel laureate Friederich Hayek and Robert Nisbet in our own had predicted that *any* State which tried such a change would eventually be brought down, and the change in Sweden has fascinated the West. The Scandinavian country is a model of a nation that appeared to have successfully combined a strong capitalist base with dominant egalitarian policies. In other words, the Swedes were said to have successfully mixed what I have called a bottom-up bonus system with a top-down handicap system.

The apparent "success" of the Swedish experiment — one by no means supported by all the people, but rather forced upon them by radicals and their cadres of social engineers (with much communist party support over the years) — was brought about chiefly by two Swedes, Gunnar and Alva Myrdal, he an economist, and she a radical feminist sociologist. Both played an inordinately strong role in the development and implementation of radical economic and social policies, which initially were directed to the preservation of the family within an egalitarian society. By the early 1970s, however, their policies, and Alva's in particular, had become much more openly socialist. She campaigned vigorously for the idea of equality, not "as the right to compete on equal terms," but in favour of an equality of results, or outcomes — "the gradual reduction of the differences in conditions of life."[1] *No longer was the family unit to be favoured in any way.* On the contrary, Sweden quickly became the first non-Marxist State to militate openly against the traditional family in its political, economic, and social policies. "All adults," in Alva Myrdal's words, "were to be treated in the same manner by society, whether they lived alone or in some sort of common living arrangement." (This was the political incarnation of the Individualism Illusion — the natural final stage of liberalism.)

Not only was the family unit not to be "favoured" in any way, *it was targeted for destruction by political, economic and social policies.* The Myrdals' report, *Crisis in the Population Question* (1934), called for "the economic independence of married partners" as a basic condition of equality, by which they meant the focus of future social policy would discourage traditional familial *interdependence*. The family unit must be disintegrated into individual units with a new dependence on the State. (Today, fully 60 percent of Swedish women who work full-time and 45 percent of those who work part-time work for the State.) An illustration of how quickly Alva Myrdal's radical views became mainstream in government can be seen in a startling statement published in 1968 by the Swedish Institute, considered a promoter of quasi-official Swedish views, under the heading "The Family Is Not Sacred": "*I should like to abolish the family as a means of earning a livelihood*, let adults be economically independent of each other and *give society a large share of responsibility for its children* . . . In such a society we could very well do without marriage as a legal entity."[2]

This was a recipe for the atomization of the family as a social unit and with it the transformation of Sweden into a true welfare — dare I say? — totalitarian democracy. Plato's Republic. It does not differ, except in completeness, from Canadian sentiments such as those expressed by feminist Mary O'Brien, an activist and lecturer at the Ontario Institute for Studies in Education, that province's quintessential factory for the production of radical education ideology. Those in Canada who wish to know what we are getting for our tax dollars need look no further to see the harbingers of Swedish totalitarianism in Canada. Here is O'Brien, cheerleading the antifamily team: "The most remarkable achievement of feminism is the breakdown of the family . . . The nuclear family is a goner."[3]

The government of Canada is drowning in mismanagement and debt, and O'Brien wants to transfer essential family duties to the incompetent, power-grasping State. The inevitable breakdown of the family this transfer requires is called an "achievement"? She is dead wrong about the end of the nuclear family, but at least she betrays herself with candour. Ironically, we the citizens and our families are being exploited by just such antifamily activists — *and we're paying them to do it.*

In Sweden, "traditional moral sentiments," especially about things like sex, "were almost completely overturned . . . by a vanguard of radical thinkers," making the 1960s a "left-wing decade," or, as the Swedes put it, *vänstervriden* (twisted to the left). Many citizens were left deeply upset by what they described as "radical egalitarianism"[4]; but once the levers of power, education, bureaucracy, and media were captured, the people could do nothing. Activists became professional grant-seekers, which is always the trend, expertly extracting the means to enforce their vision on society at large. The result, as ever: larger government, more programs, more "clients" for State therapists, more family breakdown. Scholars Heclo and Madsen summed up the consequences for Sweden when they said of this once free country that "in no other nation has a reforming party of the political left held such a grip on the State apparatus and on the public perception of policy choices."[5] Except Canada, perhaps.

In Canada, many such radical individuals, buoyed by their abstract utopian visions, have managed to control myriad positions of trust and power that help them reconstruct traditional society according to their personal political agenda. If the people really wanted this outcome, I would not say we were exploited. But the people distinctly do not. Take just one issue as an example: so-called universal daycare.

The facts are that only 17 percent of Canadian children are now placed in licensed, paid daycare for *any* period of the day (much less all day), and as for their parents, fully 66 percent, or "a whopping two-thirds," say that "the best place for pre-school children is at home with their parents" (Decima Poll, Toronto *Star*, June 5, 1991). In the same poll, only 16 percent *in any way* favoured the idea of putting children in licensed daycare centres. The poll showed, unequivocally, that even when people support government daycare, they emphatically say it should be offered *only* to the truly needy. Such programs should in no way be universal. Full stop. But because, as we have seen, universal State daycare is an absolutely fundamental requirement for the success of any collectivist ideology, all radical activists fanatically promote it. From Plato, to Rousseau, to Marx and Engels, and to Mary O'Brien, such coercive, tax-supported programs are used as a fundamental weapon in the effort to equalize forcibly the material and social conditions of all citizens, regardless of their personal ambitions, choices, or talents. These are the very "policy instruments" of the top-down State.

Swedish politicians and policy-makers eagerly embraced this new coercive idea of what "equality" was to mean: a cynical justification for transforming the classical liberal notion of government from an institution that set the rules for free people, but never played the game, to one that sets the rules, plays the game, and then handicaps all those who refused to play the same way. This overt switch from a simple equality of opportunity to an equality of outcome, or results, which necessitated — even mandated — a large-scale invasion of personal and family life, marked the beginning of democratic tyranny in the West. Tocqueville warned us of this end-condition of democracy, as did Bastiat, Schumpeter, and Nisbet [6] We have not heeded.

The wonder of it all is that such states do not crumble even faster. The reason seems to be that whereas a bankrupt business is forced to shut its doors, a State can go bankrupt with the doors open. A business is nourished by its customers, who are free to refuse to buy its product, but a welfare State feeds off its taxpayers, who are forced to pay for what the State insists they need, whether they agree or not. The result is that internal decline may very well be under way, even deeply advanced, but it is camouflaged by slowly increased tax levels, increased deficits and total debt, devaluation of currency, rigidification of business transactions through a plethora of regulation, and an inexorable movement of economic, labour, and social laws away from the kind that favour production of wealth and toward the kind that favour its redistribution. Radical labour laws are a case in point. By allowing ordinary workers to shut down a whole plant and forbidding owners to hire replacement help during a strike, such laws favour input over output, resulting in increased wage security for labour but added risk for entrepreneurs: a pure transaction of decline.

But the worst effects of decline, and often the first ones, are to be seen in the private, internal regions of family and moral life — in the "culture," broadly speaking. Here, there are unmistakable signs of the breaking of traditional community, family, and moral bonds that previously held society together with an unspoken, commonly accepted and proudly transmitted authority.

Until very recently, when its socialist government fell (September 1991), Sweden was the only remaining case of socialism anyone dared to cite. Strictly speaking, Sweden is not a socialist State (one that owns everything); it is a welfare State (one that controls everything). But the distinction is minor. Collectivists, whatever their stripe, do not have to own anything to collectivize a nation. They simply have to control and regulate heavily. This was also the method used by the National Socialists of Germany under Hitler.

Until just after World War II, Popenoe reminds us, Sweden was one of the most traditional societies on earth. But by then its Social Democratic party (there's that old euphemism for socialism) had succeeded in gaining control of every important lever of power and influence. Next it introduced far more radical programs, so that its "traditional moral sentiments were almost completely over-turned . . . [and by the 1970s] the intellectual climate, led by a vanguard of radical thinkers, had changed into a thoroughgoing moral relativism."[7] If there is any lesson to be learned, it is this: that any society can be dramatically changed by a very small number of radical activists who have learned to manipulate the democratic process, the media, and the mechanisms of government funding. In Sweden, this radicalization of an entire nation took place swiftly between 1960 and 1985. Canada always openly admired and vigorously copied Sweden, beginning with Prime Minister Lester Pearson, after whom our brand of leftism got a thumping great push from Pierre Trudeau and his government, which plunged us into massive centralization and unconscionable debt. In his 16 years of rule, Trudeau sent Canada's total federal debt into orbit, from just $20 billion accumulated since Confederation to $200 billion the year he left power. In his last year he spent fully 54 percent more than his government brought in. Such fiscal profligacy has never been seen in all the long history of our country. Apply the average rate of interest to the debt he left Canadians, and you get over $400 billion as of 1991 — which is where it stood then. (At 10 percent interest rates, any debt doubles every seven years.)

Today, Canada's governments at all three levels liberally fund all sorts of radical organizations, many of them devoted, for reasons explained, to the abolition of the traditional family. Meanwhile, the same governments refuse to fund groups devoted to preserving the traditional family. (If the State would retreat, those latter groups wouldn't need funding.) The astonishing thing is the degree to which the democratic process itself can be distorted by so small a number of radicals. A scary example occurred when a pro-family group known as REAL Women of Canada applied (against its own principles, but because it was otherwise unable to compete) for a government grant to finance its operations. The government repeatedly failed to respond to its request, and ultimately it refused on the flimsy grounds that REAL Women did not represent "progress" for women's liberation. So REAL Women sent in a new, false application, this time under the auspices of "Lesbian Mothers of Canada." At once, the government replied with a warm letter of welcome and all the required papers. And we live in a democracy?

Here's a glimpse of Sweden's "model state," with the facts gleaned from a variety of sources, including professor of philosophy Eric Brodin, a native Swede who is now a naturalized American. Those interested in the Swedish forced social experiment and who want to study it as a preview of where we ourselves are headed are encouraged to acquaint themselves thoroughly with his work. They should read as well *The New Totalitarians* and, particularly, *Disturbing the Nest*.[8]

- Swedes pay the highest taxes of any people on earth. Since 1985, the top income tax rate was 72 percent. This was recently cut to 50 percent in an effort to stem the flow of capital and entrepreneurs overseas, and to increase incentives.
- More than 66 percent of gross national product goes to government spending. (The figure is about 50 percent in Canada; it was about 30 percent here in 1960.)
- Sweden has had a VAT, or value-added tax, which taxes goods and services at every stage where value is added. When writing *The Trouble with Canada* in 1989, I wrote that "all social welfare states eventually resort to these in their effort to feed themselves." And since then, Canada has introduced, to enormous protest, a new goods and services tax (GST) of 7 percent, which, once the heat dies down, will eventually climb as high as Sweden's VAT — now over 22 percent! Canadians, only half in jest, say that GST means "go south today"!
- On any given day, 10 percent of Sweden's workforce is legally away from work on one or another kind of subsidized leave (up to 20 percent on Mondays and Fridays), totalling four million lost workdays per year.

- Fully one-third of the Swedish workforce is employed by government (Canada is closing in fast, at just over 20 percent). About 75 percent of all Canadian government workers are unionized — and they represent half of Canada's four million unionized workers.
- Between 1976 and 1982, Sweden had major currency devaluations (totalling 45 percent) and at the same time accumulated a large foreign debt, not to finance future development or infrastructure, but to pay for current consumption (much as Canada has been doing for the past two decades).
- Only 33 percent of Sweden's population provides productive work, with the resultant wages and taxes going to support the remainder of the population.
- Swedish "absenteeism" is a national scandal. The average Swede is off work "sick" for 23.4 days per year. (Canadians average 6.4 days.) Some 500,000 Swedes — known as "early pensioners" — claim physical or psychological illness. A third of them are under 49 years old. Major Swedish companies report 21 percent *daily* absenteeism — double for women (*Financial Post*, October 2, 1989.)
- "Sweden used to be a welfare paradise on earth. Now it is the sick man of Europe" (Goran Abinsonn Bruhner, in *Svenska Dagblat*, January 1990). If you use your MasterCard to pay interest on your Visa card, and vice-versa, for a very long time, you can indeed create a "paradise on earth" (the utopian ideal of the materialists). But the reality of the economic and moral processes inherent in all welfare states eventually erode them from the inside out. Canada is just now realizing it is caught in a similar web of its own weaving.
- "Ontario's industrial structure should parallel that of Sweden . . ." (Ontario's *Premier's Council Report*, 1989). Sadly, Canadians fall for the myth of industrial planning, instead of understanding how economies work: Allow people to keep most of what they earn, let them save and invest and take risks, and "the economy" will grow from the bottom up.
- A new Swedish party, The National Democracy party, which is much like Canada's Reform party (exhausted welfare states seem to spawn these), was created in February 1990, has already captured a sizable percentage of the vote, and advocates the dismantling of the Swedish welfare State — among other things. "We want to give the people space, and choice, and responsibility," says co-leader Ian Wachmeister. All this is in reaction to the fact that "their famous 'Swedish model' has collapsed." (Toronto

*Star*, June 19, 1990.) The peripatetic Richard Gwyn, author of the *Star* article, naïvely attributes this surrender of welfarism to the need to compete in international markets, rather than to the intrinsic self-defeating faults of socialism, of which he seems a blind booster.

Despite this sobering economic picture — one largely brought about by antifamily egalitarian social engineering — the Swedish experiment was the modern world's most thoroughgoing effort to install a top-down State without the assistance of the sort of physical coercion routinely used in communist states. Every other form of social control and coercion, however, has been tried: from tax policy, to educational brainwashing, to overregulation, to thought control (our own unofficial version of this, raging in the universities of the Western world at present, is called "political correctness," or P.C.). But the simple truth is that the world's most peaceful egalitarian experiment has had the predictable result of destroying local community, charitable feeling, spontaneous voluntary associations, and church and family. The root of this failure lies in the reliance of the Swedes on the Rationalism Illusion — the extraordinarily shallow liberal idea, based on human ego and pride, that life's deepest meanings and motives are only those amenable to reason and rational planning; that human beings can be made happy through the planned materialist society if only the *differences* between them (inherited, natural, or material) can be eliminated. The Swedish experiment is thus the logical end result of the Platonist, Rousseauist idea (shared by Pierre Trudeau, as well as by Ontario premier Bob Rae and his colleagues) that more government will make you free; if the State can just control all the competing intermediate allegiances (family, church, corporations, voluntary associations) and the inequalities of life and status to which they give rise, and replace them with a single set of allegiances that are the same for all — then individuals will live in an unchanging (therefore unthreatening) world, unfettered by inherited social conditions or economic differences, and will at last be free to express their natural goodness. Silly Rousseau. And silly Pierre. Silly anybody who, like a sailor who believes that the tip of the iceberg is the whole thing, arranges his charts and compasses accordingly. For any ship that steers the course of life without paying due respect to the hidden parts of the iceberg — to history, to custom, to the spontaneous natural and family allegiances of life, to the inherited institutions, prescriptions, and wisdom that have been honed over the ages by our predecessors, to the great mysteries of the circumambient universe — will surely founder. In this sense, we can think of the collectivists of the world as the cowards (and therefore the bullies) of the human species. Faced with the same unknowns as everyone else, they cope with the resulting natural anxiety not head on and bravely, but by banding together with like-minded weaklings who plot to halt threatening change and secure their personal futures by first securing the resources of others. In order to achieve this goal with some sense of dignity, they have developed a long litany of justifications about fairness and social planning.

Here are the words of a typical Swedish professor of ethnography, Ake Daun, on this note: "The source of our national pride is the country we constructed from the thirties onward, based on a strong belief in rationality and enthusiasm for science and social planning" (Toronto *Star*, April 24, 1991). Such social fabrications are doomed to failure, for to use only the tool of reason for everything would be as silly as to use only a screwdriver, which is very good for driving screws, to paint a wall. Just imagine all those social planners, screwdrivers in hand, marching out of the Central Planning Office determined to paint every wall in Sweden, and you get a feel for it. Thus, we arrive at G.K. Chesterton's wise grasp of this reality, when he remarked that "the madman is the man who has lost everything except his reason."[9] In other words, pure reason, unsupported by all the modifying cautions and wisdoms of life, which the insane have lost, will produce insane results — supported by reason.

## SOME CONSEQUENCES FOR THE WESTERN FAMILY

*The Swedish family today . . . has moved farther from the nuclear family than has the family in any other society.*

DAVID POPENOE, *DISTURBING THE NEST*

With Sweden as our guide to the future, we had best gird our loins for the coming family decline, or else resolve to resist and remove the policies that are its cause. Let us review a handful of facts culled from *Disturbing the Nest* and ask ourselves if this is what we want — and if not, just how we are going to prevent it.

Sweden is the world's most apartment-oriented society on earth. As of 1980, fully 33 percent of all households in Sweden contained but one person, and 63 percent of the residents of Stockholm lived alone.[10] This is surely a sign of the success of Sweden's welfare State in converting the basic social unit (the family) into the basic political unit (autonomous individuals).

States that rely solely on reason and materialism actively discourage the dissemination of any transcendent values that might appear higher than those of the State. Thus, as a matter of instinct do they strive to control the living church. The Swedish (Lutheran) church is state owned (as in Norway and Germany), and its employees are civil servants. This is, well . . . like taking communion from a tax collector. Thus was religion banned in the former USSR from 1917, the year modern socialism found its final form, until 1989, the year socialism died. Not surprisingly, Sweden is the most atheistic democracy on earth: In 1983 only 27 percent of Swedes said they took any strength from religion and 5 percent attended church, compared with 79 percent of Americans who took strength and about 40 percent who attended church. Only 61 percent of Canadians took strength from faith, and only 24 percent attended church weekly.[11]

Sweden has also developed many social and tax policies specifically designed to break down the nuclear family, and the State specifically intervenes in family life. In 1981, Finnish authorities took 552 children from their parents for reported "child abuse." But the same year in Sweden, with a population only three times greater, authorities took 22,000 children from their parents — and were criticized internationally on the grounds that this action was abuse of another variety: State control of families — child abuse by the State.

Sweden, as noted, is the first Western national to have the majority of its voters dependent on public funds — and thus beholden to the hand that feeds them. Sweden has the lowest marriage rate in the Western world, and the highest "couple dissolution" rate. Fully 50 percent of all live births are non-marital births. Sweden has the smallest average household size and the highest percentage of single-person households. Voluntarism and private charity have almost completely disappeared. Canadians, too, have lost much of their charitable feeling. They are half as charitable as Americans per capita, both individually and corporately. Sweden has also experienced an extraordinary "age-stratification" process whereby the old vertical family interdependencies have become horizontal stratifications, each human group quite separate from another, coddled and cosseted by the State in a womb-to-tomb cocoon. The very young are in State-subsidized daycare (where, Swedish journalist Anna Wahlgren says, many are habitually drugged); students are all in State schools; many couples live in State-subsidized housing; and the old live in State-subsidized old-age homes. Each group is effectively isolated from the other by the all-caring State, separated most crucially from the traditions, wisdom, cares, and values that might otherwise be passed down, or the joys and tribulations that might flow up. By the time such states realize they can no longer afford the programs they promise, that the unintended moral consequences of such programs are inimical to authentic values and the financial costs prohibitive, the people have lost their sense of family and community. All utopian philosophies are similar in the way they systematically destroy the natural processes of human life.

Swedish housing policy officially promotes multifamily housing (rental and cooperative) in order to discourage private family housing, which it associates with capitalism and individualist values. Units are intentionally built too small to accommodate relatives. Educational policy in Sweden (as in Canada) moved long ago to a "progressive" format, emphasizing student choice, permissiveness, a focus on social "adjustment," banishment of religion from schools, and an as yet unsuccessful campaign to remove all grading. (Ontario's "progressive" Hall-Dennis education report of the 1960s could have been ghostwritten by a Swede.) Sweden also became the first Western society to attempt to change the social and family roles of men as well as women, arguing that the man's role "must be radically enlarged" (they will have to order cattle-prodders for this job). "No longer was the family unit to be 'favored' in any way by the government" (to eliminate "family egoism"). As in Canada, laws were created to provide protection to "other forms of cohabitation," and economic autonomy became the new national standard of the good life. Radicals in Canada are pushing for this same economic standard. Canada's best known radical "sociologist," Margrit Eichler, in a flight of academic fancy, advocates a three part "Social Responsibility Model"[12] of the family:

1) Every adult is considered responsible for his or her own economic well-being. Where this is impossible, *the support obligation shifts to the State*, not to a family member. [She does not say what is to be done when the State is bankrupt.]

2) For an adult in need of care . . . *it is the responsibility of the State* (not a family member) to pay for the cost of such care. [She does not suggest simple insurance.]

3) The cost of raising children is shared by the father, the mother,

*and the State*, irrespective of the marital status of the parents. [This value-neutral format shifts the cost for illegitimate children and casual unions, to intact tax-paying families.]

A careful reader will see in this "model" every feature of the utopian top-down tradition that advocates a passing of responsibilities to the State at every opportunity. In the same fashion, the Swedish tax law in 1971 was "reformed" to prohibit joint taxation, so that the woman who wanted to be "just a housewife" was at a real financial disadvantage. (The same holds for the traditional family in Canada, as we shall soon see.) "It is widely believed that the prohibition of joint taxation was a turning point in the gender-equality issue" in Sweden. Dr. Eric Brodin, a native of Sweden, says the Swedish government views mothers who do not work outside the home as "parasites." In short, through the manipulation of tax policy by radical politicians and bureaucrats, the State succeeded in subsidizing family breakdown — a breakdown by no means desired by the masses of Swedes.

Irate that fathers are as yet reluctant to take the generous paid one-year "parental leave" (only 5 percent of fathers take it), the State is now considering *requiring* them to do so. This is the coercive humanitarianism of the welfare State in full flight. For in Sweden "family policy [is] seen as a tool that [can] be used by the government to try to change the traditional division of labour between the sexes . . . *the idea of free choice in the matter was more or less abandoned.*"[13]

The idea of free, responsible, interdependent families and individuals creating their own good life, according to personally held values, faith, and family standards, with no interference from the State, has thus been utterly abandoned, replaced with a sanitized, politically correct, State-certified life-style for all.

So we know the trade-off that Swedes are supinely prepared to make: personal freedom, responsibility, and risk will be surrendered for a putative equality of material condition; putative, because pure equality is illusory. Thus, no matter how similar we become, on no matter what measurement, the remaining differences will always seem galling to collectivists. Conversely, free people don't worry too much about inequalities, as long as they are free to be equal or unequal as they wish; if you are not free to be worse, then you are not free to be better. But in top-down states, as we gradually lose our freedom to control our own lives guided by our own values, we begin to care very much about inequalities. We begin to use our abstract "rights" to leapfrog other social groups. Tribunals are set up to adjudicate this leapfrogging process, the rules for which are so abstract as to allow decisions to swing whichever way the politically correct wind is blowing. Abstract "rights" now entrenched in our law become like magnets, attracting people and groups who use them to satisfy their personal grievances. This entire process is utterly alien to our tradition, which is anchored in the concrete common law, not in abstract Charter law concepts (see Chapter Eighteen). Whenever the law is converted from the first to the second, the people inevitably compare their condition in life to these abstract concepts, the material and moral adornments of which are supplied by their own minds. Thus does unrest begin, and we start to envy or even spy on our neighbours for fear they have been able to get more than we from the rights trough. Animals free to roam in search of plentiful food will not fight over whatever morsels are tossed to them, but once trapped in a cage, where others supply the flow of food, they soon forget their former freedom and devote themselves to a violent struggle for the scraps.

If life is inherently and naturally unequal because of the way free people and their families wish to express their natural differences, then I say let us at least have freedom and the maximum political, economic, and social mobility. Even long-standing leftists like Harvard's Barrington Moore, Jr., have shown that the so-called equality that has long been the justification for the limitation of human freedoms, and thus for so much of the horror in the modern world — the virtual devouring by socialist states not of the external enemy but of the "internal enemy" — is no different in the socialist than it is in the capitalist democracies. In short, the same human pattern of inequality shows up, but at a pitiably low level of economic wealth.[14] Sweden has avoided most of these outer horrors, and it has pressed the logic of the rational engineered society further than anyone else has been able to do without outward violence. But we must recall the words of the poet Goethe: "No one is more of a slave than he who imagines himself free without being so."[15]

What stuns in all this is the sleepy reluctance of the Swedish (and Canadian) population to see through the sweet-sounding theories to the self-serving ideology behind them, to the cynical stratagems of the State as it seeks more money, power, and allegiance by breaking the natural bonds of society. This minutely and cleverly — even deceptively — planned conversion of an authentic and free bottom-up community into an artificial national "people's home," as the Social Democrats like to call it, is depressingly routine for utopian collectivists. Plato proposed it for his "Republic"; Rousseau longed for it; Marx thought of it as a utopian paradise; Hitler called it the "Fatherland," FDR the "New Deal," LBJ the "Great Society," Trudeau, the "Just Society." Virtually all collectivists plan to bring about this insidious transformation of natural communities, or homes, into a single State "home," or communalism, either through deceptive policy and vote-marketing strategems, as in our Western democracies, or through overt totalitarian revolution in police states. The successful destruction of the traditional family is the one prior condition for the success of this campaign. As long as the family is strong, the collectivists cannot succeed in their objectives. They know it. Most of us don't. We must. Here are a few more of these inimical initiatives and their results as seen in Sweden.

If the last name of a child is not "officially" registered, the child automatically assumes the mother's name (down with patriarchy, up with poliarchy — rule by the State). The "new poor" in Sweden (and Canada and the United States) are of two kinds: intact traditional families with a lot of children, and single parents (mostly women) with children, who, on the condition they are not living as a married person, soon bond themselves to the State as a substitute spouse/parent. In Canada in 1950, fully 33 percent of family income was deductible for a stay-at-home spouse. But by 1990, this pro-family deduction equalled only 9.5 percent of the family income.[16]

In order to further impress upon private families the role of the State, Sweden (with parallels in Canada — and for that matter, in the entire Western world) introduced "children's rights" legislation in 1973, and in 1979 it enacted a law prohibiting parents from subjecting their own children to "physical punishment or other humiliating treatment." This "antispanking" law drew the wrath of the international establishment and caused Germany's *Der Spiegel* to label Sweden a "children's Gulag." All this was combined with extremely liberal laws on pornography. And State-run "sex-education" classes that effectively by-passed parental authority were, of course, instituted in all schools. All Western democracies have by now embarked on this program to imbue children with a State-approved sexual hygiene. We shall see in Chapter Eight that this innocent-seeming program has as its object the restructuring of all social values. Whereas Sweden's early sex-ed manuals (1930-60) stressed that "the implied aim of sex education is home life and its success," current manuals switch the emphasis to "sexual intimacy" as "one of the essential goals of human existence" (no mention of the sanctity of marriage or home life any more, there or in Canada, except in some religious schools).[17]

Some of the early signs of community breakdown these policies engendered were heavy increases in juvenile delinquency (according to Project Metropolitan, of 7000 Stockholm boys born in 1953, more than 30 percent had been in contact with police for lawbreaking by the time they were 26). On the white-collar level, by 1987 the "nation of cheats" was doing 20 percent of GNP in underground tax-free business (estimates are that Canadians do about $85 billion annually). After reaching a high point in the 1950s, the Swedish marriage rate dropped about 40 percent by 1975 (for women 20-24, it dropped from 194 to 91 per thousand women, or more than 50 percent). Today, virtually all Swedes cohabit before marriage (now an accepted alternative to marriage there). But the theory that premarital cohabitation would result in happier eventual marriages has been proved wrong there, and here. Perhaps the most important statistic in this entire chapter — based on the lives of 4300 Swedish women — showed that the "couple dissolution rate of cohabiting couples with one child was, on average, three times the dissolution rate of comparable married couples." In other words, legal marriage is a strong binding force that protects children. Sadly, the real victims of family decline, however we may wish the truth away, are the children, whom few seem to be defending. Fully 70 percent of Swedish divorces are initiated by women. It is about the same in both Canada and Britain.[18]

We have seen enough of family decline in Sweden, and we in Canada are living with the same trends — the same civil war of values — as we create our own "client society" in which "citizens are for the most part clients of a large group of public employees who take care of them throughout their lives."[19] Of course, once a State switches to a policy of paying formerly unpaid voluntary care-givers, through the extraction of tax dollars from the general public, it is on the way down. There are two reasons behind this pattern. First, when you tax the productive work of some to pay for the previously unpaid work of others, there will be a decisive and lasting depression of wealth. Secondly, there is and always has been far more total voluntary care given in all societies than could be paid for by any imaginable tax base. Canadians do about one billion hours of volunteer work annually, which equates to 530,000 full-year, full-time jobs.[20] But as the State increasingly takes over such functions, and the people correspondingly lose their interest in and skills at such voluntary giving, the crisis intensifies. As Popenoe explained: "Rather than drawing on a pool of family resources, the Swedish family today turns over to the state a large portion of those resources, and its members then become economically dependent on the state rather than the family. Not all of these resources are redistributed from rich to poor families; *a large portion could be said to be redistributed by the state back to the same family at different stages of the life cycle.*"[21]

Popenoe identifies four major "ideologies" as responsible for family breakdown: secularism, feminism, the therapeutic ideology, and radical socialism. But virtually all four could be subsumed under the single label of coercive humanitarianism, or utopianism, for each is based on the illusions discussed in Chapter Two, and each is a complement of the other. Here, again from *Disturbing the Nest*, is a neat summary of the radical antifamily thinking that has so controlled public policy in Sweden (and in many other Western democracies), although Popenoe says that this view may not actually be held by many Swedes. Ditto for all welfare States. These polices are unnatural (otherwise people would arrive at them voluntarily) and can be implemented only coercively by elites that have managed to secure the levers of power:

Thus the achievement of socialism requires . . . expanding whatever good there is in family life to encompass the community at large and at the same time doing away with what is "bad" in the family. *To destroy capitalism, and all it stands for, one must therefore largely destroy the family*, or at least the family as it has existed throughout history. To reach the radical-socialist ideal it is necessary to: eliminate marriage ("which provides the major legal support for the current family form"); prohibit the inheritance of family wealth by children; resist the attractions of private, domestic life (it detracts from public life); reduce the pressures (especially economic) that *compel* people to live in families; and develop alternatives to the family (such as communes) that can provide psychic security and material support.[22]

# 6

# The Family
## at a Glance

Statistics. It would be hard to find a field in which the public has less confidence, yet upon which it relies more for social policy decisions. On the subject of the family, there are some statistical contortions that are downright devious. For example, a set of figures may be produced to show high labour force "participation" by moms with young infants, but will not reveal how much of this is part-time work. Or another set of figures will confuse things by showing intact traditional families as a percentage of all "households" (in which are included all those who live alone). Or yet another will fail to include as traditional families all those whose children are very much *in* the family, but happen to be living at university.

This confusion is not surprising, perhaps, when you stop to consider that all human knowledge tends to get skewed in an opportunistic direction, especially, it seems, in family studies. After all, everything in life, and in scholarship, is a matter of attitude — much like deciding whether a glass of wine is half full or half empty. If you want more, it is half empty; if you've had enough, it's half full.

In all physical sciences, there are raw *measurements*, and then there are *interpretations* of those measurements. In the soft social sciences, however, researchers often end up measuring things they have created themselves, and thus tend to infect their studies with subtle prior interpretations of the very situation they say they are measuring. Thus, when it comes to studying the family, much depends on how the question is framed — on the questioner's attitude.

For example, if you think the natural family is a tyrannical institution and ought to be abolished, you will tend to favour family breakdown and argue that more divorce and less marriage may be healthy for society. You will therefore call a one percent increase in the divorce rate "unprecedented." But if you are pro-family, you will likely argue that the difference is "insignificant," considering the antifamily social forces at play, the breakdown in child discipline, the number of government programs that undermine family authority, and so on.

With the reader now forewarned, I can say that there are three purposes to this chapter. The first is to present the consistent attitudes of the people toward family values, as recorded in a series of polls, and compare these with government policy. Polls are not exactly high science — for the reasons I have mentioned. But when the simplest questions consistently produce the same sort of profile, we can be sure we've hit upon a basic value. Readers will see that there is a large gap between the people's family values and government policy on just about every value probed, and this discrepancy should raise very serious questions, such as: "Who is running the country anyway?" Or: "Why is there such a serious gap between national policy and national values?" In a democracy, shouldn't the two, eventually, more or less equate? The answer would seem to be yes, in a popular democracy, but no, in any top-down "democracy" in which planners persistently strive to satisfy their ideological imperatives by introducing policies specifically designed to alter spontaneous natural values and desires.

Next will come comparative international statistics on the family for basic variables such as divorce rates and illegitimacy rates. These are meant to show roughly where Canada stands between the more traditional and more collectivist nations. We will generally see that at least in the Western democracies, the more collectivist the country, the weaker and more dissolved is the family — especially if it is antireligious by policy. Paradoxically, this relationship may not hold up in the totalitarian nations, simply because the poor souls who live in them cling to family and their religion as their last bastion of meaningful values, their covert resistance to the State.

Finally, we shall look at a series of straightforward charts showing the family in Canada over the past few decades, with comparisons where possible. These will show that although still quite traditional, Canada is rapidly and inexorably moving in the direction of family decline, the prototype for which, as we saw in the preceding chapter, is Sweden.

# THE STATE vs. THE FAMILY

## WHAT THE PEOPLE WANT/SAY

```
0   10 20 30 40 50 60 70 80 90 100%
L__|__|__|__|__|__|__|__|__|__|__J
```

## WHAT THE GOVERNMENT DOES

| # | What the People Want/Say | % | What the Government Does |
|---|---|---|---|
| 1. | More emphasis on traditional family ties. | 94% | The State pursues antifamily policies. |
| 2. | An overwhelming majority believe in God. | 91% | The State legislates against religious celebration. |
| 3. | Welfare recipients should be made to work. | 84% | The State has changed the old "hand-up" to a "hand-out." |
| 4. | 6% Only 6% of Canadian children 10-19 are active enough to gain a fitness and health benefit. | | The public schools do not believe in the whole person. |
| 5. | An "overwhelming majority" believe physical education should be mandatory in the schools. | 91% | It isn't. |
| 6. | Virtually all Canadians want standardized student evaluation in the public schools. | 94% | Although we live in a democracy, the educational elites refuse to comply. The results show. |
| 7. | Children's well-being is sacrificed because both parents have to work. | 76% | The marriage tax — and taxes in general — are the greatest financial burden on the family. |
| 8. | More respect for authority. | 88% | Traditional forms of authority are weakened, replaced by "rights" legislation and bureaucracy. |
| 9. | Women say family more important than job, or career. | 78% | The traditional family is scorned. Government promotes career over family (it needs the extra taxes). |
| 10. | Morals and honesty are deteriorating. | 50% | The State promotes moral relativism. |
| 11. | The best place for pre-school children is at home with their parents. | 66% | This "whopping two-thirds" of Canadians opposed daycare of any kind. The government promotes it. |
| 12. | The people reject abortion on demand. (66% of physicians want legal protection for the fetus.) | 75% | The State — and 90% of the media — supports and promotes it. Any Canadian, or American, woman can abort a baby even as late as full term. U.S. figures are even higher. |
| 13. | A constitutional assembly, and referendums for constitutional matters. | 72% | Canada's elites persistently pursue government deal-making and social engineering. |

## POLLS

1. Gallup, Feb. 4, 1989
2. Gallup, Aug. 30, 1990
3. Gallup, Nov. 30, 1989
4. 1981 Canada Fitness Survey
5. Gallup, Jan. 9, 1990
6. Gallup, 1985
7. *Globe and Mail* / CBC News Poll, Nov. 5, 1991
8. Gallup, Feb. 4, 1989
9. National Poll, *Homemakers* magazine, March 1992
10. Gallup, Jan. 18, 1988
11. Decima, June 5, 1991
12. Gallup, June 20, 1988; also, independent poll of 10,000 CMA physicians, 1989
13. Environics, Oct. 16, 1991; also, A.J. Finkelstein poll, Sept. 16, 1990

# THE STATE vs. THE FAMILY

| WHAT THE PEOPLE WANT/SAY | WHAT THE GOVERNMENT DOES |
|---|---|
| 0 10 20 30 40 50 60 70 80 90 100% | |

| # | WHAT THE PEOPLE WANT/SAY | % | WHAT THE GOVERNMENT DOES |
|---|---|---|---|
| 14. | "Homosexuality is wrong" (U.S. figure is 81%.) | 70% | The State promotes homosexuality in the public schools. The media praise such behaviour as normal. |
| 15. | Medical students have a right to know if a patient has AIDS. | 88% | They don't. This deadly, contagious disease is politically protected by the State to shelter the "gay" lobby. |
| 16. | Courts are too lenient with criminals (1968 figure — 43%) | 78% | The State promotes the modern liberal notion that society, not the individual, is responsible for crime. |
| 17. | Cut spending, don't raise taxes. | 84% | The Consumer Tax Index has risen over 1400% since 1960 (inflation only 400%). Taxes are biggest family expense. |
| 18. | Sex outside marriage is "always" or "almost always" wrong. | 73% | Liberal sex attitudes in the schools and media are widely promoted. Sex is officially divorced from marriage. |
| 19. | Canadians declare themselves overwhelmingly of Judeo-Christian affiliation. | 91% | The nation's religious/cultural ethos is denigrated by media and education eliton. Secular humanism is promoted. |
| 20. | Canadian women say they have "little or nothing" to do with feminism. | 66% | The feminist ideology saturates the media and most institutions of government. |
| 21. | The people oppose quotas for hiring women. | 66% | The State persists in discrimination based on sex, race, and colour. |
| 22. | Women are satisfied with the "domestic division of labour." | 89% | Both media and government flay the public with endless accounts of domestic injustice and unhappiness. |
| 23. | Women are "satisfied with their lives at home" (a U.S. study, echoed in Canada). 53% of married women said "very satisfied." | 90% | We are besieged with stories of domestic discontent. The family is portrayed as a prison. The State provides tax incentives to abandon the family for work. |
| 24. | Working women would quit their jobs if they could stay at home with their children (U.S. poll). Canadians say the same. | 79% | Commercial work is promoted as better than child-rearing. The wealthy elite have no support on this. |

## POLLS

14. U.S. poll cited in *New Dimensions*, Jan. 1990; Canadian survey — R. Bibby, *Mosaic Madness*, 1990 and Gallup, Oct. 1, 1977
15. Toronto *Star* poll, Apr. 17, 1991
16. Gallup, Jan. 19, 1987
17. Gallup, March 16, 1986
18. Gallup, Oct. 1, 1977
19. 1981 *Canada Census*
20. *National Survey, Homemakers* magazine, March 1992

21. Canada-wide poll, Toronto *Star*, Dec. 10, 1989
22. *National Survey, Homemakers* magazine, March 1990
23. Gallup, Aug. 25, 1988
24. U.S. poll, Los Angeles *Times*, 1990, cited in *New Dimensions*, Nov. 1990. Canadian poll of 38,000 women showed 69% feel the same as U.S. counterparts (Federated Women's Institute, June 14, 1990)

## THE INTERNATIONAL SCENE

The pattern that emerges from these comparisons, however modest, seems to show that family breakdown, or "decline," tends to be very great in countries (or in social groups within them) where the role of government intervention is greatest, unless there is a countervailing traditional factor such as widespread religious belief. In short, the thesis outlined in Chapter One seems borne out by the data: that collectivist, or top-down, states (whether wilfully or not) actively operate to erode natural community, especially in secular nations also antireligious by policy.

Much of the work of comparing family statistics in various countries has been done by others; the rest I have had to put together. For the figures below I draw especially heavily from the excellent work of David Popenoe, both in his article "Family Decline in America" and in his book *Disturbing the Nest*.[1] Popenoe shows how various nations (or groups within them) that have been Swedenized (my term) tend to have the greatest family decline. The Canadian numbers are drawn from a variety of statistical and demographic sources to be found in this chapter's end-notes.[2]

For Popenoe, the modern family has weakened over a long period in several ways. It is internally less cohesive, and so its members depend less on each other (many rely on State income transfers). It has less control over both the sexual life and the socialization of its children (for two centuries now it has been losing power to schools and the State). Families are now smaller and are intact for shorter periods of the lifespan. And finally, the family has slowly abandoned its importance as a social unit, and has replaced it with an ethic of individual self-fulfilment (Rieff's "psychological man," or what is referred to in Part Two as "Personal Liberation Ideology").

For interest, I have arranged a variety of nations in a rough sequence to show how increasing family decline generally accompanies increasing collectivism, increasing taxation, and increasing "liberalism." The message should not be lost on us; nor should it surprise us. Sociologist L. Roussel of France summed it up at a 1986 demographic conference in Ottawa. He pointed out that while there were certain "problems" with the family in the Western world, we ought not to be surprised, for these were entirely due to developments that we had deliberately initiated, promoted, and supported. Some examples: near-perfect contraception, so people could "plan" their families; "enlightened" divorce laws, so that those in intolerable marital situations could more easily be freed from them; acceptance and encouragement of female labour-force participation, so women who so wished, or who found it necessary, could join the workforce. In other words, what we see happening all around us, as reflected in oft-cited statistics, is happening because of things we have consciously done. (By "we," he means the elite knowledge-class, not necessarily the people.[3]) Roussel, a committed social engineer, obviously approves of these changes, and opined that if the social engineers don't like it, they can develop other policies to change things again. In this attitude we clearly see once again the old left-liberal idea that man has a malleable nature, as opposed to a constant one; and the way to engineer the perfect society is to educate ignorant individuals (the masses) and change social institutions for the better. Oh, it's good fun if you're getting paid for it!

Because of the difficulties in finding firm numbers for each country for all variables (owing to different or discontinuous data), there will be some substitution in what follows, which should not harm the point to be made. Certain of these countries are acknowledged to be conservative, or traditional, from a family point of view, such as Japan, Switzerland, and New Zealand. The United States and Canada occupy the middle ground on most matters, veering toward tradition or toward collectivism, depending on the variable. The effect of collectivist programs in these nations is, however, often resisted by a relatively strong religious culture, and this inarticulate resistance creates an ongoing social tension that requires government elites to mask collectivist policies in "fair"-sounding euphemisms (to lie, that is). But, outside the formerly communist sphere, Sweden is the hands-down winner for an example of how the secular welfare State openly erodes the traditional family. It will be the watermark to measure ourselves against simply because Sweden's welfare State and family policies — indeed, the entire Swedish radical socialist ideology — found a cozy, well-subsidized home right here in Canada more than three decades ago. Until Canada's (and Sweden's) recent and quite predictable troubles began, Sweden had served as a kind of living antifamily model.

That's why it's a good bet that on most of the demographic measures shown below, Canada will soon be where Sweden is today. If we want to reverse this direction, we simply will have to find the determination to stop feeding the political radicals, governments, and quasi-governmental organizations that are responsible. But the first chore — hence, this book — is to let the people know what has been going on; to show them how, in different ways, virtually all three mainstream political parties in Canada have been supporting antifamily policies opposed to the deepest values and sympathies of the people, and utterly foreign to the political, economic, moral, and religious principles on which this country was based.

Where possible, in U.S. statistics blacks are separated from other Americans — a common practice among many U.S. sociologists.[4] The two societies are so different that if you mix them, you get neither. Otherwise, U.S. figures include both societies. In fact, I would argue that black America is a tragic example of how the welfare State can utterly destroy a human community of strong families if it really puts its mind to the job. Most people are shocked to learn that as recently as 1957, about 75 percent of black and 80 percent of white American families were headed by a married couple.[5] Since then, untold billions have been lavished on the black community in programs from President Johnson's "Great Society" to Nixon's "War on Poverty" to — you name it. In the brief space of 30 years, such programs amounted not to a war on poverty, but to a left-liberal "war on the poor" — of unimaginable consequences. The traditional system based on merit, which, however slowly, had been working for black Americans, was replaced by elite-designed welfare programs offering countless economic disincentives to work and save (and, therefore, moral disincentives to honour family commitments and responsibilities).

Someday someone will demonstrate that what such "welfare" programs have done to black Americans can be fittingly compared to what Canadians have done to their own Native people. As a group, our Native populations have a far higher single-parent rate (27 percent), unemployment rate (up to 50 percent are not even in the labour force), welfare dependency rate (up to 18 percent), and homicide, alcoholism, and suicide rate than any other Canadian group — and they are the most thoroughly Swedenized of all. It is here that we must look for explanations, simply because there are a great many other social groups in the world with far worse economic conditions than theirs, yet who have close-knit family values and social statistics the opposite of those produced among Native people in Canada. Let's not, however, hold our breath waiting for the welfare bureaucracy to vote itself out of existence in a wave of enthusiasm for self-reliance.

## The Family-Breakdown Scale

**Most Traditional**                                                **Most Collectivist**

←――――――――――――――――――――――――――――――――――――→

---

### Average Family Taxation as Percentage
### of Family Income (1989)

| Switzerland | U.S. | **Canada** | Sweden |
|---|---|---|---|
| 24% | 35% | **45%** | 60% |
| | | **(1960: 22%)** | (1961: 32%) |

---

### Total Government Revenues as Percentage of
### Gross Domestic Product (GDP) (1989)*

| U.S. | Japan | Switzerland | **Canada** | Sweden |
|---|---|---|---|---|
| 30% | 30.2% | 32% | **34.5%** | 56.7% |

\* Figures do not include borrowing

*SOURCE*: Organisation for Economic Co-operation and Development

---

### Government Current Expenditures on Goods and Services
### as Percentage of Gross Domestic Product
### (GDP) (OECD, 1989)

| Japan | Switzerland | New Zealand | U.S. | **Canada** | Sweden |
|---|---|---|---|---|---|
| 9.3% | 12.9% | 16.3% | 17.9% | **18.7%** | 25.9% |

Comment:
*This precise but narrow measure of spending gives a good comparative picture, but it does not include many items such as the interest cost of government debt.*

## The Family-Breakdown Scale

**Most Traditional**                                    **Most Collectivist**

←————————————————————————————————————————————————→

---

### Public Expenditures Per Capita (1979-80)

| Japan | Switzerland | New Zealand | **Canada** | U.S. | Sweden |
|---|---|---|---|---|---|
| $1208 | $1545 | $2373 | **$2388** | $2638 | $5184 |

SOURCE: *New Book of World Rankings*, 1984 ($U.S.).

Comment:

*If, as I believe, total taxation (the total of all taxes, visible and invisible, from all levels of government) is the surest sign of the degree of socialist intervention in a nation (socialism = taxation), then the above comparisons tell us where matters stand. With some exceptions, we can expect to see family decline, as a measure of failing social bonds, tracked by these percentages, unless there is some unique countervailing social reality, such as strong religious belief among the nation's families.*

---

### Take-Home Pay as a Percentage of Gross Earnings (1983)
### (Including Family Benefits)

| Japan | Switzerland | **Canada** | Sweden |
|---|---|---|---|
| 90% | 88% | **75%** | 73% |
|  |  | **(1960: 90%)** |  |

Comment:

*Take-home pay is a measure of the degree to which individuals surrender to the State control over the use of their own resources. These figures include "pay" received in the form of "benefits" transferred back to the taxpayer, and otherwise would be much lower. In Canada, for example, take-home pay, in the sense of the net amount of actual cash left in the hands of the average family after all forms of tax have been paid, is more like 50%.*

## The Family-Breakdown Scale

**Most Traditional**                                   **Most Collectivist**

◄───────────────────────────────────────────────────►

---

### Female Labour Force "Participation" Rate
### (For Women 15-64) (1989)

| Switzerland | Japan | New Zealand | **Canada** | U.S. | Sweden |
|:-----------:|:-----:|:-----------:|:----------:|:----:|:------:|
| 58.5% | 59.3% | 60.7% | **67.4%** | 68.1% | 80.5% |

*SOURCE:* Organisation for Economic Co-operation and Development

Comment:

*There is surely a dire relationship between levels of total national taxation and the degree to which both spouses must work to make ends meet. In addition, socialized nations, eager to assume the functions of the family and to transform each family into an atomized collection of autonomous individuals (and taxpayers), embark on programs to discourage personal childrearing, scorn housewifery, and find ways to punish single-income families through the tax code, either deliberately or by neglect. In Sweden, this has been an overt, intentional purpose of the tax code, which in 1971 eliminated the joint tax return,* intentionally *making it more burdensome economically for a wife to stay home and parent her own children.* In Canada, as we shall see, all married people are punished by the tax code, especially if they also have children under 18. *At any rate, we must be wary of labour "participation" figures. After all, women, whether inside the home or out, have always "worked," and for centuries housewives have supplemented family income through work for the outside market — ranging from sewing, to pickling, to computer work. The crucial, often-buried distinction that matters is the question:* To what degree does this non-family work for a commercial market interfere with home production and the personal parenting of children? *A mother at home typing frantically with one hand to meet a deadline, and shooing her crying infant child away with the other, is just as neglectful as a mother gripping the steering wheel with parental anxiety and guilt as she speeds to her next account, hoping her child has found the key to the house. The child loses out in both cases. Readers anxious about political correctness may, except for the event of actual childbirth, substitute "father" for "mother," if that helps to bring their blood pressure down. I do, however, argue that there is no such thing as "parenting." There is only fathering and mothering, and they are quite different, equally valuable, and both necessary to a child's development.*

## The Family-Breakdown Scale

**Most Traditional**                                        **Most Collectivist**

◀─────────────────────────────────────────────────▶

---

## Non-Marital Births as a Percentage
## of all Births (1983)

| Switzerland | **Canada** | U.S./White | Sweden | U.S./Black |
|:---:|:---:|:---:|:---:|:---:|
| 5.7% | **16%** | 20% | 45% | 60% |
| | **(1974: 9%)** | (1960: 6%) | (1971: 22%) | (1960: 22%) |
| | **(1990: 22%)** | | (1990: 50%) | |

Comment:

*Again, a clear measure of the loss of faith in the bonds of family can be seen here. Because unmarried couples dissolve at a much faster rate than married couples, the children of these unions are increasingly exposed to insecurity, change of parents, and social distress. The damage to the black family in the United States is nothing short of a national crisis of fatherless homes, the repercussions of which are bound to be severe in the decades to come and will likely be seen in vastly increased crime rates. The inimitable Charles Murray argues forcefully that illegitimacy is the most important social statistic because it inevitably means a fatherless home. All boys and girls, as we know, require role models to grow up properly, and children — boys in particular — tend to run wild in homes without fathers. Large percentages of them turn to family violence and crime as a result. Thus, a rising illegitimacy rate is a bona fide indicator of a growing underclass and of a growing crime rate.*[6]

## The Family-Breakdown Scale

**Most Traditional**                                                   **Most Collectivist**

<----------------------------------------------------------------->

---

### Unmarried Couples as a Percentage of All Couples (1983)

| Switzerland | New Zealand | U.S. | **Canada** | Sweden |
|---|---|---|---|---|
| 4% | 5% | 5% | **7%** | 22% |
| | | | **(1991: 9.9%)** | (1970: 7%) |
| | | | | (1988: 25%) |

Comment:

*These figures don't tell the whole story, because they include all couples, from all age groups. A measure of the rejection of the marital commitment is more clearly seen in the fact that in Sweden (1980), for the 20- to 24-year-old group, fully 68% of women and 79% of men lived as unmarried couples. For the next group, 25–29, the marriage rate expressed per 1000 women in this age bracket was only 78/1000 in Sweden, but 127/1000 in the United States (France: 117; U.K.: 168; Japan: 109).* Fully 36% of Swedish women born in 1955 will not have married at all by age 50!

## The Family-Breakdown Scale

**Most Traditional**                                              **Most Collectivist**

←——————————————————————————————————————————————→

---

## The Divorce Rate

| Belgium | Switzerland | **Canada** | England/<br>Wales | Sweden | U.S. |
|---------|-------------|------------|-------------------|--------|------|
| 12% | 14% | **15%** | 27% | 36% | 42% |

*SOURCE*: All figures are from Popenoe, except Canada's, which are from Statistics Canada.

Comment:

*These figures are for the percentage of those born in 1945 whose marriages are predicted to end in divorce. For Canadians born in 1960, the likelihood of divorce some time before age 80 is about 33%.*

*The United States is the world leader at divorce — but also the world's leader at marriage, and remarriage! Fully 85% of divorced Americans remarry, but only 50% of Swedes do. Fully 75% of Canadian males, and 66% of females, remarry. Also, the Swedish figure would be much higher if more Swedes married in the first place. So to test the permanence of marriage vs. common law unions, we must compare the "couple dissolution" rate of all Swedes, married and unmarried, who have children. Fasten your safety belts. The couple dissolution rate for unmarried Swedish couples with children is three times as high as for married couples with children!*

*The real story in all these figures, however, is the comparison between Switzerland and Sweden, two countries that share many similarities of climate, size, and war-free status over the past century. They have, however, diametrically opposed social policies, the first a hands-off traditional society; the second, highly State-interventionist.*

## The Family-Breakdown Scale

**Most Traditional**                                              **Most Collectivist**

◀──────────────────────────────────────────────────────────────▶

---

### Single-Parent Families (1986)

| Switzerland | **Canada** | Sweden | U.S./ White | **Canada/ Indian** | U.S./ Black |
|---|---|---|---|---|---|
| 12% | **13%** | 18% | 25% | **27%** | 53% |
| | **(1931: 14%)** | | (1960: 9%) | | (1960: 22%) |

Comment:

*Sweden's figures are for 1985. Figures are for parents made separate by all causes, such as death, divorce, and separation. Although a late-starter in the race for family dissolution, Canada is closing in on the leaders of this disaster-made-for-children. Black America has been devastated by the single-minded focus on subsidizing social breakdown. The most damning review of this tragedy, too complex to delve into here but everywhere evident in these awful statistics on black family breakdown, is Charles Murray's book* Losing Ground: American Social Policy 1950-1980.[7] *In it, he illustrates in impeccable detail how the social welfare State programs now enveloping almost the entire black population of America have adversely affected these long-suffering people. And yet this is a population which, considered as a nation, had a GNP in 1980 that was larger than all but 14 nations of the world. In fact, in 1940, Harlem had a per-capita income that ranked it fifth in the world (U.S. blacks as a whole ranked fifteenth), and as recently as 1957, fully 75% of all black families in America were headed by a married couple.[8] History will show that this microcosm of the socialist State within America virtually seduced the families of almost an entire race and culture into a pathetic helplessness, dependency, and loss of pride.*

*Many are surprised to learn Canada had more lone-parent families in 1931 (14%) than in 1990. But there's a difference. Then, many wives were left alone by early death (from war, lower life-expectancy of husbands). Today, the majority of lone parents are wives who have left their marriages.*

## THE NATIONAL SCENE

By now we have had a taste of the international scene sufficient to suggest that nations differ very greatly in many ways. The thesis of this book is that there is a complex relationship between the rise of the welfare State and the dissolution of the natural family in the West. For many reasons, this relationship is difficult to see directly, because such dissolution can be forestalled or softened by a strong religious culture, among other things. Nevertheless, we cannot wait for historians and social scientists to tell us about our own dissolution after the fact. The evidence, however murky, seems to point in the same direction: Welfare states rob the people of self-reliance and undermine moral agency. In doing so, they undermine the entire political, economic, and moral fabric of Western civilization itself.

Let us now see, in the 26 charts that follow, what has happened to the family in Canada over the past few generations. The first few charts, repeated from *The Trouble with Canada*, show the economic effect of the welfare State on individuals and families. The remaining charts show specific family trends.

**CHART 1   Putting Family First**
*Marriage is by Far the Perferred Option for Most Canadians*

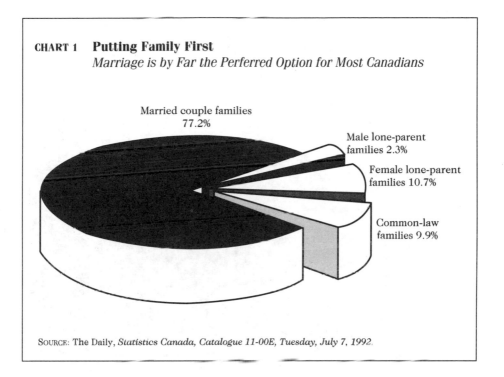

Married couple families
77.2%

Male lone-parent
families 2.3%

Female lone-parent
families 10.7%

Common-law
families 9.9%

SOURCE: The Daily, *Statistics Canada, Catalogue 11-00E, Tuesday, July 7, 1992.*

Comment:
*The chart section begins with the good news from Canada's 1991 census: fully 77.2 per cent of all Canadian families are* traditional, mother-father-children families. *If we include common-law families, then 87 per cent of all families are traditional and, as Gordon Priest, Statistics Canada's social data expert, put it, "The family is alive and well, with 86% of Canadian children under 15 living in two-parent families. . . . The old values, of men and women forming couples they intend to last, having children, supporting children, are still there.* Those who utter gloom and doom about the death of the family won't find it in our statistics." *So what's the problem? It's the trend: in 1980, that 77.2 per cent figure for married-couple families was 80.1 per cent. Conclusion? The young are increasingly avoiding legal marriage, and childbearing. As for lone-parent families, however, we had as many (12.2%) in 1936, as today—then, mostly from widowhood, today, mostly from divorce (Vanier Institute of the Family,* Canadian Families in Transition, *1992). Overwhelmingly, both in practice and as the dream expressed in every poll, North Americans seek the traditional family form—against increasing political, economic, and social resistance.*

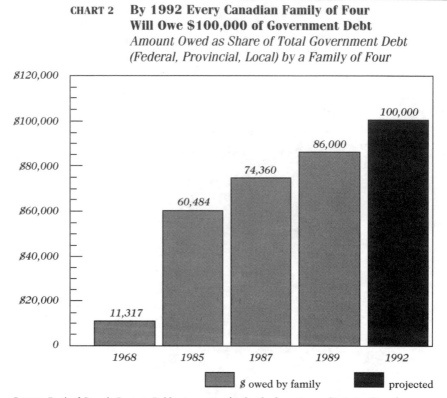

**CHART 2   By 1992 Every Canadian Family of Four Will Owe $100,000 of Government Debt**

*Amount Owed as Share of Total Government Debt (Federal, Provincial, Local) by a Family of Four*

SOURCE: Bank of Canada Review. *Public Accounts of individual provinces, Statistics Canada publication 13-001 (National Income and Expenditure Accounts), and* Canada Year Books 1970/71, 1988. *Figure for 1989 is the author's projection from the same sources. A continuation of the present trend would result in a $650 billion combined federal and provincial debt by 1992.*

Comment:

*Another title for this chart might have been: So You're Wondering Where Your Down-Payment on a First House Went? To the extent that our three levels of government must necessarily tax you higher to pay their costs and service their debts, they are taking money from you that otherwise would have been used for your down-payment, your mortgage, your car, credit card payment, a boat. You name it, they've got it. And what is not taken from you will be taken from your children. And their children. It's not that we don't get something from government. We do (we get infrastructure, such as roads, and some services we cannot supply for ourselves, such as police). But we are purchasing more than we can pay for (much of which we should provide for personally), and thus we're breaking our contract with future generations. Those who are not here to defend themselves are being saddled with the cost of goods and services we are consuming.*

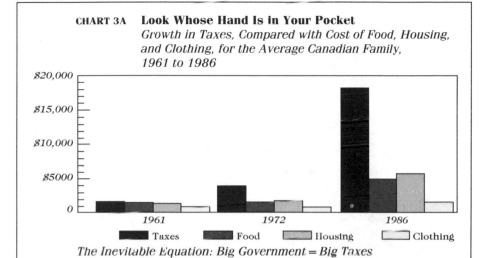

CHART 3A   **Look Whose Hand Is in Your Pocket**
*Growth in Taxes, Compared with Cost of Food, Housing, and Clothing, for the Average Canadian Family, 1961 to 1986*

*The Inevitable Equation: Big Government = Big Taxes*

SOURCE: *Sally Pipes and Michael Walker,* Tax Facts Six *(The Fraser Institute, Vancouver, 1988), Table 19, p.49.*

CHART 3B   **The Price of the Social-Welfare State Is the Erosion of the Productive Power of the Nation**
*Total Government Spending as a Percentage of GNP (5-year averages)*

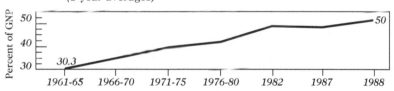

SOURCE: *Herbert Grubel, "The Cost of Canada's Social Insurance Programs," in* Probing Leviathan: An Investigation of Government in the Economy *(The Fraser Institute,Vancouver, 1984), Fig. 3.2, p.61; and Table A-1, p.129. Also* Economic Review, 1981; Bank of Canada Review, 1989; *and individual provincial Public Accounts.*

Comment:

*The average Canadian family will surely ask what has been gained by this enormously increased output of tax dollars, compared with the ratio of taxes paid in 1961. The top chart illustrates hidden costs in the three leading components of family expense. Food contains the hidden cost of marketing boards (wheat, eggs, milk, etc.) and tariffs on imported food; clothing includes the cost of tariffs and quotas on imports; housing includes the same, as well as the cost of government-guaranteed "affordable" housing, subsidized rentals, rent controls, etc. The bottom chart shows the rapid increase in total government spending since the onset of the welfare State.*

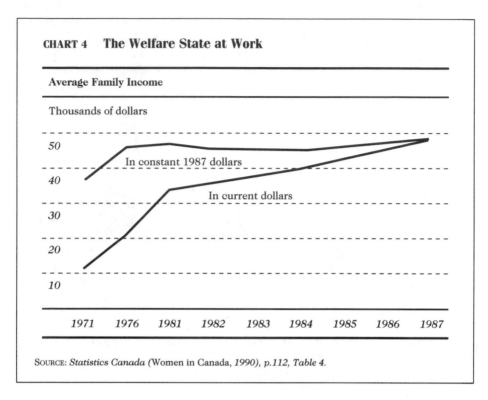

CHART 4    The Welfare State at Work

Average Family Income

Thousands of dollars

50

In constant 1987 dollars

40

In current dollars

30

20

10

1971    1976    1981    1982    1983    1984    1985    1986    1987

SOURCE: *Statistics Canada* (Women in Canada, *1990*), p.112, Table 4.

Comment:

*The inevitable economic effect of the welfare State is an increasing squeeze on personal and family disposable (and investable) income. As this chart clearly shows, average family income, for 16 years, has held about level. No real increases, in constant-dollar terms (all inflation removed), are visible. The story is more complex than this, however. For the most part, this "holding" pattern was only made possible by the contribution of female income to the family, sufficient to offset the disproportionate rise in taxes seen in Chart 3. As I have said, the welfare State creates a fiscal wedge that pries women out of the home and into the factories.*

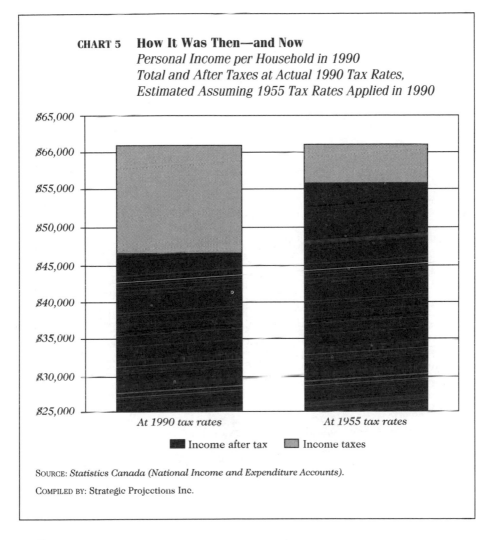

CHART 5 **How It Was Then—and Now**
*Personal Income per Household in 1990*
*Total and After Taxes at Actual 1990 Tax Rates,*
*Estimated Assuming 1955 Tax Rates Applied in 1990*

At 1990 tax rates    At 1955 tax rates

■ Income after tax    ▨ Income taxes

SOURCE: *Statistics Canada (National Income and Expenditure Accounts).*

COMPILED BY: Strategic Projections Inc.

Comment:
*This chart shows how much more of your own money you would have been able to keep if 1955 tax rates had applied in 1990. In 1990, the average household income was $60,887. Personal income taxes took 23% of this income, leaving $46,922. But in 1955, personal income taxes took only 9% of personal income. If the 1990 rate had been 9% instead of the average 23%, each household would have paid almost $8500 less in taxes. In other words, after taxes, personal income would have been 18.1% higher than it was.*

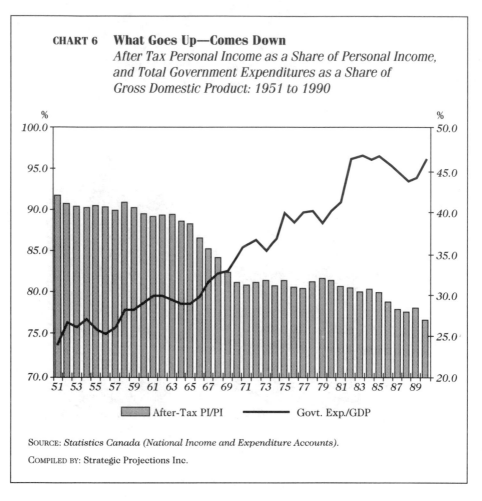

CHART 6   **What Goes Up—Comes Down**
*After Tax Personal Income as a Share of Personal Income,
and Total Government Expenditures as a Share of
Gross Domestic Product: 1951 to 1990*

After-Tax PI/PI          Govt. Exp./GDP

SOURCE: *Statistics Canada (National Income and Expenditure Accounts).*

COMPILED BY: Strategic Projections Inc.

Comment:

*Government's share of spending has been increasing steadily in
Canada for decades, and as of 1990 it was more than twice that of
1951, an indication of the State's increasing encroachment on the
freedoms, property, and privacy of its citizens. This chart gives a
graphic description of the erosion in discretionary control of
personal financial resources — and, therefore, of the surrender of
control over many personal and family responsibilities now
transferred to the State. A similar chart could be drawn showing the
phenomenal growth in the numbers of government departments,
employees, and programs. For example, Canada had only 33 Crown
corporations in 1951, but over 1000 by 1984. As of 1991, one in every
5.5 Canadians worked directly or indirectly for government (Toronto
Star, June 25, 1991).*

CHART 7   **The Breadwinner Penalty**
*Personal Taxes as a Percentage Share of Total Family Incomes
One Earner Vs. Two Earner Famlies, 1989*

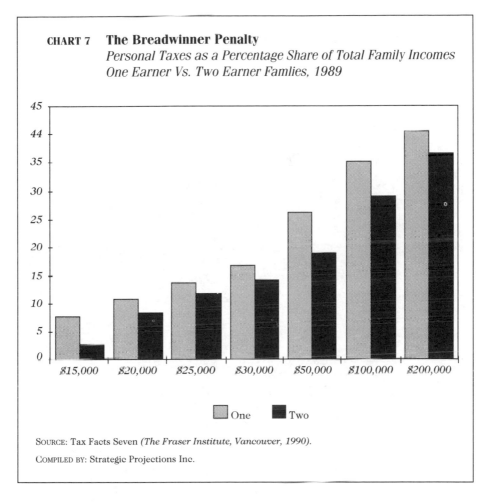

SOURCE: Tax Facts Seven *(The Fraser Institute, Vancouver, 1990).*

COMPILED BY: Strategic Projections Inc.

Comment:

*Our personal tax system also is clearly biased against the one-earner
family in favour of the two-earner family. At every level of family
income, personal taxes are lower as a share of total family income if
the income is earned by two family members rather than by one,
especially in the middle-income range of $50,000 per year. More than
any other, perhaps, this chart speaks volumes about our nation's
attitude toward families that choose to devote more personal care to
their own children than is possible if both spouses work outside the
home. In short, so-called one-earner families (with the worker
usually the male, in a traditional family) have been punished via the
tax system for their inner-directed family focus. Allowing all married
couples to split income before taxation would remove this bias. It
would also confer a much needed economic value on the work of at-
home mothers.*

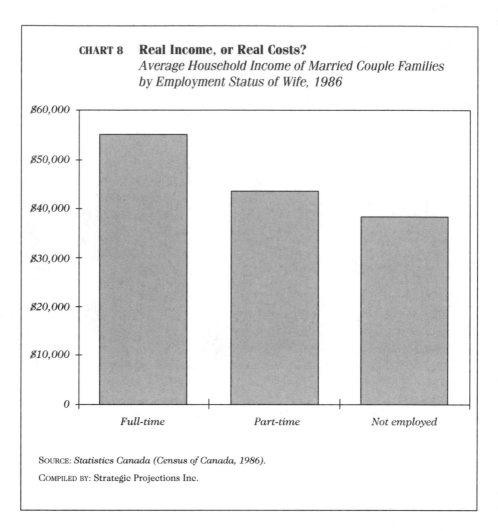

CHART 8   **Real Income, or Real Costs?**
*Average Household Income of Married Couple Families
by Employment Status of Wife, 1986*

SOURCE: *Statistics Canada (Census of Canada, 1986).*
COMPILED BY: Strategic Projections Inc.

Comment:

*The gross income of a married couple is clearly higher on average if
the wife works full-time, or even part-time outside the home, than if
she does not work at all outside the home. However, this result may
be more a consequence of socio-economic status than anything else.
Upper-income couples have higher-paying jobs. Surveys show that
most lower-income wives do not want to work, but must — quite the
reverse of the upper-income group. Of course, two-earner families
also have higher expenses. What such charts do not tell us is
anything about the emotional, psychological, or social expenses to
the nation and its families and children, caused by the modern trend
to leave the home and children for commercial work outside the
home.*

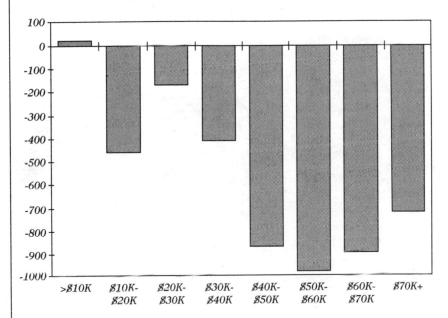

CHART 9 **Soaking the Married**
*Net Average Financial Impact of the Tax and Transfer System. Married Couples Compared to Non-Married Couples by Family Income Group in 1989 in Dollars per Year*

Source: *Richard J. Morrison and Jillian Oderkirk, "Married and Unmarried Couples: The Tax Question," in* Canadian Social Trends *(Statistics Canada, 1991).*

Compiled by: Strategic Projections Inc.

Comment:

*This chart shows the same antimarriage effect, by income groups. Compared with unmarried (common-law) couples, married Canadian couples at every income level, except the lowest, have been punished by the tax system for getting married. Those earning over $40,000 per year have really been hit (by an average of $980 per couple). Some individual couples have paid thousands of dollars more solely because they were married. Canada's proposed changes in the tax code for January 1993 ought to make these charts obsolete. We'll see. But citizens must be wary. Future governments may backslide. Socialist governments aim for this antimarriage tax result as an ideological objective, as we saw in Chapter Five.*

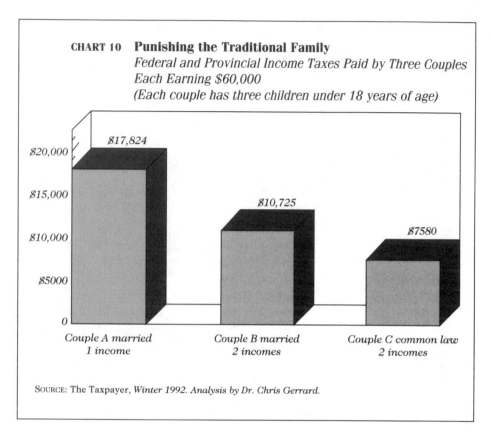

CHART 10 **Punishing the Traditional Family**
*Federal and Provincial Income Taxes Paid by Three Couples
Each Earning $60,000
(Each couple has three children under 18 years of age)*

$20,000 — $17,824

$15,000

$10,000 — $10,725

$7580

$5000

0

Couple A married
1 income

Couple B married
2 incomes

Couple C common law
2 incomes

SOURCE: The Taxpayer, *Winter 1992. Analysis by Dr. Chris Gerrard.*

Comment:

*This chart neatly presents the taxes-payable position of three different types of families in Canada. Clearly, the heaviest burden falls on the traditional, one-earner family, with mom at home. This amounts to a form of punishment for personal childrearing. Changes to come in January 1993 will make Couple B and Couple C the same. But Couple A, the traditional and most numerous, will remain disadvantaged compared with couples with two incomes. There could be no clearer example of how the "progressive" income tax system on which the welfare State is based attacks the traditional family system.*

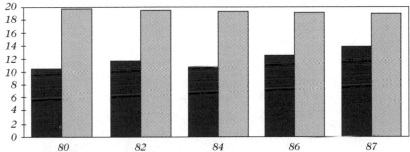

**CHART 11A Breaking the Bonds**
*Global Divorce Rates Among Males (Decrees per 1000 Married Persons), in Canada and the United States Selected Years 1980 to 1987*

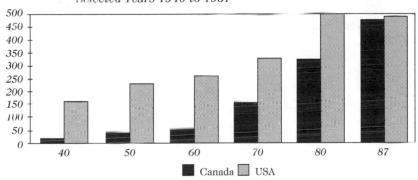

**CHART 11B** *Divorces per 1000 Marriages in Canada and the United States Selected Years 1940 to 1987*

■ Canada ▨ USA

SOURCE: *Jean Dumas*, Report on the Demographic Situation in Canada (*Ottawa: Statistics Canada*, 1990, p.87).
COMPILED BY: Strategic Projections Inc.

Comment:

*These two charts show two different things. The first shows the difference between Canada and the United States in the global divorce rate. (Of all existing marriages in the country, how many will end in divorce?) In other words, this figure shows the breakdown rate of the total stock of all marriages. How is marriage doing as an institution? The answer is, not so badly. Canada's overall breakdown rate is less than the U.S. level: currently about 14 divorces per 1000 married persons, compared with the U.S. figure of almost 19. However, over time Canada will catch up, as the second chart shows. This chart compares all divorces and marriages in a single year. On this basis, over the past half-century, especially since 1968, when our divorce laws were "liberalized," Canada has raced to catch the United States. There are now about half as many divorces as marriages in any one year.*

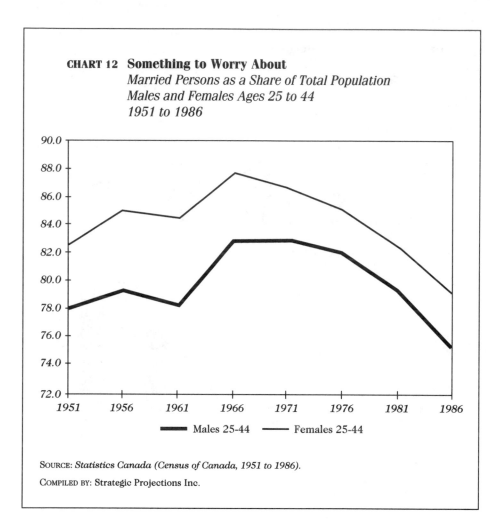

CHART 12  **Something to Worry About**
Married Persons as a Share of Total Population
Males and Females Ages 25 to 44
1951 to 1986

■■■ Males 25-44    ━━━ Females 25-44

SOURCE: *Statistics Canada (Census of Canada, 1951 to 1986).*

COMPILED BY: Strategic Projections Inc.

Comment:

*Among males and females ages 25 to 44, the percent who are married has been declining steadily since 1966, reversing what had been an upward trend. This is a trend visible throughout the developed, or "modernized," world. It is likely a result of high rates of birth control, easy abortion, and "sexual liberation," combined with tax and legal disincentives to marry. As seen in so many of the charts in this book, the erosion or decline in our way of life always seems to have begun with the creation of our welfare State in the mid-1960s. At that time our government began its political and economic campaign to force or seduce families to transfer many of their important responsibilities to the State, thus weakening family interdependence.*

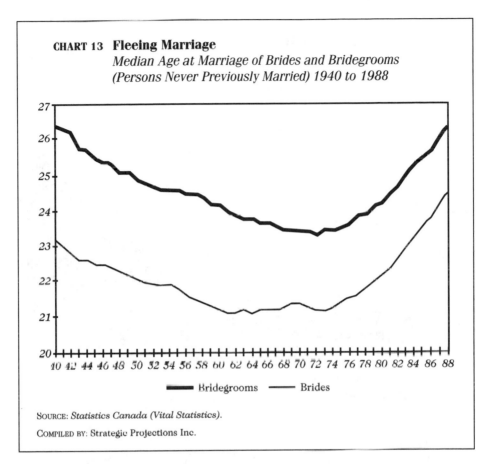

**CHART 13  Fleeing Marriage**
*Median Age at Marriage of Brides and Bridegrooms*
*(Persons Never Previously Married) 1940 to 1988*

━━━ Bridegrooms  ─── Brides

SOURCE: *Statistics Canada (Vital Statistics).*

COMPILED BY: Strategic Projections Inc.

Comment:

*This chart suggests that for about 25 years after World War II, a period of unprecedented economic expansion, marriage was increasingly desirable and economically advantageous. But with the onset of the welfare State, and the failure of child tax credits to keep up with tax increases (and other social changes), individuals began a long trend of marriage postponement. The child/dependant spouse deduction was 30% of personal income in 1950. By 1990, it had fallen to only 9.5%. We must wonder how many of today's youth would marry sooner if they expected the same beneficial tax treatment as was available in 1950. It would appear that instead of correcting this baleful trend by reducing taxes, or by restoring appropriate tax credits, welfare governments everywhere have chosen a damaging alternative. Reluctant to reduce their tax harvest, they are increasing taxes. (Ontario increased taxes 28 times between 1985 and 1990.)*

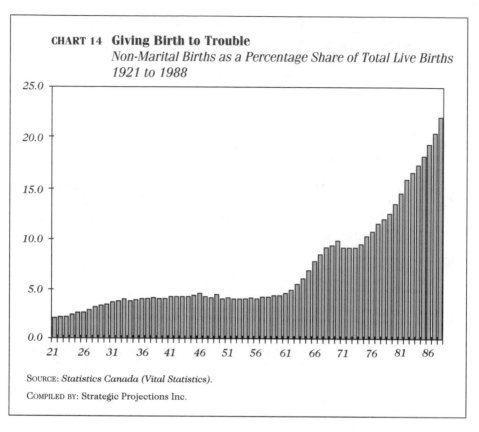

**CHART 14 Giving Birth to Trouble**
*Non-Marital Births as a Percentage Share of Total Live Births
1921 to 1988*

SOURCE: *Statistics Canada (Vital Statistics).*
COMPILED BY: Strategic Projections Inc.

Comment:

*This is surely the most disturbing chart in the whole book, primarily because, as sociologist Charles Murray has repeatedly demonstrated, illegitimate birth rates are a reliable indicator of fatherless homes and, therefore, of the creation of an underclass. This latter he defines not by lack of money, but by behaviour. The largest share of illegitimate births occurs among those of low-income; fatherless homes are homes in which children, especially teenage boys, tend to run wild. From this combination arises violent crime in society, 85% of which is committed by males, most in their late teens to mid-20s. Murray argues that the welfare State has removed the social stigma of illegitimacy, and the rewards of virtue and marriage, and has even created economic incentives for single-parenthood. In effect, single mothers are now marrying the State. It's the new paternalism. Even the cataclysmic social changes of two world wars had little effect on birth trends. It took the welfare State to produce a sudden, immediate trend toward marriage rejection and the consequent fatherless home.*

CHART 15    **Giving Birth to Dependency**
*Non-Marital Births as a Share of Total Births, by Income
Quintile in Canada in 1986 (1 = Highest Income Quintile,
5 = Lowest Income Quintile)*

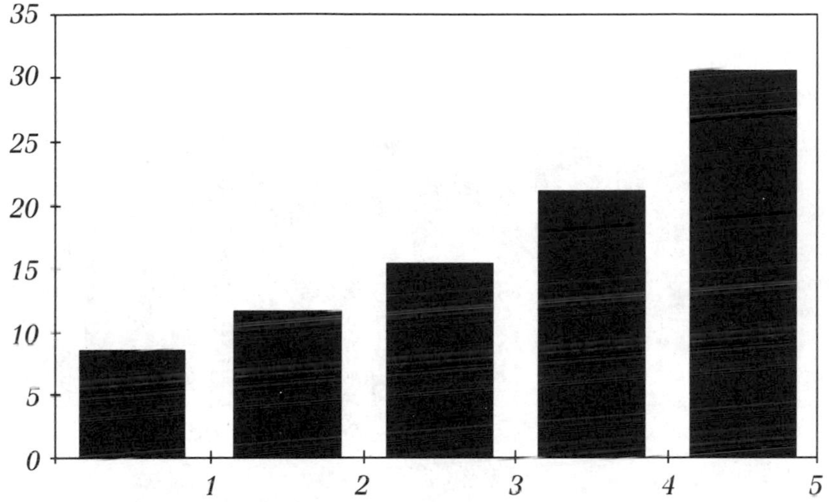

SOURCE: *Statistics Canada ("Health Reports," vol. 3, no 1, June 1991).*
COMPILED BY. Strategic Projections Inc.

Comment:

*It suffices to quote Charles Murray on the relation between
illegitimacy, single-parenthood, social class, and crime, to alert us to
the fact that we may well have created the conditions for a terribly
disruptive future: "Illegitimacy produces an underclass for one
compelling practical reason having nothing to do with morality or
the sanctity of marriage. Namely: communities need families.
Communities need fathers . . . One particular form of single-
parenthood — illegitimacy — constitutes a special problem for
society . . . (because) long-term welfare dependency is a fact, not a
myth, among young women who have children without husbands . . .
Little boys don't naturally grow up to be responsible fathers and
husbands . . . Communities break down . . . when large numbers of
unmarried women have babies . . . Men who do not support families
find other ways to prove that they are men, which tend to take
destructive forms . . . Young males are essentially barbarians for
whom marriage — the act of taking responsibility for a wife and
child — is an indispensable civilizing force" (Charles Murray,* The
Emerging British Underclass, *London: The IEA Health and Welfare
Unit, 1990).*

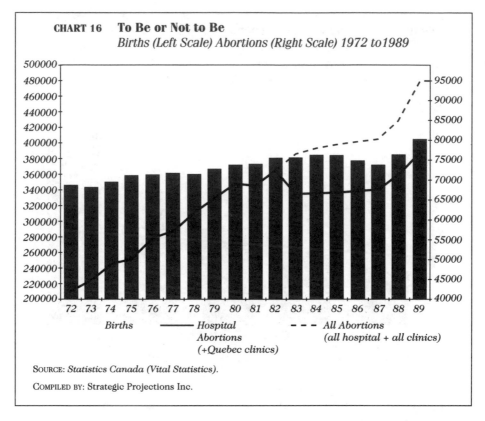

CHART 16    **To Be or Not to Be**
Births (Left Scale) Abortions (Right Scale) 1972 to 1989

Births    ——— Hospital          – – – All Abortions
                    Abortions                (all hospital + all clinics)
                    (+Quebec clinics)

SOURCE: Statistics Canada (Vital Statistics).

COMPILED BY: Strategic Projections Inc.

Comment:

*Any nation must surely find peculiar the predicament that develops when its fertility rate falls below the replacement level (the point at which the nation is failing to reproduce itself), while at the same time it is taxing the life out of legal marriages and economically penalizing child-bearing by its own citizens. Even more peculiar is the policy effort to offset the falling fertility rate by immigration from foreign nations that are increasingly alien to Canada's cultural ethos. When we add to that the sum of 94,000 legal abortions every year — 11 years would mean one million more Canadians — our policies look quite contradictory. The dotted line extension from 1982 onward shows total abortions in Canada, including all private clinic abortions (previously omitted in government figures).*

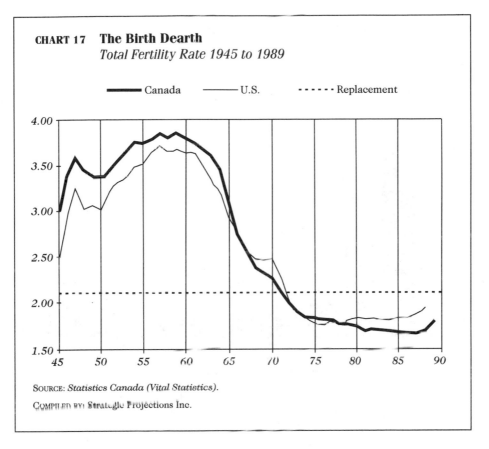

CHART 17 **The Birth Dearth**
*Total Fertility Rate 1945 to 1989*

━━━ Canada ─── U.S. ······ Replacement

SOURCE: *Statistics Canada (Vital Statistics).*

COMPILED BY: Strategic Projections Inc.

Comment:

*Canada's (and the United States's) fertility rate since the early 1970s has been significantly below the population replacement rate of 2.1 births per female. With younger people shying away from marriage and with those who marry having fewer children, this trend is unlikely to be reversed significantly in the future. If these rates continue, our natural rate of population growth — births minus deaths — will turn negative by the end of this century. The projected "population bomb" made famous by the self-styled prophet of doom, Paul Ehrlich, has never come to pass in the developed nations. On the contrary, the "birth dearth" in these nations is alarming, forcing all such nations to walk a tightrope between immigration from non-traditional sources, and a return to heavily pro-family tax and fiscal policy. Again, not without reason, the fall-below replacement rate began in the mid-1960s, just when governments began their concerted efforts to provide "cradle to grave" security to all people — a security formerly provided by large families.*

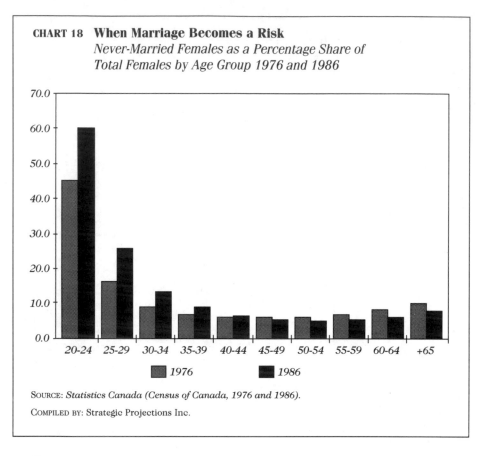

CHART 18   **When Marriage Becomes a Risk**
*Never-Married Females as a Percentage Share of
Total Females by Age Group 1976 and 1986*

■ 1976          ■ 1986

SOURCE: *Statistics Canada (Census of Canada, 1976 and 1986).*
COMPILED BY: Strategic Projections Inc.

Comment:

*The share of never-married females was higher in 1986 than in 1976
for every female age group up to the age bracket 40-44, especially
among those aged 20-29. Above the age of 45, the shares were all
slightly lower in 1986 than in 1976. In other words, a growing share
of the post-war generations is opting not to get married. Given that
the tax code currently penalizes married couples and the bearing of
children, and that modern "no-fault" divorce laws essentially
encourage the easy dissolution of marriages (regardless of the
behaviour of the spouses), marriage as an institution has become
increasingly dangerous and economically unattractive. A nation that
cared for its families and children would ensure that marriage was
the most attractive social and financial condition, not the least
attractive. This chart shows that for those in the key child-bearing
years, it is something to be avoided.*

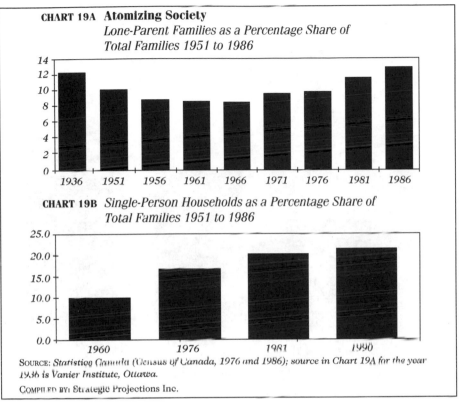

CHART 19A  **Atomizing Society**
Lone-Parent Families as a Percentage Share of
Total Families 1951 to 1986

CHART 19B  Single-Person Households as a Percentage Share of
Total Families 1951 to 1986

SOURCE: *Statistics Canada (Census of Canada, 1976 and 1986); source in Chart 19A for the year 1936 is Vanier Institute, Ottawa.*

COMPILED BY: Strategic Projections Inc.

Comment:

*Despite the catastrophism in the daily news, the increase in lone-parent families since 1936 has varied between 8 to 12% of all families. Serious enough. The real concern, however, ought to be the reasons for the existence of lone-parent families. In 1930, 14% of all families were in this category! But that situation was largely owing to the death of a spouse, or was because of some other unwanted reason. Today, much loneness of families is intentional — a rejection of marriage and family itself, or a result of irresponsible fathers abandoning pregnant women. The other, happy side of the coin is that the great majority of Canadians, over 80%, live in "traditional families." Alan King's survey of 44,700 teenagers in* The Adolescent Experience *showed that some 80% live with both parents — and 70-80% report a "happy" home life. The second chart shows the inexorable increase in single-person "households," a sure indicator that the policies of our welfare State — as in Sweden — are slowly atomizing the natural family. The U.S. figure for single-person households was 10% in 1960 — 25% by 1988* (Chronicles, *August 1988*).

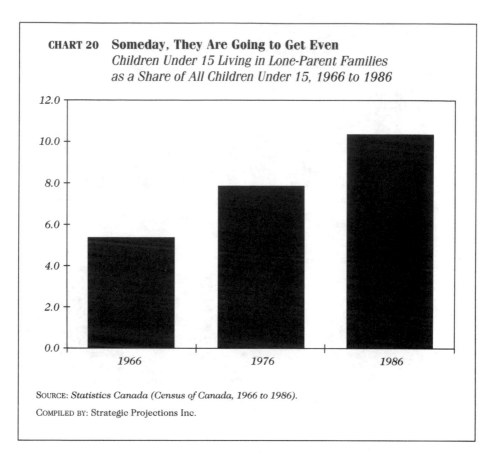

CHART 20  **Someday, They Are Going to Get Even**
*Children Under 15 Living in Lone-Parent Families*
*as a Share of All Children Under 15, 1966 to 1986*

SOURCE: *Statistics Canada (Census of Canada, 1966 to 1986).*

COMPILED BY: Strategic Projections Inc.

Comment:

*If, as I suspect, Charles Murray's predictions about the impact of lone-parent families on society prove to be true, then this chart suggests we are in for a rough time. In 1986, to take a sample year, 59,672 Canadian children woke up one day to find themselves a broken family/divorce statistic. Most of them will spend the bulk of their student years with no father at home. (Only about 20% of lone-parent families are headed by fathers.) In a decade and a half — one generation of children — this will loose about one million children upon our society who were deprived of ordinary male-female parent role models throughout their sensitive years. Many are little bombs waiting to explode. Ask any teacher.*

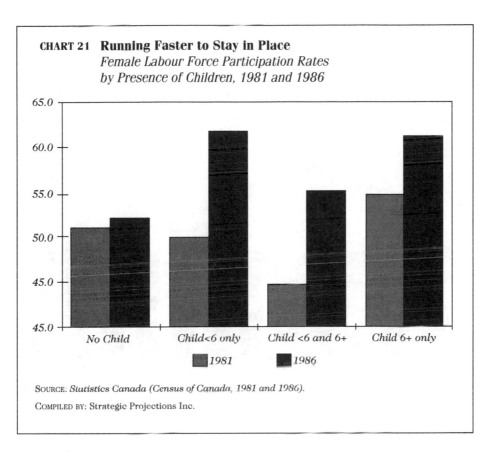

CHART 21  **Running Faster to Stay in Place**
*Female Labour Force Participation Rates
by Presence of Children, 1981 and 1986*

1981      1986

SOURCE: *Statistics Canada (Census of Canada, 1981 and 1986).*

COMPILED BY: Strategic Projections Inc.

Comment:

*Female "participation" rates among those with young children have
increased the most in recent years, especially for those with children
under the age of six and those with children both under and over the
age of six. One interpretation of the trend on this chart is that the
various costs of childrearing in our society have become so great as
to constitute a kind of economic lever, prying women with young
children out of the home in order to provide for the children left
behind. How many of these mothers would work outside the home if
their family tax and spouses/dependant deductions were as low as
in 1950? After all, the economic gain, after expenses, of a two-earner
over a one-earner family is much less than the gain would be from
lower taxation in the first place. Readers should be wary, however,
of all statistics quoting female labour "participation." The word does
not distinguish between those who work part-time and full-time, nor
does it give the age of their children.*

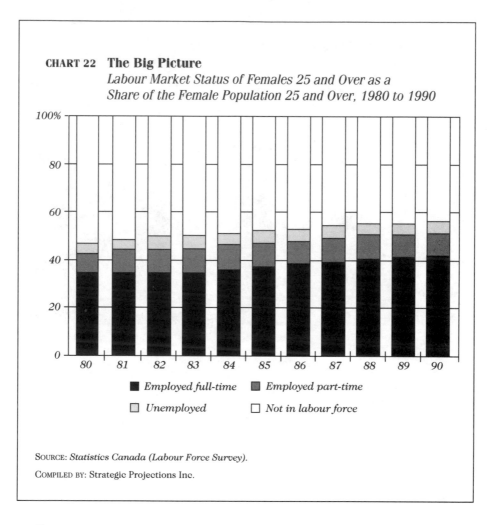

**CHART 22  The Big Picture**
*Labour Market Status of Females 25 and Over as a
Share of the Female Population 25 and Over, 1980 to 1990*

■ *Employed full-time*    ■ *Employed part-time*

☐ *Unemployed*    ☐ *Not in labour force*

SOURCE: *Statistics Canada (Labour Force Survey).*
COMPILED BY: Strategic Projections Inc.

Comment:

*This and the following chart should help to clear up the confusion
often spread by journalists — many of whom want to create the
impression that Canadian women are wholly abandoning
motherhood and their children, and flooding the labour market.
Although we do see a trend toward increased "participation," as of
1990 only 42% of all women over 25 worked full-time. As many
(42%) are not in the labour force at all. This is hardly an exodus
when you consider that the percentage employed includes all those
women who enter the job market after their children have left home,
thus giving a misleading impression that women as a whole are
ignoring dependant children. The next chart shows the age/labour
discrepancies.*

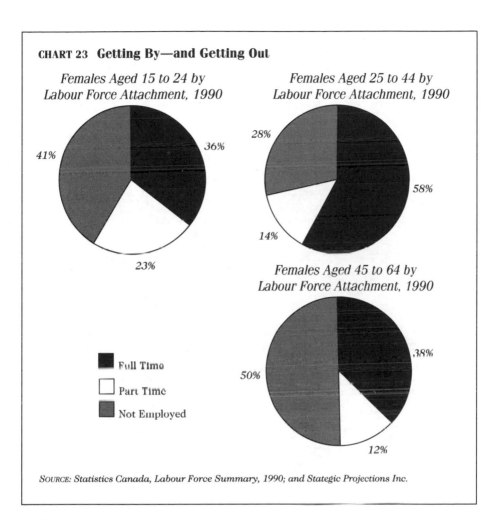

**CHART 23 Getting By—and Getting Out**

*Females Aged 15 to 24 by Labour Force Attachment, 1990*

41%
36%
23%

*Females Aged 25 to 44 by Labour Force Attachment, 1990*

28%
58%
14%

*Females Aged 45 to 64 by Labour Force Attachment, 1990*

■ Full Time
□ Part Time
■ Not Employed

38%
50%
12%

SOURCE: *Statistics Canada, Labour Force Summary, 1990; and Stategic Projections Inc.*

Comment:

*These charts tell a story. Women are working outside the home mostly in their childbearing/rearing years. This suggests — as do the polls — that they are mostly doing so not for "liberation," but for money to cover the extraordinary financial burdens of raising a family — the largest of which is the tax burden. Were this not so, then women by and large would flood into the labour market after age 45, instead of getting out of it, as they do. These charts illustrate the Frazzle Curve outlined in Chapter Eleven. If we consider part-time work unexceptional, then combined with those not employed at all, we see that after their peak years, 62% of all women retreat from any long-term commitment to commercial work. They are taking their reward. If we consider only intact families, this figure is closer to 75 or 80%.*

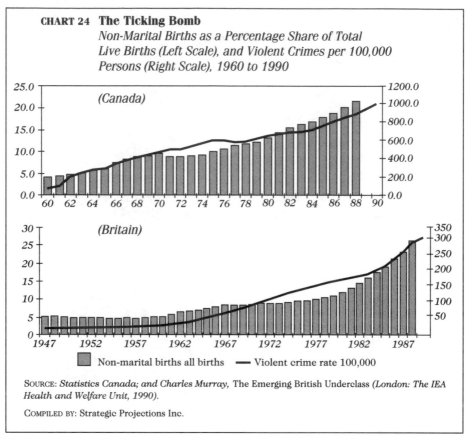

**CHART 24  The Ticking Bomb**
*Non-Marital Births as a Percentage Share of Total
Live Births (Left Scale), and Violent Crimes per 100,000
Persons (Right Scale), 1960 to 1990*

■ Non-marital births all births    — Violent crime rate 100,000

SOURCE: *Statistics Canada; and Charles Murray,* The Emerging British Underclass *(London: The IEA Health and Welfare Unit, 1990).*

COMPILED BY: Strategic Projections Inc.

Comment:

*This chart tells a story for Canada. After seeing Charles Murray's charts for illegitimacy and crime rates for Britain, I had one prepared for Canada. It shows exactly the same pattern. So does the U.S. comparison. For each nation, this juxtaposition suggests a causal relationship between illegitimacy (i.e. social breakdown) and violent crime (overwhelmingly perpetuated by young males, most from single-parent or broken families, with absent fathers). The left, as Murray warns, will spend itself unto exhaustion trying to prove that there is no causal connection here. But the people know better. In Canada, unemployment, school dropouts, illegitimacy, and violent crime, as in Britain and the United States, are overwhelmingly lower-income phenomena. (About 40% of Ontario's school dropouts are from single-parent homes.) Unfortunately, the collectivists in our midst are reluctant to face the obvious: that the best cure for all these problems is to restore the traditional family's legal and tax status while promoting the family's role in society. Poverty does not need explaining. It has been the norm throughout history. What needs explaining is wealth creation. The intact, traditional family is the engine of wealth creation.*

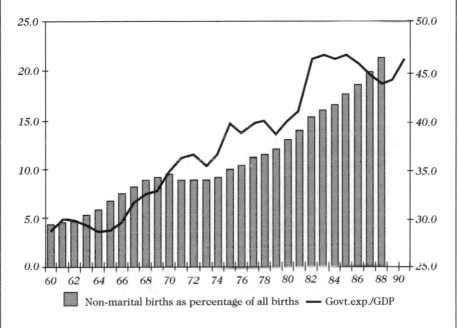

CHART 25  **You Get What You Pay For**
*Non-Marital Births as a Percentage Share of Total
Live Births (Left Scale), and Government Expenditures
as a Percentage Share of GDP (Right Scale), 1960 to 1990*

Non-marital births as percentage of all births — Govt.exp./GDP

Source: *Statistics Canada.*

Compiled by: Strategic Projections Inc.

Comment:

*This chart shows how the rising curve of non-marital births tracks the rising curve of government expenditures as a percentage of GDP. Some argue there is no relation between these two phenomena. I argue the opposite. In fact, the theme of this book is that taxation and expenditures by the State are the best indicator of the degree to which the State intervenes, in myriad ways, to transfer family functions and duties to the State. This transfer, in turn, weakens family bonds and leads to weakened sanctions against illegitimacy. Indeed, we have State subsidies that directly encourage illegitimacy, and tax policies that explicitly devalue intact family formation.*

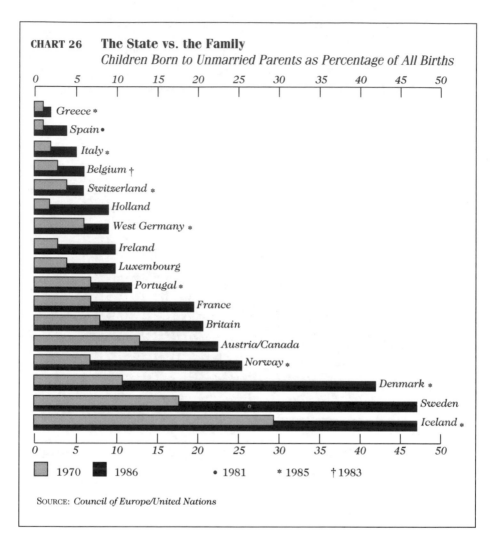

Comment:
*With few exceptions this chart illustrates well the antifamily
consequences of statism. The nations most devoted to socialist ideals
experience the greatest illegitimacy, atomization of the family unit,
and corresponding dependency of individuals on the provider State.
Canada on this chart lies even with Austria.*

# Part Two

# The Issues

# 7

# Compulsory Miseducation: Looking After Their Minds

*We believe existing [educational] institutions cannot solve the problem, because they are the problem.*

EDUCATIONAL RESEARCHERS JOHN CHUBB AND TERRY MOE,

THE BROOKINGS INSTITUTION, 1990

*I contend that the modern Canadian School is betraying the youth of this country . . . by turning [schools] into a sort of community centre which hands out shreds of whatever kind of education its average student finds most palatable and easiest to take.*

DR. WILLIAM E. HUME, PRINCIPAL AND INSPECTOR OF SCHOOLS,

TORONTO, MARCH 1, 1952[1]

The young are the future of any nation, and therefore what they learn at home, in our schools, and at work largely dictates the future. That is why teaching is surely the most noble calling, for those who teach, whether paid or unpaid, whether parent, friend, coach, boss, pastor, or professional, can be said to have a near-sacred moral duty to those taught. Any teacher is a conduit to the truths of life — or to the falsehoods. And because everything touched by the human hand, mind, or spirit is indelibly suffused with the values of the toucher, it is vitally important to know something of those values. It is especially important if they have the result of eroding a cherished society or moral system. The equation $2 + 2 = 4$ will always be the truth. It is an absolute truth. But the spaces between those objective-seeming numbers and symbols can be filled with an infinity of values. Math can be taught as the highest essential truth of the universe or as a rational illusion imposed on chaos. Or we may be told that the logic of math leads to the logic of the computer, which leads to the logic of the collectivist State. You see — it's not just a matter of $2 + 2 = 4$.

This chapter is about how there is an inherent conflict between the duty of parents and their surrogates to teach the core values of a free society, and the notion of "public" education. For when citizens are compelled to transfer this private duty (and their private funds, as taxes) to public employees of the State, every distinctive value of a free society will eventually be eroded by the counter-values inherent in public education. This is not a result anyone has to plan for. It will arise automatically as a natural consequence of the transfer. Despite the very best intentions — which is what most teachers have — public educators inevitably become contributing partners in a system that for lots of common-sense reasons tends to create mediocre results. In short, there is little difference between a collectivized, command economy and collectivized, command education. Neither can work well, and the unit cost of the product is very great — about double the cost of the same education rendered privately. The command economies of the world have fallen apart from the inside out; now many of the command education systems of the world are in deep trouble.

Let us look at the effect on the minds, spirits, and bodies of our young after a hundred years of public education in North America, and in some of our partner nations. Clearly, if public education were not an inherently blighted system, a century would certainly have been enough time to lift up the entire population on a rising tide of skill and knowledge, instead of drowning it in a sea of mediocrity.

| Spending on Education as a Percentage of GNP (1990) | |
| --- | --- |
| *Country* | *% of GNP* |
| Sweden | 7.6 |
| **Canada** | **7.4** |
| USSR | 7.0 |
| U.S. | 5.6 |
| Britain | 5.2 |
| Japan | 5.1 |
| West Germany | 4.6 |
| Italy | 4.0 |

*SOURCE:* UNESCO

This table gives us the portion of national wealth spent on education. However, we should be wary. A nation spending a high percentage of a small GNP may actually spend fewer actual dollars on each student than a nation facing the opposite situation. The United States, for example, spends a smaller percentage than many other nations, but in absolute dollars it spends the most on each student (about $4500, on average). However — surprise! — it turns out that spending figures are a red herring, because international research has failed to show any positive relationship between spending on education and academic performance.[2] If anything, it shows a highly negative relationship. The more we spend, the worse results we seem to get. Contrary to common sense, as class size falls standards seem to fall. And money — there are more teachers to pay — seems to camouflage the failure.

## WHERE WE STAND AMONG NATIONS

A standardized international test of chemistry and physics ability, administered in 1990 to the high-school students of 10 nations (Hong Kong, Britain, Singapore, Japan, Hungary, Poland, Sweden, Italy, the United States, and Canada) by the International Association for the Evaluation of Educational Achievement (IEA), showed that these nations ranged from a high score in chemistry of 77 percent (Hong Kong) to a low of 37 percent for Canada (the United States scored 38 percent). In physics, Hong Kong again scored highest, with 70 percent, and Canada second lowest, with 40 percent (the United States scored 46 percent; Italy was the lowest, with 28 percent). In a biology and physics test of 18-year-olds, more than 95 percent of the Canadian public high schools examined ranked lower than the lowest school in the best country.

A 1989 report entitled "A World of Differences: An International Assessment of Mathematics and Science," released by Educational Testing Service of Princeton (ETS), was based on a study of 13-year-olds in five countries and four Canadian provinces. We don't look too bad — until you study the data closely, to discover that we fare well only until the question level gets tough. At that point, South Korean students, the Japanese, and others whip us by scores double ours.

A fresh new Alberta study, *International Comparisons in Education*, a combined effort of government and business, focused on the quality and instructional differences in maths and sciences between Alberta — the toughest secondary school maths and sciences jurisdiction in North America — and (West) Germany, Hungary, and Japan. Despite Alberta's excellence, the results were discouraging. Alberta's cartooned science textbooks, used by many Grade 12 graduates, were judged equivalent to Grade 8 in Europe. Most telling of all: Other countries in the study relied on conventional methods of direct instruction of skills and knowledge — teach, study, test, retest — whereas Alberta (like all other Canadian provinces) had swung to a "person-centred" approach of feel-good education derived from U.S. educator John Dewey (more on this below). *Globe and Mail* education critic Andrew Nikiforuk asks how such a person-centred philosophy "reflects the character of North American capitalism" (March 20, 1992). The point, of course, is that it doesn't. It reflects the egalitarian educational goals prevalent in our schools (more on this, too, below).

Where we are definite winners, however, is in the race for least amount of time spent on homework, most hours spent watching television, highest illiteracy rates, most money spent on "education," and other such non-academic measures. Again, ETS estimated that 73 percent of American and 65 percent of Canadian 13-year-olds watch three or more hours of television each day. (The figure for South Korean children is 51 percent — but then, they must be watching it after their homework, not before). ETS also reported that only 25 percent of Canadian (and 27 percent of U.S.) 13-year-olds spend two or more hours daily on homework (Spain, 59 percent; Ireland 57 percent; Britain 35 percent). Only 72 percent of Canadians at age 17 are still enrolled in some form of formal education or apprenticeship, compared with 94 percent in Japan and 89 percent in (West) Germany (*Globe and Mail*, September 5, 1989).

The United States has a functional literacy rate of 80 percent, Canada 76 percent, Japan 98 percent, and South Korea, 100 percent, the last with average class sizes in urban areas of 55 students. In 1990, 700,000 U.S. high-school graduates could not read their diplomas (*Conservative Chronicle*, March 13, 1991), and the same number dropped out of high school — no diplomas to read! The Canadian dropout rate is over 30 percent — one of the very worst among developed nations. It is a catastrophe in Quebec, where 42 percent of Quebec males drop out (over 50 percent in Gaspé). The overall U.S. rate is 25 percent. Japan's was 29 percent in 1965, and is now 2 percent. Sweden's has fallen from 25 percent in 1985 to 15 percent today. As for spending, everywhere we see inverse relationships between success and money spent: higher and higher pay for teachers, lower and lower numbers of students taught per teacher, and worsening academic performance. The crisis is such in the United States that even staunch unionists such as Al Shanker, long-time president of the American Teachers Federation, said that "90 to 95 percent of American students who go to college, would not be accepted in any college anywhere else in the world," and that "we spend half of our money on bureaucracy, whereas the other schools in the world don't spend more than 20 percent . . . we have one teacher to every 25 kids, but one supervisor to every six teachers." He's honest enough, but he ought to look at the influence of unions on these problems. Economist Thomas Sowell estimates that "one-third of the [U.S.] money that trickles down to the schools goes for psychologists and counsellors alone," and underlines the embarrassing finding that Scholastic Achievement Test (SAT) scores are lower today than 30 years ago, and that the vocabulary of the average student contains half as many words as in 1945.

As for Canadians? In a summary article (*Globe and Mail*, October 8, 1990) all-round businessman, economist, engineer, and social commentator Pierre Lortie braced Canadians when he reported on another 1988 International Study of Achievement (again under the auspices of IEA), which surveyed and ranked the high schools of 23 nations. By Grade 5, Canadian students ranked fifth, but by the end of high school, they dropped dramatically to 22nd place.

As early as 1977, the Ontario Economic Council discovered that of Grade 11 and 12 students, only 15 percent take physics, 27 percent chemistry, and 20 percent biology (slightly more in Grade

13, but never more than 40 percent). Meanwhile, the most popular major course route chosen by Alberta high-school students in 1985 was . . . physical education. According to Canadian Tests of Basic Skills, our Grade 8 students are now a year behind the Grade 8 students of 1966 (*Alberta Report*, April 29, 1991). The American bombshell report on education, *A Nation at Risk*, said that the average achievement of students graduating from college in 1983 was lower than 15 years prior, and that, for the first time in U.S. history, "the educated skills of one generation will not surpass, will not equal, will not even approach those of their parents."

But it's not as if governments haven't been trying to buy success.

In 1991 Canada spent about $46.5 billion on education ($27.8 billion on elementary and secondary education; $9.11 billion on universities; $3.64 billion on colleges; $3.6 billion on vocational training). This amounts to between $1500 and $1800 per *resident*, depending on the province, but to much more per *student* (the more telling figure) — about $5700 for a primary student in Metropolitan Toronto, about $7400 for a secondary student. This about matches the cost for a good private day school, but in no way matches the performance or the outcome, as we shall soon see. The American average figure ($U.S.) is $4500: from a low of $2454 in Utah to a high of $7971 in Alaska (1990). In Ontario, English as a second language classes add a further $745 per user, and there are many other mandated and special programs that can add to the cost. A further $1 billion is spent annually on 2.3 million "troubled" children in Ontario — about $435 each (*Globe and Mail*, December 9, 1990).

And for this, our students are working less and less. Japanese students spend 243 days in school every year, (West) Germans 240, South Koreans 220, Israelis 216, Hong Kongers, 195, Ontarians 185, and Quebecers and Americans, 180. But students in many other nations also spend longer in school each week than do our students. A rough calculation of their weekly hours spent in class (minus recesses and lunch breaks) times extra weeks per year tells us that they attend classes 9 weeks more per year, times 12 years, which is 108 weeks, or 756 days, or *four years more schooling* at the 185 days-per-year rate. Perhaps that's why major universities of the world give French baccalaureate and British "A level" high-school students advanced placement. Dutch high-school graduates have the equivalent of two years of our university level chemistry, mathematics, physics, and biology, and many of them speak up to four languages fluently.

# THE TRENDS — DOLLARS AND NUMBERS

Here, primarily from a 1988 report for the Canadian federal government prepared by professor of economics Stephen Easton of Simon Fraser University, British Columbia, and other sources, is a disturbing trend:[3]

- Although inflation-adjusted per capita GNP grew by only 3 percent per year between 1960 and 1982, education spending rose 6.1 percent (same method of calculation). In short, we are spending well beyond our growth rate on this service.
- To educate a student today costs more than *three times as much* as in 1960, in *real* dollars (all inflation factored out). Of that increase, one-quarter is due to the reduction in the teacher/student ratio, and almost 40 percent is due to the increase in teacher salaries.
- In the United States, spending per pupil, after adjusting for inflation, has quintupled since 1945-46, when it stood at the equivalent in 1989 terms of about $900. Which means that productivity has apparently fallen by 80 percent, even assuming output quality is constant (it isn't). (*Forbes*, May 4, 1990)
- The per-student cost of administration is the most rapidly growing single item in overall expenses. In the United States, teachers represent only 54 percent of all the adults in the school system. That figure was 70 percent in 1950. (*Forbes*, May 4, 1990)
- (Take a deep breath.) Since 1960, the ratio of students to teachers in public schools has fallen steadily, *by a total of almost 30 percent* (26 students per teacher in 1960, 18.3 in 1985). The United States parallels this trend almost exactly. This change in the teacher/student ratio has boosted costs by 25 percent in real terms. The U.S. figure was 37 students per teacher in 1900. (Note: Studies show no relationship between class size and performance, although this reasoning is used widely to secure more funding.)
- Canadian teachers earned 80 percent of the manufacturing wage in 1950, reached parity in 1960, and now earn roughly 50 percent *more* than the basic manufacturing wage.
- Canadian teachers earned 60 percent of the average U.S. teacher's wage in 1950, reached parity around 1970, and since the mid-1970s have earned about 30 percent *more* than U.S. teachers.
- A far greater proportion of U.S. than Canadian teachers earn their master's degree. In fact, in 1983, 9.6 percent of Canadian teachers had a master's degree, while 53 percent of U.S. teachers had one.

(In both nations, the greatest effect of higher degrees earned seems to be on increased teacher income, not on improved student performance.)

- The net effect of unionization is to raise the cost of schooling by raising teacher's wages without a compensating increase in overall productivity.

### Illiteracy

In *Broken Words: Why Five Million Canadians Are Illiterate*,[4] a shocking $297,000 report on Canadian literacy published by Southam in 1987, we read (and swallow hard):

- 24 percent of Canadian residents 18 and older are illiterate in either official language.
- Illiteracy increases from west to east (from a low of 17 percent in British Columbia to an astonishing high of 44 percent in Newfoundland).
- Less than half of the illiterates are 55 and older.
- 6 percent of Canadians could not circle the expiry date on their driver's licence; 10 percent could not read cough syrup instructions; 11 percent could not sign their social insurance card; 13 percent could not circle a correct traffic sign; 29 percent could not circle a charge on a telephone bill; 50 percent could not locate a store in the yellow pages.
- More than half of 4.5 million illiterates (who could not do the tasks above) *said they went to high school. One-third said they had finished Grade 12.*
- 8 percent of our university graduates (5 percent if we exclude the foreign born) and 17 percent of high school graduates are illiterate.
- Americans clearly outperform Canadians in general reading proficiency, and in using everyday documents. The supposedly brightest age group of Canadians is significantly below Americans in reading proficiency. Only inner city blacks and hispanics are as liable to drop out of high school as the average Canadian.
- About 1 million of the 4.5 million illiterates are immigrants. The illiteracy rate "has risen sharply among immigrants since 1980." Illiteracy is very high among multilingual groups — 49 percent for foreign born, and 33 percent for Canadian born.
- Immigrants account for one-third of Ontario's illiterates, and "almost none of Quebec's." (This tells us once again that Quebecers have been astute in safeguarding and strengthening

their cultural heritage — they carefully select mostly French-speaking immigrants — while the rest of Canada has abandoned any effort to defend, let alone define, its heritage.)
- A survey of the general Canadian population showed that 40 percent do not know that the earth revolves around the sun (*Alberta Report*, November 2, 1990).

But here's the shocker. Most of us drift along thinking that public education may have a few problems, but, after all, it has surely produced higher literacy than the family-based local and private school systems of the 19th century. Hasn't it? There are no reliable figures for Canada, but a comparison of literacy rates in the United States before and after 1840 — the date the schools "went public" — is nothing short of astounding. It turns out that the populated northern half of the United States (a part of the U.S. comparable sociologically to Canada), as well as all of New England, *had a literacy rate of between 91 and 97 percent by 1840. That rate has fallen ever since.* (The figure for the south was 81 percent.)[5]

### The Dropouts — the Body Count

First, a note. Dropout definitions, and therefore statistics, are notoriously unreliable. More part-time students, students leaving and returning to school, poor record-keeping, no mandatory attendance, etc., make this a minefield of inaccuracy. Also, it doesn't matter how many drop out if they aren't learning anything important anyway.

Along with a few other studies, *The Ontario Study of the Relevance of Education and the Issue of Dropouts*, written by George Radwanski in 1987, provides most of the hoary educational details on Canada's richest and most populated province. Let the example serve.[6]

- "Roughly one-third of young people in Ontario drop out of high school before graduating from Grade 12." (Although we don't know how many of those ever go back and finish at some point.) Still, 33 percent is a lot.
- Encouragingly, this report, like so many others, including that of the Brookings Institution, mentioned above, heavily emphasizes the crucial role of family in the academic success of students: "The lower the income level, occupational status and level of education of his or her parents, the greater is the statistical risk that any given student will not complete high school." The decisiveness of family influence on educational success throughout the Western

world lends great weight to the need for positive political, economic, and social family policies.

- A Goldfarb survey carried out for the Radwanski study found that "fully 40 percent of dropouts lived in single-parent households."
- "Children living in mother-only homes are most likely to be children with the broadest range of teacher-assessed problems including conduct, personality or immaturity problems, evidence of socialized delinquency, and psychotic signs." (Quoted by Radwanski from an American study in Alan King's *The Adolescent Experience.*[7]) The highly respected researcher James Coleman of the University of Chicago reports the same trend for the United States, blaming much of the decline in academic achievement on the breakdown of the nuclear family, the rise of the two-income household, and the consequent disciplinary problems in the classroom ("Why Johnny Drops Out," *Forbes*, November 16, 1987).
- A good sign in King's study, however, was that of the 44,744 students he interviewed, *80 percent reported they lived with both parents*, 13 percent with mother only, 3.5 percent with father only, 3.5 percent with "other." (75 percent of boys and 68 percent of girls said they "had a happy home life.")
- Back to the dropout horror story. As in many jurisdictions, Ontario "streams" its students into three categories according to performance — advanced, general, or basic (changed to single stream in 1992). The 33 percent dropout figure is but an *average* of these. The real story is that while the dropout rate is only 12 percent among advanced level students, it is 62 percent for general level and an astonishing 79 percent for basic. And the streaming divisions parallel socioeconomic class very closely. In short, our public schools are a total flop when it comes to making education attractive to lower-class children. The change back to a single stream will camouflage this reality.
- By comparison, most private schools in Canada and the United States — only a few of which are "elite" (expensive) schools — graduate about 95 percent of their students and send the majority of graduates to universities of their choice. (More on this at the end of the chapter, where we will look at private schools for the poor — that work!)
- Astonishingly, once more, 7 percent of Ontario dropouts said they had been "A" students; 46 percent had been "B" students; 20 percent said they had never failed a high-school subject. In short, about 40 percent of dropouts had averages of "C" or better (doing well enough to graduate). Reasons for dropping out? 45 percent

say school is the reason; 29 percent say they need to work; and 19 percent give personal reasons. About 14 percent of female dropouts say they are pregnant.

* In *The Good School*, Alan King gives the percent of students within each ethnic group who are enrolled in "university-bound courses": Korean, 93 percent; Jewish, 92 percent; Chinese, 89 percent; East-Indian, 79 percent; Greek, 78 percent; English, 77 percent; Polish, 77 percent; Indochinese, 73 percent; Italian, 62 percent; Spanish, 62 percent; Caribbean, 53 percent; Portuguese, 51 percent.[8]

After one hundred years, it's not a pretty picture. Instead of quality education, we are getting intellectual mediocrity, more guns and knives at school, more teachers beaten up, more drugs, alcohol, illiteracy, and innumeracy. The people ought to be screaming. About 135,000 U.S. students take a gun to school every day (American Medical Association Report, "Code Blue"). The Centers for Disease Control say one in 5 U.S. students carries a weapon, and one in 80 a gun (Toronto *Star*, April 19, 1992). High-school gangs are booming in Canada, too. Violence by youth went up 34 percent in the four years ending in 1990 (Toronto *Star*, October 30, 1991). Eight Toronto students 14-17 years of age were recently arrested for having "an array of powerful weapons" including Uzi submachine guns, and .357 Magnums (Toronto *Star*, January 11, 1991). Vancouver's 16 high schools have 13 uniformed police officers assigned full-time. Other Canadian schools are following this U.S.-inspired trend. Teachers at some Ontario high schools are now issued "panic buttons" which alert security guards when teachers are attacked by students. Stepping back a bit, we must surely ask just how we got our children, the nation's most valuable asset, into such a dreadful situation. What exactly is being poured into their heads, and why? And what are we going to do to fix the problem? And keep in mind this question: Have you ever heard of similar unruliness at any private school in North America?

## HOW IT HAPPENED

*I received public schooling as a child, but I never let it interfere with my education.*

MARK TWAIN

*A general state education is a mere contrivance for moulding people to be exactly like one another: and the mould in which it cast them is that which*

*pleases the predominant power in the government . . . in proportion as it is*
*efficient and successful, it establishes a despotism over the mind, leading by*
*natural tendency to one over the body.*

JOHN STUART MILL, *ON LIBERTY,* 1859

History will surely show that one of the tragic links in the long chain
of Western decline was the surrender by families, to the nation State,
of control over their children's education. As Yale historian John
Demos has aptly argued, the school is one of the institutions
responsible for the long-term "erosion of function" of the family.[9]
And Stanford's Kingsley Davis writes that "one of the main functions
[of the school system] appears to be to alienate offspring from their
parents."[10] But this alienation need not have resulted, and it is
reversible. It happens, in any nation that cedes its schools to
ideologues, however implicit or explicit their influence may be, who
transmit values to children that run counter to the core values of
the nation. We shall see that many do this under the illusion they
are leading young minds to a higher truth. Would that this were so.
But it is not, and the result is a travesty. For the fact is that the public
school has often served as a powerful instrument for the counter-
socialization of the nation's children. And why not? If you were a
radical intent on changing our society, on weakening the structure
of the private family, and on replacing all the private values we hold
dear with public, collectivist ones, there would be no better way to
begin than by altering the teaching in the schools and writing
influential radical textbooks on education. In this respect, radicals
have a clear advantage over teachers, who see their primary duty as
the transmission of the skills and knowledge central to civilization.
That's because radicals don't care about skills and knowledge. Nor
do they care for civilization — at least of the traditional sort. They
care mostly about social transformation, plan for radical social
change in their sleep, and often see "the basics" as a symbol of the
wicked reality they want to alter. Basic courses in history are for
them expressions of Western capitalist exploitation. The nuclear
family model is biased against women. According to their various
theories, objective knowledge is likely warped by the exploiters, or
the capitalists, or you name it, and it is therefore secondary to their
purpose of realigning society to their point of view — most often an
egalitarian one, requiring coercive public powers.

Here is a brief look at how "education" policy in our country has
been manipulated to please the ideologues in our society, mostly
without the knowledge of the parent or taxpayer. I would suspect

that, in most cases, this manipulation has transpired even without the knowledge of the average teacher, who, brave soul, has likely marched into the profession eager to improve the world by educating children, unaware of the radical political assumptions behind much of the learning theory instilled during teacher training.

## The Collectivists at Work Again

In Canada, "by 1867, most people . . . were more or less literate," and "nearly every town or village must already have had its Grammar School."[11] And we saw above that most of the United States had by 1840 achieved literacy levels far above today's. Most importantly, local schooling reflected local values and family control.

From the late 18th century on, especially after Rousseau, many educators became infatuated with the dream of remaking society through the schools. As we have seen, it was Rousseau who argued, like Plato, that man's chains were forged of local patriotisms and authorities that inevitably lead to strife and social decay; his solution was to break down all such allegiances. Once these smaller social groupings of people were atomized, or made autonomous, or became so highly regulated as to destroy their power to create these allegiances, then, and only then, could a single allegiance be forged between a sole authority — the State — and each solitary individual citizen. As long as such a system complied with the general will, he argued, then all would be legitimate. As Robert Nisbet wrote, for Rousseau "even the family must be destroyed, for it is, of all groups lying between man and state, the most recalcitrant when the state seeks to fuse itself with the individual consciousness."[12]

The heart of the modern worldwide struggle between the conservative and the modern liberal instinct can be summed up thus: The conservative cherishes the smaller, local attachments and affections as the crucial element in the forging of human community, and sees the State as inimical to their survival; the modern liberal (and the socialist in particular), in contrast, sees such attachments as agents of social degeneration through interfamily competition and the resulting material inequities. For faith, he wants to substitute reason; for material differences, equality; for an inherited moral tradition, utopian ideals. Needless to say, *whichever of these two views permeates the schools, it plays a crucial role in determining how our children see the world.* Keenly aware of this, the schools were targeted by socialist radicals as prime instruments for the propagation of essentially collectivist ideas. The public school was to be the instrument of social change and perfection, the very best means to rid society of the old spontaneous local values and to ring in the new collectivist values. The moulding of children "was of course the key to homogenization and the key in general to the progressive vision of tight social control over the individual via the instrument of the State."[13] One of Theodore Roosevelt's favourites, progressive sociologist Edward Alsworth Ross, actually declared publicly that the role of the public school teacher is "to collect little plastic lumps of human dough from the private households and shape them on the social kneadingboard."

The greatest collectivist of all, Karl Marx, was quick to see the political advantage of state-controlled and funded education, and he made it one of the cornerstones of the communist state. After all, he knew — as anyone who takes a government grant quickly learns — that there is always a message with the money! In a less radical but no less thorough way, Western idealist sympathizers and socialists soon followed suit. Very early in the century, Stanford University professor Richard LaPierre, a proponent of the Rationalism Illusion, argued that state-run "free" public schools "would, in a generation or two, be the cure for every recognized social ill." He argued that society would break even financially on this arrangement because, thanks to the schools, young men and women students would grow up to be so reasonable and mature that prisons, jails, poor farms, and homes for the indigent would be eliminated.

Instead, education is today the largest tax burden of all property owners — about 70 percent of their bill — and there are far more poor blacks in U.S. prisons, and I suspect Natives in Canadian prisons, than there are students from either group who graduate from our respective universities. The long and short of it is that despite the success of the family/private/local education system, many groups had vested interests in passing the educational duty to the State. The big corporations needed more educated workers; the unions had an interest in reducing labour competition by keeping the young in school as long as possible; and evangelical Christian pietists saw public education as a way of "christianizing the Catholics," the immigrants, and the great unwashed in general — in fact, a way of controlling the social lives of all society.[14] So we should make no mistake. From the moment the local, parent-controlled, private schooling system was surrendered to the State, the way was prepared for endless power-struggles to control the educational curriculum and the funding process as a means to coerce conformity in social and moral values. Whether bureaucrats, paid politicians, left-wing or right-wing ideologues, teacher unions, or whatever, there is one thing they all had in common: *they wanted to use the power of the State to enforce their views.* They hoped that by controlling education, they could force people to behave in ways they would never do of their own free will.

### John Dewey and the Left

Early socialists never really believed that a Marxist or socialist workers' revolution would come to pass in the West. As a result of our strong British-derived love of individual freedom, our workers — to the great embarrassment of Marxist theory — were becoming increasingly wealthy, and anticommunist: when former Soviet Premier Nikita Khrushchev visited America, it was U.S. workers who demonstrated against him. He pounded his shoe on the table and said communism would bury the West. Now, his followers have no shoes. At any rate, because a revolution from the bottom would never work here, our dreamlanders sought instead to impose it from the top, through the "gradualism" of writing, lecturing, and teaching.

The most famous (and still thriving) society created for the implementation of socialist gradualism in the West was the British Fabian Society, established in 1884 by radical leftists. The name comes from the Roman General Quintus Fabius Maximus, whose technique was to harass his opponents mercilessly, but never join them in all-out battle. Their idea was to "permeate" the institutions of society (such as the schools) with their ideas, thus achieving a silent social transformation, unperceived by the citizens. In 1905 this society opened a branch in America, calling itself the Intercollegiate Socialist Society. John Dewey was one of the founders, and after changing its name to the League for Industrial Democracy in 1921, Dewey became its president. Its stated purpose was "education for a new social order, based on production for use, and not for profit." This directly echoes the *Communist Manifesto* as well as our own New Democratic Party's call for "planning" for a "new society" (federal convention, 1977) and for an "egalitarian society" (1983), and its frequent call to squelch free, individualism-based democratic capitalism, in favour of a coercive, publicly planned production of goods and services. The socialist belief inherent in these innocent-seeming words is that it's all right to produce goods to be *used* (according to the State's plan for their use), but not goods to be privately *exchanged* (for money, to be squirrelled away by individuals or corporations for private purposes). Socialists the world over still labour under the horrific idea that an efficient State can centrally plan all consumption by separating the true from the false needs of the people. In this we correctly smell an ancient asceticism. Thus, they hope to eliminate all greed-mongering capitalist pigs. As we know, this process instead replaces them with power-mongering socialist pigs, who hold absolute control over their people in a form of dreadful bondage. Better to have pigs whose products we can refuse to buy, than pigs with machine guns, I say. At any rate, Dewey's league eventually became the sponsor and heavy-duty fund-raiser for the radical group, Students for a Democratic Society (SDS), which ran amok over U.S. campuses in the late 1960s. Few were aware that by "democratic" society, SDS meant *social democracy*, a contradictory Fabian cover-term for plain socialism. The phrase is clearly contradictory because socialism requires a coercive centralized planning process from the top down, while democracy requires a free spontaneous order that grows from the bottom up. The two concepts, and thus the two terms, cannot lie in the same bed.

Dewey taught that there was no God (he was a sponsor of the so-called *Humanist Manifesto* of 1933), that man was merely a biological entity, a product of evolution: "There is no God, and there is no soul, hence there is no need for the props of traditional religion . . . there is no room for fixed natural law, or permanent absolutes." He wanted to use the schools as a vehicle for selling the "new society" of which he and the Fabians dreamed. The schools, he insisted, must "take an active part in determining the social order of the future . . . as teachers align themselves with the newer forces making for social control of economic forces." And, of course, he recognized the private family as an obstacle to this dream. He made not one single mention of home or family in his exhaustive *Democracy and Education*, emphasizing instead the goals of "social unity" and "State consciousness."[15] When he talked of social control of economic forces, he meant collectivist central planning, redistribution of wealth, the end of private property, the installation of a thoroughgoing top-down system, and the end of our way of life. Though he preached non-authoritarian teaching methods, he was in fact, like all collectivists, a coercive humanitarian, and his philosophy became dominant in the public schools of the West, including those in Canada. We ought to be asking how this was possible, and if this is really the attitude we wish passed on to our children.

But there are even more telling connections between Dewey and ourselves. And oh, I wish he had lived to see socialism fall apart: the tumbling statues, the retreating tanks! But like so many deluded intellectuals of the early 20th century, Dewey thought the Soviet Union was the dream society, instead of what it always was — the largest prison camp in history. So he travelled there, goggle-eyed, with his friends Bertrand Russell and Harold Laski, the socialist guru of the London School of Economics, whom our own Pierre Trudeau, another Fabian-style thinker, later held up as the most important intellectual influence on his own political thinking.

Dewey returned to Columbia (University) Teacher's College after his ideas failed in the Soviet Union. Laski ended up at the London School of Economics, and we eventually ended up with our own transmogrified Deweyite, Pierre Elliott Trudeau, who came to power in Canada. While at the London School of Economics, as Clarkson and McCall write in their best-selling biography, *Trudeau and Our Times*, Trudeau "made a surprisingly sharp turn to the left," "attached himself" to "his mentor" Laski, who had become Britain's "most powerful spokesman for socialism," and "positioned himself for the first time decidedly on the political left."[16] Rather.

Each became successful: Dewey in turning U.S. and Canadian schools "progressive"; Laski in working for a so-called New International Economic Order (NIEO) along socialist lines; Trudeau in "planting socialism," as he put it, in the Canadian provinces. Dewey's chief acolyte at Columbia, Dr. George S. Counts, in his book *Dare the Schools Build a New Social Order?* (1932),[17] wrote that "the school should be regarded as . . . an agency for the abolition of all artificial social distinctions and [for] organizing the energies of the nation for the promotion of the general welfare." All this, he said, "applies quite as strictly to the nursery, kindergarten, and the elementary school as to the secondary school and the university." You will say, he wrote, "that I am flirting with indoctrination, and my answer is again in the affirmative." Another Dewey disciple, Harold Rugg, wrote the following, which reads like a guerrilla manual for takeover of the nation through the schools: "[T]hrough the schools of the world we shall disseminate a new conception of government — one that will embrace all of the collective activities of men; one that will postulate the need for scientific control and operation of economic activities in the interest of all people."[18]

This paragraph needs to be read and reread, for it contains the germ of the progressivists' dream, then and now. By "disseminate," they mean propagandize; by "a new conception of government," they mean socialism; by the "collective activities," they mean moral individualism shall be eradicated and replaced with group-think, the anthill; by "scientific control" they mean that the folks labouring under the Rationalism Illusion will use the tools of science to steer society toward utopia; by "operating" economic activities in "the interest of all people," they mean they wish to stamp out individual initiative and free enterprise, substituting central economic planning and redistributionism. In short, they wanted to revolutionize society not through economic structures, as Marx had attempted, or through dictatorship, but through mind- and value-altering programs in the schools. Dewey called this the "method of intelligence" and he advocated a widespread intellectual infiltration of schools in order to displace moral individualism and install his brand of social planning. By 1925, Rugg and Counts reported that there were over one thousand U.S. schools, nationwide, that were engaged in "curriculum revision" aligned with "the new method"; 30 of these schools were cooperating actively with the National Education Association's (NEA) Bureau of Research.[19] Lest anyone doubt that these extraordinarily influential teachers held deeply ideological interests that run profoundly contrary to our traditional way of life, let the following quotation from Counts himself serve as a warning:

> Historic capitalism, with its deification of the principle of selfishness, its reliance upon the forces of competition, its placing of property above human rights, and its exaltation of the profit motive, will either have to be displaced altogether, or so radically changed in form and spirit that its identity will be completely lost . . . that *the teachers should deliberately reach for power* and then make the most of their conquest is my firm conviction. To the extent that they are permitted to fashion the curriculum and procedures of the school they will definitely and positively influence the social attitudes, ideals, and behavior of the coming generation.[20]

Dewey, who achieved the status of an Aristotle among his followers, felt that all educational theory was divided against itself into "traditional" and "progressive" camps. For him, the traditional system was authoritarian; it attempted, he insisted, to impose "education" on the child from without, via memorization, exercises, rote learning, the dunce hat, etc. His cherished "progressive" brand, in contrast, supposedly focused on the inner child, on the educational *process*. Is Dewey's thinking still prevalent? It would seem so. A development plan drawn up for the *Association for Childhood Education International* (ACEI, April 6, 1988) refers to traditional education as an "implicitly fascist system of instruction." Education professor Mark Holmes says Dewey-type philosophy is still all the rage in Canadian educational doctrine. Because the first camp, Dewey said, dealt with subject matter and standards of proper conduct "handed down from the past, the attitudes of pupils must, upon the whole, be one of docility, receptivity, and obedience."[21] In short, this was his argument, a very weak one, for eliminating tradition and heritage from education: it tended to get pre-packaged and then poured into the unwilling student. I am sure every student has felt this way from time to time. But let us pause here, for we can soon see that the eradication of an entire cultural tradition is a prerequisite — and a pretext — for pouring something else into the head of the student. After all, before you can teach new values supportive of the collectivist ideal, you have to discourage the old moral-individualist values. Better to clean the blackboard before you write upon it anew. For him, those "who have achieved maturity" (teachers, social planners, the knowledge class) have a "responsibility for instituting the conditions for the kind of present experience which has a favorable effect upon the future."[22] It's turgid prose — but read it carefully, and you'll detect *the duty for social reform* he lays upon teachers. Because for Dewey education is primarily a "social process," the teacher has no role as an authority, "or dictator but takes on that of leader of group activities"[23] (meant to lead us to a better world). In more explicit language, he wanted all teachers to become "change agents." By 1971, the U.S. Office of Education had published a manual, *Training for Change Agents*, and seven volumes of "change agent studies," developed by the Rand Corporation. These documents explain the psychological techniques teachers are to use: to "freeze" and "unfreeze" student values; to defuse hostile parent groups; to introduce the science of "planned change"; and to deceive the public about learning programs. If you're traditionally inclined, all this means teachers were taught how to become subversive. One detailed strategy advocated for change agents was called the "Delphi Technique," or the "Alinsky Method" for manipulating student, parent, or teacher groups into accepting the Dewey philosophy.

To make a long story short, the progressive education Dewey promoted so hard, and which was more or less encapsulated in most educational manifestos of the 1960s, including Ontario's Hall-Dennis report, is anticultural, and pro-scientific. It eschews intellectual and moral "cultivation" (and how!); it is amoral (refuses to speak of right and wrong actions), preferring instead the terms "desirable" or "undesirable" (which leads students quickly into the assertion of "rights" to get what they desire). In this sense it seeks, like all egalitarian systems, to eradicate all social and moral hierarchies, and is a key force for social entropy. It promotes a disregard for rules from external authorities — especially moral or parental rules. For Dewey, "shared activity" was the truest "measure for the worth of any given mode of social life."[24] In other words, he was a social collectivist. And so we get group this and group that; shared activities; stress on "expression," "exploration," "constructional activities," "evaluations," and what is "relevant." And so on. And we get discouragement of moral individualism and its active consequence, competition — both qualities deemed selfish progenitors to capitalism. In turn, there is a manifest disdain for grades or objective standards, and a preference for "participation" in sports. Above all, egalitarians want to avoid any "stigma" from losing, and tend to see competitive sport as a model for the Darwinian survival of the fittest and a training ground for budding capitalists. So in their system there shall be no losers or winners, but everyone will feel equally good.

Finally, and most important of all, Dewey was "ferociously amoral,"[25] arguing that the only choices that mattered were those that arose from the individual's consciously discriminating self. For Dewey, education would remove the encrustations of authority and tradition from the naturally good self encased within. Then, once freed, the good self would naturally choose the good society. He never thought the self might also be capable of evil and choose to create an evil society. So "education is life" was Dewey's motto; experience was everything; "teach the child, not the subject"; and so on. As Hilda Neatby wrote: "This has been translated into an injunction to the school to take over every part of the child's life, and every function of society."[26] We shall soon see that Dewey is alive and well in moral values education (MVE), sex education, and other modern educational theories. Let us close this bit on Dewey with a stinging summary from the eminent philosopher Russell Kirk. Dewey, he wrote, denied

> the whole realm of spiritual values . . . he propounded a theory of education derived from Rousseau, declaring . . . the child. . . . should be encouraged to follow his own bent . . . He advocated a sentimental egalitarian collectivism . . . and he capped this structure with Marxist economics . . . a planner's state. Every radicalism since 1789 found its place in John Dewey's system; and this destructive intellectual compound became prodigiously popular, in short order, among that distraught crowd of the semi-educated . . .[27]

Readers should note that all such utopian thinkers, from Rousseau onward, defend the "natural" when it serves their purposes of removing all traditional family, educational, or religious and moral ideals. But when others argue against them to defend natural gender differences, or natural parental instincts, or the bonds of the natural family, or natural moral codes, or natural sexuality, they balk and speak of totalitarian, or dictatorial, attitudes.

## The Psychology Connection

At the same time Dewey's influence was making itself so strongly felt in North American educational circles, so too was the influence of experimental psychology. Dewey himself was the pupil of G. Stanley Hall, who, like so many others, was a student of the famous Wilhelm Wundt of Leipzig University (1832-1920).[28] The Wundtians basically preached that man was a biologically determined creature devoid of spirit, or will, whose life was the direct outcome of stimulus-response experiences that, once understood thoroughly, could be manipulated through reward and punishment procedures to produce any desired human behaviour. Thus, for the psychologist, "education became the process of exposing the student to 'meaningful' experiences so as to ensure desired reactions."[29] Oh boy! Here was a "scientific" method for engineering human society, devoid of all that troublesome morality and religious stuff. As I said, it's not simply a matter of $2 + 2 = 4$. Before long, a host of "laboratory" schools devoted to the refinement of such pedagogical methods had sprung up in North America. By the time Dewey became head of Columbia's Teachers' College, thousands of public schools existed wherein

> the Wundtian redefinition of "education" to mean feeding experiential data to a young brain and the nervous system, rather than the teaching of mental skills, led to the abdication of the traditional role of the teacher as educator. Its place was taken by the concept of the teacher as a guide in the socialization of the child . . . Dewey called for a levelling of individual differences into a common pool of students who are the object of learning technicians devising the social order of the future.[30]

In the last two decades, "cognitive" psychology, which sees education as an "interactive" process between teacher and student rather than the communication of educational content, has held sway over the field. The variations don't matter, however, but what does concern us is that we are not necessarily getting education for our dollars. What we're getting instead is a lot of ideology under the guise of scientific psychology, which, as philosopher Paul Vitz has said, is the new religion. Alas, as George Radwanski has written, educational policy in Ontario "still regards education as a highly subjective open-ended *process*, rather than a product [with] clearly-defined and measurable intended outcomes." The policies are very much "child-centred," such that educators think "*it doesn't matter what a child learns as long as he or she learns something.*"[31] We parents have discovered that "something" is too often a synonym for "nothing." And we're going to get a lot more of nothing, implies Ontario's minister of education ("Province Won't Go Back to Basics," Toronto *Star*, March 18, 1992). We may justly conclude that not only is Dewey alive and well in Canada, but so is human nature: after all, any huge publicly funded bureaucracy will naturally cling to — or invent — a philosophy that helps perpetuate its vested interests while enabling all benefactors of the philosophy to escape objective criticism. In addition to its social engineering objectives, the Dewey/Hall-Dennis philosophy promotes pedagogical obfuscations that confuse the public and lead to prolonged and expensive internal philosophical debates that serve as extremely effective barriers to external criticism. What with "spiral curricula," "social promotion," "ability grouping," and systemic resistance from teacher's unions to objective evaluation, you have a veritable Rubik's cube of vested interests.

Of course, very few young teachers pause to explore these historical connections between what they learn in teacher's college and what they pass on to the young. Nevertheless, the overwhelming fact is that the majority of educators today are left-wing or collectivist in their thinking, both in the United States and in Canada. Professor Mark Holmes, of the Ontario Institute For Studies in Education, makes this fact clear when he writes that in Canada "educators, particularly educational leaders, are predominantly progressive," and that "educational history in Canada over the past twenty years provides abundant evidence of a sharp cleavage between educators and the public at large [on most educational matters]." For example, on a 1985 Gallup Poll, 94 percent of the public — but only 15 percent of educators — supported the idea of standardized student evaluation.

Of course, the term "child-centred" sounds good to a parent, until you realize that it is a licence not to teach your child anything measurable but to restructure his awareness and behaviour according to the teacher's values. Our public schools, says Holmes, "are run by people who are much more progressive in orientation than their clientele."[32] In short, the schools are a local manifestation of the elites of the top-down State imposing their views on the hapless taxpayer. They even want future taxpayers under their control sooner ("Why School Should Start at Age Two," Toronto *Star*, December 11, 1990). As for the United States, the Carnegie Foundation in 1969 asked 60,447 faculty members to state their political philosophy. In fields like psychology and sociology, it found that fully 80.8 percent identified themselves as "liberals" or leftists. A minuscule one-tenth of one percent said they were "strongly conservative."[33]

The handmaiden of educational progressivism is thus not moral education, or character building, but "psychology." As a teacher frightened to sustain traditional values, you can take refuge in the latest, most sophisticated spray-on psychological theory. This mode of analysis delivers the student, like so much putty, into the hands of the knowing educator, to be "socialized." That is to say, traditional morality, right and wrong, the classical belief in moral character as the highest pursuit, and the notion of man as a being with a spirit or soul — all standards of family, social, and religious authority to which former teachers were happy to conform — are mostly gone. In fact, these ideas are most often presented as the enemy of "progress." Today's teachers have forgotten that morality, as novelist Tom Clancy has written, is the price of civilization, and that conscience is the price of morality. We have shifted our standard of behaviour from the angels to the beasts. Man is now a mere animal, a sort of specialized ape, that has likes and dislikes and is alive mostly to maximize pleasure and minimize pain.

This is a paradigm for autonomism, for the morally fragmented society that has used the cold steel of a narrow logic to peel the living flesh from the fruit of life, leaving only the uninviting stone. Not *being* a good person, necessarily, but *feeling* good, and most of all feeling good about yourself, are the key motives of the new psychological man. Holmes says "self-esteem and self-concept" are "all the rage" in Ontario's schools just now. Thus, altruistic, other-regarding man, cherishing inherited moral values or reaching beyond himself to a difficult standard of social behaviour (there's that feared hierarchy again), has withered away. Meanwhile, self-esteem has become a cover for outrageous false-confidence. The most notorious example of this discrepancy between performance and perception is the 1988 international math achievement test on which American 13-year-olds, who scored the lowest, had prior to the test given themselves the highest math rating of all participating nations. Their Japanese and Chinese competitors, who whipped them soundly, had all described themselves as only moderately good at math.[34] This phenomenon of national self-deception, encouraged by the public schools, was aptly labelled by columnist Charles Krauthammer as "doing bad and feeling good."

Distressingly, the psychological view sees man as a product of social forces, and the *teacher as therapist* has a duty to alter this product, so as to alter society for the better. Modern parents have yet to detect in this view a belief system that runs counter to every sermon on moral responsibility they have ever uttered to their children. It's about time they did. In Canada, where ideology is easily camouflaged for a public unused to spotting it, many radicals, such as Marxist organizers, usually operating under more palatable labels ("progressives," "reform activists," "the committee for school change," etc.), actually boast that local municipalities and school boards are the easiest places to get elected to, because "that's where Canadians are asleep at the helm."[35] Toronto's school board is now resolutely controlled by socialists of the New Democratic Party, Toronto City Hall is openly leftist, and socialist Premier Bob Rae, who had already appointed known Marxist George Martell as chairman of his opposition committee on education, has installed outspoken radical activists in every Ontario ministry.

Speaking of Premier Rae, his socialist party's "Philosophy of Elementary and Secondary Education" (issued September 1990), although containing a few laudable, if contradictory, sentiments (like wanting more local control), utters every homily possible on the Deweyite collectivist society. It charges that our schools are captive to a "corporate ideology," and it wants an education system for students that "guarantees them an equality of outcome." Learning, it says, must "emphasize similarities" (the Equality Illusion — let's stamp out individuality, and differences). It wants "learning as a cooperative experience rather than a competitive one" (there's that Communalism Illusion again: let none dare strive, lest some might fail), and wants *"teachers who see themselves as advocates of change in our economic and social system"* (italics added). That's code to say that taxpayer-funded teachers must be used for a soft-socialist revolution against democratic capitalist society; in other words, against the values of the taxpayers themselves. It's a call to social revolution through manipulation of school curricula and socialization of the young. It's pure Dewey. And so, within weeks of its election, we read that Ontario's NDP socialist government "has become an over-all advocate for the child," and will ensure the child learns the "proper social values" (Toronto *Star*, November 3, 1991). And, of course, in order to get those little minds ever earlier, the NDP wants the Ministry of Education to offer "universal, affordable, quality [i.e., socialist] child-care from infancy to age 12."

Lastly, it wants students to study "the labour movement" (which is the code phrase for socialism) and the "progressive change" it has brought about in our society. For the traditions, values, and institutions of the free society it is successfully eradicating, the ministry will substitute the antifamily values of the collectivist State. This is more than a war against the family. It is a war against our entire society and all our cherished beliefs, paid for by — guess who?

We Canadians are not alone in our folly. Mr. Chester Finn, spokesman for a U.S. program called "Total Schooling," says "we cannot confine ourselves with the boundaries of what is conventionally thought reasonable for public employees to do." What he wants to do is have the schools visit and supervise home life, and "be prepared more frequently to remove children from their homes."[36] The state of Missouri in 1981 began such an interventionist program, called "Parents as Teachers," or PAT. Now operating in 40 states and eight foreign countries, PAT currently operates on a budget of $15 billion, estimated to rise to $100 billion by 1995, the year of projected full implementation. This is truly a cradle-to-grave "free" schooling system (prepaid through taxes), for which evangelical proponents recruit students even in maternity ward nurseries. Dr. Shirley McCune burbles about this new "strategic direction" for the American public school, saying that "it amounts to a total transformation of our society. We have moved into a new era."[37] PAT's "parent educators," who supervise home life, are empowered to remove children, discipline parents, and even prescribe drug treatment for children or mandatory courses for parents. The "certified parent educator" delivers an array of "free" social services, from food to mental health; yet these educators are responsible to the State, not to the parents. How the long arm of the educational-social-therapeutic bureaucracy reacheth forth! Critics suggest that such outreach programs, pushed hard by educational unions, are simply an attempt to increase their market share and social control of malleable souls, the better to protect their interests.

In the next chapter, we shall examine more deeply what those interests are, and how the public school has become a centre for the indoctrination of values aimed at restructuring our society — indeed, the whole planet!

# 8

# Looking After Their Souls: Moral Values and Sex-Ed

*The philosophy of the school room in one generation will be the philosophy of government in the next.*

ABRAHAM LINCOLN

*All that I feel to be right, is right; whatever I feel to be wrong, is wrong.*

JEAN-JACQUES ROUSSEAU, *EMILE*

Sometime in the late 1960s, the world changed. The parents of a North American society, thankful to have survived World War II, their principles of freedom vindicated, revelled in community spirit and shared values, large families, and material success. But their children, born to that success and living under the heavy shadow of the Bomb, felt differently. Our parents screwed up the world, the thinking went, so we're going to create our own world and our own values. And to give due credit, they had an argument.

In the 1960s, there was a booming industry in backyard bombshelters. One Chicago homeowner mounted a machine gun on his shelter — to keep neighbours at bay. School children practised huddling against the nuclear holocaust. Thus did the period 1966-74 quickly give way to what psychologist Edward Hoffman has called PLI, or personal liberation ideology.[1] The chief gurus of this movement were Paul Goodman, Fritz Perls, Carl Rogers, and Abraham Maslow — all of whom lived just long enough to reject publicly the moral wasteland to which their thinking, much of it distorted by their followers, had by then led modern youth.

Viewed as an extension of the Individualism Illusion described in Chapter Two, PLI basically extolled singlehood, attacked traditional family values, sang the virtues of personal satisfaction, and taught, via the Relativity Illusion, that all moral values are a matter of personal interpretation and usefulness. The focus would now be on personal, especially sexual, satisfaction, drug-altered consciousness, personal moral philosophies, awareness psychology, hedonism, growth, self-esteem, "empowerment," and "life-style." As we shall see in later chapters, PLI was intimately linked to antifamily population control, birth control (instead of self-control), and abortion (as control not really of reproduction, but of the consequences of pleasure). Books like *Ways of Growth*, *The Baby Trap*, *The New Sexual Revolution*, and *Open Marriage* specifically attacked marriage as "bourgeois" and rejected traditional moral and social values. Most of these new liberationists, while they "were undoubtedly left-of-center politically . . . saw societal liberation in mainly personal terms."[2] Given the horrible legacy of World War II collectivist morality and the failure of the established religions to attract a following, the urge to seek some form of higher individual inner truth was perhaps understandable. But in retrospect, the mortal error of this movement was that it rejected the wrong sort of authority. What it ought to have been rejecting was all statist invasions of social and private life, thus encouraging the spontaneous reconstitution of community. Instead, in keeping with the Rousseau-based naturalism taught in the schools, it rejected not only State-imposed forms of authority but also all voluntary forms of familial, community, and religious authority. Instead of finding a higher inner truth, it found a lower one.

Then as now, the schools were perceived as an attractive place to instil what was thought of as a philosophy for healthier living. In fact, Carl Rogers' colleague, Dr. William Coulson, who also later recanted, explained how he, Rogers, and Maslow "hatched a scheme" in 1963 to bring the methods of value-free, "non-directive" psychology into U.S. classrooms. The process designed to bring about this condition was labelled MVE, or "moral values education," which is by now an international movement, perhaps past its peak

224 THE WAR AGAINST THE FAMILY

but still highly influential. Regardless of the methodology used, all MVE approaches take the stance that unless values are freely chosen by students, they are inauthentic (an acceptable posture for mature adults, who already understand the formative values of our culture, but surely not for unformed children); that parental directives, no-no's, social taboos, and the like are remnants of "dictatorial" or "totalitarian" moral codes that amount to "indoctrination"; and that the starting point for all students must be a close and rational examination of the issues themselves, unfettered by the directives of others. In a 1982 American book on values teaching, James Shaver and William Strong specifically urged public school teachers to set themselves in opposition to parents who wanted to "impose" values or to tell children what they ought to believe.

In her excellent book *Yes, Virginia, There Is Right and Wrong!*, Canadian author Kathleen Gow has outlined this development in an admirably even-tempered way. Her book is must reading.[3] She tells us that by 1981, the World Congress on "Values and the School" attracted 42 nations and 900 delegates, and that one of the most popular textbooks on MVE, by Louis Raths and Sidney Simon, had sold well over 500,000 copies. It is still used throughout North America, as are the writings and books of Canadian Clive Beck. Gow outlines the three main approaches to values teaching in our schools, which travel under the labels of "values clarification," "cognitive moral development," and the "reflective approach." What ought to concern all responsible parents, however, is not the differences (or the infighting for pedagogical status) among these different procedures, but the operating assumptions underlying the whole process. If you think about it long enough, you will likely find it outrageous. Gow tells us that "the logical objective of MVE is to systematically integrate its materials into all subjects of the curriculum at all levels of education, from kindergarten to the final year of secondary school."[4] The technical term [not Gow's] for saturating all school courses with a specific ideology while remaining undetected by critics (such as parents and church groups), very clearly spelled out in 1983 by the Northwest Regional Educational Laboratory of Portland, Oregon, is "infusion," a variation on the Fabian term "permeate." The Oregon report called infusion a "key thread" in "re-education" technique, and included an "infusion grid" showing teachers how to permeate more than a dozen school subjects with a specific ideology. As early as 1974, as many as 2400 courses in MVE were being offered in New York State schools alone. Between 1976 and 1987, the Ontario Moral/Values Education Association had held 10 annual conferences for its teacher members to promote its belief "that schooling without values is not education." Right on. This statement ought to have served as a fire alarm warning parents to examine what "values" were (and are) taught in our schools. Rest assured, they are not what you likely think. Although many teachers see values education as a noble pursuit, filling the moral vacuum left by a society of dying religions and failing families, the consequences of many of their assumptions suggest that the cure may be worse than the illness. Here's why.

**Moral Values or Moral Imbeciles?**
As early as 1978, former U.S. senator S.I. Hayakawa, a distinguished professor of semantics and language studies and the former president of San Francisco State College, informed the U.S. Senate that "An educational heresy has flourished, a heresy that rejects the idea of education as the acquisition of knowledge and skills . . . [it] regards the fundamental task in education as therapy."[5] And following a study of the influence of progressivism on American education, and of the role of the National Education Association, Samuel Blumenfeld warned that "The simple truth is that the American [and Canadian] classroom has become a place where intense psychological warfare is being waged against all traditional values."[6]

Ontario's Education Act, with its 13 flaky "goals" of education, so obtuse and abstract as to constitute a primordial specimen of bureaucratese, must be read to be believed. Typical curriculum policy documents, entitled *The Formative Years* (1975) and *Ontario Schools: Intermediate and Senior Divisions* (1989), require the teacher to fill the role of values educator in the public schools. In short, most public school teachers are officially mandated to become deeply involved as a parental substitute in teaching "values" to our children.[7]

Much of so-called values clarification depends on a staged "valuing" process leading the individual to a personal decision, and teachers of this process are reminded constantly they must commit themselves to the view that *there is no right or wrong* in any particular situation. They are to respect the student's moral values, even if they disagree with them, and all responses are said to be "equally valid" (surely a recipe for budding delinquents.) As a parent you may have taught your child that stealing, say, is wrong. Period. But values clarification class will ask him if he should not steal for his starving child? You see, the reasoning goes, stealing is not *always* wrong (message: your *parents* are wrong). Therefore, the lesson proceeds, all morality is *relative*. "The point," argues Ontario's Clive Beck, is that "as total human beings we should strive to be reasonably moral, but not extremely moral."[8]

### All Great Moral Systems Are Absolute

Well, here we have a man in a position of public trust, teaching our children that in a world rife with crime and failing moral standards, aiming low is the way to get by. How wrong this is. For what is clear is that the great moral systems of the world, which will long outlive gurus Perls, Maslow, Simon, Beck, Kirschenbaum, and Kohlberg, work well *precisely because* they provide absolute standards. (In a fascinating essay, Irving Kristol makes a strong case that Jewish intellectual interest in such "value-free" systems is a reaction against the dominant Christian ethos.[9]) The wisdom common to such systems — quite opposite to Rousseau's teachings, of which these men are apostles — is that mankind is by nature imperfect, and the great mass of human intelligence is far too embroiled in the hurly-burly of life's voyage to embark on moral research at every street juncture; therefore, a moral compass is necessary. It is because we are often so morally blinded by the exigencies of daily life, and by our own emotions, that we lean with relief on wise moral absolutes. Of course, some situations may require moral fine-tuning, because few issues are black and white.

But to admit exceptions is not to abandon the rule. When we are lost in the forest, we do not proceed by throwing away our compass. For most importantly, all great moral systems are transcendent — they aim to provide moral absolutes *higher* than the dictates of any State or those of any earthly bully or MVE teacher; most of all, they are higher than one's self. They are higher precisely because they are *not* subject to revision by every teenager emerging from an MVE session, armed with a teacher-approved recipe for sociopathology. Without such value systems, the poor, the uneducated, the disadvantaged are far more vulnerable to the intellectual manipulations and depredations of any number of clever superiors, whether teachers, bosses, salesmen, or politicians. But with the strength of society's moral law for support, the person of ordinary personal or material powers can stand up to any bully and say that so and so is right, or wrong. Pure and simple. As for daily behaviour? Most real life dilemmas do not occur in classrooms or in artificial textbook exercises. They occur in the heat of work, of sexual or family life, and often in the confusion of anger or distress. Mostly, they occur in a way that provides little time for reflection or readjustment of behaviour. Amidst the smoke and looting of the 1992 South Los Angeles riot, a distraught elderly Korean pleaded before the news cameras: "It is wrong for parents to tell their kids to steal." But the kids and their parents thought it was right, and had likely been taught by their MVE teachers how to justify it.

Contrary to the idea of a reasoned reflection on values at every turn as a guide to authentic choices, great moral systems, from whatever religion (much in them is the same), function to provide their cultures with a basis for *automatic moral response*. Philosophers tucked away in their studies may reflect all they wish, but what society requires in the great mass of the people is a system sufficiently good, sufficiently high, and sufficiently automatic that ordinary behaviour is affected by it *without* reflection. Because all such automatic moral systems are other-regarding, and conceive of moral duty as something *higher* than the individual or the State, they are an integrating force for what Rieff calls "positive community." After all, no great moral system in history has ever had the individual as its primary moral focus. Quite the contrary. Such systems conceive the individual as integral but subordinate to the community.

That is why, quite contrary to MVE teaching, all moral systems can provide spontaneous moral direction only to the degree that they inhibit continuous reflection. For reflection in the midst of most ordinary life situations exposes us to the danger of our own powerful and frequently deceptive emotions. If you believe that man is rational and inherently good (and always sitting in a classroom), this is not a problem. But if you believe that most people are neither good nor bad, but capable of great extremes of either and subject always to the confusion of their own desires, then you will likely support the notion of a moral compass or consensus of some kind. Constant moral reflection, at least for those of us who do not labour under the illusion that a dollop of reason transmutes us into gods, opens most people, and especially the young, to self-deception, to the opportunity for personal gain, to the possibility of hurting others unwarrantedly. Even Maslow, who, after his granddaughter was born, did a 180-degree turn "in vain attempts to retract his earlier contentions," said that "self-actualization does not occur in young people." Thus, insofar as is possible, any society must develop as good and as automatic a moral system as possible shared voluntarily by as many of the people as possible, as deeply as possible. Left unencumbered, human communities develop such systems spontaneously from the bottom up, and thus form a powerful set of expectations — of moral, not legislated, laws. These may be imposed, so to speak, as the terms of the culture, but each moral agent has the option of accepting or rejecting them — at his own risk.

If, say, upon getting out of your car you scratch the fender of the car next to you, society is far better off if your automatic response is to find and inform the other person. But if upon reflection you convince yourself that there is no right and wrong (he has a Porsche and you a Ford, so he can afford the repair); or that in the grand scheme of things, it's unimportant (what's a little dent?); or that his insurance will pay (so why not be on your way?) — then the moral imperative of society is weakened. MVE teaches that we must be unburdened of the "guilt" that arises from not living up to the difficult external moral expectations of parents, society, or religion. I say "nonsense." Social guilt is a prerequisite for the survival of any society simply because it is the outward form of conscience, and the function of any moral system is to make you feel automatically guilty if you transgress. But if whether or not you ever feel guilty is solely up to you, well . . . it's a recipe for personal evil, isn't it? Why are our students learning otherwise? And what are we going to do about it? Let us pause to consider the effect on Canadian society of hordes of high-school dropouts — 540 dropouts every school day, 100,000 per year — many of whom cannot add a bill or read a phone book, but are nevertheless convinced through MVE thinking that the right and wrong of their behaviour, as against their parents', society's, or even the law's view, is up to them. This is a potential recipe for the direct translation of personal frustrations, angers, and fantasies into antisocial action. In 1960, Toronto-the-Good had three home security companies. Today, there are several hundred. Better order your system now.

Here are some of the extreme techniques used in moral values education to falsify ordinary life choices by confusing crisis morality with personal morality. MVE employs what skilled debaters call the "false alternative," in which the student is unaware that he is being forced to *choose* between alternatives controlled by the superior debater, or the teacher. It arrives at such false alternatives through a variety of classroom exercises such as the "Life Raft," the "Fallout Shelter," or the "Cave-in Simulation," all of which place the children in moral dilemmas. (Some of these are officially frowned upon by some ministries. But once the classroom door is closed . . . ) In each dilemma, the child must decide on his own self-worth (who should be thrown out of the life-raft to save the others?); or on the worth of others to the human race, as decided by their assigned life-roles (shall the rabbi, the biochemist, the housewife, etc., be allowed to stay in the fallout shelter?). In the case of the cave-in, they are forced to rank-order other human beings to determine who gets to leave the cave first, as determined by the class as a whole — a situation that results in a mobbing and therefore sacrificing of the weakest, or most reviled. Harvard's Kohlberg even presents as one of his 111 "dilemmas" the "swapping" exercise, in which students are asked to debate the merits and demerits of spouse swapping.

Here's an example of the technique of *rank-ordering* of "values" required of students who are presented with unrealistic choices tightly constrained by the teacher or the textbook. The student is asked to choose how he or she would want a spouse to behave if a good friend were very attracted to the spouse. The options are: clandestine behaviour, honest acceptance, or a divorce. The option of confronting the spouse with the charge of immorality and proceeding to repair the relationship is not presented (because there is no right and wrong, remember). This stuff starts when students are very young. A "discipline" sheet from the Spruce Court Cooperative Nursery School in Toronto warns parents to "make statements, not judgements. We should always avoid value-laden words such as 'good,' 'bad,' 'right,' and 'wrong.' Such words usually attack the child's self-esteem." The word "good" attacks self-esteem? Such confusion, already.

Then there is the *public interview*, in which the student is publicly questioned before the class on his or her value system, about family dynamics, happiness or misery at home (would he rather have different parents?), etc. Thus is public shame or pressure exerted, all subtly controlled by the teacher's tone and manner, nudging the bewildered student (who, we must remember, is reading and writing at an ever-declining level). Then there is the *voting* technique, in which "values" are taught as if morals were a matter of the democratic majority of the hour.

There are also specific psychological programs designed to change student behaviour. Although these are more prevalent in the United States than in Canada, educational trends tend to filter up here by osmosis. Many such "curricula" come in handsome packages with videotapes, seminar worksheets, the lot. At the least, there is little serious control over what teachers infatuated with their psychological grasp of reality are able to infuse into classroom situations. As Yale professor Lester Kirkendall advised other teachers, when faced with parental criticism: "Just sneak it in as an experimental course, and see how people react."[10] Here are a few such subjects, designed to force students to confront their "values," that ought to outrage most parents.

### Death and Suicide Education

This is a humdinger. A 1977 article in *The School Counsellor* said: "Death education will play as important a part in changing attitudes toward death as sex education played in changing attitudes toward sex information and wider acceptance of various sexual practices."[11]

Students in such courses are asked to do such bizarre things as cut out cardboard tombstones and write their own epitaphs on them, or take field trips to crematoria, or write their wills. ABC-TV reported in 1988 that one girl had to watch a teacher pick human bones from crematoria ashes. She wept that she couldn't avoid picturing her recently deceased father. Others are asked to sit in coffins, view embalmings, touch a still-warm corpse, and so on. In a scathing article, *The Atlantic* magazine wrote that such courses implicitly expect teachers to serve as psychologists, with the children as guinea pigs; that they reflect "a view of education in which the molding of the student's attitudes may be as important as, or even take precedence over, the development of his mind."

This news should not be surprising, because in 1977, the National Education Association (NEA) published "Education for the '70s", which stated: "Schools will become clinics whose purpose is to provide individualized, psycho-social treatment for students, and teachers must become psycho-social therapists." One report states that such death and dying courses "have become rather common in public schools," and may pop up in any number of different courses.[12] My neighbour's 16-year-old nephew was just asked to write his personal will as a class exercise (forget the sonnets, let's go for those creative wills). He slipped it under his mother's door as a prank. She had a fit of justifiable panic and called the police, who launched a search party for her son.

Teen suicide, more frequent in Canada than in the United States, is a small but growing cause of death. Under the guise of perhaps well-intended "suicide prevention" courses, teens are often subjected to questionnaires, videos, and assignments that probe their psychological life unwarrantedly. As with so many other value-related issues, these courses tend to promote the view that suicide is a matter of choice (there is no right or wrong) — it's up to the student. But the *Journal of the American Medical Asso-*

*ciation* (December 26, 1990) reported that such courses and materials tend to "stir up" suicidal feelings and present suicide as a possible rational solution to teen problems. Dr. David Shaffer of the Columbia University Medical School, which headed the study, warned that suicidal behaviour is "imitative." Just talking about suicide in a way that removes implicit (traditional) sanctions against it could be "playing with fire."[13] The parents of one teenager who committed suicide after such a course claimed that the prevalance of morbid subject matter in their dead son's classes and texts had provoked the death. He had repeatedly been asked to answer questions relating to the rightness or wrongness of suicide, euthanasia, the "right to die," infanticide, reincarnation, and a host of other disturbing topics.

Clearly, death education is a natural extension of the modern secular humanist agenda. That is to say, in order to promote private morality, sex, and procreation as autonomous moral choices, death too must be made "natural" and, thus, devalued, so that it is severed from any religious, social, or moral meaning higher than the yes/no choice of the individual. After all, the extension of devaluing morality, sexuality, and the sanctity of life itself is devaluing death (see Chapter Sixteen). Playing God is easier when the decisions we face have lost any vestige of moral quality. The dream of the hard-core social planner is a world filled with beings all neatly divested of any transcendent value. Then, the rationalist dream of total control may unfold, unimpeded.

### Pop Psychology and 'Self-Esteem'

Consistent with the notion that teachers are to be concerned more with process than substance, pop psychology has taken all sorts of weird and intellectually suspect forms in school courses. Psychiatrist Brian DeFreitas of British Columbia recently complained that teachers in that province were being encouraged by the Ministry of Education's *Personal Growth and Humanities Resource Book* to practise forms of hypnosis with students in exercises labelled "imagining exercises." DeFreitas rang the bell on this because induced trances, he said, can lead to all sorts of unwanted and uncontrolled after-effects in children, including self-hypnosis and escape behaviour, and warned that teachers should not be "fiddling around with children's brains."[14] The executive director of B.C.'s Ministry of Education was "unable to explain where the exercises came from." Chapter Seventeen of this book, on New Age religious beliefs, may supply some of the answer.

But this is not the half of it. The inevitable result of our loss of natural community through forced communalism is the loss of any meaningful sense of shared values — and therefore of personal value. In response to this void, the ministers of the welfare State strive to creative a cultlike worship of the "self," the autonomous entity felt to constitute the heart of our being. Now, this is an extremely loaded and confused word. Let us see it for what it is. It is a term seized upon to replace the rejected concept of the soul. It is a kind of materialist soul. After all, if religion, which requires a submission to values "imposed" from on high, had to be sacked and destroyed in order to permeate society with the new egalitarian, anti-hierarchical religion of secular humanism, a substitute for the soul was needed; a substitute that was independent, self-fulfilling, and beholden to no one and to no external moral standard.

The idea of the "self" would do nicely. This "self" is presented, in course after course, as a somewhat fugitive inner reality, or thing, that evades our awareness of it until, after much honest searching, there comes a revelation-type melding of the various fragmented "parts" of one's being into a single identifiable unit. This melding occurs ideally as a sudden spiritual manifestation. No one has explained how you really know when you've found your "self," or why you could not be fooled into believing it's the real you when it's not. But observe the inherent contradiction. How can "I" search for my "self"? In other words, how do I ever know which is the real "self": the one seeking, or the one sought after? It is a useless concept that has arisen from our vain effort to materialize our inner lives. It appeals to a morally lazy culture that has turned narcissistic, because defending the "self" requires a deep conviction only as to personal worth — and a certain amount of physical satisfaction. Self-stroking, so to speak.

Thus are our students instructed to repeat mantras derived from unctuously self-indulgent creations like Virginia Satir's "My Declaration of Self-Esteem" (this, from the wall of my daughter's classroom). Satir presents the "self" as a two-part thing divided into the subject "I" and the object "me." The lost-sheep students titillate themselves reading: "As long as I am friendly and loving to myself, I can courageously and hopefully look for . . . ways to find out more about me," and Satir assures the reader that "whatever I say and do, and whatever I think and feel at a given moment in time is authentically me . . ." A recipe for self-delusion and false confidence if ever there was one.

Satir fails to grasp the fatal flaw in this modern Rousseauism: what is one to do when two feelings, or instincts, are in conflict? The traditional answer is that feelings are almost always in conflict, and that's precisely why we need to guide ourselves by principles instead of feelings. Furthermore, experience will usually teach us that whenever a weak and a strong feeling are in conflict, our moral development is likely better served, contrary to desire, to follow the weak and not the strong feeling. For there are few pre-established good or bad instincts, but there are many good principles. It is on these, especially as children, that we must rely to guide our misleading or conflicting instincts. As C.S. Lewis put it, the feelings are just the individual notes on the piano — but the principles, the moral law, are the tune. That grown teachers, let alone young students, can actually respect such confused psycho-babble about the self is truly depressing. But . . . it fits in. It fits into the ideology of egalitarianism, moral autonomy, and disconnectedness from any sense of shared expectations. And it implicitly promotes the pursuit of self interest in a rebellion against moral hierarchy, and the repudiation of all notion of obligation, duty, or the proper limitation of freedom.

### *Global Education/Environmentalism/Multiculturalism*
Most of us have read and been astonished by reports from various totalitarian countries that practise brainwashing of their children in the schools. All communist and socialist schools have always done this. They misrepresent the facts. They even rewrite the textbooks to fit the dominant ideology, the better to engineer the social attitudes of the students and poison their little minds against political targets. In the free world we have always thought this was reprehensible, and that schools above all ought to be engaged in the pursuit and discussion of the truth. That the truth will set us free. Well, don't believe it. For there has probably never been a period of Western history in which curricula and teaching have been so heavily ideological, so pregnant with political purpose. So-called "political correctness" is now the dominant mood in schools and especially on university campuses all over the free world. Gerald J. Sykes' two books, *ProfScam* and *The Hollow Men: Politics and Corruption in Higher Education*, Roger Kimball's *Tenured Radicals*, and Dinesh D'Souza's *Illiberal Education* are a feast of evidence. We have become the passive sheep of which Alexis de Tocqueville warned. Correct thinking has now replaced the clearly failed modes of social engineering through economic modalities. The new egalitarianism is an egalitarianism not of income, but of the mind. In order to be good, to be approved by the elites,

we now must regiment our thinking. Just a few manifestations are the efforts to "globalize" student thinking; to impose a singular view of nature through "environmentalism"; and to eliminate the competitive particularity of natural cultures through "multicultural" policy. Consider the first.

Whether in textbooks or through workshops, global education has nothing to do with giving students an understanding of how the world works — good geography and history courses have always done that. Rather, "global-ed" is a politically motivated form of teaching that intentionally skews the presentation of materials toward a desired result — the modification of the students' attitudes. The U.S. Office of Education's 1967 *Behavioral Teacher Education Project*, or B-STEP, spells out the "futurist," or "globalist," goal for teachers. B-STEP makes it clear the aim is to create an elite that "plans" society for the masses and acts as a therapist for that society in the "laboratories" (classrooms) of the nation. In other words, it's not teaching at all; it's progaganda.[15] Here's how to know whether your child is being subjected to it. Mine have been.

Global-ed tends to censor or downgrade the facts of history by rewriting school textbooks, and it leaves out the important cultural facts of nationalism (deemed a destructive force), especially the distinctive features, events, and symbols of our national heritage (the Crown, British history, the RCMP stetson, and so on). It tends to discourage patriotism, flag waving, and other such nationalist expressions by preference for its dreamland concept of "one world." Global-ed claims that only ending the sovereign State will end war. It heavily preaches the "guilt" of the First World, and its alleged moral debt to the Third World, and as part of this approach also preaches a system of world redistribution of incomes to provide everyone with an equivalent standard of "sustainable" life as a "right." In other words, global-ed in the classroom is just an internationalized version of the handicap system. It is socialism in disguise. Perhaps most false of all, it tells students that the values, systems, politics, cultures, and economic ways of life of other nations are just as good as ours — only different. This is the same error of "moral equivalence" that we saw in values clarification classes. Global-ed tends to impose on students all sorts of unquestioned assumptions about the virtues of disarmament (whether we remain a free people is not a major concern, apparently), or of "world government," or of population control. The alternative arguments, that such things lead to more government and policing, are not given consideration except to be ridiculed.

Under the guise of concern for the environment, global-ed text-books often advocate abortion-on-demand. In one text, *Environmental Science: The Way the World Works*, by Bernard J. Nebel, the author actually urges students: "Join Planned Parenthood Federation or other family planning organizations and have your membership dollars provide support."[16] Whether or not you agree with abortion, a high-school textbook is surely not the place to be brainwashing children on this distressing and divisive subject.

Global-ed environmentalists also promote a funky New Age notion of nature worship. "Gaia," the earth goddess, replaces the transcendent God of religion. She is the goddess of the new Church of Nature, a kind of "feminine, planetary organism." Through environmentalism, the schools are actively if indirectly promoting a new pantheism, the cute notion that all existing things have a theological status of their own — that things are right up there with conscious beings.

My own daughter was taught about so-called "global warming," but only as propaganda. She was never told, for example, that there is deep disagreement among the best scientists as to whether or not it even exists; that even if it does, it may be part of a 100,000-year natural cycle; that the earth had much more carbon in the past and, according to many experts, is now "carbon starved"; or that even if it is true, Canada might benefit economically from global warming. But there was no debate — therefore no education. It was brain-washing.

Multiculturalism is another global-ed thrust. It generally arises from a political effort to quell interethnic strife by segmenting the voting market and urging appeal to an abstract ideal labelled "multi-cultural." All meaningful natural cultural or ethnic differences, which are subsumed under the reigning ideology by means of financial grants, are presented as equally valuable, morally equivalent virtues of mankind. In fact, they may be equally valid, but are often also intensely competitive with each other in philosophical, legal, or moral terms. Just to take one example, in Canada this has meant the extinguishing, by omission, of much of the core British history on which the nation was constructed. Teacher James S. Cunningham writes that "of the one hundred and twenty books approved as history texts by the Scarborough (Ontario) Board of Education, names like Britain, British, and England are conspicuously absent." There is no pride taught in our historic British connections; rather, we are taught shame for alleged colonial deeds. Cunningham says that barely a dozen of his hundreds of college students had ever heard of Magna Carta or the Plains of Abraham, or were aware of the British origins of the common law or those of our political institutions. A number of students even vehemently denied these things! Some recent Canadian history textbooks omit any mention whatsoever of World War II. As one letter-writer complained: "My father died twice" — killed once on the battlefield, and again by the history writers. Whether to do with radical feminism, secular humanism, globalism, peace, or the environment, much of what our students are taught today amounts to a one-sided brainwashing by teachers and textbook writers with an ideology to sell. We ought to be indignant. A good teacher ought to teach all sides of the subject, whether or not he likes all sides, after which a personal opinion is welcomed.

What is clear is that all these methods for clarifying values in fact clarify something else: that MVE is a product of the Rationalism Illusion in our society; that the values it communicates represent a revolt against established social mores; that MVE is in fact a kind of unauthorized classroom therapy that too often constitutes an invasion of student and family privacy and, because of its secular humanist bias, is an insult to the deeply held beliefs of both child and parent. At other times, it is a cover for blatant ideology of the sort found in many other school courses.

Simon and Kirschenbaum, in *Readings in Values Clarification*, clearly state that "values are relative, personal, and situational."[17] In the Deweyite vein, MVE is for them a sophisticated, process-oriented system that eschews tradition and values based on anything other than "reason," which in this case is a clever cover for teacher-led value manipulation. The fault here is that the great values of the world's societies are great not because they are particularly "rational," but because over millennia they have been found to work the best for society . . . because they are effective. The individual's morality arises from his willing acceptance of a moral standard deeper and wiser than he could have invented himself. Yet, ours is surely the first civilization in human history to teach its young to value their personal moral standard above the standards of their community.

As for values being "rational"? Some may be. Some may not. Values are correctly blind to rationalism, and therefore to rationalization. They do not seek to be rational; they seek to be good. As Irving Kristol expressed it so neatly: "Pure reason can offer a critique of moral beliefs, but it cannot engender them."[18] After all, mere reason will tell a sex-starved soldier that he ought to rape a helpless daughter of the enemy, for the world around him is lawless, his peers are all doing it, and he is unlikely to get caught. Mere reason will tell a child to shoplift, for there is plenty to go around, and no one will know the better. At Stanford, a student of mine stole a steak from a store and reasoned that corporations were "ripping off" the public with their profits. He was just getting even. Mere reason will even tell a man not to jump in the lake to rescue a friend, for it may be dangerous. The prevention of all such things comes from something often quite unreasonable — but more often very good, and very effective — called basic values. Once imbued with these — not before — we have a moral impulse, something Philip Rieff called "inner ordinances," and Irving Babbitt called an "inner check" that prevents selfish reasoning. Even where their application is not perfect, such values serve society powerfully as its very ground of social action — its moral point of departure. To imbue a student in these core values, and then tell him to hone his moral thinking, is quite different from vilifying these values, casting them out, and then telling the student to use his reason to reinvent and replace all morality. Only those who have fallen victim to Rousseau's naïve belief in the innate goodness of human beings could ever believe in MVE. Fortunately, some are aware of the danger being done.

Professor Richard Baer of Cornell University writes that values clarification indoctrinates children with "radical ethical relativism." He rightly maintains that if it is against the law to teach in the schools that God is the final arbiter of truth, it should also be against the law to teach that God is *not* the final arbiter. Because there is no rational "proof" either way, this latter statement is also a religious one (and the core of MVE teaching). Baer says that "it is intolerable in a society such as ours to have [this notion imposed] on a semi-captive audience of students in a public school setting as the sole truth about values."

In the United States, at least there is some headway: a recent federal court ruling (*Smith v. Mobile [Alabama] School Board*) declared that because secular humanism is recognized as a "religion" by the U.S. Supreme Court (*Torcaso v. Watkins*), it can no more be taught in the schools than any other religion. This decision, which will inevitably reach into Canada, led to the junking of 45 Alabama school textbooks that pushed the humanist "religion" (as the books' authors describe it themselves).

And how do we respond to naïve accusations that traditional morality is indoctrination? First, we must answer that wisdom, guidance, moral direction, and respect for the core values of our great culture can hardly be called indoctrination. Rather, I would say that failure to imbue students with such values as their firm starting point is an abdication of the role of educator. It is professional irresponsibility. After all,

> both Simon and Kohlberg also fail to avoid indoctrination. Both of their programs offer indoctrination in the "values" they take to be important — the celebration of wants and desires, the exhortation of self-gratification, and a particular ideology of rights and "special justice." Although they both claim to disavow traditional moral education because it indoctrinates, Simon and Kohlberg clearly do not oppose indoctrination per se, but the indoctrination of traditional values.[19]

## PARENTS ARE PROTESTING

Real live parents have publicly protested the creeping pervasiveness of MVE in the schools of America, at least. You can empathize with their cries of indignation by reading a small paperback entitled *Child Abuse in the Classroom*, which is the *Official Transcript of Proceedings* held before the U.S. Department of Education, March 13-27, 1984, in eight U.S. cities (published by Eagle Forum).[20] These hearings were demanded by distraught parents nationwide, who insisted that the so-called "Hatch Amendment" (formally, the *Protection of Pupil Rights Amendment*) was not being enforced. Imagine: national legislation is required to keep teachers out of the students' personal and family lives! Canadian students and families to date have no such protection. They need it, and it should be in the form of an "opting in" permission form requiring parental permission to expose a student to any course or materials having to do with private personal or family life, or behaviour modification. The U.S. National Education Association (NEA) has of course vigorously protested the Hatch Amendment on the grounds that the teachers, not the parents, are the professionals. Like most teachers' unions, they insist that teachers ought to be able to teach whatever they wish, and that the schools should not be accountable to the parents for anything. (This they call "academic freedom.")

In this clash of opinion can be seen the wider clash between the State and its schools — and the family. Parents operate under the belief that the teacher serves as the trustee of the family (*in loco parentis*), while the radical teachers' unions, minions of the State, operate under the belief that *the child's education is meant to serve the State* (Plato, and followers). In recent times, this latter philosophy dates back to the founder of social work, Ellen Richards, who chirped: "The child as a future citizen is an asset of the State, not the property of its parents. Hence, its welfare is a direct concern of the State."[21] There could be no clearer expression of the civil war of values between the top-down, collectivist State, and the bottom-up, free society, the natural moral expression of which is the family. As instruments of the State, the public schools will naturally work for the extension of the State. The task for any free society is to *take the schools back from the State* so that they can be changed back from an expression of the nation's bureaucrats and their values, to an expression of the nation's families.

My worst fear is that this radical invasion of family authority by public educators — this declaration of the public *right* to control the family — promotes anarchy and sociopathology. That's because any form of personal utilitarian (self-serving) moral teaching like MVE will inevitably result in the fullest range of human actions based, as a matter of "right," on the fullest range of human motives, including the most squalid. But don't take my word for it. Listen instead to Stanton Samenow, one of the world's foremost authorities on the juvenile criminal mind, and ask yourself if these words don't echo the ideal of the morally autonomous student.

> Criminals . . . believe that whatever they want to do at any given time is right for them . . . they regard the world as a chessboard over which they have total control . . . despite his knowledge of what is legal and illegal, the criminal decides that he can make exceptions for himself, just because it suits him at a particular time. The fact that he wants to do it, makes it right . . . Although the criminal may not accept what others consider moral standards, he claims to have his own set of morals. Just the fact that he has decided on a course of action, legitimizes it.[22]

We owe a good deal to responsible teachers who communicate the importance of transcendent moral values, freedom and responsibility, and respect for marriage and the family. But I fear that those who teach moral relativism to the young are creating tomorrow's moral imbeciles. By the time we find out whether or not this is true, it will be too late.

# HOLD THE PORNOGRAPHY — SEX-ED IS HERE!

*Educators may constantly bemoan teenage pregnancy and the frequency of illegitimate children, but their own textbooks begin fostering the notion of family without marriage in grades 1 to 4.*

U.S. SCHOLAR PAUL VITZ, AFTER REVIEW OF HUNDREDS OF STANDARD SCHOOL

TEXTBOOKS, NONE OF WHICH CONTAINED A SINGLE REFERENCE TO MARRIAGE AS THE

FOUNDATION OF THE FAMILY, OR A DEFINITION OF THE FAMILY, OR THE WORDS

"HUSBAND" OR "WIFE."

*The objectionable feature of these [sex education] programs is not that they teach sex, but that they do it so badly, replacing good biological education with ten to twelve years of compulsory consciousness raising and psycho-sexual therapy, and using the public schools to advance their own peculiar worldview.*

PROFESSOR JACQUELINE KASUN, 1987

So-called sex-ed should really be considered a category of values education, for it is surely the most powerful weapon imaginable for an attack on marriage, family, and society. Whenever we think of sex-ed, it is helpful to distinguish between the *official reasons* given for exposing very young children to such material (usually some ostensibly plausible motive, like banishing ignorance, or reducing teen pregnancy, or fighting AIDS) and the actual *results and consequences* for them and for society.

Here are some of the things your children may be reading, taken from books widely used in North America, many of them read to or by children as young as 10. The first book, *Learning About Sex* (1986), by Gary F. Kelly, was called "a must for all young people" by Dr. Patricia Shiller, founder of the American Association of Sex Educators, Counselors, and Therapists:

**On sex with animals**. ". . . a fair percentage of people probably have some sort of sexual contact with an animal during their lifetime, particularly boys who live on farms. There are no indications that such animal contacts are harmful, except for the obvious dangers of poor hygiene, injury by the animal or to the animal, or guilt on the part of the human."

**On sado-masochism**. "Sado-masochism may be very acceptable and safe for sexual partners who know each other's needs and have established agreements for what they want from each other."

**On free love**. "Some people are now saying that partnerships — married or unmarried — should not be exclusive . . . the freedom for both partners to love and share sex with others should always be present."

**On anal sex**. "Anal sex refers to the insertion of the male penis into the anus of his partner . . . because bacteria live in the rectum, the penis should not be inserted into the vagina or mouth following anal insertion without being washed first."

From the collection *Changing Bodies, Changing Lives* (1980):

**On lesbianism**. "For you, 'exploring sex' might mean . . . giving each other orgasms, or even making love . . . often this kind of sexual exploring is with a friend of your own sex."

From *Boys and Sex* (1981), by Wardell Pomeroy, Ph.D. (Pomeroy's books are full of graphic and glowing descriptions of sex positions, foreplay, homosexual love — recommended for Grade 6 children. In fact, he includes a "how to" for the whole sequence, from first encounter to full intercourse, explaining how to suck nipples, placing the mouth on the girl's vagina, putting the penis in the girl's mouth, etc. — all for Grade 6 students. Pomeroy's *Boys and Sex* and *Girls and Sex* have sold about five thousand copies in Canada):[23]

**On sex with animals, again**. "I have known cases of farm boys who have had a loving relationship with an animal and who felt good about their behaviour . . ."

From *Adolescents Today*, by John C. Dacey:

**On abstinence and self-control**. This 1984 "health" textbook, recommended as "must reading" for Grade 10 students at Norwin School District (Pittsburgh), described abstinence and self-discipline as "an improper value choice"; and homosexuality as "a natural stage in sexual development." It encouraged "autosexual activity" and recommended "gang masturbation" and masturbation as early as four years of age.[24]

A student who participated at a "sexuality fair" in West Hill, Ontario, November 1990, reported doing an "exercise," against his better judgment, in which he was asked by the teacher to open a packet of condoms, put one on a finger, and insert the "condomed" finger into a plastic model of a vagina. Students learned at the fair that "high-risk" behaviour was vaginal or rectal intercourse without a condom, oral-anal contact, sharing "sex toys" such as dildos and vibrators, and "sex acts if your partner is bleeding." The lesson was followed by the advice: "You have the right to decide and choose what you do about sex." (This message on moral autonomy was courtesy of the Bruce Grey–Owen Sound, Ontario, Health Unit.) A Florida "counsellor" told a class that a guideline to tell if a girl is old enough to have sex is if she can reach into her vagina and remove a condom if it is left in.[25]

In Ontario schools, students are regularly asked to slip condoms on bananas (it's cucumbers or zucchini in California). In a Washington State report, a scale model of an erect penis, with testicles, hair, the lot, was passed around, as the teacher giggled and smirked. *New Dimensions* magazine (September 1990) reported that the U.S. Department of Health and Human Services in 1979 circulated a questionnaire for all students of *junior high age* or older, asking: "1) How do you normally masturbate (play with yourself sexually)? 2) How often do you engage in heavy petting (playing with a girl's vagina and the area around it)?"

It also said that under the rubric of "AIDS education," which has really stoked the ardour of the therapists and educators, some students are being subjected to "excruciatingly explicit instruction in the most bizarre of deviant acts, from penile-rectal sodomy to anilingus [tongue in the anus], to 'fisting' [inserting an entire fist in the anus of a sex partner]." One pro-gay *textbook* is filled with homosexual case histories ostensibly narrated by gay/lesbian teenagers (one in ten of whom is supposedly homosexual, students are told, ad nauseam). "Rick" describes his warm feelings about undergoing receptive anal sodomy for the first time at age 15 with an older drifter — "I felt like a bride on her honeymoon," he moaned.

The Canadian Home and School and Parent Teacher Federation circulates Health and Welfare Canada material called "We Need to Know About AIDS." In it, 13- to 19-year-olds are said to need information — from teachers — on "alternative forms of sexual behaviour" (masturbation and oral sex). And Sue Johnson, author of the popular *Talk Sex* manual for teenagers, gives instruction in "how to give a good blow job" and how to get an abortion without your parents knowing, and writes that "in every school, 1 in 10 males will be gay . . ." To an objection that same-sex relationships were unnatural, she responded: "Wow — haven't you ever seen one male dog humping another male dog in the park? . . . same-sex behaviour is natural among mammals" (Ottawa *Citizen*, April 1, 1990). Meanwhile, Ottawa's two (tax-supported) school-based sex clinics offer sex info and supplies to children of any age — no questions asked. Trustee of the Carleton School Board, Judy Corbishley, said: "If you have a 13-year-old daughter, and she goes to the family physician and asks for birth control pills, she'll get them without the parents being told. Kids have a right to the kind of happiness and security we've been able to build" (Ottawa *Citizen*, June 11, 1989).

In one Calgary sex-ed class, nine-year-old boys and girls were shown a film of the female clitoris and told how it produces pleasure and orgasm; in another, Calgary Health Services officials dabbed spermicidal gel on the lips of junior high students to make them "more comfortable" with it (*Alberta Report*, November 5, 1990). In an Oregon class, a parent who was present reported that "a plastic model of the female genitalia with a tampon insert was passed around to the boys so they might understand how tampons fit," and one shy girl, reluctant to use the word "penis" in class, was forced to repeat it in class 10 times.[26] *The Children's Advocate*, a state-funded newspaper in Oakland, California, aimed at the teen market, incited a parental riot when it encouraged youngsters to have "safe sex." Its most controversial suggestion "called for children to use their mouth to put a condom on a partner" (*Educational Reporter*, May 1991).

A Calgary Health Services mimeo entitled "Questions for Exploring Sexual Orientation" is filled with loaded, presumptive questions that assume a host of false normative models, such as: "Considering the consequences of overpopulation, could the human race survive if everyone were heterosexual?" And: "99 percent of reported rapists are heterosexual. Why are straights so sexually aggressive?" (Note: So is at least 98 percent of the human race heterosexual. And . . . homosexuals have an astounding record of sado-masochistic behaviour and violence (see Chapter Thirteen). Also: "The majority of child molesters are heterosexual. Do you consider it safe to expose children to heterosexual teachers, scout leaders, coaches, etc?" And: "When did you choose your sexual orientation?"

Then there are the sex games, such as: guess how many condoms are in the bag? (winner gets a free package). Or the "condom lineup," used in many North American schools, in which young students wear a placard specifying one of the various stages of lovemaking with a condom. The kids are asked to line up, to reflect in sequence Sexual Arousal, Foreplay, Erection (lots of giggles here), Roll on Condom, Leave Room at Tip, Intercourse, Orgasm, Lose Erection, Relaxation, Hold on to Rim, Withdraw Penis, etc. Some lesson. A workbook distributed by the White House instructed students to "Draw the World's Largest Penis." The caption read: "If I had the world's largest penis . . . (make up a wild story.)"[27] One true-or-false quiz entitled "All About Cocks and Balls and Things" asked students to answer true or false to such questions as: "Black dicks are always larger" and "blue balls come from not coming." Cartoons showed copulating couples, and one assignment given was

244 THE WAR AGAINST THE FAMILY

to "draw mother and father making love." Another assignment to draw nude family members reminded students not to forget to draw "grandfather's asshole."[28]

In all such materials, students are constantly reminded: "You have some big decisions to make as you grow up, about what is right and wrong for you."[29] Parental authority and counsel are devalued throughout, or ranked along with what you hear from friends or see on television. In this antifamily vein, Canada's National Film Board embarked on a scheme with Health and Welfare Canada to market its 1989 sex-ed video, *Growing Up*, by tucking an advertisement inside the baby-bonus envelope sent to 4.1 million homeowners in November 1992. Thousands bit. The video is designed to give children aged nine to twelve "the courage to follow their hearts wherever they may lead." The video warmly presents homosexuality with the words, "two men or two women can have a loving relationship . . . they have a need for each other"; it shows explicit love-making via grinning animated cartoons, but omits any reference to marriage, gives a lot of false-confidence information about condoms, and neglects to mention any link between homosexuality and AIDS.

In sex-ed classes all over North America, students are bombarded with condomania, despite the notorious unreliability and danger of latex. Educators are recommending a potentially deadly device, for reasons to be reviewed shortly. So deadly, that various U.S. "parental consent" groups are winning liability suits against schools and teachers who promote condoms to their uninitiated children (who then got pregnant, or contracted a sexually transmitted disease, or AIDS). If you have young children, they will likely soon be asked to play with condoms, inflate them, suck them, taste them. "Condomeries" now sell flavoured condoms. A U.S. company came on-market in 1992 with a new line of condoms called Safe Play Condoms for Young Lovers, aimed at teenagers as young as 14. The six-packs of teenie-bopper condoms come with neon graphics, rub-off tattoo kits, and free condom key chains.

Very young children are being asked to find as many ways as they can to describe condoms with "sexy" and "positive" adjectives (handout sheet, Guelph Sexuality Conference); to roll them onto bananas, cucumbers, dildos, or zucchini; to handle K-Y jelly; to rehearse dialogues with imaginary partners (such as: "All my other boyfriends use a condom"); and to submit to a plethora of gender-neutral talk such as "receptive partner" and "insertive partner" — in an effort to desensitize students to traditional sex roles and encourage acceptance of homosexuality or pansexuality (the idea that everything is inherently sexual and gender is meaningless). Such conferences are also shot through with explicit and implicit antiparent and antimarriage sentiment. And the most insidious form of comment? Simple omission. A Grade 5 manual called *Facts About You*, distributed widely in schools by sanitary napkin manufacturer Kimberly-Clark, advises youngsters, repeatedly, to "find an older person you can trust" to discuss sex with. Implication? Parents can't be trusted. After all, as Ontario Premier Bob Rae said to a Toronto area high-school audience, when discussing the environment and other matters: "One of the things you can do is educate your parents — they're making decisions, and can make the wrong ones" (the *Liberal* [Richmond Hill], March 10, 1991.) There is no simpler illustration of the war between the family and the State.

## HOW IN THE WORLD DID IT ALL GET THIS WAY?

*Free Land. Free Labour, Free Love*

MOTTO OF ANARCHIST PERIODICAL, *THE WORD*

The expression and suppression of sex have always stood as powerful symbols of freedom and slavery. When Rousseau complained of the chains of authority, he had in mind, among other things, the chains of sexual authority imposed by church, family, and moral code. The English poet Shelley and his radical friends saw free love and sex as symbolic of the free spirit. Because sex is arguably the most compelling of human emotions, some ideology about it will always be found at the head of any political or religious movement. Whether repressive and exclusive for Calvinism, or expressive and egalitarian for socialism, sex always serves as an ideological battering ram. In our time, it is used to defeat those who stand in the way of the social engineering of our society. Sex, in short, is an instrument to manipulate the mood and values of the people. You can easily relieve a man of his freedoms and property if you give him more and "freer" sexual "rights" in exchange; sexual freedom anaesthetizes our desire for political freedom. From the start of their welfare State, the Swedes understood the equation. "As long as they leave me my sex," the people soon begin to think, "I don't care what else they do to me." It is cynical but true: we kiss and hug our way into a condition of political quietude.

As we have seen, Plato, Rousseau, and Marx all wanted "sexual reform," as do today's modern radical feminists. In fact all revolutionaries quickly see that to change the *social* order you first have to change the *sexual* order. The traditional family, after all, is a sexual, procreative entity that dictates much of our social reality (sexual roles, economic roles, socialization of gender, etc.). So by redefining the sexual nature of the family, we can redefine society itself. The long and short of this strategy is that those who wish to engineer society in any direction must first break all the traditional moral and religious sexual allegiances. Sexuality must be progressively divested of all its spiritual, procreative, and family meanings, divested even of its connections with romantic love (to which in our culture it has always been inferior), and in its place must be put an increasing emphasis on raw sexuality as a pure and joyous expression of the autonomous self.

All other connections between sex and loftier ideals (loftier than egalitarian ideals, say) must be discouraged. Thoroughly broken down, sexuality will be utterly narcissistic, self-directed, masturbatory, and pansexual; it will no longer lead up to God (Christian Platonism), or up to the sacrosanctity of marriage (our traditional belief), or even up to a better character (sex as an earned privilege of maturity). If you are getting nervous reading this, so am I. It's the first time the pattern has seemed so thoroughly and chillingly complete. The way to destroy the hierarchical authority of a whole social and moral order — to smash the vertical allegiances to God, family, and moral ideal and reduce everyone to a condition of hungry receptivity — is simply to attack the sexual assumptions of society. The rest will take care of itself. No master plan is required. Once a society of control turns into a society of release, the rest follows, as the night the day.

### Conspiracies of Intent vs. Conspiracies of Consensus

Such massive alterations in the moral fabric of a society do not require legions of malicious conspirators. In fact, for the most part, those who openly attempt to engineer radical change are often intelligent, well-intentioned people who happen to have radically different values from most of us. They are good people, with bad ideas. Generally, they are members of the knowledge class (teachers, journalists, politicians, intellectuals), and they are so persuaded about the correctness of their views that, against even their own personal moral standards, they are prepared to use almost any means to bring about their social vision. They see themselves as the unappreciated intellectual and moral aristocrats of humanity, and their boundless energy must surely arise from this neglect. Under-appreciated, underpaid, and unable to sell their vision in the free market of ideas, they soon become specialists in the manipulation of State power and funding to force acceptance of their faith. Such people can justly be described as conspirators of intent, because they have a specific political, economic, or social ideology they wish to substitute for the one in operation that has failed to recognize them. Their behaviour is always characterized by a pseudo-religious striving for unity, and for the central planning and funding that is needed to realize their social vision.

Conspirators of consensus are different, and most of us, certainly most teachers, fall into this category. This is the large group of practical, well-intentioned people who serve as pawns in our civil war of values. They are more interested in work than in ideas, more concerned with achievement than with ideology, and they likely have a sincere practical, but not theoretical, interest in the better-ment of mankind. Thus they are open to any ideology or belief system that will help them achieve this goal, provided it does not require a great personal effort. That is, they consent to it. They don't write Deweyite philosophy, but they uncritically absorb it. They are the foot soldiers in the civil war of values. Dewey and company knew they did not need devotion, just consent, and that such consent would be passive. Devotees would like the altruistic and euphemistic vocabulary of the radical program so much they would fail to resist words like "process," "child-centred," "fair," "self-esteem," or "equality." Because they fail to question, they unwittingly become the most potent vendors of the product. A sweet, generous-spirited, concerned elementary teacher blowing up a condom in front of her students to save the world from AIDS captures the image nicely. Let the generals do the thinking!

Here's what they have been thinking.

As early as 1928, the World League for Sex Reform was founded in Berlin by Dr. Magnus Hirschfeld.[30] It included such distinguished people as Bertrand Russell and Sigmund Freud, and a variety of fellow travellers from the Social Hygiene Movement, the Mental Hygiene Movement, and the Race Hygiene Movement, including such nuts as Wilhelm Reich, a Freudian-Marxist, who claimed that "instinct" is the deepest and purest layer of our being, and needs obeying. Reich wanted to get rid of outer and inner authority, State and conscience, all at the same time.[31] In fact, in Reich's "Religion of Energy," as Rieff called it, can be seen the very worst consequence of the marriage of Rousseauism to secular science and politics. Reich targeted the family as "the chief institutional instrument of repressive authority" and argued that just as a political revolution was required to overthrow the State, a moral revolution was required to overthrow the family. Such revolutionary sentiment underlies the entire project of sex education, in whatever banal form. To overlook this antinomian (anti-authoritarian, therefore antifamily) thrust is to misunderstand the entire subject, for "sex education becomes the main weapon in an ideological war against the family; *its aim is to divest the parents of their moral authority*."[32] And again from Rieff: "With John Dewey, Wilhelm Reich is one of the great theorists of the child as the agent of social change."[33] Reich was eventually convicted of fraud, and he died in a federal penitentiary.

At any rate, sex-ed from the start was shot through with this Rousseauistic, Reichian, utopian focus, and it has always been tinged with eugenics (perfection of the human species) plus its peculiar brand of moral and population control. There have been a lot of national leagues for sex reform in the interim, and there is no space here to delve into the tangled history of such institutions. It is sufficient to note that for lots of groups out there, sex-ed, under a variety of labels, has been or is promoted as a means to save the world either by getting rid of the unfit via forced abortion (see Chapter Fifteen) or by controlling world population. Examples of the latter include China today, where a second child may be taken from you and suffocated by the State (*Globe and Mail*, November 20, 1990); India, where sterilization is intended to save the poor from themselves; and Nazi Germany, where purifying the race was the goal (as it was, by the way, of many Americans and Canadians before them — Hitler's eugenics experts modelled their program on a 1920s California sterilization program).

The earlier sex- and race-reform activisms, having got a dirty name from wartime racial policies and concentration camp experience, quietly transmuted into one or another kind of *birth control activism*. After World War II activists ostensibly dedicated themselves to the eradication of unwanted pregnancy, sexually transmitted diseases, and control of population. In the 1945-65 period, sex education in schools was restricted to the study of basic biological knowledge (birds and bees), classes for boys and girls were separate to preserve natural modesty, and basic information on venereal disease was given. Teaching relied on lectures, drawings, anatomical charts, and the like. Terminology was rigorously medical and anatomical; information on sex was always linked to the sanctity of marriage and family; and parental authority was always respected.

The so-called "latency period" between childhood and puberty was also respected and off-limits to sex educators; and birth control information and *all sexual matters involving morals* were left to the discretion of parents and churches.[34] But, consistent with the appearance of personal liberation ideology, there came a swift change from which we still suffer.

From 1966 to the present, sex education in the schools became unrestricted, and it now includes the full range of psycho-social deviations. Special attention is given to the "restructuring" of student attitudes for eager acceptance of masturbation, oral-genital sex, homosexuality, sodomy, and even animal sex, with abortion-on-demand taught as a basic right. Discussion of anatomy tends to focus not on reproduction but on contraception, and sex as the crucial link to family within marriage is downplayed. In fact, "family" is redefined to include any group of people living together and marriage is presented as just another "option," while a strenuous effort is made to eradicate natural gender differences in the minds and behaviour of students.

Meanwhile, teaching is focused on values clarification, and all sexual morality is presented as self-determined, not parentally or socially determined. Classroom materials are intentionally and increasingly explicit, and they include acts of perversion. Street talk and obscenities are deliberately used to "desensitize" children and persuade them that sex is valued because it gives personal pleasure and fulfilment, not because it is properly linked to marriage, family, and procreation. In order to begin this process very young, the "latency period" is labelled a myth, and programs are now presented to children from kindergarten to Grade 12. Some U.S. programs (and textbooks) even encourage parental erotic stimulation of infants, and the normalization of incest between siblings. The whole North American movement has been toward explicit information on and total access to every form of contraception and sterilization — including, especially, counselling and referral services to therapists and abortionists — without parental consent. Sex education in Ontario today is "hard core," says Professor Mark Holmes.

By 1964, the key American organization for the dissemination of this new sexual philosophy was called the Sex Information and Education Council of the United States (SIECUS), the Canadian affiliate of which is called SIECCAN. Both organizations took their early lead from the Swedish model, created by Elise Ottensen-Jensen, which was formally instituted as early as 1942. Both have links to a battery of sex therapist organizations as well as to so-called Planned

Parenthood, a widespread organization that has been referred to by its critics as North America's largest contraceptive supply, abortion, and referral agency. Many of these organizations have received and continue to receive bountiful tax dollars from the State, and thus constitute quasi-governmental institutions. They regularly hold "SARS" — sexual attitude reassessment seminars — and, according to sexologist Herbert Otto, editor of the first bible of sex educators, *The New Sex Education* (1978), their "highest priority . . . must be given to teaching the teachers" via sexual attitude restructuring certification programs.[35]

Many of the original contributors to this key book were signatories to either *Humanist Manifesto I* (1933) or *Humanist Manifesto II* (1973). Canadians should know what this manifesto preaches. Although it is a highly self-contradictory document and of low intellectual value, it clearly sums up the entire philosophy of secular humanism that is today so much in the air, and it has been signed by hundreds of influential intellectual and political dignitaries, such as John Dewey, Isaac Asimov, Sir Herman Bondi, Sidney Hook, Sir Alfred Ayer, B.F. Skinner, and Sir Julian Huxley; by feminists such as Betty Friedan; by economists such as Gunnar Myrdal, architect of the Swedish welfare State; and of course by the sex-ed mafia, Professor Lester Kirkendall, Alan Guttmacher, and Canadian abortionist Henry Morgentaler (past president of the Humanist Association of Canada). I used the word "preaches" because the signatories refer to themselves as "religious humanists" (I, p. 8), founders of a new "vital, frank, and fearless religion capable of furnishing adequate social goals and personal satisfactions" to the world. The essence of this "religion," which denies any supernatural reality, is worship of man himself. The Man-god.

Following is a brief listing of the essential parts of the founding beliefs, in the signatories' own words. Reflect upon them; even though very few teachers have ever heard of this manifesto, many of these values and beliefs are today being transmitted to our children in most of the public schools of the land, as matters of fact and through the process of infusion. They are powerfully communicated via the highly charged medium of sex-ed, if not by intent then by consensus. Remember, too, that as early as 1925 there were more than one thousand U.S. schools actively involved in "progressive education," much of it steered by people in complete sympathy with the views below. The thousands of teachers in these schools, and the teachers' colleges that trained them, constituted a vast unofficial network for the promotion of so-called "humanist" values —

via the media, the bureaucracy, and the law — even though the vast majority of Canadians and Americans have never abandoned their strongly held Judeo-Christian values. The profile, "The State vs. the Family," in Chapter Six is an indication of the clash of values between the people, the State, and the knowledge class that drives the State. As Professor Holmes wrote, there is a "sharp cleavage" in values between the educational establishment and the public. If there is any doubt over the religious fervour of these single-minded folks and their eagerness to use the schools to implant their views, study this quotation from *The Humanist* (January 1983, pp. 25-26), the mouthpiece of the American Humanist Association. To me, it reads like Dewey from beyond the grave.

> The battle cry for mankind's future must be waged and won in the public school classroom by teachers who correctly perceive their role as proselytizers of a new faith; a religion of humanity . . . These teachers must embody the same selfless dedication as the most rabid fundamentalist preachers . . . utilizing a classroom instead of a pulpit to convey humanist values in whatever they teach . . . the classroom must and will become an area of conflict between the old and the new . . .

Readers should be aware (I was not) that the word "humanist" as used here has nothing to do with feeling good about other human beings. It is a specific technical term employed to describe an intentionally atheist philosophy created to invent "human" solutions to world problems (translation: with no God, but with lots of government). My commentary is in brackets.

The Principles of the Humanist Manifesto (1933)

1) Religious Humanists regard the universe as self-existing and not created. [That's it. No explanation how you get something from nothing! I can't resist sharing with readers the laugh I got when reading a graffiti inscription. The first line said "God is Dead!" and was signed "Nietzsche." The second line said "Nietzsche is dead!" and was signed "God."]

2) Man is part of nature and has emerged as the result of a continuous process. [Humanists are Darwinian evolutionists. They don't specify what we are continuous from. Current scientific challenges to evolution theory will unsettle them considerably.]

3) . . . the traditional dualism of mind and body must be rejected.
[No mention of spirit, for reasons of 1) and 2), above.]

4) The individual born into a particular culture is largely molded
by that culture. [A grounding for the Determinist Illusion, and
for the humanist reshaping of society by reshaping culture. This
is the old left-liberal belief that a change in the culture will
produce a change in the individual.]

5) . . . the nature of the universe depicted by modern science
makes unacceptable any supernatural or cosmic guarantees
of human values. [This opens the way for "values clarification"
techniques used on students. Science is the rationale for the
jettisoning of values. Humorously enough, the humanists
leave the door open to the possibility of God when they add:
"Obviously humanism does not deny the possibility of realities
as yet undiscovered . . ." After all, there are no atheists in
foxholes.]

6) Religion consists of those actions, purposes, and experiences
which are humanly significant . . . The distinction between the
sacred and the secular can no longer be maintained. [In short,
any logically consistent body of beliefs can now be called "religion." Thus, Naziism or socialism is religion.]

7) Religious humanism considers the complete realization of
human personality to be the end of man's life and seeks its
development and fulfillment in the here and now. This is the
explanation of the humanist's social passion. [It is also a recipe
for self-interest and hedonism as the goals of life. Notice the
Rousseauist, and Reichian, assumption that within each person
lies something good called a "personality," which has simply to
be uncovered by getting rid of all external repressive authority.
What humanists actually do is abolish the outer God of morals,
and substitute for it an inner God of nature.]

8) In place of the old attitudes involved in worship and prayer the
humanist finds his religious emotions expressed in a heightened
sense of personal life and in a cooperative effort to promote
social well-being. [This is an honest description of the religious
urge behind all forms of socialism.]

9) It follows that there will be no uniquely religious emotions and
attitudes of the kind hitherto associated with belief in the
supernatural. [Humanism is said to be a religion . . . but there
will be no religious emotions?]

10) . . . reasonable and manly attitudes will be fostered by education . . . humanism will take the path of social and mental

hygiene and discourage sentimental and unreal hopes and wish-
ful thinking. [As defined by humanists, of course. The word
"hygiene" ought to make people plenty nervous. Curiously, they
do not define their abstract, collectivist utopias as "unreal."]

11) Believing that religion must work increasingly for joy in living,
religious humanists aim to foster the creative in man and to
encourage achievements that add to the satisfaction of life.
[Sex-ed is a prime vehicle to steer children away from the idea
of sexuality as linked to the sanctity of marriage, family, or the
spirituality of religion, and toward the narcissism of sexual
pleasure alone. All self-control is characterized as repressive and
authoritarian.]

12) . . . All associations and institutions exist for the fulfillment of
human life. The intelligent evaluation, *transformation, control,
and direction* of such associations and institutions . . . is the
purpose and program of humanism. [Italics mine. Obviously, these
folks are not saying believe in man and live your own life. They
want to "control" and "direct." They are coercive humanitarians
in black robes.]

13) [Here's the corker!] The humanists are firmly convinced that
existing acquisitive and profit-motivated society has shown itself
to be inadequate and that a radical change in methods, controls,
and motives must be instituted. A socialized and co-operative
economic order must be established to the end that the equitable
distribution of the means of life be possible . . . Humanists
demand a shared life in a shared world. [This is pure socialism,
the works of which lie about us in failure and ruin.]³⁶

*Humanist Manifesto II* (1973) is more of the same, but there are
a few twists that pertain to the subject of education:

• We affirm that moral values derive their source from human
experience. Ethics is *autonomous* and *situational*, needing no
theological or ideological sanction. [Italics mine. This is the basis
of all "situation ethics" and of MVE thinking.]

• In the area of sexuality, we believe that intolerant attitudes, often
cultivated by orthodox religions and puritanical cultures, unduly
repress sexual conduct. The right to birth control, abortion, and
divorce, should be recognized . . . individuals should be permitted
to express their sexual proclivities and pursue their lifestyles as
desired . . . moral education for children and adults is an important
way of developing awareness and sexual maturity. [A recipe not for

liberty, but for unrestricted libertinism. Few are aware of the difference.]

The balance of the manifesto — really, a sort of bible for the faithful — calls for more State charters of "rights" (no obligations — notice that Premier Bob Rae of Ontario is now calling for a "social charter" to be entrenched in the Canadian Constitution); for a kind of popular socialism (a contradiction); for separation of church and State (although the "religion" of humanism will be taught in the latter); for central economic planning; for "moral equality" (as if this were a State-conferred attribute, rather than something we earn); for universal public education (naturally); and for a system of world law and a "world order" (yet another level for government, control, and taxation). And, finally, the humanists want a public devotion to the abstract concept of "all mankind" as "the highest commitment of which we are capable," one that "transcends the narrow allegiances of church, state, party, class, or race . . ." (In other words, one that transcends human beings in every precious and personal particularity of their concrete, lived reality.) It sounds like a recipe for control by the knowledge class, the new priesthood. Man's admiration of himself is to be the new religion.

How widespread is this thinking in Canada, as expressed in sex-ed?

Most sex-ed programs in Canada and the United States followed the Swedish model.[37] By 1960, Sweden had already mandated compulsory sex-ed in public schools (1956), and by the end of the 1960s, about 90 percent of Swedish students had been processed. As Swedish professor Eric Brodin wrote: "Sex education in the schools was a necessary preparation for a society in which the family, as it was traditionally known, was to be eliminated." So, by the end of the 1970s, one California school board had a compulsory sex-ed program for all public school children up to Grade 12, "which required children from 3-5 years to study human sexual intercourse, and children of 12 to learn the addresses and phone numbers of all family planning clinics in their neighbourhood and the bus routes to them!"[38] As for Canada, in a rapid departure from the biological-information-only approach, Health and Welfare Canada itself argued in the early 1970s that "the primary purpose of sex education was to prepare students for the permissive society by teaching them to make their own decisions"; others said that sexual skill, competence, and "well-considered attitudes" were the thing.[39]

These policies heralded the emergence of personal liberation ideology, and the new emphasis on values clarification in the schools. Owing to much resistance from parent groups, however, many sex-education courses and programs switched their names to "family life education," even while changing resolutely to the *contraceptive model* of sex-ed: ostensibly focusing on the prevention of disease, unwanted pregnancy, and *illegitimacy*. This was to become the "conventional family planning model," based on the teachings of the (Alan) Guttmacher Institute of the United States, which the research arm of Planned Parenthood (in Canada, it's Planned Parenthood Federation of Canada — PPFC — and has 47 affiliates). The model stresses contraception, coping with sexual development and orientation, information on types and use of birth control, prevention of sexual abuse, facts and discussion on abortion, and information on where to get contraceptives. PPFC is today a contraceptive supply system for society and the schools, and the largest abortion referral agency in Canada.[40] Just to take a sample year, in 1988 the Canadian federal government gave PPFC $200,000 and contributed $7 million to International Planned Parenthood (IPPF). The Canadian International Development Agency (CIDA), normally responsible for Canadian foreign aid, donated $8.9 million to IPPF, and it matched donations to PPFC (*Hansard*, December 1989). A PPFC brochure from Edmonton, Alberta (Fall 1990) advises readers that PPFC had just received funds from the Law Foundation to "ensure that rural doctors know that teens can obtain contraception without their parents' permission." Here we have tax-funded radical lawyers financing radical sex educators to undermine parental authority. This is the war against the family in broad daylight.

We shall soon see, however, that despite the widespread presence of courses with such objectives, sex-ed has been a catastrophic failure in achieving its stated objectives, and that at the same time, by pushing religious humanism, it has done irreparable harm to the fabric of traditional society and to marriage and the family — as some intended. In fact, *Canada's own Badgley Commission concluded as early as 1977 that sex-ed was a failure*, and that its findings "do not lend support for the usefulness of current contraceptive and family life education programs in the schools."[41] Nevertheless, everywhere one looks where sex-ed has been tried, we find more liberal sexual attitudes and behaviour among students and *unprecedented increases in abortion, disease, illegitimacy, and promiscuity among our youth*. As early as 1963, Alan Guttmacher himself admitted that promoting and supplying contraceptives to teens would greatly increase promiscuity.[42] In British Columbia alone, fully 25 percent of pregnancies end in abortion, and among teens the figure is 60 percent.[43] So how widely are the schools spreading the values clarification, personal liberation, religious humanist philosophy? And what is the agenda?

A 1988 survey of 245 Canadian school boards showed that whereas only 21 boards offered sex-ed programs in 1977, by 1988, 57 percent of the boards offered them (72 percent in Ontario, 68 percent in Nova Scotia, 48 percent in B.C.). A similar study has shown that 75 percent of U.S. boards offer such courses. Clearly, "sex-ed" is a growth industry.[44] The survey also showed a remarkable difference between the public and Catholic school boards in their offerings of sex-ed. The guidelines of the former, with a few exceptions, "show the influence of values clarification" (particularly in Ontario); the Catholic schools, in contrast, "stress objective moral standards against which individual views can be measured." Barely half the public boards had guidelines for such programs, and many boards reported as heavy a concentration on sex-ed in kindergarten through Grade 3 as in later years: often up to 30 hours per year, and up to 150-200 per year in later years! The survey also reported remarkable variation among public boards, some of which — particularly in Saskatchewan, and in Trail, B.C. — had rejected the values clarification approach, and others, such as Sault Ste. Marie, that insisted on parental involvement from A to Z (hurrah!). All Catholic schools stressed the sanctity of marriage and family, and insisted the role of parents was primary; one public board, in contrast, actually suggested that young people would do just as well not to marry or have children! The Halton Board discussed the marriage "alternatives" that exist, and urged students to discuss trial marriages and "open marriage" as possible life-styles. It described marriage as a "civil contract" and placed traditional marital vows in a poor light.[45]

Our babysitter's family-studies textbook, *The Living Family* (John Wiley and Sons, 1991), asks students who have finished the section entitled "Getting Married" to do only one bit of homework: find a student of the opposite sex, and "draft your own co-habitation agreement." The Ontario Ministry of Education course called "Parenting" (described as "Personal Life Management") contains no reference to marriage, mother, father, husband, wife, brother, or sister. Instead, much of the course details "children's rights" and their recourse against parents as set out in abuse legislation. The 1988 survey also said that "the sex education program places considerably more emphasis on 'values' and 'decision making' than on the study of the biological facts of life."[46]

Another example of Dewey-alive is the Dufferin County Board's advice to its teachers: teach the "process" of valuing, rather than values themselves; "there are no absolute right or wrong answers to another's value questions." Algoma Board says much the same. In short, by far *the majority of public school boards have given up the idea that moral values can be defended*. By far the majority subtly teach the children that contraception is the answer to sexual liberation, abortion is a failsafe measure, "the family" is any group of people living together, and anyway "the family" is a "constantly evolving" thing, one version of which (your choice!) is the traditional mother-father-child form. Self-control or abstinence is merely one choice among other equally valid choices, and homosexuality is just another "life-style" alternative (although Catholic boards still teach it as a perversion). A brochure labelled "Healthy Sexuality," distributed in Ottawa's Confederation High School (June 1990) and adapted from an Ontario Ministry of Health poster, shows two obviously homosexual young men smiling at and hugging each other. Asked to explain, the ministry said it was an effort to "normalize" male feelings.

Here's something really frightening: the East York Board describes abortion as "Euthenics: improving humankind environmentally."[47] Think about that one. In many boards, classroom discussion, out of "respect" for alternative "values," is heavily discouraged, and the teacher is told to "prevent the development of a class consensus on an issue." In short, *reason* can be used to arrive at personal values, but cannot be used to *rank* those values (for this would produce a moral hierarchy — something the welfare State strives to avoid). Refreshingly, almost alone among the public boards surveyed, the Swift Current, Saskatchewan, board resisted all this, arguing that there is indeed a "reasoned basis" for traditional moral values, and that sex-ed should be taught "firmly rooted in Judeo-Christian values." Based on this brief survey, however, we must conclude that the "religious humanist" values described above are almost universally proselytized by the public school boards of Canada.

## WHAT ABOUT RESULTS?

So now we know. The philosophy is everywhere.

The proponents of religious humanism in the schools, using sex-ed as the medium of transmission, have been vastly successful.

But has it delivered what it promised? Has there been a marked reduction in teen pregnancy? in teen sexually transmitted diseases? in teen abortion? Let us look briefly at a few thorough studies of the situation, much of the research drawn from the American experience — a laboratory of life much larger than our own. The United States has promoted sex-ed much longer and more pervasively than has Canada, and it is now reacting against it more strongly. Most of the information in the following section is drawn from Dinah Richard, Ph.D., *Has Sex Education Failed Our Teenagers?*, a comprehensive compilation of more than 268 studies on the consequences of contraceptive-based sex-ed programs.[48]

*Cost*. Between 1971 and 1981, U.S. public federal agencies alone (not counting local and state) spent more than $2 billion promoting sex-ed.

*Effect*. During the 10-year period, there was not a decrease, but a soaring increase of 48.3 percent in teen pregnancies, and 133 percent in teen abortions. The U.S. Senate Committee on Labour and Human Resources showed that among states with comparable demographics, *those that spent the most on "family planning" had the largest increases in abortions and illegitimate births*.

*Fertility*. The expected rate of reduction in teenage births was achieved not by means of contraception, but by reliance on abortions. Even then, Charles Murray reports that between 1955 and 1983, illegitimate births to teenage mothers jumped 288 percent (total illegitimate births jumped 450 percent).[49]

*On promiscuity*. Guttmacher, of Planned Parenthood, has already agreed that contraceptive supply leads to teen promiscuity. Dr. Robert Kistner of the Harvard Medical School as early as 1977 said: "About 10 years ago I declared that the pill would not lead to promiscuity. Well, I was wrong." The U.S. National Research Council says that there may be a causal explanation for the high association between contraceptive provision to teens and promiscuity. Many studies have shown that widespread contraceptive information tends to increased sexual activity.

*Abortion*. The *Journal of Biosocial Science* reported that repeat abortion-seekers have a better knowledge of contraception and are more regular users than first-timers. A study by the Centers for Disease Control shows "that 50 percent of teenagers who got abortions had been using contraceptives at the time of conception." Half of America's annual 1.1. million teen pregnancies end in abortion. Ten percent of those teens become pregnant again in the same year.

*Teen pregnancy*. By 1981, researchers Zelnick and Kantner

acknowledged that there was an "almost total absence of evidence" of any benefits of sex education. A Johns Hopkins study said "the final result to emerge from the analysis is that neither pregnancy education nor contraceptive education exerts any significant effect on the risk of premarital pregnancy among sexually active teenagers — a finding that calls into question the argument that formal sex education is an effective tool for reducing adolescent pregnancy." They also report that about 28 percent of teen pregnancies are intentional. Robert Ruff, using Planned Parenthood data, calculated that a girl using condoms has an 87 percent chance of pregnancy during school years.[50]

*Emotional Problems.* Dr. Melvin Anchell writes that "typical sex education courses are almost perfect recipes for producing personality problems and even perversions later in life . . . [and they] continuously downgrade the affectionate monogamous nature of human sexuality." In the past 20 years, the number of adolescents admitted to hospital for depression has tripled, and teen suicide has increased 200 percent. Dr. John Meek, of the Psychiatric Institute of Washington, says that sex-ed instruction in the lower elementary grades "is unwarranted and potentially destructive." The consensus of the American Association of Child Psychoanalysis is that "the child's development is not served by encouraging sexuality at this stage of life."

*Ethical Development.* Countless studies stress that invasion of the "latency period" by premature sex-ed information is counterproductive because adolescents function in a "concrete" rather than "formal" (adult) cognitive mode, and thus so-called "value-neutral" approaches cannot work for them.

So much for the programmatic failure. It strongly suggests that parents whose children get pregnant, or die of AIDS, or get an STD, or are shunted quietly to abortionists by teachers have serious grounds for liability suits against the public schools for handing down dangerous advice. Perhaps against politicians, too. Former premier of Ontario David Peterson gave this advice on AIDS to 420 students (grades 7-13) at Atikokan High School: "Don't get it." When one student piped up — "Are you saying, don't have sex?" — this man, supposedly a moral role model for the young, acted like a playboy medical research expert and replied, broadly grinning: "No, not at all — I'm the last one to say that." Then, after loud applause: "But practice safe sex, and that means . . . condoms must be used" (*Globe and Mail*, May 21, 1988). Grade 7 students hearing this dangerously misleading advice from the leader of their province were 12 or 13 years old.

## The Failure Rates for Teens Using Contraception

Children are often given the impression that contraceptives such as condoms and pills are good protection against pregnancy, STDs, and AIDS. Here are some of the facts:

- Planned Parenthood's own publication, *Family Planning Perspective* (Summer 1973, pp. 133-42), showed that teens who regularly use the pill experience a pregnancy rate four to five times higher than that for older women using the pill. A follow-up 1976 study set the teen rate at 5.8 percent.
- A Cornell University study reported in the *Journal of Adolescent Health Care* (September 1987, pp. 393, 395) showed an 18 percent pregnancy rate, in the first year of use, among teenagers who used the pill with a high rate of compliance. Zelnick and Kantner, in *Family Planning Perspective* (September/October 1980, pp. 230-37), showed that the failure rate of compliance was 9.9-13 percent annually.
- Side effects: 22 percent show weight gain; 18 percent have menstrual problems; 16 percent have nausea; 10 percent have headaches; 10 percent suffer abdominal pain; and if smokers, some have blood clotting. Many teens receive pills without parental consent, and therefore can give no family medical history.
- The rate of sexually transmitted diseases (STDs) among teens is three times higher than the general population. Many of these diseases, such as herpes, genital warts, and papilloma virus, are incurable. Chlamydia is epidemic at 30 percent, and females sexually active at 16 and under are twice as likely to get cervical cancer (*British Journal of Obstetrics and Gynecology*, vol. 93 (1986), p. 787).
- A recent World Health Organization report indicated that one in 20 teenagers contacts some form of STD every year ("two people every five seconds" in the United States and Canada.)[51]

### *There Is No Such Thing as "Safe Sex"*

- All sex is increasingly risky. Fischl, et al., in *Journal of the American Medical Association*, vol. 257 (1987), p. 640, showed that the rate of AIDS transmission among couples using condoms, when only one partner was infected, was 17 percent during a short 18-month period. To clarify: 17 percent of previously uninfected partners got AIDS from their infected condom-wearing partners. And we are recommending condoms to our children as *protection*?

- On June 19, 1987, Dr. Maria Crenshaw, past president of the American Association of Sex Educators, asked 800 sexologists at the World Congress of Sexology, in Heidelberg: "If you had available the partner of your dreams, and knew that person carried the [HIV] virus — would you rely on a condom for protection?" Not a single person raised a hand! So she accused them all of giving irresponsible advice to youth.

- Condoms have an overall failure rate for preventing pregnancy of 10 percent (*Population Reports*, September/October 1982, pp. H121-122) — and an even higher rate in the prevention of AIDS transmission because the virus is so small (*British Medical Journal*, October 1985, p. 1196).

- Most dangerously, condoms have a much higher failure rate in anal sex (*British Medical Journal*, November 7, 1987, p. 94), indicating all sex educators ought to be directing youth away from this practice instead of attempting to normalize it, or recommending it as safe outercourse.

- In one investigation, the U.S. Federal Drug Administration found 20 percent of condoms tested to be unreliable (FDA Medical Devices Bulletin, September 1987, p. 1). Its current pass rate is three failures per thousand.

- *A standard Health and Welfare Canada test of condoms manufactured between 1987 and 1990 reported a 40 percent failure rate* for those lots tested at the point of manufacture, based on its standard — and very stringent — three-part test of pressure, volume, and leakage. Specifically, 40 percent of the sample failed at least one of the three tests.[52] The 1991 performance reported an "improved" 28 percent failure rate.

- The general public, and surely most sex educators in North America, are unaware that the incidence of many STDs has been skyrocketing in recent years. Syphilis is at a 40-year-high level; human papilloma virus (HPV) has been found in 38 percent of 13- to 21-year-old women. This virus can produce sterility, and it cannot be cured.

- A 1988 Queen's University study, *Canada, Youth, and AIDS*, found that among 38,000 youths studied, ages 11-21, there were very high correlations between sexual activity and alcohol use, drug abuse, marijuana use, and cigarette smoking. The Queen's study established a "risk profile" for teens that ought to serve as a good indicator to teens in trouble. Instead, many school programs are promoting such high-risk behaviour.

- Gary Ingersoll of Indiana University (reported in *USA Today*, February 1991), backs up the Queen's study, above, when he reports that "sex by age 16" may reflect a "risk-taking profile," and parents should get help. Such children were five times as likely to get suspended; ten times more likely to use marijuana; six times more likely to have attempted suicide, etc., etc. And 65 percent of 16-year-old dropouts are sexually active.

- The point is, there is a strong association between comprehensive sex education and sexual activity. Parents beware! As Canadian gynecologist Stephen Genuis, M.D., has pointed out in his book *Risky Sex*: "With the illusion of liberating people from repressive attitudes and lifestyles, many now suffer the bondage of lifelong sexually transmitted diseases or their consequences, from which there may be no liberation."[53] Genuis also warns us to beware of the misleading distinction between a *theoretical* failure rate and a *practical* one. For example, 100 condom users, at an 8 percent theoretical failure rate, will over five years produce 40 real pregnancies, and after 10 years 80!

As mentioned, increasing numbers of U.S. parents whose children contract STDs or AIDS or get pregnant from following school-based sex-ed advice are winning suits against the schools, the teachers, and the boards. It's just a matter of time before angry Canadian parents catch on. After all, sex can be deadly. Drugs can be deadly. Driving can be deadly. Drinking can be deadly. But teachers don't hand out packets of clean needles; or install "pop-a-safe-dose-today" cocaine dispensers in school washrooms. They don't advise students to drive as fast as they think is right, regardless of parental advice or social norms. They don't give samples of gin and vodka to 13-year-olds at recess on the grounds that they're drinking anyway, or soon will be.

Yet AIDS, only the 50th cause of premature death in Canada in 1983, was 10th by December 1, 1990, by which time 4455 deaths had been reported. "Safe sex," in short, is a terribly dangerous message to give anyone — especially starry-eyed teenagers, because conventional, contraceptive, and abortion-based sex-ed clearly worsens the problems it was intended to solve.

But there is some good news, too. If only from mortal fear, the times are changing, and serious and respected experts are calling for a retreat.

# THE REVOLT GAINS SPEED

*The leaders of the sexual revolution . . . promised joy, liberation, and good health. They've delivered misery, disease, and even death.*
MEDICAL WORLD NEWS, AUGUST 4, 1985[54]

Spurred by the now publicly acknowledged catastrophe of conventional comprehensive sex-ed courses in the schools, Americans have revolted. President Reagan led the charge in 1981, by endorsing the passage through Congress of the *Adolescent Family Life Act* (AFLA), also known as Title XX, which at long last openly confirmed the *dependant* status of adolescents in sexual matters. Of course, this the law has always done in matters of driving, entering contracts, obtaining marriage licences, purchasing alcohol or cigarettes or pornography, borrowing money, and so on. How sexuality escaped this net of adult supervision has been the subject of this chapter. AFLA is a concerted effort to fight AIDS, rising pregnancy and STD disease rates, skyrocketing abortion, and sexual liberation by forcing schools to change their sex-ed curricula from stressing sex, to stressing family and morals-based abstinence education. It stipulates that federal funds cannot be used to "distribute contraceptives or prescriptions for contraceptives in schools without parental consent."[55] AFLA has since inspired more than 25 states to pass bills mandating that sex or AIDS education courses "stress abstinence for young people and affirm the values of marriage." Programs with names such as Teen-aid, Sex Respect (used in 50 states by 1080 school districts, and in 26 other countries), and Sexuality, Commitment and Family are widely purchased and taught in hundreds of school systems where parents and teachers have been deeply rattled over the consequences of 25 years of conventional "non-directive" sex-ed.

Predictably, Planned Parenthood and the Alan Guttmacher Institute launched a suit against the U.S. government's program on the grounds that teaching abstinence in the schools is equivalent to teaching religion. Well, if teaching abstinence is religion, what is teaching indulgence? They lost (1988). But they have not given up. Of course, the mention of teaching abstinence brings a knowing smirk to the face of the average Canadian. But Americans, with more than 125,000 dead from AIDS already (by January 1, 1992) — *almost three times the number lost in the Vietnam War* — can't afford to smirk, and soon we won't smirk, either. Many of the conspirators of intent, who are ideologically pushing religious humanism via sex-ed, have tried to get around the problem by

promoting every sexual practice *except* heterosexual intercourse . . . and calling the result "abstinence." Many of them refer
to these practices — which usually include "safe" (with a condom)
anal intercourse, oral-genital sex, mutual masturbation, and the
heavy use of sex toys — as "outercourse." But concerned parents
won't be stopped. In a New York City study, fully 91 percent of the
parents surveyed wanted their children to receive abstinence counselling.[56] The numbers rolling in are impressive. The tide, south of
the border at least, has finally turned, and there is even a ripple of
sanity in Canada. The British Columbia Centre for Disease Control
in two publications stresses that only abstinence and the complete
refusal of intravenous drug use can guarantee against HIV infection.
But it's a ripple, and it's as a result of fear of death and health costs,
not of respect for family and traditional morality.

But the Americans have passed that point, and their heavy
political, medical, and moral guns are all pointing at sexual liberation and conventional sex-ed in the schools as the culprits. Heavens!
Even loopy, libertine California, where half the people are crazy and
the other half make a living looking after them, has passed a state
law (1988) requiring the promotion of abstinence, and it further
"requires that monogamous heterosexual marriage be treated with
honor and respect in all materials and instruction."[57] Even the
students are changing. In a recent Louis Harris Poll, 87 percent of
U.S. students said they did not want comprehensive sexuality services in their schools; 67 percent did not want them in the *vicinity*
of the school. Even a poll commissioned by Planned Parenthood
itself showed that 70 percent of parents wanted sex-ed to teach
morals and to urge students *not* to have sex.[58] Study after study
shows that morals-based, directive sex-ed, with heavy parental
involvement and a stress on abstinence and the skills involved in
saying no effectively (meaning — and this is crucial — without
losing the love and respect of the boyfriend or girlfriend), is overwhelmingly successful in reducing sexual activity, illegitimacy, disease, and abortion. After two decades of conventional sex-ed, the
city of San Marcos, California, spooked by high levels of disease and
teen pregnancy, combined with parents to integrate an abstinence
program in all its schools, and in one school cycle saw teen pregnancies cut from 147 to 20![59]

## What Can Be Done?
As long as the State continues to run the schools, change can only
come when the State recognizes the horrendous failure of its sex-ed

social engineering and then mandates family- and abstinence-based programs backed up by a legal climate in which parents are not only able, but also encouraged to sue teachers, schools, and boards that promote morally unacceptable, life-scarring, or potentially deadly behaviour to the young. Currently, if a school or hospital attempts even minor invasive surgery on your child — a sliver taken from a foot, say — signed permission is required from parents. But something as serious as the distribution of contraceptives to your child, or even abortion, can be carried out without parental permission or knowledge. The threat of civil or even criminal legal suits, however, would serve to remind educators that they are granted a parental responsibility to communicate and enforce family values, not a licence to destroy the family.

Canadians need their own version of the American "Hatch Amendment," which is a "student rights" bill that basically forbids schools to require any student to submit to psychological counselling, testing, values clarification, or courses of any kind designed to modify personal behaviour, without advanced signed parental approval. It also makes all school materials available for parental inspection, and it forbids teachers from probing student or family privacy in any way.

This is an "opting in" provision, which requires not that the student opt *out* of such a class, making him feel like a dodo, but that the teacher arrange for all students to opt *in* with signed parental approval. Such a method constitutes the parents as a de facto committee overseeing the teachers. Teachers hate it. Predictably, the over-two-million strong U.S. National Education Association is trying to sue for the repeal of such laws as I am recommending here for Canadians. At its July 1991 convention in Miami, the association passed all sorts of resolutions demanding the right of teachers to determine what is taught in the schools, regardless of the wishes of parents, and the right to be "legally protected from censorship and lawsuits" (resolution C-30).[60] In her scathing new book, *A Parent's Survival Guide to the Public Schools*, author and former teacher Sally Reed (who has also authored *NEA: Propaganda Front of the Radical Left*) refers to the public schools as "indoctrination centers for collectivism." A book of the same title could be written about the various Canadian teachers' unions. We should not be surprised.

The war against the family in our society is neatly summed up in the clash between these conflicting moral and legal demands.

# 9

# Looking After
# Their Bodies

*For the ordinary Canadian child, physical fitness . . .
seems to be a decreasing function of age from the
time when we put him behind a desk in our schools.*

PROFESSOR DON BAILEY, 1973

*In many ways the fitness boom . . . is a myth. And
whatever part of the boom does exist, it doesn't trickle
down to our children.*

DON HAYDON, DIRECTOR, U.S. GOVERNOR'S
COMMISSION ON FITNESS, 1985

*Between 88% and 91% of Canadians — an "over-
whelming majority" — believe physical education
should be mandatory for all children throughout the
school years.*

GALLUP POLL, JANUARY 9, 1990

A clear case can be made that the state of the minds,
spirits, and bodies of our nation's youth is the future
state of the nation itself, for the most powerful indicator of future
behaviour is past behaviour. What they are as children, they will
likely become as adults. As we have seen, by consequence of our
lazy embrace of egalitarian ideology we have allowed their minds to
settle to the lowest common denominator, while their values, and
their spiritual and social perceptions, are invaded daily by explicit
or implicit religious humanist and therapeutic assumptions.

But what happens to their bodies, the once-hallowed "temple of the soul," in the public schools? Does the sound-mind-in-a-sound-body philosophy hold sway? The best that can be said, as we shall see, is "no." Their bodies are left to decay at the same unsettling rate as their minds and values deteriorate. Yet the overwhelming majority of Canadians — the great bulk of them parents — feel very strongly that not just physical education but physical *activity* should be mandatory in our public schools. They're paying the shot in taxes so why is it they can't get what they want?

Even the most cursory inspection will reveal that sport and fitness play an integral part in the philosophy that makes most Canadian private schools so very successful. Study after study shows that students who participate in regular and intensive sport and fitness programs are happier, better adjusted, and less depressive than those who don't. They're aerobically fitter, far less fat, stronger, and more flexible; they have greater self-esteem and they perform better academically. It's common sense. It's folk wisdom everywhere — except in the vast majority of schools run by the State. So we must now ask what effect this political and professional negligence has had on our children.

What has really happened to the health and fitness of the last generation of kids, who, during most of the 185 school days, every single year, are left in the hands of educators? And remember that taxpayers have already provided the majority of schools with sufficient capital improvements in the form of fields, tracks, equipment, and gymnasiums to do the job.

## WHAT SHOULD WE CHOOSE FOR OUR CHILDREN?

Before looking at some of the modern pronouncements on student health and fitness, remember that we ought to guide ourselves by wisdom and common sense rather than merely by science. Begin reading the literature in this area and you'll soon find enough contradictions to suggest the need for a product warning that would go something like this: "This study was performed with best efforts of all concerned, but within the unavoidable limits of funding and human understanding. It is extremely probable that some future study will modify, refute, or recast these results. We therefore recommend that any alterations in policy be carried out with extreme caution and with practical wisdom foremost in mind."

Why such skepticism about science? Simply because science, despite the hope we place in it, cannot tell us what kind of society, and values, we ought to provide for our children. So we must at all costs avoid the tendency to postpone judgment as we wait for some laboratory to grind out a conclusive answer to our problems; and we ought to realize that much of science itself is skewed by human values, even in the mere selection and interpretation of the data. So let us instead choose an instrument far more powerful than science: our own moral imagination. Let us imagine we are faced with an irrevocable choice of moving forever to one of two new countries, FitCountry or UnfitCountry, each of which is the same in every respect except in its attitude toward health and fitness. Imagine which you would prefer for your own children.

In *FitCountry* the people seem to have a deep, almost moral, interest in vigorous activity. Very few smoke (children consider it uncool). Smoking in or near the vicinity of a school during school hours meets with suspension. Almost no one is obese. The parks and schoolyards seem busy with active people of all ages most of the daylight hours. All school children are required to do an hour of vigorous activity every school day, including team sports at some level. Playgrounds ring with excitement and with the cheering (or occasional scolding) of teammates. Junk food is forbidden on school grounds. Not only are most children a bit taller than the generation preceding — the result of excellent nutrition and exercise. They are also fitter and stronger than their parents were at the same age. In FitCountry, the public philosophy of health is basically "a sound mind and spirit in a sound body." The result is that millions of the nation's children have high confidence in themselves, work at superior academic levels, and show a vigorous attitude toward life's challenges. Multilevel competitive sports teach everyone the joy of striving and improving, the humility and grace in losing, and the bonds of teamwork. The schools have negligible violence and crime, and there are few emotional problems among students. As this country's population ages, the most impressive overall health result is an extremely low level of degenerative disease among the people. Even those who do get sick tend to recover faster, and they spend far less time in hospital. The nation's health costs are lower and, therefore, taxes are lower.

In *UnfitCountry*, the people are the same in every respect as those in FitCountry, except in their attitude toward physical life. Here, you notice immediately that the young and old alike are increasingly sedentary and obese. Shockingly, the children in UnfitCountry experience a rapid loss of body strength and cardiovascular capacity from about age 15 onward. A diminishing percentage of adolescents can run a mile in a reasonable time. The children, by all biochemical and physiological measurement, are physically "old," though chronologically "young." Clearly, all school children in UnfitCountry eat increasing and alarming amounts of fatty and fried foods and refined sugars, and many have early signs of cardiovascular disease and high blood pressure. Most cannot do a single chin-up at age 14 (whereas their parents and grandparents easily could). Nevertheless, quite surprisingly the vast majority of children in the public schools are not required to do any physical exercise, and even what they do is, on close inspection, usually below the minimum level required for a positive health effect. In this country, the government controls public education and is unresponsive to parents who are annoyed and disenchanted because they cannot persuade their schools to make sport and fitness mandatory. They have given up. They cannot get their children interested in health and fitness, because "none of their kids' friends are interested." So, if they can afford it, they move their children into private schools. If they cannot, they become resigned to what they see as government-imposed educational bad luck.

Now, there is likely broad agreement that only the most jaded individual would choose UnfitCountry. And, of course, FitCountry is an ideal, a critic might argue. But then so is UnfitCountry. In UnfitCountry, the controlling ideal is least physical effort; here there is least concern for the health and fitness of citizens and least public school duty to promote physical well-being.

FitCountry is simply the opposite. It sees striving for optimal health and fitness for oneself, for one's family, and ultimately for the pleasure of it, as part of striving for excellence. It says that a school that does not strive in this way is no school at all; it is an expensive holding tank for unformed students and spiritless, unambitious teachers who have given up their ancient commitment to the well-balanced life.

## THE CONTROLLING IDEAL

We are speaking of so-called human capital here, and we are not doing much to sustain the nation's most important sustainable resource: its children. Furthermore, any nation that turns out generations of increasingly weak children will eventually reach a condition of maximum adult weakness. Is that our ideal? I say forget the reports and studies. Instead, let's have a vigorous national debate on the controlling educational ideal under which we wish to operate.

We can even forget the debate, for that matter. The people, now frustrated by the public schools, already know what they think and have already spoken, as witnessed by a tiresome litany of polls.

But if it helps at all, here's what some of the reports are telling us.

Until about 1850, most human beings died of *infectious* diseases. Then, over the past century and a half, increasingly good basic medical research, vaccination, sterilization, and so on have conquered, or have held at bay, most of these diseases — only to see them replaced by the *degenerative* diseases that spring primarily from inactivity, poor nutrition, and poor health habits. The World Health Organization has called the shocking increase in these diseases "the greatest epidemic mankind has ever faced."[1] Today, about half of all hospital beds in the developed nations are occupied by people suffering from one or another of such "lifestyle" diseases or, as some prefer to call them, "diseases of choice," meaning you can avoid them by a change in personal behaviour. Such diseases used to happen only to the very old and immobilized them against their will. Today they happen to whole societies in the measure that we shrink from regular and vigorous physical activity and spurn nutritious food. And they are striking younger and younger age groups, including school-aged children who eat poorly and do not exercise. This trend is especially strong in Canada and the United States, where fast food, high prosperity, and work-saving technology are most prevalent. Consider this:

During the Korean War, half the autopsies performed on U.S. soldiers killed in action showed heart disease and plaque (fatty deposits) in their arteries. Their average age was 22! Later, of one hundred 22-year-old soldiers autopsied in the Vietnam War, 45 percent showed medium artery damage and 5 percent *severe* artery damage.[2] These were not old men; they were of university age. But Korean and Japanese soldiers, all much leaner, fitter, and on a very different diet, showed no such traces. The point is that heart disease is not something which just "happens" to most people. It is an organic disease that most sufferers can accelerate themselves, or postpone as long as possible through life-style. The same is true of many types of cancer. At least half of all cancers are life-style-based. And high blood pressure is another killer. Many now famous studies, such as the Framingham study at Harvard and the Paffenbarger study at Stanford, have illustrated that individuals who eat a lot of fatty foods and refined sugars and burn fewer than a specified number of calories in physical activity weekly are at high risk for degenerative disease. *Such findings apply to children of all ages.*

We are just now discovering that the young arc not protected from degenerative diseases if they adopt the life-styles of diseased people.

# THE FATTENING AND DRUGGING OF NORTH AMERICA

Although it is true that North Americans have been growing taller over the last century, it is also true they are getting much fatter. Between 25 and 45 percent of the population over 30 is more than 20 percent overweight, and between 2 and 15 percent of the children (depending on age) are 40 percent over the median weight for their height. In numerous studies, the widely respected Dr. Jean Mayer of Harvard discovered in the 1950s that among young students *inactivity* — not necessarily over-eating — was the major cause of obesity.[3] In fact, some studies have shown that Americans are eating a bit less but are still getting heavier — because they are doing less than ever. Several studies have shown that obese/overweight school boys and girls *spend two-thirds less time in physical activity* than do normal-weight students.[4] Other studies have shown that many commercial dog foods are more nutritiously balanced than the average real diet of North Americans, and that there has been a dramatic increase in the consumption of refined sugars to about 140 pounds per capita per year (a 50 percent increase since 1920) combined with a 50 percent reduction in natural carbohydrate foods such as breads and fruits. And we consume soft drinks at the annual rate of 40 gallons each.

Aspirins are consumed at the rate of 40 or 50 million tablets per day in North America, and there are 200,000 different prescription drugs lining pharmacy and supermarket shelves. (Most drug-abuse deaths are from prescribed diazepam and barbiturates, and from adverse reaction to prescription drugs.[5]) From 1965 to 1980 alone, alcohol consumption in North America went up 186 percent. It has since levelled off or even fallen somewhat, with the drop perhaps related to after-effects of the fitness boom, to an aging population, and to higher taxes on alcohol. Meanwhile . . . the American Medical Association's shocking *Code Blue* report on the state of health of America's youth told us that 50 percent of high school seniors have used marijuana; 15 percent have tried cocaine. Many students are steady alcohol users by Grade 7.

**The Public Schools — Fat Farms for Children**
According to the 1981 *Canada Fitness Survey, only 6 percent of our children* between the ages of 10 and 19 are active regularly and

intensively enough to gain any true fitness benefits, such as higher aerobic scores and lower fat levels. General fitness in Canadian girls starts to level off, then decline, between 14 and 16; for boys it is between 16 and 18. At ages 15-19, only 24 percent of girls achieve a "recommended level of fitness" (itself a low standard, in my view); for boys, it is only 50 percent. Females, at all age levels, are less active than males, are more worried about their weight and health, and in general participate in fewer extracurricular activities and far fewer competitive sports. (In 1990 alone, 200,000 Canadians, mostly women, had liposuction to machine-suck fat from their bodies.) Muscular endurance starts to decline at 13 for girls and 17 for boys, and the trend indicates "that the relative strength of North American children is declining."[6] Meanwhile, the American College Testing Service (ACT) has found that the best life-success predictor for students is not grades, but involvement in extracurricular interests such as sports, hobbies, and club activities. It appears that what we have in the making is another quiet little national catastrophe, simply because the children we have consigned to the schools of the State for most of each school day are degenerating at an ever-younger age.

If we pause to consider the relationship between fitness and working capacity, we can see that a nation of weaker youths is likely going to produce a nation of weaker workers, weaker parents, weaker teachers, weaker everything. We are becoming a huffing and puffing milquetoast nation; an army of overweight armchair quarterbacks and physically slovenly couch potatoes. By pure default, we are detraining our children in the public schools. Some parents may be out jogging, but you won't see many kids beside them.

Yet in Vannes, France, as early as the 1950s, a model study was carried out that ought to have ended all debate. It had school children doing academic work only in the morning, devoting the afternoon to art, music, and sport. Students from these schools ended up superior on every personal, physical, and academic scale. A similar eight-year project in Trois-Rivières, Quebec, found much the same thing. Students receiving five extra hours of physical activity per week achieved, in addition to the other physical, personal, and social benefits, higher marks than regular-room students.[7]

Here's more. In a recent University of Toronto fitness study of 14-year-olds, half the boys and 21 of the 30 girls tested *could not do a single chin-up* (Toronto *Star*, January 9, 1990). A 1987 U.S. survey of 18,857 students aged 6-12 showed the same dismal strength levels: more than 50 percent of boys and girls could not hold their chins over a raised bar for more than 10 seconds (unlike their parents, who at that age easily achieved times double or triple that). In the 50-yard dash, the majority were significantly slower than children the same age in 1975.

Bigger. Fatter. Weaker. That's the trend.

Although Canada does not keep data to allow tracking of such trends (this makes it hard to measure the educators, too), the United States does. University of Michigan professor Gary Riess says that studies have shown "just a steady decline" in fitness among U.S. students over the past two decades (Toronto *Star*, January 5, 1987). Mandatory phys-ed was dropped in all Ontario public schools in 1969 (part of personal liberation ideology — "everything was optional"), and modestly reintroduced in 1984 with the requirement that students take one year (only) of physical- and health-ed before graduation ("health-ed" is now the class where much of the "sex-ed" occurs). In 1971-72, 74 percent of Ontario public school students took phys-ed; by 1983 that figure had dropped to 58 percent. As for the United States, students there have mandatory physical education periods once per day until Grade 10. But in Ontario, Canada's most populous province, students up to Grade 6 have virtually no serious phys-ed requirement. Anyway, much of so-called "phys-ed" in both nations is of low calibre, with students spending a lot of their time standing, lining up, watching others, or goofing around.

Recent Canadian studies, including one by University of Toronto professor Bob Goode, show that only 24 percent of time spent in phys-ed is given to actual physical movement; of that, much, much less activity is at a level intense enough to produce a *training effect* (at or above 80 percent of maximum heart rate, for a minimum of 20 minutes per day, three times per week). In one study, obese children moved for only 6 minutes in a 50-minute period — and for only one minute intensely![8] Professors Goode and Volpe state that "Canadian children and adolescents are not physically fit. They engage in substantially less physical activity than did their age-mates two or three decades ago . . . Children are not only less active, they are fatter, *and have less heart-lung fitness than middle aged joggers*."[9] They also quote studies showing that even students 11-13 years old, enrolled in ostensible physical-education programs, either do not change or actually *decline* in heart-lung fitness! Conversely, evidence from around the world shows that children of all ages, when involved in programs sufficiently *regular* and *intense*, make vast improvements in strength and cardiovascular fitness. Children at Toronto's National Ballet School, for example, who take an arduous course of studies in addition to daily workouts, showed a steady *increase* in cardiovascular fitness from age 10 to 17. In contrast, although 96 percent of our public school youth manage to meet a very low "recommended" fitness level at age 13, by the end of adolescence that figure drops to 40 percent.

## SPAWNING DEGENERATIVE DISEASES

Okay. So strength and cardiovascular health are declining in the schools while obesity is increasing. This ought to tell us that our public school system is a spawning ground for diseases related to inactivity. The U.S. data are telling for us; the sample groups are large, and U.S. and Canadian children are uncannily similar in most fitness and health surveys. Researchers at Louisiana State University have made alarming discoveries through autopsies of very young children who died in car accidents. Dr. David Freedman found children as young as 15 with high cholesterol levels and arterial plaque, and he found "fatty streaks" (precursors to plaque build-up) in the arteries of 5-year-olds (Toronto *Star*, November 21, 1985). In a study of 24,000 children, Charles T. Kuntzleman found 41 percent had high cholesterol levels and 28 percent high blood pressure. According to a Tufts University report, about 40 percent of all fat 7-year-olds will become fat adults, and 70 percent of obese teenagers will be obese adults. The same report states that there are now 54 percent more fat children age 6 to 11 than there were 15 years ago. Among 12- to 17-year-olds, obesity is up 39 percent (*Today's Health*, December 1990). At a 1988 U.S.-Canada conference on obesity, Dr. Stanley Banach named "child obesity" the great nutritional problem of North America, saying that obesity is a "national disgrace," having increased 55 percent among adults since 1960 and (again) 39 percent among children. He said that 43 percent of the British are 20 pounds or more overweight, as are 47 percent of Canadians, and 52 percent of Americans; but Canadians between 55 and 64 are more obese than Americans.[10] Dr. Wynn F. Updyke, reporting on the results of a 10-year study of 9.7 million 6- to 17-year-olds showing that U.S. children had gained weight and lost cardiovascular endurance, said the results were "ominous," because of the "clear link between heart disease, obesity, and inactivity." The best investment parents can make in the physical fitness of their children, he said, "is to insist on high quality physical education programs in their schools" (*USA Today*, September 15, 1989). Such studies simply echo findings of the 1970s that as many as 70 percent of students from 6 to 18 *already showed the beginnings of heart disease* (New York *Times*, April 22, 1979; italics added).

Is there cause for alarm? For sure. A Canadian Institute of Child Health report (1989) says that from 40 to 50 percent of school children from grades 4 to 7 eat foods high in fat; that 9 percent of grade 7 students smoke and 15 percent drink alcohol; and that 39 percent of males and 21 percent of females have had sex by age 14. Up to 15 percent of all youth death is from suicide (five times as many males as females). By age 15-19, about 11,500 children had contracted a notifiable sexually transmitted disease (1981). Some picture. Something tells me that those kids could have spent a lot more time in the pool or on the track or basketball court, developing fitness, loyalties to their teammates, and the ideals of fair play instead of developing lung disease, genital warts, and antisocial behaviour.

The widely quoted 1988 "Campbell's Survey" of 23,000 Canadians (*The Well-Being of Canadians*), a combined Fitness Canada, Campbell, and Health and Welfare effort, told the same depressing story, informing us that "one-third of the Canadian population age 15 and older may be at risk due to obesity . . ." Another report, this one on more than 33,000 Canadian students (*Canadian Health Attitudes and Behaviour Survey 1984-85*), reports on the high levels of television watching: up to 46 percent of grade 7 students watch 18 hours weekly! On this note, the *Harvard Medical School Health Letter* (November 1985) reports that of 11,000 children surveyed, the ones who watched the most TV were the most obese. Actually, Canadian students spend 1040 hours a year watching television and 900 receiving school instruction (Toronto *Star*, October 30, 1991). Although "there has been a movement in Canada to strengthen physical education programs for the young" since 1975, the Canadian survey says, the low-level types and duration of exercise that are outlined present a pathetic picture. A half-hour of "swimming," for example, gives no indication of effort expended. Nearly 25 percent of grade 10 students did nothing. Absolutely nothing. Every week. All year.[11]

Boy! The reports just roll off the presses. A recent joint project of the U.S. Bureau of Economic Research and Stanford University reported on January 2, 1992, that, compared with their counterparts from the 1960s, contemporary U.S. children were fatter, more suicidal, and more murderous, and scored lower on standardized academic tests.

Enough said. It's a terrible picture. This being so . . . how do we explain the colossal incompetence and unwillingness of our paid servants — the public school bureaucracy — to do our bidding and require a minimum of effective, vigorous physical education for our children while in their care? After all, thousands of North American private schools do it, at an average per-capita cost of half that of public schools, simply as a routine matter of school philosophy. Is there a solution? Maybe the answer is to ensure a schooling system that reflects and promotes the private values of the parents and families of the nation, instead of the public values of the educators.

Whose kids are they, anyway? That's the argument. The next chapter outlines a solution.

# 10

# The Solution: Take Back the Schools

*The Public School is [North] America's collective farm.*

LEWIS PERELMAN, THE HUDSON INSTITUTE

The people have allowed the State to take out of their hands the most important task of any nation: the nurturing of the quality of the minds, spirits, and bodies of the young. And the State has done what any State would do. It has delivered a collectivist result: runaway costs per student; an empire of academic bureaucrats; mediocre academic performance; a suppression of the core values of a free society; and hordes of overweight, unfit children. In simpler terms, we now have unsound minds and spirits in unsound bodies. Well, it's time to admit they've had their day. They tried it. And they failed. So, just as we gave the schools to the State, we ought to take them back from the State.

Let us assume our proper responsibilities instead of labouring further under the illusion that someone else can do the job better. This is one case where delegation is abdication. It won't be easy to get the schools back, mind you. The vested public interests will scream bloody murder. Teachers' unions will be up in arms, protecting their higher pay and their softer jobs. But nothing could be more rewarding for this nation. Once people see that the surrender of the schools to the State was tantamount to a surrender of our future to the State, they will see that this unhappy situation must and can be reversed, in several simple steps. The radical reconstitution of sound schools such as will be proposed here is sure to be the hottest topic of the next two decades, simply because we can no longer submit our most precious resource to the systemic bumbling of failed collectivist ideologues. It's far too dangerous, and so the people are reacting.

How serious is the reaction?

Very. That's why the most heartening recent event in the lamentable history of the public school in the West is the tacit agreement on a viable solution from two U.S. think-tanks that hardly ever agree on anything. The conservative Heritage Foundation and the left-liberal Brookings Institution have reached substantial independent agreement that public education is a dead letter, and that more money, more bureaucracy, and more legislation will not solve the problem of declining schools and standards. For the Heritage Foundation, this was no surprise. It has always promoted freeing the schools from the clutches of the State. The bombshell news, rather, came when John Chubb and Terry Moe of Brookings published their methodologically sound, thoughtful, and utterly conservative solution in *Politics, Markets, and American Schools*. Their analysis, which covered 500 schools and 20,000 principals, teachers, and students, is already a classic statement of the inherently conflicting consequences of trying to produce, in a centrally planned way, something as personal, local, freedom based, and family-value driven as education. What is unique about their book is that it advises everyone to give up on public education as we have known it, and to design a new system based on parental "choice."

Their basic message is that regardless of the best intentions, handing education (or anything else, for that matter) to the State in a democratic society will always result in an inverse relationship between cost and quality, with the various manifestations of the State itself gradually cannibalizing the very resources meant to produce the product. The very mechanics of a democratic society establish "public authority" as a prize competed for by various warring interest groups, all of them claiming to further "the public interest" — at public expense. What's new? Great conservative and classical liberal thinkers from Tocqueville to Hayek have warned of this outcome for generations. But what *is* new is the frank admission from liberals themselves. Better later than never, I suppose. The result of this turf war over the schools is that parents and students don't get the schools they want. That's because, as Chubb and Moe explain, "the public schools are *not meant* to be theirs to control, and are literally *not supposed* to provide them with the kind of education they might want."[1] In other words, public education entails, in principle, a tug-of-war over end-values which inevitably consumes the scarce resources available. That's point one.

Point two is that because public schools have a coercive monopoly on tax-supported education (compared with the private alternatives, for which tuition is paid in after-tax dollars), they have the perceived and real advantage of being relatively inexpensive, and "can attract and hold students *without being particularly good at educating them.*"[2] In fact, in rough numbers Chubb and Moe calculate that U.S. public schools as a whole cost about $5000 per child per year, about double the $2500 cost of private schools (most of which are very small and inexpensive, though we tend to hear only about the expensive elite ones). Because, in radical thinking, public schools belong to society as a whole rather than to parents and their children (a clear indicator of the war between the family and the State), "the public schools are governed by an enormous far-flung constitutency in which the interests of parents and students carry no special status or weight."[3] The parents are just the breeding machines, and the kids belong to the State. Such is the thinking, which is precisely opposite to that of private schools, of course, where the students and parents are the living centre, and far-flung society is quite incidental, even extraneous. We shall see shortly that the public school places an upward pressure on cost and size and a downward pressure on quality, while the private school does the opposite.

What all previous so-called "reformers" in the United States and Canada have tried to do is to reverse this typical structural *consequence* of a public school system, but without eliminating the *cause* that produces the consequence: the role of the State itself . . . the very "publicness" of education. Thus, the history of most school reform has been a pathetic one of trying to achieve this reversal with various forms of evasive policy: with more *money* (remember that in both nations it costs 300 percent more to educate a student in 1990 than it did in 1960 — in constant dollars!); with an altered student-teacher *labour ratio* (although there is no demonstrable relationship between such a ratio and performance); and with *curricular obfuscations* (detectable in slogans like "it doesn't matter what they learn," or in "process" programs). Keep in mind through all this that school budgets, which represent about 70 percent of every home-owner's tax bill, are largely unexamined by the public, and that the trustees themselves are utterly beyond public accountability. Neither municipal governments themselves nor parents have any means of disciplining the schools or their budgeting process. Think of the radical nature of teachers' unions and you'll see that sizable radical elements in our society have a direct, unencumbered, and unwarranted control over a significant portion of the wealth of every home-owner in our so-called free society. Although the two ideologies (top-down vs. bottom-up) are diametrically opposed, the believers in the first have a local stranglehold on the wealth of the believers in the second.

But the ultimate tactic has been the varieties of *administrative obfuscation*, such as "social promotion," "gentleman's B" grade inflation (give them a "B" because they're nice), the Deweyite switch to "child-centred" teaching, and the vigorous elimination of any standardized testing (thus enabling an escape from detection).

Other futile efforts to improve the public schools really amount to expensive *economic incentives* designed to show the increasingly angry taxpayer that public schools *really can* educate successfully. U.S. so-called "magnet" schools and Canadian so-called public "academy" schools (both offer upgraded, elite, enriched programs) are in fact quite successful — if you close your eyes to the extra cost and the fact that they exclude unqualified students (whose parents nevertheless are forced to cough up extra educational taxes). They are "show" schools run at public expense to salvage the bad reputation of the public system. Al Shanker, leader of the huge American Teachers Federation, has come up with yet another fiscal band-aid: a $500 million proposal for "incentive" schools; a plan whereby the State will reward successful schools — for doing what they are already being paid to do! Shanker wants to throw good money after bad. If this notion creeps up to Canada, we should recognize it for what it is — an *extra tax* to improve an already poor system.

Finally, the favourite technique of public educators and administrators of all stripes throughout history is a continuous use of *moral incentives* to psyche up the troops, to lead them to the light with language that implores a higher ideal. Most professional educators are stuck with this technique — because at present there is no other. At the end of a terrific critique of bad schooling you will inevitably see suggestions for repairing the damage by "persuading" educators, or "encouraging" voluntary school improvement, or "permitting" this and "rewarding" that.[4] But until the schools are taken back from the State, this is like King Canute lashing the waves. What is needed is not conceptual, but structural, reform: to align schools not with the State but with the family and the community as the key value-generating institutions of our society, and in a way that transfers real power over the schools from the State to the parents.

Although they don't go all the way, Chubb and Moe support this view and insist that the only solution possible will mean that "public authority must be put to use in creating a system that is almost entirely beyond the reach of public authority."[5] We will see that this recommendation, too, is a compromise of sorts, because it rests on the paradox of asking a public authority not to act like a public authority, which is like asking a fish not swim or a bird not to fly. But their solution would at least break the State's monopoly on educational supply and thus provide a first step in a desperately needed revolution.

### "Choice" as a Panacea

What Chubb and Moe offer is a powerful endorsement of the educational-choice movement that is sweeping North America. They declare that reformers "would do well to entertain the notion that choice *is* a panacea."[6] In essence, they advocate removing the "top-down" (their phrase) educational bureaucracy and restoring bottom-up control of the public schools, so that families have a sense of "owning" the schools. Stated another way, they advocate replacing the public operating system of the schools with a system more akin to that of private schools; for "the whole point of a thoroughgoing system of choice is to free the schools from these disabling constraints by sweeping away the old institutions and replacing them with new ones."[7] Their simple plan, easily transferrable to Canada, involves:

1. Giving parents "scholarships" (or vouchers) equivalent to the per-capita amount spent on each student from state/provincial and local sources (perhaps income-adjusted for those of low income).

2. With such scholarships, parents are given the power to send their children to the school of their choice, anywhere, and can add to the amount if they want to send them to a more expensive school.

3. The schools are restricted to, but would have full autonomy in, organization, budgeting, curriculum, and teacher hiring and firing.

4. New schools would be allowed to open in response to the new educational marketplace, and bad schools would have to shut down.

5. The State would be limited to teacher certification, the establishment of minimal graduation standards, and the enforcement of health and safety standards. It would also operate a "choice office" or clearinghouse for parent information on schools.

## Changing the Boss

Strictly speaking, what the "choice" or "scholarship" or "voucher" idea does is solve a problem inherent in any government service. Namely, whereas in free markets all producers and employees must either please the purchaser or be disciplined by him, all government employees receive their income not from the purchaser of the service but from the State. Thus, only with great difficulty can purchaser-consumers discipline a government service. The only way any public-style service can be transformed into a private-style service is by *altering the structure of the power relationship between buyer and seller of the product.* In other words, when it comes to education the trick is to *change the boss* of the teachers and administrators — from the State to the parents. That switch is achieved simply by transferring the power over the decision on where to spend educational money. Once this power is transferred to the family unit, the teacher/administrator unit quickly perceives that it's more important to please the whole community of family units that buy the educational product than it is to please the State. This is the way private schools have always operated. And the results show. A friend's son had a lousy teacher in a public school last year, but efforts to remove her were fruitless — no teacher had been fired for a decade. The bad ones simply get transferred within the system. This year the boy had a bad teacher in a private school — and his and all the other parents, having persuaded the headmaster, got rid of the teacher in the first month of school. That's the difference between pleading with the boss (the State) through an indifferent employee and actually controlling the boss yourself. The difference could not be greater.

## Private and Denominational Schools Do It Better

No one would argue that there are no good public schools. There certainly are. And they usually enjoy the special circumstances of cultural homogeneity, fairly wealthy neighbourhoods, or some other advantage over other public schools. But the real story, only now coming to light, is that in general private and denominational schools do a better and cheaper job of educating children. Perhaps the landmark study to verify this intuitive reality was published in 1987 — to much outcry from educational interests and teachers' unions — by J.S. Coleman and T.R. Hoffer. They found the same distinctions as have Chubb and Moe between "effective" and "ineffective" schools. Canada's own Professor Mark Holmes makes the same sort of distinction between "high doctrine" and "low doctrine" schools.[8] What the experts spend millions to find out, however, is what parents and students have always known about good and bad schools.

For Chubb and Moe, "effective" schools give far greater autonomy to school principals. They value academic courses highly; they focus on clear and high-level school, personal, and academic goals; and they support strong discipline, high teacher professionalism, a high degree of organization, and a lot of parent involvement. They are also highly competitive schools in which principals are rewarded by high enrollments. Nearly 64 percent of students in such schools (U.S.) are in an academic track, as opposed to only 28 percent of students in ineffective schools. On virtually every variable measured, the two kinds of schools were the flip-flop of each other.

In James S. Coleman's other landmark work on public vs. private schools — especially U.S. Catholic schools (where, in contrast to Canada, parents pay direct) — Coleman found that the "extra effect of attending a Catholic school is about a year's extra achievement over a two-year period."[9] Dropout rates are much lower, and black and Hispanic students in Catholic schools are three times as likely to graduate as their counterparts in public schools. Some 83 percent go to college, compared with 53 percent from public schools. These results held for all sorts of religiously based schools, regardless of all other social or economic factors. Such schools were paid for directly and had to compete for students, giving parents leverage against both the schools and their own children. In fact, *such schools were seen by all as agents of the parents, not of society.* Their students perform better on every measure. One of the interesting reasons Catholic schools produce better students is because they lack money and resources, and so must focus on the basics. They have not succumbed to the "shopping mall" or "cafeteria" education syndrome, whereby students are self-selecting courses from among 265 electives, as in Ontario. Good schools, Coleman says, maintain a high level of "social capital" and "functional community" that tends to glue together students, teachers, parents, and community. Finally, all such schools are distinguished by a set of beliefs of high standard, arising from religious tenets or tradition and parental involvement, usually from both.

Mark Holmes tells us that Catholic schools, French immersion schools, and private schools have all grown rapidly in Canada in the recent past (Statistics Canada reported 965 private schools in Canada in 1964-65, 1358 in 1985-86). British Columbia, Alberta, and Quebec already provide substantial funding for private schools. More than 67,000 Ontario children are educated in private schools, and private schools there have grown from 320 in 1976 to 549 in 1988 — a growth rate of about 70 percent — while public school enrollment has shrunk 12 percent. Meanwhile, publicly funded "academy" type schools have sprouted up in a variety of places in response to public demand for what Holmes calls "high doctrine" education.

By this phrase he means that while all schools in effect have a philosophy, or belief system, the key is whether the school is high or low doctrine. Low-doctrine schools tend to be based on "the minimum set of beliefs required for survival."[10] Everything is tolerated; values are entirely relative and situational. In other words, such schools have abandoned any consensus on right and wrong or on common standards of behaviour, dress, or deportment. Most urban public schools, Holmes suspects, are low doctrine. His work even suggests that low-doctrine schools are the perfect expression of the welfare State in that they discourage differences and exceptions on the grounds of tolerance — all must be treated the same, all accepted. For example, they progressively diminish the importance of academic prizes and competition in general.

High-doctrine schools encourage the opposite qualities. Consistent with Coleman's functional community and Chubb and Moe's effective school, they emphasize high standards, character, a common set of moral values, responsibility, cooperation, hard work, and the values of individual excellence and striving in all walks of life. This is what most parents encourage in their own children, and it reflects the way they want their children treated in the public schools. But that's impossible.

In short, the public school as an extension of the top-down State inevitably reflects all the values of the handicap system of socialism, while the private school reflects the values of the bottom-up society, the bonus system, traditional family values, moral agency, and responsibility.

Perhaps the litmus test of the difference in effectiveness of these two types of schools is best seen in one of the worst, most crime- and drug-infested school environments in North America, the Big Apple itself.

**Here's a peek at the drastic difference between Catholic schools and public schools in New York City (*Time*, May 27, 1991)**

|  | Public | Catholic |
|---|---|---|
| Students | 956,616 | 110,000 |
| Student/teacher ratio |  |  |
| Elementary/middle | 28:1 | 24:1 |
| High school | 30:1 | 18:1 |
| Percentage who graduate on time | 38 | 99 |
| Percentage in special education | 12 | 0.1 |
| Spending per student | $7,107 | $1,735 |
| Average teacher's pay | $39,136 | $22,550 |
| Administrators at head office | 3,930 | 33 |
| Ratio of administrators to students | 4:1,000 | 3:11,000 |

Well, that about says it all. But here are a few more gems:

- In Chicago's public schools, which are four times as costly as private ones, the dropout rate is between 43 and 53 percent. But it is less than 1 percent in its mostly black and Hispanic private Catholic schools.
- *Teachers hate public schools.* Whenever the schools deteriorate past a certain point, there is a flight from them. The rich move to the suburbs (called "white flight" in the United States). The poor are left to fill the bad schools. Result? The public school teachers themselves get desperate to protect their own kids — even from the public schools they themselves teach in!
- In a survey of nine U.S. cities representing perhaps 30 million people, between 13 and 21 percent of all children attended private schools. However, in a sweeping indictment of the public education expressed by voting with their feet, between 22 and 36 percent of the public school teachers sent their children to private schools! (American Enterprise Institute, 1990)
- Fully 69 percent of Chicago public school parents said they would put their children in private schools if they could afford it. Most telling of all: *46 percent of all the children of Chicago's city-dwelling public school teachers attend private schools!* (*Wall Street Journal*, July 26, 1990.) This is like 46 percent of all the employees at Ford driving a Honda.
- In Canada, about 4.8 percent of all students attend private schools

(1984-85; the numbers are surging). In 1977, about 188,350 students attended private schools; by 1986, that figure grew to 234,260, and the number of schools roughly from 800 to over 1300 in the same period. If we pause to consider the economic penalty of the after-tax burden of private school tuition, and the strength of family motive required to spend such sums, no more damning indictment of a nation's public school stock could be imagined than the rapid expansion of expensive private schools in the midst of declining "free" public education.

• There is a burgeoning "home-schooling" movement in Canada (and the United States). About 20,000 Canadian and 500,000 U.S. children are taught at home. (Contact Canadian Alliance of Home Schoolers, 195 Markville Road, Unionville, Ontario.)

## OBJECTIONS?

Let us hear them now. Teachers' unions in the United States and Canada aggressively resist the idea of "choice" in education or the notion of any voucher-type program on the grounds that the egalitarian ideal of a common education for all would be lost; that the rich and poor would segregate, leaving the poor to the worst of the teachers and schools; that money would go to religious-based schools that indoctrinate students; that private schools receiving public money would not be accountable to taxpayers; and that control over curriculum would be lost. These objections are answerable as follows.

Although much of the argument for the public school is that it could better educate the poor, it has miserably failed the poor. One example will suffice. Ontario, Canada's wealthiest province (though now declining under an openly socialist government) has a dropout rate for its "basic" level students — who are overwhelmingly from low-income homes — of 80 percent! So, quite the contrary to the argument of the collectivist educators, the public school system is an engine of despair that exploits the poor by holding them in a kind of bondage to lousy public education and forced indoctrination in collectivism — from which middle-income and well-off families have always been able to escape. Which is what they are increasingly doing. It is precisely to help those of low income that we need a system of choice so entrenched and widespread that such people have a chance to reconstitute their communities and values, to rebuild their hopes and dreams, and to escape their bondage to the State.

This message is not lost on the poor themselves. About 22 U.S. states have "choice" programs of one sort or another (more on this below).[11] Sociologist Charles Murray argues in his compassionate and challenging study of the poor, *Losing Ground*, that the egalitarian public school environment — always reluctant to discipline, to reward, or to promote excellence over others — ends up extracting a transfer of sorts from the better of any two students to the worst, simply through its concentration on all equally. In other words, one economically poor and disadvantaged student is compelled to surrender a part of his own education so an equally poor and disadvantaged, but more poorly behaved, student can stay in the classroom. The poor, especially the excellence-oriented black and Hispanic poor, are aware of the bondage they suffer through the educational bureaucracy. They know they are the ultimate victims of a public education system that systemically downgrades its standards to please its captive failures, not necessarily by design but by the nature of the philosophy and structure of any public system.

That's why state legislator Polly Williams from Milwaukee, Wisconsin, who is black, has been leading the charge for a voucher system for the poor — she calls it "parental empowerment" — and has won. On September 4, 1990, thousands of poor inner-city kids, each with a voucher worth $2500, marched into the schools of their choice — many of them created spontaneously to cater to the new market for vouchers. "This," she says, "is telling the public schools that if you want to keep students, fine. Just educate them. If you can't, *let's let as many hostages out of there as possible*" (*Wall Street Journal*, September 4, 1990). "Liberals," she complains, "never ask what poor people want. They have managed to create a system that rewards failure, not success, and the fitful efforts at reform . . . have benefited the middle classes, not the poor" (*The Economist*, August 4, 1990). The result? "Every private school in the inner city has a waiting list. Hundreds of low-income families want out of the public school system. There are no gang problems in the private schools, and only a two-percent drop-out rate."[12] And even businesses like Indiana's Golden Rule Insurance Company, operating in 49 states, are getting into the act by offering *private* vouchers to low-income students. The company offers half tuition (up to $800) to any student who wants to leave the public system. The only criterion is financial need. About 100 applications were anticipated in the first year. The company received 621 in the first three days! This is a program any business or charity in the U.S. or Canada could get involved in, and should.[13]

Understandably, Polly Williams' fight has created quite a furore because "the parents who want to opt out of the public school system are virtually all black, from relatively poor neighborhoods. They have watched a mostly white establishment promise reforms, changes and better days ahead for years, while their children went down each day to the same failed schools and fell behind their counterparts." So guess what? The public school folks fought back in the courts to preserve their interests. Sadly, on November 13, 1990, they won on a technicality, now under appeal. It didn't take long for a reaction from those favouring the State against those favouring the family, because, wrote Elaine Kamarck, senior fellow at the Progressive Policy Institute: "Mrs. Williams is challenging an entrenched establishment whose livelihood depends on continuing certain programs regardless of their effectiveness" (*Wall Street Journal*, June 8, 1990).

Once a "choice" system is tried in Canada, there will be the same story of courts and litigation from all the vested interests, each side using our Charter of Rights and Freedoms. But the objective is worth it. After all, why shouldn't the poor and the disadvantaged have the same opportunity as the rich to receive a good education? Why should they be held hostage to public schools? In the United States today, more than 62 percent of the population supports the idea of choice in education (*Washington Times*, August 24, 1990). Similar figures will soon apply to us, too. A choice system delivers private-type schools controlled by parents, whose values — those emblematic of the free society — radiate through the teachers, the curriculum, and the entire school. Any public school system delivers the opposite: the values of the collectivist-egalitarian State, opposed, as we have seen, to individual freedom and responsibility, excellence, and the family. We all must choose.

Educational choice programs vary from those that are really no choice at all to those that are wide open. And remember, even a choice system run with vouchers or scholarships is still a form of socialism because it relies upon forcibly extracted tax dollars. It is not true free-choice, as when you freely pay tuition at a private school, which is the ultimate goal of a free society's education system: to free the schools entirely from the State and return them to the family. The State may have some role to play in minimal *regulation* of the schools (to avoid victimization by charlatans and the like, or in funding tuition for the truly needy). But it ought to have no role whatsoever in their *operation*. Still, school choice via a tax-routed voucher system is a great step forward to the real thing.

For such a plan to work in Canada, each province would have to create its own system, because education under our Constitution is a provincial matter (despite the enormous influence of federal government subsidies). Choice systems in North America now run the gamut, dictated by how frightened the State educational authorities and politicians are and reflecting the distress of parents over the lousy quality of the product. At the basic level, choice means the student can choose to attend any public school in the same district. (Students are not "assigned" to a particular school by the authorities.) This creates healthy competition among local schools. But better yet, we should let students attend any public school in the province (eight U.S. states allow this mobility, which promotes a lot of intradistrict competition). Still better, let's allow attendance at any *public or private school* in the province (Milwaukee, Wisconsin, allows this now. Vermont has been doing it for over a century!). Or, even better, let's allow attendance at any public, private, or religious school. No U.S. state gives students public money to attend a religious school. Why not, is a mystery. After all, as the influential economist Thomas Sowell suggests, nothing forbids any citizen from *donating* money to religious organizations that he may have received from the government in salary, tax rebates, or social benefits; so why should he be denied the opportunity to *spend* his money on such services? Such small religious schools are often the cheapest and thus most affordable to poor families. Some "liberals" Sowell writes, want to forbid choice — especially to blacks — for fear of leaving only the poorest and worst blacks in the public schools. In other words, the best blacks shall be denied for the worst (the handicap system, again). Sowell, a black himself, rightly complains that "this arrogant treatment of millions of other human beings as pawns or guinea pigs would be impossible when the parents have individual choice."[14]

Some religious private schools in Canada, depending on the province, are already publicly funded — as are Catholic separate schools nationally — by a voucher-type tax-assignment form, which allows you to direct the educational portion of your municipal taxes to a particular separate school. But in this sense Canada's separate schools are really just another kind of public school because the money cannot be spent at *any* school of the parents' choice. To give parents choice, I would simply advocate an education tax-transfer system in Canada for all schools, regardless of type, provided they adhere to a simple curricular guideline to teach basic skills and knowledge. After that, they can teach what school parents want

them to teach. In the United States, Minnesota even permits qualified high-school students to attend college courses with vouchers,
and one district in California allows some public money to be
directed to home schooling — an increasingly popular option among
parents disgusted by godless, standardless, even violent, schools.
More and more students are carrying knives and guns to public
schools. But when was the last time anyone read a news story about
guns and violence in a private or religious school?

The reason even many left-liberals are promoting choice in
education today is that it permits students from poor
neighbourhoods to crash socio-economic barriers and attend better
schools — often ones in nice neighbourhoods right next to their own
depressed area. Choice gives all parents the right to escape a school
they find unsatisfactory and lets them search out — or create — a
better one. Such an alternative will not destroy public education. It
will, however, certainly destroy the worst effects of public education
by creating competition for funding between schools. Finally, in
keeping with a free society, the *producers* of education will be forced
to work for the *consumers* of it. In an untypically poor article,
columnist Jeffrey Simpson described public education as "the linchpin of a meritocratic system." (*Globe and Mail*, May 16, 1991). He
couldn't have been more wrong. The public school, as Chubb and
Moe eloquently point out, is the linchpin not of a meritocratic but
of an egalitarian system, which shuns merit in principle — educa-
tionally, morally, and administratively.

Internationally, there is also persuasive precedent for choice in
education. Britain has enjoyed the fruits of former Prime Minister
Margaret Thatcher's educational reforms, whereby local schools
since 1989 have had the right to opt out of the public system. In the
first year, 44 schools did so, and they found themselves with a 40
percent increase in applications and having 15-20 percent more
money to spend. In effect, Mrs. Thatcher designed a means for local
schools to by-pass the educational establishment entirely, though
not without howls from the unions and the school authorities.

The Dutch, however, have had true choice since 1917. Whereas
in 1880 more than 77 percent of the Netherlands' pupils attended
public schools, today, 70-79 percent (depending on grade level)
attend private schools via a voucher system. Article 23 of the Dutch
constitution ensures that any responsible group may start a school
and receive public funding without discrimination. Today, tiny
Holland has more than 6300 "competent education authorities," or
autonomous school units. Some critics have complained that Article

23, designed to prevent discrimination against religions, in fact allows white flight from schools that are filling with non-Dutch immigrants, amounting to a kind of government-financed segregation. My response is first to look at the United States, where black parents are far more worried about education than segregation. Second, most public schools there, and in Canada, are inherently segregated by virtue of their neighbourhoods. It is still far better for the parents to have choice and control; then, little prevents a minority child from changing schools, or minority parents from changing neighbourhood schools, or simply creating new and better schools. Chubb and Moe's best example is poor, drug-infested East Harlem, which, after installing a voucher-type choice system, in only a few years upgraded its students from last in most educational skills to middle ranking among all New York schools. New and innovative parent-controlled schools sprang like blossoms from the tired nooks and crannies of long-forgotten buildings.

Chicago has more than 50 such private schools that mainly serve those of low income, many of them costing students less than $1000 a year. According to *Wall Street Journal* reports on the Chicago experiment, and Chubb and Moe on the Harlem one, the students are far happier and far more successful.

The long and short of this is that it is possible for whole districts, whole regions, even whole nations to cast off the shackles of socialism in education. Let's do it.

## WHAT IS TO BE DONE?

1. Any nation wishing to liberate its young from the clutches of educational socialism must design a plan and do battle for the right to install choice in education. Such a plan will likely be a two-phase model: (1) to restore competition and parental/family control over education through a voucher, or tuition-credit, system; (2) to go one step further and free education entirely from State control of any kind. Phase 2 means not taking tax dollars in the first place. Instead, we should reduce family taxes according to the number of school-age children and allow any number of schools to sprout up in a free market for education — with all the innovation and competitive spark involved. Appropriate welfare (schoolfare?) will help the truly needy. The argument that the State must have some role in excess of the ordinary laws of the land loses force utterly when we pause to think that *for more than two centuries, Canadian and U.S.*

*private schools have never required a ministry of education* to create the most demanding curricula and the finest, most well-rounded students.

2. If we continue to be educational losers and resist the challenge to take back the schools, then this nation desperately requires some sort of standardized testing system to smoke out the incompetence and obfuscation of bad public school teachers and institutions. For the surrender of its hard-earned money, the people have a right to the control and surveillance of the schools. After all, very few citizens would freely surrender the tax money they now do to a private school that had a 33 percent dropout rate. So why, then, are they compelled to give it to public schools that perform this badly? In a 1985 Gallup Poll, fully 94 percent of the people supported the idea of standardized testing. Yet only 15 percent of the educational experts backed the idea, and they got their way. Thus do the elites of the top-down State control the people and their resources.

3. If, however, we find the courage to introduce a choice system, then no national tests are required. They may be created on a voluntary basis as a convenience and benchmark for those who wish to take them. But, as in any other market system, choice in education will automatically produce mostly good schools, just as a public system produces mostly bad ones. In a choice system, reputation and student success are almost immediately apparent. The proof is in the pudding: most private schools in Canada graduate 95 percent of their students and send a very large percentage to universities of their choice. Getting through the school itself is all the test that's needed.

4. Whether in public or private schools, Canadians must devise a means to prevent ideologically minded teachers, however well intentioned, from imposing their views on students, especially when it comes to the teaching of collectivist economic or environmentalist ideas, secular religious humanist values, or so-called sex-education. The instruments needed to prevent this are:

   a. A Canadian "pupil rights" law, equivalent to the American Hatch Amendment, that spells out the limits of teacher invasion of personal, family, and student psychological life.
   b. A "parental consent" or "opting-in" provision requiring any teacher who wishes to teach any course that counsels stu-

dents psychologically, or requires the student to give private personal or family information, to have signed parental permission from all students attending the class.

c. When it comes to an explosive subject area such as sex-ed, family authority must be honoured by the schools. The way to arrange this for any sensitive subject area is for the schools to offer the courses not to the children, but to the parents, who may in fact want help in communicating such subjects to their offspring.

5. Canada needs a minimum competence movement for public schools at the pre- and post-secondary levels similar to that in the United States, requiring, as the U.S. body does, "that no student be given a high-school diploma without first passing a test showing that he could read everyday English and do simple arithmetic."[15] Such a requirement has already had an enormously salutary effect on U.S. education.

6. Canada needs two new documents, one to control the educational product, another to control the behaviour of the students.

   The first would be a public education contract[16] to spell out what students are going to get for their money at a public school. For example: the right to privacy; to be taught to read and write English by a reasonable age; to be free of any teaching critical of private religious beliefs, or that attempts to undermine those beliefs; to be free of situational value instruction and psychological ethics games; to receive instruction in basic skills and knowledge.

   The second would be a "Charter of Student Responsibilities," which the student ought to sign each school year, spelling out agreement to standards of courtesy, of respect for teachers and for property, and of commitment to work hard, to not use foul language on campus, and to not steal, cheat, use drugs, smoke on campus, and so on.

7. Because the best way to learn is to teach, Canada should invent a simple tutorial system in which all older students must spend a portion of their day or week teaching younger students something. There is a huge difference between recognizing information and producing it. Such a student tutorial program would enliven students, likely reduce costs, and improve understanding for all.

8. Public schools must get rid of tenure. Principals must have the

unfettered right to hire and fire teachers, *and parents the right to hire and fire principals*.

9. Here are some thoughts on dropouts: In 1988, West Virginia became the first jurisdiction in North America to revoke or deny a driving licence to youngsters who do not show satisfactory progress toward high-school graduation (there are exceptions for hardship cases, and the law has no effect after a student reaches 18). Wisconsin followed suit. This is called a "no-pass-no-drive" law, and it has already cut truancy and dropout rates remarkably. Attendance rates are now above 98 percent in some districts, and 25 percent of those dropouts who lost their licences are back in school. As of 1990, eight other states are considering no-pass-no-drive legislation. At any rate, academically we have tried the worst, and failed. Let's now try the best. Secondary schools need distinct programs, with clear standards. Those students not proceeding to university levels could do a split study/work program for their last two years, and gain income and experience. At the least, a clear sequence of knowledge and skills, combined with clear exit standards, must be required of all public schools.

10. All public schools should require mandatory physical education for one hour each day, of sufficient intensity to create a training and health-protection effect for the nation's youth. Parents want it badly. They are already putting up sufficient funds for it, if you consider that most private day schools (and all the best ones) costing the same money require mandatory phys-ed of their students and teachers as a matter of their ideals.

11. Public schools should require basic inexpensive uniforms, or at the least a simple dress code. Such uniforms should be different for each school, to generate school pride. If the choice system ever becomes a reality, schools will spontaneously create uniforms in order to appeal to parents. As things stand, one of the most depressing sights possible is a gaggle of overweight public school teenagers walking down the street at recess, smoking or stuffing dripping pizza in their mouths from the local plaza, and sporting shredded blue-jeans full of holes, or revealing short-shorts, dirty fingernails, greasy hair, the works. That's a kind of uniform, too. The best indicator of future behaviour is past behaviour.

# 11

# The Feminist Mistake: Women Against the Family

*Feminist theory . . . Is passionate and salvationist in a similar way to Marxism, new religious movements, and occult enthusiasms: all of them know in advance not only the conclusions they will arrive at but the appropriate attitude toward those conclusions. Academically, it is mostly unsophisticated. A little light generalizing work is followed by polysyllabic decoration and some spray-on indignation.*

KENNETH MINOGUE, *TIMES LITERARY SUPPLEMENT*, JUNE 7, 1991

*The simple fact is that every woman must be willing to be identified as a lesbian to be fully feminist.*

THE U.S. NATIONAL ORGANIZATION FOR WOMEN *TIMES*,
JANUARY 1988

*The end of the institution of marriage is a necessary condition for the liberation of women. Therefore it is important for us to encourage women to leave their husbands . . .*

FROM THE "DECLARATION OF FEMINISM," NOVEMBER 1971

I would hate to be a woman.
My wife says she would hate to be a man.
I think this has something to do with why we have a good

marriage. I have asked my lawyer whether the local Gender Committee will charge me with "sexism" for writing this. Ah me . . .

Every age seems to have its peculiar intellectual cancers, and this chapter is meant to serve as a kind of anticarcinogen. Like so many, I find myself increasingly surrounded by strident, petty, whining feminist arguments that have by now nibbled their way into every organ of our society. If that were the limit of it, most of us would simply get on with our lives and ignore these people. But matters are far worse than the public seems aware. For in order to achieve their objectives, modern radical feminists are increasingly relying on political, economic, and legal stratagems that in any other age would rightly, and without delay, have been labelled extremist, even totalitarian.

When studied carefully, it becomes transparently obvious that their arguments, taken as a whole, amount to a virulent, cultish, man-hating, and family-hating program that threatens the fundamental health of our society, which is what it is intended to do. So we must be far more wary, because radical feminism, as we shall see, is a form of collectivism that appeals to what is lowest in all men and women, and therefore is guaranteed an endless supply of believers. The witty and trenchant critic Kenneth Minogue wrote that "the first rule in reading feminist literature is never to identify feminism with women."[1] For women as a whole in North America have *never* supported the aims of radical feminism. In a 1988 U.S. poll, a mere 18 percent of American young women described themselves as feminists, and in Canada's last election, according to Gallup (December 3, 1988), only 18 percent of women voted for Canada's socialist New Democratic Party, the agenda of which is indistinguishable from that of radical feminists.[2] Far, far more women from both nations support traditional male, female, and family roles, yet our craven three-level governments spend about $60 million annually (about $1 billion over the past decade and a half) supporting women's interest groups, many of them with outright antifamily postures.[3] This support will surely amaze future historians, attempting to explain exactly how in a democracy such small unelected minorities can control the majority, and thus how the Canadian people lost their democratic soul.

Radical feminist views are by now so pervasive and illogical, however, and the media so craven and uncritical in promoting them, that what follows must necessarily take the form of a piecemeal unravelling of their basic arguments and inherent contradictions, the better to see the pattern. Very few ordinary women who call

THE FEMINIST MISTAKE   297

themselves feminists perceive that what they may support (or support in part) is likely a segment of an interlocking structure of ideas — a cultlike belief system — the explicit intent of which is to destroy everything they hold dear. And let us be clear. Many younger women who say they accept feminism, while rejecting its radicalism, lesbianism, and antifamily ideology, are serving as an unconscious vanguard for the very movement most eager to demolish their fondest dreams. Their position is equivalent to saying that they accept Marxism but reject its ban on private property rights, free enterprise, and democratic elections; or they accept a woman's right to abortion but not killing human life.

# FAMILISM VS. RADICAL FEMINISM

## Traditional Familism

This may come as a surprise to many, but so-called feminists have not always been antifamily. In its traditional, or Judeo-Christian, form of the past century, so-called "social" or "domestic" or "maternal" feminism (scorned as a sell-out by modern radical feminists) was aggressively pro-family.[4] It was a feminism promoting femininity, motherhood, and family. It was, in short, not feminism, as we think of it today, but *familism*. The majority of activist women, it appears, even until the 1960s, generally strove to redress the political, economic, and moral imbalances of a free society in which women and children — the whole family unit — needed special considerations but did not often get them. They were extremely successful. So much so that, as many have argued, today's activists, ironically, are busily undoing the finest social achievement of the 19th century: to help women and children get off the streets, out of the factories, and into the homes of the nation, from whence children could be nurtured, fed, schooled, and sheltered from the vagaries of a market order only too willing to recruit them and their mothers.*

The inescapable conclusion to which we are led by the facts is

---

* Contrary to popular belief, it was not so much men who resisted the idea of giving women the vote. A recent study by Susan E. Marshall on "antisuffrage" politics of the 1900s finds that women constituted "the overwhelming majority of the counter-movement's leaders and members." They were women devoted to their families, who feared that the commercial market would lure young single women first into commercial life, then into political life, thus undermining the family as the basis of society.[5]

that this former feminism insisted that society be structured to protect children inside the family. The feminism we have today is, in contrast, attempting to structure society to protect women outside the family (the children can fend for themselves in daycare centres or as latchkey children in empty houses). The result is that the children have no advocate. That is why it is fair to say modern feminists are the new barbarians. In seeking equivalence instead of complementarity with males, they have adopted the traditional male attitude toward children.

The early familism fought this barbarism aggressively. It was grounded in religious and moral values that stressed the importance of character. And how could character be formed if mother, father, and children all worked outside the home? The private home thus came to be considered a kind of temple for the enjoyment of privacy and the inculcation of virtue, and the job of the family was to develop the civilized men and women of tomorrow. Surely, the State could not carry out this role, nor should it, for the State would only shape the children in its own image. So because men were mostly sweating it out in factories or fields, women took control of the moral tenor of the families, if not of the entire nation. As activists, they took a prodigious stab at the latter through the formation of temperance unions, through intervention in the homes of the poor and immigrant population (to "save" the children from ignorance and poverty), and, extensively, through their influence on the curriculum and development of the public schools.

But most important of all, unlike their modern counterparts, these earlier feminists "celebrated the differences between men and women. Women, they said, were intended by nature as nurturers, and the task of motherhood should be protected by the state."[6] In marriage, they saw the male-female relationship as one of indelible complementarity. They did not clamour for what they considered the silly and indeed damaging notion of "equal rights" — a concept roundly rejected by many European women then and now, and more recently by American women who rejected the Equal Rights Amendment (ERA) in 1979, after a decade of aggressive, tax-funded lobbying by U.S. feminists. On the contrary, they argued that because women were different and special by nature, and thus had special duties, special laws, protections, and privileges were needed. For example: Because a single factory wage was insufficient to support a wife and children, there was, they argued, a pressing need for a "family wage" — perhaps the single most important activist achievement of the time. They saw to it that laws were passed, and social conventions accepted, to protect and promote the family by raising the pay of married men with children and discouraging the employment of single women, who were seen to be taking scarce jobs from present or future working husbands and fathers. (Even today, about 95 percent of all men and women marry in their lifetimes and have families.[7]) It did not mean then and does not mean now that a woman who chose to do so couldn't go forth into the market and work. But it does mean that in a society that privileges the natural family, she might receive a lesser wage than a married man with children, and would have to cope with myriad social pressures pushing her toward a home-based life — just as the male has always had to cope with myriad pressures pushing him to marry and support a wife and children.

There was a pro-family logic to everything these earlier feminists advocated, most of it designed to keep at bay the autonomist philosophy we know today as the mix of secularism and liberalism. Women then appreciated that there is a difference between the economic order and the moral order, and that without adequate laws the first may well erode the second. We shall see that there is a crucial difference in nature between the moral order they were trying to protect and the one modern feminists value today. Then, for all men and women, the moral order rested on the family unit; today, it rests on the seemingly attractive but ultimately dangerous notion of the autonomous individual. We need to understand how radical feminism became the major driving force toward the establishment of such autonomous individualism, and, as such, the maidservant to the antifamily welfare State.

## Radical Feminism

Traditional familism lost. Badly. For two millennia, antifamily ideas, from Plato forward, had been always present but for two simple reasons were no ultimate threat to society. First there was the powerful force of humanity's spontaneous affection for the natural family (everyone could see that while nations rose and fell, the family remained). Secondly, all forms of collectivism, including feminism, require oodles of money to enforce their coercive measures; such funds were simply not available. But things had changed radically by the mid-20th century. Suddenly, the radical form of feminism found a perfect vehicle and companion to spread its influence, in the form of the modern welfare State. It would join hands with craven politicians eager for votes and more big government. The earlier forms of pro-family feminism had wanted only decent pro-family laws; otherwise, the State ought to keep its distance. But with the introduction of serious income taxation (supposedly a temporary measure to fund World War I) and the postwar, Depression appeal of the New Deal in the United States, and a similar taxation and statist thrust in Canada, vast funding became available to all sorts of special interest groups. By mid-century, the womb-to-tomb State, with its new hordes of therapists, administrators, commissions, and counsellors, was only too eager to latch on to yet another excuse to grow. Anything will do. Modern feminism was a radical cause that shared many of the aims of the welfare State itself.

So it is that the defining characteristic of this movement over the latter half of our century is its virulently socialist and antifamily nature. It has aggressively advanced the tendency of the State to atomize the family in the name of the autonomous individual (in whom all rights are said to inhere) as well as in the name of a kind of impossibly pure "equality" that has mostly to do with the modern totalitarian effort to *make* us all the same in every imaginable material way. All over the Western world this form of liberalism has been blended with vulgarized Marxist economics that have lent it a frantic and bitter tone. That is to say, it sees systemic political, economic, and social/sexual exploitation of women everywhere it looks. As one apoplectic feminist put it: "We are damaged — we women, we oppressed, we disinherited . . . We are damaged and we have the right to hate and have contempt and to kill and to scream."[8] Well, do we really think it is reasonable to describe North American women this way — women who arguably constitute the best-fed, best-educated, richest, most free population of human females the world has ever known? Unlikely. But that's beside the point, for in the radical view oppression is everywhere by definition, and nowhere is there love. "Love," declared 1960s radical Abigail Rockefeller, in shopworn Marxist terms, is "debilitating and counter-revolutionary."[9]

To such as Rockefeller, the family and private property — the two cornerstones of the free society — are said to be instruments of exploitive capitalism. They are dominated by the patriarchal father or husband. It was Gloria Steinem who declared: "Overthrowing capitalism is too small for us. We must overthrow the whole #@*! patriarch!" The male is said to be the prime social agent of this exploitation, from which all women are urged to free themselves; hence, the Holy Grail of lesbianism at the centre of radical feminism. At a recent national feminist conference in Edmonton, participant Jeri Wine declared that "the weight of the feminist movement has been carried on the backs of lesbians." Some imagery. A number of feminist organizations represented there were described as 75 to 90 percent lesbian (*Alberta Report*, November 25, 1991). Even the matriarch of feminism, Betty Friedan, worries about the "lavender menace" of lesbianism, manifest by such as the married president of the U.S. National Organization of Women (NOW), Patricia Ireland, who has a "female companion" and aggressively promotes "lesbian rights" (Toronto *Star*, December 26, 1991). We shall see that lesbianism is but the logical end-result of feminist autonomism, which, pushed further, leads to the glorification of masturbation as self-assertion and freedom from males, to self-insemination, and to single parenthood as the crowning liberty.

Whereas traditional feminism strove to unite the family, the radical form, labouring under the Victim Illusion, strives to reconstitute the entire fabric of our free society in a collectivist form — and to finance this revolution with capitalist tax dollars. We shall see that the feminist utopia is in fact being financed by the nation's productive families. Feminism attempts to abolish the natural family and then, by redistributing wealth, to provide all women with the opportunity for an autonomous (but often newly dependent) relationship to the State (via subsidized daycare, government jobs, subsidies). Thus will women be "free" of the male world.

Feminists have worked hard to further their agenda; many in positions of power and influence in Canada are outright Marxists (or "former" ones), such as Judy Rebick, president of the National Action Committee on the Status of Women (NAC), a quasi-governmental agency (*Globe and Mail*, July 4, 1990), and Judy Darcy, the "once radically left wing" new head of CUPE, Canada's 406,000-member Union of Public Employees (*Globe and Mail*, August 17, 1991). Although NAC claims to represent three million Canadian women, its ex-president apparently said it has a mailing list of only 2600 (*Alberta Report*, October 14, 1991). NAC lobbies aggressively for abortion on demand, legalized prostitution, lesbian rights, universal tax-funded daycare, and the nationalization of banks and industry, and it wants to abolish the common-law right to private property and withdraw from NATO and NORAD. Hardly the Canadian woman's agenda. It's the socialist NDP agenda. We must surely ask ourselves, if they really do represent three million women, why don't they simply request five dollars from each, for a total of $15 million annually, and get their snoots out of the government trough? Instead, the education system, the media, the unions, and most government institutions in Canada are heavily staffed with these folks. The number of radicals still in action is astounding when you stop to consider that socialism has just recently made a name for itself as the most pernicious socio-economic philosophy ever to have infected the globe. Perhaps that's why so many are now switching from economic feminism to so-called "gender feminism." Now that democratic capitalism has clearly won on the economic front they have fashioned a new gender-based conspiracy theory which, because all human and social life is sexual, is never going to disappear.

As we shall see, however, the real cause for concern is that the practical consequences of all the forms of radical feminism tried in history, ever since Roman times, are virulently antichild. Carcopino informs us that the "feminists" of third-century Rome held the motto, "live your own life"; that the serial marriages of the time became, as the Roman poet Martial described them, a form of "legalized adultery"; that there was "an epidemic" of no-fault divorces; and that many Roman marriages of the time were childless.[10] So, nothing is new.

It is bad enough that children are a low priority for men. It is far, far worse for society when they also become a low priority for women. That's why I said radical feminists are the new barbarians of modern society. The men have always been barbarians, for they vigorously pursue power and personal, largely material, goals, often to the detriment of children. But why, as Chesterton asks, would women fall for the mixed-up idea they are free when they serve their employers, but slaves when they help their husbands? That is the question. The balance of this chapter will examine in detail some of radical feminism's interlocking, and embarrassingly contradictory, assumptions, which form a kind of architecture of ideology. From false foundations, the whole structure quickly tumbles.

**Step One: They Confuse the Culture with the Law**
One of the favourite tricks of feminist debaters is to argue as if the force of culture and the power of law are the same. They are not, and societies that uncritically accept this confusion are on the high road to ruin.

Clearly, all societies maintain themselves through two basic kinds of authority. The first constitutes what sociologists call the "informal social controls," meaning the standards, habits, directives, or "expectations" of society (or "the culture," simply put); the second constitutes the actual laws themselves, which reflect, usually with a bit of a lag, most of the moral values of the culture. There are, in every society, thousands more standards and expectations — the myriad do's and don'ts of micro-social behaviour — than there are laws. We are awash in them; there is no escape from informal authority. But the secret of a free civilization is to keep such authority informal and never to allow it to be taken over, or controlled, by the State and its pressure groups. The more informal the authority, the freer we are, because although such authority may persuade us mightily, it can never actually coerce us.

Thus, when we say a minister or teacher or coach or parent speaks with authority, we mean that we are so impressed by, or perhaps fearful of, his presence or his thinking that *we voluntarily assent* to his direction. The bulk of society's work of controlling the people is of this sort. It is quite different from the laws. For when we say a policeman has authority over us, we mean that regardless of whether we assent, he can legally coerce us by using the power of the State. No culture can do that. It can only speak its fervent wishes, and we obey or we do not, each of us, in our long night of the soul, weighing the personal cost or benefit. Should I apologize, or not? Do I have sex now, or not? Should I marry, or not? Shall I defy my teacher, or not? Shall I protest, or not? Shall I accept current expectations, or invent a wholly different approach? In short, the culture sets the baseline, good or bad, of all social expectations.

Unfortunately, many people, among them most sociologists, feminists, and behaviourists, get comfort from promoting the belief that these expectations are like laws, with inherent powers that we are forced to obey. And it is true that most people, perhaps frightened to go their own way, respond accordingly. But the fact is that it's really up to us, from young adulthood on, to determine whether or not we abide by the "expectations" of society, and to decide on the degree and the style of our response. We play out our social hand for our entire lives, in the context of these informal constraints, and it is foolish to believe, as did Rousseau, that any society can get by for long without them. For the positive instruments of any culture are its high ideals, its values, and its various rewards; and the negative instruments are guilt, embarrassment, and shame. These things constitute the carrots and sticks of the culture, designed to keep us all moving in a certain direction. People who totally ignore all expectations are likely criminals and other "moral imbeciles." But those who live slavishly by petty behavioural or career expectations, as if they had no choice, are likely docile. It is the later discovery of their own past fear and docility that makes them angry and sends them in search of a present scapegoat. They are not honest enough to admit they were asleep at the creativity and personal power switch for much of their lives, and so a perpetrator must be found. Blaming a real or hypothetical daddy, or the "system" he created, is common.

If asked why they had no choice, such people will argue that they were "socialized" (for which their remedy is to change the old expectations into new ones through control of the legal or educational process). So, for example, if society is of the opinion that women should be nurses and not doctors — although there is no law against women entering either field — a woman may argue as if the expectation were a law, and tell you that is why she is not a doctor. I am not saying these powerful expectations do not exist. After all, many brave men and women throughout history have struggled against all sorts of social expectations for their dreams and achievements. But in a free country we have no right to confuse social expectations with the law and bleat that we were powerless to resist.

Everyone, in other words, must cope individually with the informal rules of the game, and only a tyrannous society would try, as we are now doing, to control individual or group outcomes from the top down. That's why those who argue for political freedom stipulate that the fairest law for a decent nation is a set of "rules of just conduct, equal for all." Social expectations within those rules are up to society, not up to the law. People will behave differently within such a free framework according to how tightly or loosely they cling to such expectations. But it is not the duty of the laws to ensure individuals all behave the same, or to direct public funds to push them in any particular direction. Female critics say that the rules of just conduct are biased against them. Perhaps. Yet surely the rules of any society must reflect that society's major moral assumptions. The evil begins not when societies reflect or guide, discourage or deter, but when they force. Prior to the initiation of laws to alter social outcomes forcefully, you have a society. After it, you have a police State.

But alas, we have succumbed. As an ideological necessity to support their case, feminists now argue that women are "victims" of social expectations, and therefore informal and formal authority must be merged. Anything less than the victim/male/patriarchy/scapegoat message would mean women can blame only themselves for slavish adherence to expectations. In our present society, a firm indicator of their public success is the presence on every campus of thought-control police in the form of human rights tribunals, gender committees, and "political correctness" officers, whose work it is to control the acceptability of social expectations while creating new ones via educational courses. As University of Toronto political science professor Jean Edward Smith wrote of these "dangerous new puritans," their aim, in a form of new McCarthyism, is "to intimidate and force the suppression of ideas with which they disagree"; and further, he warns, "a community that would encourage such action has mortgaged its future and taken a step in the ultimate direction of political totalitarianism" (*Globe and Mail*, October 21, 1991).

## Step Two: They Blame the Outside World for What Ails Them

As Professor Michael Levin points out in *Feminism and Freedom*, all forms of modern feminism rest upon a few simplistic and erroneous notions. The first, is that apart from basic anatomical differences, all men and women are the same (the Equality Illusion at work here); the second, that men unfairly occupy positions of dominance because of stereotypical socialization (the Victim Illusion: boys and girls are raised differently, owing to an exploitive patriarchal society); third, that traditional sex and family roles must be abandoned (the Individualism Illusion: life is personal and autonomous, not social); and finally, that a complete transformation of society is required to bring the egalitarian utopia into existence (the Rationalism Illusion: the idea that sufficiently prolonged social engineering will end human ignorance and will perfect faulty institutions).[11]

What the above program amounts to is a declaration of faith in the importance of environmental socialization (nurture) and a rejection of the importance or even the existence of differential biology (nature). Yet there is a overwhelming evidence from virtually every field of study that biology is destiny, and that all civilizations, including our own until now, have structured social life accordingly; and it is an accepted fact that we are manifestly a biological species through and through, and that the lives of all biological mammals are species- and gender-specific. Still, there is outraged denial of this reality. In *The Dialectic of Sex*, pseudo-Marxist Shulamith Firestone urges all women to free themselves from "the tyranny of biology," declaring that "pregnancy is barbaric."

What we are offered instead is absolutist nurture theory based on unsubstantiatable ideological assertions. The socialist utopia, to be created from reform of the present environment, is to replace nature, or biology. In short, because biology gets in the way of utopian thinking, the solution is to get rid of biology by suppressing the evidence. Feminists cannot afford to admit into their belief system one smidgeon of evidence that men and women are naturally different, else their entire argument fails. Even worse for them: If nature plays a significant role, then no amount of social engineering can radically alter society for long. Feminists are compelled to accept illogical arguments against nature as a life force. That's why feminism is like a cult.

But the radical feminists get hung out to dry on a few points of logic. Just for fun, let us accept their argument that all human beings are socialized to behave the way they do. If that is so, then surely nothing can be altered, because all behaviour is shaped by forces outside our control. Males cannot help being dominant, because they are socialized to be dominant, and females cannot help being dominated. No one can help anything. Neither can we change anything, because we are all socialized to accept everything. Ah, some say, then let's change the patterns of socialization! And I reply: Do you believe you are free to change, but others are trapped by socialization? If they answer yes, they are trapped by a bad, and elitist, argument. If they answer no, then there is no argument. Either way, they are forced to admit that our lives are a free expression of our different, if difficult, natural choices, which are based on individual inclinations and circumstances. In short, we are free to accept or reject social expectations — even to try to engineer them for others. But if we are free, then everyone is free.

Once the socialization argument is accepted, then life becomes hopeless because no matter what the world is, we are all socialized by it. We cannot escape. Even feminism is just some mysterious social force that in the future will be altered by some other force. If we accept the freedom argument, however — most of the world does, and always has accepted it — then feminists have no ethical ground to stand upon, because individuals are simply expressing their personal wishes.

So, what right do social engineers have to interfere? None, of course. That is why they resort to coercion and State control. The late Simone de Beauvoir has even argued, as many of her followers argue, that even if women are in fact free, they *should not be allowed to choose* traditional social roles.[12]

Enter feminist/socialist coercion, the iron fist in a velvet glove. Subtle intimations of these social engineers appear daily in our newspapers. I have actually seen a report of a "study" by two Ontario (male) professors arguing that women suffer more from "stress" and depression than men because women are more caring by nature, and thus they carry a "cost of caring" burden (Toronto *Star*, April 8, 1990). Boy, what a loser country we are becoming! The remedy the "researchers" propose for this horrible social problem is not to suggest that women may wish to give less weight to certain matters than they do, or attempt a bit of soul-calming meditation. No way. The study actually recommends "that programs be designed *to make men more like women*" [emphasis added]. I say let's just be happy such demagogues are confined to universities, else they'd be at our front doors with warrants to examine our domestic "gender equivalence."

There's a nasty odour of arrogant elitism in such thinking; well-off middle-class educated folks assuming the rest of the world is dumb. But, in fact, they are merely behaving like the starry-eyed adherents of any cult, or ideology. An unexamined conspiracy theory broad enough to encompass and explain all their woes and apathy acts upon them like a sudden spiritual manifestation. It is not that they believe they have found God. Rather, they think they have at last found the devil.

**Step Three: When Caught — They Change the Argument**
Whenever the logical inconsistencies in their program are pointed out, feminists respond by shifting to new ground. It takes a while, but once they realize the trap of their own logic — that the theory of socialization means all humans must be caught in an eternal immobility of action — they quickly shift ground and begin to argue against themselves by insisting that women as a gender have a special way of seeing the world, a special "female sensibility," a higher nature. Their critics call this approach "female chauvinism," for now they unwittingly support the opposite argument. By saying that the sexes have different natural traits, psychological qualities, aesthetic senses, and so on, they inherently accept the biology-is-destiny argument of their opponents, with a bit of holier-than-thou superiority thrown in. Which gets back to freedom. If by nature women are different from men, then women ought to be left alone, free to order their lives accordingly. Radicals see no inconsistency in burning both ends of the logical candle in this way. An honest and perceptive feminist writer like Germaine Greer, however, had the courage to turn her back on her earlier inflammatory work, *The Female Eunuch*. In her later book, *Sex and Destiny*, she argued eloquently, to the bleating objections of feminists the world over

who accused her of betrayal, for women's traditional role as child-bearer and mother. Betty Friedan, author of the equally inflammatory antifamily hate tract, *The Feminine Mystique*, also came a bit closer to sanity in her recanting book, *The Second Stage*, now warning women not to be trapped by a "feminist mystique" that could prevent them from experiencing the "joys of a family."[13] Now there is talk of a "third wave" of feminism. By the time the third wave washes over the second stage, we will all be eunuchs.

But mainstream unrepentant radical feminists continue to wiggle inside their own logical confusion, tightening the chains by arguing that inconsistent logic is a special female way of seeing the world; therefore, what is needed are "new paradigms" of thinking, enabling women to be logical and illogical at the same time.[14] This argument merely promotes a widespread negative stereotype of women. Some feminist literary critics actually posit "an aesthetic of repetition and illogic" as typically female. Feminist Elizabeth A. Meese declares outright: "If what I say is true, what I say is not true."[15] Well, they've painted themselves into a corner, for as writer Peter Shaw wryly observers, for such feminists, "the very use of logic . . . can qualify as a betrayal" of feminism. In other words, if what you say doesn't make sense, you qualify as a feminist.

### Step Four: They Try to Argue for Both Kinds of Rights

Thus do the contradictions in feminist reasoning produce a contradiction in their demands for conflicting types of "rights." Should feminists campaign for "special" rights because they are unlike men and ought to be treated differently? Or, because they are exactly the same as men, should they campaign for "equal" rights (and "affirmative action" until all humans are measurably equal)? It would appear they argue for both whenever it suits their purposes. This is a real dilemma for feminists, simply because if they use the equal rights argument, they will eventually end up having to support a free society. Here's how they become trapped.

The argument says that at some point in the idyllic past, all men and women interacted equally and collectively. So what was it that ruined this utopian past and subjected women to men? Supposedly, capitalism, private property, and patriarchy. (The feminists don't explain how the change happened, or how women could be so easily duped.) Regardless, modern affirmative-action-type social programs, even though they are an affront to the principles of a free society, are necessary to "correct" the political, economic, and social balance.

If you are an insecure, or angry, or conspiracy-oriented female, this is a comfortable viewpoint. However, the hitch is that after their programs of reverse discrimination have corrected the perceived imbalances in social life (as decided by tax-funded women's directorates), and all the little bureaucrats are satisfied they have adequately forced everyone to do the same things equally, then the game is over. Women who argue for sameness and equality must then drop the patronizing affirmative action, compete on equal terms with men for everything, and fulfil the same obligations, such as assuming active battle duty or entering competitions for "male" jobs without "gender norming." To be consistent and honest at that point, feminists will not be able to argue for forced equality of outcomes, but for a free society based on equal laws.

If they use the special rights argument, however, which is really the form of ongoing, built-in compensatory action (based on biology) in which all societies have historically engaged, then they defeat their own argument that biology makes no difference. Soon, society will see these blatant contradictions as the self-serving tactics they are, and will say, Enough! No one, male or female, should have it both ways.

The signs of a new sanity have been here for some time, although it will take a long while to dislodge the multitudes of entrenched, tax-funded radicals. As early as 1981, Betty Friedan announced that "the so-called radical feminists developed a lot of rhetoric against the family . . . but a lot of it was twisted, and began to be repudiation, throwing the baby out with the bathwater" (*Christian Science Monitor*, December 10, 1981). Right on her heels, Canada's Catherine Bolger called for "a renewed appreciation of the value of the differences between the sexes" (*Daily Telegraph*, December 11, 1981) — and women and women's groups around the world have since sprung up to defend their freedom, to defend women's traditional roles, and to express their annoyance at being pigeonholed by the radical feminist/Marxist view that men and women are the same, or that women are exploited weaklings. In a burst of anger that upset every politically correct journalist in Canada, Nathalie Provost, a survivor of the Montreal Lepine massacre that was roundly used by the pro-feminist press to vilify all living men, said, "I don't feel I'm a feminist. I feel like a guy does in his life. Period. Bottom line. All the doors are open before me. And, if somebody tries to close them, well, goddamn it, I'll open them" (Toronto *Star*, December 6, 1991).

# WHY THE SAMENESS ARGUMENT FAILS

## The Androgyny Hoax, Hormones, and the Inevitability of Patriarchy

*As of 1980, 72 per cent of mental health professionals . . . described a 'healthy, mature, socially competent' adult as androgynous.*
ALLAN CARLSON, "THE ANDROGYNY HOAX," IN *FAMILY QUESTIONS*[16]

A major instrument in the feminist effort to equalize sex roles in society, still used by those who insist on the sameness argument, is the assault on the whole idea of gender itself. This follows from feminist ideology. If all sex-role behaviour is just a result of social conditioning and not of biology, then in the absence of such (oppressive) roles authentic human beings would be naturally androgynous (an equal mixture of male and female). Male, and female, they say, are a myth. At the extreme, feminists even argue that God is both male and female ("Holy Wisdom" is the female persona of God. See Chapter Seventeen for details on feminist religion). And humans, they contend, can attain "spiritual adrogyny." Such ideas have ancient origins in mystical, pre-Christian (called "Gnostic") forms of thought, in which at the extreme the human spirit is said to be one with the universe, and *all* distinctions whatsoever are held to be a falsification of the unitary spirit. This sort of spiritual egalitarianism is a retreat not merely from biology, but from all social and material reality.

In his detailed and sobering work, Allan Carlson cites a bevy of serious scientists, some of them honest feminists, who show that the whole androgyny movement is ideologically motivated, has no basis in fact, and has "elevated corrupted science to the level of public truth."[17]

Beginning in the 1960s, in reaction to the "natural complement" theory of gender most people still hold (that males and females are both incomplete, and thus are a natural complement for each other), the radical feminists began to argue that women would never attain sex-role equality unless a different model of gender was created. Shulamith Firestone (who, as Carlson points out, did humanity a service by pushing feminist logic to its perverse conclusions) argued that "mom" must be eliminated, and replaced by a "socialist feminism"; that sex roles had to be eliminated, and replaced with "polymorphous perverse" sexuality (meaning anything goes); that the incest taboo had to be eliminated; and that parents should freely have sex with ready children. Bottle-feeding "technology" and daycare, she said, would end the need for natural mothering. This, she called "revolutionary feminism." Her peer, Anne Ferguson of the University of Massachusetts, argued that "androgynes," the "superpersons" of the new society (the feminist utopia), would be freed from the need for children (here's that antichild theme again, masquerading as a concern for overpopulation), by experiencing pure "bisexual love."[18] Ferguson despises natural biological parenting because it produces "a debilitating heterosexual identity" in children. Her formula to bring about the socialist society organized on feminist principles is simply to equalize the social, economic, and political power *outside* the home (with affirmative action programs). All else would follow.

Edward Tiryakian, of Duke University (a hotbed of feminist psycho-babble), insists that androgyny is a "truly revolutionary" principle for overturning both the sexual division of labour and "the present prevalent form of the nuclear family which is the source of the reproduction of heterosexuality." He advocates both revolutionary change through the perfection of a baby-bottle technology and a U.S Supreme court ruling to declare it unconstitutional to teach or reinforce heterosexuality in the schools. Ruth Bleier, another fanatical feminist academic, argues that the nuclear family must be "crushed." The bitterly hostile Andrea Dworkin argues for homosexuality and even bestiality — what she calls "other-animal relationships" — and the freeing of children to enjoy their "rights" to "live out their erotic impulses." That's what Rousseau wanted, and what de Sade did. She wants a "new kind of human being, and a new kind of human community."[19] At a recent Canadian feminist conference she actually advocated that battered women "should feel free to murder their husbands" (*Alberta Report*, May 27, 1991). However, she does not advocate that battered males murder their wives, or children their mothers.

In acceptance of this model for the new and healthier human being, Alexandra Kaplan actually argued that social pathology should be defined as "overly masculine" men and "overly feminine" women. This argument, too, follows the peculiar egalitarian illogic of radical feminism, and it illustrates their attempt to alter the foundational concepts and language of society. Another writer, Christabelle Sethna of the Ontario Institute for Studies in Education, has argued that dead animals represent patriarchal society and war, whereas live animals represent women; therefore, "meat eating is misogyny" (woman-hating), and dairying is a rampant exploitation of the female sex.[20] Without our tax dollars, such people would be reading this drivel to the walls in some asylum; but with our dollars they have a tax-funded audience. The State pays for their jobs, subsidizes their books, and funds their travel and their conventions. More's the pity. Angry, narrow-minded feminists have been extremely influential, despite the blatantly ideological, political nature of their program and their shoddy science — not to mention their perverse values. American researcher Paul C. Vitz of New York University has discovered, after intensive scrutiny of more than one hundred social-studies and history textbooks, that "by far the most noticeable position in the readers [textbooks], was a feminist one." Not a single story or theme celebrated marriage or motherhood as a positive experience. Sex-role reversals and the mockery of masculine men were common."[21] As we saw in the preceding chapters, Canadian public schools are furiously promoting the androgyny myth, or at least the notion that human sexuality is a diverse phenomenon and normal heterosexual relations, marriages, and families are no better or worse than any other kind.

This is outright tax-funded brainwashing of society through its children. But Carlson cites a host of serious social scientists who show that the whole androgyny notion is a political hoax and has no basis in fact. "Androgynous" people are in fact far more dysfunctional, more neurotic, lower in self-esteem, and more confused than normal people. There is nothing "super" about them. Researchers have shown conclusively that normal sex-typed parents make by far the best parents (androgynous parents "performed dismally"); that masculinity in males is correlated most highly with their mental health; that male psychopaths have low masculinity scores; and so on. Researcher Diana Baumrind concluded that traditional sex-typing was healthy for society and children, and that androgyny, as a positive concept, is a complete and utter failure.[22] Carlson concludes that in the United States "a small band of ideologues . . . has succeeded in imposing a fraudulent, dangerous ideology, masquerading as science, on broad elements of our public life." The same has occurred in Canada. Margrit Eichler, our most influential feminist sociologist, argues that it "is time to counter the attempts of the [pro-family] movement for the restoration of the patriarchal family . . . This requires that the feminist movement . . . [make] clear distinctions between *what types of families are seen as unacceptable*, and which ones are seen as not only acceptable but indeed deserving of social support."[23] But what are all these tax-funded prophets of collectivism — masquerading as intellectuals and social scientists — fighting against so uselessly, but so profitably? Nature itself. And in human sexual matters, this boils down mostly to the effect of hormones on individuals.

In 1974, in a once-and-for-all effort to assess whether the key radical feminist assertion of *sameness* in males and females had any grounds, Eleanor Maccoby and Carol Jacklin, both feminist academics from Stanford University, published an exhaustive two-volume survey entitled *The Psychology of Sex Differences*.[24] Maccoby and Jacklin had a lot at stake. They scrutinized thousands of works, hoping to show that all those studies showing gender differences did so as a result of design-bias, or ideological bias. But the evidence overwhelmed them. What they learned was that clear and important differences exist between boys and girls, *even before birth*. There are wide and worldwide differences between the sexes across whole ranges of physical sensitivity, proneness to illness, perception, learning, tactility, language acquisition, spatial abilities, pain threshold, and so on. Of course, there are great similarities, too — we are all human beings. But highly significant differences are detectable in all areas studied, through various stages of development. This would not surprise most parents, for as Michael Levin humorously points out, "any veteran of adolescence and parenthood still able to believe that boys and girls are born alike has already withstood more evidence than any laboratory can provide." But the one crucial difference, which serves to shatter the assumptions of radical feminism in its entirety, was "aggression," primarily because aggression affects every human endeavour. To answer the question whether sex differences have a biological foundation, they say "We contend that it does":

1. Males are more aggressive than females . . .
2. The sex differences are found early in life, at a time when there is no evidence that differential socialization pressures have been brought to bear by adults to "shape" aggression differently in the two sexes.
3. Similar sex differences are found in man and subhuman primates.
4. Aggression is related to levels of sex hormones, and can be changed by experimental administration of these hormones. ["Related" is a weak word; the relationship is overwhelming.]

For anyone who seriously considers the whole range of male/female sex differences, this sweeping survey must be considered conclusive, particularly because its two authors were working hard to *discount* the evidence for gender differences in the scientific literature. Quite clearly, there are no grounds whatever for the pivotal feminist claims that males and females are the same, and, as Michael Levin put it, "the accessibility of the immense amount of material on sex differences makes the continued respectability of feminism no less than a scandal."[25]

What this all means is that even though aggression is found in both sexes, it is much more dominant in males, who strive harder than females to reach the top of any hierarchy they encounter and even create hierarchies where none exists, simply for the purpose of climbing them. Males seem to be hormonally dominated by a desire to dominate. Boys are usually more aggressive than girls are; they are more Machiavellian in their pursuit of power, and more willing to hurt. Studies around the world show that men generally despise victims — especially their own — while women tend to take pity on them. Nothing in this male way of being is particularly admirable, in my view, but that's the way the biological world seems to work. The vast difference between the sexual and physical attitudes of the sexes was recently driven home to me by a World War II documentary showing Russian soldiers entering a concentration camp. The commentator remarked that the soldiers not only stole from the prisoners, but raped them as well — prisoners so emaciated and vulnerable it was unimaginable. With sadness and disgust I realized that no women anywhere in the world could possibly find men in such a condition sexually desirable or could wish to degrade them so, and in a flash my awareness of the vast chasm that separates the moral and sexual lives of males and females loomed large. I remember as a child reading a grisly *Life* magazine story, again about soldiers, that shocked me deeply. The conquering heroes amused themselves by tossing infant children of the enemy into the air, and competed to see if they could successfully impale the tumbling babies on their bayonets. There was a sad precedent for this in the egalitarian French Revolution, where "babies were carried in triumph on bayonets."[26] The truly large crimes of human history, sufficient to beggar the imagination, have been perpetrated by males. In fact, outside the family, violent crime in all societies of the world is an overwhelmingly male phenomenon. And anthropological studies the world over verify the reality of this male hardness and aggression, which can be induced in any female, human or primate by the simple administration of male hormones! Athletes, like my wife and myself, who have had occasion to mix with East

German, Soviet, or even Canadian competitors taking anabolic steroids, have known this fact for years. Such athletes take only *male* hormones, to increase aggressiveness and strength. If you want to *reduce* aggressiveness and violence in humans, *female* hormones must be administered, as they often are to long-term violent criminals (castration has the same effect).

Naturally, because aggressiveness is highly valued in society, men are rewarded in all sorts of explicit and implicit ways for such behaviour, which results in all sorts of secondary learning rewards for this primary behaviour. But no matter how you cut it, anthropological and biological studies the world over confirm that through hormones, men in general "are rendered more aggressive, exploratory, volatile, competitive, and dominant, more visual, abstract, and impulsive, more muscular, appetitive, and tall . . . less nurturant, moral, domestic, stable, and peaceful, less auditory, verbal, and sympathetic, less durable, healthy, and dependable, less balanced . . . more compulsive sexually and less secure. Within his own sex, he is more inclined to affiliate upwards — toward authority — and less inclined to affiliate downwards — toward children and toward the weak and needy."[27]

Fascinatingly, the beginning of all these differences, is right in the womb, for we all begin life as biological females.[28] We can become males only if the Y chromosome is present, and sufficient male hormones act upon our early development. The right chromosomes alone are not sufficient, as was clearly demonstrated by Jost, who showed that castrated mammalian fetuses will always develop as females — that nature tends toward the female unless there is active intervention by hormones secreted from fetal tissues to shift development to the male direction.[29] In other words, from the beginning of life, maleness is *difference* from femaleness. Even genetic girls, accidentally exposed to male hormones, "consistently reject most of the attempts of the culture to feminize them."[30]

What this boils down to in social relations is that because of the hormonally induced propensity for aggression, competitiveness, and hierarchical status-seeking, the tendency in all cultures of the world is for male dominance. However, just because "men monopolize leadership positions because they try harder to get them does not mean that men deserve these positions or that men do a better job in them than women would do if they became leaders. The only sense in which male dominance is 'right' is that it expresses the free choices of individual men to strive for positions of power and the free choices of individual women to do other things."[31]

There you have it. In a free society, the male aggressive propensity will express itself in status-seeking, female-seeking, money-seeking, and power-seeking behaviour. The only way to change such an outcome is to make the society unfree, to legislate some kind of "gender balance" based on a "statistical disparity" (the favourite new excuse for official discrimination policies) to counteract the different natural biological tendencies of both males and females. That is precisely what the feminists are now doing. They will have to work very hard, because as a natural result of sex differences there is no society in human history in which matriarchy has existed; nor in any way is it emerging today. In his groundbreaking book *The Inevitability of Patriarchy* (said to have a place in the *Guinness Book of World Records* for the most publishers' rejections ever), anthropologist Steven Goldberg takes scientific issue with the feminists head-on.[32] His careful analysis of every world culture has embarrassed feminists into a litany of high-pitched objections — but no serious rebuttals. In it, he shows convincingly that no world culture has ever been matriarchal, and argues that "the central fact is that men and women are different from each other from the gene to the thought to the act and that emotions that underpin masculinity and femininity, that make reality as experienced by the male eternally different from that experienced by the female, flow from the biological natures of man and woman."[33]

Goldberg argues that all cultures are aware of these differences, and thus they intentionally socialize their females to be as *unlike* males as possible and vice-versa. They teach females to develop strategies for dealing with aggressive males that circumvent the need for aggression, so that females will not constantly have to deal with males on male terms — and lose. In short, the real differences in socialization spring from real differences in biology, not the other way around. Scientists Neil MacLusky and Frederick Naftolin, from the Yale School of Medicine, underscore the same finding that there are "permanent and essentially irreversible sex differences in central nervous system function, in response to gonadal hormones secreted early in development." And Yale's Helen Lewis, a "committed feminist," was "forced to admit to her disappointed colleagues" that "the difference between having an XX or an XY as the 23rd chromosome is tremendously powerful."[34] In Canada, University of Western Ontario neuro-scientists Doreen Kimura and Dr. Elizabeth Hampson have recently concluded that the reason men and women are so different is that "sex hormones act on the brain before and immediately after birth, shaping the way the brain is organized."[35]

Anyone who doubts this finding should read *Brainsex*, which argues from reams of scientific evidence that the human brain is in fact a sex organ, in the sense that it is profoundly changed by hormones both before and after birth. This innate difference in the brain itself accounts for the countless differences in the way men and women choose to live. Although radicals have successfully suppressed this primal fact, the authors say that "virtually every professional scientist and researcher into the subject has concluded that the brains of men and women are different."[36] Recently, Dr. Sandra Witelson, of McMaster University, reported to a meeting of the New York Academy of Sciences that her research has linked differences in the anatomy of men's and women's brains to differences in behaviour. (Toronto *Star*, May 13, 1989.) But Witelson's findings "alarmed some feminists," who put out an immediate call for censorship, asking whether such work is "a legitimate area of research." Dr. Paula Caplan, a psychologist (with a political agenda) from the Ontario Institute for Studies in Education, even went so far as to compare such generally accepted findings to work on racial differences on intelligence tests. When you want to suppress something badly enough, any stretch of logic will do. Meanwhile, the word is out. On January 20, 1992, *Time* magazine ran a major story, "Sizing up the Sexes," confirming all sorts of brain- and hormone-linked sex differences, and, in June 1992, the Canadian Broadcasting Corporation aired a three-hour special called — "BrainSex."

## Admitting the Obvious[37]

My addendum to all this is simply that although the feminist argument for biological sameness is a massive failure, we should remember that *aggressiveness* and *control* are two different things. In external and necessarily hierarchical structures, like armies, businesses, or politics, the former generally leads to the latter; but in interpersonal relationships, that is not necessarily so. Everyone can think of couples where the male is more aggressive, but the female controls the relationship and the family's tenor. Nevertheless, feminists struggle to substitute political explanations for real, biologically based social differences wherever possible. Otherwise, they have no argument (unless, of course, they are arguing for the superiority of females).

What are the real effects of sex differences on society? They can be devastating — unless society undertakes to control them, principally by insisting on the key values of a free and ordered society in which the family is a privileged and legally protected institution.

But we have sown the wind of sexual egalitarianism in our time, and we are reaping the whirlwind. For as George Gilder has poignantly shown in his *Men and Marriage*, males the world over, to the great detriment of society, tend to settle for *immediate gratification* (also a key factor in the male criminal as well as the male homosexual personality). Single young men are a hazard to society and its procreative, or family health, for the following reasons. They vastly prefer uncommitted, hit-and-run sex (called "cruising"). They are wildly more aggressive than females. They drink more, more often, and have far more — and more serious — car accidents then women or married men. Although single men number only about 13 percent of the population over 14, they commit some 90 percent of the crimes.[38] Young bachelors are 22 times more likely to be committed for mental disease, and 10 times more likely to go to hospital for all chronic diseases than are married men. Single men are convicted of rape five times more often than are married men, and have almost double the mortality rate of married men and three times that of single women, from all causes.

Because homosexuality tends to be a hit-and-run phenomenon for men (distinctly not so for females), and because it suits their predilection for immediate gratification, male homosexuality is in accord with the natural sexual appetites of males. Such sexually anonymous behaviour will tend to flourish whenever a society discourages or stigmatizes distinct heterosexual roles, or confuses them through an "androgyny" program such as is dominant in our public schools. It is no simple coincidence that homosexuality is thriving in a time of sexual egalitarianism and feminism. The two go together like the two sides of a coin. Today, there is also a whole feminist cadre promoting homosexuality as "liberation" from males and patriarchy — and a lot of our tax money supports such programs. The Secretary of State, Women's Program, lists a ton of them. One such group held a tax-funded conference (August 24-25, 1985, in Prince Edward Island) and openly billed themselves as "radical lesbian feminists." There was much support there for the idea that women's centres must be restricted to lesbians, or at least to radical feminists.

But the truth is that this whole matter of sexual liberation has backfired, and it has proven a disaster for women and a special disaster for the family and its children. Men have benefited, but only in the short term, from all that uncommitted sex. Women have lost. So-called sexual liberation has caused women to lose the one sure control they have always had over their men, the one sure method that enabled women to have children, provide for them, protect them, and nurture them *personally* at the same time — all paid for by doting males — if they so desired. Now, in some despair, they are turning to the patriarchal State for this sustenance, and of course this route must always fail. The State simply does not care about individuals as beings, but as votes; moreover, it is always short of money. It can only be such a father to women either by employing them in droves (in many Swedish and even Canadian jurisdictions, up to 80 percent of the public service employees are low-paid women), or by taking from singles, and from fathers and mothers in intact families, the money necessary to support the increasing number of female-headed families. This policy is a demographic time-bomb for our society because it transfers the burden of supporting broken families to intact families, thus creating a tax lever that tends to wedge both spouses out of the home and into the workplace, and to push their children into impersonal daycare. Even worse, as Gilder explains, feminism, by default, has through its promotion of easy divorce and economic autonomy encouraged the creation of a system of legalized polygyny (what Martial, in Roman times, called "legalized adultery") — one in which the strong men, over a lifetime, can have many younger partners. Women lose out because their child-bearing years and chances of locating a strong husband are biologically confined to a few fleeting decades of their lives. If a woman waits too long, the strong males her own age are taken out of the system by other women in a pyramid of diminishing choices. Divorced women are three times less likely to remarry than are divorced men.[39]

Worse still, in societies that choose both to neutralize sex differences and to encourage "liberated" sex, the homosexual subculture always vies for normality with the core culture, destroying the core values of sexual complementarity, marriage, and (obviously) procreation. It also steals otherwise procreative males from women. For to many young men, the allure of regular, naughty, uncommitted sex (no "I love you" required), free of mortgages and children, beats out what has increasingly become the looming burden of a woman: diapers, taxes, and debts. In short, "polygyny produces homosexuality."[40] It does this both by liberalizing the choices of strong males (thus destroying the equal apportionment of mates, leaving too many men with a poor choice of females), and by setting the female ethos against the male ethos (thus encouraging a man-hating culture of sexual resentment — and hordes of uncertain males who will turn to each other for sex, instead of to challenging females). In family terms, such an ideological assault on sexual differences can only lead to breakdown. After sexual liberation, as we saw in Chapter Five, Sweden's marriage rate fell some 50 percent between 1966 and 1973 alone! And divorce rates skyrocketed, as they have in Canada.

Sexual liberation? Less marriage? Easy divorce? More homosexuality? Multiple spouses? Soaring single families? Latchkey children? A booming pornography industry? All these are interconnected and invariably undermine heterosexual monogamy and the family, which is unfortunate because monogamy is a system designed "to minimize the effect of sexual inequalities — to prevent the powerful of either sex from disrupting the familial order."[41] Which leads to Gilder's most important point: that "the crucial process of civilization is the *subordination of male sexual impulses* and biology to the long-term horizons of female sexuality."[42] In sum, Gilder convincingly argues that, because of the male/female hormonal difference in biology and aggression, all human societies must be set up to tame males and their barbaric proclivities. For without the long-term goals of women, who use the prize of sex and the promise of children to domesticate them, males would be content to enjoy their lust, to fight, to wander, to make war, and to compete and strive for power, glory, and dominance. In this view, men are inherently sexually inferior to women. For without women, men spend their lives seeking some kind of fixed purpose such as is already provided to women, who control the entirety of the sexual and procreative processes of human life. In fact, in sexual/moral terms, men are not equal to women (who are born with a larger purpose), and therefore "the man must be *made equal* by society" (must be drawn into that larger purpose). So the feminists have it tragically backwards. Instead of reinforcing the need to make men equal by drawing them more deeply into the family, feminists are trying to make themselves equal to men and to their inherently antifamily biology. But the traditional contract struck between men and women is that he provides and protects, and she processes and nurtures. Again, any woman who wants to try all four of these things, or to switch it all around, is free to try. But most, the world over, do not — because the system works. This means that men, lacking in the distinctiveness and biological determinateness of women, are "deeply dependent on the structure of society to define [their] role."[43]

Thus do women channel and confine the generalized male sexual desire in such a way as to protect themselves and their children, and in so doing teach men to subordinate their impulses to the long-term cycles of female sexuality and biology on which human society has always been based.[44] In order to avail himself of the intense and intimate sexual meaning only a woman can give to his life, because only she can give him the extension of himself into the future through family and children, a man is required to give something in return. What all cultures require him to give is "the external realm of meaning, sustenance, and protection in which the child could be safely born."[45]

### Skewing Society to Make the Theory Work

Although one can always bicker over details, or find exceptions, it is difficult to quibble with Gilder's main thesis, supported as it is by masses of anthropological studies of the world's societies. In view of the evidence, we must ask why it is that, in our present society, the State-financed influence of radical feminism is everywhere. Sex-ed classes, as we have seen, take fornication, cohabitation, and homosexuality for granted, even attempt to normalize them. Obvious and widely acknowledged male/female biological and behavioural differences are vigorously denied as "sexist." "Value-free" moral education programs are rampant in the public schools. And personal liberation ideology, or "feel-good" moral codes, are promoted over the notion of duty to spouse, family, children, and society.

At the least, readers ought to be aware that our society and the whole notion of the family in it are deeply engaged in a civil war of values at the vanguard of which are subsidized radical feminists. Also, that radical feminist theory is an unsubstantiable sham, without even the weight of simple logic to support it. Furthermore, that this is a theory that fails to grasp even the basic elements underlying the political, economic, or moral workings of a free society, and it therefore resorts to coercive methods to further its ideological aims. Taxpayers will be forced to support universal daycare; employers will be forced to pay women a higher wage, even though they cannot command it in the marketplace; and students will be forced to digest blatantly ideological textbooks that distort all natural and traditional values. That's why radical feminists are properly labelled intellectual terrorists. They are aware that neither males nor females would naturally choose the feminist's desired society, so they resort to force. This is part of their effort to achieve "the whole transformation of society," as Louise Dulude, past president of NAC, described her government-funded social revolution (meaning you and I are to pay for all of this). Her American counterpart, Sandra Harding, boasted that radical feminists "are calling for a more radical intellectual, moral, social, and political revolution than the founders of Western cultures could have imagined."

Programs such as so-called pay-equity, which are really coercive schemes for pay discrimination based on sex, have nothing to do with equity and everything to do with an assault on a free society and a free-market order. On a recent television panel, I argued that feminists are trying to substitute a political order (defined by them) for a free-market order, by *assigning* wage-values to women's jobs instead of letting the market decide. This was much like arguing that an ounce of lead and an ounce of gold should command the same price, just because they weigh the same. With great excitement, an Ontario Women's Directorate lawyer debating with me actually declared (publicly, yet), "Yes, that's it — as long as they *weigh* the same, they should have the same *value*!" I trust she is not a litigator.

The other variations on this coercion theme are essentially the same. So-called employment equity is a contrived program to "balance" the workforce, as if it ought always to reflect the current gender (or racial) composition of society. Thus do small groups lobby vociferously for changes that will benefit them, and "balance" in the workforce becomes a form of administrative acquiescence to political power. A surrender to the demands of power groups has replaced the pursuit of excellence everywhere. This is only possible when a society falls utterly for the Determinist and the Victim illusions, and attempts to engineer all social life according to the most current conspiracy theory. Such programs force employers to hire more women where they are "underrepresented," (but it will not force employers to fire women and hire more men if they are "overrepresented"). It's sick, folks. This program also extends to ethnic minorities. What to do, then, if more minorities, say, *want* to do a certain job? Well, I enjoy watching my Jewish intellectual friends squirm over this one. You can find Jews "overrepresented," in terms of their numbers in the population, in many business fields and in all the intellectual and professional fields. I say, good for them. They seem to have an astoundingly strong work and family ethic, and they deserve every bit of success in a free society. Unfortunately, however, a lot of Jewish intellectuals support the ideals of left-liberalism[46] — until these turn against them. After all, if it's all right to force employers to hire certain underrepresented minorities, then doesn't it follow that in the interests of "balance" they should fire, or refuse to hire, overrepresented minorities, regardless of qualifications? At McGill University in the 1940s, says alumnus Dr. Bill Goodman, they had something called a *numerus clausus* rule to limit the numbers of Jews because they were too smart and hard-working; if things had been open and competitive, Jews would have taken most of the spaces in medical school. And good old McGill is at it again. A recent report from the McGill "equity committee" (*The Suburban*, October 30, 1991) stated that "only women should be hired as academics" until the 50 percent level is reached. How does refusing to hire capable men because there are so many of them, differ from refusing to hire capable Jews? Watch out, folks! You can't argue for only one side of this one. Evil is evil, and coercion is coercion. The feminist *numerus clausus* is back in a sneakier form. Of course, Jews didn't take this lying down. Unlike the women's groups who, instead of competing harder, berate us and rob us of tax dollars, the Jews just put their heads down and worked harder to succeed. The same goes for incomes. The so-called male/female "wage gap" is used to argue that men are discriminating against women in our society. However, there are so-called "wage gaps" between all sorts of social groups, between the young and the old, the educated and the uneducated, the experienced and the inexperienced, the hard-working and the lazy, and so on. There is also a large "ethnic wage gap." Below is a selected list of the average incomes of some ethnic groups in Canada.

| Average Income of Selected Ethnic Groups in Canada | |
| --- | --- |
| **Ethnic Group** | **Average Employment Income ($)** |
| Jewish | 40,093 |
| Japanese | 30,750 |
| Scottish | 29,393 |
| Swedish | 29,018 |
| English | 26,968 |
| Polish | 26,754 |
| Chinese | 24,073 |
| Greek | 21,972 |
| Caribbean | 21,493 |

SOURCE: Statistics Canada, Catalogue 93-154, 1986

Now, are we going to argue that Jews, who outshine everyone with up to a 50 percent "gap," are discriminating against everyone else? Is there a "gentile gap"? Or is there a "Polish gap"? Or do these people get what they deserve? I don't see employers forced to pay Jews or Poles or Scots more than they wish. And in a free society, don't employees get paid what they voluntarily accept? It's the same for the sexes. In a free society, you have to set the rules and play the game. But rigging it for one race or another, or one sex or another, is out. If certain groups get ahead in the race without cheating — maybe they deserve it. Just remember, the sword of the Handicapper General (Kurt Vonnegut's term) cuts both ways.

In a riotous story "Pastry Cook Pay Angers 800 Nurses" (Toronto *Star*, May 18, 1990), the full idiocy of these situations was revealed. The handicappers of the State, called in to "evaluate" the work of nurses and equate it to male work of "equal value," decided, after much precision and deliberation, that a nurse's job was equivalent to that of a male pastry chef. Well, the outrage! The scandal! The "unfairness"! Florence Nightingale, a pastry chef? This was funny. So-called "pay equity" has been brought in to make pay more "fair" for certain groups of women (no men are allowed to apply for relief) who had voluntarily accepted their wages. Then, once the fairness judgment was rendered, the same women hit the streets, on strike for "Fair Pay Equity" (Toronto *Star*, October 2, 1991). The satirist Jonathan Swift must be laughing in his grave. It has never occurred to these women that if hundreds of them line up to accept low-paying jobs, they will get low pay. In a free society, pay is a function of an employer's ability to produce a product for (a) a price acceptable to consumers, and (b) the worker's willingness to accept the wage required to make the product. How could it be otherwise? Next, we will see demands for "Fair, Fair Pay Equity." (But by then the employers will all have left town.)

## HOW DO THE PEOPLE FEEL ABOUT SUCH SOCIAL ENGINEERING?

According to Malcolm MacDougall, vice-chairman of Jordan, McGrath, Case and Taylor, a large New York advertising firm, the vast majority of contemporary women want just what their mothers wanted — a home, a husband and children, and a job only to supplement the family income (Los Angeles *Times*, December 30, 1988). The firm's campaign for *Good Housekeeping* magazine (circulation, five million) refers to the modern woman as "the new traditionalist," and says that she "represents the biggest social movement since the 1960s." In a Toronto *Star* article, "Women Find Maternal Instinct Overpowers Career Plans" (March 30, 1989), we read of careerist women shocked into quitting their jobs by their desire for children. In another *Star* article ("Women Shun Jobs as Principals"), teacher

Judith Anderson says that "Women teachers don't want to become principals because they would spend so much time thinking about their children that they would do a lousy job." She argues that her own teachers' union wrongly believes that women hold few principals' jobs (13.6 percent) because of discrimination; "positions of added responsibility, sex-role stereotyping and affirmative action are simply not a high priority for the vast majority of female teachers."

As for so-called "affirmative action" to help women? A Canada-wide poll says: "Survey Finds 66% Oppose Quotas on Hiring Women" (Toronto *Star*, December 10, 1989). It seems that most people are willing to help truly disadvantaged groups improve their skills, but they don't like cheating on standards. Period. No rigging the tests, no gender or race "norming," no patronizing, no hiring people just because of their colour, race, or sex. That is the feeling. Toronto lawyer Maureen Sabia even argues that by forcing employers to hire women and artificially raise their wages, feminists are "perpetuating the myth that women are helpless victims, incapable of competing with men." Such programs, she says, simply transfer women's dependency on husbands and fathers to the State, keeping women "in the ghetto of the inadequate" (Toronto *Star*, February 1, 1988).

Meanwhile, a U.S. Gallup Poll of August 25, 1988, found that nine out of ten American women of child-bearing age were "satisfied" with their lives. Fifty-three percent of married women reported being "very" satisfied, compared with 28 percent of unmarried women, and women with children reported being the "most satisfied." Half the women said their first child was unplanned. In a *Homemaker's* magazine survey in 1990, seven of ten women surveyed said that, given the chance, they would rather stay home and raise their children than take them to daycare. Fully 78 percent said family was the most important thing in their lives, and 89 percent said they were satisfied with the domestic division of labour. More surprising, in the United States the number of working women aged 25-34 has declined for the first time in 40 years (*Conservative Chronicle*, July 24, 1991). And the fourth annual "American Family Report," published by Louis Harris and Associates, showed that fully 53 percent of working women did not want to be in the workforce at all! Another 32 percent would prefer to do part-time work, leaving only 12 percent of all *working* women who wanted to work full-time!

And Canadian female entrepreneurs are finding out it's tough sledding. Of 200 women business owners surveyed, 80 percent said their total annual business income (before paying themselves) was less than $50,000, and two-thirds had no take-home pay" (Toronto *Star*, February 26, 1991). They are working for nothing. How the times are changing. In a special issue on the family (fall 1990), *Time* led off by saying that "if there is a theme among those coming of age today, it is that gender differences are better celebrated than suppressed . . . the feminist label is viewed with disdain and alarm; the name of Gloria Steinem is uttered as an epithet."[47] *Newsweek* ran a story called "The Failure of Feminism" (November 19, 1990), and *New York Times* ran an op-ed piece entitled "Feminism, a Dirty Word" (November 23, 1990). With such statements, the post-feminist era has become the antifeminist era. *Time*'s Yankelovich survey discovered that "today's young women age 18 to 24 are more family-oriented (62 percent) than career-oriented."

Meanwhile, our media whine daily about low numbers of women in the scientific fields, and look everywhere for reasons why women do not become stockbrokers, sell cars, or dig ditches. I think it's because they don't want to. Regardless, these fields will become feminist targets for gender balance based on "statistical disparity" (a term used to justify State coercion when discrimination cannot be found). Well, Gallup put the icing on the antifeminist cake when it published the results of a poll showing that "a male boss is the preferred choice, even among females" (October 16, 1990). The same poll found that 52 percent of women "believe that married women with children entering the workforce, has a harmful effect on family life." The national figure on this opinion has not changed, Gallup reported, since 1973. And it would be a lot higher, except that personal guilt prevents a lot of mothers and fathers from admitting the truth.

# 12

# Women at War: On the Military, Daycare, and Home Fronts

Here's a look at three key arenas in which our current civil war of values is being fought. Each tells us something about what we are doing to our society in the name of a false equality.

The military is necessarily a hierarchical, authoritarian structure, and thus a prime target for feminist reform, even though minor tinkering could have a dangerous result in the face of a real enemy. The question ought to be, Will this domestic ideological warfare improve our capacity to defend ourselves, or will it not?

And of course the linchpin of all radical feminist programs is the demand for tax-subsidized universal daycare. Here we ought to be asking, Is this really best for our children?

Finally, let's look at the near-hysterical feminist effort to characterize all males and husbands as violent, and therefore to discredit the family as an institution by distorting the facts. Let us try to answer the question, What is the truth about domestic violence?

# THE NEW MEANING OF "ARMED" COMBAT: THE MILITARY FRONT

*If you persist in pushing women down into the combat area, it would destroy the Marine Corps. Simple as that — something no enemy has been able to do in over 200 years.*

MARINE GENERAL D. BARROW, *CONSERVATIVE CHRONICLE*, DECEMBER 1990

The inclusion or exclusion of women in military combat represents the cutting edge of feminist ideology (and the greatest challenge to the radical feminists' effort to feminize society), for the military is the quintessential male world. The first group of eight Canadian women combat recruits, all of whom failed to meet minimum standards (Toronto *Star*, August 15, 1988), complained of fatigue plus the discomfort, dirt, and inability to shower. The men made it difficult for the women to sleep by regaling each other with macho stories, or by awakening early — to get going. Several of the men said it was the best time of their lives.

For many of the reasons discussed above, men and women have radically different attitudes toward war, and killing in general, and no good military unit will survive in all-out battle if the two attitudes are confused in ways that adversely affect troop deployment, military strategy, or staying power while the enemy is engaged. The U.S. experience is important to Canadians, first, because we are just now trying what the Americans have been doing for years; and secondly because, as things now stand, we couldn't fight our way out of a wet paper bag, and in the event of a real war would have to beg American protection. Colonel K.T. Eddy, of Canadian Forces Command, said as much when he reported that the Canadian military is incapable of a sustained campaign against any large-scale threat from foreign or domestic enemies (*Canadian Defence Quarterly*, May 1992). As U.S. troops go, we go. Finally, this is a subject that affects families deeply, because once a nation accepts the extraordinarily indefensible and self-defeating premise that "women are the same as men and are thus as capable at war, therefore they must be drafted into service," guess who loses? The children, once again, become the victims of feminist ideology. For who will ever forget the heartbreaking photo of soldier Hollie Vallance that flashed around the world (Associated Press, August 23, 1990) as she held her seven-week-old baby to her breast and said, before shipping out for Operation Desert Storm, "I never dreamed of going into combat"? Seven weeks! Never dreamed of combat? That photo, sure to become a

classic, encapsulates the essence of the conflict between the idea of
mothers at war, and the family. Combat is all that most male soldiers
think about. They practise it with sticks and stones as children.

As it is the job of nations to protect their families, it is the job of
armies to protect nations. But by all accounts, the influence of
radical feminism on the U.S. armed services runs deeply indeed, and
is eroding the service from within. It is bound to do the same
undercover job in Canada.

By the way, I have no problem with women filling support roles
in the military. And I know that women can be good pilots and, under
certain conditions, killer soldiers. But their mere presence in training and actual combat is a subtle and multifaceted disaster for
combat troops. Even if women were every bit as good, their presence
would be a disaster for the simple reason that, contrary to feminist
ideology, women are women, and men are men. They are different.
To have women in the trenches, cheek to cheek with men, who have
wives at home, is an offence against the whole meaning of male
warfare. Mere sexual attraction between them — something drawn
to near-crazed proportions after weeks or months without the
comfort and warmth of a female body — is an enemy weapon within.
Such instinctual attraction is out of the question between rough,
smelly, unshaven soldiers, who anyway are repelled in a cultlike way
by the homosexual alternative. So they think only of war.

The idea is to drive the unsatisfied sexual instinct downward so
that it will come raging back up as the killer instinct, all the more
dangerous because it is the enemy there, over that hill, that is
keeping the soldier from his sex, his woman, his children, his
country, and all that he holds precious. In this way, female troops
in intimate action with males will always weaken the resolve of any
male soldier worth the name; for the distant aching dream called
girlfriend, or wife and home, is daily threatened and potentially
diminished by the presence of female troops. Even for those unattached, the attraction of softness, sexuality, romance, and all its
promise dissolves the killer instinct of a battle unit, softens the
hatred of the enemy, compromises courage, and impairs judgment — even badly so, if the soldier wants to protect a weaker
female instead of helping his unit. "We do not do what you do in the
United States," one Israeli general remarked. "We have to take war
seriously."

Here are a few insights from female soldiers who served in Iraq
or Panama. "It's like this: I'm a woman and a mother before I am a
soldier," sobbed Robin Williams (Spec. 4), mother of two, as she

talked about her family back home. "Out here I think more about my family than my job, and, yes, that could affect my performance if things got intense here [Iraq]" (Los Angeles *Times Syndicate*, August 1990). Her attitude could affect her whole unit and cause needless death, is what she means. Careerist and feminist soldier Lori Moore, after a week in Iraq, said, "I hate to say it, because it doesn't fit with the whole scheme of the women's movement, but I think we have to reconsider what we are doing" (New York *Times*, February 10, 1991). "Children," she rightly discovered, "are the unsung victims of Operation Desert Shield." She ought to have said that they are the unsung victims of feminism. She quit the army in mid-battle, with a less than honourable discharge, to rejoin her family. Meanwhile, Spec. Rose DeBerry, who served as a military police officer in Panama, said, "I don't think women are physically and emotionally prepared to go into combat units. Her friend, Staff Sgt. Christine Brown said, "I think the test [a real battle] would be a set-up for failure" (Toronto *Star*, March 21, 1990). Army Pfc. Sherry Kaiser, 20, who refused to be shipped out, said, "If they want to court-martial me, they'll have to, but on what grounds — that I want to take care of my baby?" Faith Stewart went into labour the day she was drafted. She complained, and got a two-week extension. The army said there were hundreds of cases like hers. There would be no exceptions. She left for Iraq, heartbroken, saying, "I feel my baby definitely needs me here" (Washington *Post*, February 14, 1991). Other mothers asked for time to wean their babies. The army said no. Some army!

Three out of four female soldiers interviewed after the Panama conflict by journalist Charles Moskos opposed the idea of armed combat for females. And that was a military operation in which even top brass lied through their teeth to cover up for two female sergeants who cried and refused to go on duty after a scary driving mission, because they were "tired out." Somehow they avoided what would have been a routine court-martial for a male. When the naval frigate *Acadia* docked in San Diego, it had 36 pregnant crew members; the *Yellowstone* had 20. A feminist navy spokesman protested that "they have a right to get pregnant."[1] But columnist Jack Anderson reported from Saudi Arabia that doctors told him their most frequent visits were "women asking for pregnancy tests" — and a ticket home. (Abortion was always on standby for after their release.)

So the feminists have won the battle, but I think they would lose the war. Everywhere one sees tears, pregnancy, and double standards of performance for men and women, utterly betraying the "sameness" idea underlying the whole fiasco. In his book *Weak Link: The Feminization of the American Military*,[2] author Brian Mitchell reveals the utterly shameful military fiasco feminism has wrought. For by now, he tells us, no other military on earth depends so heavily on women as the United States (10.3 percent). Canada is second (9.2 percent). Even Israel, after a disastrous experience using women in battle against Arabs (*The Polmach*, 1948), has not tried it since. The Arabs fought harder to avoid the shame of losing to women. Conscription is universal in Israel today, but by law women must be evacuated from the front in the event of hostilities, and women conscripts are used for non-combat jobs. No other NATO force is even close to us, and none of those forces is even remotely considering the loopy idea of sending women into bloody combat. The U.S. services themselves report that women soldiers have higher rates of attrition than men, are three times more likely to be discharged for homosexuality, miss twice as much duty time as men for medical reasons, are four times more likely to complain of spurious physical ailments, and have injury rates fully fourteen times as high as males submitted to the same drills. And someone is firing more than bullets. In any one year, up to 17 percent will be pregnant, and some small units have reported up to 50 percent.

A 1982 army study found that "barely one-tenth of Army women possessed the strength to meet minimum physical requirements" for 75 percent of army jobs — yet, 50 percent of women were assigned to those jobs anyway. Psychologically, military women were found to be less aggressive and daring, less interested in military history, less respectful of military tradition, and more likely to suffer "emotional distress," and they routinely scored lower than men on all the subjects deemed most important for military success. The one item on which they beat the men every time was: *they were better behaved!* Their continued presence in the military, Mitchell says, is owing to the fact that "women enjoy preference and protection in a variety of forms. Nowhere are women required to meet the same standards as men, and nowhere are women subjected to the military's sternest trials of mind and body that many men face."[3]

Mitchell rightly discerns that any decent (i.e. battle-effective) military is by nature contrary to every principle of feminism. It is inherently hierarchical and anti-egalitarian, and is status- and class-oriented, performance- and merit-oriented, and altruistic. Its last concern is the individual soldier and his "equal rights." Everything is geared to the survival of the hierarchical group, the chain of command. In this sense, the military is a mirror of the very values feminists are up against in an effective society, and "the feminization of the American military is perhaps the greatest peacetime military deception ever perpetrated."

Have women changed the military? You bet. The double standard is everywhere. They get shower curtains, men do not. Men get their heads shaved, women do not. They are exempt from boxing and wrestling, men are not. The military has invented all sorts of euphemisms to disguise double performance standards, speaking of "equivalent training" or "equal effort" instead of about accomplishment or performance. In all services, women have lower standards for strength testing, running, carrying heavy equipment, and the like. Only 32 percent of women could pass the standard endurance run passed by 97 percent of the males. So to avoid "stigma" to the women, the army eliminated the run. Jogging shoes have replaced combat boots on morning runs, mental pressure on plebes is disallowed (too many females broke down or cried), peer ratings to discover leaders were deemed unfair to women — so they are now out. Mitchell shows that one of the biggest reasons for women in the military schools, where women are outnumbered nine to one, is — marriage. Up to half a class is likely to marry another midshipman after graduation. So the gals are getting their Mrs. degrees, but "nothing can explain why 60 to 70 percent of the women at West Point score below the mean [average] in easy military subjects like map-reading, military heritage, and tactics, except that they do not much want to be soldiers."[4] The list goes on. When it comes to important military assets like strength and endurance, the men outscore the women by so much it's, well, dangerous (by 473 percent on leg work output). Even outside of battle, the army itself says, 65 percent of female aircraft mechanics could not perform required tasks such as changing aircraft tires and brakes, removing batteries and crew seats, or breaking torque bolts. Female missile mechanics could not lift warheads. Help!

Clearly, anyone who reads Mitchell's book will be convinced that the intrusion of feminism into the military is designed not to improve the effectiveness of the armed forces, but to advance the ideological warfare of feminism on the home front, even as it weakens the services from within. This has been a sad story, and it was not meant to demean the many courageous women who have served or lost their lives for their countries. Rather, it was meant to suggest that if we persist in having women in the military, let's do it in a way that will strengthen rather than weaken it. Let's have the same high training and fighting standards for all, and let the chips fall where they may.

Most of all, let's remember that more women in the military likely means more children getting second best at home, or pushed into the arms of aging, tired grandparents. A nation faced with this dilemma should make the smartest choice to protect itself: send the best fighters out to fight; and send the best nurturers home to nurture, but don't nurture the fighters.

## PAWNING OFF THE KIDS:
## THE DAYCARE FRONT

*Feminists have not answered the argument that day care provides no substitute for the family . . . the feminist movement . . . merely echoes the culture it claims to criticize.*

CHRISTOPHER LASCH, *HAVEN IN A HEARTLESS WORLD*

*The reality of feminism is a lot of frenzied and overworked women dropping kids off at daycare centers. If the child is sick, they just send along some children's Tylenol and then rush off to underpaid jobs that they don't even like.*

A DISILLUSIONED FEMINIST, *NEWSWEEK*, NOVEMBER 19, 1990

A little good daycare never hurt a child. And I would prefer good daycare to a terrible mother. But the fact is that nothing will ever replace even a poor mother, let alone a good one. I know . . . fathers can do it too. But who are we kidding? It's not the same during infancy. It may not be the same at any time in a person's life. Any child knows this. Any mother knows it, too, and all else is self-deception; salving the guilt. And let us not confuse daycare with the problems of the truly needy, a very small minority. That's a subject for our welfare system, which has its own problems. What needs airing, rather, is the manner in which the daycare issue constitutes the cutting edge of the feminist war against the family.

The logic of feminism, ever since Plato, says that in order for women to be equal to men, and free of their alleged exploitation in a patriarchal society, the State must look after their children. Nothing less than tax-funded, universal daycare, as a right, will satisfy the requirements of radical theory. That's why, even when government announces what would appear to be a generous new sum for daycare for the truly needy and a means test to qualify, there are howls of indignation and charges of taking daycare "back to the welfare system." That's because ideologues don't want subsidized daycare just for the poor. They want *universal, public daycare as a right* for their gender, rich or poor, in order to effect their revolution against the private family and our society. Once we understand this goal, we can understand all those seemingly off-the-wall statements by rabid feminists about "abolishing" the family. They mean it. "Money Squeeze Makes Day Care into Welfare, Aldermen Say," was a Toronto *Star* headline (October 16, 1988). "We brought daycare out of the welfare system, and now the province . . . is telling us to put it back, giving us no choice but to serve neediest families first." So the State, not the family, or the private sector, must look after all the children. "We don't want the private sector to provide the service," says Janet Davis, head of the Ontario Coalition for Better Child Care (*Globe and Mail*, August 11, 1990). She really means a coalition for "tax-funded child care." She wants a freebie, even though private providers employ lots of people and pay lots of taxes.

Well, I submit that we do not have a daycare crisis, even for spaces. There are lots of spaces. Toronto, for example, has about 5000 *empty* spaces, typical for a large North American city ("Plenty of Day-Care Space — But Only for Those Who Can Pay," *Globe and Mail*, August 3, 1988). The hitch is, no one wants to pay the price to put their children in them (from $2000 to $6000 per year), and many cannot afford to pay. No wonder. So they are making other arrangements. Grandparents, friends, co-ops, tag-team parents (working different shifts) — you name it. No. The crisis we have in this country is not a daycare crisis, but a tax and a values crisis.

Our welfare State taxation, plus inflation, is taking so much income from people they find their standard of living slipping. Panicked, they search for any available means — including coercion of others for "free" daycare through the subsidy system — to keep up their standard of living. The second part of the "crisis" lies in the fact that many "liberated" women have discovered, too late, that they have been unglamorous lackeys of commercialism. They may find themselves infertile with age; or, after an effort to raise the family's standard, they may gaze at a tax-shrunk paycheque, or a stale job, or a promotion that has passed them by. And it's too late. The only constant is their children's tears. We haven't yet learned that what this country really needs is not a *revolution*, but an all-out *reconstitution* of those values of personal freedom and responsibility — home, family, children, and the minimal State — that made us great in the first place. And women ought to be at the vanguard of that movement. It's a scandal that they are not. Yet. And it's a scandal that their husbands are not helping them. Both should be screaming bloody murder that the welfare State, singing a song of false compassion, has robbed them and their families of the means, has even undermined the desire, to stand on their own feet and raise their own children. Now, they are lackeys of the State.

We are all discovering, too late, that the State first takes the wealth of families, and then, as it inexorably grows, needs more workers to supply it with taxes. Sweden, Canada, and all other welfare states have discovered that the best way to supply themselves with more tax revenue and cheap labour is to recruit women, especially mothers, for the labour force. Janet Davis says "female labour is needed in today's work force to meet the demands of a restructuring economy" (Toronto *Star*, November 1, 1991). I'd say they're needed to meet the demands of a tax-gobbling bureaucracy. The Swedes long ago justified this by concluding that "the gain which the State makes from the taxes paid by the working woman would be greater than the cost of building out [supplying] the daycare system."[5] But the long and short of this is that the welfare society "can be financed only by taxes from a labour market in which almost everyone is working and paying taxes."[6] From this perspective, the modern liberated woman is the muttonhead dupe of the State as it creates a cycle of deceptive compassion and dependency that in turn creates more power for the State. In Sweden, staying home is officially considered an act of disloyalty to the State. Thus, Swedes have deliberately engineered very small public-housing units in order to increase discomfort, reduce family size, and exclude grandparents and relatives in a successful effort to create one-generation households. They began doing this even though only 7 percent of Swedish women said they wanted to be employed full-time. Fifty-three percent did not want to leave the home at all.[7] The aim of the socialist State, however, was spelled out with stunning clarity by the former chairman of the Swedish People's party. Canadians who value the family should pin this message on the fridge door as a reminder of what radicals here want to do with their children:

> The parental monopoly cannot be broken solely by indirect measures — the State must intervene directly, by, for example, taking the children from the parents during part of their growing up years . . . It is best for the children and society that a universal and compulsory preschool program become clearly indoctrinating, thus enabling society to intervene more directly when it comes to the children's values and attitudes.[8]

The only action that will slow this relentless cycle and raise the dignity of mothering in the home will be a loud and nationwide clamour from women for huge tax cuts and credits that will establish the care of a family with children as the career of choice. This message must be so clear that very young men and women will positively strive for marriage and children. The whole point of our traditional system is that it was intentionally designed around the biological realities of mothers. Everything in it was bent to the protection and continuance of what most women by nature cherish most. Now, everything is bent toward the world of external (commercial) action (what most men cherish most) and the institutions of the State (what politicians and socialists, most of them men, cherish most).

So the daycare issue is not about babies needing daycare space; it's about our civil war of values. Mostly, even where this is an unintended consequence, it is about "the planned spiritual alienation from kinship"[9] that is found in all states that have started the long march toward the socialist nightmare. They subsist on an inexorable chain of logic and coercive humanitarianism that by its nature must extinguish kinship in order to hold unhampered sway over the people. The daycare movement is a linchpin of this strategy. It's a direct and obvious symbol of the clash between the top-down State and the bottom-up society; between free, responsible parents, who believe their young children ought to be raised at home (mostly) by their mothers, and individuals who want to organize the "fragmented" daycare scene through a central State bureaucracy, freeze out private providers, and alter the tax code so that stay-at-home moms are pushed into the workforce. As things stand in Canada, so-called working moms (a deliberate misnomer) — meaning those who work for the market — get up to a $4000 tax deduction for children under seven, while at-home moms who raise their own kids get nothing. The system is heavily rigged against both those who make sacrifices to raise their own children and those whose taxes are used to support the children of richer two-income couples. This distortion of the basic values of our society is exactly what feminists want. It leads straight to what Joseph Sobran called "alienism," or the ideological preference for the abnormal over the normal, brought about by all collectivist public policy.

Socialist ideologues are always the first to promote universal daycare, as if this policy alone will even out the "biological handicap" of females. As the economy shifts to more State control, the State also becomes increasingly the prime employer, thus controlling wages (today's bread), pensions (tomorrow's bread), and morals (through daycare and State education). So if in a fight to preserve your private world you are sacrificing a second income, or are a "tag-team" couple working different shifts so you can raise your own children, or if you are self-employed, or are relying on parents or other relatives for help, or even pay a nanny in your own home — you will lose. For the consequence of the welfare State — one promoted by its feminist lieutenants — is to promote a *tax-forced equality of status* by taxing the natural family so heavily that you are *forced* to put your child into public daycare, thus creating yet another constituency for government. Heavy taxes at one end, "free" State-licensed daycare at the other, make up the tax pincers. The U.S. Act for Better Daycare, an extremely radical proposal for early subsidized daycare in school buildings, is based on the Connecticut model, which legislator Margaret Harris said "sketches a picture of secret policing activities generally inconsistent with democratic societies." The program is designed to send State supervisors into the homes of pregnant women, intensively monitor home life, and guide infants toward State care. At the same time, through licensing standards, it will make informal babysitting illegal without a certificate from the State. Grandma can no longer babysit your child and a friend.

But the battle is on, there and here. "Canadians don't want their tax money supporting day care for the children of yuppies," says Perrin Beatty, Health and Welfare minister (*Globe and Mail*, October 24, 1990). And a key survey prepared by Health and Welfare Canada discovered that "a whopping two-thirds of Canadians say the best place for pre-school children is at home with their parents" (Toronto *Star*, June 5, 1991). Only 16 percent favoured any licensed daycare over home care, or care by friends or relatives. Respondents also said that any government money should be used *only* to help low-income parents. It's the same in the United States, where a 1990 poll commissioned by the Los Angeles *Times*, which shocked the feminists, said that 79 percent of working American women with children *would quit their jobs* if they could stay home with their children.[10] This massive majority opinion, reflecting traditional family values, flies in the face of the tiny but strident feminist lobby for universal daycare, which is primarily an educated, white, radical, urban contingent. In May 1991, the venerable 38,000-member Federated Women's Institutes of Canada completed a nationwide survey of their rural members. Some 69 percent declared that their preference, if economic conditions permitted, would be *to stay home and care for their own children*. The consensus was against any kind of "universal" childcare funding.[11]

### Defecting Mothers: What Is Daycare Really Doing to Children?

*I'm not willing to have children and put them in daycare. I've babysat for years and taken kids to daycare centers. They just hang on my legs and cry. I can't do that.*

A COLLEGE SENIOR, QUOTED IN *TIME*, DECEMBER 1990

*Working parents want daycare. What children want . . . is their parents.*

WENDY DRESKIN, AUTHOR OF *THE DAYCARE DECISION:*
*WHAT'S BEST FOR YOU AND YOUR CHILDREN*[12]

We are in the midst of a terrible impasse. In the pursuit of economic salvation that is very real for some (the truly needy), a matter of economic choice for most (yuppie daycare mothers), and endemic in a consumer society's pursuit of a flashier life-style, we are forcing children to pay a terrible price. This is going to haunt us as long as they live, for as the old Jewish saying goes: "If you don't get up for your crying child when he's young, you'll be getting up for him when he's old." That quote came from an article by Canadian psychiatrist Dr. Elliot Barker, who has spent more than two decades working with angry killer psychopaths. He watches their anguished parents bent with sadness as they arrive to comfort their criminal sons, and he says, "I can't help wondering where they were when it mattered most."[13] Barker says that the psychopaths he treats invariably have the same history. Shortly after birth the child is separated from his mother and given into the care of a multitude of surrogate parents. From Barker, from criminologist Stanton Samenow, from legions of researchers, the evidence is cascading off the presses. We have succumbed, encouraged by the shrill goading of tax-funded radicals, to an increasing abandonment of our children.

Given half a chance, mind you, males have always had a propensity to abandon wives and children, for jobs, adventure, or war. Now, females are doing it too. But as George Gilder insightfully remarks, the "role that feminists seek is not the real role of men, but the male role of the Marxist dream, in which society does the work."[14] What all honest researchers are discovering, however, is what the popular wisdom has always known. Young children need an uninterrupted, intimate, continuous connection with their mothers, especially in the very early months and years.

## Breaking the Bonds

Quite contrary to the radical feminist insistence that "parenting" is a gender-free matter (either parent, or even a surrogate, will do), or that "mothering" is an oppressive role invented to trap women and recruit them as slaves for a patriarchal society, highly respected social scientists such as John Bowlby are increasingly reiterating the obvious: that the attachment relationship that a young child "forms with his mother is the foundation stone of personality." We are discovering much too late that when this primal attachment is missing, or is inadequate, children, especially young boys, develop into adults who lack any ability to form meaningful relationships with other people. In *Attachment and Loss*, and again in *A Secure Base*, Bowlby insists that "the young child's hunger for his mother's presence is as great as his hunger for food," and that "her absence inevitably generates a powerful sense of loss and anger."[15]

Woe betide us. An avalanche of recent "attachment studies" has shown that although fathers are terribly important to any child's development, attachment bonding is overwhelmingly a matter of the quality and continuance of the relationship between the *mother* and her children in the early stages of life. Through a variety of current experiments based on the "strange situation" used by psychologist Mary Ainsworth in the 1960s, it is now devastatingly clear that when babies are placed in "other than mother" care during the first year of life — even good quality care — "about 50 percent are insecurely attached to their mothers."[16] (The figure was 30 percent in the 1960s.) Ainsworth's technique was to ask mothers to leave their children in a room with a total stranger, abruptly and without explanation to the child (the strange situation), and then reappear some minutes later. The results were decisive. During the mother's sudden absence, and on her reappearance, the children demonstrated clear differences in attachment, ranging from callous indifference and anger, to joy on reuniting. Pennsylvania State University's Jay Belsky, who formerly argued for the harmlessness of daycare, now says that daycare erodes a child's sense of trust and order in the world. And Belsky, Barglow, and others argue that when mothers leave infant children in daycare, especially for more than 20 hours each week, children read this as parental rejection. Belsky argues that daycare weakens the father-child bond as well, because when full-time working mothers get home, they monopolize the child's attention during evenings and weekends. Belsky says he has since been "smeared" by feminists for turning against daycare, but finds that his newly critical perspective is shared by many specialists who are fearful of incurring the wrath of daycare partisans. This truth, shared quietly by many Canadian specialists, is being hidden from Canadians through an academic and media blackout. Ainsworth concluded that "it's very hard to become a sensitively responsive mother if you're away from your child ten hours a day, it really is."[17] Recently, work by Mary Ainsworth, Mary Main, and Alan Stroufe, researchers from three major but different university research centres, "has clearly and consistently shown that the pattern of attachment developed in infancy and early childhood is profoundly influenced by the mother's ready availability, her sensitivity to her child's signals, and her responsiveness to his need for comfort and protection."[18]

Jay Belsky calls extensive daycare (in the 20+ hours a week range) a "risk condition" for children — and therefore for society as a whole. Why? Because — there is near unanimity on this point — *poorly attached children are sociopaths in the making*. Such children feel anger and aggression toward their parents and other children. Study after study shows that the ranks of the aggressive, of angry children, of dropouts, of detention centres, of welfare and unemployment rolls, of drunk-tanks, of the homeless hordes, and of the jails are increasingly occupied by those who missed out. As young children they are less cooperative with adults and more aggressive in their play, fight more, cry more, hit more, cling more, are more rebellious, have far less tolerance for frustration, and are far more at risk for personality disorders in later life.

Predictably, those in the lowest quality daycare had the highest number of such disorders, and such profiles are common in low-income strata. But even children from affluent homes, left with one-to-one nannies, showed significant attachment insecurity. Psychiatrist Graeme Taylor, of Mount Sinai Hospital in Toronto, has concluded what all natural mothers know by instinct and can deny only by self-deception: that the infant–mother relationship is "an interactional system that organizes and regulates the infant's behaviour and physiology from birth," including such intimate and sensitive matters as heart rate, enzyme levels of growth hormone, thermo-regulation, responsiveness of the immune system, and upward to psychological states of mind.[19] This regulation comes about through the mother's direct and intimate attention and holding behaviour, and if it is lacking can result in conditions of physical and personality inadequacy that endure for a lifetime.

The point here is that extensive daycare serves to restructure the mother-infant relationship. If widespread, it may dangerously restructure society itself. A clear sense of the problem can be grasped from the turnover rates of child-care workers — between 40 and 60 percent per year. "Attachment" is impossible under such circumstances. I have heard that the average Swedish child has more than a hundred different "caregivers" by the age of 10. The term should be "caretakers." We can be sure that extensive daycare facilities will be matched by extensive increases in the number of divorces, social violence, psychiatric beds, and jail cells. That's why Dr. Burton White of Harvard University's Pre-school Project, perhaps American's leading authority on the first three years of life, declared daycare to be "a disaster" for children, saying that it is impossible in daycare centres to manufacture "large doses of custom-made love." "After more than 30 years of research on how children develop well," Dr. White said, "I would not think of putting an infant or toddler of mine into any substitute care program on a full-time basis, especially a center-based program . . . I urge you not to delegate the primary child-rearing task to anyone else during your child's first three years of life."[20]

### Breaking Their Bodies

As if generations of children who grow up lacking empathic capacities are not enough, daycare facilities, by their very nature, are hosts for all sorts of illnesses and diseases, some of them extremely dangerous to daycare children and their families. Dr. Harrison Spencer, chief of parasitic diseases at the Centers For Disease Control (CDC), describes a fascinating Minnesota experiment in which researchers created a video showing how a disease organism can start in a child's diaper and travel to other children and workers. A tablespoon of tapioca pudding combined with a dye that becomes fluorescent under a black light was placed in one child's diaper. The diaper oozed. One child, then another touched it, "and pretty soon it spread all over the whole room. They've got a beautiful video showing exactly how this happened. They took pictures at timed intervals which showed a gradual progression as the dye spread onto the daycare worker's hands, the furniture, and so forth."[21] Dr. Harrison said that daycare children "are at risk anywhere from two to eighteen times as much [as non-daycare kids] for certain infectious diseases that run the gamut from diarrheal diseases to respiratory and flu-like illnesses," and that "as many as 80 percent of children in daycare excrete cytomegalovirus (CMV) in their urine and saliva." Other studies show 100 percent for daycare children, compared with 50 percent for other children. Scandinavian children have higher rates than others, likely because of more widespread daycare. CMV is a herpes-type viral infection that doesn't seem to bother young children much, but can cause a mononucleosis-type illness in older children and adults, and if contracted by a pregnant woman can cause deafness, birth defects, mental retardation, and even death in her newborn.

Joanna Braithwaite, an infection expert with the City of Toronto Health Department, says daycare centres are "high risk institutions, just like hospitals"; they act as "a community reservoir" for infection — a place where bacteria and viruses are always present, ready to infect others. Winnipeg disease expert Dr. Ron Gold says the 200,000-plus Canadian children in daycare are twice as likely to get sick as those cared for at home (*Canadian Press*, February 2, 1988). There's a horrible litany of "Daycare-Related Illnesses" (DCRIs),[22] as they are called: over 70 percent of clinical cases of hepatitis A can be traced to a daycare setting, as can so many other fecal-oral enteric (bowel) diseases, including viral gastroenteritis, salmonellosis, shigellosis, giardiasis (found in 30-50 percent of daycare inmates, with an estimated 600 percent increased risk in centres with children under two), and pinworms, many of these diseases having their highest "attack rates" for children under one year. It's the same story for respiratory diseases, the various forms of pneumonia, influenza B, the various pathogenic "strep" bacteria, and the deadly meningococcus diseases.

In most cases it is useless to "isolate" such sick children in a daycare setting, because they are often badly infected long before symptoms show up and may have already infected dozens of other children (and thus their families). Even worse, their anxious mothers often resort to "masking" the child's illness with drugs so the sickness or fever will be undetected until after they are at work. Studies too numerous to mention show up to 12 times greater risk for such diseases in daycare children, and many of these bacterial and viral conditions can have sequelae like scarlet fever, nephritis (kidney inflammation), rheumatic fever (inflammation of the heart), septicemia, meningitis, septic arthritis, and osteomyelitis.

Enough said. So alarmed are some authorities that even the cautious CDC has warned that "large, *licensed* daycare centers . . . are major transmission centres for hepatitis, severe diarrhea, and other diseases." Dr. Stanley Schuman of the Medical University of South Carolina blames daycare for the outbreak of all sorts of illnesses, saying that it "is reminiscent of the pre-sanitation days of the seventeenth century."[23] More bluntly, another American epidemiologist labelled daycare centres "the open sewers of the twentieth century" (*Health*, October, 1991).

Daycare centres can also be magnets for certain types of workers. One study of sexual abuse in Michigan said 75 percent of the victims were daycare children. It didn't say whether the abuse occurred in the centres or not, but some abuse does. A U.S. senator told of a daycare centre in Florida where "dozens of children were found to have gonorrhea of the mouth."[24] The University of New Hampshire reported that from 1983 to 1985 there were 1639 *confirmed* cases of sexual abuse of children in U.S. *licensed* daycare centres; in some cases, the children were used for the production of child pornography.[25]

The current fear is that many such unattached youngsters, utterly lacking in empathy, are becoming, in a truly vicious social cycle, the angry radicals of tomorrow. Disappointed with the real world, they understandably become dependent on illusory utopian goals for the reformation of society, trying to force society to give them what they missed and punishing their parental generation at the same time. The feminists, I'm afraid, are rather cornered, and they will not succeed in reforming society to their liking through daycare, no matter how many children they sacrifice to it. A nationwide *Globe and Mail–CBC News Poll* (November 5, 1991) revealed the deep feelings of the public on this issue. A huge majority of anxious Canadians (76 percent) said "children's well-being is being sacrificed" because both parents have to work. The poll said "they have tremendous nostalgia for the way the family used to be run." So radicals would be better to reform themselves. In writing on this point for *Harvard Business Review*, no-nonsense feminist Felice Schwartz said that some women are "career primary"; following this urge, however, "requires that they remain single or at least childless or, if they do have children, that they be satisfied to have others raise them."[26] She didn't allude to the satisfaction of the children. At any rate, we cannot prevent radicals from forcing their own children into heavy-duty daycare, but we ought to prevent them from manipulating tax, legal, and social policy, effectively forcing others to make the same mistake.

## GENDER-BASHING DISINFORMATION: THE HOME FRONT

North Americans have been bombarded with round after round of explosive stories on how men are violently abusing women (and children), who then march in the streets for public funds to build shelters, pay for therapists, provide welfare, and so on. The standard feminist line is that all family violence is a result of patriarchy, of the imbalance of power in a marriage. Thus, patriarchy causes wife-battering, and the corollary is that women are violent only in self-defence. This standard line of argument is utterly, totally, and surprisingly false.

There is no doubt family violence exists. It always has and always will. And we may see more of it for the reasons outlined above. After all, human love and sexuality are nothing if not profoundly physical. It is therefore no surprise that sometimes people get hurt under conditions of peak emotion, especially under the growing influence of alcohol or drugs, which provide human beings with all sorts of illusions and delusions. Personally, I would like to see much, much tougher laws to punish men who rape, and men or women who beat up anyone. My reason for including this section is simply to show how we have been successfully brainwashed by man-hating, politically motivated feminists to believe that men are the only violent members of society, while women are their genteel loving victims. It all seems to be part of the strategy to discredit the natural family.

Human violence, like all violence in nature, is a matter of the strong taking advantage of the weak. The very strong and wicked prey on the less so. Strong men prey on women and also on weaker men; weaker men and strong women prey on women and children; women tend to prey on old ladies and children — and on some weak men. Because humans are not perfectible, society must be set up for adequate protection of the weak. No one is well served by feminist gender-bashing disinformation. Consider the following.

Merlin Brinkerhoff and Eugen Lupri of the University of Calgary, in their study "Interspousal Violence," found the same results as U.S. researchers Straus and Gelles: "[I]n marked contrast to the behavior of women outside the home, women are about as violent within the family as men."[27] And violence occurs among cohabiting couples at double the rate for marrieds. This statistic illustrates the peculiar reality of human love, since nothing in law or love prevents cohabiting individuals from walking out the door. Also curious is the fact that childless couples do more violence, and women employed full-time are more likely to do violence than are part-timers. Of 562 Calgary couples studied, 38 percent admitted spousal violence (ranging from mild threats, to slapping, to using a weapon); 75 cases were wife-to-husband violence, 58 were husband-to-wife, and 80 were "mutual." On the "overall" violence (as opposed to "severe" violence) scale, "Canadian women reportedly are more likely than men to act violently toward their partners (28.1 percent, vs. 20.6 percent),"[28] and are slightly more violent than their U.S. counterparts.

Dr. Joe Kennedy, and Donald Dutton of the University of Alberta population laboratory, sampled 708 couples, intending to focus on husband-to-wife violence, and were surprised to encounter identical levels of the wife-to-husband variety. However, in the "serious" category, "wives were twice as often the perpetrators" (wife hits husband, 4.7 percent; husband hits wife, 2.3 percent).[29] It is widely believed that wife-to-husband violence is mostly self-defence by the weaker sex; but Murray Straus, in follow-up studies of the 428 "battered" women who reported the first hitter (documented in his voluminous U.S. national survey), found that husbands struck the first blow 42.6 percent of the time, and wives 52.7 percent. Research on dating relationships has revealed identical ratios for violence, showing that "regardless of whether the analysis is based on all assaults, or is focused on dangerous assaults, about as many women as men, attack a spouse who has not hit them, during a one year period."[30] Straus concludes women commit assault and hit first about as often as men do (although men may do more damage, depending on the category). Researchers Gryl and Byrd found the same patterns held for dating relationships. In short, the women-are-only-violent-in-self-defence argument does not hold up.

As for spousal murder, Steinmetz reports that an equal number of U.S. wives and husbands kill each other every year — a pattern that has been stable over time.[31] Despite hysterical and irresponsible reporting such as the article "Women in Fear" by Canada's *Maclean's* (November 11, 1991), women as a whole are about 35 percent of annual murder victims in Canada. Men are mostly killed by, and are killing, other men. In Toronto, Canada's largest city, of 55 murders in 1990, only 16 were of women. But who is making the case for all these male victims of violence? Not the media. According to Canada's Centre for Justice Statistics, the decade 1980-89 saw an annual average of 640 murders, of which 412 were men and 228 women. Of those legally married, there was an annual average of 81 husbands murdered, and 61 wives (though not always by a spouse). Considering how few common-law marriages there are, compared with legal ones, the statistics tell us what we suspected. As measured by murder, common-law marriages are wildly more unstable — about seven times more so. For the 10-year period, many more males — and husbands — were killed than females — and wives. The truth is that while wives tend to be killed by husbands, or intimates, husbands are getting killed by wives, intimates, and by other men, too. They are doubly victimized. For the same decade, of the 510 solved homicides in Canada, legally married husbands of the victim were suspects in 14.2 percent, and wives of the victim suspects in 4.4 percent of the 510 cases. Some experts say that if guns were more available in Canada, we would likely mirror the U.S. 50-50 spousal murder figure. Any way you look at it, murder by legally married spouses is a numerically small problem.

Steinmetz also reported, however, that women are 62 percent *more likely* than men to abuse children, that boys are twice as likely to suffer at their mothers' hands than girls are, and that throughout history women are the primary perpetrators of infanticide and elder abuse.[32] Toronto social worker David Harper stated his "conviction, after 20 years in the social services field, that male children are the chief victims of both verbal and physical abuse in the home, and principally at the hands of women" (Toronto *Star*, April 14, 1992). Let us keep in mind that very small percentages of perverse or violent women do not invalidate my main agrument about the family-and-child orientation of women in general. Outside the home, women are less prone to general violence of all kinds. But in a closed, highly emotional setting, the small number who are violent easily match or exceed the violence by men, especially over their children. While this really seems to contradict the general nurturing tendency of women, we need only remember that violence any- where is rarely arbitrary. It is natural for women and men to become most loving — and therefore sometimes most hateful — toward those who constitute the emotional core of their existence. Straus and Gelles report that women tend to use weapons far more than often than men,[33] that "wife-beating" is "a political rather than a scientific term," and that violence *by* wives has not (yet) been defined as a problem in the public mind. This is a scientist's way of saying that feminists have captured the media. McLeod's studies show that whereas weapons are used in only 25 percent of severe violence against wives, wives use weapons 82 percent of the time; "clearly violence against men is much more destructive than violence against women . . . male victims are injured more often and more seriously than female victims . . ."[34] In another study by Steinmetz (1981) six different societies were examined for spousal violence (United States, Canada, Finland, Israel, Puerto Rico, and Belize), and in each society the percentage of husbands who used violence was similar to the percentage of wives; but wives who used violence tended to use greater amounts.[35]

Elsewhere, in an extensive 1984 analysis of 60,000 homes using U.S. National Crime Survey statistics, McLeod showed that 1.8 million women and 2.1 million men were victims of domestic violence. Despite these facts of life, feminists have been successful to the point of securing legal recognition of "battered wife syndrome" as "a legitimate defence against a murder charge" (Toronto *Star*, May 1, 1990), and women increasingly succeed in the use of charges of past abuse as justification for killing their spouses. If a man tried to use a "battered husband syndrome" defence he'd be laughed out of court. Clearly, radicals are "exploiting the traditional stereotypes regarding women's weaknesses and vulnerability," as one female scientist said, and this stereotype "licenses the quick use of deadly force by a specialized group [all women] and stands as an ironic contradiction both to the social equality sought by women, and to the basic aim of the criminal law."[36]

Parenthetically, U.S. data indicate that 60 percent of all *child abuse* reports are false, and that of the remainder, only 1 percent constitutes what normal people would call true abuse. Apparently, the abuse industry is up for grabs by whatever political constituency is first to the starting line. Disinformation is rampant. But news of the fallen nature of women, too, is now seeping through. Dr. Fred Matthews of Toronto recently blamed political censorship and cultural myths for the fact that "we may be creating rapists, men who are angry at women" because they were sexually abused by women and girls. He cited a U.S. study showing that 7.6 percent of boys had been abused in childhood by women (16.5 percent by men). Meanwhile, the New Jersey Department of Human Services analysed 54,366 reports of child abuse, substantiated 36 percent of them, and concluded that 67 percent of victims lived in single-family homes (mostly female-headed), where 77 percent of the crimes were committed by mothers.[37] At least one feminist writer, the American Bell Hooks, has fessed up to the colossal gender distortions on human violence (if only for her own reasons). She says women have to be more honest about female violence and must reject the "simplistic account of female experience" that once again paints women as victims of men. Her point: Until we admit women can beat up on men, children and the elderly, we won't believe they can revolt against society as a whole.[38]

And so it goes. A lot of single mothers seem to fall into child abuse, including allowing or forcing their children to have sex with their live-in boyfriends, who, along with live-ins and step-parents, account for much of the reported incidences of male "family" violence.

(Ever-broader radical definitions of the family will soon include all of society.) Published summaries from American and Canadian daily newspapers of the most gruesome crimes by women are bracing. There are accounts (reproduced here with some regret, merely to right the balance of perception on crime and gender) of women who have killed their pregnant daughters, suffocated their babies, dropped babies on cement floors, abandoned babies to die of overexposure, beat their kids to death (in one case, for falling out of a high-chair). Scalding babies to death in a bathtub is also common. Women murderers also use child starvation a lot. Some mothers simply sell their daughters into prostitution to get cocaine. A favourite trick is throwing newborns into passing garbage trucks. In prior centuries, a mother's favourite method of murdering children was called "overlaying," in which a tired mother rolled over the infant to suffocate it, and then awoke to discover the terrible "accident."

Enough said.

Clearly, the feminist effort to disrupt the family by distorting the gender-relations record is irresponsible, an abomination of dishonesty, in which our lazy-minded media are fellow travellers. A shame. However, the truth is that men and women are in this together, and we'd best stop the gender-hatred stuff and get on with a concerted effort to reconstitute our society. Every study of violent behaviour shows that the very best protection against crime is the intact, traditional family, especially where there is strong religious faith and no drug or alcohol use. You just need to read a bit of the literature comparing divorce-, crime-, and drug-infested Nevada with its neighbouring Mormon state of Utah to see the dramatic difference. Utah is the mirror image of Nevada on every imaginable demographic and health scale.[39] The single factor that protects Utah residents is their moral strength and determination to uphold family values. It is the same with Japan and Switzerland, two very traditional, family-based nations in which violent crime is very low. During the past two decades, while crime has soared internationally, it has actually *fallen* in Japan. There are more murders committed in New York City in one weekend than in all of Japan in a year.[40] Societies with strong family values have less crime, and within all societies ethnic groups with strong family values commit less crime (such as the Japanese and Jewish cultures in Canada).

To conclude, blaming men for the problem of family violence in order to discredit the natural family is a vicious tactic. This is especially so when the alternative proposed is more State intervention, more male hating, more retreat from marriage, more childlessness, more divorce, more cohabitation, and more taxes and grants that enable women to fix upon marriage to the State as their best alternative to the real world. In the long run, the State is the worst master of all.

## Let's Tell the Truth

The truth is that the great majority of women (and men) in our society, by and large, have it pretty good. North American women are demonstrably the best-fed, best-educated, most materially well-off group of women that has ever existed. And Canadian women live in one of the safest, most free nations. North American women experience daily the greatest latitude of personal, family, and career choice among peoples of the world. To say they are an oppressed and exploited class is intellectually vulgar.

Rather, it is arguable that in our society, any woman who *at least* graduates from high school, gets and stays married to a good and stable provider, and has a child or two will surely be living the universal dream life. Consider this. With a loyal and committed husband (as most husbands are), she will be assured of lifelong income and material security, will not have to consign her children to impersonal high-turnover daycare paid for by others, will be her own boss for life, will be in control of life's and society's most valuable work, and will thus be freer in her career as homemaker than most men ever imagine in their careers. Finally, thanks to what I call the "frazzle curve," she may, if she wishes, spend the rest of her life after the children have departed — some 20 or 30 years — on interests of her choice.

Men, by contrast, must bend under the male millstone until 65, and as they die much younger, may only look forward to a mere nine years of devotion to personal interests, which will most likely be spent in failing health. The "expectations" laid upon males to provide and protect are as strong as any laid upon women to nurture. And males, if they were silly enough, could make an excellent case for social victimization. In Canada, males, as we have seen, are by far the more numerous victims of violent assault and murder. Also, 80 percent of suicides are male. Men suffer four times as many work injuries as do women, and 97 percent of all occupational deaths are male. As for other forms of "discrimination" and bias? Men suffer from court bias (longer, tougher jail sentences than equivalent female criminals), support bias (males are expected to pay), power bias (they are widely expected to compete), custody bias (courts give children to wives), alimony bias (they are jailed for non-payment, but wives are not), an abortion/support bias (it's a jingle: "if she aborts, he has no say, but if she doesn't, he has to pay"). It's a long list. We could even argue for male "retirement equity" compensation from the State, and affirmative action forcing women to shoulder more of the economic stress of society until there was a "gender balance" in retirement years available. Maybe men could even sue the State for compensation, using discrimination based on "statistical disparity" as their Charter defence — a favourite feminist trick. And somehow we blithely overlook the fact that about 100 million men, not women, have been drafted and sent to their deaths in war in this century alone — to defend country, wives, and children. Now that would make a nice little class action against the State — and women — for discrimination based on sex, wouldn't it?

**The Frazzle Curve, the Female Padlock, and the Male Millstone**
The frazzle curve looks like this:

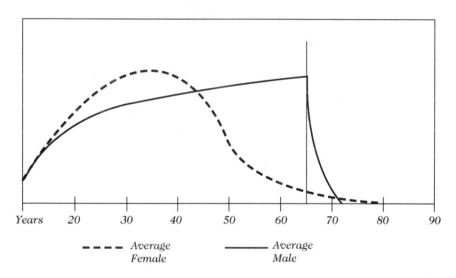

It basically shows what happens to most women and most men in terms of the amount of frazzle, or externally imposed stress, they bear throughout their life cycles. We can see that there is a stage in a woman's life (at least for those with lots of children) when she is indeed bearing most of the at-home frazzle, to be later compensated with her just reward of freer time. That is to say, a home with only a husband to look after is just not a full-time job. In fact, most women begin to experience the relief of significant free time once all their children are in school full days (most are like males, though: as the externally imposed burdens diminish, they create new, self-imposed ones).

The male, meanwhile, has a more continuous frazzle curve, which continues until he is 65 years of age, during which time, despite what feminists write, society continues to expect him to wear the male millstone of provider. Many men who retire early even say they feel a lot of guilt about no longer working. Unlike women, the great majority of men live their lives (if you like this sort of language) oppressed and exploited by their bosses and companies — by the "system" (to speak like a feminist). Males are oppressed by the social expectations of the lifelong provider role. In many cases, what they earn, where they live, and the like are controlled by others. During this time, they are largely working for their wives and children, not for themselves. The evidence for this is straightforward. Bachelors of all ages in North America earn half or less the income of married men with children — simply because they don't need the extra income themselves and lack the natural trepidation and therefore the motivation underlying the demands of family survival.

Contrary to the feminist line of argument about domestic "sharing,"[41] I would argue that to the extent her husband is on-track at work, and on an earnings curve sufficient to provide for the long-range future of the entire family, she *ought* to be bearing the domestic load, and he the external, financial load, and that these two loads, at least where the provider is experiencing significant job pressure and financial risk, cannot be equated. Of course, whether the husband or wife is the provider is a question for the couple to decide, not the society. And because of the female padlock — the biological deadline on her procreative life — most couples will opt for traditional roles. That's their business. My point simply is that if the couple wants to get ahead, to be efficient as an economic unit, they should preserve their specializations, not erode them. In short, any couple that tries to break down the specialization of labour which is the hallmark of the traditional family is working against its own economic self-interest. As economists like Gary Becker have shown, a sound marriage finds its economic justification only in the "exchange" of specialties brought to it by the husband and the wife. Whenever husband and wife arrange things so that both share everything, specialization is lost, and only a changeable affection remains, unsupported by other needs. Then, much of the basis for the marriage is lost. The whole point of a binding marriage is that each member of the unit not only should want each other, but should *need* the other in a complementary sense.

Conversely, a husband who holds back at the job, because he has more work waiting at home, is going to underperform at the job. He gets X number of hours to go all out, *at a speed and intensity dictated by others*. If he fails to give 120 percent, he will be replaced by someone willing to do so. In fact, an equivalently skilled go-getter husband with a traditional wife at home will beat him up the success ladder, because the go-getter is being pushed up by his family's expectations; the loser is being discouraged from working to the limit, and is pulled back into the work of the home. Of course, her work can be very stressful, too. But at least, once the high-demand baby period is over, she gets to control her own organizational world, is her own boss, sets her own deadlines, and so on. And she is not likely to get fired (but is more likely to quit).

Sure, it is pleasant for him to help out where he can. But it is not in the economic interest of any couple to bicker about sharing the diaper-changing at home, because they then fail to see that in terms of the economic success of their unit, they are far better off to organize their domestic lives around the provider's economic effort — to pressure him (or her) like crazy to succeed — than to turn the efforts of both inward. For the breadwinner to hold back is counter-productive. If they want more money (or fish, or potatoes), they should send the best earner/provider out to get it. This is a lesson we will soon be learning as a nation, as we continue to debilitate our families, our corporations, and our society with phony egalitarian squabble, most of it feminist-inspired. For if, as I suggest, the family supplies the economic motive to males, and the driving economic power to society, we are witless to erode the traditional unit. It would appear, however, that we are already doing so. As low-earning wives work more for the market, their much higher-earning husbands are working less (wives are working about 10 percent more, husbands about 5 percent less from 1975 to 1988, according to the *U.S. Statistical Abstract*, 1990). Another study has shown husbands working 12 percent less.[42]

So the trade-off goes something like this: Women who want the natural fulfilment of family and children must live with the innate knowledge that their procreative purpose is born with them and will soon live within them. Most crucially, they must plan according to a biological deadline. Males are the opposite. They early become intensely aware of their expected role and duty to family and society, and it is surely true that if we argue that women are in bondage to their biology and the home, then men are in bondage to their biology, to their provider role, and to the market. This means that most women will instinctively choose a life that permits the full expression of their female nature, and will tend instinctively to avoid a career track that denies this natural expression. My own wife (and now also my eldest daughter) consciously did this. They sensed the looming conflict between their instincts and the careers available. Their bottom line was home and family, not boss and taxes, and they chose accordingly. Men normally do the opposite. From the age of first mature awareness, they worry like crazy about what they are going to do with their lives. Conversely, most Canadian and American female high-school students even today, after decades of bombastic feminist propaganda, still say that what they want most in life is a good husband and children, and that *they do not expect to work for more than five years* after graduation.[43] Even when women do work in the market, they tend to utilize far less of their "earnings capacity" than men, are far more likely than men to leave their jobs, and do so far more frequently.

They're not stupid. They know that a traditional family is the most meaningful arrangement available. In our society, at least, we are wealthy enough that having fulfilled their biological imperative, the majority of women can turn their energies to more personal or public tasks at a relatively early age. This is sadly not so for those of low income, who must abide by the female padlock and also bend under the male millstone, as they have in every prior century. That's why radical feminism is simply not supported by the poor, or by low-income immigrants. For them, as for most, the dream is to get *out* of, not *into*, the labour market. To them, feminism is a rich-bitch phenomenon. Feminist scholar Jean Beth Elshtain admitted this when she wrote that of the feminists pushing for equal rights, almost all were "upper middle class and relatively affluent," while their female opponents were "lower middle class, and ethnic, religious, and racial minorities," who saw in feminism "a move to impose on them an alien vision of personhood and family." Black Americans, in particular, "cannot relate to the desires of white women to enter the labour force . . . or to be freed of child-care responsibilities . . . to many black women who are heading households, a [providing] husband would be a welcome figure."[44]

The facts are that any half-intelligent young woman in a free society will likely do her own cost-benefit analysis on life as she sees it, and say: A husband? Legitimate sex? Children of my own, to raise myself? Maybe a small house and a car? And if my marriage is economically successful, a good shot at experiencing the highest forms of civilized life, such as the arts, the hobbies, some relaxation, perhaps some charity work — all this will be mine to explore? Point me in the right direction!

Chart 23, in Chapter Six, tells us that this is exactly what they are doing. Fully 50 percent of Canadian women ages 45 to 65 are not in the labour market at all! With a small but growing number of exceptions, many of whom are being supported by the taxes sucked from intact families, Canadian men and women are overwhelmingly basing their lives on the realities of the frazzle curve, and the complementary trade-offs between the female padlock, and the male millstone.

# 13

# Radical Homosexuals vs. the Family

*The heterosexual family unit — spawning ground of lies, betrayals, mediocrity, hypocrisy and violence — shall be abolished.*

GAY COMMUNITY NEWS[1]

*All we are trying to do is take the moral connotation and judgment out of homosexuality.*

MARIE LAING, NDP MEMBER OF THE ALBERTA LEGISLATURE[2]

*[I have] a healthy commitment to depravity.*

GERALD HANNON, TORONTO GAY ACTIVIST,<br>GLOBE AND MAIL, APRIL 4, 1992

Just in time for Christmas, 1978, "Gay Bob," the world's first homosexual doll, toting his own closet, a blue earring, and a California tan, was placed gingerly on the toy shelves of New York and San Francisco (Associated Press, August 4, 1978). His sterile gaze met the confused eyes of thousands of otherwise happy children, as their parents struggled to explain the inexplicable. But his inventor, Harvey Rosenberg, who sold over 2000 Gay Bobs in the first two months, had no trouble explaining it. The impetus behind his creation, said Rosenberg, feeling "an internal ecstasy" over Bob's popularity, was the philosophy that everyone ought "to have the courage to stand up and say 'I have a right to be what I am.'"

Gay Bob was, however, more than a money-making venture. He was a pathetic capitulation to modern pansexualism — the idea, promoted most strenuously by the worldwide homosexual movement and by many "sexologists," that all consenting sex, no matter how, or with whom, or what, is good. The presence of Bob on the shelf for the highest celebration of the Christian year was a direct assault on normalcy as perceived by children, an affront to the values of millions of families, and a symbolic expression of the civil war of values raging throughout the Judeo-Christian world. It was also very clever. Propagandists the world over waste little time on the present generation. They go straight for the fresh young minds, hungry for approval and eager to digest whatever belief system adults wish to feed them.

Should human sexuality be intimately interwoven with life's higher moral purposes, protected and directed in the service of procreative, social, and spiritual goals? Or is all human sexuality, and therefore much of what constitutes human values, solely a personal matter, with no wider purpose in which society ought to have a say? The answer to this question is the answer to how a people lives.

By the time Gay Bob appeared, the U.S. "National Gay Rights Platform" (spelled out in 1972 and supported by Canadian homosexuals) had already changed the way people think about sex and about homosexuality. Their increasingly strident platform called and still calls for many things, among them:

- the abolition of all laws governing "age of sexual consent," thus enabling adults to have sex with consenting children of any age or either sex;
- the repeal of all laws against sodomy and adult or child prostitution;
- the homosexual right to legally adopt and have custody of minor children;
- the repeal of all laws that restrict the sex or number of persons entering into a marriage unit.

As a general comment to this chapter, I should state my view that as citizens of a free country, homosexuals ought to have the same legal *protections* as any other citizen, as long as they keep their proclivities to themselves, but never the same *privileges*. And I know that there are a lot of respectable, kind-hearted, talented homosexuals out there. But that's not the issue here. The issue is that homosexuals have broken the implicit pact of a conservative society, which has always been to tolerate unnatural private behaviour, but never to approve of it; nor allow it any public weight; and certainly never to force acceptance of it upon the citizens at large. But by using concepts of individual (Charter-supported) rights against the larger society in the name of legitimizing unnatural behaviour, homosexuals are intentionally attacking this pact, and the concept of the natural family it was created to protect. Tired of the stigma of the unnatural, radical homosexuals now argue that protection is not enough. They want affirmation of their values and behaviour; they want the same social and legal privileges that accrue to those who follow society's moral dictates, and are determined to get them by changing public morality itself, even if it means destroying traditional society. So this chapter is not about homosexual individuals who are minding their own business. Nor is it intended to hurt the feelings of otherwise proper homosexual citizens, many of whom are themselves extremely distraught by homosexual behaviour and the radical agenda. Rather, it is about the terribly destructive effect of the homosexual lobby on our most treasured social and moral institutions. It's a counter-attack on the whole process and philosophy of homosexuality.

Unbelievably, radical homosexuals have become so influential and mainstream ever since about 1960, that by 1977 the U.S. federal Commission on Civil Rights actually called (so far unsuccessfully) for a lowering of the age of consent for all sexual acts, from the current 14 for heterosexual and 18 for homosexual acts, to age 12 for both. Such a law would have given anyone the "right" to sexually use consenting children in any way they pleased without fear of parental interference. In other words, under such a law, you couldn't legally prevent a 40-year-old from seducing your "consenting" 12-year-old son or daughter. In Holland today, the age of consent for homosexual sex is 12 — as long as the parents do not formally object. Such laws, wherever they may arise in history, always represent a blatant retreat by the State from its traditional protections: of the family, of sound parental authority, of children from bad parents, of the sexual exclusivity of the family, and of normal procreational life. And the pressure continues apace. How can it be that the basic principles of Western liberalism have been co-opted by such special interest groups who, with the help of the top-down State, have turned these same liberal principles against the family as a social institution? Here is just one example of how it works. Homosexuals argue that under the Canadian Charter of Rights and

Freedoms it is discriminatory to have different ages of consent based on "sexual orientation." Top-down Charter vs. bottom-up morals.

Well, after two decades of stunning success in the homosexual revolution against society and the family, neighbours were not surprised when, in August 1988, one Terry Pagel of Port Angeles, Washington, was picked up by police for sodomizing a 13-year-old foster child legally placed in his care — by that state's Department of Health and Human Services. The department had known all along that Pagel was homosexual, and it was also aware that a 16-year-old boy, also placed in his care, had some months prior been convicted of sodomizing the same 13-year-old in Pagel's home. However, a department spokesman, apparently a passionate defender of so-called gay rights, said the department had "absolutely no intention of changing its policies" on placing troubled children with known homosexuals (*New Dimensions*, January 1990). Pagel argued in his own defence that he had not coerced the seduction of the younger by the older boy, and therefore, his reasoning went, he had done no wrong. Notice that he used the defence of "free choice" in his attack on tradition. The year prior, 42-year-old David Allen Lindsey of Florida, a "father" who had "adopted" 11 young boys, was discovered to have routinely sodomized them. He said on his way to jail, "I get more out of the boys than out of freedom."[3] Homosexual Robert Tucker, who died of AIDS at 57, had legally adopted 17 boys along the way (Philadelphia *Gay News*, March 8, 1991).

There are those who say that lots of ordinary heterosexuals abuse children in this way, so why am I upset when homosexuals do it? I answer, Yes, a disturbing number of such cases have always occurred (although homosexuals proportionately are far more prone to such abuse, as we shall see). The young are vulnerable to adult abuse and perversion by either sex. However, until about the 1970s, society always tried to protect its young by developing stringent moral codes — and laws — *against* the proliferation of such acts by defining them as *unnatural*, and punishing them severely. But now, for the first time in the history of modern civilization, we have become so morally weak — so cowed by an aberrant notion of "rights" (based on a notion of freedom unconnected from responsibility, or duty to society) — that homosexuals have actually been able to redefine such acts as natural and acceptable. Thus, we now enact laws to protect such acts, or — amounting to the same thing — we remove laws to forbid them.

There is quite a difference, after all, between doing something you know is wrong, and doing something wrong but defending it as right.

But this is the direction of our moral drift. As a nation, we are shrinking from the hard job of facing and dealing with an increasingly abnormal society. We have decided to cope not by reconstituting our traditional responsibilities, but by permissively redefining the problems, and then enshrining protection for these redefinitions in various social charters. This latter half of the coping mechanism enables us to walk about with our heads held high under the assumption some invisible legal power has blessed our aberrant behaviour. How such a conflict between morality and the law is possible in democratic nations where huge majorities on survey after survey declare that homosexuality is wrong and abnormal is rather extraordinary. About 81 percent of Americans on a recent National Opinion Research survey said that homosexual relations were "wrong";[4] in Canada, 70 percent say they "do not approve of homosexuality."[5] Most human beings everywhere have always said this throughout recorded history. Yet, both nations have been transformed at an astonishing pace into homophiliac societies that, in the name of a putative "equality," are busily undermining the natural family.

### How Equal "Rights" Undermine Social Values

Of course, homosexuals are correct about unfairness. All social groups, and society as a whole, are *intentionally unfair* to all who fall outside their norms. That's why all social groups and society at large — a group of groups — have standards of cohesion and rules of conduct. They serve as an organizing principle for group survival, and are based on affinities between members that are by definition exclusionary. Private girls' schools exclude boys; black soul-music stations hire blacks and play black music; armies have always fought with men, not women; private malls exclude bums; francophone clubs exclude anglophones; corporations shelter only their own employees; nations protect only their own citizens; and societies based on the political, economic, and legal privileges of the heterosexual family unit refuse to privilege outsiders — such as the unmarried, bachelors, or homosexuals. And of course homosexuals have all kinds of exclusive groups, clubs, and services. Christopher Street Financial Services in New York City is a financial firm "catering exclusively to the gay community" (*Globe and Mail*, December 1, 1991). The Los Angeles City School District has asked the local gay and lesbian association to operate "a boarding school for homosexual teenagers" (Washington *Times*, November 11, 1991).

A key point of this book, and of this chapter, is that all social groups, positioned as they are between the individual and the State — exist and survive in the first place precisely because they are exclusionary. They are real-world expressions of some common and distinctive underlying set of values. But we must be wary. The sad history of our times is that through the use of government-imposed charters and other legal interpretations that often "find" individual rights where none are written, we are rapidly destroying our cherished institutions. Into the vacuum will rush the ever-ready State. This is the destructive dynamics of totalitarian democracy: Rights and freedoms originally meant to protect the individual against an oppressive State increasingly become used — in the name of equality — by individuals against privileged social groups. The right to be treated equally by the State is transmuted into the right to have equal privileges from society — privileges formerly reserved for those who earned them.

For all social groupings are based on an authoritative hierarchy of particular moral values. But when their exclusive privileges are destroyed with the weapon of charter-based individual rights, they themselves are destroyed. Then, new groupings arise, which are based not on morals but on political power. In short, political power-groups destroy traditional social groups by using the notion of individual rights as a battering ram to demolish all legal privileges. Such is our present dilemma.

In these campaigns, exclusionary institutions (the family, the church, private clubs, etc.) that do not treat everyone equally — even those people who have none of the characteristics on the basis of which the institution was formed in the first place (nor any reason to join), must be destroyed. This attack will lead to the eventual homogenization and therefore ruination of all traditional social institutions, because it will gradually dissipate their founding purposes and their basis for action. They will erode at an alarming clip. (There is a good argument that some groups, with violent or anti-social purposes, ought to be destroyed. These are of a separate class altogether.) Male (or female) schools, clubs, teams, societies, or business groups will be forced to include the opposite sex (and vice versa); male armies will be forced to use women in battle; private malls will be controlled by public bureaucrats and increasingly redefined as public spaces; language- or culture-based groups will be forced to include outsiders who want access; groups with age limitations will be forced open to all ages; churches will be forced to ordain atheists and homosexuals; apartment owners will be forced to rent to smokers, or to people whose behaviour offends their religious beliefs. Even sororities will be forced to accept men.

In the end — and it will be the end — all positive social institutions, increasingly redefined as negative, will be forced by law to reconstitute themselves based not on social or moral affinity, but on a bureaucratically defined and controlled model of an egalitarian society. This culmination will be the ultimate in our modern endeavour to bury differences, hierarchy, and exclusionary social affinities and the values that gave rise to them. At this stage, every social entity is first expected, and then required by law, to reflect the larger whole. All smaller social institutions are forced to import the appropriate decreed mix of social groups (and tensions) to be considered non-exclusionary. The judges and courts of the land go insane attempting to adjudicate the impossible. Standards of fairness and right and wrong become based on demographic and judicial bean-counting. In the end, we will stare at our reflected social selves as we disappear into an infinity of sameness, a reflection reflected. Entropy, at last.

The great sadness of this socially suicidal process is that we have confused the moral and social debate. For the test of a good society should not be the question what is fair and what is not, but rather, which, of all the unfair systems, is the best, since none can ever be fair to all. Clearly, in the case of homosexuality, it is far better for a normal society to be unfair to homosexuals in the name of its own social health, than to be unfair to the entire society in the name of fairness to homosexuals (or any other pressure group).

At any rate, radical homosexuals want to destroy the natural family because its very existence defines them by exclusion as unnatural. And yet, in the same breath, they clamour to be defined and accepted as "family" themselves. Obviously, the only way they can have what they want is to redefine what is natural. This means they need a campaign to eradicate all differences between themselves and all other people who have normal sexual and social habits.

## Getting the Same Rights

On October 11, 1987, 200,000 homosexuals marched on Washington, D.C., demanding that their sexual liaisons be recognized as legal marriages (Toronto's homosexual Metropolitan Community Church now offers "blessing" rites for homosexual couples, or "holy union"); the right to joint income tax returns; the right to adopt children; that young children be taught homosexual acts in the schools; and so on. They want the same health, bereavement, insurance, pension, adoption, inheritance, hospital visitation, tax, veterans' benefits, residence, and even frequent-flyer travel rights as legal married couples.

As a direct result of this homosexual assault, the historical privileges of the natural family are crumbling at a frightening pace. In October 1990, Canadian Justice Joseph McDonald "found" sexual "orientation" in the equality section of the Charter of Rights and Freedoms (where it is not mentioned). On October 3, 1990, the City of Toronto decided to extend medical benefits to same-sex "spouses" of its employees. The Province of Ontario then gave job benefits, bereavement leave, medical benefits, and insurance benefits to civil servants' homosexual partners. "Starting today," the media boasted, "the term 'spouse' . . . has been extended to include [heterosexual] couples who are cohabiting . . . or homosexual relationships" (Toronto *Star*, January 1, 1990). And California recently enacted a "domestic partners" policy to provide its burgeoning homosexual population (as well as cohabiting heterosexual couples) with all the rights and benefits of normal married couples (Toronto *Star*, May 12, 1989). Homosexual prisoners in Canada now have rights to "conjugal visits" with friends (*Globe and Mail*, November 7, 1989). Toronto's socialist (NDP) City Council has voted to "ban" the Salvation Army, because it opposes homosexuality. Whether or not they demand "rights" to join the military or the boy scouts, or so-called "employment equity" hiring to teach young children in the schools, homosexuals will soon have them.

Ontario's Government Services minister articulated the underlying theme of family destruction in all this when she declared, in a burst of self-righteous egalitarian rhetoric, that "the major consideration in the changes is the principle that all of Ontario's laws and programs must treat people fairly, regardless of their personal relationships" (Toronto *Star*, December 21, 1990). There could be no clearer statement of the manner in which the Individualism Illusion has operated to annihilate the special social status of the family: how marriage and the family, conceived as a social unit with a *higher* value, status, and purpose than that of a mere individual, is rapidly being atomized in the name of individual rights. This is the "lowering" process of which Philip Rieff spoke. In its name, but oblivious to the consequences, the minister, seeing herself as a warrior in the fight against injustice instead of an agent of social decay, commenced a rampage to hunt down and change "at least 79 [laws] that define 'spouse' as a member of the opposite sex." Acting as an agent of social decay ought to be peculiar for a socialist, but in fact it is routine, for it is precisely the ministers of any egalitarian State who make this their special priority. This is exactly what Tocqueville, Nisbet, and so many others have warned would happen once any democracy succumbed to that powerful tandem, the Equality Illusion and the Rights Illusion. They knew that the minions of the State would attempt to increase the power of the State by diluting the privileges of all intermediate, spontaneous associations, because these are the very ones that tend to generate values opposed to those of the State. So they must be hobbled. This technique is essential to any modern program of sexual revolution, and it emerged early in the first instance, the French Revolution, where "'sexual liberation' and casual sex were from the very beginning weapons . . . intended to destroy the *ancien régime* of human nature, family, religion . . . and usher in the age of bliss"[6] of which all utopians and social engineers dream.

This demolition is accomplished not by directly *removing* any special protections for such groups, but by *bestowing* similar rights on all those not formerly included, thus equalizing, and therefore dissolving, all semblance of social privilege by spreading it equally among the masses. This insidious process leaves individuals, who formerly identified with and found their natural bonds of community within such freely formed entities, naked before the edicts of the State, with only a broken shield against it. Thus do the people, starved for bonds yet deprived of spontaneous community and privilege, turn hungrily to the State for identity and solace once the family unit has been all but demolished. To a great extent, the homosexual movement has been the vanguard of this destruction. For homosexuals have mounted a powerful campaign to exact from society not merely a legal tolerance of their habits and behaviours, but public approval and affirmation of them — a very different thing.

The only way the movement could achieve this goal was through the dilution of social definitions and legal privileges. This process is now widespread in our society. It starts in kindergarten and pervades our school textbooks, universities, government bureaucracies, and law.

The basis of their strategy, consistent with that of the top-down State, has been a clever campaign to avert attention from their unnatural *behaviour* (to be described below; brace yourself) by forcing us to focus on their individual *civil rights*, or legal status, instead. They are successfully attempting to position themselves under our Charter as equivalent to blacks or women in society — as just another visible minority that happens to be a victim of discrimination and prejudice. A Toronto *Star* article, "Gay Couple Go to Court to Fight for Right to Marry" (May 19, 1992), illustrates this point perfectly. The frustrated "groom" said, "I think in this country if blacks were denied the right to marry . . . or Jews or French Canadians, there would be an uproar." To achieve their desired result, they push the Victim Illusion and the Tolerance Illusion to the hilt, striving to make society at large feel so guilty about its "intolerance" of their civil rights that it will finally yield and give them what they want. "Teach Tolerance of Gays, Toronto Schools Urged," we are admonished, again in the Toronto *Star* (November 30, 1991). But a careful reader will soon see that the article is not pushing tolerance; it is pushing approval. It wants to force school children to approve of homosexuality by "making the discussion of homophobia mandatory." Of course, there is nothing in the article about making the discussion of the natural family and heterosexual marriage mandatory, or discussing the familyphobia of homosexuals.

But the huge difference between homosexuals and other victim groups is that the others are defined by some non-behavioural characteristic, such as race, or colour, or gender, *whereas homosexuals are defined by their behaviour alone*. To use legitimate civil rights grounds for behaviour choice is wrong. As a U.S. black activist put it, "The freedom bus that went to Selma, was never intended to go on to Sodom." For to allow this confusion means that any group that likes to practise a certain type of behaviour can blame it on some cause beyond its control, muster sufficient political (or junk-science) clout to frighten politicians and the media, then claim protected status under the law and the Charter. In this insidious capitulation to the demands of a tiny minority with peculiar appetites, we can see the process of a cascading legal approbation, from the formerly grand heights of a moral society downward to mere behaviourally defined minorities. Thus have the top-down State and the homosexual-egalitarian agenda been bedfellows. They have together dissolved our respect for the only institution of society — the family — that has historically protected us from State power, and from homosexuality.

The point is not that all families are good. Of course they are not. For that matter, most people, although imperfect by nature, are not good, or bad, by nature. They behave the way they do because of a social and moral reality that confines them by presenting a menu, so to speak, of what is acceptable and unacceptable. But history does suggest that when the natural family fails, all other methods for ordering human life tried in its place are far, far worse, because their only ordering principle, in the end, is power. Thus does humanity tend to drift toward political, economic, and moral chaos. That is likely why the specific purpose of the *privileges* of the natural family has always been the generation of invisible but powerful moral carrots and sticks to guide disparate, purposeless individuals into a social and moral order deemed best for society and the procreation of the human race. It's as if at some unconscious level wise societies have always known that the general sexual energy of humanity, unconfined by any hierarchial moral order, will always seek approval for what is essentially narcissistic, masturbatory self-indulgence, and be loosed to maraud against the larger social order.

Let the record of history also show that in the measure that the machinations of the top-down State erode the bottom-up society, aspirations to moral order eventually dissolve. Hard-won values and family privileges then capitulate, as myriad social groups mire themselves in an escalating struggle for political power fuelled by spurious rights to social privileges and the ever-diminishing resources of the State. The sexual order, or disorder, of society is thus like a bellwether of the general social condition. Rampant divorce, illegitimacy, serial polygyny, latchkey children, widespread pornography, the legalization of sodomy — these are the fragments that clothe us in the end.

## Born, Made, or Homosexual by Choice?

There is great frustration over the exact cause of homosexuality. For throughout human history homosexuals have been considered abnormal, and therefore persecuted, excommunicated, or even killed for their behaviour. The term "faggot" comes from the ancient practice of throwing them on bonfires. They have reason to be nervous, for historically they themselves have always born an animus against normal society; in their unending campaign for self-respect they have rightly identified the natural family as their enemy.

### Born Homosexual?

The hope latent in the modern homosexual strategy for acceptance is thus to find some "natural" cause of their behaviour. This is what lies behind their push to have what various laws and charters call *enumerated rights*, which normally extend only to race, colour, or gender — to those who are "born with it." After all, if you are born with a condition that causes you to behave in a certain way, then you cannot be said to have chosen that behaviour. It is "natural," and therefore you cannot be charged with immoral conduct. In the United States, some sex educators in a few states have already gone right into the schools with this message. Through a program called "the Link," telephones are installed in the classroom, connecting students to "value-neutral" sex and drug information. The program says homosexuality "is not a choice. It's a given. Like left-handedness. It's determined before birth." The tape then refers curious students to the National Gay and Lesbian Crisis line.

The difficulty with this view, however, is that no one has ever found a single replicable genetic, hormonal, or chemical difference between homosexuals and heterosexuals.[7] Furthermore, even if there were a natural physical cause, it ought to be found evenly throughout the populations of the world. In fact, in 1984 the Institute for the Scientific Investigation of Sexuality found that children raised in non-religious homes had a 450 percent higher chance of choosing the homosexual life-style.[8] And there is apparently little or no homosexuality in China, in the former Soviet Union, in Israeli kibuttzim, or in various religious sects such as the Amish. In other words, culture, belief systems, and plain old strong morals can protect society against growing homosexuality. In this vein, University of Toronto Professor of Psychiatry Joseph Berger writes: "I have never come across anyone with 'innate homosexuality.' That notion has been a long-proclaimed gay-activist political position, intended to promote the acceptance of homosexuality as a healthy, fully equal, alternative expression of human sexuality. It has zero scientific foundation, though its promoters latch on to even the flimsiest shreds of atrocious research in their attempts to justify the notion" (Letter, *Globe and Mail*, February 26, 1992).

Regardless of how many studies are generated on this topic, the debate is pointless, for the following reasons. First of all, if it were true that homosexuals are born genetically so, then a calculation based on genetic replication or natural selection suggests their numbers would diminish fast, not multiply, simply because they do not reproduce. More tricky still, it is dangerous for them to argue that they are born homosexual, because what they do has always been universally despised. If homosexuality is found to have a physical cause, then society will likely set about to root it out. The offending gene, or whatever, will get excised at birth. So they had better not argue that way if they want to preserve their habits. But the search for scientific evidence homosexuals are born that way is a dead-end, politically. For example, one controversial German researcher, Dr. Gunter Dörner, has argued that homosexuality in humans is a direct function of the precise timing of greater or lesser prenatal doses of male hormone. But he also claims that with prenatal hormonal injections, homosexuality can be prevented.[9] This argument has predictably sparked ferocious anger from homosexuals, who accuse him of equating their condition with a disease. They would rather argue that it is natural.

But the "gay is natural" argument doesn't work either, simply because lots of things that are bad for us or bad for society are "natural." Many cancers are natural. So are heart disease, tuberculosis, and sexually transmitted diseases. Society is not required to encourage or protect things just because they are "natural." On the contrary, it tends to sort out the natural good from the natural bad and then organize for self-protection, whether against physical, social, or moral threats. Neither can we argue, as Toronto "sexologist" Sue Johansen has done, that homosexuality is natural to the beasts. According to W. Gadpaille, writing in the *Archives of General Psychiatry* (1980), "preferential homosexuality is not found naturally in any infrahuman mammalian species."[10] In fact, the best argument against homosexuality, other than those found in the great religions of the world, is that it's utterly contrary to every natural law of human and animal life, and counter to the morals, purposes, and institutions of a procreative society. There simply is no good argument for homosexuality. There are lots of bad ones, though.

### Made Homosexual?

Some psychiatrists argue that homosexuals are made, not born; that human sexuality is a non-directed drive steered by society into heterosexual pathways, and homosexuals have somehow strayed from the right path.[11] Mothers and fathers mostly get blamed for this, and in the heyday of Freudian psychology it was the standard view that all male homosexuals had domineering, seductive, manipulating mothers (who sheltered them with sissy love) and ineffectual, often absent fathers (weak male role-model). Irving Bieber maintained that in none of the cases he treated or studied had there ever been a normal father–son relationship. A Toronto psychiatrist told me that all the homosexuals he treats have had "unsatisfactory relations" with their parents. About 40 percent of all lesbians have dead or divorced mothers.

The permutations and combinations of these various theories are mind-boggling. They lead all sorts of social scientists and psychiatrists to experiment with the social environment in the hope of discovering the exact dynamics underlying this "condition." But homosexuals don't like these theories either, because the implication is that pathology is present — that they are sick — and therefore society is correct to shun their ways and seek a cure. They have visions of State supervisors seeking them out as infants and placing them in re-education clinics. In this respect, one of the most chilling suspects as a spawning ground for increasing homosexuality must surely be long-term daycare. That's because developmental psychologists have discovered that the 18- to 24-month period of life is crucial in the formation of sex-role identity. Some psychiatrists see homosexuality in females as an effort to make up for inadequate mothering in childhood, a striving to recover "the ecstatic conditions of infancy."[12] The British psychologist Elizabeth Moberly argues convincingly that "the homosexual love-need is essentially a search for parenting." She writes that "[t]he central factor in all cases is that needs that should have been met through the parent-child attachment, remain yet to be met. What the homosexual seeks is the fulfilment of these normal attachment needs, which have abnormally been left unmet in the process of growth."[13] If Moberly is correct, then from the egalitarian/feminist drive for tax-funded universal daycare we can expect to see a horrendous unintended consequence: tax-funded centres for sexual pathology.

At any rate, most parents strongly feel that homosexuals are made, not born, and they don't want their kids around them. In 1985, the Institute for the Scientific Investigation of Sexuality (ISIS, renamed the Family Research Institute in 1989) found that 97 percent of heterosexual males and females reported that their first sexual experience was heterosexual, while 85 percent of homosexual men and 29 percent of lesbians said their first experience was homosexual or bisexual.[14]

What both explanatory models have in common is a reliance on the Determinist Illusion: the idea that something outside ourselves is responsible for what we are and therefore, by extension, for our behaviour and our moral choices.

### Homosexual by Choice?

Once the first two models are rejected because they suggest a curable pathology, homosexuals are left with only a free-choice model. This makes them most uncomfortable of all, because it states that all human behaviour is an outcome of personal values, self-control, and character. This means that faced with the option to charm or to yield to someone of the same or of the opposite sex, there is always a decision point — a point at which they can accept or refuse their own urges, curiosities, temptations, or lusts. Most of all, there is a point at which they are able to direct, or redirect, the outcome of their own lives based on values they freely sustain or refuse. They are choosing their own behaviour. And in choosing their own behaviour, they are behaving as moral agents in society, and bear some responsibility for all social outcomes. This was Immanuel Kant's argument: that even in the absence of a religious moral code, humans can guide themselves by what he called a "categorical imperative." This imperative — I am paraphrasing — takes the form of a single serious question to be asked whenever we undertake any act, namely: "What kind of world will be created if everyone does what I am doing?" In other words, Kant argued that by choosing certain behaviours, we *legitimize* them for all others. But even the most radical homosexual cannot make a sound moral argument that the world would be a better place if everyone chose his way. For one thing, there would be no one left in the world to enjoy it. It is thus ludicrous to argue that homosexuality can be legitimate, or life-affirming, behaviour. So they are caught on the horns of a moral dilemma.

Nevertheless, faced with sexual appetites they want to satisfy, in a world that has elevated personal gratification to a near theological status, some homosexuals take this position defiantly. They are choosing their behaviour because it is good. Thus, proponents of the activist group Queer Nation go public, feverishly chanting: "We're Queer! We're Proud! We're Fabulous!" and threatening, like Toronto member Greg Pavelich, that "we're not going to be good little boys and girls any more." Greg said he felt "a great sense of power" while deep kissing his gay partner in public (Toronto *Star*, January 21, 1991). What he more likely felt was the short-lived burst of relief that always arises whenever human beings confuse strength in numbers with moral strength.

As it turns out, however, most homosexuals reject the choice model for political reasons, simply because it puts the onus on them to explain why they have chosen unnatural behaviour that is bad for society. The fact that about 60 percent of all homosexuals agree that they "could be changed to exclusive heterosexuality" further underlines their political stance (C. Williams and M. Weinberg, 1971).

### The Author's Model
My view is that any human population could be made homosexual under certain extreme conditions. For example, a group of young

children with no prior sexual knowledge, raised on a desert island by a homosexual, would likely end up fancying homosexual behaviour themselves. In other words, it is quite possible to train a young population to like homosexual behaviour. What prevents this from happening on a large scale are the social sanctions against it. Societies intentionally suppress homosexual behaviour so that such extreme situations cannot arise.

Secondly, there may be very small numbers of people with a predisposition, however caused, to choose homosexual behaviour. Notice that I used all the models here. Some may be predisposed, in the way an alcoholic may be predisposed to drink if drink is available. But nothing except personal desire makes the bottle (or the penis) jump into his mouth. After all, all societies have people with predispositions to all sorts of weird appetites and behaviours, whether homosexuality, suicide, drunkenness, killing, stealing, overeating, or bad temper. This has always been so, and it is not going to go away. We are only going to exhaust ourselves trying to figure out why, and we likely will always wind up in a conflict of expertise in which biased experts with warring political agendas dispute each other's findings for eternity. It's a dead end.

So my third point has to do with the enabling structure of personal liberation ideology, as follows.

### The Inner God of Nature vs. the Outer God of Morals
Much of the modern social dialogue really seems to boil down to a change of gods. At the high point of our Judeo-Christian world (remember, about 90 percent of Canadians — and Americans — still declare that they belong to this religious group), our God was distinctly a moral God, standing outside His creation at the apex of a hierarchy of values that provided a clear moral ranking of all human behaviour and a system of reward and punishment, forgiveness, and redemption. All high cultures of the world have had such a God — or gods — of morals, serving as a brake on human abandonment to self, appetite, impulse, and violence.

What people in weakening cultures like our own seem to do is to seek a justification for abandoning themselves to their own senses by attributing a kind of religious virtue to the very appetites that cause the trouble. This is achieved first by a systematic effort to abandon all outer ("imposed") notions of "right and wrong" that flow from the moral residue of the old moral God; and then by swearing allegiance to the newly crowned inner God of nature. In the measure that the old outer moral faith, which provided us with stern standards but left us free to rise or fall on the basis of our conduct, has waned, the inner faith has taken over. The inner God of nature now dictates what we shall be, and every predetermined alternative (or orientation) is good. Well, what a relief! There's no longer any need to worry about personal moral standards or behaviour, because no longer can we do wrong.

In other words, if you don't like the judgment, you just get rid of the judge. High self-esteem is everything, says the new dogma (no longer must it be earned), and it will result from obeying the inner God of nature. Most of all, as Gay Bob put it, let me "be what I am." Things have changed a lot. When Shakespeare's Polonius warned, "This above all: to thine own self be true," he meant that we should listen to moral reason and not deceive ourselves with our own desires. But the first commandment of the new cult is: Be Thyself. There is no need for a commandment to be good, since whatever constitutes your self — it's your decision — is now good. It's a tautology, or a circular argument. The new therapeutic and educational goal is therefore not to teach the moral way, but to eliminate all self-doubt, recrimination, and guilt.

Of course it follows that any difficulty we experience in becoming one with our inner God must have arisen from the "imposition" of bad social conditioning, either by parents or by a patriarchal society. So we no longer talk of higher values, but only about "conflicting" values. And psychiatrists will not discuss homosexuality as a sickness (far too judgmental) unless the patient thinks it is one (then he is said to be "egodystonic," meaning, in self-conflict). Well, the tail seems to be wagging the dog here. Today, the good doctor's job is to make the patient feel at ease with his inner God, which is a metaphor for the patient's own feelings. The task now is not to help the patient align with the core hierarchical values of the culture, but to make him feel less in conflict about his deep (but authentic) desire, say, to sodomize little boys. If we can only get rid of the law against it, he will likely feel just fine. Thus, we have the professional sanctification of narcissism and evil (for only $75 an hour, prepaid through taxes). Shake off all imposed moral standards, and ye shall be free. We have arrived at the Man-god. It's a dangerous, thoroughly professionalized, farce.

So my last point is merely that we don't really need the ultimate truth about homosexuality, or any other weirdism. What we need is to allow society to defend itself in values and law against the likelihood of such behaviours as homosexuality, simply because they are unnatural and antisocial in all the ways mentioned. The vast majority will always reject homosexuality, and for this reason alone society must be allowed to structure its political, economic, and legal institutions to strongly discourage such tendencies and opportunities wherever they may arise. Any society will always need some means to protect itself against the hordes of individuals walking around with the nefarious idea that they are obeying the dictates of an inner God of nature. The real danger comes when such individuals end up controlling the major institutions of society itself. Some insight into this process can be gleaned from one of the most astounding facts of criminal life, which is that the overwhelming majority of vicious sex murderers, after multiple convictions for crimes so heinous you would be ill just to read of them, *still see themselves as morally upright*. Multiple murderer Charles Manson insisted on this point in his March 1992 appeal hearing. Ordinary people think he is crazy; but in fact he is obedient to a tightly structured inner logic supplied by his inner God. Such people are bewildered that we do not agree with their assessment of themselves. So we must do what is suggested here to protect especially the young, whether inside or outside the home, because under optimal circumstances they are the most easily persuaded or converted.

Homosexuals know this. That's why they insist on getting into our schools and teaching our children about proper anal sex procedures (under the pretext that they will protect the young from AIDS; however, one is most likely to contract AIDS from anal sex). An integral part of the 1972 "Gay Rights Platform" (point 6) calls for "encouragement and support for sex education courses, prepared and taught by Gay women and men, presenting homosexuality as a valid, healthy preference and lifestyle, as a viable alternative to heterosexuality." The platform also wants to "repeal all laws governing the age of sexual consent." And that's why the slogan of the North American Man-Boy Love Association (NAMBLA) is: "Sex Before Eight, or Else It's Too Late!" (They mean eight years of age, not eight at night.)

David Thorstad, a spokesman for NAMBLA, says his organization "takes the view that sex is good, that homosexuality is good, not only for adults, but for young people as well." He talks of the "liberation" of children (from traditional and family values), saying that NAMBLA members want to help all children "break the yoke of 'protection' . . . imposed on them by adults — their family, the schools, the state, and prevailing sexual and social mores."[15] The image-marketing group for NAMBLA, called the Task Force on

Child-Adult Relations (TFCAR), pursues these same goals, but in its own lists (read this carefully), said they wanted "Liaison with feminist and other groups to establish the principle that the goals of all liberation groups are essentially the same: the elimination of sexist, authoritarian regimentation of human lives; and that *the liberation of children is the sine qua non of all human liberation.*"[16]

A similar but sicker organization, the René Guyon Society (founded 1962), has about 5000 members and believes that adult males ought to be able to have sex with boys and girls as young as four. It claims that such pedophilia, done "correctly" with love and affection, will help children grow up without guilt, and thus reduce social problems and costs. Get it? This is actually a debt-reduction program in disguise.[17]

If this is not a declaration of war against the family, via our children, I don't know what is. Such people want to create little islands of influence wherever they can, and must be stopped at every turn. We are talking about the cult of the inner God here, and the best way to stop them, besides through strongly enforced laws, is through pervasive moral and social values that on the one hand establish clear distinctions and privileges for normal behaviour (and for the natural family), and on the other create distinct and forceful stigma against public homosexuality. In a compassionate society, we should also do everything we can to help such people recover normalcy (they will protest, absurdly, that homosexuality is "normal," too). In fact, there are many organizations, most religion-based, such as Exodus International, New Directions for Life (Toronto), and New Beginnings that specialize in this very chore of helping homosexuals recover. Masters and Johnson achieved a 71.6 percent success rate (five years "straight") for a group of 300 homosexuals. One psychiatrist achieved a 100 percent success rate.[18] New Directions tells me that by its tally, "about 60 to 70 percent" kick the habit. The prestigious *American Handbook of Psychiatry* (vol. 3, 2nd edition) states that "approximately one-third to one-half" of all patients who seek a return to heterosexual life through therapy are successful. About half of all homosexuals claim to regret their habits, and the same percentage would "become upset" if their child became homosexual (Bell and Weinberg, 1978). Toronto psychiatrist Dr. Daniel Cappon, who has treated more than 450 homosexuals, says they are "as curable as anyone else."

This amounts to saying that all human societies have engaged in — and must continue to engage in — a civilized *repression* of socially unsavoury behaviour as a matter of course, for the sake of self-protection and child protection. Some, like China and other socialist states, actually engage in *oppression* of such behaviour, which seems to do the job. But as proponents of democracy, we believe that civilized repression is adequate; that, as stated at the beginning of this chapter, we should allow homosexuals the same legal *protections* as every other citizen, no more and no less, but not the same *privileges* reserved for social groups who conform to society's highest ideals. And we should stipulate honestly and openly that their behaviour is socially unacceptable. In most nations sodomy, for example, is still illegal. However, the United States has dropped its law against sodomy in 24 states, and Canada dropped its antisodomy law in 1968. Anal intercourse is legal in Canada today, in private, but not in public, between *any two* (not more) consenting people over 18 (lowered from 21, in 1985). There it is. Once such behaviour is legalized, other citizens cannot legally object to it, nor can they protest by withholding their services, nor can they any longer tell their children it is illegal. Had the people, instead of their political representatives, been asked directly, this legalization could never have occurred. (Most politically elite groups are notoriously "liberal" on this subject.) Sadly, homosexuals and their egalitarian-minded supporters have used the very decency of a democratic society — the decency inherent in our willingness to ignore them, that is — against society, and are vigorously calling for approval, normalization, public affirmation, and direct influence over the schools. This is the way of modern liberalism. Everything must be politicized and dragged into the public arena, because man is said to be perfectible. Therefore, with the right policies and enough tax-dollars, all social groups must be made equal through the termination of social and legal privilege. More conservative folks argue that man is imperfect by nature, and so the task is not to distort society to accommodate these imperfections but to tolerate, while discouraging them. Homosexuals do not like the conservative attitude, because it implies that they are sick. So, about 20 years ago, they decided to get rid of the sickness.

### Storming the APA and Intimidating the Doctors
The first and likely most important strategy for making the abnormal normal was to attack the doctors who had defined homosexuality. So, in a deliberately planned campaign of intimidation and disruption, the U.S. National Gay and Lesbian Task Force (NGLTF), declaring that "psychiatry is the enemy incarnate,"[19]

actually managed to force a 1973 convention of the American Psychiatric Association (APA) to declare homosexuality, theretofore defined as deviant, "a normal condition." One protester told Dr. Irving Bieber, an eminent expert on homosexuality, that if his book "talked about black people the way it talks about homosexuals, you'd be drawn and quartered . . . " He was being called a racist for what was in effect a clinical diagnosis describing behaviour. Another lecturer was accused of using "Auschwitz" techniques for treating homosexuals. And psychiatry itself was accused of waging "a war of extermination" against homosexuals.

As a result, the APA's *Diagnostic and Statistical Manual of Psychiatric Disorders* — relied upon extensively in Canada — today contains no entry for homosexuality. A small but well-organized political lobby had actually succeeded in first changing, then totally eradicating, a medical diagnosis (although only 58 percent of APA members who voted — only half did so — agreed with the change). It is conceivable that every other group defined in the manual could do the same — and there would be no manual at all. (This might be a cost-effective way to make the whole world healthy.) But it was a lie. Even four years later, a survey of 2500 psychiatrists found that 69 percent believed homosexuality was "a pathological adaptation." About 18 percent disagreed; 13 percent were "uncertain."[20] And homosexuals tended to feel the same way about themselves. About 25 percent believed their behaviour was an emotional disorder, and 37 percent answered that they were "emotionally disturbed." Young male homosexuals (14-21) commit suicide at two to three times the rate of heterosexuals (*Pediatrics*, June 1991). For all ages, their rate is six times that of heterosexuals. This encapsulates the mentality: morbid, disturbed, and no future or posterity in sight because of the initial choice to reject the procreative natural direction of human life. Against happy families, respecting the past and embracing the future, we have sad homosexuals, hating and condemning the past, with no future to embrace. Despite this reality, homosexuality in North America is now officially a psychiatric non-problem. In a news story bragging about Canada's two most "prominent" public-servant homosexuals, member of Parliament Svend Robinson and broadcaster Laurier Lapierre ("Medicine's Changing View of Homosexuality," Toronto *Star*, March 15, 1988), Dr. Noel Doig, then chairman of the ethics committee of the Canadian Medical Association, said, "It's a sexual variant, a matter of orientation" (meaning: all moral choices are equivalent). In the same story, Dr. I.A. Kapkin, president of the Canadian Psychiatric Association, said, "In our nomenclature, we don't have it as a mental disorder as long as it's preferred behaviour" (meaning: as long as they are obeying the inner God of nature). The American Psychological Association has actually made working for "gay rights" an "ethical requirement" of its members. However, while euphemisms may mask reality, they do not eliminate it. In the February 1989 issue of *The California Psychologist*, Dr. Joseph Nicolosi said "many members of our profession still privately express the opinion that homosexual development is not normal. The 1973 ruling did not resolve the issue — it simply silenced 80 years of psychoanalytic observation." (You could say the shrinks need some counselling themselves on how to stand up for what they believe.)

After this victory, all that remained for homosexuals was to change the public perception of the problem by changing public language itself, thus altering the terms of the discussion.

### Queers* and Quirks, or "Gayspeak"

The anthropologist Benjamin Lee Whorf some decades ago demonstrated the language/thought connection in his book *Language, Thought and Reality*, wherein he showed that language heavily influences perception, that reality is "to a large extent unconsciously built up on the language habits of the group."[21] Language serves as a kind of perceptual instrument, or filter, either to detect or to mask certain aspects of reality. The Inuit, for example, can identify only specific kinds of snow, for which they have specific words. But they do not have a general word for snow, because only specific kinds of snow are of any use to them. An everyday example of linguistic masking used to hide some aspect of reality is the common euphemism. Calling something "pork," for example, hides the fact that we are eating a dead pig. Just so, by altering the word-labels that describe their world, homosexuals hope to make their behaviour invisible, or at the least so "normal" it won't be noticed. This is part of their campaign to morally desensitize the public.

In 1987, the New York *Times* "finally capitulated and authorized [use of] the word *gay* without quotation marks."[22] This was hailed by some editors and reporters as "inching into the 20th century." In reality, it was inching further into moral chaos, and was also the

---

* As an outgrowth of their new candour, homosexuals persist in calling themselves "queers" publicly. The most offensively radical group labels itself "Queer Nation." "Queer" is increasingly the authentic homosexual term of reference.

culminating point in a long and continuing homosexual campaign to alter the way the public thinks, by controlling the way it is allowed to speak and to read. Public acceptance of the word "gay" has been a great victory for homosexuals, for the word "homosexual" had always been a negative term to denote those who preferred to copulate with their own sex. But what homosexuals wanted was a word that elevated their behaviour to an admirable status, and they achieved this by taking a perfectly good English word — now off-limits to normal people — and appropriating it for their specific use. To them, the word "gay" suggests carefree, happy-go-lucky individuals, who have a culture and a way of being all their own, which may in some secret way be superior to the hum-drum, sometimes ungay world of the rest of humanity. The word suggests a special in-group with access to happiness the rest of us lack. But the important thing this appropriation of an English word achieved for them was tactical control over the public definition of what they are. In the past, you could ask anyone what a homosexual was. But no more. Now, you are expected to defer to a "gay" person to tell you what "gay" and "gay culture" mean. What they now mean is that "within the homosexual subculture, 'gay' is a magical word that has a creative power of its own . . . the key indicator for today's liberated homosexual," it signifies not simply those who are attracted to the same sex, but "those who also *celebrate* this attraction."[23]

Those who wish to defend the natural family and the core values of our society should strenuously resist the use of this word, and publicly replace it with the word "homosexual," which is more honest. After all, most of these people are the furthest thing from "gay." Twenty-five percent of homosexuals themselves say they have an emotional disorder, one-quarter to one-third are alcoholic,[24] very high percentages are in fact physically sick much of the time from sexually transmitted diseases, and when asked sincerely by a young person about pursuing the gay life-style, they counsel against it, four to one.[25]

But that doesn't stop the political agitation for normalization. Once they have defined themselves anew by rejecting society's generic "homosexual" label and established the "dignity" of being "gay," the next choice was to position normal people as frightened, bigoted, and irrational. This was achieved by inventing the nonsensical but extremely effective word "homophobic" and using it like a grenade to throw at anyone who dared to utter the slightest negative opinion. Most people, of course, are not afraid of homosexuals at all. They're disgusted by them. What they are frightened of is being accused of not being nice; of being a bigot, "intolerant"; of "discriminating" against someone. (They are also justly frightened of the diseases homosexuals seem to generate.) A handful of brave faculty at Claremont College in California were recently accused by their own deans of "rampant discrimination" against homosexuals when they protested a "gay rights" parade on campus. However, these same self-righteous deans stopped short of approving a student attempt to mount an "incest and bestiality awareness week" (The *Proposition*, April 1989). Oh well, maybe next year.

Are we really discriminating? Sadly, Canadians seem to be wimpy moral fence-sitters, for what this nation needs is a good dose of judicious intolerance. We need to be far more *intolerant* of lots of things, including (and just ask yourself in how many ways the following are connected): overtaxing, overregulating governments; failing public schools; haughty, politically biased media; bad-mannered, foul-mouthed kids who lack all respect for their teachers and elders; violent criminals and the soft-headed parole boards who let them out to rape and kill again; violent movies, videos, music, and television; radical, tax-funded lobby groups out to revolutionize our values and our society; and . . . homosexuals who are out to destroy the family. After all, most people who strongly dislike homosexuality do so because of decent, constructive, family- and community-building moral or religious principles, and not out of fear at all. It is a pathetic sign of weakness that our society speaks only defensively of its values. What we ought to be doing is going on the offensive. After all, the truth is that it is not we who are homophobic, but rather homosexuals who are "heterophobic," "moralphobic," and "familyphobic."

But the major thrust of the homosexual movement in our society — and in this respect it is a movement of the liberal left — is to destroy all moral hierarchy so that homosexuals can escape criticism. Those who want to fight back and preserve the moral dignity of our society will have to begin by refusing publicly such words as "gay" and "homophobic," for to accept and use them means to accept the assumptions they denote.

Perhaps one of the most insidious victories of the homosexual movement can be seen in the broad acceptance of the term "sexual orientation," now used widely in our schools and in sociological and government documents. It was coined to replace the phrase "sexual preference," which suggested that homosexuals were choosing their behaviour and therefore were responsible for it — an implication most of them now strive to avoid. They needed to find a word which suggested that just as the magnetic forces of the earth pull the compass needle to North, something called "sexual orientation" directs homosexuals to indulge in the behaviours they enjoy as if those were a natural fact of life. You have your orientation, I have mine. Homosexuals have thus imported the notion of "moral equivalence" into the "orientation" dialogue, and even attempt to justify it scientifically, as we shall soon see. The public would do well to reject this word, too, and to talk about "sexual choice" instead of "orientation." And everywhere they see the former phrase, they should insist on the use of the latter, both privately and publicly. For the truth is that even if you are predisposed to admire those of your own sex, a moral choice must be made to indulge in homosexual behaviour with them. After all, there may be millions of people out there who, in their most private moments, have had a passing sexual curiosity about those of their own gender. But because they understand the importance of moral and family life, they have chosen to repress such thoughts or feelings. Homosexuals have chosen the opposite.

As U.S. congressman William Dannemayer points out in *Shadow in the Land*, homosexuals have been aggressive and successful in changing the language. They talk about "exploring one's sexuality," as if sex behaviour were an internal, self-directed impulse and all you have to do is give in to it; capitulate to that inner God who will make all decisions for you. The same false attitude of moral equivalence drenches the phrases "alternate life-style," and "family partner," and others like them. Homosexuals strive to get rid of the stigma of exclusion by forcing society to include them as family, or "domestic" partners. They have succeeded. After all, what radical homosexuals really want is to encourage young people to leave the whole idea of the natural family behind and join the "gay" world. What better way to encourage this than be redefining "family" out of existence, making any "family" seem normal? The authors of *The Overhauling of Straight America* declare that their objective is "to desensitize the public," to help it view homosexuality "with indifference." When are we going to wake up? Some indication of this agenda can be seen in the following antifamily diatribe by homosexual Michael Swift, which was published in *Gay Community News* (February 15, 1987):

We shall sodomize your sons . . . we shall seduce them in your schools, in your dormitories, in your gymnasiums, in your locker rooms, in your sports arenas, in your seminaries, in your youth

groups, in your movie theater bathrooms . . . wherever men are
together . . . All laws banning homosexuality will be revoked . . . Be
careful when you speak of homosexuals because we are always among
you . . . the family unit . . . will be abolished . . . All churches who
condemn us will be closed. Our only Gods are handsome young
men.[26]

## Kinsey's "Grand Scheme"

Much of the founding philosophy for the attack on the Judeo-Christian values of our civilization was initiated in the labs of the most
famous modern "sexologist" of all, the American Alfred C. Kinsey.
In a remarkable recent book, *Kinsey, Sex and Fraud*, authors
Reisman and Eichel provide what can only be described as a chilling
exposé of Kinsey's "grand scheme," as he called it, to reshape
Western values through sex research, much of it, as it turns out,
fraudulent.

Even when Kinsey published his famous *Male Report* in 1948 (the
*Female Report* came out in 1953), only his closest associates were
aware of his values and his agenda. And as Reisman and Eichel point
out, Kinsey and his two volumes of "scientific research," more than
any other documents in history, "shaped Western society's beliefs
and understandings about what human sexuality is. They have
defined what people allegedly *do* sexually, thereby establishing what
is allegedly *normal*."[27]

Based on reams of data taken from 6000 men and boy interviewees,
Kinsey claimed that 85 percent of U.S. males had intercourse prior
to marriage; that nearly 70 percent had sex with prostitutes; that up
to 45 percent of husbands had extramarital intercourse; and that 37
percent of all males have homosexual experience between adolescence and old age. Most disturbing of all were his "findings" that
small children were "sexual beings" even from infancy, and that they
could and, he maintained, *should* have pleasurable and beneficial
sexual interaction with adult "partners."[28] His surveys were said at
the time to "explode traditional concepts of what is normal and
abnormal, natural and unnatural in sex behavior." Which is what
he wanted to do. Kinsey persistently insisted that what is *done*, is
natural; that what is statistically common, is right — and out of
whack with the commonly understood Victorian moral code. His
idea, in other words, was that moral life should be a matter of
democracy. If most do it, it must be good; a fallacious equation
much like saying that if everyone kills, then killing is morally
acceptable.

What he didn't say, however, was that the bulk of his results were obtained by skewing, selecting, and omitting data, and designed "to provide a scientific base for his pre-existing radical sexual ideology." Even his most influential co-workers, such as Wardell Pomeroy, "were chosen *for* their bias; biased samples were *knowingly* used . . . [and] *criminal experimentation* was the prime source of Kinsey's childhood sexuality data." And on it goes. The authors conclude that Kinsey's research is "the most egregious example of scientific deception in this century."[29] It turns out that it was based not on random sampling of the population, but largely on volunteers, many of whom came to him for help with their problems. This introduced an immediate "volunteer bias" to the findings. This group, the authors say, "was so overtly unrepresentative of society, then or now, that the fact that a group of 'scientists' defined the 'normal' sexual behaviour of U.S. males from this sample is astonishing in retrospect." Wardell Pomeroy, in a later book, revealed that "possibly a quarter" of Kinsey's volunteers were in fact *convicted sex criminals*, and a Kinsey co-worker told author Eichel that about 44 percent of those prisoners had had homosexual experiences in prison. Most of the high school boys Kinsey interviewed included an unusually high percentage of homosexuals. About 64 percent of Kinsey's sample were college-educated (vs. 12 percent of the population); of the group aged 30 to 50, 55 percent were widowed or divorced; and fully 80 percent of his sample were "inactive" in their religion. More damning still, Kinsey apparently directed experimental "research" on several hundred children between the ages of two months and 15 years. These children "were orally and manually stimulated to orgasms by a group of nine sex offenders." Attempts were actually made to "produce" orgasm in babies of two to four months of age. (Where were their mothers and fathers?)

**Pansexualism and Modern "Sexology": "All Orgasms Are Equal"**
Kinsey was basically a social revolutionary disguised as a scientist, in the same way that many such revolutionaries today are disguised as sexologists. What is common to social and sexual revolution is that they are both anti-authority in the extreme. They represent the end-point of liberalism, manifest in the Individualism Illusion and the drive for self-fulfilment. Socially, such modern liberalism expresses itself in the simplistic idea that all authority is bad, all (sexual) liberation, good. Kinsey, as his biographer Paul Robinson pointed out, strongly rejected the entire Judeo-Christian tradition of morality. He had early adopted the viewpoint that "being involved in all types

of sexual activity would represent freedom from the cultural conditioning which society imposes and which leads to artificial distinctions such as 'right and wrong,' licit and illicit, normal and abnormal, acceptable and unacceptable in our social organization."[30] Kinsey never spoke of morality. He was strictly a biological materialist who, in order to understand the meaning of life, attempted to reduce all human experience to the raw, biological level, which utterly fails to explain the powerful mysteries of human sexual involvement.

Stuck as he was with the simplistic premises of materialism, Kinsey argued that the best model for humans was animal sexual behaviour, because animals are not influenced, he decided, by cultural conditioning. In fact they are, and their sex lives are highly controlled by ritual. But let us not confound bad theory with good facts. Robinson says Kinsey "even sought to invest [sexual relations between humans and animals] with a certain dignity by suggesting they could achieve a psychological intensity comparable to that in exclusively human sexual relations."[31] In other words, he thought human sexuality, in the absence of repressive cultural conditioning, was simply an appetite, which could express itself through any available and adequate "outlet." To him and his followers, then and now, all sex is good sex, and all orgasms are equal. He coined the term "outlet sex" to describe this idea. His was basically a version of the mechanical, stimulus-response world view used by behavioural and educational psychologists (discussed in Chapter Eight). According to this thinking, there is no reason to give social priority to heterosexual relations, as these preferences are merely the result of socially prescribed "inhibitions." Here's the Kinsey bottom line: "We suggest that sexuality, in its biologic origins, is a capacity to respond to any sufficient stimulus . . . this is the picture of sexual response in the child and in most other young mammals. For a few uninhibited adults, sex continues to remain sex, however they have it."[32]

In Kinsey's scale of values, ordinary heterosexual intercourse, compared with other modes, was an inferior (because culturally conditioned) form of sex. One of his acolytes, sexologist John Money from Johns Hopkins University, actually talks of "obligative heterosexuality," implying that those who practise this form of sex exclusively are somehow brainwashed by a repressive society.[33] Kinsey even felt that virginity before marriage and sexual exclusivity within marriage were unnatural and therefore, in a sense, immoral. Such thinking is an outgrowth of biological materialism, which insists that appetites should not be restrained by conventions, and that what is, is good. It's a view of human sexual behaviour stripped of all social, moral, and emotional context. Even today, something called the "Kinsey scale" is used in many schools to rank the sexual "orientation" of children. But the simple fact is that no moral or sexual code in history has ever endured as a sliding code. The whole point of such codes is that their effectiveness in controlling deviance (and diseases) springs from their all-or-nothing nature. To pretend otherwise is to mislead. It is because we know that people do not wholly abide by them that such codes must be clear and strict. It's a question of social damage control. For a sliding moral or sexual code is no code at all; it is a licence. Thus, the optimum choice on Kinsey's seven-point scale is "bisexuality," which is in the middle, and which Kinsey advocated as the most "balanced" form for normal, uninhibited people (although Kinsey himself assigned most prominence to masturbation and homosexuality, and had "a tendency to conceive of the ideal sexual universe according to a homoerotic model"[34]). Kinsey's ultimate ambition was to create a pansexualist universe in which all human beings, including children of any age, would engage in whatever kind of sex they enjoyed, including with animals. He also maintained that 10 percent of males are "normal" homosexuals — a figure that has been wrongly treated as authoritative for more than 40 years and is used hysterically to help calculate such things as the spread of AIDS (even by prestigious organizations such as the Centers for Disease Control, which has had to downgrade drastically its original estimates by millions, while wiping the Kinsey egg off its face).

The enormous influence of the Kinsey reports has been felt everywhere in our society, particularly in our schools, where children learn today that heterosexual love is just one "option," that 10 percent of every class is "gay" (more accurate, honest studies such as the 1990 University of Chicago Survey, put the figure at 1 or 2 percent); that bisexuality and homosexuality are normal variations open to them; and that multiple partners are encouraged. Manuals, programs, courses and video-tapes, produced by sexologists attempting to normalize homosexuality and stigmatize "homophobia" as intolerance, have flooded the educational market. High-schoolers at a U.S. airbase in Yokota, Japan, have a "cross-dressing day," in which boys wear dresses and high heels, and girls wear shirts and pants — all part of their sex-education program (*Pacific Stars and Stripes*, October 22, 1991). Even television is featuring homosexuality in response to pressure for "gay equity." But the people aren't buying it — yet. A "Thirtysomething" program showing two gay men in bed cost ABC

$1 million in sudden lost advertising when "half of the episode's commercials were pulled." A second segment showing the same actors merely talking at a party cost the network $500,000. But the advertisers are at it, too. A recent "Trust Trojan Condoms" television ad in Canada, run ostensibly to prevent AIDS, shows two people wriggling under the sheets. But "because the people's sex is not revealed, the ad is targeted to both heterosexuals and homosexuals" (*Globe and Mail*, January 13, 1991).

But as if to ensure the success of the pansexual ideology, the Canadian government wants to suppress such public outrage. So, on November 23, 1991, the Canadian Radio-television and Tele-communications Commission (CRTC) officially ruled that any "abusive" comments about homosexuality would be banned on all Canadian radio and television. The article announcing this decision added that many such comments, according to Ronald Clark, who initiated the complaint that led to the ruling, may be abusive even though they do not "directly mention homosexuality." Now, just try to imagine every sensitive soul with a favourite cause forcing the CRTC to ban all "abusive" comments about a cause "not directly mentioned" — and you've got a recipe for totalitarian telecommunications. For a religious person, for example, it is abusive to *praise* homosexuality. Next, people will be forbidden to write, publish, or buy books like the one you now hold in your hand. This is surely a most damning indictment of a supposedly free country in which over 70 percent of the people say homosexuality is morally wrong.

As for how we will think in the future, people like SIECUS (Sex Information and Education Council of the United States) co-founder, Professor Lester Kirkendall, are predicting (in the *Journal of Sex Education*, Spring 1985), that sex-ed programs of the future will "probe" so-called "cross-generational" sex and "sexual expression with same-sex partners" (meaning pedophilia, sodomy, and lesbianism), and that such programs will be easier to introduce because of a "diminished sense of guilt."[35] We're already there. The Project 10 course (meaning, "10 percent" are gay) used in some California high schools (taught by a lesbian) shows 13-year-olds an extremely explicit video of two homosexuals copulating. Disgusted students are made to watch it again and again until their feelings change to acceptance. Mary Calderone, co-founder of SIECUS, lectures widely about the "vital importance of infant and childhood sexuality." Sex-ed author Gary Kelly's book describing how to have anal intercourse, and "non-harmful" sex with animals was voted onto the American Library Association's Best Books for Young Adults list (he demurs, saying, "I cannot judge the rightness or wrongness of any of these behaviours").[36] I agree. He has disqualified himself from such an important task. And Wardell Pomeroy, whose books *Boys and Sex* and *Girls and Sex* have sold "about 5000 copies in Canada in the last two years — mostly to schools and teachers,"[37] blithely describes every moment of oral sex and anal intercourse, and tells his teenage readers that one out of five boys who live on or visit farms have intercourse with animals: " . . . ponies, sheep, pigs, even chickens or ducks. Dogs are also commonly used, but cats rarely . . . [Some boys] build a strong emotional attachment to an animal . . . [even] a loving sexual relationship with an animal and felt good about their behaviour until they got to college, where they learned for the first time that what they had done was 'abnormal.' Then they were upset and thought of themselves as some kind of monster."[38] Notice that he speaks approvingly of such "relationships" (because he sees them as natural and therefore good) and blames college (society) for making the poor farmboys feel like monsters. His clever use of quotation marks for the word "abnormal" signals the child reader that what the boys are doing is really O.K. and is only said to be bad by colleges, society, parents, religions, and the like. Not to worry, Junior, if you feel the urge, just whistle for the dog!

Pomeroy still maintains the view that adults having sex with children is not a problem, and he has opined that he "would not counsel one of his patients who was having sex with a minor to stop, but would ask why [the patient] felt guilty about such activities?"[39] Pomeroy also claimed that when he worked on the Kinsey interviews, "many beautiful and mutually satisfying [sexual] relationships between fathers and daughters" were found. Gebhard, another co-worker, refers to such instances as "positive incest." And Kinsey's *Female Report* tells us that we ought not to worry about such incest, as his researchers found "only a few instances of vaginal bleeding," in young girls, and, well, "it is difficult to understand why a child, except for its cultural conditioning, should be disturbed at having its genitalia touched . . . or at attempted intercourse." Kinsey blamed the child's upset on prudish parents and teacher "hysteria" and referred to those who frown upon pedophilia as "moralists." I say we need more moralists to protect us against such people and their teachings. In April 1989, Peter Reinharz, New York's Juvenile Prosecutor, revealed on CBS's "Face the Nation" that eight- and nine-year-olds in New York are now engaging in rape, sodomy, and sexual assault of three- and four-year-olds. But . . . he says he's too busy with the drug war to deal with it.[40] Some world.

This is all very hard to believe, but it's not made up. It is enough to say that the Kinsey influence on sexology and sex education has been powerful — and extremely damaging. Kinsey's co-workers, like Pomeroy and Gebhard, and their friends, Kirkendall, Calderone, and Calderwood, and the organizations and sexology programs they spawned to teach the teachers, like SIECUS in the United States and SIECCAN in Canada, have touched every aspect of sexuality training in both nations. Modern sexology is extremely antireligious, antisocial, and pro-homosexual. It springs from a simplistic, romantic, Rousseauian belief, utterly consonant with the presence of the top-down egalitarian state, that everyone is equally good by nature and naturally pansexual (pansexualism is just the sexual equivalent of socialism), and differences, whether in sexual behaviour or in gender, are simply caused by social conditioning. So the idea is to change the conditioning. Kinsey and his followers are motivated by an anti-authority, antifamily utopian vision of a "liberated" world full of similar pansexualists, and thus do we get bombarded by their aggressive promotion of homosexuality. They know that to desensitize people to what disgusts most is to desensitize them to all lesser matters. To radical sexologists, heterosexual preference is part of an oppressive, property-owning, patriarchal system, and must be ended. That's why they encourage pedophilia — so that all human beings can enjoy mutual sex, regardless of age and free of parental or social constraints. For them, pedophilia will prevent patriarchy. They say that because there is no such thing as "normal," sexual deviance is purely a moral term. And the hidden gay agenda in all this is recruitment: to reach boys and girls "before they are affected by societal 'restraints' and rescue them from the supposedly pathological norms of exclusive male-female relating."[41] Hence, the effort to eliminate from the lexicon of public school courses words like "monogamy," "nuclear family," "marriage," and "right and wrong". On November 14, 1990, Toronto City Council voted (11-3) for the Board of Education to introduce gay and lesbian issues into the curriculum "to deal with homophobia early in life." Notice that there is no such program to support the natural family and protect children from recruitment by homosexuals. In May 1988, the same board decided to develop a "sexual orientation" course for its schools. Did they ask normal parents to help with all this? No. The trustees consulted the Gay and Lesbian Task Force, whose representatives sat on the curriculum committee — and promptly voted against any parent sitting on the same committee.

This entire feverish tax-funded sexology industry has really stoked the fires of the homosexual movement and given it the semblance of scientific support. In early 1973, when sexologist William Johnson "announced to the nation's press that homosexuality is a 'natural,' and by implication normal sexual act or sexual condition . . . he raised the status of the anus to the level of the vagina . . . what was until then a purely excretory organ [became] a genital one — by decree."[42]

It was the same year the APA had declared homosexuality to be "normal." Thirteen years later, in 1986, Gary Kelly's book *Learning About Sex — A Contemporary Guide for Young Adults* explained in detail how school children should perform oral and anal sex if the spirit moves them, and advised that "there are no special medical dangers associated with anal sexual contact."[43] Medically, that's about as responsible as advising children who are thirsty to drink sewer water.

As a writer and the parent of five children, I now have an unpleasant duty. We are all being grievously misled by an extremely accommodating media, and a dangerously silent medical and educational profession, into believing that homosexual behaviour is just a harmless variation on normal sexuality. But this is far from the truth. People need to know exactly what it is that most homosexuals do, and what moral, social, and medical dangers arise from their behaviour. If homosexuals stayed in the closet, there would be less need to go into detail. But as they are out in the open promoting their "life-style" as good for your kids and mine, they've declared war against the family.[44] We must therefore strike back. Some argue that heterosexual people do lots of the things detailed below, too. And some do. But very few. And whereas a normal couple may engage in some unnatural behaviour as a matter of a temporary detour or experiment, or in a fit of passion, or while intoxicated or using drugs, radical homosexuals choose such barren behaviours as a matter of routine and ideological preference. In doing so, they position themselves as alien and opposed to the human enterprise. Such behaviour can never be stopped, of course, but it can be largely limited if we manage clearly to oppose the normalization of it, and take steps to protect ourselves from the political, medical, and moral dangers that flow from it. What follows is the worst-case scenario, and, lest those who admire such behaviour wax resentful, they should remember that much of this information has been published by homosexuals themselves.

## What Some Homosexuals Do —
## and What This Does to Them — and to Society

### Molestation and Violence

Although homosexuals represent only between 1 and 4 percent of the entire population (up to 2 percent exclusively homosexual; and 2 percent casual bisexuals), studies based on ample U.S. data tell us that they perpetrate between one-third and one-half of all child molestations (Los Angeles *Times* survey, August 26, 1985), and that homosexual teachers commit between 25 and 80 percent of all pupil molestations. They are 12 times more likely to molest children than are normal people, and seven times more likely to molest pupils. About 31 percent of those claiming molestation by men were homosexually assaulted. Fully 35 percent of British boys (and 9 percent of girls) say that they have been actively approached by adult homosexuals (2 percent and 1 percent, respectively, say they "succumbed"). A British Columbia study of 2099 child sexual abuse cases, although never mentioning the word homosexual, found that 50 percent of victims were boys, a majority were under 12, and 94 percent of the perpetrators were male.[45] A national study by the Canadian Centre for Justice Statistics, covering the decade 1980–89, found that 91 percent of perpetrators of sexual assault on children were male, and 46.5 percent of victims of sexual assault and "other sexual violations" were boys.[46] Both studies tell us that homosexuals (at 4 percent of the population) are proportionately vastly more likely than heterosexuals to abuse children. A 1985 study in *Psychological Reports* stated that homosexuals were up to 100 times more likely than heterosexuals to involve themselves sexually with child pupils.[47] Homosexual New York teachers recently agreed such acts were improper on school property — but reserved the right to "have relations" with children after school.[48] In its 1987 study, "Murder, Violence and Homosexuality," the Institute for the Scientific Investigation of Sexuality (ISIS) reported that of all multiple or serial murders in the United States in the two decades after 1970, homosexuals killed at least 68 percent of the victims, were implicated in 41 percent of the total sets of crimes, and committed 70 percent of the worst 10 sets. Other studies arrive independently at the same, roughly two-thirds, figure. C. Allen's *A Textbook of Psychosexual Disorders* (1969), and J.P. de River's *The Sexual Criminal* (1956), say much the same. Convicted homosexual murderer Jeffrey Dahmer, who raped, killed, then raped them dead, and ate parts of 15 boys and young men, will swell this number greatly (Toronto *Star*, February 16, 1992).

And from whence does all this arise?

Fully one-third of all homosexuals admit to sado-masochism — a rate about 600 times greater than for heterosexuals (Gebhard and Johnson, *The Kinsey Data*, 1979). Homosexuals frequently use whips and leather straps to tie up and beat, or "punish," their partners. They enjoy violent pornography, and sometimes they use an array of peculiar items such as metal rings around the genitals, or metal clips on the nipples to give pain. Also popular are various sex "toys" and dildos. A favourite group activity is sex orgies with total strangers at the "baths"; also, "slave auctions" in which naked men are publicly beaten and "sold" as a sex slave to the highest bidder. The San Francisco Bulldog Baths' auction poster showed a naked man on his knees, tied to a railing, beneath the caption: "Where the Men Are Hard to Beat!"

Other weird and degrading behaviour is carried out in "dungeons" or "torture" rooms. About 20 percent of homosexuals report sado-masochism in which their partner is hurt, scratched, bruised, and/or bloodied ("What Homosexuals Do," *ISIS*, 1987; and *The Gay Report*, 1979). As a surgeon for 15 years and former chief of surgery at San Francisco General Hospital's trauma unit, where many sexually injured homosexuals end up, Dr. Lorraine Day stated that "much of gay sex is of the harmful, sadistic and/or masochistic variety. Gays hurt each other. They also hurt themselves."[49]

Readers should not miss the connection between homosexuality and pornography, either. Run down to your local corner store and you will see all sorts of magazines showing female homosexuals in action, something unthinkable in a mainstream porn magazine even a decade ago. While arguably such lesbian scenes are meant to titillate heterosexual males, they are a tactical step closer to pansexualism. Next we will see male homosexuals in action — at present, something deemed a bit too daring for the general public — although such magazines are easily available from homosexual bookstores and are protected as free "speech." But it's all part of a Pandora's box process. After acceptance of homosexual sex, it will be sex with children (openly depicted in Danish porn magazines). Already, mainstream "adult" magazines use "teasers," or what Reisman calls "pseudo-children": women allegedly over 18, dressed up as little girls, sometimes with shaved genitals. Then comes human sex with animals, already normalized in some widely used sex-ed books in North America and easily available as pornography in many European, especially Scandinavian countries. Finally, at the depths of barbarism and social decadence, at the end of a long chain of successive normalizations of the abnormal, of which homosexuality is merely the first link, comes sex with killing. British authorities recently raided an underground video business with international connections, specializing in "snuff" movies recording real murders, torture, mutilation and cannibalism. One of the ring's hottest-selling videos shows a sexually excited man slicing open a pregnant woman and eating her baby.[50] Psychologist John Preiesaik, a staffer at Jackson State Prison, tells of a prisoner who, when asked why he had to stab his victim 23 times, replied: "That's the number of times I needed to get an erection."[51]

Of course, most homosexuals are not violent. But it is important to appreciate the depths of the underlying commitment of the hard-core homosexual/porn movement to the demolition of traditional morals and sanctions. The *Playboy-Penthouse-Hustler* type of "soft" publication is available to any minor who can reach the shelf level — or talk a taller friend into buying a magazine for him. And the public must disabuse itself of the naïve idea that pornography is merely an issue of free speech. Far from it. It's mostly steered by multi-billion-dollar organized crime interests who seek, and often get, control over corrupted public officials.[52] Such first experiences with sex are now encouraged by cable T.V. sex, dial-a-porn telephone sex, and growing numbers of "XXX" video shops with hard porn for rent — all approved, in Ontario, by the Ontario Film Review Board (by liberal standards that happen to clash with Canada's Federal Criminal Code). And computer porn is big business. Computer groups such as Internet supply "millions" of enthusiasts with personal porn. Among pictures recently featured was "a photograph of a woman having sexual intercourse with a dog" (*Globe and Mail*, July 20, 1992). But there is a greater clash coming between parents who want local community control, and the educated elites who approve of pornography and its laissez-faire message as "free speech." The whole pornography issue is a microcosmic example of the clash between the bottom-up society and the top-down State. Ontario basically says that if there's no violence or true weirdism, then it's O.K. Think again, Ontario. A book that will clarify the perversity of the pornography connection (which is supported through the magazine advertising of an astonishing array of *Fortune* 500 companies) is, again, by Judith A. Reisman, Ph.D., *"Soft Porn" Plays Hardball* (P.O. Box 53788, Lafayette, Louisiana, U.S.A.,

70505). Send for it. Her view — against the civil libertarians — is that both soft and hard pornography are far from harmlessly confined to the end-users.

Porn has tragic spillover effects and thus imposes on society at large a conception of women and children (and men, I might add) that encourages violence, sexual abuse, and deviance. In fact, the pornography market actively works to engage the fascination of millions of younger and younger boys and girls, the better to alter their values and secure their purchasing power. This porn-marketing program is abetted right in your local school, where "sex-ed" teachers and programs are designed to assure your Grade 4 child that all consenting sex is good sex. This is the two-century-old murmur of Rousseau: Sex is good, because we are good. At the least, school is where the kiddies learn that sexual values are up to them, and the values of teachers, religions, and parents are inconsequential. Harvard homosexual writer Marshall Kirk criticizes this moral values education (MVE) sentiment, explored in Chapter Eight, when he says the problem with modern sexuality is that " . . . everyone has the right to behave just as he pleases . . . everyone [is] to decide what [is] 'right for him' — in effect, to make up the rules as he [goes] along."[53] The problem of pornography is not a problem of personal freedom or of choice. It is a problem of society at large. The same is true of all other personal choices made in human communities. Choice is always personal, but the consequences of choice are always social.

### Promiscuity

Male homosexuals are a living argument for George Gilder's thesis that the male sexual energy, untamed by the domestic forces of society, will seek out promiscuous, polygamous — by definition, *uncommitted* — sex. By contrast, female homosexuals are far, far less promiscuous than men. What follows is mostly about homosexual men, many of whom live discreet private lives. But most do not.

Most homosexual sex exchanges occur between total strangers. In Bell and Weinberg's *Homosexualities* (1978), and in Gebhard and Johnson's *The Kinsey Data* (1979) — corrected — about 70 percent admitted to having had sex only once with over half their partners. Other studies report that homosexuals average 20 to 106 new partners per year. The average had 300 to 500 partners in a lifetime. "Cruising" for sex with total strangers was the preferred pastime. Bell and Weinberg state that fully 28 percent had sodomy with over 1000 partners in their lifetime, about 43 percent with over 500.

Some report thousands of partners.[54] One homosexual wrote in *Gay Report* that he had over 4000, based on a diary cataloguing two or three per week, and ten or twelve every time he goes to the baths. A British survey appearing in *British Journal of Sexual Medicine* (April 1987) reported two London homosexuals who had 500 partners in one year, and twelve who estimated 5000 in their lifetimes to date. By the early 1980s, many homosexuals "reduced" the number of new partners by about a third, from an average of 70 down to 50 per year, for fear of AIDS. Some precaution.

### The UAS Syndrome

Part of the stimulus to such frenzied sex is the uncommitted anonymous sex (UAS) syndrome, in which a deliberate inverse relationship is established between the desired objective sensual experience and the subjectivity of the persons involved. We are talking about the cult of pleasure, now, which is what provides the connection between homosexuality and pornography: at the extreme, the sensual effect of each is diminished by normal human affection. The reason for this relationship is fascinating. Male homosexuality and pornography can succeed only by repelling natural emotional sensitivity or amorous feeling of any kind, because these emotions detract from the pure sensual experience. The reason they detract is because the arousal of human affection spontaneously transforms any sexual relationship and suffuses it with a hierarchy of emotional and moral values. All of a sudden, caring, love, jealousy, respect, or, especially, shame may enter the scene, or rise up without warning. Once such emotions and values enter a homosexual or pornographic experience, they invoke the immediate possibility of judgment upon the act, and therefore upon the actor, ruining the sense of uncommitted, anonymous pleasure. They make difficult the treatment of the other as the pure object of one's personal satisfaction, which is the aim of all promiscuity — both hetero- and homosexual — and of pornography.

Thus, every care must be taken to ensure that no such emotions can be created. You may do lots of kinky things with an anonymous partner, who will never tell, which you would never do with a lover or spouse from whom you crave respect. This dynamic of homosexual and pornographic experience explains why there is no such thing as a pornographic love story or movie. Such a story could never succeed, simply because pornography and love contradict each other. Either the love is ruined, debased by the vulgarity of pornography, or the pornography is shamed, and ruined, by the purity of love. This dynamic of mutual exclusivity explains the inherent evil in the two forms of decadence, and why they are both dangerous to society. Women are quite correct to complain that pornography demeans them. It demeans us all. But this is not simply due to the violence, as they suggest, for the violence flows from the object-status, not the other way around. Violence is impossible in conditions of true subjectivity, which is why male homosexuality and pornography both rely on maintaining the object-status of the participants and their pleasures. It is wrong to believe that male homosexuals are psychological failures because they copulate with so many strangers. That is the whole point of all promiscuity. It is in fact this very novelty, objectivity, repetition, and anonymity that provide the heightened excitement, unavailable to them in normal heterosexual love (which creates the opposite of all these things). Homosexuals are hooked on UAS, which is autoerotic by nature. That is why they spurn monogamy. Of those Kinsey interviewed, 60 percent said they would not want a monogamous relationship (no fun). And Harvard's Kirk and Madsen wrote that "what Joe Gay is looking for . . . is a 'hassle-free' relationship, in which his lover isn't 'overinvolved' . . . a handsome . . . sort of low-maintenance household appliance." A popular San Francisco metaphor for the perfect homosexual relationship was Kleenex: "One blow, and out you go."[55] As I said, they want an object, a thing. And that is why their special pleasures are inhuman, and antisocial. And that is why they cannot be whole human beings, for whom the highest relationships are subjective.

Of course, there are a few heterosexual music, movie, or sport "stars," surrounded with myriad dewy-eyed groupies, who perform at the same sexual output, for the same reason. The UAS syndrome is the perpetuation into adulthood of the masturbatory adolescent male sexual dream, normally given up for family, marriage, and wholeness, which is why the syndrome flourishes only in corrupt societies, in the seamy underworld of perversity, or in the unrealistic swoon of adulation. Thus, so-called "gay marriages" last an average of two or three years, most homosexuals engage in sexual relationships with others about halfway through the relationship, and so-called monogamous homosexual partners admit to having a minimum of one other new partner each week.

### Anal and Oral Sodomy

Over 90 percent of homosexual men participate in anal sodomy, a practice that carries great risk for them and for all society. It is the furthest thing from "safe sex," as we shall see. The human bowel is meant to excrete feces through the anus, not to receive a penis. Accordingly, it is a steaming jungle of dangerous bacterial organisms which, when they come into contact with other human tissues ill-equipped to deal with them, cause dire health problems. Some bath houses that pretend to be more than sex-hotels offer showers fitted with a diverter and a plastic nozzle for irrigating the anus, which is part of the process of converting it into a vagina. Surgeon Lorraine Day, in describing the multiple traumatic injuries to homosexuals she treated in her trauma unit, said, "We see prolonged and repeated physical abuse and resulting trauma to very vulnerable body parts. We see a lifestyle where hygiene is nil, thanks to shared bath house hose nozzles and feces. Urine and semen flow onto the floor and onto each other."[56] There is not much question that all the sanctions against such behaviour in human societies have arisen from historical experience with bowel-generated diseases that have devastated large pools of humanity at various historical periods. In the following chapter, we shall see how dangerous this behaviour is.

Human fecal bacteria can easily travel up the urethra and cause severe bladder infections and chronic prostatitis. And human sperm alone deposited in the rectum via anal sex is a known immuno-suppressive agent, causing homosexuals to be at far greater risk for infectious diseases. As for oral/penile sex — the danger with homosexuals is they seldom stop to disinfect, and thus ingest fecal material as a matter of course.

### *"Rimming" and Eating Feces*
The ISIS report "What Homosexuals Do" (1987), says that about 90 percent of male and 65 percent of female homosexuals report enjoying oral/anal sex activity, by way of licking or inserting their tongue in their partner's anus ("rimming"); about 75 percent and 25 percent, respectively, report this to be a regular habit. Seventeen percent of homosexuals admit to eating their partner's feces (called "scat," from the Greek word for dung), or rubbing themselves with feces ("mudrolling," sometimes done in groups); this is officially called "coprophilia," meaning "love of dung," and a "scatophagian" is an eater of dung. It has a long history. Probably the most notable coprophiliac ever was the Marquis de Sade (1740–1814), who made the variations of this disgusting habit famous in his book, *The 120 Days of Sodom*, wherein he declared: "If it is the dirty element that gives pleasure in the act of lust, then the dirtier it is, the more pleasurable it is bound to be."[57] The oft-imprisoned de Sade "made famous the argument that since both sexual deviation and criminal

acts exist in nature, they are therefore natural."[58] His modern name is Alfred Kinsey. In de Sade's work, and that of Kinsey and his followers, we can see this equation and the moral equivalence such people always try to defend between the queer, the criminal, and the "natural," all of which are justifications for worship of the inner God of nature, all battering rams to destroy the notion of moral hierarchy and the interfering love and judgment that will always bring the ruination of their pleasures.

Ironically, along with "urophilia," such mental disorders, under the cover term "homosexual," are "protected disabilities" both in the United States and Canada, which means you cannot refuse to hire such people for jobs like food handling. In fact, under so-called "employment equity" laws, which are really a form of employment apartheid (legalized preferences for some classes of people), you may soon be *required* to hire a certain percentage of them.

Homosexual men, on average, ingest some fecal material, always bacteria-laden, and often infected, from about 23 different men per year. About 19 percent of male and 4 percent of female homosexuals report urinating on their partners (called "water sports," or having — or giving — a "golden shower") or defecating on them. In one survey, a group of so-called monogamous homosexuals (with a high awareness of health guidelines) themselves reported that during a single month, 5 percent drank urine, 25 percent urinated on their partners, 33 percent ate feces, and 59 percent received sperm in their rectum (*American Journal of Public Health*, vol. 75, 1985, pp. 493-96).

### *"Fisting," or "Handballing"*

"Fisting," or "handballing" is the rather astounding practice of inserting an entire lubricated hand and forearm into the anus of a partner. This practice, as well as repeated anal sodomy, soon leads to enlarging, slackening, or tearing of the anal sphincter muscles. Afflicted homosexuals end up having to wear a diaper to catch the embarrassing dribbling of anal secretions. Sometimes damage is irreparable, and so a colostomy operation is required. Many homosexuals have surgery on their anus to tighten them up again to help them contain feces, phalluses, fists, and other items. Surgeon Lorraine Day reports she and her colleagues have had to remove "light bulbs, vegetables such as zucchini and cucumbers that have already started fermenting, Coke bottles, dildos, vibrators, and shaving cream cans." She even saw an X-ray of one homosexual's rectum with "a 3-inch by 12-inch plastic tool box . . . the tools were still inside," and she reports that a famous actor had to have a dead gerbil removed.[59] In relaying similar stories, homosexuals Kirk and Madsen, of Harvard, say homo-haters have dug up the truth, "our lifestyle — is the pits," and they advocate "social censure" to deal with it, urging the public to "speak up!"[60]

### Sex in Public Places

> But I have to admit there's a perverse side of me that would love to see queer theater for kids.
>
> MARY ROGERS, TORONTO PLAYWRIGHT, TORONTO STAR, OCT. 15, 1992

To the argument that homosexual behaviour is their own private business, we can answer that they have not kept it so. They have made it a matter of public business, for they largely practise their weird habits in public. According to Gay Report, the favourite places to practise homosexual behaviour are public restrooms, service stations, bus stations, public libraries, college restrooms, public parks, beaches, public baths (or "health clubs"), pornographic "peep" shows, and gay bars. Some homosexuals enjoy cutting "glory holes" in public washroom and wall partitions through which to give or receive oral or anal sex. The particular high here arises from the utter anonymity of this masturbatory act. It is the UAS syndrome perfected. The U.S. Department of Health and Human Services survey of where homosexual encounters took place listed city parks (80 percent), gay bars (62 percent), theatres (61 percent), and restrooms (33 percent). Some 28 percent of those surveyed said they had known their partner for only a week (New Dimensions, January 1990). American and Canadian students are currently complaining about having to witness homosexual acts in college washrooms across the continent. Ohio State University's Scoreboard Alert complained that the university's main library had to embark on a major cleanup of dried semen and urine stains on the floors, walls, and books of the library. UCLA actually posted signs in campus washrooms pleading that such behaviour was "inappropriate" in university washrooms (New Dimensions, January 1990).

Inappropriate? A word too calm by a good measure. Now that the politics, tactics, rationalizations, and habits of the homosexual movement have been reviewed, let us turn to the next chapter to see just how this "private" behaviour is a public danger to our society through the often fatal diseases it generates and spreads.

# 14

## The Gay Plague
and the Politics
of AIDS

*It is much more important to know what sort of
patient has a disease than what sort of disease a
patient has.*

SIR WILLIAM OSLER

In view of what we saw in the last chapter, it is not
surprising that U.S. surveys show that about 78 percent of homosexual men have had a sexually transmitted disease
(STD). In August 1984, Buchanan and Muir blew the whistle on the
homosexual disease epidemic in an article entitled "Gay Times and
Diseases," published in *The American Spectator*. The public was
shocked, and the newspaper was besieged — by more than 90,000
requests for reprints of the article! As in many similar articles in the
*New England Journal of Medicine*, the *Journal of the American
Medical Association*, and *Annals of Internal Medicine*,[1] and a
variety of books published over the last two decades, the looming
shape of the gay plague is finally all too visible.

"*Gay bowel syndrome*" was a phrase first brought to the public's
attention by Buchanan and Muir's article. It describes a well-
documented collection of bowel diseases that lead to a mechanical
dysfunction of the lower bowel tract. Most of these diseases were
previously thought to occur only in tropical climates. However,
largely unknown to the public because of a near-total pro-gay media

blackout, they have now reached epidemic proportions in North America, and all of them long preceded AIDS. These include:

- *Amebiasis* — a disease of the colon caused by parasites. Results in dysentery, sometimes liver abscess, and is spread by fecal ingestion or contamination of food.
- *Giardiasis* — also prevalent in daycare centres because of wandering fecal material; a parasitic disease that produces diarrhea and inflammation of the bowel tract. Spread by fecal ingestion and contaminated food and water.
- *Salmonellosis* — a bacterial disease causing food poisoning and gastroenteritis, vomiting, severe diarrhea in infants and the elderly. Can lead to death by dehydration. Spread by fecal ingestion and contaminated foodstuffs.
- *Shigellosis* — an acute bacterial infection like salmonellosis, it can lead to a diarrhea-induced dehydration death in infants and the elderly. Infected individuals should not handle food.
- *Hepatitis A and B* — a viral liver disease spread by fecal contamination (A), or by blood (B). The latter type is considered to be transmitted "by 'parenteral injection' of saliva or semen positive for B antigen through breaks in anal or oral mucosa during anilingual (tongue/anus) contact or proctogenital intercourse (penile/rectal sodomy)" (*New England Journal of Medicine*, 1980, p. 302).[2]
- *Tuberculosis and syphilis* — these are charging back since the beginning of the 1980s, in both the United States and Canada, among other things, because of AIDS and cocaine use, the latter because it promotes high-risk sex activity, often performed in exchange for the drug. Officials express huge concern because syphilis sores provide an easy route of entry for the AIDS virus (*Globe and Mail*, June 7, 1991). As for tuberculosis? AIDS patients are particularly vulnerable because of weakened immune systems. Nearly half the AIDS patients in some New York State AIDS clinics have the disease. The North York, Ontario, public health department has reported "a one hundred per cent increase" in 1991. No reason given.

Most of these diseases do not normally occur except through food or water contamination. However, they are endemic to the homosexual population. Physicians from the Johns Hopkins School of Public Health note in their recent study of 388 homosexuals that male homosexuals are "at high risk for Gay Bowel Syndrome" because of what the doctors euphemistically refer to as their "distinctive sexual practices."[3]

- *STDs* — In addition to the above, rates for standard sexually transmitted diseases like syphilis, gonorrhea, genital warts, herpes, chlamydia, and human papilloma virus have been soaring for the past two decades. Some STDS are bacterial and can be treated. But the majority are viral, will remain for the lifetime of the patient, and can be transmitted by skin-to-skin contact, even by breastfeeding (AIDS). A recent World Health Organization report stated that "about two people are infected every five seconds" in the United States and Canada. Twenty percent of the 14-40 female age group have HPV; syphilis is at its highest level in 40 years in both nations.[4] Male homosexuals are responsible for up to one-half of all U.S. cases of syphilis.[5]
- According to a wide range of medical and scientific journals and reports, male homosexuals have the following diseases or conditions more frequently than heterosexuals by the following multiples: syphilis — 14 times; gonorrhea — 3 times; genital warts — 3 times; hepatitis — 8 times; lice — 3 times; scabies — 5 times; penile-contact infection — 30 times; oral/penile infection — many hundreds of times; AIDS — 5000 times.

But the most important message the public is *not getting* is that all the following behaviours or substances were known to be highly immunosuppressive long *before* AIDS became widely known. Namely, there is an immunosuppressive response to semen following anal intercourse; to recreational drugs like nitrates ("poppers" and "snappers"); and to "speed," or the "speedball" (a mixture of heroin and either speed or cocaine). Some of these enable a perpetual erection combined with orgasm suppression, and thus are perfect for continuous promiscuous sex. Also immunosuppressive are chronic antibiotic drug use (often associated with promiscuity); opiate drugs; multiple transfusions; anesthetics; malnutrition (often caused by "gay bowel syndrome"); Epstein-Barr virus; and hepatitis B virus. All the above substances and behaviours are highly associated with AIDS, and are life-style related.[6]

Of late, the AIDS virus (HIV) has been detected in the bowel epithelium of patients with gastro-intestinal problems.[7] And the reason anal sex is so dangerous is because while the vagina is built of tough platelike cells meant to withstand sex and childbirth, the urethra and rectum are made primarily of columnar cells, which rupture more easily and allow infected semen more readily to enter the blood supply, causing immune system havoc.[8]

AIDS is thought by some to have been communicated to man from animals, particularly from the green monkey. A British scientist has recently found evidence that many people were injected with monkey blood in the course of malaria research "experiments" during the past 50 years, carried out to see if malaria could be passed from animals to humans (Toronto *Star*, November 28, 1991). This discovery has given relief to Africans, who have been outraged by the suggestion that Africans may have had sex with monkeys, and thus brought the world AIDS.

## THE GREAT AIDS COVER-UP

AIDS is the first politically protected disease in modern history, and it is overwhelmingly related to high-risk homosexual behaviour. So much so, it was initially labelled gay cancer, or "GRID" — gay-related immune deficiency — before being changed, through political pressure, to remove stigma from homosexuals. In all other ages, human societies have used whatever means were available to protect themselves from threatened extinction due to a virulent disease. For the most part, they were failed by inadequate understanding and technology, not by public or political will. It is different with AIDs. The process that governs what we know about this disease, that prevents us from knowing the unvarnished truth, is purely political.

Everyone has a hand in the pot. The left is using the fear of AIDS to push its antidiscrimination, social-equality agenda, as well as its sexual liberation programming for the public schools (the deadly condom/"safe-sex" scam); the right, and all sorts of fundamentalists, are using the AIDS scare as a moral lever to discipline their children and society at large (AIDS is the work of God, wrathful vengeance wrought upon a sinful world); the major research institutions are using the AIDS scare to extort more money from governments (give it to us now, or the whole world will die). Of all these groups, the fundamentalists may end up with the best case, simply because it is highly likely that AIDS, which is not a new disease but really a collection of old ones, has been here before. Professor Robert Root-Bernstein, of Michigan State University, one of only a handful of researchers who have bothered to search historical medical records, says that AIDS may have a new name but it is not a new syndrome. He confirms that he has found hundreds of such cases as far back as 1872, and insists that AIDS is largely a "life-style" disease.[9]

Homosexuals know this. That is why AIDS is being used politically by their lobby groups to distort information, fool the public, hide the truth, spare themselves stigma, and promote their own sexual agenda. It's a dreadful mess. I don't think anyone really knows what's going on, and I'm certainly not going to pretend I do. However, this brief segment on AIDS belongs in this book because, as I have argued, homosexuality is an antifamily phenomenon, and AIDS in North America is still overwhelmingly a homosexual disease. Encouraging more of one will bring more of the other. What we are allowed to know about it will affect our judgment as parents and citizens, how we react to public policy, and what is taught to our children. Clearly, we ought to be a lot more skeptical of what we hear and read, and a lot tougher when it comes to demanding the truth about this horrendous, and horrendously political, disease.

## SOME FACTS ON THE FAST TRACK TO AIDS

Michael Fumento, the man homosexuals love to hate, and author of *The Myth of Heterosexual AIDS* (1990) — a book I have never seen reviewed in Canada — pointed out in *Commentary* magazine (December 1991) that the estimates, projections, and conclusions surrounding the AIDS epidemic have proved completely wrong. (Readers must be wary. The human immuno-deficiency virus, HIV, though still thought by most to be the "cause" of AIDS, is under increasing scrutiny. The lag between infection by the virus and succumbing to full-blown AIDS can be over 10 years. The two conditions — the virus and the disease — should not be confused.) As late as 1987, many authorities, informed and otherwise, predicted that many millions of North Americans would be infected by 1990, and a 1987 cover story in *U.S. News and World Report*, saying "the disease of *them* is now the disease of *us*," treated AIDS as a general heterosexual disease. By 1989, various prestigious U.S. medical and governmental authorities made predictions for AIDS of between half a million cases (Surgeon General Koop) to 1.5 million (the Centers for Disease Control) and even 4 million. The World Health Organization (WHO) predicted 100 million cases worldwide by 1990. One British estimate was for 1 million in the U.K. alone, by 1991. Alistair Clayton, director general of Canada's Federal Centre for AIDS, confidently predicted that 20,000 Canadians would develop AIDS by 1990, with 16,337 new cases appearing in 1989 alone. Dr. Norbert Gilmore, of Canada's National Advisory Committee on AIDS, predicted 105,000 cases by "the late 1980s."

Fumento gives the official U.S. AIDS tally as of August 1991: 188,348 total cases, of whom 121,196 had died.

U.S. heterosexual cases, including Haitians and Africans, came to 10,279.

Of whites with the disease, a mere 727 cases, or *less than one-half of one percent of all cases*, is listed as having contracted the disease by heterosexual means! A SIECUS report on U.S. AIDS cases states that among heterosexuals with the disease, about 80 percent are black and Hispanic IV drug users (Ottawa *Citizen*, October 6, 1991).

The current heavily revised CDC estimate is for 1 million U.S. cases, total. As for the rest of the world? There have been only about 4000 cases reported in all the U.K., in the whole 10 years of the "epidemic." The WHO has scaled down its 100-million projection, to 8-10 million. Health and Welfare Canada reported that by October 29, 1992, 6889 Canadians had developed AIDS, ever since 1979 (not 20,000, or 105,000). Of these, 4370 (63 percent) had died. Of the total, living and dead, 360 are listed as adult females (the vast majority from high-risk groups), 38 as boys, and 36 as girls, most of whom presumably got it from their mothers, or from blood transfusions.

Heterosexual activity accounted for only 5 percent of all cases. Half these cases were from "pattern II" countries (see below), and the other half had "sexual contact" with a person at risk. Although entire schools are running AIDS conferences to communicate the AIDS "plague" to students, in the entire history of the disease in Canada, there have been only 24 reported cases of AIDS in the 15-19 age group, 17 of whom had died by October 29, 1992; the vast majority got the disease at birth, or from blood transfusions (Toronto *Star*, October 6, 1991). Dr. Maura Ricketts, medical epidemiologist for the Canadian Centre for AIDS, says, "The Canadian epidemic is largely driven by Gay men" (same *Star* article). For a whole decade, the federal government has "consistently misled Canadians about the risk of getting AIDS," says Toronto epidemiologist Eric Mintz. The University of Western Ontario's Dr. Ian MacNeill maintains the same. There has been a massive deception and disinformation program mounted by the State, which has finally admitted that "there is no evidence of spread into the general heterosexual population" (Ottawa *Citizen*, September 6, 1991). Fumento says that more white heterosexual males with breast cancer are diagnosed each year than those with heterosexually transmitted AIDS.[10]

AIDS, Fumento tells us, is at present declining in all risk categories, and was "flattening" long before any therapy was available, following a normal "saturation effect" common to all such diseases. He says that despite the media and educators' hype, so-called safe-sex has played only a minuscule role in the rate of decline of infection. He also says that the CDC has found that up to 30 percent of cases labelled "heterosexual" in fact belong to other categories, and that U.S. "national statistics on heterosexual transmission, low as they are, are significantly overstated." Fumento also says that, after some minimal effort to protect themselves, as the disease now wanes, U.S. homosexuals "have gone back to engaging in the riskier activities." So have Canadians. An Edmonton study of 205 homosexual men "revealed that most engaged in extremely high-risk sex; more than half (59 percent) reported practising 'insertive' anal intercourse without a condom." A Chicago study reported that fully 90 percent of homosexuals there thought their chances of contracting AIDS were either "some chance" (50 percent), or "small" (40 percent).[11] We are talking about loaded guns here. Dr. Paul Cameron, an AIDS researcher at the Washington Family Research Institute, says pointedly that AIDS activists have capitalized on public fear "to democratize the disease." He says that what is essentially a disease contained within the homosexual and drug-user community has been portrayed as everyone's disease. That portrayal, says Dr. Cameron, has enabled the gay community to continue promoting its risky life-style without objection. However, he adds, "it's not a lifestyle, it's a deathstyle."[12] In February 1990, the CDC reported that male homosexual, male bisexual, and intravenous drug users still account for about 90 percent of AIDS cases, and about half of the remainder have had contact with them. About 3 percent have been accidentally infected through treatment with blood, or blood products. (The official party line for almost a decade was that AIDS could not be transmitted through blood banks. Many innocents have already died, and more are yet to die, for that self-serving opinion.[13])

To the question: How about Africa, where so many cases are found among heterosexuals? the answer is not clear. Many argue that the unsanitary conditions, high prevalence of multiple STDs, heat, promiscuity, prostitution, lack of sewage control (the pattern II profile), and unadmitted anal intercourse among Africans of both sexes create a disease envelope, or biological environment much like what is found in North American homosexual bath houses, where fecal material, genital fluids, saliva, blood, contaminated water, heat, and oral/anal sex are regular features. Gay bowel syndrome is really a collection of "tropical" bacterial bowel diseases common among many Africans, and also among children in daycare centres everywhere. That's why an American epidemiologist recently declared that "daycare centers are the open sewers of the twentieth century" (*Health*, October 1991). He could have included bath-houses in that description. Regardless, most agree that AIDS, wherever found, in the absence of such conditions, is largely a "behavioural disease."

Fumento says there is not a thing we can do about individuals who insist on engaging in high-risk behaviour, and that AIDS "cannot be socially engineered out of existence." The best that can be done, he says, "is to tell people exactly how the disease is transmitted and, especially, who is at greatest risk." This, he says, is exactly what the AIDS establishment "has so far tried desperately *not* to do." He cites a (U.S.) $30-million advertising program targeted "at people who still think AIDS is someone else's problem . . . at white middle-class heterosexuals." And he comments: "Here we go again."

In fact, we are spreading extremely dangerous disinformation to the public and especially to school children, because they are being told that homosexuality is normal and are not vigorously counselled against such behaviours. But because AIDS is so overwhelmingly associated in North America with what homosexuals do, this message is close to a counsel of death. In fact, there is currently a looming controversy about the whole matter of AIDS causation, in that many serious international scientists, including Luc Montagnier, co-discoverer of the AIDS virus, are adopting a "modified" view of AIDS causation that links it with multiple co-factors of "immuno-suppressive behaviour."[14] Montagnier, Root-Bernstein, and about 50 other scientists met in May of 1992 in Amsterdam at an "alternative" AIDS conference, where they assailed the "HIV dogma" for its shortcomings, and focused on life-style "co-factors" and various newly suspected micro-organisms.[15]

Despite what we may have been led to believe, AIDS is a very small, but very expensive, disease (about $60,000-$100,000 per patient). And everywhere, huge sums of money are being spent on AIDS research, and far, far less on the real killers. It's time to consider that we are diverting precious financial resources from the major diseases we can largely prevent, to a minor one only potential sufferers can prevent.

Every year in Canada, more women die from breast cancer (about 4500) and cervical cancer (about 600) than the *total of both sexes* who have died of AIDS since 1979. Every year, close to 3000 Canadian males die of prostate cancer. More than 54,500 Canadians die of cancer annually (about 600,000 Americans), and about 77,000 Canadians die every year of cardiovascular disease (about 775,000 Americans). Meanwhile, in 1991, only 330 Canadians died of AIDS — a free-fall drop in mortality from the peak year of 792 deaths in 1988 reported October 29, 1992. But in Canada in 1991, breast cancer, for example, got only $1.6 million worth of cancer research dollars from Ottawa, while AIDS got $16 million in 1991-92; $138 million in the five-year period ending March 1993. Diseases like cervical cancer are *totally preventable* if caught early.

According to Canada's Federal Centre for AIDS, of all male victims ever diagnosed, 87 percent report themselves as homosexuals, bisexuals, intravenous drug users, or some mix of these. Understandably, even such figures are low because many fear the stigma of homosexuality. Guesstimates are that between 12,000 and 29,000 Canadians were HIV positive as of 1991. (It is assumed that most who have the virus will die from AIDS.) Fumento maintains that because AIDS is so behaviour-related, which we cannot (or decline to) control, and it cannot at present be cured, the millions of Canadian and billions of American dollars spent on AIDS, most of them transferred from other medical research or social programs, are nigh futile, and "a great many people will die of other diseases because of the over-emphasis on AIDS."[16] What about the argument that AIDS deserves more funding because it is contagious, while heart disease and cancer are not? Listen to this bit of truth from *Commentary* magazine: "In fact, AIDS is contagious almost exclusively through behaviour, and modification of that behaviour could in theory reduce future AIDS cases virtually to zero without another penny spent on research and without a single medical breakthrough."[17]

## Politics and Public Health

There is cause for worry, because the politics of AIDS, which seems to be largely controlled by homosexuals wherever there are "AIDS committees," government overseers, or media watchdogs, is preventing a full public examination of the relevant facts. In what follows, questions are raised that are not being answered or even aired in the media because of political fear — and now, the threat of fines. This is an abuse of public trust.

Many AIDS epidemiologists argue, as above, that AIDS is extraordinarily difficult to catch if you don't indulge in high-risk behaviour.

The danger arises from the fact that liberal "experts" are trumpeting the virtues of "education" and "counselling" to ensure not that the young, say, abstain from such behaviours, but that they engage in them "safely." But what, exactly, is "safe," and how does the public find out? After all, apparently "1 in 5 MDs fear AIDS in classroom," says an article informing us that of 2000 doctors surveyed, 20 percent say they would "pull their children out of class" if they knew a classmate had HIV (Toronto *Star*, April 17, 1991). Fully 88 percent of medical students say they have the right to know whether or not a patient is infected before a physical examination.

## SOME FACTS ON THE SLOW TRACK TO AIDS

*Never Let a Fool Kiss You, or a Kiss Fool You*

OLD SAYING[18]

In a blow to prevailing opinion, the *Journal of the American Medical Association* reported that the AIDS virus can "theoretically" be passed on while kissing (*JAMA*, January 13, 1989), and a 1989 advisory from the CDC warned U.S. dentists that "blood, saliva, and gingival fluid from all dental patients should be considered infective . . . Hemoglobin — and therefore blood — is normally present in the saliva of about 50% of subjects. This percentage significantly increases after teeth brushing, and after passionate kissing . . . [therefore] passionate kissing cannot be considered protective sex for the transmission of human immunodeficiency virus infection" (*New Dimensions*, Special Issue, 1989).

In one Italian study, 80 percent of 45 people studied had blood in their saliva after brushing their teeth, and 91 percent had it after passionate kissing. On December 8, 1991, Kimberly Bergalis, 23, of Fort Pierce, Florida, who contracted AIDS from her bisexual dentist, died at her family home. Her dentist had died the year prior, but doctors, who initially had rejected the idea of infection by the dentist, determined that Kimberly's particular strain of HIV almost identically matched his virus (Associated Press). He reportedly infected four others who will also die.

Am I now arguing against myself by saying, above, that AIDS is tightly confined to the homosexual community, and then warning about the risk of getting AIDS from heterosexual or casual or household contact? Not really. For it is entirely possible to argue both points. Although AIDS is mostly confined to male homosexual, male bisexual, and drug behaviour, where it is communicated with a wildfire certainty, it may also possibly be communicated, although with much greater difficulty, through casual contact among people outside such groups. This we cannot discover through epidemiology, which is purely retrospective. Epidemiologists tell you very accurately how many horses and of what type are coming out of the barns of the nation, and when. But they didn't go into the barns, so to speak. And they have no way of knowing if there are tunnels connecting some of them. Consider the following.

Fully 256 Canadians infected with AIDS report they have *no idea* how they got the disease, and have "no identified risk factor" (Health and Welfare report, October 29, 1992). In the United States, in 1990, 1848 people with AIDS had "no identified risk factor."[19] That's a lot of people.

If the AIDS virus, with up to a three-year "negative window" of undetectability and a 10-year period for full-blown AIDS, is commonly communicable, even if with great difficulty, a creeping plague could indeed be under way. If so, a special hazard for children everywhere are schools and daycare centres, where young children kiss each other, sneeze, cough, eat each other's food, suck on toys, bite each other, sometimes bleed on each other, and generally get saliva and lots of microscopic fecal matter on everything. And it's not just physicians who are nervous. In Saint John, New Brunswick, a man with AIDS was given a two-year sentence for biting another man (*Globe and Mail*, January 23, 1992). And British doctors say they have diagnosed the first case of AIDS transmitted during a fist fight (between a wedding guest and a gate-crasher — *Globe and Mail*, January 25, 1992). And a 25-year-old Italian soccer player got the AIDS virus after colliding with an infected player.[20]

Dr. William Haseltine, a prominent Harvard researcher, has warned that "anyone who tells you categorically that AIDS is not contracted by saliva is not telling you the truth. AIDS may in fact be transmissible by tears, saliva, bodily fluids, and mosquito bites." (*New Dimensions*, February 1990.) The CDC itself admits there is plenty of evidence that the virus is present and active in tears, saliva, semen, breast milk, vaginal secretions, urine, cerebrospinal fluid, and amniotic fluid.[21] Whether or not it is *easily* transmissible is another matter. As recently as 1980, no one thought blood transfusion could transmit the disease; now it's common knowledge. Many have died from such denial. No one in 1980 thought needlesticks could transmit HIV. Now it's common knowledge. Today, no one thinks saliva can do it. But tomorrow? Clearly, until we know for sure, there are millions of health-care workers at potential risk of accidental death from AIDs.

## A Hardy Virus

British AIDS expert Dr. John Seale, of the Royal Academy of Medicine, said in 1987 in a report to the British parliament that "the AIDS virus is unusually stable outside the human body . . . it retains almost all its infectivity after seven days in water at room temperature, and some after being kept dry for a week. A virus with this degree of stability, which persists in the blood and is shed in saliva, cannot fail to be transmitted in many ways apart from sex." The virus can even survive freezing. This expert worries about the growing incidence of pneumocystis pneumonia, because patients cough aerosols (spray) containing saliva and blood; about the fact that people are being misled everywhere about "safe sex" and the protection offered by condoms; about the cruel deception that the blood supply is safe (24,000 to 30,000 Americans have got the AIDS virus from unscreened blood; the French are involved in a huge scandal over contaminated blood — about $2.8 billion from a class action court settlement has been divided among thousands of the contaminated). Yet those who tried to warn of AIDS from blood supplies were scorned as alarmists. The blood-bank tragedy seems to be an extension of the general scandal, which is that homosexual politicking has prevented the true dimensions of the plague from being known. Some radical homosexuals have even indulged in, and publicly advocated, "blood terrorism," which is the wilful infecting of the blood supply — to get even with society. A writer in the *Dallas Gay News* (May 20, 1983) said, "[I]f research money [for AIDS] is not coming, all gay males should give blood . . . whatever action is required to get national attention is valid. If that includes blood terrorism, so be it."

Journalists at *New Dimensions* magazine probing the politics of AIDS found that scientists almost everywhere were very open and forthcoming with the shocking news on AIDS infectivity. But the public does not hear the story, because homosexual groups effectively filter the news. Dr. Seale testified that "homosexual men have been the most determined and effective in distorting the truth about AIDS." He concluded that "by equating sodomy with sexual intercourse, the impression is given that homosexuals have just been unlucky to get infected before heterosexuals. In reality, homosexual activity has spread the virus through the population at a vastly greater speed [the fast track] than normal sexual intercourse would have achieved" (*New Dimensions*, March 1990). In the same issue, Dr. Lorraine Day, former chief of orthopedic surgery at San Francisco General Hospital and the author of *AIDS: What the Government Isn't Telling You*, complains that throughout North America health workers and physicians can have patients routinely tested and, if necessary, quarantined for all sorts of non-fatal infectious diseases — but not for AIDS, which is fatal. How do you explain that? She justly complains that health workers are at high risk because they are forced to work with patients who may have AIDS, but are not allowed to know this in advance. She says that the AIDS virus can be found in aerosols created by high-speed drill bits used in surgery (Stanford University research), and that the virus is so small it can go through a surgical mask like a BB pellet through a tennis net. Researchers at the National Institutes of Health did high-powered X-ray examinations of latex surgical gloves (similar to condom latex) and found lots of holes 5 microns in diameter. The AIDS virus is 0.1 microns, and can pass through such "protective" latex without even touching the sides of the hole.

Day continues to be attacked in the media for exposing the politics of the homosexual/AIDS lobby. She was the first one to call public attention to the scandal of allowing homosexuals in San Francisco to donate blood on a "self-screening" basis, which, she and others complain, is useless and dangerous, because of "silent AIDS." This is the recent discovery that a significant number of high-risk groups may actually have HIV for up to three years *before* showing positive on current standard tests.[22] Something called a PCR test has even detected AIDS infection up to 42 months prior to detection by standard means (*New Dimensions*, Special Issue, 1989).

Dr. Day, who has operated on thousands of homosexuals but has now quit surgery altogether, says that even 70 percent ethyl alcohol cannot easily kill the virus quickly. She says we may have reason to fear dried urine on toilet seats, and dried blood, saliva, or semen, and that we should be wary of daycare centre work. She convincingly argues that although so far we have few recorded cases of AIDS transmission from contact with other body fluids or aerosols, there has been a virtual blackout on research into this area, so we cannot know the truth. How can you calculate general infectivity, if no one will produce the data? AIDS, she says, is a retrovirus that actually becomes part of the replicating system of DNA in the body, and it is unlikely a cure will readily, if ever, be found; intact skin, she says, is supposed to be a barrier to the virus, but there really is no such thing as intact skin. Tiny cuts, abrasions, hair follicles, and so on could provide a mode of entry. But, again, research is not being done here, nor is it being carried out in the area of transmission through foodstuffs, sneezing, and other marginal modes of transmission. Dr. Day laments that political forces are still blocking research into general infectivity of this deadly virus because homosexuals fear public alarm and a consequent call for quarantining homosexuals. Thus, they are desperate to persuade the public that this is a general (not behaviour-related) disease, and that "safe sex" will solve all problems.

### So the Beat Goes On . . .

Toronto's fourth bath house, the Cellar, opened in May 1991, but — "now they're tolerated . . . even encouraged, because they promote safe sex" (*Globe and Mail*, June 1991). The Ontario Public Health Association, an influential health lobby, in 1989 recommended giving condoms to the poor and recognizing the rights of homosexual "spouses." The *Globe and Mail*, in a scandalously irresponsible article, "Safe Sex: Defusing the AIDS Time Bomb" (July 4, 1991), utters all the common "advice," including wear a latex glove for "activities" such as "inserting the hand into the rectum."

Meanwhile, in "Protesters Hold Die-in over AIDS," (Toronto *Star*, December 2, 1990), homosexuals complained that "people still try and pretend AIDS is a disease of gay men." One ultra cheerful egalitarian politician, Ontario's "citizenship" minister, Elaine Ziemba, was even reported to have "bent over backwards in her attempt not to appear homophobic." The first thing she did was "to dismiss the idea that homosexuals are connected to the AIDS plague. She called this a 'myth'" (*The Interim*, March 1991). What planet is she living on? Epidemiologist Eric Mintz says Canadians have been "terrorized" by unfounded warnings about getting sex through vaginal intercourse (*Globe and Mail*, October 10, 1991). "We've been given the big heterosexual scare," he said, "told that all unsafe sex is of equal risk." Mintz says that the reason the disease is slowing down in Canada is because all the gay and bisexual men most at risk already have the disease. In the same article, John Blatherwick, chief medical officer of Vancouver, says that "we totally allow ourselves to ignore that a major transmission of AIDS is via anal intercourse." And *Globe and Mail* science editor Stephen Strauss says the same: "I believe a massive overplaying of the risk to women feeds into this awful ignorance because our medical coverage and public awareness programs criminally underplay the overwhelming gayness of the plague." He's right. It is criminal. Because it means that lots of innocent people, including children, are going to die, simply because the homosexual lobby is politically powerful enough to ensure that normal public health protection is not introduced. It remains powerful because the public, the media, and the educational establishment are morally cowardly and frightened to condemn homosexual behaviour. Many will pay the ultimate price.

### The "Gay" Lobby

For reasons strictly relating to the perpetuation and "normalization" of homosexuality, the homosexual lobby everywhere is powerfully united in its effort to distort and filter what the public gets to know about AIDS. Here's their strategy.

1. They oppose automatic testing of all high-risk groups such as hospital patients, because they want to avoid "stigma." This means hundreds of thousands of health-care workers are unduly exposed to potentially deadly risk. Dr. Day says she is allowed to test a patient for any disease known to man, except AIDs. And as a patient, you have a right to know practically everything about your surgeon — except whether he or she has AIDS.
2. They oppose laws requiring physicians to inform sex partners of patients who have AIDS. (Which means the decision to infect another is up to the infected party. We can place little faith either in the morals or the mental condition of such diseased individuals.)

   Public health officers, paid to protect us against death and disease, are normally *required* to inform anyone who may have had contact with a diseased person. Yet they are *not allowed* to inform the innocent victims of AIDS patients, unless those names are volunteered by the transmitter. Ontario physicians must decide for themselves whether to report, and then only if they believe their patient will put others at risk. ("Honest, Doc, I'm a nice guy.") In short, if there are homosexual physicians involved, you are not likely to be told if your lover or spouse has AIDS. AIDS patients are like people walking around with loaded guns that can go off any time.
3. They oppose even confidential reporting (although Ontario and

British Columbia are now mounting "self-reporting" programs that guarantee confidentiality to the homosexual).

4. They oppose barriers to blood donation. Donating blood, they argue, is up to them, and they can self-screen responsibly, just like other people.

5. They oppose "contact tracing" to inform unknowing former partners that they had relations with an infected person. (Some jurisdictions have an anonymous method whereby the infected person gives names to a public health officer, who then informs the contact, without revealing the partner's name.)

6. They have successfully lobbied in the United States and Canada to have people with AIDS treated as a "protected disability." You cannot fire or refuse to hire or to work with anyone who has AIDS, and you can't insist a person be tested or object if he is your child's teacher or classroom playmate.

## The Liberal Illusion

What all this boils down to is that carriers of this deadly virus have persuaded politicians and public health officials to rely on "self-reporting." The assumption is that once infected persons are informed, and given enough educational counselling about their responsibilities to their past and future partners, they will do the right thing. It's the liberal illusion in flesh and blood. Reason shall prevail. Education will solve everything. The vices of mankind can be washed away by a rational approach to moral and social problems.

But what is the truth?

Deadly. On January 9, 1992, the *New England Journal of Medicine* reported that "only 7 per cent" of newly infected homosexuals had been notified voluntarily by their infected partner. Canadian doctors said they were "alarmed" by the study, and one physician said it was "terrifying." This almost nonexistent rate of notification was recorded "despite in-depth counselling about the best method of breaking the news to their partners." Despite this bleak reality, Ontario, for example, has "no specific guidelines for partner notification." Jay Browne, that province's AIDS coordinator, said the province "relies on the good-will of those infected by the virus to pass on the news" (*Globe and Mail*, January 9, 1992). The news! He also said, "we take the word of the patient." Classic liberal assumption clashes with eternal reality of human behaviour, with deadly consequences. Our "public health" policies are killing innocent citizens.

But the people may be stirring. Some "health officials say they now fear losing the power to curb a deadly disease and protect unsuspecting people from becoming infected" (Toronto *Star*, April 21, 1991). When people like Magic Johnson get AIDS, or a 24-year-old woman who later died of AIDS reveals she slept with 50 NHL players, likely victims clamour for protection, and we read: "Athletes May Face Mandatory AIDS Test" (*Globe and Mail*, December 4, 1991). After all, hockey players bleed all over each other when they fight (between brief bouts of hockey). People in buses get sneezed on. And, of course, it is true that AIDS can be passed heterosexually — but it is impossible for an infected heterosexual person to get AIDS through normal sex unless his or her partner has had contact with a high-risk group; namely, homosexual or bisexual men, intravenous drug users, or heterosexuals who have sampled such behaviour.

The shocker is that if you have *any ordinary infectious disease* in Canada or the United States other than AIDS, you will be controlled by law for the sake of public health. In fact, you will likely be quarantined. But if you have AIDS, which is deadly, you will be treated as if you do not have an infection. All laws and public policies governing AIDS are for the benefit of the infected person, not the uninfected. This is true even though we know that about 80 percent of people with AIDS eventually suffer severe brain damage, and at least half will have clinically apparent signs of this effect, called HIV encephalopathy, or "AIDS dementia complex."[23] Such people are a danger to others when they fly aircraft, work with heavy equipment, drive school buses, and so on. But you can't protect yourself or your loved ones from them.

Meanwhile, this protected group of people, whose unnatural behaviour has caused most of the spread of AIDS, rather than *changing* its behaviour is exerting every effort to change the public's *perception* of its behaviour. Of course, some homosexuals are "responsible." But that is beside the point, because the public is not allowed to distinguish these from the many who are blatantly irresponsible, if not morbidly careless. Scary. In a typical example of this, "Toronto Gays Practising Safer Sex, Survey Finds" (*Globe and Mail*, September 21, 1991), we read, ominously, that condom use has "increased dramatically" among gay men. (Just not so, and anyway, were the researchers in the room with them? At any rate, condoms are notoriously unsafe, as we saw in Chapter Eight.) However, (here's the agenda): "There will have to be extensive education of teenage boys before they become sexually active if the

AIDS epidemic is to be controlled." The two "researchers" said that previous school-based AIDS awareness programs had "wimped out" on dealing with questions of homosexuality. This is code for them wanting to tell very young boys explicitly about anal sex: "There is a real danger if we don't start now, when people need to hear the information, before their sexual patterns are established." Get it? They call it an "epidemic" (meaning, it'll get you if you're not careful, as opposed to, don't do such things in the first place); "education" is their answer (meaning, nature must have its way, let's just make sure it's safe). And by "sexual pattern" they mean sexual orientation is inbred and not a matter of choice, so rather than talk of moral character, or impressing upon the young the unnaturalness of choosing homosexual behaviour, we should put the inner God in a condom.

A March 1991 "safe sex" story in the Dalhousie *Gazette* (Nova Scotia), featuring an explicit photo of a man performing oral sex on another man, explained: "Telling our stories of wild safe sex serves to make us all aware of the myriad possibilities for lust and passion in our lives."

Such a near-hysterical shriek of self-indulgence may well serve as our moral, cultural, and national epitaph.

# 15

# The Invisible Holocaust: Abortion vs. the Family

*"Abort God!"*

A PRO-ABORTION PLACARD, 1991

*The Victorians used to hide the pregnant woman. Now we hide the child. Permanently.*

MARTHA CREAN, *TORONTO LIFE*, FEBRUARY 1991

Just about everyone you care to ask has a firm, deeply felt opinion on abortion, one way or the other. And it is very likely that a great many people reading this book either have had abortions themselves or have approved of them for their spouses, children, or friends. In Canada, we are all implicated — by government decree — because, whether we approve of them or not, we are forced to pay for abortions through taxes. In short, there are a lot of closet aborters out there. Including me. As a young man, I helped a 20-year-old friend who had a considerable command over my pulse rate obtain an illegal abortion. She had conceived with her fiancé, who then ran off. Unwilling to have her end up with a back-alley abortionist, I dragged her to confess to her (as it turned out) understanding father, who provided ample funds. I figured it was just a microscopic bit of tissue anyway, and argued vigorously that she should free herself from an unappreciative lover's legacy.

When it comes to abortion, very few really know, or want to know, what is going on out there. The preferred approach is to consign the whole subject to a kind of diplomatic pouch in the hopes that private options may be preserved at public expense. Once the full truth of this subject is pulled from the pouch, however, most people engage in a kind of instant intellectual contortionism to adjust their moral assumptions. This response has told me that all is not well in our fair land, and that we seem collectively to have drifted seriously off course. For it is impossible to speak or write more than a few words about abortion without taking some kind of moral stand.

Neutrality, after all, is really just a coward's vote for the confusion of the status quo, so I beg of the reader a willing suspension not of all judgment, of course, but of all *prior* judgment, until the end of this chapter and the following one as well. That is a difficult but essential effort, because in sharp contrast to the prevailing dogma, this subject has a moral importance far beyond the interests of any single individual. The abortion/euthanasia issue — the two cannot be separated — is like an unforgiving prism that refracts and reveals the moral conscience of society and the quality of our whole civilization.

## WHAT THE PEOPLE THINK

### The Great Religions

Whether in the world's great religions, the legal code, or public polls, past or present, the great majority of human beings from all civilizations have always strongly rejected what we would call abortion on demand. Mankind has universally sought "to balance a concern for the mother with a concern for the fetus," and where there are exceptions made for rape, incest, terrible deformity, or for the life of the mother, these have always been carefully limited "and in no way predicated on the notion of a woman's right to do as she pleases with the fetus in her womb."[1] Most religions have always considered abortion a sin, or a crime — but not always murder. This is because historically they did not consider the fetus to have a soul until after "quickening," the point at which the fetus first stirs. Then, under one name or another, "ensoulment" or "hominization" is deemed to have taken place, the spirit of God is said to enter the person, and killing the fetus becomes an irremediable evil. In 1869 the Roman Catholic church became the only absolutist faith regarding abortion, and since then it has considered the fetus human from conception. In the middle ages, St. Augustine even argued that abortion was much worse than murder, because it deprived the fetus of baptism and thus denied a human soul entrance into heaven.[2] In the sense that one of the main functions of all religions (prior to the rise of the so-called religion of "humanism") is to harness and direct the sexual energies of society to higher ends, all faiths universally reject abortion as an "affront to the procreative meaning" of marriage, as well as a "subterfuge for sexually immoral conduct."[3] They disapprove of what we now call contraceptive abortion. In Augustine's eyes, abortion was like trading defenceless lives for personal carnal pleasure.

As the lights dim on our civilization, we can move back in time and reflect with some pride that it was very likely the absolutist nature of Judeo-Christian love, especially for the weakest, most defenceless members of society, that drove the paganism out of the Roman Empire. For Christianity, despite whatever else it may have done, essentially elevated the moral and legal value of human life beyond the reach of all but the most deliberate tyrannies, especially those perpetrated by the State itself. Because a Roman infant was officially a non-person until its father declared the child wanted (the mother had no say), unwilling mothers often would leave babies exposed by open sewers, hoping they would die of some vile disease. Just as surreptitiously, other women, "grieving over their barrenness, would hasten no less secretly to snatch the baby, hoping to palm it off on a credulous husband as their own, and thus with a supposititious heir, to still the ache in his paternal heart."[4]

By the beginning of the third century A.D., however, under the influence of a swelling Christian spirit, the first laws were passed forbidding infanticide and pagan ritual. This new moral focus, the first to put a brake on Roman barbarism in three centuries, formed a crucial distinction between Roman and Christian society.[5] The authorities of the empire, desperate to control the aimless and often hungry urban population, had for centuries offered them a kind of welfare in the form of bread and "circuses" (*panem et circenses*). At their height these huge affairs, originally designed to display military and athletic prowess, ended by offering huge crowds the most abusive and inhumane exploitations of women, slaves, prisoners, and animals. Death in the Coliseum, approved by the highest authorities and administered in ways designed to titillate the blood-lust and sexual passions of the eager crowd, was the highlight of each day. Slaves or prisoners were often substituted for actors at the decisive moment of a play, and, to the roar and goading of the insatiable crowd, they were mutilated, crucified, beaten, or even mauled to death by wild animals. At the peak of decadence, the Circus Maximus amphitheatre in Rome seated over 255,000 spectators, and such events filled over 150 days of the Roman year — or about one circus day for every workday.

Our modern and extremely explicit pornographic videos are a kind of post-Victorian version of those ancient spectacles, available to millions in the privacy of their homes. It is worth mentioning again that British police recently cracked an international "snuff movie" ring selling thousands of videos of live murders, torture, and mutilation, with such titles as *Cannibal Holocaust*, *Human Experiments*, *Blood Baths*, and *Blood Sucking Freaks*. One video showed a man cutting open the belly of a pregnant woman and eating the fetus (*Globe and Mail*, May 28, 1992). Arguably, barbarism in a post-Christian age merely hides itself in the more dispersed and comfortable amphitheatre of the private home.

The Christian religion from the start was on a collison course with such a pagan (or secular) State, because Christianity passionately defends the idea that because every individual has immeasurable value in the sight of God, *all are essentially equal*.[6] This is a point to which we will return, for it means that man and woman, parent and child, slave and prisoner, *regardless of any earthly differences*, have equal status in the eyes of God.

## The Great Civil and Medical Codes

The great civil and medical codes have always followed the great religions. The Sumerians condemned abortion about 2000 B.C., as did Hammurabi some 300 years later.[7] As for science, about 500 B.C. Hippocrates created his Hippocratic Oath, which for the first time in human history completely barred physicians from their ancient freedom to kill, if they wished. The oath neatly encapsulated the whole notion of the sanctity of life and enjoined all physicians to use every means at their disposal to protect the lives of all patients, especially those of unborn children (" . . . I will not give a pessary to cause abortion . . ."). The Hippocratic Oath controlled the ethics of Western medicine for almost 2500 years, until the 12 years of the Third Reich, when, for the first time, the oath was banned as "obsolete," thus freeing German medical scientists and doctors to engage in "exterminative medicine," as doctors had always done in pagan times. On the decreasing number of occasions on which the Hippocratic Oath is taken by medical students today, the sections on abortion and protection of life in general have been deleted.[8] Nevertheless, the Declaration of Geneva, adopted by the World Medical Association in 1948, in response to Nazi atrocities committed by modern pagan doctors uncontrolled by the oath, states specifically: "I will maintain the utmost respect for human life from the time of conception." And the United Nations Declaration of the Rights of the Child (1959) declares that the child needs special legal protection "before as well as after birth."[9] (The United States supported this U.N. commitment; Canada refused.)

Why have modern physicians surrendered their role as protector of all human life? It's astonishing, when we remember that very late in the 19th century North American physicians complained widely that the clergy was silent on abortion; the American Medical Association (AMA) even urged doctors "to visit every clergyman within their districts in an effort to persuade them to come out against abortion."[10] How times change. Where then aborters were expelled from the AMA as "executioners," today many physicians the world over eagerly perform abortions for handsome fees. There is one explanation that explains this change satisfactorily: Whenever a society worships the Rationalism Illusion, and the corollary illusion of "progress" that requires massive social engineering to get us all to dreamland, physicians must be given the right to kill. The legalized eradication of certain forms of human life deemed to inhibit social perfection becomes part of the "solution" to social progress.

**The Polls, Since Time Began**
No matter where polls are taken, or by whom, whenever the public is asked a straightforward honest question, they repeatedly condemn elective abortion. A Gallup poll of June 20, 1988, showed only 25 percent of Canadians favoured unlimited abortion (even though very few understand what that means legally, or know exactly how abortions are performed. When they are told, the numbers drop significantly); 59 percent said they would grant abortion only in very limited circumstances (such as a serious threat to the mother's physical health, or for cases of rape or incest); and 15 percent said abortion should be illegal in all circumstances. An American Gallup poll of February 1991 revealed that even most respondents who described themselves as "pro-choice" opposed abortion in most circumstances, and according to legal scholar Victor Rosenbaum, "an overwhelming majority of Americans do not know what is allowed under current law." Fully 83 percent of respondents said

the parents must be involved in any abortion decisions for children under 18, and 75 percent said they considered abortion to be the taking of human life.

Huge majorities opposed abortion for school-related (66 percent), financial-related (66 percent), career-related (76 percent), or gender-selection reasons (91 percent). A recent Los Angeles *Times* poll found 85 percent of the people wanted parental consent laws for girls under 18, and 58 percent insisted on spousal consent laws (rejecting the idea that a mother alone has the right to abort a couple's child). As for physicians? In a 1989 poll of 10,000 Canadian physicians, 66 percent wanted "legal protection" for the fetus and opposed the broad "health" reasons for abortion endorsed by their own association.[11]

## How the Truth Is Filtered
The public's views are, however, not reflected in the media. A recent *Media Watch* study showed that the labels used by the media to describe anti-abortion activities were 79 percent negative, while those used to describe so-called "pro-choice" (pro-abortion)* activities were 97 percent positive.[12] Typical of such bias is a Toronto *Star* story describing how the failed campaign of "pro-choice" Ottawa political candidate Maureen McTeer was targeted by "a noisy rump of anti-abortion activists" (March 8, 1992). The editorial pages of most major newspapers support abortion on demand, and two major U.S. media studies have shown that up to 90 percent of U.S. journalists favour so-called "abortion rights."[13] Canadian surveys of media show the same. This is perhaps the most dramatic example of the civil war of values raging between the knowledge class and the people, a war reflected widely in the "State vs. the Family" chart in Chapter Six. When journalists (90 percent of whom support abortion) write about it for a public (where up to 75 percent disapprove), we can be sure we are not hearing the truth.

## The Rankings
How is Canada doing in the abortion rankings? Officially, there were over 94,000 abortions performed in 1990.[14] On a per-1000 women (age 15-44) basis, here's how we compared to other countries in 1989: Canada: 10.2; England and Wales: 14.2; Israel: 16.2;

---

* I use the terms *pro-abortion* and *anti-abortion* throughout this chapter because the issue concerns what happens to unborn babies, not semantics.

Japan: 18.6; Sweden: 19.8; United States: 28.2; Hungary: 38.2; Soviet Union: 111.9 (*Globe and Mail*, February 20, 1991). When we read that the average Soviet woman has half a dozen abortions in her lifetime, and that many Canadian and American abortions are performed on two- or three-timers, Augustine's warnings ring more solemn.

But let us not get buried in the numbers. They flow from the morals of the story, and the key governing moral has always been whether or not the fetus is considered a full "person" or "human being" in religious, civil, or criminal law. This question has always been subjected to a confusing series of value-gradations, and it still is, as we shall see below. Until very recent times, however, these were always *value*-gradations, never *non-value* gradations.

What we seem to ignore, at our peril, is that only four crucial and very simple elements are necessary to fuel the fires of barbarism, ancient or modern. The first is the phenomenon of *progressive* moral degradation. Rome's took only two centuries to reach its basest level. The second is the *official sanction* of such behaviour by the highest authorities. Third is the idea that all potential victims of barbarism (slaves, women, children, prisoners) must be officially defined as *non-persons*, as a class, under the law (this definition protects those engaging in such acts from either public or self-censure). And fourth comes the belief that designated classes of elites (politicians, physicians) may be empowered to *substitute* their judgment for that of the victims, because non-persons are deemed either unworthy or incapable of exercising personal judgment.

All four of these elements have come into conjunction in our own time, and we reap the consequences. Except for the most evil dictatorships, for regimes that have attempted genocidal war against another race, or in the writings of "scientists" or racists who have advocated eugenic manipulation of breeding to achieve a master race, no people in the history of modern civilization has ever rested upon the belief that the unborn child has no value whatsoever — until the last three decades of this century.

Let us at least ask how has this happened.

If the great religions oppose it, if the vast majority of the people oppose it, if all the moral codes of the world have always spoken against it, then how is it possible today for any Canadian or American woman to walk into a public hospital and request a legal, tax-funded abortion, even at nine months' gestation, even right up until the minutes prior to natural birth? How is it possible that a woman today, without public outcry, has total control over the life or death of a baby until the moment of birth, without regard to the father's interest, or society's interest — not to mention the interests of the child itself?

In ancient Rome, under the law of *patria potestas*, the father had complete control (rarely exercised) over the life or death of the child, until the Christian State — our own moral heritage — intervened to block his, *or anyone else's*, power over life. Today, a mere 1600 years later, the father is impotent. In his place the mother, with the blessing of the law and the State, has absolute control over the life or death of the child, a control exercised about 270 times every day in Canada, 4200 times daily in the United States, and 150,000 times daily in the world as a whole. It is said to be her "reproductive right" to destroy the child (even if the father is willing to raise his child alone); and also her reproductive right to keep and raise the child and sue the father for 18 years of child support — if he does not want the child. Women who objected to being owned by men are now successfully claiming to own the unborn. For the child, nothing much has changed. Many argue that a fetus is not cognizant of its own death and, furthermore, feels no pain (we'll get to this later). But as one writer, who herself had an abortion, said: "If a killer creeps up behind you and blows your head off with a semi-automatic, you will feel no pain either, nor will you be cognizant of your death" (*Commentary*, November 1990).

## HOW IT ALL GOT THIS WAY

A series of closely connected political, economic, and moral changes over the past three centuries has resulted in the replacement of religious and moral public views by mere secular and legal ones. Following is a very brief overview of these interconnected changes, which collectively form a kind of envelope of opinion, or expectation, within which we daily make decisions. A key argument of this book is that very little of this change could have come to pass without the advent of the top-down State in the modern period. The major moral evil of our time is not so-called "individualism," as many like to think, but rather "autonomism." (This difference was detailed in Chapter Two, under the Individualism Illusion.) Individualism, properly considered, entails the exercise of individual moral agency by all citizens and results in a spontaneous community of shared values. Autonomism arises in proportion to the action of the State as it progressively promotes the transfer to itself of family and community functions and responsibilities, thus gradually destroying effective moral agency among the citizens. The individual stands alone with the morals of his family, his community, and his God, but the autonomous citizen stands alone before the secular goals of the welfare State. There is an iron chain of logic leading from the ideology of the welfare State, to that of the communist State and its devaluation of life, to the fact that China and the states of the former Soviet Union, combined, average about 30 million abortions per year. This is more than the entire population of Canada in abortions, every year.[15] Let us examine the intellectual process precedent to the modern practice of wholesale abortion on demand.

## Changing Minds: Rousseau and Nietzsche

As mentioned in earlier chapters, Rousseau was a scurrilous, egotistical man devoid of the capacity to love women or children. He surrendered his own five children to an orphanage, where they surely died. He preferred his own ideal of abstract man (under the utopian State) — to real people. Like Plato (who favoured abortion and selective breeding), Rousseau hated social inequity and change. He was determined to eliminate all agencies of change, in effect by establishing a dictatorship based on what he called the General Will. He wrote that "the most ancient of all societies, and the only one that is natural, is the family."[16] He was keenly aware that the values it generates are private and normally linked to transcendent religious ideals beyond the reach of the State. Therefore, along with all religions, especially Christianity, the family had to go, for both institutions inhibit unquestioned obedience to the sovereign leader. In the place of the private family, he wanted to create a single public State "family" with its uniform collectivist ideals. This public family was designed to replace all the competing local ideals that Rousseau maintained always led to social decay. The State would replace all other values, and all religion. Rousseau thus wanted "to change human nature, to transform each individual . . . into a part of the larger whole from which the individual receives, in a sense, his life and his being . . ."[17] The reader will correctly see in Rousseau's ambition a template for both the fascist and the collectivist, or communist, State.

But perhaps the most telling feature of Rousseau's thinking is that he denied the inner struggle of good and evil in the souls of men, which is the focus of all religions. He declared, in effect, that because we are all naturally good, then goodness arises simply from giving way to our own natures or feelings — by unfettering ourselves. Anything bad in us must have come from the outside world, and it is there we must look both for the cause and for the solution. The standard of goodness thus is not the moral law handed down to us (which is said to be authoritarian), nor is it something measured by our inner deliberations on virtue. Rather, goodness comes from obeying our inner natures. This is the new standard of personal truth and authenticity. So in the place of the moral law, even of the civil law, Rousseau put the personal will. That is why pro-abortionists today argue that abortion is strictly a matter of individual choice; of the personal will. The mother's will, over all other wills.

As we saw in Chapter Eight, our young are learning to combine personally created values and the idea of the personal will, right in our classrooms. As a nation we must be wary of this trend. As one of our few original philosophers, George Grant, has written: "It is the very heart of fascism to think that what matters is not what is true, but what one holds to be true," because what one holds to be true "can produce that resolute will, tuned to its own triumph."[18] In other words, absolute belief in personal truth creates tyrants.

The arch-prophet of the modern will was Friedrich Nietzsche (1844-1900), who went beyond Rousseau to argue that all moral systems are really just rationalizations for the "will to power" of certain groups (within nations and, of course, between them); therefore, all morality itself is relative, an artifact of power. His was a rejection of all absolute moral standards of any kind. There is, he said, no absolute right and wrong. He hated bourgeois democracy (because right and wrong in it are the outcome of a vote); the idea of equality (because the power he admired requires subordinates); and Christianity, which he labelled a "slave morality" (because it promotes loving the weak). He spent the last decade of his life hopelessly insane.

It was Nietzsche who combined the idea of the personal will with the idea of science and technology, and reinforced the notion of asserting control over the world around us. Later, a pseudo-Nietzschean named Adolf Hitler insisted, like Rousseau before him, that each person within the National Socialist State, once aligned with its ideals, would find liberation in unity, becoming freed at last from the pull of conflicting values.

Today, however, rather than admit our modern fondness for the triumph of the will, we clothe it in the inspiring language of personal rights and then create charters to guarantee these rights to ourselves at the expense of others. In this vein, George Grant reminds us, it was U.S. senator Huey Long (who knew lots about political power), who said that "when fascism comes to America [and Canada] it will come in the name of democracy."[19] And Grant convincingly argues that the modern women's liberation movement has adopted this same language to reinforce its claim that "biology is not destiny." That is, in order for the radical feminist to escape the bonds of biology, she must rid herself of the "otherness" that lays claim to her body — the fetus. She achieves this by using the language of democratic rights to successively devalue the thing which blocks her freedom, then asserts a higher right in order to dominate the thing. She ends by describing the fetus as a kind of meaningless parasite that inhibits her freedom, and must be gotten rid of. The triumph of her will is thus achieved through the euphemisms of the language of rights, which free her, as Grant puts it, from traditional restraints against killing (as the same sort of language freed the Romans).

This justification is only possible because in its relentless attempt to create a simple connection between the individual and the values of the State, unmediated by higher value systems, the State confers upon all its autonomous citizens an "equal right" to the expression of the personal will. This is a very sneaky process that explains why there is no talk in our various charters of duties, obligations, or responsibilities — just a feast of rights in exchange for allegiance to the State and its ideals (and taxes). The Faustian bargain is struck. Those who cannot provide votes, or whose mere existence blocks the pure cultivation of the autonomy and allegiance necessary to the State, simply get defined out of existence, their official nonexistence propounded in the highest courts of the land. Slaves in America and everywhere else they were (or are) held; Jews under Hitler; and in our own society the fetus — all fall into this class. Thus has the way been prepared. Thus do millions upon millions of young women today insist that abortion is not a moral matter, but simply a matter of personal preference. In order to say such a thing, you first have to kill the child in your mind. Moving the discussion beyond good and evil is a way of altogether avoiding any debate on good and evil.

## PLI, Self-Esteem, MVE, and Sex-Ed

How have Rousseau and Nietzsche come down to us? Very simply, in the various forms of pop psychology and philosophy that focus on personal liberation ideology (PLI) and so-called self-esteem, and of course in the ubiquitous teachings of moral values education (MVE), the crucial offshoot of which is sex-ed. Young people learn very early that right and wrong are a matter of personal choice. In fact, many of the moral "dilemmas" used to engage them in such discussions focus on abortion or euthanasia (called, by some, "pediatric euthanasia").

Rousseau and Nietzsche are incarnate in such classrooms, where every popular illusion of collectivist ideology is purveyed, then combined with the language of rights. Students are assumed to have natures which, once unfettered from authority and especially from family tradition, will conform to the liberal view of "the good," which is presented as natural. This belief requires "the reform" of all sorts of social institutions and forms of thought outside us that inhibit the expression of self. Such reform efforts are visible in textbook redefinitions of the family, marriage, and society, and in the many kinds of thought-police rampant in North America. "Education" is proposed as the answer to all forms of ignorance and evil, so students are told in their classrooms (and in their music) to "get in touch with themselves" (at which point they will be expressing the inner God of nature — their own feelings). Because there is said to be no absolute right and wrong, homosexuality, abortion, and indeed all morality are matters of "orientation" or preference. Pansexualism is the reigning and ultimate ideal of sensuality. Anything narrower is defined as intolerant.

In the feminist pantheon of values, auto-stimulation is very big, and what women decide to do with their own bodies is solely up to them. Stimulate themselves? Empty their wombs? What's the difference? Abortion is presented in sex-ed classes as a simple technological (Nietzschean) solution to inconvenience. In reality, however, the PLI philosophy, in the euphoric language of self-actualization, camouflages a whole range of secondary spillover effects for society at large, even as it proceeds to uproot all traditional values. It does this, willy-nilly, through a progressive disconnection of the individual from any sense of moral duty to an entity or set of values higher than self (or other than self). Even with no plan at all, this single fact of modern life, this process, unresisted, is sufficient to destroy us.

**The Contraceptive Mentality**
Another fact of modern life that has accelerated the devaluation of the fetus ever since the 1970s is the widespread use of contraception. Canadian philosopher Donald DeMarco, of St. Jerome's College in Waterloo, Ontario, is the leading exponent of the view that a "contraceptive mentality" has evolved from our reliance on technology, leading to a mental, and therefore a moral, disassociation of

intercourse from conception, and from there to the increased public acceptance of abortion.[20] Basically, this mentality arises when the separation of intercourse from conception becomes taken for granted through repeated use of contraceptives. People using them begin to feel that they have done their responsible best to prevent unwanted responsibilities, and if a pregnancy arises from contraceptive failure, it is not their fault. It is the fault of the contraceptive. Responsibility has been shunted from the subject to an object. Since technology has failed, then the answer must be . . . better technology. Abortion will simply finish the botched job of contraception, goes the thinking, and we'll be more careful next time.[21]

## The Radical Feminists: "Biology Is Not Destiny"

*Abortion has become the central organizing issue of the women's movement.*
MARTHA CREAN, *TORONTO LIFE*, FEBRUARY 1991

The most virulent voices promoting abortion on demand, under the rubric of the liberal idealism of the Freedom Illusion, are those of the modern radical feminist movement. They offer quite self-contradictory arguments, but it is important to understand the source of their convictions. Their argument is essentially that men and women are basically the same, but women have always been oppressed victims of male patriarchy because they are stuck with unequal social and domestic duties that arise from the fact that they bear and nurture children. Radicals have aggressively attempted to change this "inequality" by spurning the duties associated with child-bearing — and rearing. Their aim is to harness males and, if necessary, force or cow them into sharing more of this duty; or, preferably, to pass the most burdensome part of the duty (in terms of time and cost) onto the State in the form of universal free daycare. Only then, they say, will women be as free (and as uncommitted) as men. Plato pushed it. Rousseau and Marx pushed it. All utopians and statists push it. An essential element of their platform is the unequivocal, unquestioned demand (now called a right) to "control their own bodies" via tax-funded abortion. Some will argue that maybe they ought to have controlled their bodies a little better before they got pregnant; that what we need to tell our children is less about birth control, and more about self-control. At any rate, the male life is seen as the ultimate model, based on the uncommitted anonymous sex (UAS) syndrome. In the end, everything radical feminists promote can be understood best as an attempt to reorganize our biologically based society along male economic and technological lines by persuading the State to accept the responsibility for the so-called unequal female burden. Keep the frazzle curve (Chapter 12) in mind as you ponder this connection between the feminist and abortion rights movements. It explains why they combine so forcefully to convert the bottom-up society into a top-down State. The heart of the first kind of society is free, individualist, moral, biological, and hierarchical. But the second is coercive, collectivist, secular, utilitarian, and egalitarian. The first is utterly pro-family and based on emotional, economic, and legal interdependence. The second is inherently antifamily and based on whatever emotional, economic, and legal autonomy can be squeezed from the tax-funded programs of the welfare State.

Readers may be pleased to know that all is not insane, however. There is actually another "feminist" movement out there called "Feminists for Life." Its members accept feminism in general, but reject the abortion rights dogma that goes along with it. They argue that feminism is, or ought to be, part of a larger philosophy that values all life; that all human beings have inherent worth, and this worth cannot be conferred, or denied, by another. They recognize the interdependence of all living things and "reject the male world view that accepts violence as a legitimate solution to conflict."[22] They say abortion is violence against another human being that denigrates the life-giving capacity of women, and that "feminists who accept abortion have agreed to sacrifice their children for the convenience of the male world view." Radical feminists, they say, rather than rejecting the patriarchal worldview, have swallowed it whole, and have thus capitulated to the male desire to rid themselves of responsibility for children and family. Well, that's refreshing, isn't it? But in the antifamily welfare State, this attitude is anathema. Radical feminist organizations that promote "abortion rights" get millions of our tax dollars every year. Feminists for Life gets nothing. Personally, I think all lobby groups ought to be cut off. But if the State funds feminist pro-abortion groups, how come it doesn't fund feminist anti-abortion groups?

### The Language of Abortion
Part of any political struggle is the campaign to disguise one's objectives in euphemistic or misleading language and slogans. Once radicals discovered that the public did not approve of unlimited rights to abortion, as shown by every poll in history, they dropped the "pro-abortion rights" theme and searched for a higher ground.

It was their hope to neutralize and disguise the real purpose of abortion by an appeal to higher aims, and they have done so.

## *"Freedom Means Choice"*[*]

The radicals have cleverly shifted the entire issue from one of *abortion* rights to one of *civil* rights, wrapping the debate in the inspirational language of freedom. In the previous chapter, we saw how homosexuals use this technique. It consists of using the Victim Illusion to posture oneself as someone whose noblest ambitions are denied expression. This has the effect of categorizing as intolerant all who oppose one's hidden agenda. Hence, the phrase "pro-choice" is designed to imply that if you are against abortion for any reason whatsoever, then you are against freedom. It is sad that our public monologue on abortion has absorbed such a transparent subterfuge: the post-liberal belief that "no objectively established code should force an idea of what is good on the individual, 'good' can be only what each chooses according to her conscience . . ."[24] Readers will see the connection between this belief and so-called moral values education in the schools (Chapter Eight). The evil in it is the idea that each human being lives in a private universe of values and choices, off limits to others, yet has the right to public funds and legal support for the consequences that arise from that privacy.

A moment's thought reveals, however, that all human beings not only have "choice" in everything they do, but are indeed forced by daily circumstances to choose between competing and often difficult alternatives. But a freedom to *choose* between available options in life, however meagre, has never meant that we are able to *dictate* outcomes, or that we are free to evade the biological, social, or moral consequences that arise from our choices. Feminists, like the rest of us, have always had the right to choose — including choosing

---

[*] The three slogans critiqued in the headings of this section were originally invented by Bernard Nathanson, M.D., founder of the U.S. National Abortion Rights Action League. After 60,000 abortions performed, he has turned against abortion on the grounds it is the killing of human life, and he says: "I remember when we made those slogans up . . . We were looking for something sexy; catchy slogans to capture public opinion. They were very cynical slogans then, just as all of these slogans today are very, very cynical." Nathanson also said in his book, *Aborting America*, that he and others lied through their teeth about the number of maternal deaths from abortion prior to legalization: "I confess that I knew the figures were totally false."[23]

whether or not, when, and how carefully to have sex in the first place. The fact that any free exercise of personal choice may have natural consequences we later wish to reject is, however, another matter. For it is false to cry freedom when it is precisely our use of our freedom that has given us an unexpected result. And after all, in a public context, as legal scholar Iain Benson reminds us, "most of our criminal law is based on moral notions of what is 'right' and 'wrong,' on the effects of one person's behavior on others in society and on the principle that such rules of right and wrong should apply regardless of the views of individual citizens."[25] In other words, the act of choosing in itself means nothing. What does matter is what we choose, how we uphold the responsibility for all our choices, and how our choices affect others. What pro-abortionists want is not the freedom to choose; they already have this. They want the freedom to deny the natural consequences of their own actions or, if you prefer, to undo their original choices. They want Godlike powers. We shall see that they have been given them.

Pro-abortionists like Faye Wattleton, president of Planned Parenthood, even insist that moral questions "lie outside our purview"; that it all boils down to "women having a choice . . . women should have nothing less than full autonomy" (*Vogue*, January 1992). It's a silly mantra that utterly divorces the idea of freedom from the idea of responsibility for how one's freedom is used. A simple response from the other side is that all that is wanted is full autonomy for the unborn child. In the same interview, one of her colleagues, intending to describe Wattleton's coolness under fire, uttered a slip that will surely stick when he said: "If she were an axe-murderer, no one would tell you."

These are the same people who argue that although abortion is strictly a personal choice, with no public consequences, the choice to read pornography is not defensible (because, they say, this exploits women); nor is the choice to abort because your baby happens to be female (because this discriminates against women). In this latter case, they argue that nature ought to be allowed to take its course — which is what anti-abortionists have always argued for pregnancy in general (that's why they chant: "A woman's choice: a live baby or a dead baby"). Another irony, of course, is that feminists who have complained for a generation that men do not care enough about parenting utterly exclude fathers from the life-or-death decision to abort a couple's child. (And then, if they change their minds, they turn around and sock the fathers for 18 years of child support.)

These incompatible positions are linked at a deeper level by the combination of the Individualism Illusion and the top-down State.

### *"Every Child a Wanted Child"*

*That every child born be a wanted child, who can receive love and affection.*
DR. HENRY MORGENTALER, STATING THE GOAL OF HIS ABORTION-ON-DEMAND PROGRAM,
*GLOBE AND MAIL*, APRIL 8, 1981

Dr. Henry Morgentaler, Canada's most notorious abortionist, who performed an abortion on nationwide television — on Mother's Day, 1973 — relies on the dangerous "desire = value" equation, primarily because there is no other grounds enabling a nation's law to permit the elimination of some babies, but not others. At least Denyse King, of the Canadian Abortion Rights Action League (CARAL), is more honest. She says that "every woman who is pregnant knows that she is pregnant with a human being." And abortion? "Of course it's discriminatory," she says. But "it's at the woman's discretion."[26] The Swedes preceded her by 20 years. They have long had billboards mounted about their country declaring: "Children, Yes — But When We Want Them." I am reminded of the charming woman who responded to her adolescent child — the last of six — who had complained he was a "mistake." "My dear," she said, amused, "you were all mistakes. Glorious mistakes!" (Half of all North American women say their first child was "unplanned.")

But surely the notion of justifying anyone's right to live on the grounds that he may or may not be "wanted" by someone else at a particular moment is morally bankrupt. It is a dangerous formula for granting some a Godlike control over the lives of others, solely for emotional reasons. Even medical opportunists like Dr. Morgentaler cannot fail to see that this kind of social standard for life or death, based as it is on whether or not we are loved by others today, is a licence for convenience killing. That's why he is desperate to deny the reality of the living child: "There is no child there," he protests. "If there was a baby, women wouldn't have abortions."[27] Only a man could say that.

History shows that everywhere it has been tried, convenience killing that begins as the choice of the individual always ends as the choice of the State, which soon becomes the final arbiter. This process usually starts with abortion, proceeds to infanticide, and ends with euthanasia, initially adopting the idea, as Professor Janet Ajzenstat put it, that "only those who are loved deserve to live."[28] But this is self-delusion, for it is precisely love that aborting women fear. (Hearteningly, the vast majority of women denied abortion proceed to have their children — and end up loving them.) They know that if they don't hurry, they will soon grip the child in a lifelong embrace. Perhaps "every child a wanted child" ought to be replaced by "every mother a loving mother." If every pregnant woman were a cause for social joy, the problem would seldom arise.

Once any grounds for killing human beings as a convenience are established, however, they tend to spread from the most pressing case at hand to the marginal ones — and eventually encompass all undesirables in a wider and wider net. In a fine article, lawyer Robert Nadeau details the stages involved.[29] He cites the compelling American columnist Joseph Sobran, who describes the social and moral evolution of abortion as a three-phase process. First, the activists admit that abortion is evil, but argue that since it is happening anyway, we'd best legalize it and protect women from unsafe abortions (the safety argument). Then, as anti-abortionists reveal the gore behind it all, they switch to the argument that abortion should be a private matter decided between a woman and her physician (the free-choice argument). And finally, the activists describe abortion as a positive public good, or a civil right that ought to get public support (it does). Nadeau cites a number of eminent scholars and scientists to show the moral gradualism built into the process. He explains how in Germany a situation evolved where a community of physicians and scientists who began by defending all life ended, a mere generation later, by killing all citizens deemed unfit and by starving and gassing millions of Jews. Dr. Leo Alexander, medical consultant to the Nuremberg trials, tells us that among physicians it started "from small beginnings . . . with the acceptance of the attitude, basic to the euthanasia movement, that there is such a thing as a life not worthy to be lived . . ." Nadeau cites some truly scary people, just to remind us (especially those who have a disability or disease of any kind) that there is no shortage of experts in any country willing to purge society of its impurities and inconveniences. In 1972, Stanford University "philosophy" professor Michael Tooley wrote that "the practical moral problem [of abortion, deformity, and disability] can be satisfactorily handled by choosing some period of time, such as a week after birth, as the interval during which infanticide will be permitted."[30]

I can hear it now. Irascible, slovenly, hung-over George wakes up to the cries of his newborn, and shouts to his wife: "The little son-of-a-bitch is driving me crazy! Why, I do believe he's got some kinda goddamn *crying disease*. We only got two days left to decide, you know. Better just shut him up for good. I need my sleep, really I do." His despondent, frightened wife answers: "Fine, George. Just hand me the pillow."

In a 1973 issue of *Time* magazine, Nobel prize winner Dr. James Watson, who with colleague Dr. Francis Crick decoded the DNA molecule, said that "if a child was not declared alive until three days after birth, then all parents could be allowed the choice [to kill their child] that only a few are given under the present system." There it is, you see, the argument that such "choices" ought to be extended to wider groups. Not to be outdone in his own passion for purity, Dr. Crick wrote that "no newborn infant should be declared human until it has passed certain tests regarding genetic endowment . . . if it fails these tests, it forfeits the right to live."[31] I think these two ought to forfeit the Nobel prize.

We simply cannot avoid the fact that humans do not deal very well with relative moral or legal systems. Under the influence of their own emotions, they tend to create the most fantastical rationalizations for cruelty of all kinds. The first warming to evil of the utilitarian rational mind is evident in its embrace of "substituted judgment." This is the notion that one human has the right to judge the value of another's existence and exercise power over it — only for benevolent reasons, of course. In 1990, during the infamous Chantal Daigle case in Quebec, Daigle actually declared she underwent her abortion "to protect the fetus." And Thomas Loker, former superintendent of Grandview school for girls, who forced Toronto's Becky Davis to have an abortion in 1970 when she was 14 (she insists the baby was briefly alive after the abortion), said his decision to make her abort was made with her "total health" in mind (Toronto *Star*, February 28, 1992).

So there it is in action. Once human life is devalued at its core, a chain of devaluation begins that travels outward from the source and cheapens all of life. This chain is not visible in any single person's decision. From legalized abortion, to child abuse and infanticide, to convenience killing of the disabled, to passive euthanasia, to active euthanasia, to State funding and promotion of all of these — there is no moral stopping point. And so we open the newspaper and read, ominously: "Manitoba Probes Deaths of 8 Babies." The prosecutor said these deaths are "cases where children have died and there are no suspects and no charges and they have clearly been murdered" (Toronto *Star*, January 4, 1992). Well, it's very hard to allow one citizen to kill her baby a minute before birth, and condemn another for doing the same thing a minute after, isn't it? Once you tell the citizenry that the decision to preserve or end a life is up to them, you can expect them to exercise this prerogative — a lot. Nothing is new. A century ago Toronto had 19 "baby farms" where mothers, some as young as 15, "lodged their unwanted babies" ("Wholesale Murders," *Evening Star*, January 13, 1894). Apparently, hundreds of such babies perished mysteriously, many of them slaughtered wholesale with doses of paregoric, opium, and aniseed. Many young women from the surrounding countryside flocked to Toronto "because the city furnished exceptional facilities for the disposal of unwelcome babies." It still does.

### "A Woman Has a Right to Control Her Own Body"

This is another slogan of the abortion movement, which again invites the reply that she ought to have controlled her own body before jumping into bed. After all, there is a "presumption of possible consequences" in most human action. People who dive into shallow water, or touch open flames, or make love thoughtlessly, invite certain predictable consequences. However, in a tortured piece of argumentation, lawyer Alan Borovoy actually argues that the "occupation" by the fetus of a mother's womb is a form of "coercion" of the mother, and that no fetus has a "right of sanctuary" there.[32] Interestingly, Borovoy's very use of the term "sanctuary" strongly implies the existence of a separate being already existing in its own right, separate from the mother's body. This image dissolves his argument about a mother controlling her own body. The issue is really her desire to control someone else's.

We can argue just as vigorously that in the eyes of society and the law, the very act of any male and female making love, regardless of their expressed intentions, is a de-facto presumptive act in favour of the creation of human life that forms an implicit contract between the parents. Because the function of the law is to protect the weakest members of society, any new life that may result from this contract therefore has an overwhelming legal right of care and protection, by both parents and society at large, until age 18.

The truth is that the idea of using the law to enforce personal "control" over others is a pathetic symbol of the end-stage of twisted liberal thought. It embodies a conceptual attempt to sever one's natural actions and appetites from their natural consequences, and to define the general good according to personal motive only, whether before or after the fact. This is the Rationalism Illusion run amok, a denial of all organic truth, and of all truth or mystery beyond the immediate facts of personal experience.

Furthermore, it is specious to argue for "control" over one's body when in fact all human beings are, throughout their lives, almost wholly controlled by their own natural biology and physiology. We breathe by remote control; our biology dictates that we eat, and excrete, or die; and we often experience uncontrollable grief, anger, fatigue, desire, or fear. Yet in order to control these things, we do not resort to tax-funded technology. We do not demand surgical excision or computerized control of our breathing centre; we do not submit to surgically implanted colostomy bags so we can "control" the emptying of our bowel at will with a tap; and we do not demand neural surgery so that we will have more "control" over our emotional lives. So why do we resort to surgery to "control" the consequences of our sexual appetites and actions? The desire for absolute legal and physical control over a child's life as a retroactive solution to a failure of personal control is a poor rationale for abortion.

Finally, modern biological and genetic science has established beyond a sliver of doubt that the fetus is a separate being from its mother. Whether or not and at what point it is maintainable separately from the mother is beside the point. For every fetus (with very few exceptions) is viable, or living, until it is made non-viable by someone else. And whereas a potential mother and father are free to refuse the act of love, a child is not free to refuse the act of its own conception. Both the child's life and its very temporary residence in the womb are imposed by the will of others. The act of conception thus imposes a primary moral duty on both parents to provide continued sanctuary and nurture until adulthood.

As a test of the interdependency of human life, try this mind experiment — I call it the kangaroo test — on a female pro-abortionist, and see what she says: If, as a fact of nature, all babies were conceived as they are, but then at the end of the first two months a mother had to transfer her baby to a kangaroo-type pouch on the father — who would carry the child for the balance of the term — would you support the father's unilateral "right" to abort, and thereby control his own reproductive life? I vouch all honest women would say "no."

## WHAT THE LAW SAYS

Here's a hypothetical situation that should serve to illustrate the extremely narrow legal arguments made in favour of abortion on demand.

Susan and Betty become pregnant on the same day. Six months later, Susan has a premature but healthy baby. Betty is still pregnant. One week later, however, each woman decides she doesn't want her baby. Why should Betty be allowed by law to kill hers, but Susan not? This dilemma nicely reduces the key factor not to the morality, legality, or practicality of the issue, but to the will of the mother alone. We cannot escape the dilemma by saying that one baby has been born and the other has not, since this point merely relates to where the baby is located. At issue, in other words, is not the *existence* of a separate being, but the *value* of that being, and whether or not that value should be decided by the mother alone or by society at large. The question we must therefore ask ourselves is this: Is it sufficient for a civilized society to base the value of human life on the will of *any* single individual, whether father, mother, physician, politician, or the local baker? Are we content with a situation in which any individual may act as saviour or executioner of human life, with personal inclination as the sole justification? Surely the value of human life, if we do not believe it derives from God, should at least be determined by some kind of community consensus (and then reflected in the laws of that community). But it seems that for the first time in our history, we have surrendered both our religious and our community standards.

Professor Ian Hunter of the University of Western Ontario tells us that Canada, since January 28, 1988, "has been unique among countries of the Western world in having no law on abortion," despite the fact that "more than two-thirds of Canadians favour legal restrictions on abortion, and perhaps as few as 10 percent of Canadians favour abortion on demand."[33] Professor Hunter lays the blame squarely at the feet of the Supreme Court of Canada and the Canadian Charter of Rights and Freedoms, which "in less than a decade has fundamentally transformed Canadian life." He then explains how Pierre Trudeau, as justice minister under Prime Minister Lester Pearson, shrewdly promoted a whole package of so-called criminal law "reforms," including liberalized lotteries, homosexuality, and abortion, and rammed them through Parliament in an omnibus bill in 1969. Trudeau later admitted this bill contained so many diverse issues it would lead to "psychological inertia" and thus make the passage of liberalized abortion easier. Whereas many democratic nations take such important moral matters to national referendums (where abortion rights would fail), Trudeau's omnibus bill turned out to be Canada's first experience with a kind of political and moral dictatorship to which the people would soon become accustomed. Little more than a decade later, the Charter itself was pushed down the throats of the people by the same man, in the same deceitful, unilateral fashion.

In the new 1969 formulation, altering an 1803 law that had rigorously protected the fetus, *from conception*, abortion in Canada was henceforth to be decided by three hospital physicians allowed to certify abortion if a pregnancy endangered the mother's life or "health." Hospital committees all over the land quickly latched on to the definition of "health" used by the World Health Organization, which is "a state of complete physical, mental, emotional, and social well-being and not merely the absence of disease or deformity." As Hunter wryly observes, this is a definition "of such fathomless flexibility and absurdity that its literal application would exclude from 'health' nearly every human being since time began."[34] In Canada, Britain, and the United States today, about 95 percent of abortions are carried out on grounds of extremely loosely construed social and psychological "health." The word itself is thus debauched. And abortions are permitted in all three countries (the United States is currently moving to greater restriction) right up to the point of natural delivery (though about 90 percent of all abortions are in the first trimester). Abortion has been made easier by the lack of definition of the "person" or "human being" in the law, and most disputes over the justice of abortion have hinged on this matter.

## What Is a Person?

*A more or less civilized society has to be based on a minimum of respect for the person. The destiny of the person is linked to the destiny of love and the destiny of politics.*

OCTAVIO PAZ, MEXICAN POET

Everyone knows, surely, that when you put a live sperm and a live egg together, you get a live fetus. As writer George Jonas put it: "If a foetus were not alive, it would not have to be killed." The question, again, is not whether the fetus is *alive*, but what *value* ought we to give it? Value, as it turns out, is conferred by a name — a label — that carries with it certain legal rights. We shall see that most of the modern twisting of the law — against the will of the people and their religions — has been aimed at denying the fetus the label of "person" or "human being." This act of legal denial is the bedrock of the pro-abortion case, and we will see that our Charter, the highest legal document in the land, has been used vigorously to deny the fetus such a label, even though in our common-law civil tradition (and in Quebec law) the fetus has had strong and growing legal rights for centuries.

Accordingly, as historian Ian Gentles puts it, "there exists today a grotesque contradiction at the heart of our legal system as it touches the unborn child."[35] He explains that unborn children in Canada have a realizable right to inherit property (as when a parent leaves an unborn child money); they can sue a third party for injuries sustained during their time in the womb (say, if a driver hits the mother and injures the child); and they can even sue the mother, or a third party, for abuse or neglect of them while in the womb (as when a child born with a disability sues his mother for having used drugs during pregnancy, or sues a company for supplying her with toxic medicine). All these rights are strongly and almost unequivocally supported by the laws of Anglo-Saxon countries. In fact, support for such laws is growing, not weakening. And yet the one right that is not supported, on which all these other rights depend, is the right not to be killed. Now really, how can someone be a "person" or "human being" in the civil law, yet be a non-person under the criminal law? As William Prosser, the dean of American tort law, says: "The unborn child in the path of an automobile is just as much a person in the street as the mother."

This undermining of our bottom-up Anglo-Saxon common-law experience, one that reflects centuries of life-affirming family and community values, came about with deceptive simplicity through the imposition on Canadians of a top-down Charter, filled with abstract rights, that has been used by ideologically motivated lobby groups and judges to change the legal and moral spirit of the nation. (See Chapter Eighteen for a discussion of law versus family.)

In the United States, the *Roe v. Wade* Supreme Court case (1973) basically claimed that all abortion laws invaded a woman's constitutional "right to privacy," *even though there is no explicit protection of privacy in the U.S. Constitution*. This right was "found" there by the judge, who said, in what was surely the most ludicrous thing ever spoken by someone of his profession, that the privacy right was "an emanation issuing from a penumbra" of the Constitution.

In Canada's *The Queen v. Morgentaler* case (1988), the Supreme

Court struck down section 251 of the Criminal Code, which prohib-
ited abortion. Although the Court did not argue for a Charter right
of "privacy," it irresponsibly stretched the meaning of the Charter's
section 7 guarantee of "security of the person," using it to invalidate
section 251 of the Criminal Code. Interestingly, anti-abortion activists stretch the same section 7 of our Charter to defend the right to
security of the person of the unborn child. However, this is a case
the Supreme Court has yet to hear. In striking down section 251,
the Court basically left Canada without any law to adjudicate, one
way or the other.

Nevertheless, as Professor Gentles points out, such constitution-
alism contradicts a long tradition of common-law defence of the
unborn child, such that today in Canada and the United States, "it
is clear that no one has the right to kill the unborn child, to injure
her, or deprive her of her property. No one, that is, except her
mother."[36] For the mother, this right is unrestricted. Said otherwise, in Canada and the United States the common law of the people
defends the child, while the Charter/Constitution, an instrument of
the courts, defends the mother. Gentles cites a number of eerie but
utterly possible outcomes of this clash between the civil and the
criminal law. One is the case of a mother whose husband dies during
her pregnancy, leaving his money to be divided between her and
their child. Obviously, if sufficiently greedy and heartless, she can
now simply abort the child and keep all the money for herself. A
further anomaly is that of a child who is taken out of the womb for
surgery, at which moment he has all normal civil rights as a person,
and then is returned to the womb, where he re-enters "a free-fire
zone," subject to the mother's (Charter-supported) absolute will.
Perhaps the ultimate absurdity is that under our present laws "a
mother may not neglect or abuse her unborn child. But she may still
legally kill her."[37]

### The "Born Alive" Rule

Even more confusing, Canada's Criminal Code says that a child in
Canada becomes a human being when it has "proceeded alive" from
its mother's body (section 223) — this is the so-called "born-alive"
rule. But section 238 then declares that "everyone who causes the
death, in the act of birth, of any child that has not become a human
being, in such a manner that, if the child were a human being, he
would be guilty of murder, is . . . liable to imprisonment for life."

According to Robert Nadeau, if Canada's higher-court justices
really did their homework, they would soon discover that "recent

scholarship has entirely discredited the [born alive] rule as an outmoded legal fiction, a legal anachronism that is now obsolete and primitive."[38] It was originally a simple evidentiary standard required by physicians and the courts to determine the outcome of certain legal suits at a time when medical technology could not tell whether a fetus was alive or dead. In its origins, Nadeau writes, the born-alive standard "was never intended to constitute part of the substantive definition of 'person' or 'human being.'"[39] The effect of what he rightly calls this legal hocus-pocus is that the law is "in the anomalous position of protecting the legal rights of one who is considered to have no legal right to live."[40] Thus, as he puts it, there is a legal advantage to be gained in being sure you have killed the unborn child, and have not merely injured it.

## The Charter and Abortion

The cloudiness of all this evaporates once we understand that the abortion issue is but a microcosm of the larger civil war of values twisting our nation. This war of values was described in *The Trouble with Canada* as a conflict between the (English-derived) bottom-up style of community-generated family values, reflected in the common law and the workings of a free parliamentary system; and the contrary (French-derived) style of abstract values, imposed on us in the form of a Charter and designed to permit top-down control of social policy (and therefore of community and family values) by the courts. The result is that although the people do not want unrestricted abortion, and although the common-law courts of the land defend a multitude of civil rights of the unborn child and grant it the full status of a person — we have abortion on demand. Indeed, all laws of the land restricting it have been struck down. How did this become possible?

Fundamentally, control over the moral decisions of the nation, as reflected in the meaning of our laws, has passed from the hands of elected legislators into the hands of unelected judges. Most importantly, this change has meant that if interest groups of any stripe want to alter the meaning of a law, they can now do so by trying to influence judges instead of their elected member of Parliament. In other words, our Charter has provided all sorts of groups with an opportunity to change the moral direction of our democracy — by explicitly ignoring democratic methods.

Many political groups, but feminists in particular, worked very hard to influence the drafting of the Charter itself and then lobbied (using tax dollars) for its adoption. The process is detailed by

University of Calgary professor of political science F.L. Morton, and it's a scandal.[41]

As Morton suggests, "any interest group with enough money to hire a lawyer can have their interest claim transformed into the rhetoric of rights."[42] (Might makes right.) That's why Americans — and now Canadians — fight so bitterly to place judges with specific ideological preferences on the bench of the Supreme Court. As one U.S. jurist said: "The constitution means what the judges say it means."[43] Otherwise, how could a "right of privacy" be found where none is mentioned; or "security of the person" be interpreted to mean killing babies? Unelected judges have no authority from the people to create a right where none is specified. They justify this authority, however, on the grounds that the Charter is a "living" document that *ought* to protect certain unmentioned rights; and then they stretch the meaning of the document in order to enforce their world view. And whether you are liberal or conservative or socialist, this is a dangerous situation for any democracy. That's why Charter skeptics like myself say that when the Charter is silent on an issue, the judges ought to be silent, too. But Charter experts in Canada are far from silent. Most are relatively young and politically left of centre, and they see the Charter "as a valuable instrument for achieving social and political reform."[44] In other words, it's viewed as a tool for replacing the bottom-up society with the top-down State. An example of their influence was visible in the days following the Morgentaler case, when the media "relied heavily on interviews with women lawyers and law professors almost all of whom were active feminists."[45] In effect, many judges, emboldened by the Charter and deluded as to their own wisdom, now constitute a new political force, or what Morton describes as "the Court Party." They have "become active players in the political process."[46]

And the process stinks. In fact, an almighty ideological odour emanates both from some of the judges involved and from various deceptions of the public. For example, whether for or against abortion, the people surely cannot condone the stacking of a jury such as occurred in the *Morgentaler* case; stacked juries are the surest sign of a corrupt democracy.

## Pushing Canadians Around
In the *Morgentaler* decision that struck down Canada's abortion law, the Chief Justice of Canada wrote, oddly, that such laws were "a profound interference with a woman's body and thus a violation of the security of the person."[47] But let's think about it. How can a

law *against* an action be a *violation* of the person acting? The judge has it backwards. Such laws are prohibitive, not imperative. They say the person *must not do* something illegal. They require no positive action. That is, a prohibitive law cannot violate anything; but a person — and only a person — can violate such a law. The judge would have been correct if our abortion law *forced* a woman to abort (as it does in China), for then it would violate both her person and the person of her child. The law, however, did not interfere with anyone's body. Rather, it forbade any interference. He said the law was "forcing [her] to carry a foetus to term . . ." But on the contrary, the law was silent on if or for how long she was to carry a fetus. It simply said that if she did carry one, she was not allowed to kill it. The Chief Justice's logic suggests that all Canadians are currently being *forced* to do the opposite of everything specified by the thousands of prohibitive laws of this country — an absurd notion. A law that says you cannot eat in a store is not "forcing" you to eat anywhere else, any more than a law that says you cannot walk on the grass is forcing you to ride in a car.

At any rate, as the dissenting Justice McIntyre put it: "All laws . . . have the potential for interference with individual aspirations and priorities. In fact, the very purpose of such laws is to cause such interference."[48]

Professor Ian Hunter clearly shows how feminist ideology utterly controlled the *Morgentaler* decision. This was typified by Justice Bertha Wilson, whose majority judgment was described by Hunter's legal colleague, Professor Ben Hovius, as "a manifesto issued by a pro-choice group."[49] Justice Wilson publicly declared half the human race (all males) incapable of forming an opinion on abortion, despite the fact that delicate and persuasive opinions both for and against abortion have been argued by males for centuries; that the four Supreme Court justices who sided with her were male; and that the fathers of all unborn children are male. To deny the simple power of empathy to half the human race is ridiculous. By extension, such a denial implies that a woman cannot understand the agonies of a man with prostatic cancer, or that a man cannot understand those of a woman with breast cancer. Hers was a sexist declaration of emotional and therefore civil and moral isolationism of the most antihuman kind from the highest bench in the land.

But perhaps the worst scandal of all was the actual *Morgentaler* jury selection process, which reads like something from the old Soviet Union.[50] One reason the jury system usually works very well,

Professor Hunter explains, is that "we have not hitherto allowed members of a jury panel to be questioned about their beliefs, habits or opinions." We are supposed to take 12 good people from the street, so to speak. But Hunter shows that for Canada's *Morgentaler* trial, 132 people were "interviewed" and "screened" by a U.S. firm from Washington, D.C., using pro-abortion "consultants" in such a way that precluded a jury chosen at random and resulted in "a jury predisposed to acquittal." This predisposition was further reinforced during the case by an address from defence lawyer Morris Manning, who, as Hunter put it, "invited the jurors to disregard their oath, the trial judge's instructions, and the clear language of the Criminal Code." In fact, the defence lawyer told the jury it was their *right* to disregard the law. In short, the selection process weeded out anyone with religious beliefs, anyone who might in any way have opposed to the concept of abortion on demand, and anyone who *agreed with the Parliament of Canada* and its Criminal Code.

But the fact is, our law does not require that a juror be neutral as to the offence. For "no juror would be excluded from a murder, rape or robbery trial because he or she believed that murder, rape or robbery was morally wrong." And the Criminal Code itself, as Hunter explains, by making something illegal "has conclusively pronounced on the wrongfulness of the conduct," and "jurors should regard with abhorrence the offence with which the accused is charged" (but should be open-minded about the evidence, pro and con, and about whether or not the crime was actually committed, the accused fairly charged, and so on). The standard of *indifference* is supposed to mean "impartiality between the adversaries, not indifference to the offence." As it turns out, the firm used to select the jury acknowledged afterward that its purpose had been to exclude "regular churchgoers, housewives, young people and older professionals."

There could no clearer example of the perversion of justice, and of the way in which top-down ideology succeeds in suppressing the will of the people, as is clear from the polls.

But just as it was judicial activism in the United States that enabled the imposition of abortion on demand on an unwilling public, the Americans may lead us back to a point where abortion policy becomes a matter of the voice of the people. On July 3, 1989, in *Webster v. Reproductive Health Services*, the U.S. Supreme Court basically ruled that abortion is a matter that ought to be settled locally, at the state level, in response to the will of the people. Several states quickly passed laws restricting abortion. Canada will likely eventually follow suit. So, in an ironic reversal of its original outrage over illegal and do-it-yourself abortions, the radical National Organization of Women (NOW) is currently teaching U.S. women how to perform "at-home abortions" (*Globe and Mail*, January 23, 1992). About 42 U.S. states have by now enacted parental involvement or consent laws, some a decade ago. Minnesota found that in the years immediately following its 1981 parental consent law, teen births dropped 23.4 percent, abortions decreased 40 percent, and pregnancies declined 32 percent among 15-17 year-olds.[51]

To this point, we have seen how widespread abortion on demand is possible in a post-Christian society only if a certain sequence of events is enabled first. This sequence goes from an initial atomization of the family and its values (which is a natural consequence of the rise of the welfare State) to a values vacuum that is filled by a form of dependency on the State and its largesse, ironically promoted as a kind of amoral economic autonomism and freedom — a cradle-to-grave security. The schools and the media express it as personal liberation ideology, but what it really amounts to is the rejection of all external moral standards. The way is then paved for the rise of the personal will. This, combined with the contraceptive mentality and the use of mostly Latin euphemisms (fetus, embryo, etc.), enables a denaturing of the unborn child itself and encourages a shunting of responsibility for this "thing" onto technology (for failure of the will to achieve its aim efficiently) and onto the State (to cover costs for the failure). The next-to-last stage in this process involves the invention of legal fictions to devalue the unborn child and the entrenchment of the ideology of autonomy through manipulation of the courts. The courts in turn assist in the top-down canonization of these new rights, usually in opposition to the will of the people, as is clear from the polls.

In what follows, the reader will get a glimpse of the realities of abortion on demand, and through it some sense of the effort to commercialize abortion and even salve our guilt by turning this invisible holocaust to the benefit of others.

But first, a warning. Readers who are squeamish had best not proceed. While most abortions are not carried out like the ones described here, there is surely a causal link between these ugly facts and the moral decay at the core of our society. Let each judge.

# THE HORRIBLE TRUTH

*We believe abortion technology to be perfectly safe and effective for women.*
JUDY REBICK, PRESIDENT, NATIONAL ACTION COMMITTEE ON THE STATUS OF WOMEN,
TORONTO *STAR*, NOVEMBER 26, 1990

*Pregnancy is a venereal disease, treated by evacuation of the uterine contents.*
PLANNED PARENTHOOD PAMPHLET, 1971[52]

## Risks to the Mother

In 1972, the year prior to *Roe v. Wade*, the U.S. case that legalized abortion on demand, there were about 100,000 illegal abortions per year in the United States,[53] and 28 deaths reported from those illegal abortions.[54] In Canada, according to data derived from the *Badgley Report* (1977), the average number of self-induced or illegal abortions in Canada before legalization was about 10,000, and the maternal death rate from illegal or self-induced abortion was about 12 per year.[55] Immediately following legalization in the United States, however, there were about 175 deaths from legal abortions, and 17 from illegal ones over a four-year period.[56] So the argument for legalization on the grounds of saving maternal lives is rather flimsy. Today there are close to 1.6 million abortions performed annually in the United States (25 million since 1973). When all hospital, private clinic, and offshore abortions are included, the figure is about 95,000 annually in Canada (likely well more than 1 million since 1969), of which 25 percent are performed on teenagers — many of whom are encouraged by teachers to "enjoy safe sex" and ignore parental and religious advice as "authoritarian." Some 23 percent are performed on women who have had at least one previous abortion. Expensive contraception, I'd say, paid for by the neighbours.

In his detailed study *Grand Illusions: The Legacy of Planned Parenthood*, prolific U.S. author George Grant (not the Canadian philosopher quoted above) details a number of studies from some of the finest medical research institutions in the world. These arrive at a consensus that "there is no such thing as a safe and legal abortion." Researchers in nine countries and seven U.S. medical schools, including Cornell, Vanderbilt, and U.C.L.A., concluded that "abortion was found to dangerously risk maternal mortality, perinatal fitness, congenital malformation, and future fertility."[57] Dr. Horton Dean, of Los Angeles, says that 15 percent of first-trimester, 40 percent of all mid-trimester, and 90 percent of all late-trimester abortions result in problems demanding serious medical attention. Grant says that every technique used is dangerous. The "mutilated, violated, and uninformed mother" is the other victim of abortion, which is, according even to Planned Parenthood, America's largest provider, a "risky business."

Even the simple-sounding technique of *menstrual extraction*, most often used for rape victims, can result in urinary tract infections, cervical trauma, sepsis, peritonitis, endometritis (inflammation of the uterus), and salpingitis.

*Suction aspiration* (used for 85 percent of U.S. abortions in the first trimester) requires a vacuum tube 30 times more powerful than a home vacuum. In addition to the above complications, it can produce uterine laceration, renal trauma, pelvic inflammation, embolism, thrombus, and even sterility.

*Dilatation and curettage* (D&C) involves the insert of a sharp, loop-shaped scraping knife to scrape away the child and the placenta, and can lead to all the above complications as well as to bowel laceration and pelvic abscesses.

*Dilation and evacuation* (D&E), a popular second- and third-trimester method, relies on the use of a forceps instrument to pull the child to pieces and remove it bit by bit, followed by a vacuuming and swabbing of the uterus. After this procedure, a high number of subsequent births tend to be of low weight, or are stillborn, of ectopic implantation, or congenitally malformed.

*Saline amniocentesis*, used less often today, is for babies after the 16th week. A long needle is inserted into the womb and a saline fluid injected, which the baby must breathe, leading to a slow death, after which the mother goes into labour to produce a corpse. Complications can include blood clotting, pulmonary thromboembolism, erosive gastritis, hemoglobinuria, and active renal failure.

*Prostaglandin abortions*, activated by hormones sold as Prostin® F2-alpha (banned in the United States, but available through Upjohn Canada in Don Mills, Ontario), Prostin® E2, Prostin® 15M®, Cytotec®, and their variants induce violent labour and premature delivery, often of live babies. This has been shown to cause many of the above complications, including cardio-respiratory arrest, strokes, epilepsy, and acute kidney failure.[58] The newest drug, RU-486®, is accompanied by a whole litany of complications, including extensive bleeding, hemorrhage, and some cardiac anomalies; some "patients" need blood transfusions and follow-up surgical abortions.

Babies who survive RU-486® are often born with abnormalities (*Lancet*, December 19, 1987).

The *hysterotomy* procedure is basically a Caesarian section that is performed for fear the mother cannot deliver a large dead baby, or because a Caesarian section permits the convenience of performing other simultaneous procedures, such as sterilization. Such live babies are therefore left to die from thirst and lack of attention, before disposal (I have discussed this gruesome reality with Canadian nurses who have participated, usually against their will).

Enough said. Grant details the personal experiences of hundreds of outraged mothers, many of them made sterile, and some ill for life, who ask poignantly: "Why didn't somebody tell us?" Even Planned Parenthood, which now runs a $380 million per year abortion/birth control business in North America, in 1963 published a booklet (before it came out in support of abortion) that warned women: "an abortion kills the life of a baby after it has begun. It is dangerous to your life and health. It may make you sterile so that when you want a child you cannot have it."[59] Women who seek abortions in our society are not being told this or provided with many other critical facts about abortion. We shall see that the practice of abortion, especially where free-standing private clinics are allowed, is often a duplicitous and dangerous business, subject to the same commercial pressures as any other economic enterprise, selling the benefits and hiding the risks. Most businesses soon get punished by the marketplace for shoddy practices. But abortion profiteering — and there *is* big money in abortion — is deemed, by most people, a morally shoddy enterprise and therefore it seems to attract low-grade, hustler-type physicians and rip-off artists.

### The Back-Alley Problem

Much of the rhetoric surrounding the drive to legalize abortion centred on the cruelty of "back-alley" and "coat-hanger" abortions. While it is true that fewer mothers are now dying from abortion than before legalization — some say 40 percent fewer — it so happens that fewer mothers are dying from pregnancy-related problems, period. This trend, attributed to the wider use of such things as antibiotics, had been established long before the legalization of abortion. Still, in the place of the mothers, a lot more babies are dying, and the back-alley problem has not gone away. In Canada, the free-standing clinic has until recently been strongly resisted (about 25 percent of Canadian abortions are done in such clinics).

Even our most notorious aborter, and promoter of safe abortion, Dr. Henry Morgentaler, had his licence to practice suspended in 1976 by a Quebec disciplinary committee. The committee said that Morgentaler conducted no valid interview with the patient before an abortion; that there was an almost complete lack of case history; that neither pregnancy tests nor blood tests were taken; that pathological examinations were not performed; and that there was no follow-up care. Morgentaler's attitude, his colleagues said, was "primarily directed to protecting his fees."[60] Morgentaler even reused polyethylene "vacurettes" on patients, against the manufacturer's advice, a dangerous practice because diseases such as viral hepatitis, tetanus, STDs, gaseous gangrene, and herpes II can be transmitted. A Honduran woman who changed her mind at the start of her Morgentaler abortion said that he gave her no painkiller and did not respond to her pleas to stop the abortion. When she began to scream, "an assistant shut her mouth, and another forced a sanitary napkin into it" (*Globe and Mail*, January 14, 1985).[61] As Professor Gentles writes, Morgentaler is regarded as a "model" abortionist, and so we can rightly expect that a proliferation of such clinics in Canada would duplicate the U.S. experience (where 90 percent of all abortions are done in clinics).

What has that experience been? In 1978, barely five years after the U.S. legalization, the Chicago *Sun-Times* carried out an intensive five-month undercover investigation of only four city clinics. What the newspaper found was shocking. Dozens of "abortions" were performed on women who were not pregnant; many women became infected because of unsterile conditions or rusty or encrusted instruments; blood-stained sheets were often unchanged between patients; many patients required emergency hysterectomies afterward; a number of doctors were moonlighting for cash, were drinking beforehand, or had no licences; many performed the operation in less than two minutes, and before painkillers had taken effect; in one clinic, the nurse's dog came into the clinic and lapped blood from the floor; and pathology was ignored, specimens were often mixed up; and vital signs were falsified. Unknown to authorities, 12 women had died at these four clinics. Doctors often went from one abortion to the other without washing their hands; some women had dead tissue left inside them, or had perforated uteruses, and lacerations; crisis cases were simply bundled off the table and sent to a local hospital by ambulance. Common to all clinics were high-powered selling and marketing techniques used to corral vulnerable, often frightened, mothers. It's a scandal. And always, the *moral equation* is ignored — the trade-off between mother-deaths and baby-deaths. To crow that fewer mothers die now, when millions more babies die, begs the question.

Nurses from other cities, quoted in *New Dimensions* (October 1990), have said they were trained by professional marketing directors in how to sell abortions over the phone, how to "hook the sale." One particular worker, they said, "was very good. She could sit down with these girls during counselling and cry with them at the drop of a pin . . . draw them out . . . whatever their pressure point was, she would magnify it." Abortion was there as the answer to a girl's every worry. In short, the back-alley abortion continues to exist — in what is now the upfront alley. An organization called Women Exploited by Abortion (WEBA), operating in all 50 U.S. states and 8 foreign nations, exists to help women who have concluded they are abortion's "other" victims. (WEBA's telephone number is 214-366-3600.)

## The Reality of Abortion

*If you've ever seen an abortion . . . nothing comes out except a bunch of blood. It's like a menstrual period.*

MOLLY YARD, PRESIDENT OF THE (U.S.) NATIONAL ORGANIZATION OF WOMEN (NOW),
QUOTED IN *NEW DIMENSIONS*, OCTOBER 1990

Most people believe the quotation above, and prefer to think of abortion as a quick, harmless, safe procedure to eliminate a piece of lifeless microscopic tissue. I used to think that way. And, in the immediate few days after conception, when the initial combination of cells is changeable, the image may apply. But modern science is rendering such arguments increasingly obsolete. You could say there is a race on today between two groups: the mostly feminist radicals, who want to entrench their abortion right to kill what they define as the non-person life within them; and medical science, which is redefining the beginning point of "human" life as something that occurs much closer to conception than was thought a decade ago. So we have to stop fooling ourselves. A life-size photo shows that a six- to seven-week-old "fetus" contained in its tiny transparent sac is about the size of a large cherry. At that age, its heart has been beating for three weeks, and, as Dr. Paul Rockwell described it, "within the sac was a tiny human male swimming extremely vigorously in the amniotic fluid. This tiny human was perfectly developed with long, tapering fingers, feet and toes . . . the baby was extremely alive and swam about the sac approximately one time per second." Genetics professor Jerome Lejeune says that "you can use a hair and tickle the baby's upper lip and at two months of age he's already able to remove his whole body to escape the stimulation." At 19 weeks, the baby can open his eyes, hear and recognize his mother's voice, has fully formed limbs, and weighs about one pound. And animal lovers who are picketing laboratories because experimenters cause pain to rats and rabbits may now have a new cause. An article by Harvard medical researchers has definitively proven not only that the fetus can feel pain, but also that he feels it more so than when older (*New England Journal of Medicine*, November 19, 1987).

What is happening is that the religious, moral, and medical views are powerfully converging, reinforcing one another for the coming clash with modern liberalism. Science alone is converting hundreds of former abortion activists into anti-abortionists. The most famous of these is Dr. Bernard Nathanson, who, along with Lawrence Lader, started NARAL (the U.S. National Abortion Rights Action League) in 1969. In its first year of operation, on a budget of only $7500, NARAL managed to strike down a 140-year-old New York law against abortion.[62] Today, NARAL has a budget of $3.5 million. But it doesn't have Dr. Nathanson. After personally performing or supervising over 60,000 abortions (120 per day in his clinics, staffing 35 doctors and 85 nurses), he became persuaded by the scientific evidence that he was killing human life. So he got out — along with a lot of other physicians. By 1990, only 2 percent of American physicians would agree to perform abortions, compared with 4-5 percent in 1985. Immediately, Nathanson wrote two books: *Aborting America* and *The Abortion Papers*. He is now a much sought-after speaker travelling the world in the hope of reversing the invisible holocaust he helped start.

Dr. Nathanson says that *real-time ultrasound*, which gives a moving picture of the child in the womb; *electronic heart-monitoring*, which detects fetal heartbeats at 17 days; *brain-wave monitors*, which track brain activity at 5 weeks; and especially fetoscopy, which allows a physician to "actually eyeball" the baby, simply astounded him. Such techniques as *cordocentesis* even allow medical diagnosis, treatment, and surgery *in utero*. "There was nothing religious about it . . . I finally came to the conviction that this was my patient. This was a *person*! . . . This was purely a change of mind as a result of fantastic technology . . ."

Soon after he published his new conviction, he was, as he put it, summoned before a kangaroo court and "discharged from the pro-abortion movement." He did not lose sleep. Instead, he fastened an ultrasound machine to a woman undergoing an actual abortion at 12 weeks, and produced *Silent Scream*, a film that justly horrified the nation. It showed the "fetus" trying desperately to move away from the intruding vacuum, and then . . . its body parts were successively sucked off. The film produced a massive campaign of defamation against Nathanson from pro-abortionists. This only made him more determined, so he decided to show an abortion from *inside* the womb, at 19½ weeks. He attached a camera to a fetoscope and inserted it during a D&E abortion. The resulting film, entitled *Eclipse of Reason*, was sickening, and he commented that

> this procedure involves dilating the cervix, rupturing the bag of waters, taking a large crushing instrument and introducing it way up into the uterus, grabbing a piece of the baby, pulling it off the baby, and just repeating this procedure until the baby has been pulled apart piece by piece. Then the pieces are assembled on a table, put together like a jig-saw puzzle, so the abortionist can be sure that the entire baby has been removed. This is a shattering film.

I have seen photographs of the pieces of a baby aborted in this way, and they are so disturbing I chose not to include them in this book. The four photos, published in *New Dimensions* (October 1990), show the remains of a 28-week-old "fetus" (now widely known as "baby David") aborted at the Houston Women's Pavillion abortion clinic, one of a chain owned by Dr. Douglas Karpen. The 16-inch-long baby was literally ripped apart. One photo shows the perfectly formed face and head, with eyes closed, mouth open, tongue gasping, bruised, and bloodied in a nurse's rubber-gloved hands. Another shows a delicate, fully severed arm and hand that was pulled out first. The last shows the whole headless body, one remaining arm resting on the hospital pillow, fist clenched.

In Canada, where the number of free-standing clinics is growing (there are perhaps 20 now), but where 75 percent of abortions are performed in hospitals, we have yet to experience the panoply of abortion-related horrors such as we read about in the United States or in Europe — especially Eastern Europe. But read we must, for we are catching up. The worst is included here, simply because from it we get a glimpse of what is in store for us. History shows best that no society is immune from the corruption of morality that seems to follow the cheapening of human life, either at its beginning or at its end.

Some 100,000 babies in the United States and 5000 in Canada become "mid- or late-term" abortions, performed after 16 weeks.[63] Many late abortions are done with saline solution, which is injected into the womb. The baby swallows it, beginning a violent, slow death that takes about an hour. The salt actually burns the baby badly, and often strips off its skin. As nurse Debra Henry describes it, "the mother feels everything . . . because the baby starts fighting violently for his or her life. He's just fighting inside because he's burning." Sometimes saline-aborted babies are born alive anyway, and they finish their short lives outside the womb in front of the nurses and the horrified mother. One such mother, Bethany de Grassi, said "the baby was gasping when it came out. It was awful. I started screaming. The doctor was cursing. And the nurse didn't seem to know what to do. It was a nightmare."[64]

Pretty, wistful 14-year-old Gianna Jessen, in Ottawa recently for an international conference for a growing number of "survivors of abortion," managed to procure California hospital records to show that she survived a saline abortion at 29 weeks gestation. She says that under California law a girl needs parental permission to get her ears pierced, but may get an abortion without a parent's knowledge. She said she came to Ottawa to show that there is life inside the womb, and no one has the right to take it away (*Globe and Mail*, February 14, 1992). Outside that conference, when berated publicly as the Roman Catholic who created abortion on demand in Canada, Pierre Trudeau retorted: "Proud of it."

But there's no need to worry about survivors with the D&E procedure, says former abortionist Dr. Anthony Levantino. "You never have to worry about a baby's being born alive . . . as a doctor you are sitting there tearing, and I mean tearing — you need a lot of strength to do it — arms and legs off of babies and putting them in a stack on top of the table." Levantino quit. He reported a gradual decline in his self-esteem before he realized that, as he put it, "I'm killing somebody's child." He said he had come to feel like a paid assassin, a "hit man."[65]

Nurse Carol Everett recalls that her job was to "tell the doctor where the parts were, the head being of special significance because it is the most difficult to remove. The head must be deflated, usually by using the suction machine to remove the brain, then crushing the head with large forceps." She says that although doctors always "sized" the baby at 24 weeks (in free-standing private clinics, clients pay more according to the size of the baby), "we did an abortion on one baby I feel was almost full term. The baby's muscle structure was so strong that it would not come apart. The baby died when the doctor pulled the head off the body."[66] In an El Paso, Texas, incident, a mother went home after her abortion — and delivered her baby's head three days later.[67]

Calgary nurse Lorraine Keess tells the same sad tale. She worked 179 days in a pathology lab, analysing 10 abortions per day, before she quit. The vast majority had "tiny parts . . . human parts . . . arms, legs, intestines, rib cage, lungs, liver and heart . . . No one in the lab [her first day] is aware I am numbed by the sight. I choose an arm and cut off a hand for the microscope." Opening the next bag, "I sense my heart quicken, my chest and throat tighten . . . This one is enormous."[68]

In Canada, Nurses for Life has campaigned hard for the right of nurses to refuse all work related to abortion without fear of losing their jobs. But they have a difficult chore. Hospitals have clauses on employment application forms that say, for example, "I further agree that my personal opinions, and private or religious beliefs in respect to certain hospital procedures will not prevent me from carrying out my assigned duties and responsibilities" (Toronto's Women's College Hospital). As most Canadian hospitals are government-operated, here is a further instance of how Charter-mandated "rights" gained by ideologically motivated lobby groups and judges are legally imposed on individuals trying to defend traditional religious, moral, and family values — those shared by the majority of Canadians.

### Getting Rid of the Evidence

All hospitals and clinics in Canada are governed by some sort of Human Tissues Act, and, in a normal hospital setting, whatever is removed from the mother's womb is directed to a pathology laboratory for analysis to make sure the mother was indeed pregnant, the baby was aborted, and nothing was left inside the uterus. In all mid- or late-term abortions, as we have seen, there are quite visible body parts that must be analysed and accounted for. After that, the so-called "products of conception" in Canada are usually sent to hospital incinerators. In free-standing clinics in most other countries, however, unless disease is present or the physician wants to protect himself against liability, the pathology stage — deemed an unnecessary extra expense — is skipped. Then, the aborted child is disposed of in other ways. Says nurse Nita Whitten, of Dallas: "If they were small enough, we hardly ever sent anything to the laboratory . . . We basically put them down the garbage disposal [garburetor]."[69] Her colleague, nurse Kathy Sparks, says: "Often-times, second-trimester abortions were performed and these babies we would not put in the little jar with the label to send off to the pathology lab. We would put them down a flush toilet — that's where we would put these little babies."[70] A Winnipeg pathologist said most hospitals use very large incinerators, but "even large babies are no problem for a garbage disposal, because the babies come out in pieces, and a good machine that can chew up the likes of a pork-chop, can easily handle a baby."[71]

More horrifying yet, and fraught with historical tremor, is a copy of a brochure from an Austrian firm promoting the sale of its "mini-crematoriums." It shows three backyard-barbecue-sized, gas-fired ovens that generate temperatures up to 1150 degrees Celsius. The banner over the photograph says: "If You Want the Highest Efficiency!" The underlying specifications state that these ovens "have the capability to burn one or two baby corpses within one hour. Larger ovens can burn up to 3 kilograms of human material (20 to 30 preborn babies)."[72]

For *Babies for Burning*, a book that scandalized Britain but was — not surprisingly — quickly savaged and ignored by the media, authors Michael Litchfield and Susan Kentish, wearing hidden tape-recorders, toured a number of British abortion clinics, posing as a worried but reluctant couple. All clinics were positively hungry to perform the "termination." All reported Kentish pregnant, though she was not. Some even reported her pregnant from samples in which Litchfield's urine had been substituted for hers. Then, posing as a manufacturer, Litchfield approached a gynecologist who reportedly sold fetuses to cosmetic companies, which were said to process them for fetal fat. European women apparently prize fetal fat for its supposed anti-wrinkle properties, and also favour fetal cells for their putative youth-giving properties. "Cell therapy," in which animal and human fetal cells are injected into humans, is reportedly fashionable at some European health spas. According to Professor Chris Bagley of the University of Calgary, "fetal fat is much in demand by the cosmetics industry,"[73] but I hasten to add I have found no proof of this in Canada. At any rate, Litchfield's gynecologist said:

> You see, I get some very big babies. It's such a shame to toss them in the incinerator, when they could be put to so much better use. We do a lot of late terminations . . . I do them at seven months without hesitation . . . many of the babies I get are fully formed and are living

for quite a time before they are disposed of. One morning I had four of them lined up crying their heads off. I hadn't the time to kill them there then because we were so busy. I was loath to drop them in the incinerator because there was so much animal fat that could have been used commercially (*Times*, January 23, 1975, p. 16).

Subsequent to the publication of this book, the *Sunday Times* ran a detailed article attempting to discredit both authors, as well as the publisher (who stands by the book). The several libel suits launched by the clinics have been unsuccessful. Whether completely true or false, however, there are enough gruesome stories around to suggest that the citizens are not fully informed by pro-abortion media. One huge manufacturer that ought to be typical, Nu Skin International, claims it uses placental products only from hospital sources, and that 80 percent of "harvested" fetal material goes to medical research. Many women may be shocked to discover, in their own cupboards, cleverly labelled items such as "Placentyl" cosmetic cream. Canadian cosmetic companies say they use only animal fetal products, for items such as "collagen" protein. But my daughter has a cream made by Hask, of Montreal, advertising the use of "human placental extract"; and Perm Repair, "for troubled hair," advertises the use of "lyophilized human placenta" (whatever that means).

Charles Low, head of the Canadian Cosmetics, Toiletries and Fragrances Association, says he would like to know the truth himself. He has been unable to find any evidence of the use of human fetuses by his industry. And other than these few examples, the Canadian industry seems to deal only in animal collagens. But elsewhere? The European Parliament, Brussels, issued a report suggesting that some "cosmetic research" uses dead as well as live fetuses, mostly clandestinely, and saying the fetuses "are removed whole and live, then dissected to remove certain organs which are then frozen" (*International Child Welfare Review*, 59, 1984, pp. 45-47). It then recommended against this practice, but no law has yet been passed. The *Times* of London (December 16, 1983) has written that fetuses are frequently used in both Europe and North America for cosmetic purposes.[74]

**Fetal Harvesting, and "Designer Fetuses"**
Dr. Nathanson says there is "a flourishing commerce in the sale of fetal tissues and organs, such as at the Hana Biologics Institute, in Berkeley, California." He describes how all sorts of fetal products are currently being used to help older patients sick with diabetes or

Parkinson's disease. (Many "healthy" aborted babies are needed for these brain cells.) Such cells are also much in demand to treat Huntington's chorea, spinal cord injuries, leukemia, aplastic anemia, and radiation sickness. China attributes its success in such treatments to the aborting of *30-week-old* babies (*Medical Post*, February 10, 1990). Hana forecasts sales of $3 billion a year for insulin derived from fetal pancreases, and $8 billion a year from fetal brain tissue for Parkinson's treatment. Margaret Somerville, of McGill University, describes and warns against "designer fetuses" aborted for the correct genetic match with a patient. But the new eugenics already "has quietly slipped in the back door," says Jeremy Rifkin of Washington's Foundation for Economic Trends,[75] as scientists experiment with embryos and fetuses for answers to the genetically perfect human. They vie with moral fervour for the right not only to excise disease-producing genes, but also to implant superhuman ones.

An aging population can be expected to exert increasing commercial pressure for the new trade in fetuses, *the most useful of which must be harvested alive.* Neither science nor business has much use for a dead baby. Quick freezing of a live baby means healthier tissue to sell. On November 7, 1980, Hans Perukel published an article, "U.S. Government Funded Gruesome Experiments on Live Aborted Babies" (*International Life Times*). The story says Dr. Peter Adam, of Cleveland, Ohio, received $600,000 from the U.S. government for work "on live aborted babies that are kept alive for the sole purpose of medical experimentations." The live babies were purchased through a Helsinki hospital. As Dr. Paul Ramsey, of Princeton University, said in the same article: "U.S. doctors are going abroad to do research which would cause an uproar in this country." In January 1984, Olga Fairfax, Ph.D., published a story entitled "101 Uses for a Dead (or Alive) Baby." She reported that babies were sold for research for $25 a bag, or $5.50 a pound, and showed photos of "just a few" of the thousands of dead babies curled up in containers, ready for commercial sale, found behind the house of abortionist Marvin Weisberg. She reported vaccines grown with cells from aborted children, and a sizable trade in fetuses sold to drug companies.

In 1973, Dr. Robert Schwartz, chief of pediatrics, Cleveland Metropolitan Hospital, travelled regularly to Finland for fetal research disallowed in the United States. Dr. Schwartz says that after a fetus is delivered, while it is still linked to its mother by the umbilical cord, he takes a blood sample, severs the cord, and then, as quickly as possible, removes organs and tissues, while the heart is still beating.[76] In 1977, the U.S. Environmental Protection Agency approved a $300,000 project that used 100 aborted babies for testing the effects of pesticides on living tissue (Chicago *Sun Times*, July 26, 1977). Research carried out at Canadian hospitals in the 1970s involved the dissection of 54 intentionally aborted babies, from 10 to 25 weeks gestation, for sex steroid research.[77] At Stanford University in the 1960s, Dr. Robert Goodlin cut open the chests of live aborted babies to study their heart action. All died within 11 hours.[78] In another project, the live beating hearts themselves were taken out of intentionally aborted babies, and their continuing contractions were studied while in a nutrient solution.[79] In a macabre Finnish experiment, a U.S. doctor, Peter A.J. Adam, of Case Western Reserve Medical School, harvested 12 babies by hysterotomy abortion, cut off their heads while the babies were still living, and attached the heads to a special machine that perfused them with various chemical substances for study.[80]

The reason there is a market for fresh fetuses is because diseased or dead babies are of no use to researchers. The most desired cells are those that result from the deliberate, planned killing of babies in what one pathologist describes as "high-tech cannibalism." Dr. Bernard Badley, President of Victoria General Hospital, Halifax, says that the tissue from miscarried fetuses "is usually not as good as that of an aborted fetus" (*Daily News*, Halifax, February 21, 1990).

Canada's limited research work on unborn babies is carried out mostly at Victoria General Hospital under Dr. Alan Fine, of Dalhousie University. Remember, this is Canada, not Nazi Germany. Each pregnant woman signs two blanket consent forms, one for the abortion, and one for the research use of the fetus. (This is curious, considering the baby is a non-person. So why does the mother have to give permission?) A medical research team stands by when the baby is taken out, because live, warm tissue is the best, and after four hours the baby cells are useless. The desired cells (brain, liver, pancreas, whatever) are quickly "processed" for immediate use. "Just down the hall," as one critical physician put it, "there is a patient with, say, Parkinson's disease waiting, with a tube stuck in his head for cell injection." Four or more unborn babies may be required for each Parkinson's patient. Dr. Fine ingenuously writes that moral problems might exist if such research were "the sole reason for abortion," or if the fetus were living. He dispels any moral qualms with the rationalization that the "caseload" of aborted fetuses is "independently motivated." In other words, as long as women choose to provide him with aborted babies, the morality is not his problem. He adds that dissecting and transplanting fetal tissue cannot constitute an abuse to the dead, fragmented fetus, although all this work would be "simplified by use of an intact [living] fetus removed from the uterus by hysterotomy."[81] His exact arguments were used by Nazis who cheerfully herded prisoners into gas chambers ("I'm just undressing them"), or shovelled them into incinerators ("they were already dead"). He's just so very pleased that one out of 10 cases of routine suction-curettage abortion can supply live, identifiable fetal midbrain cells not macerated by the procedure.[82]

Apparently the Swedes, under Dr. Olle Lindvall of Lund University, have perfected a "lo-flow suction" technique. It allows them, during a normal abortion procedure and carefully guided by ultra-sound, to stop the abortion and suck the baby's head off for brain-cell harvesting, before tearing out the rest of the body. Researchers there also report that such implant research is performed on "dead" fetuses, but that's because this form of vacuum decapitation kills them. It is now routine in many hospitals of the world to keep new-born anencephalic (born with no brain) children alive with respirators, giving time to remove their organs for transplant. Spooked by their own actions, the Canadian Paediatric Society bioethics committee in 1988 recommended a moratorium on such transplants. But many doctors argue passionately for the creation of what would be human organ farms, where babies would be grown from anonymously donated human eggs, and harvested.

The American George Grant says especially our media are a huge moral failure. They do not bother to investigate or report that

> the very kinds of atrocities we roundly condemn Hitler's doctors for are today practiced routinely by upstanding physicians and researchers in [North] America's hospitals and universities. Babies that survive abortions are subjected to bizarre and barbaric live experiments. Human tissue is bought and sold on the open market for everything from cosmetics to pharmacology. Fetal organs are often artificially sustained and then later "harvested" for commercial consumption.[83]

Vancouver columnist Trevor Lautens, however, gets close when he writes of "the 'great and terrible horror' of abortion," and asks "How close to Nazism can you get? How close to what the historian H.R. Trevor-Roper once called, in another context, 'the posthumous triumph of Hitler from the grave'?" (*North Shore News*, March 20, 1992).

Meanwhile, frightened by it all, in 1989 West Germany banned all such embryo and fetal research, surrogacy, and related matters, and argued for limits to the freedom of scientists when their experiments affected the dignity of the human race, adding that "we Germans have a special responsibility because of our history to act in an exemplary way on these ethical questions" (Toronto *Star*, February 11, 1988).

But Nathanson forecasts widespread use of fetal bone marrow for marrow transplants, fetal skin for those who have been burned, corneas for the blind, livers for the "factor 8" used in hemophilia, and so on. "Don't you see what is going to happen?" he asks. "After they are through selling us fetal tissue for vital uses — for those who are diseased . . . they will then go on to sell us non-vital tissues. Is your sex-drive failing? How about a fetal gonad transplant? Is your hair going? We'll sell you some fetal scalp. Are your teeth going? We'll implant some fetal teeth for you." Nathanson sees the enormously powerful impulse behind this kind of trend as surging from the human desire for somatic immortality. In a materialist society, those who have lost a God who promised a calming afterlife seek heaven on earth. Don't think it's crazy, he warns. "Thirty years ago, when I was a medical student, *in vitro fertilization* was a lunatic concept."[84] Today, it is routine.

As a Jewish physician, sensitive to his cultural heritage, Nathanson sees abortion as a tragedy made possible by the very same forms of moral, legal, and political self-deception that led to the Holocaust. Robert Jay Lifton, in his heartbreaking book *The Nazi Doctors: Medical Killing and the Psychology of Genocide*, tells just how thousands of ordinary German doctors allowed themselves to be swept up in this process. Pediatric euthanasia — legalized abortion — is always the first stage, because it's easier for the people to justify bumping off an invisible "fetus" than bumping off parents or a spouse. What we must heed is the warning that *it's all part of a single process*. For the Nazi doctors, weaned from the Hippocratic Oath, the deliberate separation of "research" from healing was a crucial factor. Then came acceptance of the idea that some lives are "unworthy to be lived." Once a certain class of human beings is accepted as unworthy, disposal of them can be linked to the concept of a higher ideal — for the Germans, the nationalist ideal of the German *volk* (the people) and their vaunted purity. As long as what they did was camouflaged — couched in euphemisms and medicalized — the doctors and scientists saw their actions as serving an ideal higher than the individual. At the International Congress of Genetics in Toronto (August 22, 1988), German geneticist Benno Muller-Hill reminded us that "Auschwitz was a monument and shrine to science and technology," carried out, as he warned, in a "vacuum of values."[85] He said that in view of what is happening today, the Nazi murder of newborns for genetic research was simply "anachronistic" — an idea ahead of its time.

One particularly scrupulous doctor of the Nazi era actually agonized whether gas was a "medical" means to euthanize people. Hitler answered that if it is more humane than other methods, like suffocation, and also cheaper, then it must be good. The relieved doctor then saw himself as professional, using heroic efforts to save the state money, which could now be put to higher military uses. His fanatical colleague, Dr. Pfanmuller, said "the idea is unbearable to me that the best, the flower of our youth must lose its life at the front in order that feebleminded and irresponsible asocial elements can have a secure existence in an asylum."[86] He saw himself as essential to the highest cause as he hungered to euthanize the "asocial elements" and divert the savings to the war front. Thus did all moral actions in the Nazi State eventually become ordered solely around service to abstract State ideals.[87]

### Perverting the Liberal Ideal

What is the parallel for us? What is the *abstract good* that now orders all moral actions in our own society?

Surely it is the ideal of "choice" and "rights," divorced from duties and responsibilities. In a welfare State such as ours, where all physicians are already State employees, where medical budgets are strained and the population is aging, we can expect increasing pressures to define all sorts of people as having lives not worthy to be lived. Our justification will be the exercise of "choice" — and the dollars saved. After all, a $400 abortion costs the Canadian State a lot less than the $80,000 of welfare needed to support a teenage single mother for 10 years.

Remember: there are already about 6 million abortions performed annually in the 22 Western capitalist nations,[88] about 70 million worldwide. China does 16 million abortions per year, many of them forced. It also uses infanticide for those many who give birth illegally, and some provinces publicly shame, fine, and even cane couples who attempt to have more than one child, forcing them to sign abortion contracts.[89]

Citizens must be wary, because in the final stage, the State simply steps into the moral and legal vacuum it has helped create, with "rights" of its own, all easily justified in the name of the "public good" — by then the only remaining motive for action. All motives become utilitarian. Cost and value become one. At this point, with the remaining intermediate associations legally weakened, the State can define whole classes of human beings as unworthy of the protection of life itself (the unborn), or ineligible for basic health care (those deemed too old), or a burden to the State because too costly (the terminally ill, or others requiring expensive treatment).

As we have seen, all welfare States seem to destroy themselves financially through unlimited claims on the public purse, combined with the banning of private incentives in the name of equality. Because medical costs are so large a part of budgets, such states begin gradually to formalize a procedure for medical triage. Certain groups are deemed worthy of care from, or life saving by the State; others are not. The State of Oregon already has such a limiting procedure, but use of one's private funds is permitted there. Canada, too, has a limiting procedure, but it is illegal here to purchase many basic medical services privately. The simplest form of triage every-where it is introduced is silently achieved through *rationing by the queue*. Many patients who line up for "underfunded" services, and are forbidden by law to purchase that service with their own money, are likely to die before receiving it. Ultimately, they will be openly denied service. (For a sense of how the process works, see Chapter Eleven, "Medical Mediocrity," in *The Trouble with Canada*.)

Although many Western aborters, like the younger Nathanson and our own Dr. Morgentaler, are Jewish physicians, they do not seem readily to see the link between the devaluation of life, and the camps. (Dr. Morgentaler is a survivor of a Nazi concentration camp.) And as a measure of how ideology can be made to fit one's morals, Morgentaler even characterizes the anti-abortion side as "anti-women philosophies . . . akin to the fascist, dogmatic movements that resulted in the Holocaust" (*Globe and Mail*, June 12, 1992). Arthur Cohen, perhaps the world's leading Jewish scholar on the Holocaust (Orthodox Jews oppose abortion), says the modern abor-tion holocaust is a *mysterium tremendum* — an utter mystery to the human mind, something so unutterably diabolic as to be literally unknowable to us.[90] But in the modern democracies we are seeing an increasing awareness that there is a chain of progressive moral devaluation. That chain, more subtle than but with chilling parallels to the one found in Nazi, Stalinist, Maoist, and Kmer Rouge genocidal programs, goes from the political insistence that the autonomous individual — the political unit — is also the highest social unit; to the uniformitarian consolidation of all such units under constitutions or charters; to the official devaluation of "the other," over which the individual craves dominance through an exercise of free choice (the "Jew," the "fetus," the slave, the black, or the woman as non-person); to the stripping of all rights and status from the devalued being; to the identification of the non-being as "the enemy"; to the heavy marketing of negative labels reinforcing the correctness of this behaviour; to the promotion of the commercial "usefulness" of the exterminated "other" as a moral virtue.

What, after all, is the practical or moral difference between taking gold teeth or tissue or organs from a freshly gassed Jewish child, and taking a pancreas or the brain of a freshly aborted Canadian baby? Just as "the Jew" was re-marketed as the evil, "unwanted" thing, as "dirt" or "Jewish garbage" ("Jüden sind hier unerwuenscht" — "Jews unwanted here" — said the German schoolbooks, in a cartoon form of ridicule),[91] so "the fetus" is now the unwanted thing. German kids got their school cartoons negating the value of unwanted Jews; our kids get their sex-ed classes negating the value of unwanted babies. The final stage is the call for elimination of the evil thing as a positive good, even as a public duty. Abortion, and other forms of genocide, are then equated with personal freedom, "choice," the defence of inherent rights, and the pursuit of a glorious and heady life-style in the permissive welfare State. Many Canadian women are flown, with escorts, all expenses paid — up to $4000 each — from outlying regions to abortion clinics in Ontario. There they receive this service as a "right" (Toronto *Star*, February 29, 1992). At the ludicrous extreme we have reached in Canada, abortion clinics are even granted charitable tax-exempt status by rulings of our highest courts (*Federal Court of Appeal re: Vancouver Everywoman's Clinic*).

**Killing Babies Will Save the World**
This chain of moral devaluation is illustrated by the child-as-enemy image. The population movement — a huge variety of environmental and national- and international-aid organizations — has been promoting this image for decades: the unwanted or unexpected child as the "cause" of poverty and economic hardship around the world. Thus the perfectly healthy fetus may be described as a potential danger not only to the mother (to her "health," to her career), but also to the whole world, because too many people supposedly means

the end of the planet. So via the chain of moral devaluation, it becomes a heroic public duty to abort the fetus to help lower world population. It was a heroic public duty, too, to cleanse the earth of Christians in Roman times or of Jews in Hitler's time, or to send millions of non-believers to the Soviet Gulag.

We are encircled by this same chain of devaluation. Mary Calderone, who was medical director of Planned Parenthood in 1968 and has been instrumental in the developing of sex-ed programming, has said: "We are unable to put babies in the class of dangerous epidemics, even though that is the exact truth."[92] Modern feminist writer Carol Gilligan actually argues that the decision to abort is an "occasion of growth" for women who do not flinch from the knowledge that abortion is a decision to kill a baby. Is this morally any different from the statement made on October 3, 1943, by Heinrich Himmler, in his speech to death camp staff, when he praised them by saying: "Many of you know what it means to see a hundred corpses lie by side, or five hundred, or a thousand. To have endured this and to have remained decent . . . in our history, this is an unwritten and never to be written page of glory."[93]

## Margaret Sanger, Feminism, Planned Parenthood, and the Population Scare

At the end of the 20th century, it is difficult for us to appreciate the feverish embrace, at the end of the 19th, of theories promising a progressive improvement in the human race. But then we remember that fundamental to the evolution of modern liberal thought is the idea that there is no such thing as a permanent human nature. All human progress must come from an aggressive social engineering to shape human beings — especially through public school programs — and through the changing of faulty political, economic, and social institutions. Given this secular urge for heaven on earth, it is not surprising that many liberals and utopians fell for the idea of biological manipulation of the population; the notion that, through widespread birth control, sterilization, and abortion, populations everywhere could be "improved." The poor, the imbeciles, and the criminal elements could be gradually eliminated, and the perfect society could be achieved in the space of a mere generation or two. Irresistible.

This belief spawned the "eugenics" (or "good birth") movement, which drew heavily upon and often misinterpreted the 19th century works of Malthus, Spencer, and Darwin. Malthus argued that growth in population would inevitably outstrip food supply (it hasn't);

Spencer coined the phrase "survival of the fittest"; and Darwin the term "natural selection." All their theories were used, though often in distorted form, to push the idea of achieving social "progress" without the need for traditional morality or religion. In other words, the works of these thinkers became the bible of secular humanists (many of whom are so devoted to their ideals, they call themselves "religious humanists"). The first International Congress of Eugenics was held in London in 1912. Winston Churchill, as well as the presidents of Harvard and Stanford universities, were vice-presidents.[94] Churchill, as home secretary in 1910, was worried about "moral degenerates" and other "inferior" classes outbreeding the educated classes, and he hatched a plan, unsuccessfully, to sterilize 100,000 British subjects (Toronto *Star*, June 20, 1992).

But certainly the most powerful influence behind the movement for eugenics via birth control, and all the elitist and racist ideas it implied, was Margaret Sanger (1883-1966), the radical feminist founder of Planned Parenthood (1942) and of the International Planned Parenthood Federation (IPPF, 1948). Sanger devoted her life to the worldwide birth control movement. In 1916 she said: "Our business is unlimited sexual gratification without the burden of unwanted children." This could well stand as a motto for all modern abortion-rights activists. But she also wanted "more children from the fit, less from the unfit — that is the chief issue of birth control." She called for "birth control — to create a race of thoroughbreds." By 1917, about 30 U.S. states had passed mandatory sterilization laws for their "unfit." These laws, especially California's model, designed by the U.S. Human Betterment Foundation, are said to have inspired those written by the Nazis. It was Sanger who said "blacks, soldiers and Jews are a menace to the race" (in *Birth Control Review*, 1933, a journal she started).

Sanger was an advocate of "voluntary motherhood" (an early version of the "pro-choice" phrase), and she became a committed socialist. She also preached an early form of "situation ethics," or subjective morality, adapted from Ellen Key, a Swedish feminist (who had adapted it from Nietzsche). ("Situation ethics" still travels in our public schools, under the names moral values education, and values clarification.) Sanger advocated free love and called the marriage bed "the most degenerating influence in the social order."[95] This was certainly true of hers — although married, she spent much of her time in other beds.

She began her career by hoping to assist the poor through socialism, but quickly turned away from them, from socialism and from anything that threatened the freedom of the educated elite. She soon was referring to the poor and ignorant as "human weeds." Under sexologist Havelock Ellis (her lover), she came to believe in a kind of selective breeding by the most capable people, thus echoing Plato and presaging the *Lebensborn* breeding houses proposed by Hitler to improve the Aryan race. She promoted sterilization of the "feebleminded," among whom she counted 70 percent of America's population, and felt all government officials should be hand-selected by Plato-type philosopher kings and queens, since democracy could only deliver a system in which a moron's vote was as good as the vote of a genius. (Such thinking seems strange and remote to us until we remember (Chapter Eight) that one school board in Metropolitan Toronto describes abortion as "Euthenics: Improving humankind environmentally.")

Sanger declared publicly that "the most merciful thing that the large family can do to one of its infant members, is to kill it." She railed at the public about the huge cost of maintaining "human waste" (undesirables). Although the overt eugenics language is gone now, Planned Parenthood thrives, and annual awards are given out at PP functions in Sanger's name. In 1983, Faye Wattleton honoured Sanger's 100th birthday by calling her a courageous leader and saying that "abortion is only the tip of the iceberg."[96] Predictably, by 1974 the decline in fertility was steepest among blacks, Native Indians, and Hispanics (U.S. Census Bureau), and women on welfare were twice as likely to be sterilized. By 1975, rates of abortion in the United States were much higher for blacks and lower-income Americans, and "an estimated 100,000 to 150,000 low income persons were involuntarily sterilized." Dr. Mildred Jefferson, the first black woman to graduate from Harvard Medical School, says Planned Parenthood's heavy targeting of poor communities is "a class war against the poor."[97]

It is sufficient to say that much of the thrust of the antipopulation movement today is eugenic. It is directed at the Third World and the poor. Abortion, sterilization, and euthanasia are part of that movement. "Abort, not support" is a common economic theme rallying the activists, and the slogan gives us a clue about the modern movement. It is not biological any more. That is not popular. Instead, it is economic. The underlying thrust of the modern feminist and abortion-rights movements is economic- and career-oriented. Babies cost money. The way to become economically elite, to escape poverty, or to preserve your financial status is to eliminate unwanted babies. The first thing honey-tongued abortion-sellers ask of unsure pregnant teenagers, always careful to objectify the baby, is: "How are you going to afford it?" One Planned Parenthood brochure said: "Babies are *not* sweet things. They wet and dirty themselves, they get sick, they're very expensive to take care of."

Today, both Planned Parenthood and the IPPF are big business. They are together the world's largest providers of contraception, sex-ed, and abortion services. Planned Parenthood has a budget of $380 million, most of it from government, about 30,000 employees and volunteers, and 172 affiliates in the United States (and about 50 in Canada). It operates 879 clinics that counsel about four million people, mostly youngsters, every year. It is a highly ideological organization. It pushes open, non-exploitive sex, whether in or out of marriage (it is pansexualist); it promotes only contraceptive-model sex-ed classes, even for the very young; and it tries to normalize homosexuality. It has aggressively brought legal action against *parental consent* laws (although 76 percent of Americans support them), against requiring aborting physicians to inform the parents of minor daughters, and against the requirement to give full information on the developing fetus to abortion seekers. Still, PP insists it does not *advocate* abortion. It ensures, however, that school children get the names of local abortion clinics, and it even has an "abortion bus" that regularly picks up students at some U.S. schools.[98]

In the early 1980s, the U.S. government, while auditing federally funded clinics, discovered that Planned Parenthood clinics referred women for abortion (35.2 percent) far more often than other clinics did (5.7 percent). One clinic referred 86.4 percent of women who had tested positive for pregnancy. In one survey of women who had their abortions through Planned Parenthood, 89 percent said PP was strongly biased in favour of abortion; 95 percent said they received little or no biological information on the fetus they carried (often described as just a "pink blob"); 80 percent said PP counsellors gave little or no information about risks to the mother; and fully 90 percent said that had they not been so strongly encouraged to abort, *there was a strong chance they would have chosen against it.*[99] Recently, even Planned Parenthood has admitted that about 90 percent of women suffer some form of post-abortion physical and/or emotional trauma, and another recent survey of about 200 women backed this fact up: 94 percent said they definitely suffer psychologically; 73 percent, "severely." And to the question: "Knowing where your life is today, would you still have chosen abortion?" — 94 percent answered no.[100]

By the early 1960s, the eugenics movement resurfaced as the Campaign to Check the Population Explosion, an organization created and promoted vigorously by Hugh Moore, founder of the Dixie Cup fortune. "People pollute," was his favourite slogan. He allowed Stanford University scholar Paul Ehrlich to use his other catchy phrase, "the Population Bomb," for the title of a 1968 book that sold millions of copies and, as we shall see, was arguably one of the most misleading and irresponsible documents ever published.[101] The U.S. government, the population catastrophists, and the sex-ed and abortion movements seized upon this new and fashionable motive with a vengeance. Ehrlich predicted the end of the world's food and resources supply, and said "massive famines will occur soon, possibly in the early 1970s, certainly by the early 1980s."[102] They utterly failed to materialize. Those African famines that have occurred have been purely political in origin. We see one famished state beside a self-supporting one, although each has the same agriculture and climate.

But the pseudo-theological thrust of this movement has never let the facts slow it down. The widely propagandized and mostly government-funded imagery of the new antipopulation movement described the earth as a "lifeboat" (Garrett Hardin) or as a "spaceship" (ecologists). The "two-child" family became heavily promoted throughout the world as the responsible ideal, along with ZPG, or zero population growth. There is even an NPG movement, pushing for negative population growth.

Population and environmental catastrophism and propaganda were, and still are, everywhere. No sooner had the population scare begun than sex "educators" started banging the drums for more funding to control the "crisis" — nationally and internationally. Mary Calderone, founder of the Sex Information and Education Council of the United States (SIECUS), wanted family planning and contraceptive practice used with "total effectiveness" for "control of population growth," which, she said (1968), was crucial to socio-economic development and world peace. Human fertility must be reduced, she said, or "disaster is inevitable."[103] U.S. sex educators Burton and Meek (1975) told their student readers that "the population explosion" is "the greatest problem in the world today." Not bringing it under control, they said, would result in "mass starvation by the year 2000."[104] SIECUS co-founder Lester Kirkendall preached the same message of fear, urging "special treatment" (sterilization) for "lower class families." As Jacqueline Kasun says, local curriculum guidelines for school sex-ed programs are "riddled with the horrors of overpopulation." She's right. I checked my own children's school curriculum. The same, tired, and utterly false propaganda is still there. Contraception and abortion can save the world from mass starvation, goes the equation.

But none other than Alan Guttmacher, founder and head of the Guttmacher Institute, the government-financed and coddled "research" arm of Planned Parenthood, got egg on his face when much sounder research revealed, first, that virtually all teenagers coming for abortion already knew more than their peers about contraception, and second, that teen pregnancy (and abortion) soared wherever his contraceptive model was tried, especially so in states with the most sex-ed funding.[105] So-called "experts" like Calderone and Guttmacher don't know the slightest thing about world trends in population — because no one does. They have simply used the popular perception of a "crisis" to promote their pansexual, liberal agenda. Thus, school textbooks continue to present students with moral "dilemmas" asking them to choose what they would do to save an "overcrowded" planet (choices vary, but include options such as: use contraception, have an abortion, have no children, become a homosexual). Some choices. Much of the focus, once again, is on teaching children to become "responsible" through birth control, abortion, and population control, and to become "emancipated" from their parents, the better to take on the values of the new planned society.

This same thrust is overwhelmingly apparent in the way U.S. and Canadian foreign aid is delivered. For two decades now, much foreign aid has been "tied" to the willingness of foreign nations to demonstrate their "commitment to progress" through "control of population growth."[106] In the 1970s, the governments of many Western nations began preaching the "duty" to promote the two-child family model around the world, sometimes with awesomely large "family planning" programs encompassing as many as 30,000 villages in countries like Indonesia, where both sterilization and abortion are often introduced as "choices" in exchange for food, money, medicine, or water supplies. International agencies such as UNICEF ("UNICEF Urges Better Family Planning," Toronto *Star*, December 17, 1991) send little kids collecting on Hallowe'en, then turn around and finance the supply of abortifacient drugs, sterilization, and abortion services in foreign countries. The World Bank and the World Health Organization do the same. The UNICEF "Children's

Fund" saturates its programs with the equation: contraception + abortion + sterilization = survival. Not surprisingly, many of the local people see this as a form of bribery promoting genocide. They do not share in the population scare.[107]

It surprises most people to discover that many of the largest charitable organizations, such as the United Way and the March of Dimes, are also heavily involved in contraception and abortion ideology. In *Grand Illusions*, the American George Grant musters conclusive evidence that the United Way directs "millions of dollars" to Planned Parenthood every year,[108] and the March of Dimes, an organization originally dedicated to helping the disabled, is "at the forefront of the Planned Parenthood movement." Since the 1960s, "it has increasingly turned its attention away from *curing* genetic disorders and birth defects to *detecting* and *eliminating* them."[109] The March of Dimes (U.S.) funds what Grant calls "search and destroy" missions through massive funding for amniocentesis and abortion programs: 88 percent of all U.S. March of Dimes geneticists favour abortion on demand, and "a large number even revealed that they were involved in live fetal experimentation and fetal harvesting."[110]

Let us ask ourselves why we still put up with near total ideological infiltration of our schools and society by sex educators and environmental catastrophists, who continue to devalue human life by referring to it as a form of uncontrolled plague and who subtly promote abortion on demand as a means of "defending" ourselves. Against what?

## The Population Scare

> *The answer to anyone who talks about the surplus population is to ask him whether he is the surplus population, or if he is not, how he knows he is not.*
>
> G.K. CHESTERTON, INTRODUCTION TO *A CHRISTMAS CAROL*

Consider this: The entire 27 million population of Canada could stand up in just over one square mile of flat land. Even more dramatic: the Grand Canyon is 10 miles across, rim-to-rim, and just over one mile deep. Allowing the space of an average coffin per person, the entire population of the world could be packed into a crate just over a mile square. Shove it over the canyon's edge, and you would still have to look down to see it.

Now consider the following, all carefully presented by Jacqueline

Kasun in her book *The War Against Population*, which pulls together the work of hundreds of scholars:

*We have more food than ever:*
- The world food output has continued to match or outstrip population growth ever since 1977, especially in some of the poorest nations. (Ehrlich said, "Population is far outstripping food production." *The Population Bomb*, p. 177.)

*There is very little real hunger in the world:*
- Only about 2 percent of the world's population suffers from serious hunger (Harvard Center For Population Studies). (Ehrlich said "more than half of the world is hungry," p. 177.)

*Political tyranny, not people, is the problem:*
- War, political despotism, and socialism are the great destroyers of food supply in Africa, and everywhere else, not climate or natural agriculture.

*World agriculture is underproductive:*
- The world's farmers use only half the arable land. The world has vast, untapped productive capacities.

*The world can support many more people:*
- Colin Clark, of Oxford University, writes that using current best methods, the world could easily support 35.1 billion people (we are at about 5.5 billion).

*The worst cases have potential to be the best:*
- Roger Revelle (Harvard) estimates Africa alone could support 10 billion; Indian economist Raj Krishna says India's arable land could be doubled and sufficient food grown there to feed the entire world.

*Humans live on a tiny portion of the earth:*
- Scholars Doxiadis and Papaiannou calculate that only three-tenths of one percent of the land surface of the earth is used for human settlements (Kasun, p. 37).

*Civilization is not crowding out good land:*
- Arable land has been increasing in the world, not decreasing.

*All basic resources are abundant, and increasing:*
- None of the predictions of resource exhaustion has come about, and world basic resource prices (the best indicator of scarcity) have fallen, not risen, in the past century.

*More population is good, not bad:*
- There is no evidence that densely settled nations tend to have lower levels of per-capita income. Quite the opposite is true. Kasun, and Julian Simon before her, show that *with few exceptions, wealth tends to increase with population density.* Japan, the United States, Hong Kong, Germany, the Netherlands, Britain, and Korea are examples. Exceptions are traceable to political repressions. Both the distinguished P.T. Bauer of Britain and Simon Kuznets of the United States have shown "the advantages of population growth to economic development." At the turn of the century there were about 6 "wealthy" nations; today, there are about 35. Communist, and therefore underdeveloped, China has about 280 people per square mile, while free and rich Taiwan, a tiny crowded island, has about 1400. Manhattan, far wealthier still, has about 67,000 people per square mile. Very wealthy Hong Kong has 248,000 per square mile. Even Canada (8 people per square mile) is far wealthier in its crowded cities than in rural areas.

As for the vaunted two-child family the West has promoted? Kasun says that the "simple reason why people in the less developed countries have larger families than people in the more developed world is that they want them."[111] She says "there is no evidence that people in any country are having significantly more children than they want." Widely reported studies of "unwanted" children are defective because they fail to distinguish between the terms "unwanted" and "unplanned." Our very willingness to believe in "the problem of overpopulation" may be evidence of our paired belief that too many children cause poverty. In fact, in most of the world women and families want more children, not fewer, and higher population correlates with higher wealth. Bangladesh is the only notable exception, and even there a recent study has found that 82 percent of the women "hoped for a family of five to seven." Three-quarters of Nigerian women want a family of "at least six children." It seems that if left to their own devices, and protected from political — especially collectivist — tyranny, most human communities see children as wealth and tend to get wealthier as they grow in size, especially if permitted to create free markets.

However, many modern environmentalists and critics of population are plainly anti-capitalist or outright collectivist in their sympathies. They are called "watermelons," because they are green on the outside, but red on the inside. Instead of focusing on the errors latent in their utopian ideas, they fix on population as the reason collectivism has failed. In their minds, economic control, birth control, and abortion (instead of democratic capitalism and the free market) are the best "solution" to low economic standards. Instead of getting rid of the dictators and their oppression, pogroms, forced famines, and endless wars, they get rid of the babies. This is a natural mistake caused mostly by ideological wilfulness. From their top-down thinking comes their pernicious view, as Kasun writes that "the traditional concept of the value and dignity of the individual human being must be overhauled," replaced by a planner's view of what is good for the species.[112] My heart sinks. In 1920, Alfred Hoche, one of the intellectual architects of the Nazi euthanasia movement, wrote: "A new age will come which, from the standpoint of a higher morality, will no longer heed the demands of an inflated concept of humanity . . ."[113] There is a terrible echo in these words, which proclaim the supremacy of the collectivist ideology — always eager to convert subjective humans into manipulatable objective things — over the moral agency of the individual and the family.

So where has the two-child, ZPG ideal led us? Ben Wattenberg, in his carefully researched book *The Birth Dearth*, presenting numbers carefully vetted by statisticians at the U.S. Census Bureau, argues that the West is in for an awful surprise. Fertility in the West has been falling for more than a century (except during the post-war baby boom). The 22 Western democracies he studied have, since about 1970, been *reproducing below replacement level*,[114] which is at least 2.1 babies per woman, thus producing a "birth dearth." (See Chart 17, Chapter Six, for a snapshot of Canada's replacement problem.) Well, what a surprise to us all! Everyone simply assumed that once the two-child model was achieved, the world would thrive and poverty would disappear. No one anticipated that reproduction rates would continue to fall . . . right through the bottom; or that entire nations might begin to die off. But at the (West) German rate of 1.3 babies per woman, (West) Germany's 60 million will be 50 million by the year 2000, and 16 million by the year 3000. Fertility in the Netherlands has plunged 53 percent since 1970. These two nations are wealthy, but as they age, and the old consume the wealth of the working young who are not being replaced, disaster brews. The French rate has dropped 32 percent in the past decade. Here is French Prime Minister Chirac's prediction for the modern European nations: "Europe is vanishing. Soon our countries will be empty." If the present underreplacement rates continue, Western Europe will be smaller by some 200 million souls within one century, and falling. As for the whole world? It would be fair to say that the experts are confused. The United Nations Population Division (1992) has published world population estimates for the year 2150. The projected high is 27 billion people. The projected low is — 4 billion (1.5 billion fewer than in 1992).

In the corridors of power of the developed nations, however, the panic has already started. That's why some major nations, including Canada, have embarked on heavy-duty immigration programs. (You skim from the overpopulated nations, and top-up the shrinking ones.) Third-Worlders are good breeders, First-Worlders are not. But it's of no long-term use, because once the post-boomers' children reach their fertile years, the slide will really start, as they in turn produce fewer children and their parents die off. No immigration program will be able to counter the free-fall resulting from this duplication effect. That's why we may soon expect to see panicked governments embarking on pro-family, anti-abortion, pro-natalist policies. Quebec has already taken an initiative by offering up to $7500 cash for new babies, thus raising the birth rate there 18 percent over two years and reducing the abortion rate by 37 percent. Almost half of all babies born in Canada in 1990 were born in Quebec, at a rate double that for the nation as a whole (*Globe and Mail*, April 20, 1991). And the United States, as mentioned, has recently reacted legislatively by permitting states to restrict abortion. This technique always raises birth rates, not only from the abortions spared, but also from after-effects of the positive, pro-family moral message. Failing such action, as we continue to vanish we will be hard-pressed to explain to our diminishing offspring the logic of why we spent half a century legalizing and promoting an invisible holocaust against the unborn in the name of freedom.

# 16

## Killing with Kindness: Euthanasia vs. the Family

*Euthanasia is concerned with the responsible termination of life. The more we can relate these two movements [abortion and euthanasia] practically, the better . . . We've added death control to birth control as part of the methods or lifestyle of our society.*

DR. H. PITNEY VAN DUSEN, 1968

*Beyond 60-65 years of age, man . . . costs society a lot of money . . . indeed from society's point of view, it is preferable that the human machine should stop suddenly, rather than face progressive deterioration . . . The socialist logic is freedom, and the fundamental freedom is suicide; therefore the right to suicide, either directly or indirectly, is an absolute value in this type of society.*

M. JACQUES ATTALI, PRESIDENT, THE EUROPEAN BANK

In *Le voyageur français* (1748) there is an awful description of a death in an Indian tribe around Hudson Bay. Two men dug a grave for their ailing grandfather. Then they placed him in it, and with two rawhide ropes around his neck, they pulled in opposite directions until he was dead. Then they covered him up. This custom, along with the eating of babies when necessary, was supported by the tribe as a means of preservation in the face of scarce food. Other tribes did not believe this was right. The central point to be observed is that nothing other than collective opinion — which varied from tribe to tribe — protected the babies or the old people in a particular tribe from the group intention to kill them for utilitarian purposes.

If we consider life as a process of living from beginning to end, in which we are conceived in a human body, and expect to be nurtured in our parents' arms and die in our children's, the central question to be asked is, What protects our children from us, and us from them? Reflection will reveal that nothing whatsoever can protect a single human soul from the ambitions of a group, except for the obedience of the group itself to some higher inviolable standard of behaviour that declares each soul to be worthy of preservation and dignity. This protection is further strengthened if it is deemed to flow as a fixed directive from a higher being. But when faith in the higher being is aggressively challenged, many such protections erode, and the motives for all social action become increasingly utilitarian. At that point, all group values change according to whoever controls the group. Tribal elders? Dictators? The Supreme Court? You name it.

History shows that all societies have experienced this process of despiritualization, in which a transcendent value system is abandoned for a secular one. This process signals the beginning of barbarism, and if barbarism has any meaning at all, it springs from the willingness of a people to benefit by consuming or sacrificing its own kind. This act may take a pure physical form, as in outright ritual cannibalism or sacrificial offering to pagan gods; or an ideological form, as in abortion on demand for personal convenience; or a political form, as in genocidal movements; or an economic form, as in euthanasia of all those deemed to be parasites on the economic body of the State. As one writer put it, there's not a great distance from the pro-abortion slogan, "every child a wanted child," to "every granny a wanted granny."[1] We shall soon see the similarities.

## What Do We Mean by Euthanasia?
Euthanasia is another example of an issue that has been clouded by distortions of our language, which lead to distortions of our values. So let us keep in mind that all political struggle begins as a struggle over language.

Practically speaking, there are only three ways to die. You can let nature or fate take its course and die on your own (natural death); you can kill yourself, with or without someone's help (suicide); or you can be killed by someone else, with your knowledge and consent, or without your knowledge or consent (murder). All religions and most societies have always banned the last two forms, and even those that have allowed suicide have usually done so only for ritual reasons, such as to glorify a god, or national life. So the so-called "mercy-killing," or "euthanasia" (meaning "good death") movement has tried to alter these simple categories by altering the language, and therefore the values, surrounding the ways to die, hoping to authorize the different forms of killing. It is easier to understand what they are doing if we can see that they take transcendent concepts, or protective absolutes such as the commandment "Thou shalt not kill," and argue that if the victim is agreeable to having his life ended, or if in one's eyes the victim's life is "unworthy to be lived" (a deformed newborn) or of "low quality" (a suffering patient, or a mental defective), then this is not killing, or murdering — it is a form of mercy. In other words, before you can legally murder a person, you have to murder the language and the values of society, and then impose these, top-down, on others. As it turns out, the traditional permanence of the language and the many values it expresses are still, though far less securely, controlled by the permanence of basic principles.

**What Do the People Want?**
In poll after poll, Canadians and Americans say, quite reasonably, that they do not want to be trapped inside a maze of technical contraptions against their will if they are dying or if they decide their life is not worth living. And the medical establishment has certainly been guilty of trapping too many people and causing lots of extra suffering this way. But neither do people want to be unwilling victims of physicians or relatives who decide to do away with them against their will. Beware. All poll questions are loaded in the way they are asked. Nevertheless, here are a few indicators. In one Gallup poll (Toronto *Star*, July 24, 1989), 77 percent of respondents thought a competent physician should have the legal right to end the life of a patient who endured "great suffering" from an incurable disease, if the request had been made in writing. Other such Gallup polls show that the young (78 percent) are far more in favour of such final solutions than the old (58 percent) (Toronto *Star*, November 25, 1991). Hmmm . . . Other polls show majorities who say that

legalization should be opposed if the patient is incompetent, or others have to make the decision for him. One U.S. poll said that 70 percent of Americans asked to imagine themselves gravely ill said they would decide against life-sustaining treatment. Most of these responses seem normal. The difficulty is this: Can human beings be trusted to use proper safeguards? What is a "competent" physician? How do you weed out unscrupulous family or estate financial interests? And most important, how do you keep at bay the representatives of the State itself? These are important questions.

Death is an irrational, anxiety-provoking enigma felt as the highest insult to the ordered rational mind driven by a desire for utopia, a symbol of the uncontrolled darkness that has always plagued the human spirit. So . . . you attempt to control the anxiety by controlling the meaning and moment of death. And the death controllers are everywhere. The University of Iowa recently drafted a model "Aid in Dying Act," which it said would bring "quality control in the termination of life." The Act authorizes the killing of individuals with an "intolerable condition" (a pianist who has lost the use of his hands, is one example); and the killing of the "incompetent" (which could include anyone in a mental institution). The Act also envisages "telostricians" — physicians trained to administer a sweet death. A *New England Journal of Medicine* article advocates euthanasia for the "pleasantly senile," and a Dr. Ronald Crawford, in the same article, appears to use the need for spoon-feeding as the cutoff for a decision on withdrawing food and water from patients. (Too much trouble? Better to starve them.) There would appear to be no perfect answer, but some basic questions sure need asking. As columnist Don Feder wrote, "When healers become hit men, society should shudder."[2]

### Will It Be Eros or Thanatos?

There are so many agonizing dilemmas in human life, and enough bothersome exceptions to every rule, that most societies have wisely decided to ignore the exceptions and rely instead on basic principles. The individual "rights"-based euthanasia movement is attempting to erode those principles by forcing a confrontation between two conflicting principles in modern civilization: the political principle that an individual has the right to control his body, including his death; and the contrary ethical principle that society has a right to forbid and punish all killing directed against its own members. This is really a conflict between the end-stage of liberalism as manifested in the Individualism Illusion, in which personal "freedom" is

asserted as of a higher value than any social or ethical obligation —
and the conserving force of society (formerly always considered
higher than any individual) as it struggles for self-preservation.
On the conservative side, society claims the right to preserve all
life, regardless of what any individual may think. On the liberal
side, the individual seeks to place his personal will above the
social will (as distinct from the State, which coerces both individual
and society).

But in the end, a society can only, and indeed must, decide
whether it is for life *in general* or against it. No society can opt to
decide in favour of life for one, and against for another. A society is
always forced to choose in general, and in the abstract, between
*Eros*, or the life principle, and *Thanatos*, or the death principle. *Eros*
dictates that all human action must be directed toward caring,
nurturing, and preserving; that all human beings, by virtue of their
existence, are irrevocably bound by a common interest in the
support of life. *Thanatos* dictates the opposite: that individual life
is utilitarian and expendable, and must be bent to serve whatever is
deemed useful. Individual life, under they sway of *Thanatos*, that
is, has no higher meaning. When the *Thanatos* principle is widespread, it even declares that the meaning of life itself — is death.
And wherever widely supported politically, it inevitably becomes
joined to the enterprises of the collectivist State. In Nazi Germany,
death — especially the death of others, such as Jews, intellectuals,
the infirm, the elderly, homosexuals, the deformed, and those of low
intelligence — became a symbol of pure devotion to the higher
causes of the State. Japanese kamikaze fighter-pilots were emboldened by the same ideals. The death of the pilot was seen as a glorious
contribution to the future of the State. And the incalculable horrors
of socialism in the communist nations were and still are carried out
under the banner of the State. Whenever *Thanatos* supplants *Eros*
as a principle of a society, everything subtly changes; the laws of the
land become written to conform to this basic principle, and to justify
it. So we must look not to the laws to see what is right, but beneath
them, to see what is valued.

### What Is Euthanasia, and What Does the Law Say?
There is much wilful confusion promoted over the exact meaning of
"euthanasia." Expressions like "death with dignity," "self-deliverance,"
"passive euthanasia," "the right to die," or "aid-in-dying" are slogans
used by death-control activists to lead the public to an acceptance of all
euthanasia, and to obscure the central fact underlying it, which is this:

*Euthanasia always involves someone else making you die.* There is no euthanasia without killing. As one critic, Rita Marker, director of the Anti-Euthanasia Task Force, said about sick patients: "making a patient die either by doing something (commission) or by not doing something (omission) *with the purpose and intent of killing the patient*, is euthanasia."[3]

In other words, refusing to render simple help to someone who will die without it, for the sole reason that you want him to die, or eliminating the help once he has it, because you want him to die, or doing something to actually kill him, like suffocating him or giving him a lethal injection or a cup of tea laced with arsenic — all this is euthanasia. The legal and moral definitions of these actions as wrong have nothing to do with what the patient wants. Consent of the killed individual has nothing to do with it. As the telling analysis of Leon Kass expresses it, all societies have decided that certain acts are abominable, and society reserves the right to judge its members guilty if they commit these acts.[4] This is true for many other abominations as well. For example, consent cannot transform incest, adultery, cannibalism, or slavery into acceptable acts. But the prevailing liberal technique for transforming formerly immoral or illegal acts into acceptable ones is to legitimize them under the rubric of choice, or consent. Groups like the North American Man-Boy Love Association, as we have seen, argue aggressively that mutual consent and privacy justify pedophilia, incest, and bestiality.

At any rate, in addition to religious sanctions against it, euthanasia has always been judged wrong on a simple secular principle; namely, the notion that life must be based either on *Eros* or *Thanatos*, the life principle or the death principle. There can be no middle ground, simply because the law must head in either one direction or the other. Life and death are absolutes, and they require absolute laws to defend or deny them. If someone is in a situation where a decision from society is a critical factor, and if he cannot voice an opinion, then society and its agents (doctors, nurses, citizens) must fall back upon a basic principle, either: love of life or love of death. There will be sacrifices either way. In the *Eros* culture, a few *individuals* may be kept alive against their will through sometimes heroic care. And the notion of "heroic care" is vital, because those giving it do so in the service of a noble ideal that generates selflessness. This alone is sufficient reason to prefer *Eros* over *Thanatos*. But in the *Thanatos* culture, whole *classes* of people are killed against their will by elites whose heroic devotion is not to those individuals, but to some notion of the State. We must choose what sort of culture we want, as we cannot have both. Traditionally, owing to an historical suspicion concerning the motives of the State, or those of some individuals within it (who may have heinous personal motives, unknowable before the fact, to wish others dead), we have opted for the life principle as a protective device.

It so happens that until now our own laws have reflected this choice, one not always available to members of other societies. In his brief and lucid work, *Euthanasia: Charting the Legal Trends in Canada, the United States, and the Netherlands*,[5] Canadian legal scholar Robert Nadeau shows the evolution of the laws and, I fear, proves how vulnerable they are to abandoning sound principles and following fashionable fears.

In Canada, the euthanasia issue has been framed and defined not so much by the courts, as in the United States, but by the Law Reform Commission of Canada, which in 1976 began an intensive study of the matter. As Nadeau writes, however, the law in Canada today is "just as vague and muddled" as when the commission began. He concludes that in both countries the courts have focused upon the difference between "voluntary" and "involuntary" euthanasia, a distinction that has to do with the attitude of the killed person. In voluntary euthanasia, the person must be rational and give a clear and unequivocal direction of his wish to have someone else end his life. Involuntary euthanasia is carried out without the patient's consent, or even against his wishes. Right away, we can see the problems. Some examples: A patient has given a clear consent, but was in pain and not fully informed of available pain-control treatment; or he has had such information withheld by professionals or by greedy relatives; or he is depressed and not truly rational; or he is burdened by guilt over the costs of care. In short, these two forms of killing, separated only by the cloudy nature of the *intent* of the victim (as opposed to the intent, or basic principle, of society) are easily confused. At any rate, in Canada and the United States, the courts have "widely rejected" the whole idea of involuntary euthanasia (phew!). They have also (so far) "refused to authorize withdrawal of treatment against the express wishes of a patient."[6] The only real legal debate has been over the question of decriminalizing voluntary euthanasia (allowing us to kill others if they wish to be killed).

As for the terms "active" and "passive" euthanasia, these refer not to the presence or absence of consent of the one killed, but to the *method* of the killer. Did he actively do something to end another person's life, or did he refuse to do something he ought to have done, as a duty, to maintain that life? In Canada, so-called "active" euthanasia is classified under the Criminal Code as culpable homicide, and the *motive* of the killer of the victim is irrelevant. You can see why. Courts cannot sit in judgment on what might or might not have been in two consenting people's heads at the moment of a crime, especially since one of the people is forever absent. Also, they do not want to encourage the wanton fabrication and proliferation of motives for the spirit of "mercy."

And as for "passive euthanasia"? The law is less clear. But at least it has decided in favour of the life principle, for it requires all of us who undertake to do an act (such as providing medical care) *to continue to do so if an omission to do so would be dangerous to life.*[7] The law is written this way to prevent some from killing others by omitting treatment when they could easily have administered it. The law wants to deter the young niece who stands to gain from the death of rich Uncle George from "mercifully" underfeeding him, so that he "falls asleep" and dies. The life principle in our society has been put in place to deter those who prefer the death principle, or no principle at all. This does not mean that individuals are required to give "heroic" treatment, but they currently have a duty to give such ordinary care and treatment as would reasonably be provided in the circumstances.

As the proponents of "choice" advance, however, using the lure of freedom for coercive purposes, they influence the courts, so that today many courts are rethinking whether even food and water are "ordinary." As Nadeau points out, however, if death results from withholding food and water, it happens from starvation or dehydration and not from the underlying illness. Citizens must be alert to these niceties. They may support such vagueness for others, but what about for their own children, or parents, or spouse? In his book on genocidal medicine (1986), Robert Jay Lifton describes the elaborate ruses used by the German government, always ennobled in elaborate medical terminology, to mislead families who had entrusted their loved ones to hospitals and physicians. As we saw in the last chapter, in many hospitals of the world perfectly healthy babies who have survived abortions are simply left unfed to die. Others are intentionally aborted alive, sold to scientists, dismembered, disembowelled, or frozen for science. Many elderly or disabled people are let starve, or are drugged against their will to hasten death. Under German national socialism, doctors put drugs (*lumin*) in the deliberately inadequate rations of "defective" young children until they got drowsy, could no longer cry of hunger, and died of malnutrition. But the doctors refused to admit they were killing the children. They said they were "putting them to sleep." Now, we think of those dirty old Nazis as vicious, unfeeling folks; not kind, gentle, and civilized, like Canadians. Right?

Meanwhile . . . Ontario's Dr. Robert Sliwowicz has defended using heavy doses of morphine in the deaths of 15 disabled patients at the Christopher Robin home in Ajax, Ontario. He said it was "to ease the child's distress in dying." When the examining lawyer asked him why no one tried to *save* the children's lives, he replied, "because of the philosophy of the home" — which was "do not resuscitate" and to drug the children "unless parents have stated otherwise." But many parents were not consulted, or told that 12 of the 15 had pneumonia. So large doses of morphine were administered to all 15 children, despite its being a known respiration-repressant drug. The doctor attempted to argue that pneumonia is a "terminal disease" (Toronto *Star*, March 6, 15, 1992). But U.S. expert Dr. Leslie Rubin was "scathingly critical" and testified that pneumonia does not cause pain and the doses of morphine used were "excessive, to potential lethal levels." He said decisions at the home not to resuscitate were "glaringly inappropriate," and he was enraged by the treatment the children received (Toronto *Star*, April 7, 1992). Another expert, from Toronto's Hospital for Sick Children, said a 1½-year-old victim received "overdose, after overdose, after overdose." As she held her dying 2½-year-old daughter Melissa, Mrs. Irene McGrath sobbed at the trial that Melissa "was so weak that she'd kind of lose her breath and her eyes would close." She was unaware at the time that 18½ hours earlier Melissa had been given 10 milligrams of morphine. Mothers at the inquest said they knew nothing of the "comfort care" philosophy at the home; they had been told their children "would get whatever [they] needed." They did. The home acted according to the classic dual presumptions of "substituted judgment," and the death principle, to determine their "needs." Comfort care, as one grieving parent's lawyer, Harvey Strosberg, pointed out, was "a nice way of saying we're going to allow helpless children to die."

In the wake of a recent police probe into the death of a Timmins, Ontario, senior citizen given a lethal injection without her knowledge, Ontario Chief Coroner James Young issued a red-alert warning that "palliative care" for the dying in Ontario had gone to the point of providing enough medication to end the patient's life (Toronto *Star* December 17, 1992). One month prior, an employee at Toronto's Wellesley Hospital had been charged with first-degree murder after a 77-year-old patient died of an alleged lethal injection. And Randy Pritchard, a former patient of the Penetanguishene Mental Health Centre, an institution currently under investigation for abuse, told a news conference "the truth is going to be told here," following reports that the staff used towels to choke patients unconscious (Toronto *Star*, December 17, 1992).

All who fear falling victim to euthanasia enthusiasts using the law must ask: Does the law of Canada support the life principle or the death principle? Encouragingly, the Law Reform Commission has said, "Preservation of human life is acknowledged to be a fundamental value of our society . . . The Commission believes that any reform having to do with human life must begin by admitting *a firm presumption in favour of life*."[8] And, "[I]n the absence of reasons to the contrary, the patient should always be presumed to want to live, and that the patient would prefer life to death *even when unable to express that preference*."[9] Here, society is substituting its judgment for that of the patient, and it has quite properly opted for the life principle.

**But What If the Patient Wants to Die?**
Nadeau makes it clear that Canadian (and U.S.) common law have "long recognized an absolute right of a [competent] patient to refuse medical treatment," however foolish such a decision might be and even if it results in death.[10] In short, *competent* and fully informed patients can refuse medicine, and even food and water, if they wish to die. This is a right they have had for a long time. They can even sue a doctor for assault if he attempts to force treatment on them. The question of the *incompetent* patient has not been clarified in Canada, however, except that the Law Reform Commission has distinguished between "treatment" and "care," and implied that while medically useless treatment may be withdrawn, care and comfort may not. But it is, however, a short step indeed from saying that a competent patient may refuse even food and water, to withholding these basic necessities from incompetent patients. (The case of the United States, below, demonstrates the shortness of the step.)

The commission has repeatedly and unequivocally rejected legalization or decriminalization of both voluntary and involuntary active euthanasia,[11] and it has urged that any such "mercy killing" be treated as murder. It also firmly rejected the decriminalization of "aiding" suicide, and has said that whether for the purposes of active euthanasia or aiding suicide, the "right of self-determination" does not imply the right to *require* that some other person put us to death, nor does it confer a right on a sympathetic third party to assist in a suicide.[12]

So far, it seems, we Canadians are relatively safe. But for how long? A revived Bill C-203 (defeated in Committee in February 1992) could, as Professor Ian Gentles wrote of the original, "open the door to active euthanasia" (*Globe and Mail*, November 19, 1991). That bill basically authorizes physicians to use measures "intended to eliminate or relieve the physical suffering of a person," even though such measures "will or are likely to shorten the life expectancy of the person" (C-203, section 217.1(c)). In other words, the bill proposed that Canadian physicians be free of all liability if they decide to eliminate the pain — as well as the patient. Had the bill passed (one liberal is reportedly about to propose a bill even worse), no patient would have been safe in a Canadian hospital. All our hospitals, take note, are desperate to reduce their costs.

And the "Nancy B." case in Quebec illustrates the trend in Canada. Nancy won a court case allowing her to "discontinue medical treatment," and the press widely trumpeted that she had won the "right to die" with dignity. But let us be clear, for the sake of honesty, whether we agree with euthanasia or not. Nancy was "heavily sedated" by her physician for a reason (*Globe and Mail*, February 14, 1992). It was to prevent her from reacting by reflex to the suffocating feeling of lack of oxygen once the respirator was turned off by her physician; to prevent her from screaming to turn it on again, which, like anyone else, she would certainly have done. So what Nancy actually won was not the right to die, but *the right to be killed* by someone else, and to have the person who killed her exempted from charges of murder. The doctor killed her legally. Period. What Canada's head of Dying with Dignity, Mr. Don Elliott, of Cheltenham, Ontario, said was that she was "entitled to make that choice" based on her assessment of her "quality of life." This is the sort of simplistic justification often heard from those frightened by or unable to fathom moral complexities. For every choice has a context; and our "quality of life" has a lot to do with what is both inside us and outside us. After all, who, suffering the miseries of a brief illness, has not briefly felt like dying, or at least understood how easy such a decision to end one's own life would be? Then, surging upward on the mend, who has not felt that burst of joy in renewed strength and love of life and said to himself, "It's amazing how pain or misery can change the way you see your whole life"?

Consider the case of two patients with identical diseases. One is surrounded with loving and caring family, well-trained support staff, appropriate medicines for pain and mood, excellent therapists, and a world that wants her specific gifts, however limited. The other has none of these things, languishes in a dismal hospital with cold, lazy staff, has no future in sight, nobody to care for her, is reminded daily how expensive her care is, and maybe even has a few greedy relatives awaiting her end and other, less ill patients, for her bed. You ask them both if they want to live. The first is very likely to say yes; the second will likely say no. So before proffering such "choices" and hastening to find physicians willing to kill, let us as a society ensure that everything reasonably possible has been done to promote the presumption in favour of life. If we don't, every temporarily depressed or ill citizen will have a lot more to worry about from those who confuse the so-called dignity of dying with the sanctity of life. You only have to imagine a society full of mean or greedy relatives, cash-starved hospitals, and witless philosophers of death to realize that it's incredibly easy to create an environment in which the "quality of life" for the sick or disabled is permanently absent.

**The U.S. Precedent**
In the United States, the same *Roe v. Wade* case that found a "right of privacy" in the U.S. Bill of Rights, thus opening the door for abortion, or pediatric euthanasia, has led Americans further down the road to adult death control. (There is a connection between these different forms of euthanasia, and between the people who promote them. Alan Guttmacher, of the pro-abortion group Planned Parenthood, in 1972 was on the board of the U.S. Euthanasia Education Council.)

But in what will surely rank as the most loopy legal argument ever rendered, if it were not so tragic, Justice William O. Douglas said Americans had a right of privacy because specific guarantees in the U.S. Bill of Rights " . . . have penumbras, formed by emanations from those guarantees . . . "[13] As Nadeau illustrates, this generalized right of privacy became the right to refuse extraordinary medical care, whether the patient was competent or incompetent. This extension of the meaning of "privacy" has gone so far now that such a right does not have to be exercised by the patient himself, but can be exercised by a legal surrogate. From this decision issued the further right (of the surrogate) to refuse *any* medical treatment, and from this the right to refuse food and water (ordinary care). In one case Nadeau cites, a U.S. court gave a wife the right to withhold food and water from a perfectly healthy husband — who happened to be comatose.[14]

### The Doctrine of Substituted Judgment

What the wife did was to substitute her judgment not only for that of her husband, but for that of the State as well. In effect, in the United States the State has moved over to allow related third parties to make personal life and death decisions for others in its place. Clearly, this is the first of the two crucial steps in the long process of change from a life-affirming to a death-affirming culture: The law effectively takes the traditional and exclusive right of society to define and defend the worthiness of life itself, and transfers or surrenders it to separate, disparate individuals. Thus is the value of life relativized. Thus is the philosophy that all values are personal and relative written large in the land.

The easier, second step begins at the moment the rising State — having abandoned its general protection of life and successfully relativized its value — in one sudden move strikes to assume for itself the power of substituted judgment. Clearly, in free countries, it can assume such a role only *after* the people themselves have accepted a utilitarian standard for the value of life. So what the State does is to teach the standard, in the name of choice, autonomy, and equality, and then turn around and use this utilitarian (primarily economic) argument against whole classes of citizens. Fanciful, you say? In a 1984 speech, Richard Lamm, former governor of Colorado, announced to the senior citizens of his State that they had "a duty to die and get out of the way." They were, he said, "wasting precious resources that the other society, our kids, need to build a reasonable life." He likened the elderly to leaves falling from a tree, and "forming the humus for other plants to grow up." This is chilling when you recall the various totalitarian movements that have actually used humans for fertilizer.[15] Right here in Ontario, morally confused people like the former Anglican minister and now columnist, Tom Harpur, justify physicians killing patients with lethal injections on the grounds that such physicians are "fulfilling their total responsibility towards the patient's well-being" (Toronto *Star*, December 8, 1991). Death is well-being? If death is well-being, what is life?

Meanwhile, on March 7, 1991, 26-year-old Conley Holbrook of Lexington, North Carolina, his mother by his side, awoke suddenly from an eight-year coma — and immediately identified the two men who had tried to beat him to death. "It's been like hell," he said, and then asked for his favourite food and said he wants to walk again (Toronto *Star*, March 7, 1991). You could say it's a good thing he wasn't married to the same kind of wife as the fellow above, or living in the same state.

## Confusions of Language and Concept

*Newspeak: language designed to make lies truthful and murder respectable.*
GEORGE ORWELL

What follows is a meditation spurred by Leon Kass in his moving article, "Death with Dignity, and the Sanctity of Life" (*Commentary*, March 1990). As he clearly indicates, "death with dignity" is a moot phrase. Think about it. Death itself cannot be dignified. Only the way we face death can be dignified, and that is determined by the values we uphold in facing it, our courage, our love, and our respect for its meaning to ourselves, to those we love, and to our entire culture. The philosopher Kant, with his concept of the "categorical imperative," argued that in the absence of a religious standard of conduct, we should choose to behave in a way we would have others behave. In this sense, we must see our behaviour as *legitimizing* the behaviour of humanity, and such a notion gets us back to the question of our basic principles. For even in dying, we can affirm life or affirm death, and in our personal way of dying we inevitably give a message to the living. Kass rightly maintains that no one wants to be an object trapped in a machine, for this confinement indeed deprives us of freedom. But neither can we gain dignity by pre-empting death. What is wanted, he says, is not death with dignity, which springs from our response to our own mortality, but "death with decency," which springs from the way we are treated. We must find a better way to keep the eager doctors off us with their fancy contraptions, if these are unwanted. Fine. But that's a far cry from authorizing them to kill us or, worse, to kill others.

All human dignity springs from ourselves; but it is only human decency that allows us to be dignified. The "death with dignity" slogan is just a clever trick to make people think that dignity arises from our material conditions instead of from our values and our attitudes. Dignity is perfectly compatible with letting die, but utterly incompatible with killing. Worst of all, the phrase has been joined, as has abortion, to the idea of "choice," to the idea of "controlling" (your own death/body). Of course, right up until you are physically incapable, you are free to kill yourself — and maintain control. Most, however, are frightened to kill themselves, so they wait until they are unable, then implore others to do it for them. In the last stage, they demand the right to be killed nicely by another.

Phrases such as "the right to die," however, cannot impose a duty on another to kill you. This is just another slippery phrase. We already have a common-law right, as we have seen, to refuse treatment and be allowed to die naturally. Everyone supports that. But demanding a right to be killed is a different matter, for it imposes a duty on another, or on society, to kill us. Under such a regime, physicians fret about committing acts and being sued for "wrongful survival" if they refuse to kill a patient (just as with abortion; some U.S. physicians have been successfully sued for "wrongful birth" — refusing to abort a child).[16] The two perspectives expose the clash in our culture between values controlled by contract between two human beings, and values controlled by conduct — by a transcendent ideal or a basic underlying principle. Euthanasia enthusiasts push for contract. In the name of freedom, they attempt to legitimize private killing. But euthanasia is not a private act. It is very public indeed. That's why those frightened by euthanasia supporters, or of the State itself, push for the ideals and laws to protect us from them. What I hope to show is that mere contract is a poor basis for a moral society, because it springs from moral relativism and leads to totalitarianism. After all, no physician can accurately distinguish between the subjective suffering of one patient who wants to live, and of another in the same predicament who wants to die. So to legitimize private killing for subjective reasons merely legitimizes all killing. Period. However, the most compelling reason for a principle such as the sanctity of life is that "the sacredness, whatever it is, inheres in life itself . . . To say that sacredness is something that can be conferred or ascribed — or removed — by solely human agreement or decision is to miss the point entirely."[17]

But once the State has eroded any allegiance to transcendent ideals by virtue of its mere presence, invasiveness, and educational programs, it then easily sweeps in as a ready partner with myriad soulless citizens to control death in countless ways. Those of us living under a regime of socialized medicine such as Canada's must be wary, for the temptation of the State to economize at our expense, using the language of rights (the rights of the State, at this point), will be overwhelming. As Kass reminds us, our culture has always upheld the sanctity of life. It has said that it is wrong as a matter of principle to kill the willing, the unwilling, or the non-willing (the comatose or the incompetent). It has said that the sanctity of life is utterly independent of any individual will. And after all, how could we live otherwise? Is "the life of another human being to be respected only because that person (or society) *deems* or *wills* it respectable? Or is it to be respected because it *is in itself* respectable?"[18] I should say the latter. It is from this inherent respect that the sanctity of life springs, and it is contradictory to say that we can bestow dignity by removing dignity. As Kass tells us: "One does not come to the defense of diminished human dignity by finishing the job, by annihilating the victim."[19]

If Canadians proceed with a revived Bill C-203, citizens had better reserve a space in a private nursing home now. At least private homes have a vested interest in keeping you (and your monthly payments) alive. But public hospitals will find a hundred ways to shorten your life, because you are only an expense against their limited budgets. Again, what is private will tend to support the bottom-up society, family values, and moral and economic agency. But the public hospital as an arm of the welfare State will impose a top-down utilitarian morality on all its patients, who will increasingly be seen as mere integers on a reporting sheet. In every totalitarian State in history, many of the worst crimes against humanity have been carried out under political directives from educated elites and professionals. The hospitals and other such institutions (homes, asylums) become killing centres; the research laboratories become centres for bizarre medical experiments in which some lives, deemed unworthy, are used to help others, deemed useful. This is possible only once the State has abandoned the Judeo-Christian principle of the sanctity of all human life from conception and replaced it with a relativisitic utilitarian principle based on the power of surrogates to substitute their judgment for others. From here, the State then declares whole classes of human beings first as non-persons, then as people having lives unworthy to be lived, and finally as a form of waste or parasite. Next, the State proceeds to kill, dismember, mutilate, and experiment with these "things." That's why Gloria Steinem argued (September 9, 1981) that a woman should have the right to abort, to remove "any parasitic growth" from her body. And that's why Vancouver artist Rick Gibson created a sculpture of a woman's head wearing freeze-dried human fetal skulls as earrings. And it's why a popular rock group called "Day-Glo Abortions" has a song called "Feed Us a Fetus." And that's why Hitler called the Jews parasites, and sexologist Havelock Ellis referred to the fetus as "a parasite performing no function whatsoever," and psychiatrist Natalie Shainess likened the fetus to "a parasite" with the capacity "to murder its mother."[20] It is such initial gross distortions of language that make eventual murder "respectable," opening the way for the laws to uphold the new ethics. It is chilling to remember that the Hippocratic Oath obliging all physicians to respect human life has been rejected only during two historical periods since the fourth century B.C.: during the 12 years of the Third Reich, and during our own post 1960s period.

In 1945, at the Nuremberg trials, Professor Julius Hollervorden said: "There were wonderful materials among those brains . . . where they came from and how they came to me was none of my business."

In February 1990, Canada's Dr. Allan MacDonald, of the "ethics" committee of Victoria General Hospital in Halifax, said: "How the [aborted] individual from where the tissue is obtained dies, is not directly germane to the use of the tissue" (*Chronicle-Herald*, February 21, 1990).

And fetal "researcher" Dr. Martti Kekomaki of Finland regularly slices open the stomachs and cuts off the heads of deliberately aborted live babies, without anesthetic. "An aborted baby is just garbage," he says, and that's where it ends up."[21] Kekomaki says "the fetuses are fully alive when we cut their heads off . . . " Then he explains how he extracts "nutrients" from the brains of these fetuses to help premature babies — his noble cause. One can always be found.

When will we understand that just as the "health" of the mother is the justification for abortion, so the "health" of society is the justification for the State's interest in euthanasia? If those with families want to protect them, they'd best understand that the State has a powerful financial and political incentive to support abortion and euthanasia, both of which are compellingly inexpensive and profoundly antifamily.

After all, some argue, we put down animals who suffer, so why not be at least as merciful to humans? Peter Singer, a prominent U.S. animal-rights activist, argues that medical research ought to be conducted on human babies, instead of an animals, and that there is "no morally relevant difference" between experimenting on a dying dog and a dying human baby. The dog, he writes, "is the more intelligent, sensitive, and autonomous being."[22] But we don't do this, as Kass poignantly explains, because we are not animals. First of all, humans and animals can have only a subject-object relationship. (I know, I know, your pet, like mine, is almost human.) Whereas human dignity can spring only from a subject-subject relationship. When that is over, we can easily hate. Wish the other dead. (Ask any divorced person.) In fact, all human evil springs from the subject-object relationship, all human goodness from subject-subject. Any intent to kill, regardless of motive, requires that we relate to the other as an object, as someone we are going to make into a non-subject. In this sense, no form of euthanasia can be authentic,[23] for "It is precisely the absence of dignified humanity that invites the thought of active euthanasia in the first place"[24] — the will to forcibly substitute the object for the subject. So above all, we must resist this temptation of the State to objectify all human life. Unfortunately, as explained in *The Trouble with Canada*, socialized medicine is already a form of objective, veterinary-like medicine for human beings (see Chapter Eleven, "Medical Mediocrity," in that book). Whereas humans ought to be able to control and to spend whatever of their own resources they wish on their own health care, animals are treated as objects, controlled by the command and the budgets of their masters. They have no say. As it turns out, Canadians, by law, are forbidden to spend their own resources on their own basic medical care, too.

In 1992 in North York, Ontario, a scandal was created when an uncharacteristically entrepreneurial public hospital technician, faced with an exhausted budget and obliged to refuse further human patients, decided to raise a little cash by accepting pets for CAT scans. Red-faced hospital officials reacted to the pet-owner lineups by refusing the animals, too. Better for both owner and animal to die, was the inherent reasoning, than to accept private funds. If we don't watch out, the State will soon justify putting us down like animals. At that stage, no one will be safe. In the end, it is impossible to relate authentically to those who have the unfettered option to kill you. So I say the real dignity will come from escaping the death control of the State.

But the way is now being cleared for this control. How will we stop it?

### The Dutch Example

The experience of euthanasia in the Netherlands — as practised openly there for over a decade, though it has never been legalized — ought to serve as our test case. The Dutch example clearly shows "that a practice that starts out being voluntary, can quickly become involuntary."[25]

With surprising candour, that government's Remmelink Committee (by Professor J. Remmelink, attorney general of the Supreme Court of the Netherlands), charged with reporting on the practice of euthanasia, revealed some shocking — though entirely predictable — results. The committee's two-volume report, "Medical Decisions Concerning the End of Life," was released September 10, 1991.[26]

Notice it was not entitled "Moral Decisions" about the end of life. The report is extraordinary because, while brutally candid in presenting the data, it is wholly political in its interpretation of them.

The report defines euthanasia extremely narrowly as "the deliberate termination of another's life at his request," and determines "scientifically" that 1.8 percent, or about 2300 of the 130,000 annual deaths in the Netherlands, are by such voluntary euthanasia, with only 400 cases of so-called assisted suicide. The report also estimates that about 1000 Dutch people per year are killed *involuntarily* (about three per day), and says that 25 percent of these patients were mentally competent but were not asked to give consent, and all were enduring grievous suffering. The remainder, also very old, demented, incurably ill, or in grievous suffering, were euthanized at the request of the family or the physician, without their knowledge. It further states that a "notification procedure" is in place to block abuse.[27]

But the Remmelink report should not get off so lightly, and the Western democracies should pay strict heed to the numbers. The committee has been roundly attacked for political bias, and the raw numbers have been reanalysed by Dutch cardiologist Dr. Richard Fenigsen, among others, with a shocking result.[28] The prestigious British medical journal *The Lancet* also analysed the data with findings almost as alarming.[29] Dr. Fenigsen was in turn vilified by the Royal Dutch Medical Association in a paper that defended the committee's very narrow definition of euthanasia, restricting it once again to purely voluntary cases (perhaps in order to avoid a feared international reputation of Dutch physicians as "killer doctors.")[30] This effort only ensured the association would sink faster in a bog of verbal quicksand, as when it wrote that death as a result of a pain-relieving drug was a "side-effect."

The truth is yet to come out, but let us mark well Fenigsen's warning. He relies on a comprehensive and strict definition of euthanasia to include all cases where a patient has been directly killed by a doctor, or other such person, or has had treatment withdrawn or excessive drugs administered with the *intent* of ending life.[31]

In addition to what the committee reported, above, Dr. Fenigsen's analysis of the public data showed that there are in fact 25,306 cases of true euthanasia in the Netherlands annually. Of the 25,000 cases in which life-prolonging treatment was withdrawn or withheld *without a request of the patient*, 8750 were carried out with the specific intent to kill. Of the 22,500 deaths from overdoses of morphine,

8100 were carried out with the intent to kill (the others gave death as a "side effect"). The total of 25,306 cases constitutes fully 19.4% of all deaths in the Netherlands. In summary, by an overly narrow definition, the committee excluded fully 23,006 cases of euthanasia from its description, though not from the data. Further analysis shows that 14,691 people in the Netherlands are killed annually by involuntary euthanasia. That is to say, far more people die in the Netherlands from involuntary, than from voluntary euthanasia. (It is fair to say they are executed by agents of the State.) Of the 8100 who died of overdose, 61 percent were killed without their consent, with the death listed as "pain relief." About the same number were killed by stopping or withholding treatment without consent. In one group of 5800 patients so dealt with, only 82 percent actually died when the machines were turned off. (You rather wonder how the doctor said "good morning" the next day to the ones who lived.) And these figures do not include all cases of euthanasia of newborns with disabilities, children with diseases, or psychiatric patients.

Even more ghastly, 14 percent of the cases, or 140 people a day, were involuntarily killed even though they were *fully competent*. A "low quality of life," or "the family couldn't take it any more," were listed as typical and most frequent reasons. A shocking example of the antifamily mentality of the State is that 45 percent of those killed in hospitals were euthanized without the knowledge of the family. In 27 percent of the cases of morphine overdose, the patient was fully competent but not informed of the physician's intent to kill. And 86 percent of all hospital orders for "do not resuscitate" are given without the patients' knowledge or consent.

As for the guidelines? The Netherlands by law demands patient consent for voluntary euthanasia (the only kind it condones). Yet, almost 6000 cases a year of involuntary killing had no such consent. About 20 percent of physicians do not bother to consult another physician for voluntary killing, as required by law, and 60 percent fail to do so for the involuntary type. About 54 percent decide not to record the procedure at all, 74 percent admitted that they conceal the voluntary procedure in the records, and none stated the truth about involuntary killing. Fenigsen ends on a sober note. If you subtract the 43,000 sudden deaths from cardiac arrest, accidents, and the like, you discover that in 56.5 percent of *all* other deaths in the Netherlands, physicians took decisions that hastened the deaths of their patients. These findings are very close to other Dutch surveys of euthanasia, such as the Holland VARA poll, which put the total figure at about 40,000 annually.[32]

Ironically, a system meant to give patients control over their own lives has ended by giving control to physicians, as agents of the State. The Dutch percentages applied to Canada today would mean about 30,000 to 50,000 Canadians killed every year by agents of the State, without their prior consent or that of their families. Currently, the Canadian Association for Community Living estimates that there are about 1000 euthanasia cases annually in Canada, likely a very low estimate. But the knives are out. In a 1983 *Maclean's* feature article, Dr. Scott Wallace, among others, argued that we need a national referendum permitting the elderly to volunteer for euthanasia to free up hospital beds.[33]

As for the predicted brutalization of civilized sensibilities that euthanasia is predicted to follow and aggravate? In a poll of Dutch economics students as early as 1972, 90 percent supported involuntary killing of specified groups of people in order "to streamline the economy."[34] And so-called medical experts argue, as did J.H. van den Berg in an influential book in 1969, that doctors have a duty to kill those whose lives are meaningless; if a family resists, the death should be imposed anyway, by a committee of doctors and laymen.[35] Soon Canadians will make the same arguments. In 1989, the Dutch Medical Association advocated the "right" of children to kill themselves. One Dutch cardiologist, describing frightening examples of how the practice of euthanasia has changed and cheapened people's attitudes, cites cases of the elderly refused surgery, or anesthesia for surgery, or even hospital admission; of a chef allowed to die because "the patient is an unmarried single person"; of a physician who advised against treatment because his patient is "a lonely widower."[36] But how do the patients feel?

A survey of Dutch nursing homes (more accurately, killing hostels, perhaps) found that 60 percent of the residents feared involuntary euthanasia.[37] So to fight the death principle at work in the Netherlands, the Dutch have formed a patients' rights organization. Its primary purpose is to warn the public that sick people are being killed in the Netherlands, in all the ways mentioned here.

**What Does the Future Hold?**
The signs are not good. In 1984, Helga Kuhse, speaking at the World Federation of Right to Die Societies, spelled it out: "If we can get people to accept the removal of all treatment and care — especially the removal of food and fluids — they will see what a painful way this is to die, and then, in the patient's best interests, they will accept the lethal injection." The "they" here is, first, the patient. Then the

patient's family. Then physicians or bureaucrats who presume to speak for both. And finally the State, which presumes to speak for us all as it sets about defining and ranking classes of citizens in terms of their right to life and health care — and their corresponding duty to die for the health of others. A particularly gruesome story is that of Toronto's Matthew van Geffen, a quadraplegic with muscular dystrophy. St. Michael's hospital and Matthew's physician were cleared of murder charges. But his friend Elizabeth Hardy, and his neighbour Linda Hearst, both in the death room at the time, testified at the coroner's hearing that Matthew, with a tube in his mouth that prevented his speaking, was shaking his head to indicate that he did not want the respirator removed. He shook it again even as a priest administered the last rites.[38]

Alas, there is a chain of logic revealing that when we try to gain control of the tree of life (by death control) through the tree of knowledge (medicine), we end up inevitably at the hemlock tree. In September 1991, American Derek Humphry, a British journalist and the founder of the U.S. Hemlock Society, published *Final Exit*, a book about the practicalities of killing yourself or helping others to kill themselves. It has sold over 200,000 copies in the United States, over 10,000 in Canada (June 1992).

Rita Marker tells an interesting story that connects with Humphry. She had recently become close friends with a woman diagnosed with breast cancer. This woman had turned to Rita because her husband, instead of reaching out in love and support, abandoned her as soon as he learned of her cancer. Marker says the husband persistently put pressure on the wife to commit suicide. She finally did so, and left a note to her husband, saying, "You finally got what you wanted." Signed: Anne Humphry.

Anne was Derek Humphry's second wife of 13 years. She had marvelled to Marker at "what subtle and not so subtle pressure could be put on people to die and get out of the way."[39] Before committing suicide, she brought a $6 million suit against him, charging that his actions were "timed and calculated to exploit [the] . . . weakened condition of the plaintiff, to induce her despair and her suicide."[40]

Well, it turns out that Humphry's first wife, Jean, had also committed suicide, and Derek always said he had helped her "deliver" herself to the grim reaper. Maybe. But Anne, in a note she sent to Rita Marker, says he "did not help his first wife commit suicide. Jean actually died of suffocation . . . Derek is a killer. I know."[41]

But how shall anyone really know — when both witnesses are gone?

And so how shall we prevent having ourselves, our parents, or our children Humphried?

First, let us put aside our personal wishes, and resolve to reconstitute the great and enduring values of our civilization. Let us ask not what is good for ourselves, but what is good for the next generation and for human civilization.

Quite obviously, what is good for the next generation is the life principle, or what the lawyers call a presumption in favour of life. We have to understand as a society that this principle must be securely in place not to protect some individuals, but to nurture and protect all. Whether under the life principle or under the death principle, some individual sacrifices, so to speak, may be an unavoidable consequence. Under the life principle, some of the living may be inconvenienced or caused personal suffering to guarantee the life principle for all. But it is better to inconvenience a few living individuals — through denial of abortion or euthanasia — than to kill whole classes of victims — the knowing or the unknowing, the willing or the unwilling, in the name of personal, social, medical, or economic comfort.

In matters of abortion, we must fall back upon our ancient standard of agreeing that all life begins at conception. If abortion is permitted at all for special reasons — because a young child has been raped, or to prevent a mother's death — it is always a matter of deciding to kill human life. We then weigh one life against another. Let us end the falseness of pretending otherwise in language and law.

The false liberal principle of choice-in-a-vacuum has to go, along with the fetal harvesting and experimentation, the murder of live babies, the burning of killed ones, the selling of fetal parts to laboratories or cosmetic companies, the sex-selection aborting. Yes, the whole, grimy, sad, twisted, political, legal, medical, and commercial mess will have to go. We must admit that, because we are imperfect human beings, we have lost control. O.K., there were some good intentions. But these transgressions of the moral law inevitably fail because they always end up substituting the death principle for the life principle. So let's admit we have failed miserably to control the uncontrollable, and that moral relativism and gradualism have been a disaster for our children and our society. Let us try to regain our humanity.

It's the same for adult euthanasia. Let us respect the wishes of the dying to be made comfortable, as pain-free as possible, and surrounded with as much love as possible; or to die by refusing care, if they wish. But so-called "living wills" designed to control one's death — as if contract could replace conduct — are near-useless.

For one thing, they cannot possibly anticipate the whirling complexity of emergency or disease, or the fact that a piece of life-saving equipment may be required only for a few hours; or that the living will proves too vague or too detailed for anyone to follow; or that the patient may change his mind at the last minute (then, how do you decide if he means it or not?). And what if the family disagrees with the patient's instructions? Suppose the patient is unconscious, but the will is stale-dated and the doctor or family knows he would have changed his mind? What if the doctor complies and the family sues him? Or he does not comply, and the patient sues him?

Rather, the best bet if you have reasonable worry about medical assault is to ensure that your loved ones agree with you, and that your doctor agrees, too. The rest is a matter of trust in these people to let you die peacefully if you want to and in a society with a life principle. Such a society will prevent others from killing you for what they think is a merciful reason — when you don't. For once doctors become legal killers, the people need protection. There exists a protective medical decisions document (PMDD), which patients can now sign to ensure nothing will be done by medical personnel to cause death, and to ensure that health-care providers are not immune from culpability for acts of negligence. In these two opposing documents — the living will to ensure we are killed, the PMDD to ensure we are not, can be seen a caricature of modern liberalism.

Alas, dignity cannot arise from killing, or from being killed, regardless of how merciful the reason may seem. The legal and moral distortions required to enable the exceptions deemed merciful end up distorting all the values of human society. From this greater death no society has ever escaped.

# 17

# Blessing
# Our Trespasses:
# The Church vs.
# the Family

*. . . as a mainline [liberal] bishop has explained to me,
"The mission of the church is to build the kingdom of
God on earth, and the means of the mission is politics."*

RICHARD JOHN NEUHAUS, 1984[1]

*They only want to love their neighbour if he is far
away, like in Nicaragua, not in their own spare bedroom at home.*

REV. KENNETH HAMILTON, WINNIPEG, 1991[2]

*. . . Same-sex covenants, the future of Canada, the
economic blockade of Cuba, and Columbus' voyage to
the Americas . . .*

A PARTIAL LIST OF TOPICS TO BE SOLVED AT THE ANNUAL
REGIONAL MEETING OF THE UNITED CHURCH OF CANADA
— TORONTO *STAR*, MAY 2, 1992

The contention offered in this chapter is that, of all our
institutions, it is especially the mainstream Christian
church which ought most vigorously to defend the family in society
and avoid all worldly intellectual or political seductions from this

path.* After all, the most important Divine relationships in Christianity are family-based. The primal family model of father, mother, son, each revered as an essential part of this eternal triangle and truth, and thus indelibly embodying the first of all Christian families, permeates Christianity. And just as the church defends — or ought to defend — eternal values, the natural family is the primary universal human institution in which those values take root. The family is trans-historical in the sense that it precedes and survives all other institutions. Yet almost all the rapid and debilitating changes in modern church thinking — only some of which can be explored here — are resoundingly antifamily. The church, which should be defending this value-generating and value-perpetuating primal structure called the family, is participating in contemporary social decay.

A notice posted on the door of a Toronto church in 1960 listed the following church activities for the coming week:

*Sunday*
9 a.m. — Sunday School
9:30 a.m. — Worship Service
11 a.m. — Worship Service
7 p.m. — Evensong

*Monday*
6 p.m. — Confirmation Class

*Wednesday*
6 p.m. — Bible Study

*Thursday*
7 p.m. — Choir Practice

A notice posted on the same church door in 1990 listed another kind of activity:

*Monday*
7 p.m. — Sex Addicts Anonymous

*Tuesday*
6 p.m. — Women Church
8 p.m. — Liberation in Practice

*Thursday*
7 p.m. — Creation Theology, Native Myth and World Spirit

*Friday*
The Church as an Instrument of Social Change

Despite whatever intellectual interest any of the topics on the second notice may hold, they are bound by a common denominator: any one of them — unlike those on the first — can be discussed,

---

* This chapter is mainly a critique of the liberal mainstream Protestant churches and the activist, left-leaning element within the Roman Catholic church. However, even conservative Protestants and Catholics, who are traditionally pro-family, ought not to excuse themselves too lightly in their avoidance of church politics in the name of religious privatism. They, too, may be slowly and subtly altered by unresisted policy.

debated, or taught outside the special moral purview of the church. They have everything to do with political, economic, and social relations, very little to do with the church and theology, and not much at all to do with the worship of God, or with individual souls. In the 30 years between these two notices, most mainstream Christian churches in the Western world have gone through two monumental, and surely not unrelated, changes. First, they have progressively lost followers — or, for those commercially minded, market share; and second, they have reacted to the decline by railing against heaven, having reasoned, in understandable desperation, that lack of "relevance" was the cause of their thinning flock. If the God of judgment and tradition seemed unduly harsh, or the absolute standards of religious morality appeared too difficult, then perhaps the answer was to domesticate God.

This strategy has been a disaster for the church.

It has led to a new, church-inspired death of God, this time among the faithful, without stemming the exodus. Mind you, as Anglican archbishop Lewis Garnsworthy of Toronto pointed out: "It's not that they're leaving; it's just that they're not coming!"[3] In his widely read book *Fragmented Gods*, Reginald Bibby writes that Canadians, like Americans, whose religious behaviour we largely mirror, are not giving up their affiliation with the various churches. But they are not attending, either. Bibby's analysis shows that although for many years *numbers* were up, in fact — because the population was growing so rapidly — the *proportions* of the church-attending population were down. High attendance was in part a baby-boom demographic illusion that has now become a bust for the churches. The overall picture appears in the box below.

From what follows, it will be difficult to avoid the conclusion that most mainstream denominations of the church have become ideological, largely captured by the radical left. A recent U.S. article showed that mainstream churches there are urging not Big God, but Big Government. Widely respected sociologist Peter Berger of Boston University referred to the "grimly humorless ideology of the mainline churches." Almost all have discovered, through recent surveys of their flocks, that although 69 percent of congregations are conservative, 61 percent of church leaders are left-liberal.[4] In a probe of Canadian clergy and congregation on the bellwether left/right issue of homosexual ordination, Bibby found a huge rift between sheep and shepherds. Only 12 percent of conservative Prostestants approved, with the highest approval rate being only 38 percent, for the "liberal" United Church. In short, almost regardless of the issue, modern

On the 1981 census (1991 census is yet to be published), Canada reported itself to be about 50% Roman Catholic (U.S. 28%, U.K. 14%); 40% Protestant (U.S. 57%, U.K. 73%); 1% Jewish (U.S. 2%). Less than 1% report Hindu, Islamic, or Buddhist, and the balance report no affiliation. In short, Canada is an overwhelmingly Judeo-Christian nation (91%).

### Percentage Attending Church in Previous Seven Days (%)

|                      | 1946 | 1956 | 1965 | 1975 | 1986 | 1990 |
|----------------------|------|------|------|------|------|------|
| Protestants          | 60   | 43   | 32   | 25   | 27   | 22   |
| Roman Catholics      | 83   | 87   | 83   | 61   | 43   | 32   |
| "Other" Religions    |      |      |      | 17   | 13   | 16   |
| "Never" attend church|      |      |      | 17   | 18   |      |

Bibby's updated "Can90" survey said 35% of Americans and 23% of Canadians "worship regularly." However, he notes a remarkable drop in the percentage declaring themselves Roman Catholic, now about 41% of Canadians, and he writes that the drop is almost wholly due to more Quebec Catholics declaring "no religion."

traditionalist congregations find themselves forced to listen to liberal preachers who are disdainful of the "less learned" flock.

That's likely why Bibby says only 37 percent of Canadians have "a great deal" or "quite a bit" of confidence in their religious leaders. As we shall see, the church has gullibly accepted and promoted most of the false doctrines of our time, and it is now paying the price. It is liturgically, intellectually, morally, and scripturally confused and weakened, swarming with strident radical feminists (male and female), homosexuals (ditto), modern Gnostics (explained below), and failed economic theories (mostly Marxist — how embarrassing), and encircled by harping witches and goggle-eyed New Agers burdened with magic nostrums, potions, and cures. To this list we can add environmental catastrophists, one-worlders, collectivists, and utopians eager to align the whole wide world under new gods and regimes of their own invention.

But how new is all this, really?

Not very. In fact, it is mostly a sad repeat of the same old human confusions, with just one difference. This time, the church is promoting them instead of resisting.

# WE ARE SPIRITUAL CREATURES

There has been an historical contest to describe the one most distinctive feature of the human race in fancy Latin terms, such as *homo sapiens* (intelligent man), *homo erectus* (upright man), *homo laborans* (working man) or, *homo economicus* (economic man). But they are off the mark. Arguably, the most accurate single description of the human race would be *homo spiritualis* — spiritual man. Again, and despite much talk of modern nihilism, surveys repeatedly indicate this is so. Even though church attendance is down, the spiritual quest is ever up. A recent European values survey of such attitudes showed that "belief in heaven" is very high in most countries (Ireland: 86 percent, United States: 81 percent, Canada: 67 percent) and religion is "important" to 79 percent of Americans and 61 percent of Canadians (of whom 86 percent say they "believe in God").

Another survey by Bibby showed that 92 percent of Canadian Roman Catholics "accept the existence of God," and 82 percent believe in the divinity of Jesus.[5] His Can90 survey said 92 percent of Americans and 90 percent of Canadians "identify with a faith." And fully 88 percent of Americans and 86 percent of Canadians still label themselves Christian. Fully 70 percent believe in life after death — and in heaven, specifically — and 50 percent believe in hell. Fully half the population believe they have personally experienced God's presence. Only in the highly socialized nations, where the State in effect competes with the churches for spiritual allegiance, are such profiles consistently low. But it is highly probable that in foxholes, all these figures would approach 100 percent rather smartly.

To say we are "spiritual" does not mean we are all innately good, or any such thing, but it means we all have a spiritual hunger — we spend much of our lives seeking ultimate meaning, explicitly or implicitly, in most things we do. Even those who deny all spiritual aspects to life nevertheless seek such ultimate meaning in the material world — in a roundabout way — by sublimating their search, or by projecting into the frenzy of their status-seeking lives some fleeting semblance of eternal value. What everyone commonly craves is, simply, an ultimate explanation.

Most of modern cosmology (scientific theory about the origin and workings of the universe) is an intense and intriguing example of this search. Famous cosmologists, such as Sandage, Hoyle, Hawking, and Peebles, are really searching the skies, and contesting one another's theories of the universe, for one reason: to find the meaning of life, or what they call the "singularity" — the ultimate physical explanation for how the universe could have been created from nothing. (Two recent books, *Lonely Hearts of the Cosmos* and *Origins* provide a good sense of this theoretical, and essentially theological, pursuit.[6]) As one famous Princeton astronomer complained, cosmological theorists are "theologically promiscuous."[7] The English physicist Stephen Hawking concludes his worldwide bestseller, *A Brief History of Time*, by saying that to know the ultimate working of the universe is to "know the mind of God."[8] And the American Allan Sandage, who has charted much of the course of modern astronomy, summed up the current disarray of cosmological speculation by saying that the main lesson of cosmology is that the heart of existence is a mystery that cannot be solved so much as savoured.[9]

## THE LOCUS OF REALITY: IS IT INNER OR OUTER?

At a less scientific but no less urgent level, the ordinary human quest for the meaning or truth of reality seems to take the form of a much deeper effort to determine where reality is located. Is it inside us or outside us? I call this the search for the *locus of reality*.[10] It is ordinary because it is the search most people undertake, whether or not they ultimately turn to a theological solution. And the question of location is a good one. After all, with enough argument and sophistication you can show that human consciousness is a dreamlike illusion; or that only consciousness is real, and the external world of things is an illusion, made up by ourselves. These are the grand themes of the quest for the locus of reality. Shakespeare's line from *The Tempest*, "We are such stuff as dreams are made on, and our little life is rounded with a sleep," illustrates the first position. And the highly imaginative world of deep physics and relativity, where physical "reality" is just an idea, or a matter of evanescent probability, illustrates the second.

But whether in secular or in theological terms (they will be considered in that order, below), the ordinary spiritual quest seems to travel back and forth in a pendular way, seeking to establish and defend reality either as part of our inner world of consciousness, or the outer world of things. There is an ongoing swing between the subjective world inside us and the objective world outside. At various historical periods, one explanation or the other seems to win out, but, after a time, becomes banal, the solutions appearing too rigid. Then people literally lose faith, and the long travel back to the alternative begins again, ever seeking. If the truth inside disappoints, then we search again outside ourselves. Same journey, different clothing.

In the secular, or non-religious, world, this to-and-fro tendency is most evident in what is called the history of ideas, especially artistic and literary ideas. There, reality is sought either in the feelings and perception inside us, or in some code or set of rules outside us. In the world of theology, or religion, the spiritual quest takes the form of a swing between popular preference for either an inner, or outer God. Since it is easier to see this pendulum-like movement by surveying past travels, let us start with a sketch of the history of ideas on secular ground, and then move to theological ground. To study the pattern of movement, we must enter the pendular structure at some point, and the Classical or ancient world of our heritage seems as good a place as any.

## THE CLASSICAL, OBJECTIVE, OUTER WORLD

The Classical world of the ancients was dominated by a belief in fixed universal absolutes, which ancient philosophers aggressively opposed to the flux and degeneration of life (the latter venerated by their philosophical enemies). This view of nature and reality prevailed from the time of the Greeks until the middle of the 18th century.

Classical thinkers were interested in the general, the normal, and the universal, not the particular, the abnormal, or the personal. Plato and Aristotle, both of whom in their different ways argued for immutable, fixed categories of existence (Plato's idealistic, Aristotle's concrete), won out over philosophers such as Heraclitus, who argued that all life was flux. In other words, they said that the fixed truth of the universe is to be found outside the perceiving person (the subject), and they warned against the distorting influence of emotion and sentiment. Plato, we saw in Chapter Four, even argued for stabilizing ever-changing societies under fixed social programs and philosopher kings, so as to resist otherwise inevitable decay. In this way, he set the framework for all utopian, collectivist, and antifamily regimes.

The point here is that for such Classical thinkers, the locus of reality lay outside the subject, where it was to be discovered and affirmed by the individual. Classicism established rules for the understanding and ordering of this reality. These rules, to be learned by all children, were for the most part hierarchical in nature. Students learned not only to appreciate them but also to understand the steps by which they themselves could rise, through obedience to such rules of understanding, to a higher wisdom. In the arts, again, rules dominated. The Classical sculpture upheld the perfectly proportioned body, later made famous in the Renaissance drawing by Leonardo da Vinci (which he drew from a text by the first century Roman general, Vitruvius) showing a man, limbs outstretched, inside a square, inside a circle. Until very recent times, this proportioned circle was used in all art schools of the Western world as a formula for the perfect human figure. In drama, rules dictated that external reality be accurately copied by preserving the "unities" of time, place, and action. In other words, you weren't to write plays or tell stories dependent on fantasy or the unreal, or in which time was compressed or skipped, or in which physical locations were altered unrealistically. That was considered lying, or distorting normal external reality, which was the truth.

For art to be true, Classicists argued, all that was ephemeral and idiosyncratic must be purged from this process. Thus, the image and symbol for the Classical period was the *mirror*. (The clearest explanations of how widespread was the mirror's power can be found in Meyer Abram's book *The Mirror and the Lamp*.[11]) The artist, the mathematician, the student, and the child all were counselled to see *through* the deceptive illusions of human emotion and perception to life's truest, most enduring aspects, and then to hold up an imaginative mirror to capture this reality — first to reflect, then to *imitate* it. All famous Classical drama, poetry, and sculpture obey these rules and this vision of reality.

This Classical vision, which utterly dominated the ancient world, was resuscitated after the Middle Ages in the Renaissance and rose to power again in what became known as the neoclassical period, which peaked in the 18th century. During this period, the Italians, the French, and the British mostly tried to impress their audiences with their own versions of ancient art and principle. The epitome of the neoclassical style is Alexander Pope's sober poem, "Essay on Man," which in measured rhyming couplets recapitulates ancient wisdom. The poem is a kind of lesson on life, teaching that all art is meant not merely to please, but to instruct us in the truth outside ourselves.

Importantly, the artist's social and moral role in such a society is to support, not criticize, the perceived external truth, employing his special powers to communicate this truth broadly. By wide agreement, he was allowed poetic licence and the illusionary tools of art only to perpetuate the objective truth, never to distort or deceive. The Classic thinker's ideas may initially sound authoritarian to our individualist ears. It is, however, important for us to understand that he firmly believed that only through classical ideas "can genuine individual fulfillment be found. For [Classicism] regards man's feelings as by themselves helpless, blind, and eminently susceptible to dictation of some sort"[12] (and therefore to dictatorship). The Classical theory of reality was also a theory of politics. They said then, as they say today, that you can't be a truly free individual until you know, and learn to live by, the outer truth.

Some clue about how this theory fits with religious belief can be found in a remark by the trenchant critic Irving Babbitt who, in writing of these things, said that "the man who aspires to live religiously must no less than the humanist look to some model set above his ordinary self and imitate it."[13] We shall get to this religious parallel shortly.

## THE ROMANTIC, SUBJECTIVE, INNER WORLD

About the middle of the 18th century, the external rules and standards of Classicism came to seem formulaic, rigid, and empty of meaning, and this vision of truth and its hierarchy of values began to break down. Babbitt talks of a "recoil" from stale Classicism, but I venture that the pendular swing described here is more than a recoil. It is a typical turning away from the failed outer realm to the inner realm, attributable to a deep, if unexpressed, spiritual dissatisfaction — an unsatisfied hunger. (The shift was paralleled by a turn away from religion and the church.) It was not recoil from staleness, but from meaninglessness that fuelled the search to fill the spiritual void.

So by the middle of the 18th century, the pendulum began slowly to swing (again) the other way. Famous thinkers and poets soon were arguing that the locus of reality could not be outside, but must be inside. By the end of the century, this continuation of the human search for meaning emerged — forcefully — -as the Romantic movement (our modern term for it). It appeared in a burst of poetic glory under the familiar names of Keats, Wordsworth, Byron, and Shelley in the English tradition, and flowered as well in the work of their equivalents in many other European countries.

But this movement, although it certainly has roots in romance, is not merely about love. The essence of Romanticism is the belief that external reality is entirely secondary to the truth of the inner world, which is about feeling and the spirit. The symbol for this world is not the mirror, which reflects an outer truth, but the *lamp*, which burns with an inner one. In other words, the truth of life emanates from the person; it is not something outside, to be reflected. At its limit, Romantic art explores the extremes of emotion and declares that feeling itself is the one truth. All else is false. In fact, even the basic use of the cold, rational faculties "came to be condemned by the romanticists as inimical to the imagination."[14] It was Wordsworth, in rebellion against the rules and subjects of Classical poetry, who insisted that all good poetry springs not from obedience to artistic models, but rather from "the spontaneous overflow of powerful feelings." To the Romanticist, the feeling person becomes the measure of sincerity. Once spontaneous inner desire and sentiment are deemed more true to life, external imposed standards gradually become rejected — along with all moral, artistic, or religious tradition — as false. At their peak, such "inner" movements promote millions of insular realities. And each reality, provided it is sincerely felt, is said to be as good as the next one.

Whereas the objective external pole always breaks down because the rigid outer rules become cold, imposed formalities and no longer seem to satisfy human needs, the subjective inner pole eventually decays and is abandoned because societies simply cannot cope with multiple, competing moral or aesthetic realities. As the poet Yeats wrote it in his poem "The Second Coming," "the centre cannot hold," and so "mere anarchy is loosed upon the world." This alternating dance of the soul plays itself out repeatedly in our history. The choreography is always the same, the costumes different.

Romanticism began to pall because, as Addison warned, "without steadiness and direction to some end, a great fancy is one kind of madness."[15] Without some external code, imagination runs wild, spawning all manner of moral and social evils. So a new belief system was needed, and now thinkers and artists began to move outward to the external material world of "Realism," a form of thinking and writing exemplified by Balzac and Flaubert in France, and many Victorian writers in Britain. Rather than internal emotion, external processes and the forces of social and economic life, or even whole social classes, were said to "determine" the lives of their characters. External reality became dominant once more. In Balzac's novel *Le Père Goriot*, the characters seem literally to emanate from the furnishings. Zola's characters seem like puppets dangling from the strings of the social forces that control them. The painters of the period were devoted to the lower classes (said to be more authentic) and were mostly "realist" or "naturalist" in their depictions of the external world. The extreme of such externalized determinist thought can be seen in Marx's utopian mixture of Hegel and ersatz economic science.

But these external explanations of truth themselves soon grew stale and tiresome, failing to satisfy the spirit, so at the end of the 19th century artists and philosophers once again dove inward and downward to arrive at the truth through "Impressionism," which both in painting and in the novel once again explored the world as filtered by the emotions of the perceiver. Truth was said to be subjective, the external world not a fixed reality. For painters like Monet, Seurat, and Manet, truth was evanescent and shifting. And for novelists like Woolf, Proust, and Joyce, highly personal, idiosyncratic, and intense internal worlds — as depicted in "stream of consciousness" writing — became the new measure of artistic truth. Their writing aimed to tap right into the unfolding consciousness itself. The emphasis in their novels was not on the "story," but on intertwining emotional, lyrical, and symbolic themes, linked by the subjective experience of both the characters and the reader. In philosophy, we can see this probing of the inner life in the work of Henri Bergson, and even in various schools that attempt to base all morality not on absolute standards, but on personal choice. The end of such subjectivism was the weirdness of the Symbolist and Surrealist movements, played out by the first quarter of the 20th century, which exhausted themselves trying to establish or recombine ever more strange new symbols of inner human reality as the fixed truth of human nature. Most artistic movements since have alternately exploited the agonies of the inner emotional world as truth (Bacon, Munch) or the minute details of the outer one (Andrew Wyeth, Bateman), or some variation of abstract personal perception (Picasso, and a million imitators).

## WHERE ARE WE NOW?

With astonishing speed and surely accelerated by the dissatisfaction of the young who saw religious and moral standards so contradicted by the wars and moral confusions of their parents' and grandparents' generations, all semblance of external truth in our time was thrown overboard. The 1960s spawned a neoromanticism of the most widespread order, and once again society experienced the big dive inward for personal truth, often alluded to in this book. This current swing of the pendulum has been accompanied by all the paraphernalia normal to such movements: drugs (Baudelaire and others were heavy users of drugs in the earlier Romantic period); mysticism and myth (Romantic and Symbolist poets relied heavily on both); rejection of external authority and tradition via the "counter-culture" and an attempt to create an ideal worldly order (Shelley, Blake, and many of their associates were well-known utopian radicals).

Yet surely the most crucial characteristic of all such inner movements is that the artists, philosophers, and moral leaders of society no longer support historical and traditional moral and religious values. Rather, aggressive rejection of these values becomes part of the duty to the new inner truths, and an essential aspect of personal "liberation." Our era is currently awash with books and gurus promoting self-empowerment, personal liberation, moral relativism, and situation ethics as the highest truths. Indeed, the most common saying is: "No one else's truth is necessarily better than mine."

## THE LOCUS OF REALITY IN RELIGION: GNOSTICISM AND THE SOCIAL GOSPEL

What does this inner/outer pendular movement in the world of secular ideas have to do with religion? More particularly, what does any of it have to do with the family? Very simply, this same movement is visible throughout the history of theology. What will be shown here is how the preference for placing the locus of reality inside the person leads, in theology, to a chain of reasoning that seduces the church into accepting political, economic, and moral policies which eventually erode the family structure.

The Judeo-Christian tradition has long struggled to maintain itself as a religious institution based on the idea of a transcendent God, from whom flow fixed moral absolutes. The Christian God is a *Deus absconditus* — a hidden God — *of* this world, but not immanent, or *in* it. He is a God external to us, not internal (He created the universe, but is not part of its substance), and from this externality flows a whole hierarchy of fixed values, and moral authority. All humans are deemed inherently imperfect because only God can be perfect. Personal salvation through adherence to the hierarchy of values is the desired aim of all believers. There is recognition that natural man needs a guiding moral framework, for as Babbitt put it, echoing Pascal, "a man's imagination will run away with his judgement or reason unless he have the aid of divine grace."[16] So the church is the institution meant to control the interpretation of these values and support their observance among the faithful. You can see how this system works: If God is not within us, then we cannot know His law directly. Rather, it must be taught to us and protected by ordained spiritual specialists.

From earliest times the Christian, especially the Roman Catholic, church has struggled to maintain this vision of an external, authoritative God against those who fought for the opposite. The key here is to remember that for such faiths, God and his law are external, absolute, hierarchical, and authoritative, and descend from above. God's law represents the normative, universal, objective value. Human salvation and bliss are obtained through adherence to this law, and are rewarded, after death, in a moral utopia above this earthly realm. All theological truth is necessarily external to and above the individual's personal interpretation, which must eventually conform to the external Word, else the individual is shunned, or even excommunicated.

But from the beginnings of the Christian era, there have been periods of energetic rebellion against this view of an outer God. As the Canadian theologian Kenneth Hamilton clarifies in a fascinating book entitled *Earthly Good: The Churches and the Betterment of Human Existence*,[17] the church has been bedevilled since ancient times by pseudo-Christian sects such as the so-called Gnostics, which, in the first two centuries after Christ, became so strong as almost to replace Christianity.[18] Some scholars even argue that Christianity itself arose from Gnosticism, struggled with it, and won. Hamilton shares the view of many commentators that "contemporary attempts to make Christianity acceptable to man today are understandable only when they are seen as a revival of ancient gnosticism,"[19] a quasi-religion that seems to reappear, newly clothed, in every age.

Gnostics (from the Greek word for "knowers," as opposed to "believers"), despite their many differences, are united by a few basic beliefs that continue, in barely altered form, to our time. The Gnostics who posed such a threat to the young Christian faith began by claiming, against the authority of the church, to *know* the true meaning of Christianity. The essence of their complicated Gnostic myth, which they opposed to the Christian myth, included a messenger from the cosmos, or the kingdom of light, who came to earth and, before returning, left sparks of light in certain "elect" individuals. More of this light, or knowledge, remains available to others, who may now "awaken to self-consciousness of their essential nature as pure spirit."[20] The Gnostic myth divided the universe into an opposing two-part reality of light and dark, spirit and flesh. All humans, until freed, are supposedly caught in the struggle between these two opposing forces.

Gnostics also believe in a demiurge called the dark god, a Satan-like creature in control of the earth, and hold that escape from the earth and the flesh can be gained only through special mystical knowledge (gnosis). Gnostics consider earthly existence meaning-less (because the world is imperfect) and reject traditional Christian concepts of sin, salvation, and resurrection, primarily because these teach acceptance of the world as it is, while calling for personal salvation according to how truly the person adheres to the author-itative Word of God. Gnostics reject all outer authority and chase the inner light instead. So they reject the Bible, and they say Jesus was not a god; his resurrection was a trick. What they stress is the personal spiritual encounter with Christ, or "Christ consciousness." In short, they by-pass church and biblical authority. Their rejection of history "turns religion into a wholly subjective phenomenon which exists largely at the will of the individual."[21]

A curious element of the Gnostic myth is that the body and the spirit are opposed (whereas in Judeo-Christian thinking they are one). Most Gnostics even express a kind of revulsion for the body as just another form of evil matter, a product of an evil world. Some become ascetics and may even refuse to reproduce. Others, con-vinced there is no connection between body and spirit, become worldly libertines, indulging the meaningless flesh. But both types see the light of the personal spirit trapped in the body, and the body in turn trapped in the imperfect world. So this much is familiar: The truth for Gnostics, as for Romantics, lies within. This general revulsion for physical life often results in a masochistic or a purging element that prepares the way for cult beliefs in witchcraft, magic powers, sacrifice, and substituted judgment (by which Gnostics see themselves as "releasing" others from their earthly entrapment). A life trapped in the body is spiritual death for a Gnostic. This should cause us to reflect upon the matters of modern abortion and eutha-nasia, and the practice of medical genocide, reviewed in the preced-ing chapters. Hitler's powerful propaganda film promoting euthanasia, *Ich Klage An* ("I accuse"), is prototypical, and shows an extremely emotional husband in court after killing his beautiful but ill wife. He accuses the world that forbade him to kill her of "trapping her in her body." You can see the appeal of this mind-set to radical feminists, too, for whom "emptying the womb" via abortion gets rid of the "parasite" living there, that will otherwise "trap" them in motherhood.

Even more important is the concept of spiritual bliss. For the Christian, an eternal life of spiritual bliss is something promised by God in heaven, a place from which the flawed human is removed in space until death; for the Gnostic, however, bliss arises from the spirit awakening to a consciousness not of God's nature, but *of its own nature* here on earth, gained by shucking off the imperfections of the body and the world. First you mentally reject the physical self, the imperfect body imprisoning the spirit. Then you reject the imperfect world, which is the imperfect body of all humanity. Finally, once enlightened, you take active steps to change the imperfect world. Modern theologians who embrace Gnostic-style thinking conveniently argue that until very recently God did very little for the world. Now, however, He has opened up a new creative process, allowing humans to do something meaningful to meet the needs of others; hence, the notion of "social salvation." As Hamilton explains so well, the Gnostic heaven is promised not in space, but in time. It is a future condition of social perfection. God's work of correcting the demiurge must be done here on earth. Salvation is not *personal* ("the elect" are already enlightened), but *social* (it's a matter of awakening others still in spiritual darkness). Thus, both ancient and modern Gnostics, unlike traditional Christians, have contempt for the created order and feel quite justified in reordering it. Thus also do they shun the real world, preferring the abstract, utopian one that the ancient Gnostics called the *Pleroma* — the whole, the all — a kind of mystical union with perfection. Modern Gnostics differ from ancient ones only in that they pull this ancient concept of the *Pleroma* down to earth and speak of earthly utopias, or divine societies. It is no happenstance that the Gnostic forces of utopian collectivism are strongest in our cities, where Christianity is weakest, and weakest in our rural areas, where Christianity is strongest. They are contradictory theologies.

Thus does the "knowledge class" today see as its role the "education," or deliverance from ignorance, of all people who are trapped by imperfection. For Gnostics, "liberation" is earthly, not heavenly, and so in modern times they strive to promote myriad interest groups who seek to be freed from the various forms of oppression they imagine. Modern Marxism was arguably the most dangerous and widespread form of Gnosticism ever, since it promoted an earthly paradise free from the entrapment of social classes and capitalism — a utopia on earth — and specifically denied any divine authority. That's why the influential scholar Eric Voegelin described totalitarianism as "the existential rule of Gnostic activists." What unites Gnostics, in keeping with the inner/outer distinction above, is that the spiritual, for them, is not outer and hierarchical. Rather, it is inner, personal, and diffusely collectivist. Gnosticism is thus a kind of formalized Romanticism, just as so-called "liberation theology" — mostly Marxist in its economic theory of oppression — is the modern church's economic Gnosticism. It was Engels who declared, "God is man," and Marx who said that human consciousness is "the supreme divinity — by the side of which none other shall be held."

German theologian, Professor Jurgen Moltmann even argues that God has not arrived yet (because a perfect God would not make an imperfect world), and is therefore not responsible for this world, but will make his appearance when his creatures have perfected this world.[22] Very clever. His follower, Karl Braaten, is even more direct when he says that the coming theology will not go from above to below but from the future to the present, by "creating a new tomorrow through revolutionary transformation of the world."[23] As Hamilton points out, this is a vision of nothing authoritative above and everything inspired from within; it is aimed at salvation brought to imperfect others by the perfect spirits already here, through action on the imperfect world. It's a sure recipe for social revolution and collectivism, in which secular hope replaces religious faith; the lamp of emotion replaces the mirror of objective truth.

Hamilton clarifies how all forms of Gnosticism result in a revulsion for all that is traditional, authoritative, or from the past, because they attribute all worldly evil not to personal sin or to imperfection, but to an oppressive reality that needs to be changed. In this crucial sense, Gnostic thinking relies utterly on the Determinist Illusion, sees human imperfection as caused by external factors, and therefore spurns the idea of moral agency that underpins Judeo-Christian civilization. Whereas the church used to condemn the perpetrators of personal sin (the extortionist, the unjust, the adulterer, and so forth), it now takes aim at the oppressor (the capitalist, the First World, the polluter). That's because for Romantics and Gnostics, we are all inherently good; thus, sin must simply be "imperfectly developed virtue" or our "mistaken good intentions."[24] For you are either enlightened, or you are not. Goodness is not something you *earn* through moral behaviour, but something in yourself, to which you become *awakened* by others. Readers will see that Gnosticism is just a romantic, theological version of modern liberalism, in which the enemy is anyone still under the sway of the oppressive status quo. It thus becomes a religious duty to attack the enemy and free him (that is, after attacking and freeing one's own "oppressive consciousness").[25] Sin, under this belief, is never individual, but social. In the recent Toronto church trial of the homosexual Anglican minister James Ferry, Bishop Douglas Blackwell said "'sin' is a word we try to stay away from."

## THE SOCIAL GOSPEL

In his book *Stones for Bread: The Social Gospel and Its Contemporary Legacy*, Harry Antonides presents a tidy explanation of how the social gospel movement, which peaked early in this century and has been revived in our time, is connected with Romanticism and Gnosticism.

The social gospel movement is based on radical subjectivism, and it "locates the centre of religion in man, not in God."[26] It focuses on the *usefulness* of religion to man, not of man's usefulness to God. In fact, it equates the two. This focus is of course the great danger of all Romanticism and all mysticism. Once you place God in the centre of the person, you make the person into God.

In what Antonides calls "the Great Turnabout" that began in the middle of the 18th century, Western religion, influenced by the Rationalism Illusion, swallowed the notion that reason and the self were the best guides to Christian truth and right action. From here, it was but a short step to conclude that human happiness on earth was God's will. The elimination of human ignorance and the invention of new social programs were regarded as commandments of God to man; and since, as Rousseau put it, humans were naturally good, it remained but to calculate solutions and put them into effect. Antonides cites the Frenchman Condorcet, who said "there is no limit to the perfecting of man's powers." He explains how the joining together of this type of messianic rationalism with Romanticism and Gnosticism gave rise to the social gospel. It was Rousseau, in particular, who argued that man himself, and the nature in which he was embedded, are worthy of worship. Nature was seen as "Providence," or as a "Friend who cares." Such people wanted to believe that the "Power behind Nature" was benevolent, and devoted to man's interests and ideals.[27] Once again, romantic intuition and the idea of "becoming oneself" was everything. This idea of *religion as feeling* (and then as social action) was popularized long ago by

Friedrich Schleiermacher (1768-1834), who held that religion was but a form of "cosmic consciousness." For Romantics such as Schleiermacher, feeling was everything, and truth and falsity were irrelevant to religious life.[28] We see this attitude today in the moral values education, self-esteem, and radical environmentalist movements promoted in our schools; in each of these, whatever is natural is good, even holy. Soon a whole flock of messianic and romantic Germans, such as Ritschl and Feuerbach, developed a number of "religions of humanity" advocating a kind of Gnostic self-transcendence and escape from all religious tradition.

Eventually, liberal Christians who found themselves attracted to this new form of Gnosticism, in which church authority was suspect and God was essentially internalized, effectively developed a concern for "Christian socialism," à la Ritschl (1822-89), for whom all true religion was basically ethical, social, and political activity. Such people see the face of Jesus in the poor, and by reflex offer them socialism.

Antonides sums up the essential elements of the social gospel, which I paraphrase here: The social teachings of Jesus are reliable for individual and social life; God is immanent in history — He is in the world (not above us, or absent); man is basically good and perfectible (this from Rousseau and Romanticism); men of good will can establish the Kingdom of God here on earth (the Gnostic belief); sin is not a personal thing, but is primarily selfishness, and it can be overcome by an improvement in the social setting and especially by education (the theme of all collectivists); the Bible in this view is just a human product, not divine revelation, and is to be studied like any other book; and finally, reason and science are the most reliable sources of truth (not faith or moral tradition).[29]

Antonides gives a finely detailed description of just how these fundamental assumptions led the majority of mainline Canadian churches, through a variety of conferences and publications in this century, to accept, nay, to swallow whole, most of the secular and socialist assumptions of worldwide collectivism. (Or how, to borrow from a United Church document, the church "became concerned with the redemption of society and worked for the development of Christian civilization" and strove "to transform those agencies and institutions of society which are foreign to that spirit."[30]) At their silliest, churchmen actually saw "the Spirit of Jesus at work in Mao's [Communist] China,"[31] and at a 1977 Saskatoon conference they argued that "theology is at its best when political."[32] All speakers at the conference favoured "a socialist reorganization of society" and considered Marxism to be "a superior ideology."[33] Talk of "oppression" and descriptions of Canadians as "slaves of capitalism" (the Gnostic dark god) were everywhere. Bewildered radical intellectuals like the theologian Gregory Baum attempted, as Antonides writes, "to declare the struggle for justice in society itself to be the means of salvation and the way to participate in the divine."[34] This is the Gnostic ideal. God is within, and salvation is achievable in the here and now. Gnosticism is salvation on the instalment plan. It is strange these people couldn't figure out why it is that the socialism they considered so Christian is, and has always been, ideologically opposed to all religious, and essentially Christian, values. It is primarily the socialist governments of the world that have specifically jailed, tortured, and murdered masses of Christians.

Happily, in 1991 the Roman Catholic church came to its senses and published *Centesimus Annus*, an encyclical that spurns socialism and collectivist economics and (finally) concedes the wealth-creating power of democratic capitalism as the optimal economic arrangement. Offering something less than a perfect understanding of the true workings of free enterprise, the encyclical was nevertheless a major event for modern Christianity, signalling a rebuff to Christian socialism and an official rejection of liberation theology. The collectivist clerics are still there, however, singing their song of failure disguised as pity for the poor. If the church really wants to help the poor economically, it should stop inflaming them against the Gnostic demiurge and also stop arguing for the redistribution of capital they don't know how to create in the first place. It would be better to offer courses on free enterprise and entrepreneurship, on the meaning of saving, hard work, independence, family, private property, and voluntary association and exchange, and on the principle of subsidiarity. Alas, once the church abandons the outer God, it becomes just another social service agency, competing with all the others by preaching flawed secular doctrines.

Economics? I'd like to see Gregory Baum go up against Milton Friedman on the subject of wealth creation. Marxism as a cure for the poor? How come so many former and all current communist countries are desperately poor and can't feed themselves? And still, Edmonton Catholic archbishop Joseph MacNeil says, "The early Christians were the first communists."[35] And William Sloane Coffin, formerly of Yale, said that communist revolutionary movements "were the essence of Christian faith," and communism itself was "a page torn from the Bible." And Walter Farquharson, moderator of Canada's fastest-shrinking Protestant denomination, the United

Church, travels about preaching "community" and social action. And Ted Schmidt, a Toronto lay theologian, embraces a "socially conscious faith";[36] meaning, if you are a Marxist, you're O.K. Meanwhile, these self-important people were silent as hundreds of thousands of faithful Christians, Jews, and Muslims languished for generations in communist gulags just because they had a religious faith. Alas, Baum and his ilk offer only a recipe for disaster and death for the poor. The world has seen that the best liberation of the poor is achieved through free-market economies and the classical principles of a free society. So why do we listen to preachers who advocate totalitarian systems? We don't. Hence, the empty pews.

The environment? We read the headline "Church Leaders Demand Action on Global Warming," calling this phenomenon a "special moral challenge" (*Globe and Mail*, January 29, 1992). Maybe. Are the bishops environmental experts now, too? Well, there are expert scientists on both sides of this issue. Briefly, any honest scientist will admit that so-called global warming has not been proven. Even if it exists, there are good arguments that it occurs naturally in 100,000-year cycles; that the earth is carbon-starved (plants thrive on carbon) and needs much more of this element; that the economic benefits of warming far outweigh the costs; and that it may be the result not of man-made gases, but of solar effects and radiation. The fact that there was an ice age here a mere ten thousand years ago — and that forests of oak trees once grew in the arctic — will tell you that the bishops are far from environmental prophets.

Social issues? Instead of arguing aggressively for the sanctity of life, for the traditional family structure, for the communication of Judeo-Christian values in the schools, and for normal heterosexual love, what do we get from them? Moral cowardice. Except for the Roman Catholic bishops, too many mainline church leaders are *silent* on abortion on demand and euthanasia; *they are silent* on the disappearing legal and social privileges and protections of the traditional family; and, despite the strongest sanctions against it from their own Holy Book and their God, *they are silent* on, or tolerate or promote, homosexuality by morally reconstituting unnatural acts as a form of divine love on earth. Interestingly, when you reflect upon the homosexual rejection of reproduction, combined with frequent sado-masochism, multiple partners, and disease, you can make a decent argument that homosexuality is itself a kind of sexual Gnosticism flowing from a profound disrespect for the body and a refusal to procreate. So what is the church doing? Some are now "blessing" homosexual marriages, arguing that Jesus did not specifically condemn anal sex (he didn't have to; everyone agreed it was abominable), and they support their peculiar blessing by further arguing that homosexual marriage will reduce homosexual promiscuity and contribute to fighting AIDS. (In May 1992, the United Church ordained its first active out-of-the-closet homosexual minister.) Most transparently, they defend such blessings as "authentic expressions of interpersonal commitment" (Toronto *Star*, March 11, 1992). Perhaps. But that is beside the point. Traditional marriage is not about interpersonal commitment. It is about commitment to the future of human society and its values. This, no homosexual couple can give, either in theory or in practice.

Meanwhile, these church leaders *are silent* on rampant pornography, on widespread drug use, and on the salacious and vicious rock and reggae music lyrics and videos that are rotting the minds of children. For example, when's the last time we saw a church leader marching against the rock group Judas Priest, or one of its hit songs, like "Eat Me Alive" (I'm gonna force you at gunpoint/to eat me alive"); or against the group The Dead Kennedys and their song, "I Kill Children" ("God told me to skin you alive/I kill children, I can hardly wait for yours")? And *they are silent* on the proliferation of secular humanism that helped produce most of this strange new *religion* in the schools of our 90 percent Judeo-Christian nation, despite the fact that this so-called humanism is anti-God and antifamily.

A major sign of their overall weakness is their retreat from their faith into the supposed universality of religious "multiculturalism," the adoption of which always results not in a better understanding of any faith, but in a worse understanding of all faiths. In October 1991, in Cincinnati, Ohio, a rabbi asked permission to erect a ceremonial menorah near the city Christmas tree. The tolerant judge ruled in his favour, even though Judaism and Christmas don't exactly mix. Well, next the Ku Klux Klan demanded the "right" to burn a cross publicly. The city agreed to a cross, provided the Klan didn't light it. The irate Klansmen then sued the city to eliminate beards from all the city's Santa Clauses (*Maclean's*, January 7, 1991). And the schools? All over, they are abandoning Christmas carols in favour of "Frosty the Snowman," and rejecting Christmas plays about the birth of Jesus in favour of a multicultural "festival of lights" where kids chant about the "universal" within us. Some such festivals actually substitute a kind of pagan breaking of bread. Children inside a circle are surrounded by nature symbols and chant mantras about their common goodness and humanity. It sounds to me like, well, Gnosticism.

In 1991, Edmonton Catholic high-school students painted a popular mural entitled "Your Will Be Done," depicting revolutionaries and Marxists. Included were portraits of Karl Marx, Che Guevara, Malcolm X, church "liberationists" Gustavo Gutierrez and Leonardo Boff, the spiritists Teilhard de Chardin and Mathew Fox, Winnie and Nelson Mandela, and Fidel Castro. Regina archbishop Charles Halpin said he was "touched by it." The art teacher, Hank Zyp, who supervised the project, spoke with a 2000-year-old Gnostic voice when he said: "We are not just waiting around for the eternal reward. We are co-creators with the Creator to make it a better world. Marx, for example, helps the church in its mission. These figures all helped the process to create the kingdom."[37]

To summarize, the church in our time has largely transformed itself from an agent of personal salvation to an agent of social revolution. It has been led to do so by accepting the Gnostic myth of personal spiritualism and earthly perfection, and therefore it has had to reject external religious authority and moral standards. It has thereby also surrendered most of the moral ground for a defence of the natural family. Modern church Gnosticism has started the church upon a chain of reasoning that leads it inevitably either to accept forms of moral liberalism that discomfit its flock mightily, or to recant and give up modern Gnosticism. But it is almost impossible for those who count themselves among the enlightened, to return to what they believe is darkness. So alas, once opened to the inner-God idea, the church becomes involved willy-nilly in a defence of a worldly litany. It tolerates or even promotes personal and pagan mysticism in the form of New Age "religions"; it defends many anti-authoritarian and antifamily movements such as radical feminism (now heavily into the feminization of God and the practice of witchcraft); and last but surely not least, by following the Gnostic urge for earthly perfection, it ends up defending utopian and New Age notions of world government. The early Gnostics would have been pleased. I have included such discussions here because in their ultimate effects these forms of thought, if unresisted by churches professing an outer God and a firm moral hierarchy, will simply erode the whole political, economic, and social/moral order of our Judeo-Christian civilization — and hence, the family. And the signs are not good. Ari Goldman, a top graduate of Harvard Divinity School, says of his 1985 experience: "The mere mention of God — an omniscient God, God as a transcendent being — when I was there . . . would be guaranteed to produce snickers."[38]

## NEW AGE PSYCHOBABBLE

*You're god in your universe. You caused it . . . What you're doing is what god wants you to do. If you keep saying it the way it really is, eventually, your word is law in the universe.*

WERNER ERHARD (FORMERLY JOHN PAUL ROSENBERG),

FOUNDER OF EST (ERHARD SENSITIVITY TRAINING)[39]

Let us begin with a brief overview. So-called "New Age" thinking is a loose conglomeration of modern Gnostic assumptions attractively packaged to appeal to the secular appetites of the materialist 20th century. It is aimed at those who have lost faith in traditional religious or spiritual authority, and are therefore especially vulnerable to, even hungry for, ersatz spiritual nourishment. Like ancient Gnosticism, New Age thinking offers an explanatory model for "spiritual" unity stripped of the old burdensome moral constraints, combined with a do-it-yourself ease that provides something for everyone. New Age bookstores have upward of 5000 titles.

Like its ancient Gnostic model, New Age argues that human civilization is at a time of crisis (the world is fallen). Therefore, all humans must work to make the transition from the current age of Pisces to the New Age of Aquarius. The old age, followers say, is typified by fragmentation, materialism, rationalism, greed, war, political disorder, personal crises, and the separateness of all things. Unless corrected, this assortment will lead to disaster. Devotees don't sound all that far off — at first. Come to think of it, that's what most mainstream religions say. But what is the new corrective?

New Agers insist that "the central reality of our existence is unity, wholeness, harmony, integration, and interdependence";[40] in a short phrase: All is One. External divisions and separateness are illusions. All separate beings must therefore strive, as Antonides puts it, to be reborn into the one cosmic, universal self. The universe New Agers envision is not mechanistic, but spiritual; and, like the divine spark of the Gnostics or the spontaneous overflow of powerful feeling of the Romantics, its being is formed utterly of "energy," a word and concept that reappears constantly in New Age writing as a panacea-explanation. One successful New Age guru even refers to the money she makes from her teaching as "green energy." Convert Heather Skelton explains that "our lives are managed by an intelligent force who exists as pure energy" (*Globe and Mail*, June 9, 1990). Let me see now . . . this is physics personified and deified, and so we can live on cruise control. But it gets much more arcane. Antonides explains how New Age is based on a few basic concepts: that man is God, and is therefore immortal; that there is no right and wrong; and that each person creates his own world.

Here is the chain of assumptions. Because All is One, God is simply a part of the All. This is a form of immanentism common to all pantheistic religions. It is the belief that all things — rocks, trees, water — are in fact spiritual things, some perhaps invested with the powers of special gods of their own. But here comes the important leap. This kind of belief, one that denies the outer God and promotes the inner one, essentially says that because all things are spirit, and God is in them, then God is in us, too. *Therefore we are all gods.* New Agers set themselves the task of "freeing" the power of God within everyone (they don't explain how we can be "managed" and "free" at the same time). The Toronto *Star*'s "ethics" writer, former Anglican minister Tom Harpur, burbles on in the same vein, in an excellent example of earnest confusion. In his article "The Power of Creativity Flows Through Us All" (Toronto *Star*, February 16, 1992), he advises us to "become what we are." (But if you "are" something already, how can you "become" that?) Being "like God," he says, means being "creative" and finding ways to "get in touch with our innermost selves, and the God-given sources of 'energy' within." (If we are seeking our "selves," which is the real self: the seeker or the sought after? And if there is 'energy' within us all, why is it hidden? If it's not hidden, then we don't need to find it.) Harpur suggests there is an "inner voice" or "vision" that will say things to us, or through us. (But how do we know whether or not to trust it?) We are told to be true to "whatever allurements and glimpses we discern in ourselves" (surely a recipe for emotional abandonment) if we are to discover what is "at the core of our being." (Tom, really . . . how do you know it is the true core, and not an illusory core, with another core inside that? Or even a false core, meant to throw you off?)

Well, let's not ask too many questions, now. For the truth is, the appealing assumption behind all concepts of the inner God, new or old, is that the inner God is always presumed to be good. Thus, there can be no alienation from this God, or any displeasing him/her/it, or any notion of sin or repentance or of the need to work to understand God. All these barriers to purity, which flow naturally from any concept of an outer God, evaporate the moment we switch allegiance to an inner God. The outer code of religious morality vanishes, too. Whoopee! Free at last! No need to please any but myself. Down with all that self-discipline stuff! As the *Globe* journalist above put it, a New Ager can flit from one cure to the other "in a relentless self-centred search for healing, empowerment and instant redemption." It follows that there is no punishment for wrong behaviour, because all action and all morality are determined from within. The chore is simply to make each person aware of his own "divinity." That's why spaced-out Shirley MacLaine sputtered: "You must never worship anyone or anything other than self. For you are God."[41]

What people caught up in such amoral euphoria forget is that if all meaning is personal, then it is also arbitrary. And when it is arbitrary, we become vulnerable to the powerful, who will quickly organize society according to their will. For in any such world, it's my meaning against yours, so to speak. The New Age answer to this moral dilemma is to unify the whole world under the same thinking — and hence the New Age penchant for collectivist, universalist, or "globalist" politics. But all such solutions to morality fly in the face of a free, bottom-up society based on private property, moral agency, tradition, local custom, the family, and the rule of law. The last was designed specifically to control people who believe their meanings are better than those of others — and to prevent them from gaining power over the weak.

Another quick-sell idea flowing from the New Age concept of the Man-god is the belief that everyone is immortal and, upon physical death, will be reincarnated. This belief neatly avoids the whole idea of earning one's way into eternity through good works. Eternity is a given, and all is good. (Where there happens to be some evil "karma," it's no one's fault; not to worry, it will be worked off in successive reincarnations.) All forms of Gnosticism offer this short-cut to heaven essentially by relocating it inside the person. We are supposedly able to communicate with divinity or other kindred spirits through "channelling," "mediums," "spirit guides," and the use of occult methods such as mantras, chanting, meditation, crystal gazing, and "centring." You can see how this belief springs from Gnosticism and from Romanticism. Each rejects the idea of evil as something springing from faulty morality. Evil is said to be created by human ignorance or by faulty social institutions. Therefore, for us to arrive at a perfect world, it is enough to remove ignorance by enlightening others through education, and to reform social institutions.

And because nature and all humanity are inherently good, there can be no ultimate right and wrong. It is of course this aspect of

Gnosticism, Romanticism, and New Ageism that is most disturbing, for this belief is the root of all social destruction. Whenever you identify the good with personal feeling, or with an *abstract* concept of love, you detach it from all concrete good and evil and, eventually, from all legal concepts of right and wrong. When that happens, the big and little Hitlers and Charlie Mansons of the world — who always identify their political objectives with abstract love, as defined only by their feelings — flourish. Manson sacrificed Sharon Tate to the pleasure of occult "spirits" he saw as good. For love of the German people, Hitler (who had a serious interest in the occult) wished to eradicate the "evil" Jew (his version of the Gnostic "trickster" who spoiled the world) and thereby purify the "good" Aryan race. Herein lies the great danger of all forms of Gnostic and New Age belief: They are conveniently divorced from any external moral control.

The end-stage of this chain of reasoning is the Nietzschean will to power: the idea that we are like gods, able to re-create the world in our own image. New Age writing is filled with statements of "empowerment," of "human potential," of "self-actualization." Courses such as Lifespring, Insight, Silva Mind Control, Transcendental Meditation, and the Forum, all basically promise God-like control of the almighty self — in exchange for a tidy fee, of course. Florida "channelling" expert Jack Pursel (alias "Lazaris") runs a $16 million business inviting clients to "travel" in search of the "forces" that have shaped their personalities. And currently hordes of believers are falling for would-be aboriginal gurus like Pa'Ris'Ha (Patti) Taylor, who says she is part Cherokee. She organizes the Toronto Raven Band and the Ohio White Buffalo Society. One of her followers, Joanne Sustar, recently died during a live "sand burial." (She was placed alive in a sand grave with only a snorkel to breathe from.) Raven Band member Bill Powlesland of Orangeville, Ontario, says sand burial is "a way to be totally in touch with oneself and hear that God within." As for Joanne? Bill says that "this time she chose not to come back . . . you always have a choice between life and death and this time, Joanne chose to follow that light — death." Ring a bell? Death is the Gnostic spark of light; release from the body. The police didn't have enough evidence for charges of manslaughter. And real Indian leaders say Patti is a fake. There's no "R" in the Cherokee language — and besides, true Indians do not advertise their religious beliefs and certainly don't charge for them. But Patti solicits offerings of "green energy" for everything, including a $10 course fee for babies and much more for investments in her real estate holdings (Toronto *Star*, June 10, 1990). In the supposed native tradition, drumming, sweat lodges, chanting, fire-walking, shield-making, and pipe-smoking are big. A survey of 500 California companies showed that over half had resorted to some kind of "consciousness-raising" technique.[42] Stanford University's Graduate School of Business offers a seminar on "Creativity in Business" that relies on "dream work," meditation, chanting, tarot cards, and discussions of "New Age Capitalism."

Lest the conclusion escape us, all New Age thinking, as the New York *Times* reminded us on September 29, 1986, is based on a curious blend of Eastern mysticism and Western occultism. At its foundation is "a complete rejection of Judeo-Christian belief in God as the author of eternal moral values, and a substitution of 'create your own religion' in which man can do no wrong, so there is no sin or guilt."[43] As Erhard put it to his followers, "life has no rules."

New Age is based on: self-discovery; experience as truth; and God as nature (sometimes called "Christ consciousness"). It comprises all good and bad, balanced in one. Human evolution to perfection is the plan of the universe; man is said to have a divine nature and can attain God-likeness; and feelings are utterly authoritative. Cleansing, fasting, and meditation supposedly eliminate the corruption of the world and put us in direct touch with our unsullied inner divinity. All things "natural" (organic foods, etc.) are symbolic of the goodness of nature itself. When we ingest them, by extension we suffuse our physical and therefore our spiritual being with their goodness. Hydroponic lettuce replaces the Christian eucharist; physical cleansing replaces moral cleansing. The enormous attraction is surely that a concentrated focus on the self, as part of a belief that we are all dissolved in the same spirit, removes the painful moral labours of truly coping with different human beings and conflicting moral and social obligations. In short, New Age is an escape from the real world based on the promise of spiritual bliss to be gained from an undemanding inner God — oneself. It is a kind of ceremonialized narcissism, in which personal sanctification replaces personal sacrifice.

But Christianity, and all other world religions based on an outer God of morality (I would argue that this aspect distinguishes a true religion from one based on magic), believe the opposite. For these religions, the important thing is not self-discovery, but God-discovery; not personal experience as holy, but obedience to the holy law; not nature as divine good and not god-in-nature, but God as separate from His creation, of which humans are stewards. God, for Christians, is not a spiritual amalgam of all good and bad, yin and yang, and so on, but is the one highest good. In this scheme man has a human and an imperfect nature, not a divine nature. By adherence to the moral law, we may partake of divinity, but never be divine ourselves. In all outer-God religions, the height of human evil is the belief that humans themselves can be gods or have God-like, usurping powers. The story of Adam and Eve is about the sin of falling for this temptation.

Inner-God religions glorify the purity and beauty of human feeling, while for outer-God religions feeling is a poor guide to spiritual goodness or moral behaviour. Why? Because, more often than not, we are misled by our own feelings and therefore require a moral law to help us from falling victim to selfishness. And reason cannot help save us from this end, because reason is merely an instrument we use to help rationalize evil or goodness according to our will. The cleansing we need is not the rejection of traditional wisdom; nor does it come through fasting or eating organic food. We need a cleansing of evil thoughts and of wrong behaviour. And then, to help us build a better character, we need to incorporate the moral laws of the outer God. Without such laws, Gnosticism seems to lead to witchcraft, Romanticism to the guillotine,[44] and modern collectivism not to the God within, but to the gulag.

## The History of It

We have seen how ancient Gnosticism, Romanticism, and New Age "religion" emerge in the inner-God belief. Many of their shared ideas are actually subtly promoted by Christians themselves, or by entertainments like the 1966 rock musical *Hair*, or by churches that are unaware of the clashing theological values and principles. For example, on February 4, 1990, the weekly *Catholic Sunday Church Bulletin*, used in many parishes, quoted from Ram Dass, a famous New Age "channeller" who was not identified as such.[45] Even the Archbishop of Canterbury, "aware that New Age thinking corresponds better to the spiritual needs of a new generation than orthodox Christianity, has urged his fellow theologians to take it seriously" (*Globe and Mail*, June 9, 1990).

He's joined an ancient crowd, for the roots of New Age are old and run deep and wide. In 1875, the so-called Theosophical Society was founded in New York City by the Ukrainian Helena Blavatsky (1831-91). Madame Blavatsky was followed in loose succession by admirers such as Alice Bailey, David Spangler, Barbara Max Hubbard, Elizabeth Clare Prophet, and Marilyn Ferguson, whose 1980 book *The Aquarian Conspiracy*, a kind of manifesto for New Agers, "took off like a rocket." Marilyn chirps that "heretics are gaining ground, and Christian doctrine is losing its authority. Knowing [gnosis] is superseding belief."[46] All of them share Blavatsky's hatred of monotheism (outer-God religions), especially of traditional Christianity, and promote most Gnostic beliefs. A confused form of Darwinian evolution toward wordly perfection is also a stock item, as is one or another "plan" for a new world order, headed by "Lucifer." Lucifer (meaning "bearer of light"), the name of Satan before his fall, describes those who would usurp God's power. Venus (although actually a planet), commonly known as the morning star, is also called Lucifer because it is the second-brightest light in the heavens (cast out by the sun). Blavatsky's books are still published by Lucis Trust in New York, the earlier name of which was the Lucifer Publishing Company, founded by her in 1922. The first periodical published by this society was entitled *Lucifer*.[47] Oh yes: Lucis Trust is affiliated with the United Nations as an NGO — a non-governmental organization.

Most New Age leaders claim their prophecies were dictated to them by "spirit masters," and many promote a belief in the coming of the last and greatest "Christ" of all, whom they call "Lord Maitreya," a kind of multicultural messiah who will "fulfill the expectations of all religions for their own anticipated Teacher"[48] and solve all the religious, social, racial, and environmental problems of the world — leading us into the Age of Aquarius. This will be achieved at a single moment through telepathic communication with all peoples, and "spontaneous healing" will ensue. In sort, Lord Maitreya will dissolve the tower of Babel and end the conflict of religions. New Agers organized World Peace Meditation Day on December 31, 1986 (which was followed by Tiananmen Square, the Iraq war, and the crumbling of communism). August 16, 1987, was supposed to produce a worldwide "harmonic convergence," projecting humanity within 25 years into "an evolutionary domain" at present unimaginable. "Earth Day" was April 20, 1990. It was uneventful (except that Mount Pinatubo blew up shortly afterward and poured more "greenhouse gases" into the atmosphere than all the gases created by man since the Industrial Revolution). So at 11 p.m. on November 11, 1990 (called "11:11"), they tried again to "open the doors to global harmony" by trying to stop the flow of time and concentrating on the "flow of energy from themselves into the earth." Following the movements of a Virginia-based spiritualist named Solara, the group "symbolically ended time, space, and all divisions between people to create what they described as a oneness"

(*Globe and Mail*, November 4, 1990). One crystal-laden member, Mala Sahan (shucking one's real name, like Mary Smith, is part of this scene), stood outside the moaning circle of time-stoppers to serve as a "pillar of light" to focus the "energies" in the hall. Similar groups gathered at the same moment at the great pyramids of Giza, at Grouse Mountain, B.C., and at the South Sea islands of New Zealand, which are considered "the vortex for cosmic energies at this time." Sounds like a spiritual washing machine.

Theosophists and New Agers say that Lucifer, in the tradition of the dark God of the ancient Gnostics, even has ultimate control over Lord Maitreya. So they call for a "Luciferic Initiation" into the New Age, many holding to a medieval doctrine that it was really Lucifer who created the world before suffering injustice at the hands of a despotic power. According to this myth, man frees himself from God's "oppression" by joining Lucifer (a symbol for all us downtrodden folks) in his struggle for unification under the *doctrine of wholeness* — central to all New Age belief. This doctrine says that because man is separate from and broken apart by feelings of guilt and sin, all "creedal" religions (from an outer God) must be attacked. Then, all people will be "fused" into "one humanity," which adherents call "Lucifer's gift of wholeness."[49]

Local manifestations of this thinking can be found in most of the world's 400 Waldorf schools, which were inspired by Rudolf Steiner. Calling himself an anthroposophist, Steiner fancied himself an "awakener of men" and wrote on the occult, reincarnation, karma, socialism, and his private version of moral individualism. He held the ego to be the unique spiritual centre of man, and the outer God he characterized as a "tyrant." Much of his early work was published in a journal called *Lucifer-Gnosis*.[50]

Now when you stop to consider that there is an unbroken line of preaching from Gnosticism, to Rousseau and Romanticism, to New Age, to the religion of secular humanism, to the imbuing of school children with so-called moral values education, and that the one thing common to all of them is the idea that the outer God and external moral standards are to be despised in favour of the inner God, do you not wonder where it is all leading?

Perhaps some answer can be gained from our crumbling society. One informal survey of 100 probation officers from Toronto attending a seminar on handling cults, reported that 70 percent of Ontario probation officers "have encountered a young offender with a serious interest in Satanism." One expert, Robert Tucker, said "these cases are coming up all over Canada and the U.S.A." (*Globe and*

*Mail*, November 7, 1990). Tucker said the satanic philosophy "glorifies murder, suicide, mutiliation and rape, along with rituals such as the ingestion of feces and animal intestines, and the drinking of menstrual blood." He sees kids coming in with the satanic pentacle symbol on them. The seminar was "jolted" by a presentation showing the relationship between Satanism and heavy-metal rock music. Why jolted? Because they don't listen to it.

But millions of teenie-boppers do, and it all flies under the flag of "free speech," even though the full lyrics published in a book would be banned. Here's the rock group Rigor Mortis, in its song "Demons": "We force you to kill your brother/Eat his blood and brain/Shredding flesh and sucking bone 'til everyone's insane." Or, how about the group King Diamond, with "The Oath": " . . . my persistent archangel, Prince Lucifer. . . . I deny Jesus Christ, the deceiver, and I abjure the Christian Faith." Or the group Venom, with "Possessed": "Look at me, Satan's child/born of evil, thus defiled . . . I drink the vomit of priests/make love with the dying whore." Many rap songs are nothing but violent sexy lyrics set to numbing music. So, is social violence so surprising?

Tucker warned that because of the spread of such popular media, "we are going to see more and more violence, involving younger and younger children." In return for performing the rituals, he said, which often involve heavy doses of violence and group sex, followers "believe they can be granted power to shape events or their lives." When asked why most youths involve themselves in Satanism, Tucker answered: "Because it feels good." He added that a number of them have parents who dress in full satanic regalia and who involved them as children — as young as three — in forced satanic ceremonies or in sexual and physical ritual abuse.

Some examples? There are about 60,000 people in North America who go "missing" every year. Most of them are runaway kids who eventually go home. But many remain missing, some forever. Some have undoubtedly been raped, murdered, or sacrificed, or eaten in satanic rituals. At the time 18-year-old James Tobin murdered 21-year-old child-care worker Christina Sepp, of Midland, Ontario, he was directly involved in Satanism (Toronto *Star*, November 7, 1990). So were the three 14-year-old Lethbridge, Alberta, boys found hung in a home. One of them, Chilton Thur, had the words "to live is to die" written in blood on his naked body.[51] More than 2000 Canadians — mostly women — have in the recent past stepped forward with claims of abuse in satanic cults, and many police forces now include courses on Satanism. Dr. George Fraser, a psychiatrist at the University of Ottawa, says "these stories are coming from everywhere. Across Canada, across the United States, Australia, England, the Netherlands" (*Globe and Mail*, November 27, 1990). And most experts believe that, after accounting for faulty memories, kooks, trauma, and plain silliness, there is a hard core of true satanic crime at work in our societies, in the form of youth gangs and cults.[52] The church of Satan claims 10,000 members worldwide; some cults adhere to the Gnostic Catholic church, or another such group; "black mass" is often read — to mock Christianity; communion with animal blood is served, and "sex-magic" indulged. Priestess Patricia, of Edmonton, where there are believed to be five covens, declares: "We believe Satan is a spiritual being who liberated men from moralistic systems . . . We look forward to Hell because at the end of history, Satan will defeat God."[53]

On the gang side, serious crimes, often hard to prove, seem to occur. These include child sex abuse, rape, and child sacrifice. Some satanic families are said to breed their own children for sacrificial ceremonies that include murder, suicide, eating feces, and drinking urine and human blood. A special investigative unit of the RCMP is in charge of such investigations. In a notorious 1989 Hamilton, Ontario, case, Judge Thomas Beckett accepted the evidence from two young girls of satanic ritual abuse by their own parents, which included pornography, graveyard orgies, cannibalism, and murder of babies and adults. Dr. Fraser, above, warns the public not to blind itself to such stories or dismiss them totally, saying: "I believe that there are people out there organizing together, abusing children on a cult-like scale, and some of them using satanic props [as a] good stage setting for their activities" (*Globe and Mail*, November 28, 1990).

At the root of it all is plain old Gnosticism, evident in the violation of the body and the hatred of this world, in sexual violence, and in the rejection of any moral system, in the secrecy and symbol common to Gnostic sects, and in the reversal of standard religious ceremony as a form of repudiation.

## The Future and "The Plan"

There are many loosely interlocked organizations and movements united by a New Age belief. Die-hard New Agers believe that when the fabled city of Atlantis was destroyed, the "ascended masters" of the "white lodge" left the world temporarily in control of the "black lodge" — the source of the despised Judeo-Christian tradition. The New Age of Aquarius will be initiated by the former when they come back with their plan for a new world order. Christianity and its restrictive laws and commandments are blamed for "holding back this evolutionary spiritual process."[54] (This notion is quite correct, because like all outer-God religions, Christianity is based on privatism, family, adherence to a transcendent set of moral laws, and the corollary belief that a flawed humanity can never, and should never, unite in obedience to any worldly collectivist power.) Banal examples of such antifamily, anti-Christian thinking can be found in the likes of popular guru John Bradshaw, author of *Bradshaw on the Family*, who says "96 percent of all families are 'dysfunctional' . . . and 'poisoned' by unhealthy and demeaning rules of unquestioning obedience, denial of emotion and shame." He maintains that the United States (with a population of 250 million) has 131 million "addicts." With half the population young children, that makes every adult an addict of something. He lectures widely on the "vital lies" that are "drummed into kids at home, at school, and at church" (Toronto *Star*, June 17, 1991). I would say the fellow who murdered Sepp needed some rules, and a goodly dose of unquestioning obedience and shame.

It's all very confusing and complicated, but let us focus on the basic danger here. New Age philosophy is inherently socio-political because, like all forms of Gnosticism, it envisages a perfect world order brought about by the Man-god. It is precisely this unitary perfect order that threatens the life of the Western family as we know it, because it requires the breakdown of all social groupings, including the families of the world, and their reformation into one egalitarian "family." You cannot have a new world order if the families in it owe allegiance to a transcendent outer God, rather than to the order itself. You can see the thrust of it all. By breaking down allegiance to moral absolutes, you render mankind malleable, ripe for spiritual allegiance to a unified earthly order.

What kinds of groups and movements are directly or indirectly involved? For starters — any group that is "globalist" in its thinking or thrust shares much of New Age philosophy. Some examples are Planetary Citizens, the World Federalist Association, many environmentalist and ecology groups such as Greenpeace, the Tara Center, the Club of Rome, Global Education Associates, the Freemasons, and many radical feminist groups. There are over 10,000 such groups, most of them small. But others are large religious organizations. The Maharishi Mahesh Yogi and Canadian magician Doug Henning have reportedly teamed up to build a $1.5 billion "heaven on earth" theme park near Niagara Falls, Ontario, based on the "seven steps to enlightenment," on the "Veda" land. Veda, which means knowledge (gnosis), refers specifically to "cosmic intelligence that structures the laws of nature" (*Globe and Mail*, March 19, 1992). At the press conference announcing this grand project, Henning's wife "slipped into another state of consciousness." At the same time, about half the press corps "slipped out the door."

At the core of most such cults is the idea of "universal brotherhood," a condition in which all distinctions, nationalisms, hierarchies, and divisions are suppressed. Mankind, for all one worlders, is to be united under one church, in one nation, and as one family, under one government — nominally a form of socialism. When this is properly accomplished, all world problems — which cannot be solved by warring, separate nations — will be resolved. At their most air-headed, one-worlders promote the idea of the consolidation of the whole planet in universal godhood, or divinity, directed by those with paranormal abilities. They will tap the "global brain" and initiate all matter into godhood. Peter Russell's book *The Global Brain* explores this theme (with accompanying video "for a new age") and promises to "reconnect" people with their deeper intuitions and inner visions. Spiritual growth (in the video) is shown to be "no less than the forces of evolution working through the human mind," It's quite weird. Clearly, the choice for the faithless is between a life spent as a free moral agent, attempting to improve one's character while guided by unchanging religious and moral values, or a life controlled by something like a global brain. The decision shouldn't be difficult.

Once the church forsakes the outer God for the inner, however, anything can happen. It has been my purpose to show that the false chain of reasoning by which even many in the Christian church have accepted Gnostic beliefs, always leads to one form or another of universalism, which is in turn always necessarily antifamily. In its failure to reject these Gnostic forms, and through its willing embrace of witless doctrines about generalized human love as a form of divinity, the modern church has erred grievously. During his February 1992 Toronto church trial, homosexual minister James Ferry insisted "this is a matter of love and not a matter of law and technicalities." Poor James. He missed the point. Jesus, the Bible, and the church have, until recently, been quite firm that there is good and bad love, and that those sufficiently under the sway of their own emotions will always seek to attribute their bad motives to good "love" and then turn around and condemn those who attempt to distinguish between the two. Ferry, defiant, said that "to stop him from loving another person is beyond the scope of any human being, including a bishop" (Toronto *Star*, February 6, 1992). So there. Alas, for him, as for anyone, generalized love is an all-too-convenient cover for the exploitation of personal desires. Unguided by any standard of virtue outside ourselves, we soon end up with a mere love of our own appetites. Certainly, the homosexual penchant for multiple partners suggests this. Civilizations and their religions are supposed to be wise enough to maintain an external moral standard so that we do not fall victim to our own sleight-of-heart.

## From Morals to Magic

*Superstition is the religion of feeble minds.*

EDMUND BURKE, 1790

Underlying all Gnosticism and New Age thought as it forsakes the outer God is the aggressive abandoning of morals for magic (New Agers call it "magick"). After all, it is difficult for most of us to adhere to outer moral standards that we are powerless to alter, and real prayer is tough because it's a form of confessional, or a beseeching of some divinity beyond our control. But magic makes the false promise of direct control over ourselves and others, according to our whim instead of God's will; hence, its appeal. If magic fails, we are counselled to try harder, to go deeper into the "source" of our own divinity. Magic, we could say, is really a vulgar form of prayer, offering the promise without the pain. This is why New Age spiritualism is replete with seers, forecasters, palm readers, crystal experts, diviners, out-of-body and re-birthing experts, tarot cards, centring, channelling, and the like. These have in common an absence of any moral imperative. In its place is found a magical, paranormal quest for personal unity with the benevolent "energy." New Age is appealing because it transforms morality into magic, and the heavenly into the human.

Just how widespread is this movement? The sociologist of religion, Reginald Bibby, says not very. Yet. Seventy percent of Canadians say they are "unfamiliar" with New Age thinking, and only 8 percent say they are familiar and interested. Still, that's close to a million adults. Phillip Whitten, editor of *New Age Journal*, says he has 180,000 subscribers. Some authors say the movement is a "world-wide coalition of thousands of organizations" (Gaverluk and Cumbey, *New Age Movement*, p. 18). Witches in the Victoria, B.C., area have recently been given money to build a "church" in Sooke,

B.C., "accessible to witches, pagans, and followers of earth religions" (Toronto *Star*, November 4, 1990). Salem, Massachusetts, has a Witches League for Public Awareness, with 2400 witch members. A 1988 Gallup poll found that 29 percent of U.S. teenagers "believe in witches" (*Globe and Mail*, May 1, 1991). Canada has its own "Wiccan Church" on Vaughan Road in Toronto — with about 100 full members. According to Bibby, almost 50 percent of Canadians say they have experienced precognition, 23 percent say it is possible to communicate with the dead, and 25 percent say they expect to be reincarnated. Well, it's a fertile field for those marketing pseudo-religions. Sizable percentages of Canadians (66 percent) have an absolute belief that "everything's relative," and 50 percent say that "what is right or wrong is a matter of personal opinion." I wager they don't tell their children that. Or the judge.

### From Convent to Coven
That's the title of a telling chapter in Donna Steichen's *Ungodly Rage*, a detailed, blow-by-blow account of the feminist "theological" boondoggle.[55] She gives a chilling view of radicalized women — especially nuns — working to bring down the entire Judeo-Christian tradition from the inside by using the well-honed techniques of their Marxist brethren, who are still thumping the broken drums of liberation theology. Liberationist Paulo Freire is their favourite, because he outlines a complete methodology for "conscientizing," or awakening students to the need for revolution.

Instead of expressing their dissatisfaction with a "patriarchal" Christianity by leaving it alone for those who enjoy it and setting up an alternative religion and church of their own, radical feminists have rather successfully set about revolutionizing Christianity from the inside. Their special target is the Roman Catholic church, which to this day refuses, for traditional reasons, to ordain females.[56] What they want, says feminist Naomi Goldenberg, who teaches religion at the University of Ottawa, are "not minor alterations" but "major departures from tradition" that will "shake [Christianity and Judaism] at their roots."[57] Feminists characterize the Christian church as patriarchal, hierarchical, oppressive, and non-egalitarian, and therefore sinful, and they tend vigorously to promote (religious) humanist goals. To facilitate their effort, they have infiltrated the church (largely by converting nuns to their view) and have adopted their own "non-sexist" *Women's Bible* (written by Elizabeth Stanton, in the late 19th century) and their own "liturgies." They aim to alter the sex of God (they prefer Maitreya, of androgynous Buddhist

534 THE WAR AGAINST THE FAMILY

origin), and to suffuse Christianity with pagan ritual and witchcraft (which they say is a "woman's religion" of the earth).

They say all monotheistic, hierarchical religions (based on an outer God) are male and "linear" instead of female and "process-oriented," and thus they fail to capture the true cyclical spirit of religion (non-judgmental and earth-based). For them, a true religion would grant "equality of opportunity" and allow total freedom for women in personal life, including contraception, abortion, divorce, and of course lesbianism. Feminist "witches" of the Dianic school claim that "about 90 percent of Dianic witches are lesbians."[58] For history, they substitute "herstory," with which they "undermine" and "revoke" scripture and tradition. Their statement of "theological" purpose, as outlined in *Women of Power* magazine, defines spirituality as "a world-wide awakening of woman-power whose vision is the transformation of ourselves and our societies," and includes "the activation of spiritual and psychic powers; the honouring of woman's divinity; reverence for the earth, and the celebration of her seasons and cycles."[59] Well, that's a pretty good definition of paganism, and heresy. Goldenberg candidly admits that "very few people working for sexual equality within Christianity and Judaism realize the extent of their heresy."[60]

Let me see, now. Earth worship? Woman as divine? Celebration of the seasons? Lesbianism? Psychic powers? No moral absolutes? A political "Bible"? Magic? Pagan ritual? Well . . . it sure sounds like a recipe for evil. And that's where the chain of revolt leads: to "magick," witchcraft, and pagan celebrations. Steichen amply outlines this evolution and revolt against the outer God and the programmatic feminist effort to worship the inner God. There is little to distinguish these radicals from New Agers, except for their political program. Just listen to a bit of it, and ask how this is going to straighten out the world.

"Every person has a right to their own beliefs and convictions . . . you can come to your own truth," exudes Patricia Bartscher, who with her academic colleagues cheerfully discusses ways to corrupt their students and relativize their value systems, even justifying incest, and defending "extremely erotic, very fulfilling sadomasochistic relationships."[61] When one observer at a conference Steichen attended asked, "Where do morality and ethics fit into Women-Church?" (the label for the feminist church), one Keller-Maresh answered: "Trust the goddess within you."[62] This is just the old Gnostic heresy, in drag. Steichen, who attended many such conferences, attests to the ever-present effort to ritualize feelings with pagan- and witchcraft-type ceremony. Most sessions seem to draw from the preaching of the eclectic and compelling Mathew Fox, who dabbles in any "spiritual" thinking that will motivate his audience. A handsome, warm man with an unctuous manner but confused intellect, Fox seems the ultimate spiritual snake-oil salesman. Pressed to resolve the moral and philosophical absurdities of his sweet-sounding thoughts, he quickly skates to new territory by globalizing everything: Morality is only a problem because we refuse to acknowledge our universal spiritual community. Fox is especially moved by "sexual mysticism," and he exalts homosexual lovemaking as a religious pursuit."[63] He declares that the androgynous "Cosmic Christ" gets very excited when lovers make love, and is "saddened" when people "moralize." In short, underlying Fox's adoration of indiscriminate sensuality-as-divinity is the Gnostic ideal of escape from morality. He states that homosexuality is superior to heterosexuality and that "there is no better birth control," claiming there is "cosmological merit" in the fact that it is not productive.

In "The Hands That Would Shape Our Souls" (*Atlantic Monthly*, December 1990), journalist Paul Wilkes, who intensively interviewed the religious at 15 American seminaries, says there are big problems with "lavender rectories." Seminaries generally are failing to attract top students. In fact, they are filling with bad ones. The Roman Catholic church in the United States had over 40,000 seminarians in training in 1968, but only 8000 in 1989. Canada's enrolments are falling, too (from well over 600 in 1988 to about 560 in 1989). It's the same with ordained priests; Canada had 7498 in 1977, but there are only 6599 today, despite a much higher population. The story everywhere is that heterosexual students are leaving and homosexual students are applying and staying. As one student put it: "The balance is being tipped in their favour. Claiming celibacy is a wonderful cover for gays, and let's face it, the seminary presents a marvellous area of opportunity for them." Wilkes says estimates are that the Catholic church is 20 to 40 percent gay. A Yale scholar says that for seminaries and the church, homosexuality is "a powder keg." Radical bishop John Spong of Newark, New Jersey, while in Toronto to defend James Ferry, said: "I could name 16 of our bishops who are gay" (*Globe and Mail*, February 22, 1992).

So Fox's vision is unfolding everywhere.

His pseudo-pagan novitiate, "Starhawk," a popular paganist-nativist (born Miriam Simos, of St. Paul, Minnesota), is much quoted by feminists and witches, who get a rush from her pansexual message: "All acts of love and pleasure are my rituals."[64] Starhawk, who teaches at Fox's Institute for Culture and Creation Spirituality, calls the feminist goddess movement "a New Age revival" of witch-craft. Now this is scary stuff, precisely because it is Gnostic and is unanchored by any outer law. Witches are fond of "sacred circles," and "centring," and "raising energy," which is "directed" through a "cone of power" to the "magick" object. They enjoy nude dancing, celebrate menarche and menopause, and have adopted a host of pagan and druidic rituals, the underlying message of which is rejection of the Old Testament and all spiritual hierarchy, and devotion to "the divine within." Kolbenschlag, another radical, says that the first sign of the "ultimate religious experience" will be "the liberation of God."[65] This makes you wonder about the size of her ego. Everything in feminist theology is designed to bring about "spiritual androgyny" (also a Gnostic belief) and is based on what one critical theologian, Robert Grant, described as "a passionate subjectivity." Well, that sounds a lot like Wordsworth's "spontane-ous overflow of powerful feeling," ratcheted up a few notches and deified.

Steichen does a service in drawing our attention to critic James Hitchcock, who alerts us to the presence of Gnostic thinking in many walks of life. Hitchcock, a Roman Catholic historian, says all such movements have "an exaggerated sense of their own historic importance; an anti-intellectualism that exalts instinct and imagina-tion over reason." They express hostility to all moral and church hierarchy and promote a new, "invisible church" centred in the "sovereign, infinite self." These movements also claim that "self knowledge is tantamount to knowledge of God" and that their authority arises from direct inspiration by the spirit." Finally, they all reject a "narrow" objective notion of God and promote a utopi-anism that "absolutizes a single view of social justice" that never-theless coexists with their wide support of relativism.[66] The aim of such internalizing of the spiritual is the radical sacralizing of the self (and, by extension, of others). The aim is to dissolve all outer material and moral absolutes, thus engendering a complete freedom *of* instinct, and *from* judgment. Here is the old illusion that the self "creates its own reality"[67] and it is antisocial in the extreme. Far from melding all spirits into one, it dissolves all material and moral absolutes, the very instruments of moral cooperation and law that make human life possible. Without them, evil sprouts everywhere.

Why? Perhaps because once such anti-hierarchical, antisocial, anti–outer-God cults succeed in eroding the rule of law and the

community of morals that permitted them to exist as fringe curiosities, the real trouble sets in. Crime, moral imbecility, extreme
relativism, voodoo, hexing, ritual murder, human sacrifices, increasingly explicit pornography, cannibalism, violent group sex,
and so on take root because there is no inner or outer ordinance
left to stop them. The thirsty spirit searches for meaning in the
unrestrained personal passions and uncontrolled fears of the ages.
Many countries in Africa, and elsewhere in the world, still engage in
*muti*, or ritual murder based in witchcraft. This a form of sacrifice,
usually of someone close, who, as anthropologist Harriet Ngubane
puts it, "has personal qualities needed by the group" (Toronto *Star*,
December 1, 1991). In November 1990, about 80 people in one
northern South African territory stood trial for participating in
witchcraft-related murders. In *muti*, various body parts are valued
for their magical qualities, or for casting evil spells, and many young
"disappear" for this reason. Businessmen believe good luck can
come from burying human body parts under their establishments.
Ngubane, a typical anthropologist, for whom whatever is, is right,
explains that African medicine "embraces the possibility of cutting
the living flesh from a selected living person who is then killed." As
I said, magic is amoral, so it always leads to a war of magic rights.
That same November, 20 local youths were charged with killing
witches with whose hexes they disagreed.

Well, when you add up clerics who have given up the outer God and
promote a bevy of wrong-headed antifamily social and economic
policies, feminists who are successfully remaking the church, and
radical humanist teachers who fill the heads of our youth with belief
in the Man-god, you've got a quiet revolution in the making. Anyone
who reads school textbooks and curricula will be able to find
widespread interest in the "no right and wrong" morality, in "self-
esteem" and personal-empowerment discussions, and in guided
imagery, meditation, fantasy role-playing, socio-drama, psycho-
drama, and occult influences, such as in the widely used *Impressions* reading series from publisher Holt, Rinehart and Winston
of Canada (since cleared of this allegation by a U.S. district court).
At the 1984 U.S. Department of Education hearings to investigate
invasions of privacy by teachers, a host of parents complained about
the imbedded presence in many subjects of satanism, the occult,
and witchcraft, often offered to gifted students as a kind of lure. But
the courts, themselves overtly liberal, approve. Many recent school-
based "stress" courses (labels like "stress" and "self-esteem" are

often cover terms for New Age teaching) compel young children to engage in New Age rituals such as deep breathing, "centring" (in which kids are told to fill the "space" inside them with "energy"), or group hypnosis, or advise them to "consult a wise man living inside you" (instead of God, parents, or clergy). Some U.S. courses, sure to find their way here, come complete with video-taped lessons in "stress reduction," based on hypnosis, transcendental meditation, psychoanalysis, bio-feedback, and "visualization" techniques asking students to lie prone on their desks and engage in out-of-body experiences, or "quieting reflexes."

Soon, they will be able to place last in mathematics asleep, as well as awake.

From the followers of the ancient Gnostic inner light, to the Romantic worshipper of emotion, to the modern-day searchers for the wise man inside . . . The priests and priestesses of tomorrow will be arriving in increasing numbers.

# 18

# Turning Wrongs into Rights: The Law vs. the Family

*The religious vision of Heaven, a land beyond time and morality and very far off, has been replaced by a Utopian vision of an egalitarian society, to be obtained through Charters, Commissions, Affirmative Actions, and Legislated Codes of Behaviour.*

IAN HUNTER, LAW PROFESSOR, IN "WHAT'S WRONG WITH
HUMAN RIGHTS?" *THE IDLER*, APRIL-MAY 1985

*It is not true that the function of law is to regulate our consciences, our ideas, our wills, our education, our opinions, our work, our trade, our talents, or our pleasures. The function of law is to protect the free exercise of these rights, and to prevent any person from interfering with the free exercise of these same rights by any other person.*

FREDERIC BASTIAT, *THE LAW*

*Lawful (adj.): Compatible with the will of the judge having jurisdiction.*

AMBROSE BIERCE, *THE DEVIL'S DICTIONARY*

In all liberal democracies the law eventually becomes an agent of social dissolution in direct proportion to the power of the State, and to alterations in the law that favour abstract individual rights over the traditional rights and privileges of social institutions such as the family. Why should this be so? And how can the law, which ought to protect human society, end up as chief agent of its downfall?

It's a two-century-long riddle, but the brief answer seems to be that a successful society is a whole which is far more than the sum of its individual parts. For whenever people gather together freely to form groups, they create and enforce myriad written and unwritten conditions for group inclusion — and therefore exclusion of those unwilling or unable to qualify. This tendency is likely because they recognize intuitively, as well as practically, that one's agreement to conform to the expectations of a social group demands two things: a restraint on personal passions and claims, and a commitment to the future of the group that solitary individuals are not expected — and cannot be asked — to make. In short, membership in any group implies some degree of personal sacrifice for group ideals, and thus confers status on its members. This sacrificial limitation of one's liberty in the service of the group ideal represents a social contract and becomes the bonding force within all groups. A "society" is thus an aggregate not primarily of individuals, as we are led to believe, but, more importantly, of all voluntary groups formed by free individuals, which then interact to make up society: married couples, families, enterprises, religious congregations, clubs, charitable organizations, sporting teams, and so on. In other words, between the State at the top, which governs us, and the unformed random mass of individuals at the bottom, from which members are drawn, lies society itself, a composite of interacting molecules formed from individual atoms. Individual freedom and responsibility are of crucial importance to democracy, of course. But they are more important to *society*, because only such free individuals can form voluntary associations, or community groups. Because these groups have a higher social status than the individual, they need legal protection, both against envious individuals and against the State itself. Western societies have traditionally provided such groups the protection of special political, economic, and legal privileges. But once individual freedom is defined only in relation to and guaranteed by the *State*, it always ends up redefined as rights against society, and thus destroys community.

The error of egalitarian democracy is that in order to garner votes and deliver not freedom, but equal outcomes, it must subordinate such freely formed groups to its own project of controlling individuals through the promise of equally apportioned abstract rights.

However, the key to the survival of a democratic community has always been the specific *privileges* such groups have enjoyed in exchange for their commitment to the social project. Such commitment marks these groups as important to the health of that civilization. The protection, status, and privilege they have in turn induce individuals to form and enter such groups. That is why all free communities develop fairly clear and decisive unwritten rules of right and wrong behaviour established not merely as legal rights (contracts), but as voluntary and reciprocal bonds of civility (conduct).

As the quasi-religious ideals of egalitarian democracy evolve and the State transfers more of these group functions to itself in an attempt to extend its mastery equally to all, the legal privileges of social groups are increasingly attacked in the name of individual rights. The assault is mostly advanced by political interest groups who use the law as a weapon to weaken the privileged social groups that exclude them. Until recently, for example, a husband and wife could not testify against each other. Special tax status in the form of generous deductions for child expenses used to be standard, as were social protections in the form of specific legal definitions meant to exclude the unqualified from receiving "family" privileges. Examples of privileges for other groups include tax-exempt status for churches and charitable organizations. In the very recent past, courts have enabled individuals to attack and dissolve such privileges in the name of individual rights and freedoms. Thus does the craving for equality erode community, and democracy evolves into a genteel, but despotic, collectivism.

## FROM CONDUCT TO CONTRACT

We are changing from a society in which the hierarchical authority of an unwritten, evolved standard of conduct is the core binding value to one in which contractual arrangements between individual citizens, as defined by written "rights," is uppermost. Once the traditional, carefully crafted and slowly evolved legal protection of cherished groups is eroded, the groups themselves decay and falter under the attack of rights legislation. Then, understandably, we lose all motivation to change from atom to molecule.

The key instrument of such decay is, without question, the law, which since the Romantic period has increasingly been used to attack the authority, privilege, and legal protections of social groups in the name of the freedom, autonomy, and privacy of the individual.

Because the privileges and rights of those who agree to form the social whole are attacked and removed when the same rights and powers are granted to those who refuse these conditions, the whole is weakened and dissolved. Tragically, a democracy then moves from conduct to contract: from a defence of the individual's immeasurable worth, to an egalitarian insistence on sameness of treatment; from a determination to leave individuals alone in their freedom to form whatever voluntary associations they desire, to abstract principles designed to enforce conformity under the law. Society is turned upside down when common-law "spouses" receive the same tax treatment as legally married couples (it is in fact far better) or are provided tax-free welfare funds denied to an equivalent married couple. Or when homosexuals, who refuse the human procreational project, are granted married status and benefits; or young women are rewarded by subsidies for bearing and raising illegitimate children; or healthy young people are paid not to work; or a disloyal — even abusive — spouse seeking "no-fault" divorce has an automatic right to half of all marital assets against a partner faithful to the marriage. In such cases, the right and wrong of human conduct exist no longer; they have been replaced in the minds of the people with mere notions of contract. At this sad point, the law ceases to serve society; rather, it destroys society to serve the State.

**What Will Be the Sorting Factor?**
The more a society loses its natural confidence in some kind of unwritten moral law that promotes self-control and civility, it seems, the more it turns as a substitute to abstract human laws and declared rights. Such a shift is a sign of moral desperation. To make this point, it is instructive to look back once again to Rousseau and the French Revolution for the first calamitous harbinger of our present practices. Although there is no point in drawing unfit equations between different histories or periods, we may well compare many similarities of mentality, for the same syndrome is identifiable in the history of all democracies. Perhaps our only duty to history itself is to attempt to understand present errors in the light of past ones.

It is no coincidence that Romanticism, as discussed at various points in this book, gave attitudinal rise to all modern revolutions; that the template for all modern collectivisms was born there. Just as Romantic idealism sought to cast off all outer controls on the self, so the French Revolution it fostered sought to cast off all traditional social, political, and religious controls on the citizen (but only to replace them with despotism). Both succeeded in this project, and we live today in the wake of each. At the personal level, there is evidence for this inheritance everywhere, especially in our schools, where we see a focus on the philosophy of natural goodness and its consequent moral relativism, or unearned self-esteem, and on pansexualism — even though, as Babbitt put it so trenchantly, "the faith in one's natural goodness is a constant encouragement to evade moral responsibility."[1] That is simply because responsibility is always the more difficult path, whereas man's secret desire is ever to follow the path of least resistance. Modern hedonism, or the unbridled pursuit of one's most basic instincts — including the instinct for violence and perversion — is a clear manifestation of this ancient trend, all too well reflected in modern rock videos and progressively more explicit pornography, failing public civility and rising crime, government and corporate scandals, and, simply, our intensely commercialized society.

**Filling the Void**
On the impersonal, collective level, the turning away from outer controls, from outer God to inner God, left a rather immediate spiritual vacuum that most modern societies have attempted to fill with utopian ideals, euphemisms, and legislated rights, and with the worship not of anything authoritative or divine, but of man himself, and above all of his faculty to reason. This approach would not be so objectionable if we had an example of any human society in which it had worked, but there is not one in all human history. So it is important for us to focus on the way these seemingly unconnected threads form a knot tight enough to strangle us. In fact, if there is a single lesson to be learned from our long heritage of failed rational philosophy, it must be that it cannot produce a workable morality. This can arise only from custom, values, and tradition.

In 1927, in response to the political, economic, and social chaos that followed the second devastating revolution to convulse the modern world, namely the socialist Russian Revolution of 1917, the Russian writer Rozanov, aware of the common dynamics of terror that flowed from French to Russian [and later German] socialism, lamented the frenzied utopic violence and decay of the West, saying: "The deeper reason for all that has happened is found in the fact that vanishing Christianity has created enormous cavities in the civilized world and now everything is tumbling into them."[2]

Babbitt's imagery explains these "cavities" and helps us understand why the Romantic urge and the revolution — all such revolutions, it seems — always fail. It's because reason, like a shovel, is but an instrument — not a moral faculty. You may use it to dig a foundation for a home, or to beat someone to death. Reason will always be used to justify one's actions, good or bad. The most common trait of sociopathic killers is that they refuse to admit they were wrong (unless applying for parole). What they did "made sense" to them, and does still.[3] Many of the best-educated henchmen of the Third Reich, even today, insist dogmatically on the rationality of their motivations. That's why we must remember G.K. Chesteron's marvellously wise insight that "the madman is the man who has lost everything except his reason." The "everything" of which Chesterton spoke is the human composite of restraining civility, custom, and morality. Chesterton's "everything" normally prevents us from falling victim to our own sweet-sounding reason, which we quietly commandeer in the service of one or another of our active passions (political, sexual, or material) and use to justify them. For to worship reason really means we are worshipping the personal passion it disguises. Babbitt describes reason as standing sandwiched between and ready to serve, either our spiritual nature, above, or our instinctive nature, below. Both spirit and instinct vie for the help of reason, recruiting it to justify whatever direction we have already chosen.

Well, then, what determines the direction we choose? The answer is — the imaginative will, guided by the compass of virtue. But whenever people cast aside the protective residue of custom, tradition, and civility, they expose themselves, as Charles Murray put it, to the risk of taking direction from "sudden, random impulses" rather than "from an underlying, *coherent concept of virtue*."[4] Then most get into trouble. Deep trouble. For without such a concept, nothing can protect us from ourselves. Thus do our passions become our law. The dominant reality of most human beings, as Babbitt explains, is not their ability to reason, but their tendency to use reason for self-deception.

Once a people wilfully cuts itself loose from "the infinitely complex web of felt obligations and bases of mutual respect and motives for generosity that make up a civilized culture,"[5] it immediately requires some replacement code of conduct — some new outer standard. (It's a reflex response, surely based on fear.) Hence, if the law of God is deemed a failure, we turn to the law of man. Man's law then substitutes for the dead, rejected God, and the promise of earthly utopia (described in that law) replaces the promise of heaven (described in religion). The difficulty for all late democracies is that the law alone cannot hope to provide the spiritual bonds that generate right conduct. On the contrary, *just as right conduct conjoins us, the law always separates us.* It then attempts to compensate for this failure with ever more frenzied legality, forcing the entire society into increasingly contractual relationship, with accompanying litigation. The people then seek the missing bonds of community in the disappointment of abstract legal words. This dreadful legality increases as the State succeeds in equating freedom with political power, planting in the public mind the false idea that more government will make you free because the State will provide more of what you want.

With the storming of the Bastille prison in Paris on July 14, 1789, this devastating new — and far from exhausted — egalitarian religion of the modern period burst forth as a culminating synthesis of two strains of thought.*

The two strains that combined so powerfully were the *Cult of Reason* and the *Cult of Nature.* The former promotes the idea that because religion is an oppressive myth and society a shackle, clear reason will follow revolution to create a better, more egalitarian world. The latter promotes the corresponding Rousseauian notion that man is basically good by nature.

The new tablets of Moses, first proposed on July 11, 1789, were the articles of the French Declaration of the Rights of Man and Citizen, adopted August 26, 1789, and much influenced by the 1776 American Declaration of Independence. The articles were basically a list of "inalienable rights" of the individual. (Duties, after some debate, were omitted by the framers.) They were a signal that perfect legislation could invoke true obligation, mutual respect, and generosity (deemed absent from inherited culture). Thenceforward in the liberal democracies of the West and with ever-increasing powers, judges could replace Jesus, Lady Justice would take over from the Virgin Mary, and the articles of our various abstract bills of rights

---

* To the "victorious" mob's surprise, there were only seven prisoners within the Bastille. Recently transferred was the Marquis de Sade, the first modern pansexualist and the archetypal moral relativist, who, like all radical leftists, had a strong hatred for the family, which he characterized as "individualistic." For true fraternity, he advocated that the State take all children from their parents, and that incest be mandatory between all brothers and sisters.[6] Such coercive measures always flow naturally from world leftism. Sade's prescriptions are simply a smutty version of Rousseau's dictum that all citizens who refuse to obey the General Will "will be forced to be free," by which he meant, equal. Forced incest breaks family bonds and produces forced equality (*The Social Contract*, Chapter 7).

would stand in for the ten commandments. In a mere 200 years, this new strategy for producing virtuous civilizations by legislative decree has grown — and grown more frantic — with the spread of nationalism in the world and especially with the overweening presence of the State in the lives of the people. It has produced the unitary, or "identitarian," State, where deviations from State values are tolerated less and less. In nations with no democratic tradition to serve as a brake on collectivism, what begins with a drilling of the mind usually ends with a drilling of the body: mass calisthenics performed to State anthems, with the people blindly chanting hymns to the unity of the national "family." Canada's version of the French declaration, called the Charter of Rights and Freedoms, became law on April 17, 1982. Are we to expect such fanatical identitarianism here? Yes, and increasingly so. Keen analysts such as Tocqueville, Schumpeter, and Nisbet have predicted this as the outcome of liberal democracy, which places an increasing egalitarian pressure for uniformity at every level and features soul-deadening worship of a precisely equal material welfare.

Both Canada and the United States are already rife with citizen-staffed tribunals with truly extraordinary powers. They act as language police, employment equity police, pay equity police, price police, human rights police, thought police, homophobia police, media police, and myriad other kinds of police, fully backed by the highest laws of the land to fine and even imprison citizens who dare to contravene their egalitarian edicts. The drilling of the mind is aggressive here. My own personal physician, from Richmond Hill, Ontario, was summoned before an ethnic- and gender-balanced tribunal of the Ontario College of Physicians and Surgeons to defend herself against charges — triggered by a patient — that she kept "sexually abusive" reading material in her waiting room. A five-hour grilling came at the end of two years of worry and legal costs. She was narrowly acquitted. The offending document was a copy of the Toronto *Sun* daily newspaper.

Canada's first prisoner of conscience, a 69-year-old man named John Ross Taylor, was imprisoned for a full year in 1979 simply because he refused to stop communicating his opinions, which the court said offended the "spirit" of human rights (although no one was forced to agree with his kooky ideas).[7] The purpose of these tribunals, all of which operate on the principle of guilty until proven innocent, in flagrant violation of the most cherished legal value of a free society, is simply to enforce conformity of human thought and behaviour to an elitist view of the egalitarian good. (After all, the best remedy for so-called hate literature, and kooky ideas, is the boredom that accompanies the freedom to ignore it.) Since this fore-ordained good cannot be bad, those not sustaining it in any way are automatically guilty. All criticism is evil. Where grounds for conviction cannot be found in the evidence, they are justified on the grounds of offence to the "spirit" of the law, or on a "statistical disparity" between one's practice, say, in hiring, and the ideal. A current favourite is to style any unpopular opinion as "abusive." At the extreme are offenders who, as was the prototype Marie Antoinette and the many who followed her to the guillotine for no legal crime, are simply vilified as "essentially impure in body, thought, and deed."[8] This was essentially Taylor's sin. We are far removed from guillotines, but free citizens ought to be aware of the deadly connection between coercive uniformitarian thought, democratic failure and chaos, social breakdown, the invocation of martial law, dictatorship, and then the final stage, which produces the identitarian State itself — with its powerful appeals to nationalism, purity, conformity, scapegoating, and violence.

The energizing thrust of all this is the religious-type drive to achieve the universal brotherhood of all peoples. At a citizenship ceremony on April 13, 1992, Prime Minister Mulroney told 567 new Canadians from 85 different nations that "the country is very much like a family." This was official support for the modern, and quite desperate, "multicultural" policies sweeping the Western world — an everyday manifestation of the abstract ideal of universal brotherhood. Such policies survive for a very short time on the lunatic idea that we can derive unity by reinforcing and rewarding diversity. But as community increasingly fails in the concrete, it is promoted and enforced more fanatically in the abstract. The humorous democratic prototype for this fanatical universalism was also established in France on June 19, 1790, when the self-designated "orator of the universe," Anacharsis Cloots, a wealthy disaffected aristocrat, led a motley rabble of representatives into the National Assembly. Representing "the oppressed nations of the universe," they were dressed in different ethnic costumes, each wrapped in the French flag. There was much pontificating about all mankind existing in a "family pact," brought about through the alliance of truth with reason.[9]

However, in order to sanctify the new abstract ideals, you must trash the old, in a ceremony of destruction and creation. In addition to guillotining thousands of dissidents, nobles, intellectuals, clerics, and their families, *none of whom had committed a single legal crime*, the French revolutionaries embarked on a whole program of "dechristianization." This was designed to topple all allegiance of the people to ideals higher than those of the State and its charters. It included toppling steeples, smashing church symbols and windows, desecrating cemeteries, forcing priests publicly to declare themselves charlatans, and even dragging an upside down cross through the streets for the people to spit on. There is a chilling parallel between this last act and the recent publicly funded art exhibit in North America showing André Serrano's *Pisse-Christ*, a photograph of a cross immersed in a tumbler of urine. The French had their "Directorate" to promote such desecration; we, and the Americans, have our more subtle State-funded ministries of culture, arts councils, and human rights tribunals.

My purpose in detailing such things is simply to warn that all welfare states eventually embark on a program to oust competing ideologies, insistent that the truth of the State, which always ends in abstract legalisms, is the highest truth. In the French Revolution, Thuriot declared all traditional religions to be but inventions of man, and said: "It is *the moral order of the Republic*, of the Revolution, that we must preach now, that will make us a people of brothers." And the recanting priest, Gobel, declared that "there should be no other public cult than liberty and *holy equality*." Holy equality!

The crowning act of dechristianization surely came when Notre Dame Cathedral was renamed the "Temple of Reason." Inside, a gimcrack Greco-Roman structure was built of linen and papier-mâché, and a toga-clad opera singer playing Liberty sang and bowed to the flame of reason. In the Cathedral of Saint-Jean, a "Feast of Reason" featured supplicants singing antihymns celebrating "Reason as the Supreme Being."[10] The connection between this political mania to substitute abstract reason for God, who has betrayed us by creating an imperfect world, and the Gnostic myth (discussed in the previous chapter), which entails a repudiation of the real world, gives pause for thought. Socialist utopianism suggests the same motive.

Take note. On December 10, 1990, the same year all religious celebrations, notably for Christmas, were banned from schools in most Canadian provinces — our own brand of dechristianization — the Alberta Human Rights Commission declared a "Human Rights Day" on which all schools were to celebrate the anniversary of the publication of the United Nations' Universal Declaration of Human Rights (December 10, 1948). The instructional brochure says the U.N. document is "the basis upon which every human may fulfil the potential that is his/her birthright." Get it? Fulfilment is to flow from external legislated abstract statements, not from personal virtue, and this fulfilment is a "birthright" — meaning someone (inevitably the State) has an obligation to ensure it for you, whether or not you are worthy. Students are instructed to create a ceremony within a circle of tables surrounded by an outer circle of banners bearing the 30 articles of the Declaration. Flowers are to be placed in a large open vessel mounted on a pedestal in the centre, and the class, with accompanying music, is to break and eat bread, drink water, and take salt. Well, this is a kind of cardboard Stonehenge combined with a traditional Christian communion, performed by devoutly bowing kids before a nature-altar of flowers. Professor Norman Ingram of the University of Alberta objected that this ceremony was an attempt "to give a metaphysical justification to human rights," and rightly called it "ersatz paganism," and concluded that such rituals are tied to a "modern perception of the perfectibility of man; that through politics man can be elevated from the quagmire of depravity."[11]

As it happens, so-called "human rights" really amount to a set of obligations on a State only too happy to take everything you have in order to give you everything you want. In short, obligations formerly incumbent upon each of us, according to our spontaneous human relationships and moral responsibilities, are now incumbent upon the State and *theoretically* producible in exchange for our taxes. This radical change in the nature of human expectations became possible because of the general acceptance of the Romantic idea that the source of evil is not the individual (the view of mainstream religions), but the institutions of society. Hence, the need for revolution. You clear the decks of the old authorities and start over with the new tablets. A heavy-handed State with taxing power will ensure that the new rights are provided. This philosophy makes the State grow proportionately as the moral sense of the people shrivels. It attempts to combine the two utterly conflicting ideas of freedom and equality, the latter soon coming to mean equality not of opportunity or of legal protection, but of condition. This combination cannot work, because if you want more of this kind of equality you need more government; and if you want absolute equality, you need absolute government. In its final stages, this now very "democratic" philosophy produces a massive uniformity of opinion and expectation that manifests itself in an increasingly indignant mood of "collective righteousness." (The current antiracism hysteria is an example.) So in late democracies we no longer debate ideas. Rather, we attempt to intimidate opponents of our fixed assumptions by declaring how "extraordinarily offended" or "outraged" we are. The righteousness of our issue is assumed.

For true debate, we substitute emotion, by the strained expression of which we demand what we think is ours by right. This stage is followed by increasingly frenetic and contradictory regulation of human freedom and enterprise. For example, to counter alleged racism, the State must officially classify the entire population by race. The effort to achieve righteousness, now defined through group attitudes and not by personal behaviour, becomes a core function of the State, as does the attempt to stamp out all nonconforming ideas and remove all impurities, and to control all information, media, academic institutions, and legislative institutions — and all funding that flows to or from them. The Ontario Human Rights Task Force recently published an advertisement coyly entitled, "Let's Talk About Human Rights Enforcement" (Toronto *Star*, April 16, 1992), asking citizens to help the Task Force design ways to spy upon and punish individuals and corporations that fail to conform to its egalitarian guidelines.

Finally, if such a nation falls into political and economic collapse, there follows, as the night the day, the violence and terror that always flow from abstract utopian schemes. In the measure that imperfect men recruit reason to bolster their dreams, the ends envisioned soon justify any means; and the more passionately felt the ends, the more thorough, desperate, and violent the means. In short, the pursuit of heavenly or earthly perfection (there is no difference to the collectivist mind) eventually justifies any sacrifice. And so a formerly free State may end by sanctifying the seriousness of its causes through the bloodiest of crimes against its own people. It was Robespierre himself who said "surely it is necessary that a small number perish so that the mass of the people may be saved?"[12] The Third Reich justified the sacrifice of Jews to save the purity of the Aryan mass. Radicals defend the sacrifice of healthy babies to procure for the mass of modern women an equality in the workforce. This is the connection, as Harvard's Simon Schama puts it, between blood and freedom. Violence and death soon become "the source of collective energy" of any revolution.[13] Once blood is drawn, both ideals and violence grow more extreme to justify the initial blood. What will be next? Are Canadians so benign as to believe that violence, terror, or even martial law or dictatorship cannot happen here, or in the United States, as has long been predicted?

It does seem unimaginable. And in what follows I do not wish to suggest that Canada or the United States is currently equivalent to the French terror. But I do want to suggest that the mental and moral processes that in the name of abstract ideals lead to the victimization of citizens — then, under the right conditions, to terror — are much the same for every democracy. The process always begins with genteel, democratic justifications, but ends in moral decay and social and political chaos in the measure that servitude expands through the surrender of freedoms for rights. Then anything can happen. We ought to be keenly aware of the fatal direction of this process on our own soil, the better to ensure it does not proceed to its natural culmination, and, if possible, to reverse it.

## THE STAGES: HOW WE GET FROM FREEDOM TO COLLECTIVISM

### Stage One: Divorcing Rights from Duties

In the name of egalitarian freedom based solely on individual rights, divorced from duties, comes, first of all, violence to morals. Then, in the name of the myth of natural human goodness, all spontaneous outer authority is purged from the community. Next, the family is weakened through inducements to surrender its vital functions to the State. And for the sin of offering values higher than those of the State, religion is converted into a multicultural curiosity — often assisted by the religious themselves, who imbibe the new substitute religion of humanity. So-called religious humanism, or worship of the inner God, becomes the order of the day, and the entire population is taught that it is the beneficiary of a cornucopia of "rights" equal for all, since all are equally good and worthy. As success in life is now deemed to be something conferred upon us by the State, all must receive it equally — even *forced* to receive it. (Swedish bureaucrats, for example, want to force reluctant fathers to take parental leave.) The logic of all this compels the creation of an ever larger, more coercive provider State, as the passion for equality feeds on growing envy.

### Stage Two: Legislating the Provision of Equality

Next comes violence to ordinary freedom and to the important natural differences freedom normally exists to nourish. At this stage there is a tremendous growth of tribunals, commissions, supervisors, and courts of all kinds attempting to stamp out all the natural differences spawned by freedom, which are now perversely redefined as resulting from discriminations of every kind, visible and invisible. From 1867 until 1982, Canada's Constitution said nothing whatever about human rights, and for the entire period the people carried on as a tolerably peaceable kingdom among nations of the world. But following World War II, there came an avalanche of bills of rights and human rights codes created both by the provinces and by the federal government, as if to stanch the bleeding heart of civil society. Some codes, like Ontario's, declared a comprehensive "right to equal treatment" in almost every aspect of life. That is, rights and privileges were promised to individuals, no longer to the social institutions they had always cherished, such as the family. These institutions were now deemed the primary (albeit uncon-fessed) competition for allegiance to the State. They were to be tolerated, but certainly not privileged in any way (and sometimes they were to be punished). That's how the idea of egalitarian rights based on the individual alone became a recipe for total government. Tocqueville said that the welfare State "every day renders the exercise of the free agency of man less useful and less frequent; it circumscribes the will within a narrower range, and gradually robs a man of all the uses of himself." And Professor Ian Hunter tells us that in "little more than two decades, Canada has gone from having no statutory protection of human rights, to having ten provincial Human Rights codes, a comprehensive federal Human Rights Act, a Canadian Bill of Rights, and an entrenched Charter of Rights." It's astonishing. And he is correct to ask, "Has this frenzy of legislative activity enhanced our freedom? Are our lives or property now more secure? Has the enactment of this legislation abated the public clamour about rights? Is Canada a less divided, a more harmonious country in which to live? Have these statutes diminished injustice and oppression?" His answer? "I do not believe that liberty can be legislated."[14]

Professor Hunter cites the American jurist Learned Hand, who wrote that the spirit of liberty " . . . lies in the hearts of men and women; when it dies there, no constitution, no law, no court can save it; no constitution, no law, no court can even do much to help it; and while it is alive it needs no constitution, no law, no court to save it."

**Stage Three: Eliminating Differences**
At this stage we get the creation of special laws empowering the equality-seekers (freedom is now defined as equality) to *disadvantage* all citizens deemed to have advantages. This announces the legislative dominance of the handicap system in society, and it always signals the end of true freedom. This stage of the process is

inherently antifamily, because the family and the moral independence, private property values, and free enterprise it promotes create real differences — inequalities — based on individual effort. Canada entrenched the handicap system in its Charter in 1982, by way of sections 1 and 15.2, among others, which permit the State to discriminate against some groups in favour of others (although citizens who do the same are said to be breaking the law). Merit and effort under such systems are demoted as a principle of virtue, replaced by public cynicism and official tokenism. Virtue is soon equated with equality, and equality with the official extermination of all differences and provision of equal outcomes. Nice, egalitarian democracy exterminates differences. But when such democracies get nasty, as they must to enforce equality, they may quickly transform themselves, under the pressure of their own frenetic logic, into a mob that exterminates not simply the differences but the different people themselves. Then, we have democratic despotism. As the heat of collective righteousness rises, all those who oppose it are branded as disposable. First you send old men to jail, then young men. Then, for the egalitarian purists, jail is not final enough.

A national slogan such as the French cry, "liberty, equality, fraternity," if unbridled, is guaranteed to produce terror when followed to its natural conclusion, simply because the first two terms of the three are mutually exclusive, and so the fraternity they are meant to produce must be enforced.

It is instructive to follow what happens when this process is unchecked, as it was in France. During the terror, the entire Vendée region of France was liquidated — though all inhabitants were French citizens — simply because the people there, who accepted the revolutionary ideals, resisted the dictatorship required to enforce them. This extraordinary and disgusting terror, carried out in the name of resurgent democracy, was wreaked primarily against French families. Whole towns were burned, and mothers and babies were raped and killed by zealous defenders of equality; some children were fried in butter, others roasted in baker's ovens; and residents of entire villages were tied up and bent over open graves they had dug, and shot — the wounded left to drown in blood or to be buried alive. Some 250,000 people of the Vendée were exterminated in Year II of the French Jacobin Terror in the name of the Republic of Virtue and the Cult of Reason. The revolutionaries even urged the liquidation of dissidents with chemical gases, but they failed to produce the technology.[15] The people they slaughtered in the name of liberty and equality were not foreign enemies. They were mostly ordinary people who resisted the decimation of their freedoms, and thus became defined as internal enemies of the egalitarian State. If they belonged to a wealthy family, or a learned family, or a religious family, or a merchant family, or an aristocratic family — they were automatically suspected of inegalitarian sentiments. The search for those who offended the spirit of revolutionary freedom was carried out against targeted families and all those connected with them. Blood connection became the mark of treason. First the property-owning landlord was guillotined, then the baker who had dared to sell him bread. In the end, all identitarian states create their own internal enemies, and the family (based on blood relations) is always the targeted institution around which terror is organized. As we know, the same intellectual template of utopian values has produced mass genocide and desecration during the century.

### Stage Four: Enforcing Political Correctness
By this stage, if the evolution into violence has been checked, there have usually been years of intellectual domination of the nation's cultural, political, and legislative organs sufficient to create an oppressive and overwhelming uniformity of opinion. All meaningful social, cultural, and intellectual functions are now directed, funded, and therefore censored by the State. So-called "political correctness" becomes the manifestation of this stage and, like a boil bursting through the unassuming skin of civility, is a clear sign of the illness beneath. It is the intellectual, or knowledge, class — huddled in the universities and the media, and prone to utopian idealism — that most vigorously promotes and justifies such correctness and effectively suppresses dissidents.

The great worry for the West will begin when the unresisted attitudinal sclerosis of late democracy creates the conditions for violence, following a well-worn path: from increasingly abstract individualist ideals, to legislated equality, to breakdown of all privileged social institutions, to attitudinal domination, to fear and force. Informal and formal censorship in North America now looms everywhere in the drive for conformity. All textbooks are regularized to fit the new ethos, and history itself is rewritten. All legal jurisdictions struggle to "align" their policies, from highest to lowest administrative body, even, as we shall soon see, from the United Nations to your living room via documents such as the United Nations Convention on the Rights of the Child (see below).

## Stage Five: The Law Replaces Morality

At this stage, there is a lot of public condemnation by administrative tribunals that make a habit of constructing evidence based on their own indignation and righteousness.

The steps are: from a focus on *freedom*, we move to a focus on *equality*, to a focus on the *enforcement* of equality, to the enforcement of the *provision* of equality by the State. From there, the process moves to *qualifying* for equality (being of low-income, or from a certain ethnic or gender group, etc.), to *disqualifying* whole segments of the population from State jobs and largesse (too qualified), to legally *entrenching* the qualifications for equality in various charters and codes, to surrendering to unelected judges the last vestiges of democratic self-governance and control over the law. At this stage, the democratic will is entirely replaced by abstract utopian concepts, and the populace is divided against itself into groups based on language, gender, ethnicity, income — or even behaviour, as in the case of homosexuals. From here, the emphasis shifts from democracy, to control of power, which means control of how the abstract rights are interpreted. At this point, a society has arrived at a kind of genteel fascism by dividing itself into warring groups; freedom and morality have now been replaced by rights defined by the State. Some professors at the University of Toronto actually tell their graduate students they should leave Canada because they will never get a job in academe if they are white, male, and English-speaking. Ability is subordinated to officially defined equality.

At this sad stage, whatever is legal is deemed right, and morality is a dead issue. If the court says a baby is not a human being, then it is not. If it says homosexuality is natural and right, then it is. If it says it is right to pay someone more than he is worth, or to hire someone just because of his skin colour, or to grant early parole to a vicious rapist, then it is. Lights out at this point. The ship is heading to the bottom.

We like to believe we will never reach such a stage. (That's what the civilized French, Russians, and Germans believed, too.) But if there is sufficient perceived economic inequity — or perceived group differences — or multiple ethnic allegiances — or perceived poverty, combined with egalitarian fervour, North America will not be exempt from such human frenzy . . . the various steps precedent to terror have already been taken; all safeguards gradually weakened. The illusion that it cannot happens to us, that we are too civilized and too good, is precisely what allows the process to begin. Once we dare admit it is here, it is too late. The levers of righteous power have been captured, the student sheepishly unthinking; and correctness — and fear of incorrectness — are everywhere, all honest differing opinion squelched. Remember, the largest occupational group of Germany's National Socialist Party was — educated elementary school teachers.[16] And the major radical forces behind the French Revolution were not the people, as we are led to believe. France's new revolutionary ideals and utopian schemes of universal brotherhood were "monopolized by a relatively small intellectual elite" who "were all devotees of Reason and votaries of Virtue."[17] As Tocqueville warned of the French Revolution: "It was not want, but ideas, that brought about the great revolution . . . chimerical ideas . . . doctrines of ultra-centralization which had at last persuaded large numbers that it depended on the state not only to save them from want, but to place them in easy, comfortable circumstances."[18] Sounds to me like our knowledge class at work. That's why U.S. Senator Huey Long said, as mentioned earlier, that fascism will come to America in the form of democracy.

## It Begins at the Top

*You know I don't think society is an end in itself. I think a person is the most important thing. Anything else is there to assist the person to fulfill one's life . . . everything else is subordinate. Even collectivities."*
ANTONIO LAMER, CHIEF JUSTICE OF THE SUPREME COURT OF CANADA,
*GLOBE AND MAIL,* APRIL 17, 1992

Well, in what amounts to a stunningly simplistic — and garbled — statement of our current value system, the Chief Justice — no Tocqueville, he — said it all. He thinks the fulfilment of the autonomous individual is the highest good, and that the highest Court of law is there to assist in the fulfilment of the individual by means of abstract rights interpreted by philosopher kings such as the Chief Justice. We must be as clear as possible about what this thinking means, for the judge and his colleagues are the vanguard of our new legalistic and antifamily world.

The top-down State, in a vain effort to ensure egalitarian outcomes for all, and votes and control for itself, establishes charters and bills of rights designed to dictate and provide equal outcomes to individual citizens — the voting masses. At this point, there is produced an inherent clash between the rights of autonomous individuals and the traditional privileges of protected groups. Right and wrong cease to be moral matters and become, increasingly, merely legal questions decided not within the person, but by outside judges and tribunals. Freedom is no longer a matter of doing whatever you wish, provided you do not break the law; rather, it is living according to behaviour dictated by the law. At this point the law, instead of simply telling you what you cannot do, increasingly tells you what you must do. As this style of democracy advances, any special protected status formerly afforded to groups such as the family gets attacked by those who see such groups as discriminatory, or exclusive, or conferring special tax, legal, or social privilege to some (such as the married) and not to others (such as the unmarried). Then, because final concrete decisions on abstract rights are controlled from the top by the judges who interpret the charters, and because equality is the highest goal, all intermediate groupings may be seen as discriminatory (or hierarchical or patriarchal) institutions that need aggressively to be stripped of all privileges. As Justice Lamer said: "Everything . . . is subordinate" to the individual.

What happens in the final stages, then, is that the sole legal relationship is between the State and the individual, controlled by judges who are now called upon not to *apply the law, but to judge the laws* themselves. They are now asked to make what Justice Lamber describes as "a political call," for which a judge has to be a "socially and politically well-balanced person" (*Globe and Mail* articles, above). Well, if you incline toward planned, egalitarian societies, you will believe free societies in which natural individual, family, and group differences are allowed to flourish are not well-balanced. Right?

And so it is that the civil war of values discussed throughout this book culminates in a clash between radically different concepts of what is good law — a clash that affects our lives at every level. In the final, sclerotic stages of such egalitarian societies as we have created, advocates of abstract rights attempt feverishly to permeate every level of personal, social, governmental, commercial, (and now "environmental") life with a network of total legislation and regulation, in the face of which any irregularities are deemed unbearable, subject to increasingly harsh penalties and absurd justifications. Worst of all, powerful lobby groups, financed by the State itself, vie to influence the meaning of abstract rights in order to shape society from the top down. Inevitably, this process produces a ludicrous world in which contract gradually replaces conduct in daily life, and human sexual, business, and social relations become emptied of moral standards and filled with legal ones. The effect of all this? Increasingly wary citizens see one another and all professional relations as potential legal crises; and then each citizen, each lover, each teacher, each spouse, each entrepreneur retreats inwardly, withdrawing from the kind of commonly understood behaviour made possible only through a consensus on civil conduct. We end up with a kind of legal separatism that stifles such conduct and creates a litigious society.

Let us now turn to four examples, at the personal, community, national, and international levels, to see how the Law, increasingly based on contract, first subordinates, then dissolves the inherited standards of just conduct of a democratic society as it strives relentlessly to enforce the fulfilment of abstract individual rights.

## THE PERSONAL LEVEL

### "No Means No" . . . Maybe

> I know it's wrong [sexual harassment] when it makes me feel sour afterward, when it makes me feel squishy or uncomfortable.
>
> FEMALE NEWSPAPER EXECUTIVE, TORONTO STAR, OCTOBER 18, 1991

The boss tells a female employee: "You're a very exciting woman." If she is offended, she will call this "sexual harassment." If she likes it, she may end up his wife.

It is a tragic fact of modern life that as the law weakens with respect to true rape, a vicious offence for which not very long ago men were properly hanged, ordinary sexual relations between men and women are now trivialized by such expressions as "date rape" and garbled phases like "no means no." So in the past, when the sexual conduct of females and males was more guarded and respectful by custom, men swung for their impetuosity. And it was primarily males who, to protect their women, insisted on such punishment. But now that the levellers have their way, and crime is said to be caused by society, true rapists walk the streets after only a few years in jail — and a bit of therapy — to try their luck again, as almost all rapists do. Having denied the biological differences of nature in the interests of egalitarian policy, and now properly frightened, our permissive elites attempt to forge laws to govern the most intimate sexual relationships of innocent people who have forgotten how to behave. Their idea is that you can eliminate rape by first creating sex contracts for males and females, and then educating the judges in how to interpret them. This notion has resulted in what the meticulous sociologist Neil Gilbert called a "phantom epidemic," with dynamics similar to those of the Salem witch hunts.

By confusing contract with conduct, and the law with moral behaviour, we are luring thousands of young people into an emotional free-fire zone exploited by equal numbers of careless or even unstable men and women, and worst of all are teaching decent young women the dangerously false view that human biological conduct is a matter of egalitarian legalisms and explicit intent; that if they say the right words, danger can be avoided. The predictable result is more rape, real and false, and more trials. The much-promoted egalitarian idea of sexual freedom based on contract, instead of conduct, is a trap for both young men and women, and it diminishes the meaning and horror of real rape. It is also a misleading extension into our times of the cult of reason and the cult of nature, the devotees of which always attempt to reduce complex human behaviour to a few extraordinarily inadequate premises.

Just think about it. "No means no" is a silly phrase. First of all, if it clearly meant no, we wouldn't have to say it twice. But we do so because sometimes we aren't sure we mean it, or that others who say it mean it. After all, language is a powerful tool precisely because it is so fluid and potentially deceptive. When someone rushes up to tell us he is getting married, and we say "No-o-o-o!," we actually mean we're amazed and delighted. We don't mean "no" at all. Often when our children or grandchildren ask beguilingly for a treat, we say "no" at first because we don't want them to take treats for granted, though we may have every intent of giving in eventually. We are using the word for behaviour control, not for denial, and usually they know it, too. In tough negotiations we most often start with "no," knowing full well that we are being unreasonable and may have to back down to some compromise. "No," is a powerful bargaining chip often used to manipulate, even to heighten emotional response. In short, the communication power of language springs not solely from its clarity, but also from its marvellous ambiguity. Radical lawyers, feminists, and ministers of justice who walk about insisting that when "women say 'no' they mean 'no,' and it's up to men to understand it" (Justice Minister Kim Campbell, *Globe and Mail*, December 13, 1991), are blinded by legalisms and need some education in semantics.

The ultimate meaning of all language is determined not merely through denotation (the narrow literal meaning), but through connotation (the total context of meaning), which may be internally or externally controlled. For example, if a woman gives a clear "no" with obvious sternness of voice and demeanour as she pushes the man toward the door, she confirms the dictionary meaning of the word; but if she says "no" with a slip of a smile or taunting tilt of the head, or as she coyly lifts her door key from her pocket, it has another meaning entirely. Same word. Different meaning. The test of consent ought to be not what she says she meant, but what a disinterested bystander would reasonably interpret from the situation.

Or again, take the external context. She may say "no" after torrid foreplay, pulling her date forward physically even as she denies him — and herself — verbally. In fact, much of the excitement of sexual love can arise from such sexually contradictory messages, ones in which the denier herself may find simultaneous self-denial and yielding — and control of the male — auto-erotic. After all, no one except perhaps a feminist lawyer would think that the true passion and vertigo of love have any necessary or direct relationship to explicit language. In love and passion, it's all innuendo. Never mind the kinky world of sado-masochistic personalities, where pleasure is specifically derived from contradictions between pain and pleasure, denial and consent.

And anyone familiar with the history of romantic love in the Western world, from the medieval *Romance of the Rose* to Molly Bloom's famous soliloquy in *Ulysses*, knows that the whole secret to this powerful tradition may be found in the role of calculated, diminishing resistance and denial by the female in the context of her eventual submission to the adoring male in a final "yes, yes, yes." Delicious. It is precisely this female resistance coupled with the charm of seduction that excites and drives the amorous male to higher levels of ardour — eventually a boon to both parties. Most self-respecting men, when faced with a woman who says "yes" to their initial advances, instead of the appropriate "no" that means "try harder, I'm no pushover," look for someone a little more challenging. A clear "yes" in the place of an ambiguous "no" is often the sign of a too-easy woman (ask any woman).

Alas, in a world of failing conduct, we prefer administrative, contractual sex to the real thing. In Gilbert's follow-up study of the 6195 women *Ms* magazine defined as "rape victims," three-quarters of whom denied they had in fact been raped, 42 percent later engaged in consensual sex with the men who had allegedly (according to the *Ms* definition) "raped" them, as did 55 percent of the male "rapists" with their putative victims.[19] In a recent *Chatelaine* article, a social worker said that many of the women who phoned her rape crisis centre did so to ask, "Was I raped?"[20]

Contrary to the hysteria of radical rape catastrophists (one such radical declared that "yes" sometimes means "no"), who shout that one in every two women has been raped, Gilbert showed these were "advocacy figures," designed for "consciousness raising." In other words, they are lies. The real rate, based on the U.N. index and corrected for underreporting, is 114 per 100,000 people for the United States, and 30 for Canada. As writer Barbara Amiel succinctly puts it, feminists "define date rape in a mischievous manner to include any situation in which a woman is persuaded to engage in sex she later regrets."[21] Amiel neatly summarizes the problem when she writes that "the criminal justice system is being used [by radicals] to monitor the sexual arrangements between consenting heterosexual adults in [North] America"; and the result has been "to outlaw and stigmatize normal courtship patterns." She further insists that much of the thrust of this hysteria has its origin in the lesbian male-hating — and family-hating — politics of radical feminism — a politics that attempts to cast all women as virtuous, self-controlled wee things, incapable of either connotative or self-contradictory behaviour, and all men as uncontrolled violent rapists. Nonsense.

Mind you, it's a lot harder to stop a heated bull than one that's grazing. Everyone knows that. That's why all societies based on conduct instead of contract are chock-a-block with moral cautions, especially to girls, from the mothers of the world. Such as: "Any girl who goes to a man's apartment alone is asking for trouble." (Fifty-five percent of the women in the *Ms* study had been drinking.) Or, "If you were both drinking, what do you expect?" Or, "Don't walk down dark alleys." Fathers, too, have warnings for sons, such as: "Remember, a stiff member hath no conscience." (That one from my own dad, when I was 18 — to watch out for girls wanting babies. Even though they said "no," they may have wanted to force you into a marriage.)

Alas, we are seeing the end-state of egalitarian legalism as it invades even our most intimate relations in the name of autonomism. "The bill says women have a right to be autonomous with respect to their bodies," pronounced the justice minister (Toronto *Star*, April 8, 1992). But as Alan Borovoy, general counsel for the Canadian Civil Liberties Association, said, from the original "no means no bill," one could apply the word "rape" even to "teenage petting." Such a law signals that a new sexual terrorism has enlisted the law of contract to compensate for the failure of conduct. But conduct is the only sure safeguard. Age-old sanctions against sexual looseness — not walking alone at night, not drinking with strange men in their apartments, and saying "no" at the door instead of when your panties are off — are still valuable admonitions. You can be sure that officials like Marion Boyd, Ontario's minister responsible for women's issues, either has no teenage daughters or is suffering from ideological myopia when she writes that "a woman has the right to say — or convey — no to sexual involvement. It doesn't matter what she wears, who she talks to, or what she drinks" (Toronto *Star*, April 7, 1992). Oh? Tell our neighbourhood high-school teacher that. She is appalled at teenage female students who arrive for class with bosoms spilling from their blouses, and shorts so high cut, she says, you can see the bare creases of their fannies. The minister's shallow notions are just another move away from personal responsibility.

But the people are not fooled. In a poll, 48 percent of Canadians said "Women are sometimes or often responsible for their own sexual harassment because of the way they dress or behave" (*Globe and Mail*, December 4, 1991). In short, no one disagrees that a woman has the *right* to say "no"; but everyone knows it's possible to say one thing and mean another, and possible to indicate that meaning connotatively through voice tonality, facial expression, or dress. That's what a "teaser" does — and other women are the first to recognize and condemn such behaviour. Feminist Marian Botsford Fraser of Ottawa writes that the law "should impress upon men that they do not get to act first and ask later."[22] Agreed. But it also ought to impress upon women that they do not get to act first and deny later. As Professor Robert Martin of the University of Western Ontario's law faculty says, the contract-law model of offer and acceptance is inappropriate for sex. "I would think that any adult is perfectly aware that it doesn't work that way" (*Globe and Mail*, June 16, 1992).

The real subject at issue here is not whether a woman has said no, but *when* she ought to say it. The rules of conduct always made that clear, because they were always based on common-sense acknowledgment of the basic sexual differences between males and females. But because radicals, especially feminists, refuse to acknowledge these differences, they invoke the law of contract to force equality, despite the danger to young women. Since the rules of conduct fail us, however, the rules of contract must rely on the intent of the parties, which is necessarily private and never very clear. So instead of helping society reconstitute the protections afforded by traditional sexual conduct, then prosecuting the hell out of true rapists, the law sides with the modern egalitarian religion of abstract rights and denial of sexual and biological differences. It allies itself with the revolt against social authority in the name of a unisex utopia.

The height of legal idiocy was surely reached when Sheila MacIntyre, of the radical feminist (and handsomely government-funded) Legal Education Action Fund (LEAF), intoned: "Consent at a minimum must be overt words or gestures which unequivocally convey [to a reasonable observer] affirmative agreement to sexual action" (*Globe and Mail*, November 21, 1991). Well, what's a "minimum"? And how about covert words, ironic words, demur words, entreaties, double entendres, sarcastic words, sly words, flirtatious words, coy words, coquettish words, and so on? And who does all this with a "reasonable observer" in the room? And what is reasonable, anyway? And who decides exactly how unequivocal? Or how affirmative? And what constitutes sexual "action?"

Well, when we have to hand out blank legal contracts to our sons to co-sign with their dates, or when public officials like the assistant dean of Vassar College actually condone false accusations of date rape on the grounds that this will force young men to re-evaluate their relationships with women,[23] I say the law has wholly assisted with the demolition of ordinary personal conduct.

## THE COMMUNITY LEVEL

### How Fair Becomes Foul
Perhaps the most obvious example of the clash between the egalitarian ideals and laws that support the welfare State, and those supportive of the family, is found in community welfare policy. Clearly, such law could be designed to foster either family formation or individual autonomy, but not both. Although many welfare documents in our welfare State still give lip service to the idea of family formation, the actual effect of much social policy — something controlled and dictated by the law — is to create individual dependency on the State by adversely taxing marriage and family formation. Here are two examples from Ontario — a typical North American jurisdiction — that speak for themselves. We need look no further to discover why the family-based civilization of the West is threatened by the egalitarian State.

### The "Spouse in the House"
Whenever a person applies for welfare assistance in Ontario, the question of need is assessed according to total family income and

assets of the applicant, spouse, and dependants. Married status is defined either by legal marriage or by "co-residence" in a spousal relationship for three continuous years.

However, if the co-resident is not a legal spouse (the definition is very slippery, as we shall see), the income and assets of the co-residing partner are not considered in any assessment of "need." This means that if you are legally married, your chances of getting welfare assistance are fewer than if you are a single parent or are co-habiting. Here's how it works for two hypothetical families, one married, the other not.

The Smiths have been married for five years, have two children together, and pay $1000 a month rent for a townhouse. Mr. Smith earns $35,000 a year, and his wife raises the children at home. They are not eligible for welfare assistance because their *total family income* is too high.

Next door to the Smiths lives Miss Jones. She has two children born out of wedlock, and also pays $1000 a month rent. She has lived with a man for the past year who is not the father of her children. He happens to work with Mr. Smith and also earns $35,000 a year. However, solely because Miss Jones and her partner *are not married*, she is eligible for approximately $1200 a month welfare assistance. This raises the Joneses' total household income to $50,000 a year, $14,400 of which is tax free. To add insult to injury, if Miss Jones gets a job, she can hire her partner to care for the children while she is working, and get reimbursed for her daycare costs — which she could not do if she married him.

The advantage to the unmarried household persists because the definitions of "family" and "spouse" in the law have become so loose, and the will to privilege the legitimate family so weak, that welfare policy ends by establishing a powerful economic incentive to avoid the commitment of marriage. In other words, if you want assistance from the State, you are a fool to marry. In large measure, this counsel is intentional, and ideologically driven. The ancient animus against the family, from Plato onward, is fuelled, as we saw earlier, by the egalitarian/utopian drive to eliminate all differences between individual citizens and distribute the goods of society equally to all, irrespective of personal effort. The moral justification, remember, is that all persons are equally good or deserving, and were social conditions the same for all, an equitable world would prevail. That is why modern social radicals, liberal judges and, in particular, feminist lobby groups have striven to commandeer the resources of the State to eliminate the "dependency" of women — especially mothers — on the family. For interdependence, they want independence or autonomy. That is why legal groups, radical lawyers, and charter-supporting judges have intentionally interpreted or designed the law to focus on the individual, not on the family unit. And that is why a single woman or man today may live as a married one, enjoying the income of a partner while drawing a single-person's income from the State. (There are some 850,000 "lone-parent" families in Canada.)

There are some frightful examples of how reality is distorted to accommodate this shift in morality. One Ontario judge (in *Pitts v. Commissioner of Social Services*, 1985) really stretched things. This case involved a boyfriend who visited the applicant woman daily, frequently stayed overnight, vacationed with her, used her home as his mailing address, and gave her some financial support. The judge decided that all this was no different from being a "close friend" and allowed her claim for support. In another case (*Szuts v. Commissioner* [etc.], 1985), the judge was so keen to provide assistance to a woman who had a working live-in partner for over 16 years, that he actually ruled she was living both as a "single" person *and* as a "spouse" at the same time — but not enough as a spouse to deny support.

And as expected, the radical lawyer's group, LEAF, has launched Charter legal challenges against the whole idea of defining welfare need on the basis of marriage and the family, on the grounds that welfare regulations discriminate on the basis of sex and marital status (section 15) and therefore deny single parents the right to life, liberty, and security of the person (section 7). Notice that there is no section of the Charter defending "security of the family." Oh, and as a final ploy such challenges assert that the supervisors of the State are too snoopy. Investigations into the personal life of a recipient living on welfare are deemed to violate the right to privacy. The idea here is to use the Charter to convert welfare into a guaranteed income supplement as a right; no questions asked. As discussed, such arguments stem from the belief that all economic differences are caused by a bad system (free enterprise) and have no connection to individual merit. Welfare payments are seen as a reparation to those badly treated by the system. Therefore, how a person of low income lives, or spends the money provided by others, is no one else's affair. Individual responsibility in such a system is not a topic for discussion.

A welfare "family" will be viewed not as a single economic unit, but as *two separate units that happen to be cohabiting*. Precisely what the levellers have always wanted.

### How the Law Encourages Dependency

This is a summary of just one Ontario program, called Support Towards Employment Program (STEP), designed to encourage welfare recipients to work without being cut off from welfare. What would you do if you were in the position of either of the two women below?

Each earns $30,000 a year, has two dependent children under 12, and pays rent of $680 a month. *Both work full-time*. The first woman has decided it is not right to apply for welfare at her income level. The second figures you take what you can get, and has applied for social assistance through STEP.

| *First Woman* (Refuses welfare assistance) | |
|---|---:|
| Gross earnings per month | $2,500 |
| Less all applicable taxes/deductions | 700 |
| Less daycare costs | 400 |
| Net income | $1,400 |
| | |
| *Second Woman* (Gets welfare assistance) | |
| Gross earnings per month | $2,500 |
| Less applicable taxes/deductions | 700 |
| Less $175 per month (deducted through STEP) | 175 |
| Subtotal | $1,625 |
| Less 25% of subtotal (through STEP) | $406 |
| Less daycare costs | $400 |
| Net income (after all STEP adjustments) | $819 |

At this point, the second woman is worse off than the first, whose net income is $1400. However, watch what happens as the welfare assistance clicks in.

Assistance due to the second woman is calculated (1992 figures)[24] by taking what her welfare assistance would be if she were not working at all ($1347) and subtracting her after-STEP-deductions income shown above ($819), to arrive at what she will now get from welfare: $1347 - $819 = $528 per month, or $6336 per annum, not counting extras — such as winter clothing allowance, back-to-school allowance, etc., etc. But because the $528 is tax free, its real value is, say, $600 a month, which means her total net *after-tax* income is now $1947 per month, or $23,364 per annum (from a gross income of $37,000). In short, she ends up with $547 per month more disposable income than the first woman, merely for having applied for welfare. If she combines this with the spouse-in-the-house situation, above, she can live very well indeed. She is then being handsomely rewarded for refusing marriage and claiming dependency on the State.[25]

### Other Antifamily Weapons of the Law

There are many more ways in which the law is antifamily. Here are a few, based on the 1992 tax year. Some of the ways, we are told, will be eliminated in 1993 (indicated with an *), but all warrant attention. The contrasts are glaring, and the examples bear watching because another government may simply reverse any new provisions. The examples suggest how a society that forgets the importance of the family soon creates the tools with which to demolish it. Hear this: Although some current tax and legal privileges of common-law spouses will be eliminated, this change merely has the effect of providing the government with more tax revenue. Such changes *do not increase the privileges* or reduce the costs of the legitimate family vis-à-vis single persons, as they should. They merely remove some of the former benefits received by couples pretending to be married, who paid none of the costs of marriage.

**Principal Residence.*** Surely the greatest tax-free windfall in the life of most Canadian couples is the exemption from capital-gains tax on a married couple's principal residence. This is the family nest-egg and retirement bonus, all in one. But a married couple can claim this exemption only on *one* residence, even if two are owned — say, a home and a cottage — as long as they are married. However, if they are an *unmarried* couple, they can claim both the house *and* the cottage as principal residences, and gain handsomely indeed. Over the past few decades, this provision has likely meant many millions in bonuses for non-marriage.

**Income Splitting.*** Under section 74.1 of the Income Tax Act, married couples may not "split" income or capital gains for the purposes of lowering the higher earnings (and therefore taxes) of one spouse. Unmarried couples have been allowed to report separately for a long time, giving them the same effect as splitting income. Incidentally, I would propose that all, and only, legally married couples in Canada be allowed to split their incomes before taxation. This would have the simultaneous effect of lowering total family taxation and strongly validating the wife's homemaking role in the legal and tax codes of the nation — something long overdue.

**Registered Retirement Savings Plan (RRSP) Rollovers.\*** An RRSP is one of the few tax shelters available, and although the estate of a deceased spouse is normally deemed disposed of, and therefore taxable, surviving legal spouses are permitted to "roll over" RRSP money to a spouse's RRSP and avoid taxation. As of June 12, 1990, this provision was also offered to common-law spouses, or to those who are unmarried but are the parents of a common child. This provision, which has the effect of granting married privileges to the unmarried, will be eliminated, as it should be.

**Child Tax Credits.\*** In the calculation of child tax credits, the income of both married spouses is considered (and higher income means lower credits); if, however, a couple is unmarried (whether or not one, or both, are the natural parents), only the income of one parent is counted — a clear bias in favour of the unmarried, which, happily, will be eliminated.

**Alimony and Separation Payment Deductions**. A separated or divorced husband may deduct from his own pre-tax income all support payments made to his former wife. This makes some sense if he is also supporting a second family. But the provision is applicable to a single divorced husband as well — as long as he stays divorced. If, for example, he later wishes to remarry the same woman, he will lose the deduction. So many divorced men say, "If I can deduct the costs of a family when I'm divorced, why couldn't I deduct it when I was married?" (My proposal to allow income splitting for all married couples would give such a benefit in a different way.)

Even more bizarre is that unmarried partners, as we saw for Ontario, may have a right to support if they have lived together "continuously for a period of not less than three years" or in a relationship of "some permanence . . ." Well, this wording has been rather liberally interpreted, to say the least. For example, on-again, off-again lovers are deemed not to have broken the continuity of the relationship if there was an "intent" to keep the relationship alive. As for "permanence"? In one case, *Labbe v. McCullough* (1975),

1. Deadbeat Dads →
2. Males - ① refuse to pay - not fair.
① paying makes k.

TURNING WRONGS INTO RIGHTS   569

support was awarded to the "spouse" even though the couple lived together for only four weeks, broke up, then tried again for a further two weeks, for a total of six. Needless to say, homosexual couples are lobbying hard to have all such legal support provisions applied to themselves. Under the force of the liberal antifamily methods, the courts are bending.

**"Trusts" and Property.** Part of the law's movement away from the defence of the family unit and toward the defence of the autonomous individual — very strong in recent years — is the creation of so-called "trusts," which deem property to belong to both parties, even though unmarried, and attempt to calculate the "unjust enrichment" of one party (usually the man) due to the "free" services of the other (usually the woman).

For example, the courts sometimes construe that a "resulting trust" has evolved between unmarried partners if, during a "marriage-like relationship," contributions toward the purchase of an asset have been made not just in money but in things like "services," rent, or groceries, and if there was a common intention to share the property equally. This is a way of conferring assets of an unmarried partner as if the partners were married. Its effect is to dilute further the privileges of, and the pressure to commit to, legal marriage — in this case, property privileges — by making marriage unnecessary to obtain the privilege.

In the event there was no common intention to share equally (tough to prove in a breakup), then the courts fight even harder to dilute legal marriage by creating something called a "constructive trust," which means that regardless of any common intentions, the provisions of "services" by one person to another, even the provision of household services alone (as in *Sorochan v. Sorochan* (1986)), can constitute the basis for a constructive trust. In short, the courts will deem a marriage-like right to another's legal property if you have cleaned house for him or her.

The courts have reduced much of this issue to one that is purely commercial by applying to live-in arrangements commercial concepts like "quantum meruit," which in employer-employee situations allowed the courts to determine the value of a service rendered and then compensate a person according to standard labour costs. In other words, the courts establish a contract price for the service. In *Chrispen v. Topham* (1986), a female applied for compensation on the grounds that she had provided "housekeeping" services to a man with whom she had lived for one year. The court awarded her a lump sum based on the minimum wage, discounting 50 percent for the fact that she would have had to clean house for herself anyway and thus would have benefited from her own services.

Thus do we mire in frivolity. Obviously, she would not have cleaned only half the house had she lived alone; nor did she claim for his "services" to her. When two people decide to live together, each will calculate personal costs and benefits that cause the relationship to continue, or to end. In the absence of an explicit contract between two free people, the law should not intrude to invent one.

On top of all this, the courts have liberal powers to award an unmarried partner of a person now dead an annual income from the deceased's estate, a lump-sum payment, a transfer of property, or possession and use of the property. Legal marriage is inessential to such gains. The same is true for pension rights.

One last matter. As a further demonstration of the law's antifamily bias, children as young as 16 may (in many jurisdictions, like Ontario) have a dispute with their parents, leave home, and apply for generous social assistance. This support may be given regardless of the opinion of the parents, without their consent, and regardless of their income. In short, sons and daughters of millionaires may, if they choose, live on the efforts of other citizens. Eligibility for this age group is only a matter of each case-worker's administrative discretion, based on whether undefined "special circumstances" exist that necessitate the child's living away from home. Students who claim welfare may do so regardless of the financial condition of their parents, and teachers (paid by tax dollars extracted from the same parents) are not required to tell those parents of their runaway children's whereabouts. In fact, teachers are required to inform the welfare worker, but not the parents, of the child's behaviour and progress. This is an example of the collusion of the State, the schools, and the law versus the family.

Such things are permitted to happen because of the manner in which the law is written and interpreted. For the fact is, all laws discriminate. The question for our nation to decide is whether such laws should discriminate in favour of the individual and against the family unit, or in favour of the family unit and against the individual. Our Charter is worded in such a way that there is ample room to do either. Which way we go depends on who advances the legal challenges, and on the values and ideology of the judges who interpret them.

# THE NATIONAL LEVEL

## The Court Party

On April 17, 1982, Canada was changed from a democracy, which reaches for perfection yet often fails, to a plutocracy, which is by nature flawed. On one day, and owing to the compulsive efforts of a single prime minister, with nary a scrap of input from the citizens, or their approval (it was not sought), Parliament, formerly the elected lawmaker of the nation, became a mere proposer of laws to a bench of unelected scholar kings and queens.

Now these are harsh words, especially to the ears of ordinary Canadians, who still think the Charter a good thing. Why do they think so? Primarily for the reason that it sounds good. Why should we not have great affection for a document that proposes to protect us from the evils of tyrannical government while showering us with a cornucopia of benefits, thus guarding us from the slings and arrows of outrageous fortune (as Hamlet put it)? There is only one good reason, which is that it does nothing of the kind. In fact, no charter can offer what ours proposes simply because all charters and constitutions are filled with hopelessly abstract concepts and intentions. They all but beg judges to fill them with their own meanings. That is why — and how — the Declaration of the Rights of Man and Citizen, as well as the Constitution of the Soviet Union — two of the noblest-sounding documents in all of human history — became in practice licences for the instigation of unspeakable injustices at the hands of the prevailing powers. So the historical lesson is clear. Charters, codes, and the like do not provide rights or freedoms; they merely predicate how those things shall be disposed in society by the powers that manipulate the charters. Once we rid ourselves of the understandable but dangerous misconception that the words on the page are the things themselves, we can ask how it is that the Charter has altered the way in which we enjoy our democracy and our freedoms.

## *Common Law vs. Charter Law: Freedom Planet vs. Rights Planet*

Imagine yourself landing on a new planet, like Earth, you believe uninhabited. The feeling of freedom is wonderful, for there is no one to tell you what to do. But you are suddenly met by a delegation of friendly beings who inform you that this is Freedom Planet, and that others have come before you. The rules are that you will be allowed to live there entirely as you wish, except for a set of laws of mutual restraint, specifying what you cannot do. The extraordinary thing about life on Freedom Planet is that so long as you do not break any of these simple laws, you will never hear of them again and can do exactly as you wish for the rest of your life. This is how the common law, painfully evolved over centuries in British-derived countries, was intended to work. The rules are made in common by elected citizens, and changed as needed in a Parliament that expresses the will of the people, for mutual benefit.

One day, after many happy years, you are invited to fly to Rights Planet, nearby, and you do so. This planet is inhabited by beings who tell you that there are common laws here, as on Freedom Planet. However, lest you mistakenly start thinking you are as free as there, you need to know that Rights Planet also has a charter document. The charter, you learn, defines all your freedoms in specific words, the meanings of which are controlled neither by yourself, as on Freedom Planet, nor by people you have elected, but by a group of unelected lifetime judges. In short, on Rights Planet your freedom is completely qualified, may from time to time be subtly altered without your permission, and may even entail your being made to do specific things or behave in certain ways to ensure that the lives of others — as defined by such judges — are no worse than your own. In other words, not only are the so-called rights and freedoms here conferred by the State (and therefore may be withdrawn by it), but as well, the language of the charter may actually *compel* you to behave in certain dictated ways.

By this example we can see that whereas the common law simply allowed society to *evolve* lawfully according to the sum of all individual wills, charter law fully intends to *direct* the evolution of society according to certain pre-determined abstract concepts — a rather large difference.

Modern charter law is a system that was first visible in modern times in the French Declaration. It was built on French notions of the *dirigiste* (directing) State and has since spread all over the Western world. It has greatly subdued and hobbled the common law almost everywhere — except in the United Kingdom, where common law first arose by custom and which still has no written "constitution." You might say that just as the common law was the perfect embodiment of the free bottom-up society, charter law is the perfect embodiment of the controlled top-down State. Needless to say, charter law is preferred by the intellectual, or knowledge, class of educated elites because it enables them to alter society in a utopian direction without having to appeal to the broad democratic mass of the people, whom they generally disrespect. How does it do so? Very simply, and through what Professor F.L. Morton and others call "the Court Party."[26]

### Kings Without Crowns

The Court Party is a phrase coined to say, in no uncertain terms, that the Charter — with its entourage of supporters and judges — constitutes a political party additional to mainstream Canadian parties. Under common law, judges simply applied the laws of Parliament and interpreted them as they thought Parliament meant them to be. In contrast, under charter law they judge the laws themselves, comparing them to the abstract words of the Charter to ensure they measure up, and then either modify them according to their personal interpretation, or strike them down. The abstract Charter words inevitably constitute a camouflage for the judge's political, social, and moral views (what Justice Lamer termed the "political call").

For this reason, as Morton says, Canada has passed from a nation that lived under *parliamentary supremacy* (of the people) to one that now lives under *judicial supremacy* (of the judges). Not the Charter itself, but how the Charter is interpreted now controls how all law in Canada is interpreted. Sadly, political interest groups can therefore circumvent the entire democratic-parliamentary process and apply pressure directly to the judicial process at every conceivable level. Instead of trying to persuade the people to support their views, Charter activists can pass over the people and transform those views into law simply by challenging Parliament through the courts; hence, the crucial importance for interest groups (as in the United States) of placing sympathetic judges on the Supreme Court.

As it turns out, judges faced with legal words on the page always have an option. One choice — favoured by centuries of legal tradition until very recent times — is to restrict the meaning of the words to the intent of the elected representatives who wrote the law. This is called the "original understanding" approach.

Another option is to be very liberal and read all sorts of things into the words they think the original framers missed, or ought to have intended, or would have intended had they lived today, and so on. This is called the "living tree" approach. Conservatives, who believe that out of respect for parliaments and the democratic tradition judges should *apply* the law and not *make* the law, prefer the former approach. As Robert Bork put it, a judge should "never make new constitutional rights, or destroy old ones. Any time he does so, he destroys the limits of his own authority and, for that reason, also violates the rights of the legislature and the people."[27] But liberals, who want to direct social outcomes and therefore have a vested interest in violating the wishes of the people, vastly prefer the latter method, and in fact delight in making new rights (leading to utopia) and destroying old ones (which aren't egalitarian enough, or are too privileged). In fact, Canadian judges have endorsed the liberal approach by holding that "the spirit of this new 'living tree' planted in friendly Canadian soil should not be stultified by narrow technical, literal interpretations . . ."[28] In essence, they argue that as philosopher kings, judges ought to be allowed to apply the law not according to what is "legal," but according to what their sensibilities tell them is right. Spectacles such as the savage U.S. Supreme Court nomination hearing of Judge Robert Bork are an example of the clash between the two schools of thought. It was the civil war of values fought out before the cameras by the Court Party in the United States, and it is occurring daily in Canada in a less public but no less insidious way.

The Court Party is basically made up of all the constitutional stakeholders, who amount to "an emerging new power structure"[29] that is profoundly antidemocratic. Far from conferring rights on the people, it robs them of that most basic democratic right of all — to make and change their own laws. Morton details several of its approaches. Most often the Court Party leans on the egalitarian defence of individual "rights" levelled against the privileges of established political, economic, and social institutions (the family, for example). It achieves its aims directly, through legal argument (as when a group litigates or intervenes in a Charter case); and indirectly, through Charter scholarship, by influencing judicial appointments, and through nefarious "judicial education" seminars — all of which lead to what constitutional scholar Alan Cairns labelled "Charter imperialism."[30] Professor Morton cites the feminist Legal Action and Education Fund (LEAF), which has sapped millions of taxpayers' dollars to advance its causes through the courts, as the prototypical example of such imperialism. In 1984, a spokeswoman confessed this imperialism, saying that LEAF stressed "litigation as a vehicle for social change."[31] LEAF has been joined by a whole bevy of groups that fancy themselves disadvantaged, or victimized, by discrimination, most of whom, Morton stresses, "want to reform society as a whole." They are revolutionaries who succeed with reform only by appealing through the courts for more State action, funding, or services, for the people themselves would never support them. One LEAF litigator aptly said that "the promotion of freedom" calls for the absence of government regulation, but "the promotion of equality" calls for governments "to take positive action." Hence, the enormous growth of the welfare State.[32]

Morton details just how the Court Party is supported by and permeates the welfare State: in public funding agencies, in court personnel and human rights commissions, in the "Charter clearance" process in government itself, and through public funding of the universities that supply so much of the Charter scholarship written by "charterphile" scholars. He also cites the new status of the Attorney-General's office as a "Charter clearance-house" and the influence of in-house government lawyers, administrative tribunals with their thousands of adjudicators, and human rights acts — the policy agenda of which "is not so much to protect society from the state, as to reform society through the state in the name of equality rights."[33] The process is all compounded by reams of charter "scholarship," which, as Cairns has described it, is "purpose driven and laced with advocacy."[34] This "scholarship" in turn has led to "flooding the law reviews" as a strategy for influencing judicial interpretations — and of course for influencing the media.

What all this means, essentially, is that once a country is charter-dominated it becomes changed from the top (primarily through a process of elite influence) and not from the bottom (primarily through a democratic process, as before). As Morton writes: "Whereas previous reformers sought the electoral support of the masses to challenge the power and privilege of the few, for Court Party reformers, the masses are the problem that needs to be reformed."[35]

What are some examples of the way in which Charter challenges have been used to demolish traditional society and the family? Here are a few. Regardless of what we may feel about it, abortion on demand in Canada was brought about not by the will of the people, but by a Charter challenge brought against Canada's abortion law, which succeeded in striking the law down strictly on procedural grounds. Now Parliament, which would formerly have made a new law through the elected representatives of the people, must await direction from the court. This important matter is out of their hands. In Ontario's *Askov* decision, 40,000 people charged by the police with offences — many guilty of very serious crimes — were released solely on Charter grounds that they suffered because of the lack of a "speedy" trial (there was no mention of speedy justice for their victims). In the *Schecter* case (which provided maternity leave for adoptive fathers, but not for natural fathers), *the Court actually ordered the government to spend money* (ours) for a social cause — a right formerly reserved for parliaments. Several U.S. courts have also recently ordered municipalities to raise taxes to fund new social programs. Here's more. Despite the fact that the people want to ban prostitution in their communities, the Court ruled that this violated a prostitute's Charter right to "freedom of expression," a perfect example of top-down law eroding bottom-up community and local family values. (When the phrase "freedom of expression" can apply to philosophical debate, as well as to sex for pay, it becomes a recipe for social anarchy.) As for criminal matters, section 24(2) of the Charter has freed untold numbers of guilty individuals and released them into the community without punishment, for paltry procedural reasons. In Canada today, it is possible to be apprehended for murder, confess to it, yet be acquitted under section 24(2) because — to name only one possibility — the weapon you used was improperly discovered by the police (who may have entered your house, say, with no warrant to catch you).

Even more chilling, Charter law, nationally and internationally, is slowly but aggressively intervening between parents and their children. It does so simply by considering minor children as adult "individuals" at an ever younger age, thereby enforcing their "rights" against their parents, whether in claims for welfare or in access to restricted information, pornography, or abortion — you name it. More and more the law is directing us to listen to and obey the child. There could be no more poignant example of the way in which the egalitarian State, in its constant search for an ever wider constituency, uses the law to convert the key social unit into autonomous political units. Remember, throughout the work of Rousseau and the Romantics (and the John Dewey types in our education system) runs the idea that the child is a special embodiment of natural goodness. So the aim is to nurture this goodness — to prevent it from becoming tainted by an authoritarian world (family, capitalism, religion) that may suppress the inner God in each of us. The Deweyites promoted "process, not product"; they said "teach the child, not the subject" — and ended up teaching neither. It is vital to understand that while this ideology runs through most "rights" thinking, there is never talk of responsibilities or duties. The assumption is that once equalized by rights, all citizens will naturally want to perform duties.

Needless to say, this entire tradition is offset by the contrary idea, found in the work of Freud and most psychoanalysts, in great novels like *The Brothers Karamazov* and lesser ones like *Lord of the Flies*, and in works by all great conservative philosophers and religious thinkers: that in fact each human being, from childhood on, is a seething mass of contradictory passions and illusions which, unfettered and uncontained by discipline and moral authority, may easily wreak havoc upon the world. The child-as-naturally-good view promotes the idea of the child standing alone before the State with a bundle of rights under his arm, prepared to challenge parents with the help of the State. The child-as-needing-moral-discipline view promotes the family as guardian of the needy child, and arbiter of family authority. We must ask why the State, through its charters and its Court Party, is neglecting the latter view and increasingly adopting the former. The two views are in deadly conflict, which again sets the State and the law against the family.

An extraordinary example of this attack upon the privilege of family is found — in all its hallucinatory scholarly splendour and moral distortion — in Professor Bruce Ryder's essay, "Equality Rights and Sexual Orientation: Confronting Heterosexual Family Privilege."[36] Regardless of the subject (regrets for having to discuss this again), this essay, misleading facts and all, stands as a remarkable example of how the Charter is being used by a member of the Court Party to attack family privilege. (You could counter-write Ryder's entire article as a defence of family privilege, and cover the ground very well.) A thorough study of this author's fanatical antifamily argumentation reveals how, in the name of individual equality, the status of the family as a privileged social institution is being dismembered by the liberal ethos of late democracy; and how, consequently, our society is being reformed from the top into special interest groups, each guarding its own rights. The writer complains that heterosexuals and the natural family in Canada are both privileged, and he charges that this is discriminatory (rather, as explained, it is a form of differential status and protection proffered by society on those who commit to social purposes). An example he sorrows over is that the age of consent for homosexual anal intercourse in Canada is 18, whereas for "other sexual acts" (meaning between heterosexuals) it is 14. He argues that because the sexual needs of all humans are the same, treating some differently from others just because they are male and female, or man and wife, is wrong, and he threatens that an evolving jurisprudence is going to end this privilege. (It is.) He writes that the idea that those whose choose to live together must do so in a monogamous, nuclear, patriarchal, heterosexual family unit is (are you ready?) "authoritarian." But society, we might respond, does not prevent him from living in any other way. It has simply said it cannot approve of it or grant similar privileges, because to do so is not productive for society. But this radical is clear about his methods. He states that the purpose of lobbying to prohibit discrimination is "to remove heterosexual privilege," and he wants the State to provide egalitarian sex education in an "even-handed" manner, "avoiding heterosexual indoctrination." He insists that "the legal hegemony of the heterosexual family will continue to be challenged." I'm sure it will be. The Toronto *Star* notes that in the Charter case of homosexuals Pierre Beaulne and Todd Layland, who claimed the right to marry (and compare their plight to discrimination against blacks): "It's the first time the Canadian rules of marriage have been challenged using the Charter" (May 19, 1992). Ryder is teaching the young at Osgoode Hall, once Canada's top law school. I say cut off his public funding.

## THE INTERNATIONAL LEVEL

### Changing the Family from Afar

It is a strange but telling fact that the very same interest groups that characterized the Free Trade Agreement between Canada and the United States as an oppressive invasion of Canadian rights and freedoms, welcome with open arms international treaties that propose to restructure Canadian social and family life along liberal egalitarian lines. International law has become the new focus for dreamlanders and one-worlders hoping to collectivize all humanity.

Two notable treaties that Canada has recently signed and ratified are already having a powerful effect on our nation, and they bid fair to further weaken the bonds of family life throughout the free world. Both these documents are a good read, and it is possible they may have some beneficial effect in tyrannical nations or where social conditions are deplorable. (But do tyrannical nations really care what anyone else thinks?) In a free country such as our own, however, they spell only trouble and more top-down control from meddling bureaucrats.

The first is the United Nations Convention on the Elimination of All Forms of Discrimination Against Women. Canada co-sponsored the initial resolution for this convention, which was subsequently adopted by the U.N. General Assembly. Having played a large role in drawing up the convention, Canada felt pressure to ratify it, which it did on October 21, 1981. It is a matter of some curiosity how such conventions, which are binding on signatory nations, manage to get ratified with no national discussion whatsoever. (This one was heavily promoted and steered by ubiquitious radical feminists.) Once ratified, all other national laws must be aligned with the treaty. Well, no one likes discrimination, so why complain? There'd be no problem, except that such abstract documents always seem to constitute a licence to invade society. So we need to ask about the ideological thrust of the convention, and about what it directs Canadian lawmakers to do.[37]

Well, does this sound like it's focused on discrimination against women?

The preamble of the convention calls for a "new economic order," which is a tip-off to its redistributionist, socialist mentality. Not shy about begging, these people. It also calls for "general and complete disarmament and in particular nuclear disarmament," but it does not mention how we are to protect the peace. And there's even a list of wish-fulfilment about racism, colonialism, and so on. The preamble calls not for equal opportunities for all women, but for "maximum participation of women on equal terms with men . . ." (etc.). There is no mention whatever of the millions of women around the world who prefer to stay home to raise their children and look after their families. Every single health and welfare benefit mentioned in the convention applies only to women *in the labour force*, and there is no mention of part-time employment. There is an obsessive thrust in this document to the effect that women of the world ought to leave their families and enter the workforce full-time as autonomous economic units, fully protected by the State. Gender quotas will be created to enforce this effort. The egalitarian edicts of the convention are so broad that they could mandate all women for military service and authorize the end of single-sex institutions such as schools, convents, and prisons, all in fulfilment of the badly flawed androgynous ideal.

Other articles promote State daycare for all, and order the State to provide "family planning services" as a right to all women. This edict means free contraceptives and abortion, as a right. Planned Parenthood has already jumped on the bedwagon with its international document "The Human Right to Family Planning." However, if as a parent you don't wish your 13-year-old daughter to be provided with such things, your authority is now effectively undermined by busybody bureaucrats at the United Nations. The convention in fact committed Canada to providing free access to abortion. Get it? This policy was imposed on Canadians at the top, and filtered down. It was not decided by the people from the bottom up. The Court Party looks to conventions like this for guidance on such matters, not to the voting citizens. Furthermore, the convention calls for measures to "modify the social and cultural patterns of conduct of men and women . . ." to achieve egalitarian aims. In short, this is Big Brother via the U.N. So-called "antisexist" programs of "re-education" are proposed to break down "stereotypes" of the traditional family. This task includes purging all school textbooks that in any way promote traditional sexual and marital patterns.

Curiously, the "Committee of Experts" from 23 nations, appointed to monitor compliance with this convention — to police it — included 19 dictatorship and 14 nations black-listed by Amnesty International for the use of torture. During a January 1985 review of Canada's "progress," a whole range of countries from this international "committee" chided us, encouraging us to get moving. The Soviet Union said more had to be done to change traditional stereotypes in Canada (maybe concentration camps would do it?), and that men had to be "directed" to do more parenting. Rwanda wanted us to do more to "protect homosexuality" (Rwanda ought to know); Mongolia complained about limited access to abortion in Canada (does Mongolia have a hospital?); East Germany complained of "limited child care" here (when the Berlin Wall came down, did all the Germans run to the East?). Well, there was much more of the same, mostly from countries world-famous for incompetence.

### Sentimental Pawns and the Triumph of Force

*The possibilities for advocacy flower exponentially . . . [this is] a benchmark that you can hold in your hand and take to a municipal council and read in the federal House of Commons and use as supporting material in Charter cases before the Supreme Court of Canada!*

STEPHEN LEWIS, COMMENTING ON THE 1989 U.N. CONVENTION ON
THE RIGHTS OF THE CHILD, TORONTO *STAR*, MAY 8, 1991

This is the image of the revolutionary. Stephen Robespierre Lewis, frothing with indignation and righteousness, waving a piece of paper filled with utopian rights and invoking the power of the State. It's an archetypal scene. This time, it's about giving children "rights" and enforcing them. Please note, there has never been a resolution or a convention at the United Nations to create a charter of family rights, or of parental rights, for one good reason: Egalitarians, as witnessed throughout this book, hate the family. Don't be fooled by the language of their quest, because there can never be any such thing as "children's rights." Children are too young to exercise rights, so someone must always exercise these for them — against their parents. So the only possible rights here are those of the State against the authority of the family.

Now in some times and places, these powers could be a good thing. And it would be wonderful to cleanse the world miraculously of all injustice to children, surely the most sorrowful of all forms of evil. It would be especially nice if we could cleanse the world of all injustices to children brought about by the State itself. Among these, one could number almost every famine in the history of the world, all wars and genocides, revolutions, concentration camps, tortures, and almost limitless other indescribable infamies carried out in the name of "the Sparta of their dreams" as Babbitt described utopian schemes. The family has been the victim, never the perpetrator, in all these things.

So let's look at this convention, too, and ask how it is that Canada's prime minister rushed off to sign it (on May 28, 1990) with no discussion from the nation's 5.7 million families. At present, Canada and its provinces, and about 150 other countries, are adjusting their laws to be in *full compliance* with this convention, which, on September 2, 1990, "took on the force of international law in all ratifying countries."[38] Canada's signing, authorized by Order in Council (Cabinet), required no debate from the Parliament of this land — a land based on freedom, family, free enterprise, and faith; and there was (and is) little knowledge of it among the Canadian people. Nevertheless, all our courts are bound to take the convention into consideration as a guideline to interpreting Canadian statutes. The question, again, is simply this: How can a treaty that will eventually reach into every home in the nation and restructure most parent-child relations be signed and ratified without the full knowledge of the people of Canada?

Here are just a few remarks on some of the more meddlesome provisions. Article 13 grants children "the right to freedom of expression, including the freedom to seek, receive and impart information and ideas of all kinds . . . either orally, in writing . . . in the form of art . . . or through any other media of the child's choice." This wording means that parents will have no enforceable right to control such matters as the type of sex education offered to, or sexual experimentation by, their own children; nor will parents have the right to control what television programs, movies, pornographic magazines, videos, or books their children are allowed. As you can imagine, this is a "children's right" eagerly supported by the mega-billion-dollar North American entertainment, magazine, video, and music industry. And Planned Parenthood is already using this right to prevent concerned parents from halting the free distribution of condoms — through schools and sex clinics — to their underage children.

Article 14 says "parents shall respect the right of the child to freedom of thought, conscience and religion." Parents are only allowed to "provide direction" to the child in the exercise of his rights. This means you no longer will be able to require your 10-year-old to go to church, say grace at the table, or take religious training at Sunday School. It may also mean you will have to censor passages of the Bible; for example, when it condemns homosexuality, sodomy, or adultery. Mustn't offend those little minds with decency. This Article also means that if your sweet little Amanda decides to become a satanic cultist, engrave swastikas all over your house, and hex her little brother, you will have little to stand on in court when it comes to prohibiting her. "Amanda, dear, I'd like to give you some direction today . . ."

Article 15 grants the child the right "to freedom of association . . . and peaceful assembly." This is no problem if 14-year-old Junior wants to join the Boy Scouts, of course; but it may quickly become one if he chooses the Hell's Angels, instead.

Article 16 grants children a "right to privacy," and privacy rights can be used for all sorts of things. Your little darling may decide that what goes on in his bedroom is his own business, not yours. "Dear, what was that acrid odour drifting from your room last night, and all that groaning when your friends came over . . . and, was that glass I heard breaking? You know, you haven't allowed me in your room since we bought this house five years ago. Couldn't I have a look, please?"

Article 17 charges the State with the job of encouraging the "mass media" to disseminate information to the child, even though our children already spend more time in front of the television than they do in the classroom. Article 18 says all parents have the "right" to "child care services" from the State — more mandated socialism from the U.N. Article 24 *orders* the signing states to develop "family planning education and services" — a euphemism for tax-funded abortion on demand, and supplied contraceptives. This provision basically lends international support to legions of sexologists and abortion counsellors, vacuum tube in hand, saving humanity from itself. Despite the fact that the preamble to the convention says (at the insistence of the United States, Ireland, and the Vatican) that "the child, by reason of his physical and mental immaturity, needs special safeguards and care, including legal protection, before as well as after birth," Canada refused to make such a commitment. Article 27 is a catch-all feel-good clause promising the ever-present socialist panacea: the "right" of children to a good standard of living "adequate for physical, mental, spiritual, moral and social development." This would normally make one feel warm all over, except that it means more taxes; legions of inspectors, counsellors, supervisors, therapists, and welfarists; and general interference with the family. (From what I have discovered about public education, an inexpensive way for Canada to bring about all these mandated conditions of adequacy for our children — and pay off the deficit at the same time — would be to privatize all the public schools.)

Do parents have anything to fear from such meddlesome articles concocted by egalitarian bureaucrats so far away? For sure. On May 4, 1991, in Vancouver, British Columbia, a 12-hour event was organized at the provincial courthouse to "educate" children about their rights (much of it passed off as rules needed to help the children of India). Many schools in the nation arrange to have United Nations representatives explain these children's rights. Soon the knowledge class will be all geared up to infiltrate the education system and the media, with the news that children are no longer to consider themselves as living under the authority of their parents. Then, who will sweep in to influence our children?

Here is a partial list: statists selling the idea that the State knows best and that the home is just an extension of the school; overzealous social workers eager to demonstrate "abuse" by parents or punishment they think too severe (harsh words may qualify here); sexologists, the homosexual lobby, and the like, who will be empowered to spread their influence further. Textbook producers will reinforce their one-world, universalist agenda. Bureaucrats who want to limit home-schooling and religious schools will become strident. Abortion rights activists pushing "reproductive care" will be energized. State child-care advocates will try harder for grants, of course. And the purveyors of pornography and salacious music will cite freedom of information for children as a right.

We have seen how, from the most intimate personal relations to community, national, and even international levels, much of the law today is antifamily. But is the law inherently antifamily? The answer is no. As someone once said, "the law is an ass, upon which no man has ever sat." A donkey. It will do work for whoever drives it hardest with the whips and prods of ideology. In other words, like reason, the law is ultimately only an instrument of the reigning will. It can be used to fortify freedom, family, and free enterprise against the State; or it can be used for the reverse. After more than a thousand years spent working for the family, the law recently and abruptly has been driven by radicals to the aid of the autonomous individual seeking shelter under the wing of the welfare State. It is time to drive it back to the aid of the family. For as G.K. Chesterton put it so trenchantly: "This triangle of truisms, of father, mother and child, cannot be destroyed; it can only destroy those civilizations which disregard it."

# 19

## A Call to Action: The Choices Before Us

If we consider a human society to be the sum of every-thing that human beings do voluntarily, including the institutions through which they do them (all that is not the State — such as the family, the church, community groups, and so on — but which may in varying degrees be controlled by the State), then there are only three ways to exist as a society.

A society may be a spontaneous creation of the people, operating according to their own values and within a set of firm rules they themselves have chosen, equal for all; or it may end up as a product of State planning, according to the values of the planners; or it can be some combination of the first two forms.

All free, democratic societies are based on the first model. All collectivist regimes are based on the second. All modern "liberal" democracies (no longer free, or liberal, in the original sense) have been gradually moving from the first to the second, and thus are living examples of the third.

For any civilization based on the principles of freedom, family, free enterprise, and faith (the four Fs), such as ours, the first way is natural and, provided these four Fs are preserved under a rule of law that allows them to flourish, will always be successful. The second way, always justified on the basis of community, inevitably leads to communalism — the ant heap — and has been a manifest failure throughout history. The third way, however, which as we have seen leads back to the second, is inevitably self-contradictory and therefore destructive.

This is so because the four Fs of Western civilization constitute its great moral heart, and all these principles are grounded in a concept of the individual moral agent. It is precisely this moral agency that nations based on the second method must extinguish in order to establish themselves.

It follows that if any people wishes to live by and perpetuate the four Fs, it can do so only by establishing rules of just conduct that are equal for all, specifically designed to allow the flourishing of freedoms and natural differences. Such rules will be primarily prohibitive. That is to say, they will prevent, or prohibit, one citizen from harming another, or from interfering with another's freedom within those rules. That great ideal has been the heart of Western democracy, from Athens forward, and it is still sufficient to stir our souls.

Crucial to this freedom formula, however, is leaving the people alone once the prohibitive rules are established. The people must be left alone because they will then spontaneously create a community, or a society, based on their rules of just conduct and will naturally seek to protect, and to grant privileges to, the social institutions that perpetuate that society and those values. These privileges will be like bonuses designed to lure individuals into the great projects of that society: work, marriage, procreation, family, loyalty to social ideals, and so on. And they will not be available to individuals who spur such objectives. In this sense, all spontaneous free societies will end up as a social matrix of *functional inequalities* designed to maintain core values. In a healthy free democracy, the rules dictate that *the State must not interfere with these functional inequalities*. On the contrary, as guardian both of the values and of the rules, the State and its courts must protect and nourish such natural inequalities because they are the signal guarantor of a free society.

But as democracies progress they seem to forget these principles, grow intellectually and morally lazy, and progressively surrender the most important individual, family, and community tasks to politicians and bureaucrats, whose central aim is to garner votes. Whenever this lassitude sets in, the people are ripe for the advent of the planned society, which can succeed only if all citizens, by now craving not equal opportunities but outcomes, are willing to abandon allegiance to their society and transfer it to the State. To be equal in the egalitarian sense, they must be equally compliant, equally subjected to coercion, and bitterly opposed to social privileges of any kind and to any differences between individuals, however natural. In short, a planned society can succeed only by contravening each of the four Fs. In such a society, ever greater resources, in the form of taxes, must be forcibly extracted from the people to fund the egalitarian ideal. A late democracy may be defined as one that has forgotten the four Fs and replaced them with egalitarian ideals drawn from the second model.

This point is reached when the State becomes powerful enough (and the people sufficiently supine) to use the rhetoric of freedom against their own society in the name of State-supervised equality. At this stage — we are deeply into it now — there is a rapid disassembling of the core values in all customs, in schools, and in law (these institutions themselves increasingly controlled by the State), thus enabling the State to misrepresent itself further as the great defender of freedom when in in fact it is the great extinguisher, or what the novelist Kurt Vonnegut called the Handicapper General.

Regrettably for the values of Western democracies, the special target of the State, once this turning point has been reached, is the family, together with other voluntary and formerly privileged institutions that remain standing and thus constitute an insult to the State's simplistic egalitarian ideal. So, to demolish all social institutions that confer privileges of any kind (and in the State's eyes make noncomforming individuals "unequal"), special documents, courts, and tribunals are used aggressively, even fanatically, until not one shred of natural difference is visible. At this point, natural society, in the sense described above, is suffocated, and individuals, now bereft of natural allegiances, turn hungrily for more of whatever the State has promised to provide. Since no State can long survive in this fashion, social decay in the form of illegitimacy, divorce, family dysfunction, and crime loom increasingly. Meanwhile, the State itself founders in a sea of red ink, managerial confusion, and moral and fiscal corruption; it is soon devoid of any fiscal means of control and bereft of any values that stir the hearts of men.

This book has examined the result in key areas of our society.

If we have any hope of return to core values, the people must be prepared to argue vigorously for the reconstitution of society. Conveniently, and paradoxically, this reconstitution does not mean planning very much. Mostly it means affirming the core values — which never change — and then getting rid of big government, big taxation, and big control of the people and their communities. It's a deplanning process that returns resources to the people and allows them to create their own society, with all the attendant rewards and risks. Painfully, for those who have become hooked on the narcotic of big government — most of Canada — it also means a return to self-reliance and family interdependence as the active principle of our democracy. It means clinging to freedom, family, free enterprise, and faith, and actively spurning all that erodes them.

Here are some suggestions for reconstitution. They are informally divided into political, economic, and social actions, though each is inevitably mixed with the others. Some people tell me these suggestions are themselves radical. I respond that you can think so only if you are a collectivist. In themselves, they are plainly and simply traditional, designed to defend the family and, therefore, a free society.

## Political Action

For the nation as a whole, there are a number of procedures for reconstitution, detailed in the last chapter of my earlier book, *The Trouble with Canada*. They are broadly based, and will be only briefly reviewed here, to be supplemented below by specific pro-family measures.

In order to reconstitute Canada on the basis of the four Fs, Canada must first be radically depoliticized. Like Switzerland, a multilanguage, multireligion federation of provinces, our federation — any federation — needs only seven federal departments to do its national business, not a Cabinet of close to 40 overseeing 28 departments and 15 subdepartments, such as we have.* And no federal government should be allowed to create more ministries without the permission of the people, given by referendum.

Such depoliticization must be enforced by a wise, family-based people aware that big government is inherently antifamily. With such a small federal government, there is no need for a Hollywood-style political contest for the office of prime minister. The Swiss don't have such an office, and if a democracy is set up properly, there is no need for one. Such an office wrongly distorts political life and gives the illusion that our well-being is directed from above, instead of from below — from the people themselves. Like the Swiss, we need a simple cabinet of the seven necessary ministers, whose job it is to run the government, not to engineer the behaviour of the people, or to interfere in the nature of their society, or to attempt an egalitarian assault on the functional inequalities the people deem

---

* The seven Swiss departments are: Justice and Police, Defence, Interior, Finance and Banking, Economic Affairs, Transportation and Energy, and Foreign Affairs.

necessary for the preservation of their social institutions. Such a cabinet simply rotates the job of chairman on some mutually agreed formula.

Integral to the above is the all-important matter of the devolution of power, contained in a crucial principle called "subsidiarity." That's a fancy word to say that in a free society, all human needs must be answered, and all political power exercised, at the lowest possible level first. Only if a lower level fails may an appeal be made to the next highest political level. This important principle is a safeguard for the four Fs, and arguably it would be impossible to protect them from the encroachment of the State without having subsidiarity as a controlling principle. Everything about this principle cries out for local control, not central power. It is a principle that says "hands-off" to all higher powers of the State. It is the principle that guided the original Greek, American, and Canadian democracies and is specifically entrenched in the Constitution of Switzerland. Modern Canadians have entrenched the opposite principle, by which the federal powers are specifically mandated to interfere with and equalize the economic and social life of the regions.

Once subsidiarity is firmly understood, defended, and entrenched as the most important political instrument for the protection of local and family control, we may, like the Swiss, refederalize.

Refederalization means a return to the proper meaning of federalism, which pertains to a collection of states, or provinces, bound by a few simple rules of conduct called a federal constitution. Firmly based in subsidiarity, such a true federation operates as a collection of free states bound by a common will, instead of as a collection of administrative jurisdictions of the central power. In such a system, all so-called "residual" powers — those not specifically delegated by the constitution — belong to the states, not to the federal power. In a true federal system, central solutions, apart from those associated with the seven basic ministries, are a sign of the failure of localism and, therefore, of society.

In a proper federal system, what binds the people, ultimately, is not a charter or a set of laws, but a common love of freedom, self-reliance, and local control of their own destinies. Once this bond is eroded by top-down control, however, the love disappears, and then so does the love of the federation. At this point, all may end in constitutional wrangles and bitterness in which the parts fail to find adequate rationales for remaining in the federation. Once properly refederalized, however, a free and democratic people needs instruments to control and preserve that democracy. The vote alone is not sufficient once all parties implicitly collude to impose collectivism on the people. More direct democratic means of control are needed.

The best instruments of popular democracy are *recall* and the *referendum*. The first allows a people to fire a politician midstream for lack of integrity, or for failing to support their wishes. With recall in force, a politician will always be representing the people, not the party. The Americans have used this instrument five thousand times since 1950, half of those times successfully. The last time recall was seen in Canada was in Alberta in 1936, when Premier William Aberhart brought it in for noble reasons. But when he discovered the people wanted to use recall to dislodge him, he had it removed!

The referendum — what the great constitutional scholar A.V. Dicey called "the people's veto" — is used by Americans, Australians, the Swiss, and many other people. Properly designed, it allows the people to authenticate the choices of their leaders by popular approval, or to reject them. Certain forms of referendum even allow the people to create laws directly. The referendum can turn the whole nation into a kind of people's parliament and enable the people to "own" their democracy.

Other instruments of popular democracy include the "fiscal guillotine," which enables the people to control government spending, effectively barring the State from robbing the families of the future. One such simple device would be to allow the people to trigger an election whenever the government fails to meet its budgets for two successive terms. The Swiss use the referendum for this purpose, and the Americans use devices such as California's Proposition 13 and their federal Gramm-Rudman Bill. Various forms of term limitation, which prevent professional politicians from making a career of legal plunder, are also possible. The tax system, perhaps, is the most powerful device for restricting the tendency for central government to grow. A proper federation should not allow the central powers to tax the people directly. Rather, the states, whose incomes are controlled by the people via the referendum, should in turn fix an annual proportion of their incomes for the central power.

The effect of all the above methods is to reinforce subsidiarity, local control, freedom, family, and free enterprise. A particularly nice result of this philosophy of democracy is that all notions of equity between regions are largely abandoned (as in Switzerland). Each participating state fends for itself and controls its own life. And the people? As always throughout human history, they will migrate internally to the best regions. The positive effect is that each state vies with each of the others for high-quality, low-cost services, forcing local governments to be competitive rather than collusive. The result of this system for the Swiss has been the highest standard of living and the best government services at the lowest cost — a total average family tax rate of about 24 percent, of which only 5 percent is federal. Not bad, compared with Canada's total rate of 50 percent and Sweden's 60 percent.

To further cement the pro-family basis of our civilization, either we ought to get rid of our Charter, for reasons outlined in Chapter Eighteen, and return to our traditional common-law society, or, if we haven't the foresight to do that, we ought to entrench in the Charter a pro-family declaration, detailing natural, inherent family rights and privileges. The United States has created its own "Family Protection Act" for this purpose. It seems clear, however, that even such laws are Band-aid measures, because charters of any kind are inherently antifamily, for reasons reviewed in this book. They empower egalitarians to destroy the natural functional inequalities and privileges of our most sacred social institutions; charters inevitably destroy community and replace it with the ship of State, with judges at the helm. Charters thus become the chief instrument for the erosion of the four Fs. With subsidiarity firmly supported, you don't need charters.

For reasons outlined in the four chapters on education, a key pro-family action is to take back the schools from the State. This means total privatization of the school system by way of vouchers, or some such means, enabling parents to send their children anywhere they wish. Only if parents control the schools themselves can we ensure that these institutions reflect the values of the local community — of society, not of the State.

Schools also ought to be required to teach the pro-family model. However, if they are privatized, there is no need for such a course, because private schools, when the bureaucracies leave them alone, generally become expressions of the family. If we continue with our socialist-style State schooling, however, we will just get more of the same antifamily messages, however veiled. Perhaps until we are brave enough to privatize the schools, we should require such a course. Until that happens, we could simply deny school funding to any public school that fails to honour traditional family and marriage, or uses textbooks that do the same.

Another necessary measure that springs from reconstitution is the need to reject, even denounce, all international treaties and conventions that have as their purpose the control of local or family life of free nations and their families. These are meddling treaties designed by dreamlanders for top-down control. By their nature they are repugnant to all who cherish freedom and responsibility, and are usually created and feverishly promoted by people with the policing temperament.

The laws, too, need reconstitution on a family basis. A pro-family society must define marriage in the law very strictly as a socially privileged institution for the joining of man and woman in society's procreational project, thus establishing the natural family as the ideal model. All efforts to loosen this definition in law must be resisted and treated as absurdities proposed by opportunistic individuals attempting to gain advantages they have not earned.

In order to make this model attractive, society must be allowed to design whatever protections and privileges are deemed necessary. For example, given that a key element in social decay is the existence of homes without fathers, irresponsible fathers must be constrained, with the full force of the law, to honour their family commitments. Those who do not or cannot pay, may be forced to work for the local community, with pay sent to the wife, until they have acquitted themselves of their obligation. This is not social engineering, but enforcement of ordinary duty.

At the same time, the laws of any pro-family nation must reflect the equal responsibility of both father and mother for their offspring. It is an outgrowth of twisted liberalism that a mother, if she chooses to keep her child, without marrying, may enslave the father to the child's support for 18 years; yet a mother alone may decide to kill her unborn baby. As further pro-family support, until the abortion issue is resolved, tough laws should be passed to ensure parental consent for any child under 18 who seeks an abortion (42 American states have such laws), and spousal consent should also be required for all married and common law couples — perhaps for all couples. It is impossible to rest a society upon family and procreational ideals if we give males the message that the children they help conceive are not their responsibility.

As a final point on political matters, our parliamentarians must be allowed free votes on all issues of conscience, or on issues in any way touching the family, without regard for party policy. If their conscience conflicts with the considered wishes of their constituents, they should leave politics. However, this eventuality is unlikely if referendums and subsidiarity are entrenched. Through such mechanisms, local values will erupt into law and policy from the bottom and will no longer be imposed from the top against the people's wishes.

## Economic Action

The taxing power is a powerful device for steering individuals into, or away from, various social arrangements, simply because even the most unsophisticated citizens can tell whether a situation brings them more money or less. So they tend to organize their efforts — and sometimes also their morals — accordingly.

Here are a few suggestions for reconstituting society to reflect the four Fs through the tax system. The details can be easily worked out by tax experts. What is of greatest importance is the national will to design such incentives for the citizens to form and support families.

The first important method for assigning value to the work of homemakers and undoing the damage of the welfare State is to allow all legally married couples to "split" their incomes before taxation. In other words, married couples should be taxed as a family unit and not as individuals. A wife who earns no money at all should be allowed to report half her husband's income as her own, thus reducing his reported income and yielding a much lower tax rate for the family. This proposal flies straight in the face of what the radicals want, of course, because it amounts to an incentive to homemaking and home childrearing. What I like about the method is that it confers a recognized income value to the wife's work in the home. She can say, "I earned this money" and feel her work is valued by both society and the State. The difference in income retained is about $8000 per year for a family earning $60,000.

In order to further validate legitimate families, significant child deductions should be allowed, of, say, $4000 per child under 18 (the current system of tax credits allows $400 to $800, depending on the child's age). In 1942, Canadians were allowed to deduct up to 75 percent of their weekly wage for all dependants. By 1950 this figure fell to 30 percent. By 1992 it was about 9 percent. The truly needy who may have too little income from which to deduct such amounts can demonstrate why they need a temporary subsidy (from their local community, not from federal transfer payments back to the provinces). Nations that really want to boost baby-making and family will also likely have to consider sizable maternity bonuses of some kind, such as Quebec has done (up to $7500, for the third child). These programs would amount not to welfare, but to familyfare. I am in principle against them, because the best way to help the family is to leave it alone, which means not plundering the money of families for spurious collectivist purposes. But until such time as we decide that the four Fs are better than the four Gs (Government, Groups, Grants, and Grabs), we could at least direct our tax dollars to winning propositions such as the family, instead of to losing propositions such as economic autonomism and welfare dependency. It goes without saying that all so-called "universality" must be ended and officially spurned as a collectivist vote-getting sop that robs the people of self-reliance.

As further economic incentives, legally married couples with children should be allowed to deduct mortgage interest on their homes until their last child is 10 years of age. This policy is outright positive discrimination against both singles and childless couples, which is quite justifiable because they don't have child expenses. I can think of few economic incentives as powerful for encouraging and rewarding intact families to stay together and to have a lot of children over a long period of time.

As a general tax measure for all the people, from which families would benefit most, all taxation should be indexed against inflation to avoid the "bracket creep" that pushes earners into higher tax brackets solely for inflationary reasons, though their real earning power has not increased.

As well, joint registered retirement savings plans (RRSPs) should be designed to allow higher contributions from married couples than from individuals, regardless of which spouse earns the most income. Married couples would lose this right if they divorced, and further contributions would be disallowed until the married-bonus sums were absorbed at the single contributor's rate. This scheme would be a powerful family-savings device. The point here is to have people see that the best route to financial security for them is getting married, having kids, and staying married. Joint family wealth can have a powerful positive effect on discontent. A lot of phantom disputes get solved in advance because the cost of raising them is too high.

Other forms of familyfare (also unnecessary if tax rates are appropriately low) would be a deduction allowed for "same-home" care of parents or grandparents. Americans have an "individual retirement account" plan for this purpose. This deduction would encourage family cohesiveness by making the care of elders less financially burdensome, and it would help "re-verticalize" society by eliminating the collectivist tendency to separate the generations from each other and rearrange them into State-dependent classes.

As a further incentive to family interdependence, no welfare should be given to individuals from wealthy families. The idea here is to force individuals to go first to their own families for help, then to their communities, and last of all to impersonal, higher State bodies. This, too, is in keeping with the principle of subsidiarity; and because there is always a message with the money, so to speak, families and local communities, whose money is being used directly, will be the best arbiters of true need — and the best guardians of the honesty and effort required to escape from need.

As for the economics of daycare? If any funding is provided — and there should be little need, if the measures suggested above are implemented — it should go to the parents in the form of vouchers, and not to the daycare centres themselves. This way, the centres must compete for the vouchers, making collectivizing daycare almost impossible (I am happy to say) and further frustrating the top-downers and social engineers.

Finally, because family business, based on free enterprise and private property, is the foundation of wealth in a free society, some thought should be given to special banking privileges for families and family businesses. In a nation like Canada, where the banks specialize in giving you an umbrella only when the sun is shining, the fear of entrepreneurial risk-taking could be mitigated by a plan to insure bank loans to legally married couples, much as the State now insures a percentage of bank deposits. If banking is ever freed up for competition, as it ought to be, such plans would not be needed, for we would see a proliferation of smaller banks falling over each other to help entrepreneurs.

## Social Action

We ought also to rid ourselves of the idea — one that springs from the devaluation of marriage — of so-called no-fault divorce, at least for those marriages that have produced children. One idea would be a five-year delay for marriages with children. Tougher divorce laws engender less frivolous entry into the commitment, and a much tougher exit. Most of all, they define divorce as a wrong, and assign blame on the grounds that where there is a wrong there is a wrongdoer. There is no perfect system, but no-fault laws, like most other modern liberal policies, remove the fault from the person and assign it to the system. No fault means no responsibility. Combined with equal rights to property, such no-fault laws become incentives to the least, rather than the most, morally fastidious.

Another pro-family social policy with merit is adoption. The fact is, there are no unwanted babies in Canada or the United States. Or let's just say that while their moms may not want them, many other people, desperate for a child, do. We ought to encourage a national adoption philosophy consistent with valuing families and children.

This would also constitute what someone has called an "internal immigration" program by which population would increase from our own families before resorting to baby-making by immigrants or even importing babies for adoption. (Currently, for example, the United States does 1.5 million abortions per year, and adoptions there are 30 percent foreign; not enough babies to fill the home demand.) To bolster such a program, increased tax deductions could be offered to families caring for adopted children, again placing a value on adoption.

Consistent with this program, our nation ought to turn its back on the growing "illegitimacy chic" and on abortion on demand. And if abortion is offered at all, if we haven't the moral strength to ban it, then it should be allowed only for the time-honoured reasons of true life-threat to the mother's health, rape, incest, or a child so badly deformed it is incapable of sustainable life. This measure would at least vastly limit the abortion rampage of our time. A time-honoured community jury system can decide such things, and thus we can return to the important idea that the community, not the individual, decides on the value of life. And it goes without saying that ghoulish medical experimentation with unborn babies must be brought to an end, as well as any commercial trade in their flesh.

Further, to help sustain family values — and again consistent with subsidiarity — all moral policy ought to be decided locally, not nationally. Again, there is no perfect answer to such things as rampant pornography and the violence on T.V., in rock music, or the movies. But it is better to have local control — and the matrix of different standards this system would produce — than one national policy controlled by, say, egalitarian pansexualists (or, at the other extreme, rabid fundamentalists). Under the matrix of localism, people would either change the standards in their community, or move to one they prefer. This choice creates an intercommunity competitive pressure for higher standards instead of lower ones, because no community wants to exist for long with a sleazy reputation. And localism gives the people a sense of ownership in the standards of their own community. Young people brought up in such communities are less likely to breach such standards, for the same reason delinquents are far less likely to kill a policeman they have known all their lives, than one they don't know at all. The same spirit applies to sex-ed in the schools. Let local communities control it, instead of far-flung ministries of education overpopulated with collectivists holding zany ideas.

And as long as we have lost our sense of conduct, and opted for more contract, then let's start emphasizing that all contracts are two-sided. Never mind human rights. We know all about those. In fact, most of us are sick to death of them. How about human, family, student, and social *responsibilities* and *duties*? It would do no harm at all, for example, to have a Charter of Student Responsibilities drawn up by the parents, teachers, and senior students of each school and signed by all students. In a free society, such charters of responsibility ought to reflect the four Fs in every detail.

Having said this, human history is a sad lesson in how moral standards fail in the absence of moral absolutes. For this reason, we should restore our Judeo-Christian roots and allow prayer in any school that wishes it. Let each community decide. This point usually gets the knees jerking (although — surprise! — the Ontario Ministry of Education has actually recommended it). However, I raise it here because we are already teaching ersatz religion in the schools in the form of secular or religious humanism. And we will discover, as we revisit our own democratic roots, that the so-called separation of church and State was clearly never intended to forbid prayer in the schools. It was intended to prevent the State from telling people how to pray, from gaining control of religion, or from banning religion. In other words, it was a doctrine designed to provide freedom *of* religion, not freedom *from* religion.[1] The framers of the Canadian and American nations would have been horrified at the idea of forbidding children to pray in school. They believed in the four Fs, and they knew the importance of personal allegiance to a moral power higher than the State — else the State becomes the only higher power.

**Personal Action**
There are a host of other possible political, economic, and social incentives, laws, and policies that we as a people could design to allow the growth of spontaneous community and encourage the family health that I have advocated. What ought to be clear from this book is that the antifamily model has seriously eroded our civilization and its values. It is time to fight back.

People passionate about these family issues and eager to help reconstitute them often approach me and ask what they, alone, can do. The problem seems too overwhelming. And after all, they are working hard and raising their own families. I answer that they don't have to do much — but they have to keep doing it. Think of the nation as a billiard-table, I say, with thousands of motionless billiard balls. All you have to do is get yourself moving with the aim of hitting two of those balls, and giving them the same idea. Soon, the whole table will be moving.

There is nothing worse than feeling useless to a passionate purpose, and nothing quite as rewarding or as much fun as making a difference in this life. So my attitude is, just get a few like-thinking friends and go to it. That's what I did. And that's why my two books happened.

For those who want a bit of help getting started, there's a fine little organization (American, wouldn't you know?) called the National Center for Public Policy Research. It publishes a $10 course in the form of a set of manuals to help people get started reconstituting the great values of Western society. This organization has manuals to show you how to write effective letters and run letter campaigns, and how to handle talk shows, write press releases, form community groups, demonstrate, and so on. Amy Moritz, the president, says her organization would welcome your letter or phone call (300 Eye Street, N.E., Suite 3, Washington, D.C., 20002, U.S.A.; telephone: 202-543-1286).

Meanwhile, I'm going to hit some more billiard balls. Since members of the media seem shy to talk about the things that really matter, and since most of them are singing the same political song anyway, I'm going to start a monthly newsletter to give people news and views they're not likely to read elsewhere. I hope it ends up in every home in the country. If you have been patient enough to get this far and would like to know more about it, please write for information to *Newsletter*, 255 Yorkland Boulevard, Suite 220, Willowdale, Ontario, M2J 1S3, Canada.

And let us close by remembering the admonition of the philosopher Edmund Burke (1790), that "the only thing necessary for the triumph of evil is for good men to do nothing."

He did not mean that evil comes from good people doing bad things. He meant that if they stop doing good things, evil things will take their place.

# Notes

*Emphasis in all quotations has been added*

## 1 / THE STATE VS. THE FAMILY

1. Quoted in "The Goading of America," *Chronicles*, May 1991.
2. Robert Nisbet, *The Quest for Community: A Study in the Ethics of Order and Freedom* (San Francisco: Institute For Contemporary Studies, 1990). This is a profound book that appeared in 1953 just as the awful totalitarianism of Eastern Europe was taking hold. It reorients the classic debate of the left, which holds that the individual is alienated and diminished by the forces of impersonal markets (and therefore requires the benevolent State). Nisbet argues instead that natural, free man creates community spontaneously, and that the unitary State can dominate only by eroding this community.
3. Tatyana Tolstaya in her review of Francine du Plessix Gray, *Soviet Women: Walking The Tightrope* (New York: Doubleday, 1990), in *New York Review*, May 31, 1990.
4. See my *The Trouble with Canada* (Toronto: Stoddart, 1990), Chart 21, p. 191.
5. The "French style" has ancient roots, from Plato onward, and any thorough study of modern collectivism always leads back to the French rationalist, collectivist tradition as its ideal model. I am indebted to Irving Kristol's fine treatment of the differences between the French and Anglo-Scottish enlightenments in his essay "Adam Smith and the Spirit of Capitalism," in *Reflections of a Neoconservative* (New York: Basic Books, 1983), p. 139. See also Alain Peyrefitte's elaboration of these differences in his *The Trouble with France* (New York: Alfred Knopf, 1981). For historians, Simon Schama's *Citizens* (New York: Alfred Knopf, 1989) provides a thorough overview of the effect of French millennialism on French society, as does Erik von Kuehnelt-Leddihn's *Leftism Revisited* (Washington, D.C.: Regnery Gateway, 1990), on

Europe as a whole. See also Robert Nisbet's *The Quest for Community*, note 2 above, for the effect of Rousseau on this collectivist process. An intensive and fascinating treatment of the effect of Rousseau on prerevolutionary thinking and the politics and morals of our time can be found in Irving Babbitt, *Rousseau and Romanticism* (New Brunswick, New Jersey: Transaction Publishers, 1991), originally published in 1919. To my mind, this is the best and most profound analysis of the Romantic mentality in its relation to political thinking.

6. A finely detailed treatment of this process by which true federalism became centralism in the United States can be found in Felix Morley, *Freedom and Federalism* (Chicago: Henry Regnery, 1959). For the Canadian process, see Kenneth McDonald, *Keeping Canada Together* (Toronto: Ramsay Business Systems, 1990).

7. F.L. Morton, "The Charter Revolution and the Court Party," prepared for the Roundtable Conference on the Impact of the Charter on the Public Policy Process, organized by the Centre for Public Law and Public Policy, York University, Toronto, November 15-16, 1991.

8. Alain Peyrefitte's *The Trouble with France* gives insights into the economic and moral differences between Catholic South America and Protestant North America.

# 2 / THE POPULAR ILLUSIONS

1. James Burnham, *Suicide of the West* (Washington: Regnery Gateway, 1985). First published in 1964. See especially Chapter 7.

2. The best short treatment of this subject is by Alan Macfarlane, *The Origins of English Individualism* (London: Basil Blackwell, 1978). This is a dry but crucial read that argues for the presence and importance of individualism in Britain since the 12th century, based on the existence of clearly defined individual property rights of a kind that existed in no other European nation until six or seven centuries later. (And only in the Soviet Union as of June 1990!) Also instructive is Paul Johnson, *A History of the English People* (London: Weidenfeld and Nicolson, 1972).

   For examples of how individualism can effect the course of entire nations, even continents, I heartily recommend Michael Novak, *The Spirit of Democratic Capitalism* (New York: Simon and Schuster, 1982), and also Alain Peyrefitte, *The Trouble with France* (New York: Alfred Knopf, 1981). Both show the intricate connection between individualism and political, economic, and moral life. A more direct economic view can be gained from Nobel laureate F.A. Hayek, *Individualism and Economic Order* (Chicago: University of Chicago Press, 1948).

3. Reginald Bibby, *Mosaic Madness* (Toronto: Stoddart, 1990), p. 14.

4. Michael Novak, *The Spirit of Democratic Capitalism* (New York: Simon and Schuster, 1982), pp. 63-65.

5. Michael Novak, *Free Persons and the Common Good* (New York: Madison Books, 1989), p. 31.

6. Jean-Jacques Rousseau, *The Social Contract* (New York: Dutton, 1966), p. 15.

7. This is the great intellectual fault of leftists and Marxists — that they fail to distinguish between seduction and coercion. These two things may have the same result, but the moral and philosophical difference between them is everything. Human beings can be seduced; but only humans made into non-humans can be coerced. Even sensitive critics like Christopher Lasch are seduced by this error.

8. Roland Huntford, *The New Totalitarians* (New York: Stein and Day, 1972), p. 326.

9. David Popenoe, *Disturbing the Nest: Family Change and Decline in Modern Societies* (New York: Aldine De Gruyter, 1988), p. 173.

10. Jessica Pegis, Ian Gentles, L.L. de Veber, eds., *Sex Education: A Review of the Literature from Canada, the United States, Britain, and Sweden* (Toronto: Human Life Research Institute, 1986).

11. Gertrude Himmelfarb, *Marriage and Morals Among the Victorians* (New York: Vintage, 1987), p. 79.

12. Stanley L. Jaki, *Chance or Reality* (Lanham, Maryland: University Press of America, 1986), p. 66.

13. Cited in Philip Rieff, *The Triumph of the Therapeutic* (Chicago: University of Chicago Press, 1966), p. xvii.

14. The role of Saint-Simon, in particular, in the development of the theory of the social welfare State is well detailed by Nobel laureate F.A. Hayek, in *The Counter-revolution of Science* (Indianapolis: Liberty Press, 1952).

    Of course, there were famous British utopian planners such as Jeremy Bentham (1748-1832) and William Godwin (1756-1836). The best brief treatment of the social and personal distortions to which such abstract reasoning can lead when applied to human communities may be found in two delightful essays by Gertrude Himmelfarb: "Bentham's Utopia" and "Godwin's Utopia," in *Marriage and Morals among the Victorians* (New York: Random House, 1975).

15. Donald Johnston, ed., *Pierre Trudeau Speaks Out On Meech Lake* (Toronto: Stoddart, 1988), p. 45. The phrases "national will" and "une volonté générale" are frequent in Trudeau's speaking and writing.

16. Pierre Elliott Trudeau, *Federalism and the French Canadians* (Toronto: Macmillan, 1968), p. 127.

17. F.A. Hayek, *New Studies in Philosophy, Politics, Economics, and the History of Ideas* (Chicago: University of Chicago Press, 1978), p. 6.

18. Himmelfarb, *Marriage and Morals Among the Victorians*, p. 144.
19. Ronald Hamowy, *The Scottish Enlightenment and the Theory of Spontaneous Order* (Illinois: Southern Illinois University Press, 1978), p. 3.
20. In Christopher Lasch, *Haven in a Heartless World* (New York: Basic Books, 1977), p. 14.
21. Sigmund Freud, "A Difficulty of Psychoanalysis," in *On Creativity and the Unconscious* (New York: Harper and Row, 1958), p. 4.
22. Himmelfarb, *Marriage and Morals Among the Victorians*, p. 79.
23. Freud, *On Creativity and the Unconscious*, p. 8.
24. A compact and informative review of Rieff's work (from which this quotation is drawn) is by Jerry Z. Muller. "A Neglected Conservative Thinker," in *Commentary*, February 1991, pp. 49-52.
25. Those interested in these matters will enjoy a nice slant to this story. One of the most famous public newspaper debates over free will and determinism occurred in 1903-04 between G.K. Chesterton and the columnist Robert Blatchford. Chesterton argued for free will as God's gift to man; Blatchford fought for determinism. Some say Blatchford won this titanic intellectual struggle. But an ironic twist threw the victory long afterward to Chesterton. In 1921, Blatchford converted to the spiritual view because the theory of relativity, as he saw it, put an end to the mechanistic idea that the universe operated according to cause and effect in the old Newtonian way — like a clock. Since it obviously operated not like a clock at all but according to chance, its outcome, he reasoned, could be known only to some higher being than man. Jaki, *Chance Or Reality*, p. 8.
26. Dennis Overbye, *Lonely Hearts of the Cosmos: The Scientific Quest for the Secret of the Universe* (New York: Harper Collins, 1991), p. 185, 429, and 420.
27. Michael Denton, *Evolution: A Theory In Crisis* (Bethesda, Md.: Adler and Adler, 1986). Another book making many of the same points as Denton's is by lawyer Phillip Johnson, *Darwin on Trial* (Washington: Regnery Gateway, 1991), in which the theory of evolution is subjected to the rigours of legal argument, and found wanting.
28. Arthur O. Lovejoy, *The Great Chain of Being* (New York: Harper and Row, 1936), p. 184. Lovejoy called this idea "the sacred phrase of the eighteenth century, playing a part somewhat analogous to that of the blessed word 'evolution' in the late nineteenth."
29. The case was over the murders of San Francisco mayor George Moscone and Harvey Milk, on November 27, 1978, by Dan White, in which lawyer Donald Lunde used the "diminished capacity" defence. White got only seven years and eight months for manslaughter, with early parole, instead of life imprisonment for murder, all by eating Twinkies.

# 3 / THE TRADITIONAL FAMILY SYSTEM

1. David Popenoe, *Disturbing the Nest: Family Change and Decline in Modern Societies* (New York: Aldine De Gruyter, 1988), pp. vii, 35, 36. Popenoe's book is the single best study of family decline in modern societies that I have found, for he not only amalgamates the disparate statistical findings, but also manages, despite what would appear to be his personal statist leanings, to preserve a semblance of ideological balance as he pushes through the thicket.

2. The journals surveyed were: *Canadian Family Law Quarterly, Canadian Journal of Women and the Law, Canadian Sociological and Anthropological Association Journal, Society, Family Perspective, Family Relations, Journal of Family Therapy, Marriage and Family Review, Journal of Family Issues, Journal of Marital and Family Therapy, Journal of Comparative Family Studies, and Canadian Journal of Family Law*.

3. Popenoe, *Disturbing the Nest*, p. 10.

4. Christopher Lasch, *Haven in a Heartless World: The Family Besieged* (New York: Basic Books, 1977), p. 23. Lasch is an interesting, if somewhat convoluted, writer of the reformed pseudo-Marxian sociological vein who, like so many other influential leftists of the past 30 years, such as Collier, and Horowitz, has recanted considerably and discovered his own neo-conservative instincts. In *Haven*, he fingers all the correct symptoms but lays much of the blame on the capitalist system; unlike Robert Nisbet, who assumes that capitalist phenomena are largely an aggregation of choices made by millions of consumers, while the real villain is in fact the coercive, invading State.

5. Lawrence Stone, *The Family, Sex and Marriage In England 1500-1800* (New York: Harper and Row, 1977). A point to be made here is that the polarization of debate in family history and sociology is so extreme that any earnest lay reader will find himself the ham in the proverbial intellectual sandwich. Stone and Alan Macfarlane likely represent the extremes of this debate, and each has written reviews of the other's work more withering than any I have seen in any other field. This simply bolsters the point I hope to make throughout this book. Namely, that family matters are too important to be left to scholars.

6. I am indebted to Alan Macfarlane for his review of Stone's work in *History and Theory*, 18 (1979), pp. 103-26, which gives a thorough overview of the conventional view paraphrased here. Also worthy of mention, for its overview and championing of the family, is Brigitte Berger and Peter L. Berger, *The War over the Family: Capturing the Middle Ground* (New York: Anchor, 1983). The Bergers' view is that so-called "modernization" may very well not be possible without what they call the "bourgeois family" that creates the values that give rise to modernization. Neither, happily, do they see

any "viable alternative to the bourgeois family in the contemporary world" (p. 134).

7. Alan Macfarlane, *Marriage and Love in England: Modes of Reproduction 1300-1840* (London: Basil Blackwell, 1986). This is the book so roundly criticized by Stone (*TLS*, May 16, 1986), for being, among other things, "neo-conservative." In this classic interpretational struggle between Stone and Macfarlane can be seen an academic version of the "civil war of values" I have described, manifested in scholarship.

8. Linda A. Pollock, *Forgotten Children: Parent-Child Relations from 1500 to 1900* (Cambridge: Cambridge University Press, 1983). Pollock strongly supports the Macfarlane side of this debate.

9. The best case for this view is again Alan Macfarlane, in his earlier book, *The Origins of English Individualism* (London: Basil Blackwell, 1978). In it, Macfarlane makes the case, again from detailed primary sources, that England alone among the nations of Europe has, since the 13th century at least, had a deep tradition of individualism and free market economic relations (land was not held communally, or by families, but by individuals).

10. Pollock, *Forgotten Children*. The comments from Pollock are primarily drawn from chapters 2-5.

11. Ibid, p. 271.

12. Le Roy Ladurie, *Montaillou: The Promised Land of Error* (New York: George Braziller, 1978), p. 30. The original french version was entitled *Montaillou, village occitan de 1294 à 1324* (Paris: Gallimard, 1975).

13. Ibid., p. 31.

14. Ibid., p. 47.

15. Ibid., p. 199.

16. Ibid., p. 209.

17. Ibid., p. 210.

18. Jerome Carcopino, *Daily Life in Ancient Rome: The People and the City at the Height of the Empire* (London: Penguin, 1941), p. 94. (Translation by E.O. Lorimer.)

19. Ibid., pp. 104-106.

20. Michael Novak, *The Spirit of Democratic Capitalism* (New York: Simon and Schuster, 1982). A must read, this book supplies the essential political, economic, and spiritual foundation of democratic capitalism.

21. Leonard Liggio, *Chronicles*, October 1990, p. 22.

22. Ibid.

23. Thomas Fleming, "The Facts of Life," in *Chronicles*, October 1990, p. 15.

24. Liggio, *Chronicles*, p. 23.

25. Gaston Bachelard, *La poétique de l'espace* (Paris: Presses Universitaires de France, 1967).

26. The quotation is from the grand master of the philosophy of freedom, Nobel laureate F.A. Hayek, in his *The Fatal Conceit* (Chicago: University of Chicago Press, 1988), p. 33. To him, so much is owed. An excellent specialized treatment of the evolution of private property rights in our tradition can be found in Richard A. Epstein, *Takings: Private Property and the Power of Eminent Domain* (Cambridge, Massachusetts: Harvard University Press, 1985), especially pp. 9 ff.

27. E.P. Stein, *Takings*, p. 13.

28. The figures on the United States are from Frank Tilley, IMI Horizons, 54 (Spring 1988), Geneva. On Canada, from Aron R. Pervin, Pervin and Co., "Special Report on Family Business," Toronto, undated. In personal conversations, Mr. Pervin kindly updated my U.S. figures as well.

29. See my *The Trouble with Canada* (Toronto: Stoddart, 1990), Chapter 10, especially p. 287, which cites a 1987 Statistics Canada study, "Earnings of Men and Women," showing that for all but the youngest age group, never-married women actually earn marginally more than never-married men in Canada.

30. I owe a great deal to a number of fine publications of The Rockford Institute, among them *The Family Wage: Work, Gender and Children in the Modern Economy* (Rockford, Ill.: The Rockford Institute, 1988); also, *The Retreat From Marriage*, ed. Bryce Christensen, 1990. Those interested in family research would do well to subscribe to the Institute's excellent monthly newsletter, *The Family In America*, and can do so by writing to the Institute at 934 North Main Street, Rockford, Illinois, 61103, U.S.A. Tel.: (815) 964-5811.

31. Summarized in a paper by W. Keith Bryant of Cornell University, "The Economics of Housewifery," and presented to a Conference of The Rockford Institute, Rockford, Illinois, June 6-9, 1991.

32. Fleming, *Chronicles*, October 1990, p. 14.

33. Charles Murray, *In Pursuit of Happiness and Good Government* (New York: Simon and Schuster, 1988), p. 288. This is more than a good book: it's a lesson in life, and how to live it.

34. George Gilder, *Men and Marriage* (Gretna, Louisiana: Pelican Publishing, 1986), p. 5. This book was originally published as *Sexual Suicide*. Gilder was a thinker ahead of his time, who deeply influenced the conservative revival in North America with his subsequent book, *Wealth and Poverty* (New York: Basic Books, 1981). In fact, this was the book that first got me interested in the subject of economics and social policy.

35. Gilder, *Men and Marriage*, p. 10.

36. Ibid., p. 12.

37. Novak, *The Spirit of Democratic Capitalism*, p. 165.

38. Pollock, *Forgotten Children*, p. 39.

# 4 / THE ANTIFAMILY TRADITION

1. Alexis de Tocqueville, *Democracy in America* (New York: Random House, 1990), Volume 2, p. 319.
2. Michael Oakeshott, quoted in Gertrude Himmelfarb, *Marriage and Morals Among the Victorians* (New York: Vintage, 1987), p. 220.
3. Karl Popper, *The Open Society and Its Enemies: The Spell of Plato* (London: Routledge and Kegan Paul, 1945). This two-volume set, the first on Plato, the second on Hegel and Marx, is worth more than a whole year of undergraduate education in political philosophy. There are some excellent writers, such as Robert Nisbet, who dislike Popper's recasting of their hero's thinking and either suggest that Plato was not serious in his construction of a utopian republic or hold open the hope of a "totalitarianism of virtue" (Nisbet, *The Quest for Community*, San Francisco: Institute for Contemporary Studies, 1990, p. 258). I believe Plato was serious, for his Republic is the logical outcome of the structure of his ideas and of his values. They point to it and travel along it like a train on iron rails. Nevertheless, regardless of what Plato himself thought, his utopian thinking has been used as a template for collectivist thought in the West, and so has done its damage.
4. Plato, *The Republic* (London: Penguin, 1955).
5. Popper, *The Open Society and Its Enemies*, p. 84.
6. Plato, *The Republic*, p. 239.
7. Ibid., p. 241.
8. Popper, *The Open Society and Its Enemies*, p. 82.
9. Ibid., p. 103.
10. Ibid., p. 87.
11. Nisbet, *The Quest for Community*, p. 258. Nisbet never actually explains what a "totalitarianism of virtue" is.
12. Popper, *The Open Society and Its Enemies*, p. 102.
13. Ibid., p. 102.
14. Ibid.
15. Ibid., p. 107.
16. Paul Johnson, *Intellectuals* (New York: Harper and Row, 1988), p. 23.
17. Few Canadians, even today, realize that their former prime minister was a confessed socialist. In his *Federalism and The French Canadians* (Toronto: Macmillan, 1968), he makes repeated allusion to the techniques Canadian socialists must use to govern Canada. For this purpose, he wrote, "Federalism must be welcomed as a valuable tool which permits dynamic [provincial] parties *to plant socialist governments in certain provinces, from which the seeds of radicalism can slowly spread*" (p. 127). Although he may misunderstand the term as used by Rousseau, Trudeau frequently refers to the

concept of *la volonté générale* in his *Pierre Trudeau Speaks out on Meech Lake* (Toronto: Stoddart, 1990); see pp. 63ff.

18. Johnson, *Intellectuals*, p. 24.
19. Colin Campbell, *Governments Under Stress*, quoted in my *The Trouble with Canada* (Toronto: Stoddart, 1990), p. 103.
20. Paul Johnson, "Is Totalitarianism Dead?" in *Crisis: A Journal of Lay Catholic Opinion*, February 1989.
21. Bryce Christensen, *Utopia Against the Family* (San Francisco: Ignatius Press, 1990), p. ix.
22. Ibid., p. 5.
23. Gertrude Himmelfarb, *Marriage and Morals Among the Victorians* (New York: Vintage, 1987).
24. Ibid., p. 141.
25. Ibid., p. 143.
26. Ibid., p. 145.
27. Ibid., p. 146.
28. Ibid., p. 162.
29. Paul Johnson, *Modern Times: The World from the Twenties to the Eighties* (New York: Harper and Row, 1983).
30. "Karl Marx: Howling Gigantic Curses," in Johnson, *Intellectuals*, pp. 52-81.
31. From Michele Barrett, Introduction to Friederich Engels, *The Origin of the Family, Private Property and the State* (London: Penguin, 1986), p. 26 (first published in 1884).
32. Ibid., p. 87.
33. Ibid., p. 105.
34. Ibid.
35. Ibid., p. 107.
36. Simone de Beauvoir, "Sex, Society and the Female Dilemma: A Dialogue Between Simone de Beauvoir and Betty Friedan," *Saturday Review*, June 14, 1975, p. 12.
37. Michael Levin, *Feminism and Freedom* (New Brunswick, New Jersey: Transaction Books, 1987), p. 26.
38. Ibid., p. 18.
39. Ibid.
40. Nicholas Davidson, *The Failure of Feminism* (Buffalo, N.Y.: Prometheus Books, 1988), p. 15.
41. Kate Millet, *Sexual Politics* (New York: Avon, 1969), p. 69.
42. Ibid., p. 175.
43. Mavis Gallant, "A Couple and Their Family," in *Times Literary Supplement*, September 14-20, 1990. (This is a review of several works on de Beauvoir.)
44. Millet, *Sexual Politics*, p. 92.

45. Philip Rieff's books, *The Triumph of the Therapeutic* (1966), *The Feeling Intellect* (1990), *Fellow Teachers* (1972), and *Freud: The Mind of the Moralist* (1959), are all published by the University of Chicago Press.
46. "Reflections on Psychological Man in America," in Rieff, *The Feeling Intellect*, p. 3.
47. Ibid., p. 5.
48. Ibid., p. 7.
49. Ibid., p. 9.
50. Rieff, *Triumph of the Therapeutic*, p. 3.
51. Ibid., p. 15.
52. Ibid., p. 11.
53. Ibid., p. 17.
54. Ibid., p. 25.
55. I am indebted to Rael Jean Isaac and Virginia C. Armat, for *Madness in the Streets* (Toronto: Collier Macmillan, 1990), an excellent book that clearly details the process by which radically politicized psychiatrists emptied the institutions and filled the streets with people needing help.
56. Ibid., p. 29.
57. R.D. Laing, *The Politics of the Family* (Toronto: CBC Enterprises, 1969), p. 8.
58. Ibid., p. 57.
59. Quoted in Donald DeMarco, *Today's Family in Crisis* (Saskatchewan: Marian Press, 1982), p. 1.
60. Credit is again due to Isaac and Armat for their overview of the Szasz phenomenon.
61. Christensen, *Utopia Against the Family*, p. 35.
62. Ibid., p. 35.
63. Ibid., pp. 35-36.
64. Ibid., p. 38.
65. Frederick Jarman and Susan Howlett, *The Living Family* (Toronto: John Wiley and Sons, 1991), p. 5.
66. David Popenoe, *Disturbing the Nest: Family Change and Decline in Modern Societies* (New York: Aldine De Gruyter, 1988), p. 42.

# 5 / THE SWEDISH LESSON

1. Most of the information and insight into Swedish family decline is drawn from David Popenoe, *Disturbing the Nest: Family Change and Decline in Modern Societies*. New York: Aldine de Gruyter, 1988). Readers who wish a detailed survey of how the socialist ideology was implanted in Sweden by the Myrdals will find it in Allan Carlson, *The Swedish Experiment in Family Politics* (New Brunswick, New Jersey: Transaction, 1990).
2. Popenoe, *Disturbing the Nest*, p. 147.

3. In *Alberta Report*, April 22, 1991.

4. Popenoe, *Disturbing the Nest*, pp. 134-37.

5. Quoted in Popenoe, *Disturbing the Nest*, p. 156.

6. See in particular Frederic Bastiat's *The Law* (Irvington-on-Hudson, N.Y.: The Foundation for Economic Education, 1981), which is surely the best short lesson on the evils that befall any people once the law becomes a social engineering device instead of a protection from such devices. Also, see Joseph Schumpeter, *Capitalism, Socialism, and Democracy* (New York: Harper and Row, 1942). Tocqueville's *Democracy in America* (New York: Vintage, 1990), first published in 1835, was a clarion call to freedom; it warned Americans of the tendency of all democratic states to become totalitarian, not so much in their outward forms as in their tendency to control the inner lives of the people once the state had successfully atomized society and placated the intellect with material plenty. But perhaps the best general warning comes from Robert Nisbet in his classic work of 1953, *The Quest for Community: A Study in the Ethics of Order and Freedom* (San Francisco: ICS Press, 1990), which explains in historical detail the process of social erosion brought about *as a natural phenomenon* in all states, whether totalitarian (where the process is overt and intentional) or democratic (where it is as certain, if slower and less conscious). In short, the shift from a bottom-up to a top-down condition is not unusual but is the most prevalent condition and direction of human societies. The framers of the American Constitution were aware of this and, unlike the Canadian framers, put in place a variety of instruments and checks (not wholly successful) to forestall this inevitability.

7. Popenoe, *Disturbing the Nest*, p. 134.

8. Roland Huntford, *The New Totalitarians* (New York: Stein and Day, 1972). This book, which is promoted on the jacket as "a terrifying portrait of an ideal society that has destroyed democracy," created a furore in Sweden and the rest of Scandinavia when first released — but no serious rebuttals of which I am aware. I have drawn Brodin's comments from two articles published in *The Freeman* (Irvington-on-Hudson: The Foundation for Economic Education, December 1980 and March 1987). Popenoe's *Disturbing the Nest* remains the best examination of social and familial decline using Sweden as the bellwether nation.

9. G.K. Chesterton, *Orthodoxy* (Garden City, New York: Doubleday, 1936), p. 19.

10. Popenoe, *Disturbing the Nest*, p. 175.

11. The Canadian figure is from "Religion," *The Globe and Mail*, September 25, 1991.

12. Margrit Eichler, "The Limits of Family Law Reform or, The Privatization of Female and Child Poverty," in *Canadian Family Law Quarterly*, 7, pp. 60-84.

13. Popenoe, *Disturbing the Nest*, p. 149.
14. Barrington Moore, Jr., *Authority and Inequality Under Capitalism and Socialism: USA, USSR, and China* (Oxford: Clarendon Press, 1987), pp. 8-9.
15. Quoted in *Chronicles*, August 1991. (I have been unable to locate the original source.)
16. Calculations supplied by Kids First, Edmonton, Alberta.
17. Popenoe, *Disturbing the Nest*, p. 154.
18. For England, see Lawrence Stone, *Road to Divorce* (Oxford: Oxford University Press, 1990), p. 420.
19. Popenoe, *Disturbing the Nest*, p. 205.
20. Doreen Duchesne, *Giving Freely: Volunteers in Canada* (Ottawa: Statistics Canada, 1989), p. 60.
21. Popenoe, *Disturbing the Nest*, p. 209.
22. Ibid., p. 236.

# 6 / THE FAMILY AT A GLANCE

1. David Popenoe, *Disturbing the Nest: Family Change and Decline in Modern Societies* (New York: Aline de Gruyter, 1988); also, see his "Family Decline in America," in Blankenhorn, Bayme, Elshtain, eds., *Rebuilding the Nest: A New Commitment to the American Family* (Milwaukee, Wisconsin: Family Service America, 1990). Although Popenoe himself hesitates to judge family decline, he defines it operatively and shows not only that it is real, but also how it is worst in the most interventionist welfare States.
2. Although written in an oppressively radical style that surely must hinder the author's intellectual equilibrium, John F. Conway's *The Canadian Family in Crisis* (Toronto: James Lorimer, 1990) has usefully presented the numbers on Canada from the left-liberal point of view. I have also drawn from the *Canada Year Book 1990*, from Roger Sauvé, *Canadian People Patterns*, and from Jean Dumas, *Report on the Demographic Situation in Canada 1990*. Readers interested in pursuing these matters are encouraged to check these sources, as I have not wanted to clutter the text with footnotes.
3. From *Transition*, March 1987, p. 10. This is a publication of the Vanier Institute of the Family, an Ottawa-based institution that combines compassion for the family with a disingenuous, fence-sitting promotion of the sort of left-liberal views that are sure to bring it down.
4. The first newsmaking analysis of this kind was Daniel Patrick Moynihan's *Family and Nation* (New York: Harcourt, Brace, Jovanovich, 1987), which publicly shamed the U.S. administration and showed how policy was itself a cause of black family breakdown. Charles Murray's *Losing Ground* (see note 7, below) is devoted to this very theme; and more recent analyses, such as by Herbert L. Smith, "Current Trends in Nonmarital Fertility and Divorce,"

in Bryce J. Christensen, ed., *The Retreat from Marriage* (New York: University Press of America, 1990), are obliged to split black from white society in order to make sense of the numbers.

5.  See note 8, below.

6.  Charles Murray, *The Emerging British Underclass* (London: The IEA Health and Welfare Unit, 1990). Murray makes an important distinction between the *poor* and the *underclass*. The latter is distinguished not by its low income, but by its behaviour, which generally includes illegitimacy, refusal to join the labour market, use of drugs, and violent crime.

7.  Charles Murray, *Losing Ground: American Social Policy 1950-1980* (New York: Basic Books, 1984).

8.  The figure on black percentage of GNP is found in Michael Novak, *The Spirit of Democratic Capitalism* (New York: Touchstone Books, 1982), p. 220. The Harlem figure is from Edward C. Banfield, *The Unheavenly City Revisited*, in Charles Murray, *Losing Ground*, p. 271, n. 2. The figure on families headed by married couples is found in his Table 24, p. 262.

# 7  /  COMPULSORY MISEDUCATION

1.  I am indebted to the sound and well-written critique of education by Hilda Neatby, *So Little for the Mind* (Toronto: Clarke Irwin, 1953, p. 276), for this quote, taken from *Maclean's*, and for her general discussion.

2.  John E. Chubb and Terry M. Moe, *Politics, Markets, and America's Schools* (Washington, D.C.: The Brookings Institution, 1990). Because it was published by a highly respected but predominately left-leaning think-tank, this book has been a bombshell in the world of educational reform. This is so primarily because it was based on a careful analysis of a monumental data base, which led the authors to conclude that "existing [educational] institutions cannot solve the problem, because they *are* the problem . . ." The authors reiterate the well-known conclusion that spending and educational success are unrelated, with the exception being that better U.S. schools have more money to afford better teacher student ratios. This would seem to be a dubious source of success, however, because many of the nations that whip us academically have teacher/student ratios far in excess of our own. South Korean classes in urban areas commonly have 55 students, and they regularly place first in international academic comparisons. At least in the West, as class size diminishes, standards seem to fall. Professor Eric A. Hanushek of the University of Rochester reported in *Journal of Economic Literature* on his review of 65 studies, 49 of which showed no statistical relationship between spending and student performance. Of the 16 that showed a relationship, 3 were negative. Of another 112 studies of teacher/pupil ratios, only 23 showed any relationship — 9 positive, and 14 negative. (Reported in

Edwin G. West, "Restoring Family Autonomy in Education," *Chronicles*, October 1990.)

3. Stephen T. Easton, *Education in Canada: An Analysis of Elementary, Secondary, and Vocational Schooling* (Vancouver: The Fraser Institute, 1988).

4. *Broken Words: Why Five Million Canadians Are Illiterate*, published by the Southam Newspaper Group, 1987 and 1990, Toronto, Ontario, Canada.

5. Barry W. Poulson, "Education and the Family During the Industrial Revolution," in *The American Family and the State* (San Francisco: Pacific Research Institute for Public Policy, 1986), pp. 138-39. Poulson writes that "the overwhelming evidence is that American families from the very outset provided the vocational and social skills that enabled their children not only to function, but to achieve higher levels of income and wealth than their parents" (p. 139).

6. George Radwanski, *Ontario Study of the Relevance of Education and the Issue of Dropouts* (Toronto: Ministry of Education, 1987). This excellent report advocates a moderately traditionalist view of education (high expectations, an emphasis on results, standard exams, etc.) that echoes the opinion of the people — but not of the educational establishment. It has been virtually ignored.

7. A.J.C. King, *The Adolescent Experience* (Toronto: Ontario Secondary School Teachers' Federation, 1986).

8. A.J.C. King and M.J. Peart, *The Good School* (Toronto: The Ontario Secondary School Teachers' Federation, 1990), p. 3.

9. *The Family in America*, vol. 2, no. 6, June 1988, p. 3.

10. Bryce Christensen, "Schools vs. the Family," in *Utopia Against the Family* (San Francisco: Ignatius Press, 1990), p. 87.

11. Egerton Ryerson, quoted in Neatby, *So Little for the Mind*, p. 4.

12. Robert Nisbet, in his foreword to *The American Family and the State* (San Francisco: Pacific Research Institute, 1986), p. xxv. As usual, Nisbet succinctly formulates the war against the family in this interesting book. His trenchant analysis of Rousseau's influence is best seen in his *The Quest for Community* (1953).

13. Murray N. Rothbard, "The Progressive Era and the Family," in *The American Family and the State* (San Francisco: Pacific Research Institute for Public Policy: San Francisco, 1986), p. 116.

14. Ibid., pp. 127-28.

15. *The Family in America*, vol. 2., no. 6, June 1988, p. 3.

16. Stephen Clarkson and Christina McCall, *Trudeau and Our Times* (Toronto: McClelland & Stewart, 1991), pp. 49, 121. It continues to astonish how few Canadians have actually read anything Pierre Elliott Trudeau wrote, particularly prior to his political career. His elegant, but intellectually thin, *Feder-*

*alism and the French Canadians* is an elaborate program for installing piecemeal Fabian socialism in Canada. Although he never called himself a socialist (because of the plethora of confusing varieties), he leaves no doubt in his writings that his political and economic preferences are socialist. It was the role of the State, he often argued, to bring the people ordered freedom. The political equation he clearly relied upon in all he did was derived from Rousseau's notion of the General Will, and resulted in the contradictory belief that more government will make you free.

17. George S. Counts, *Dare the Schools Build a New Social Order?* (New York: John Day, 1932).
18. In Paolo Lionni, *The Leipzig Connection* (Sheridan, Oregon: Delphian Press, 1988), p. 84.
19. In the 26th *Yearbook* of the National Society for the Study of Education, 1926.
20. Counts, *Dare the Schools Build a New Social Order?*, pp. 102-104.
21. John Dewey, *Experience and Education* (New York: Collier-Macmillan, 1963).
22. Ibid., p. 50.
23. Ibid., p. 59.
24. Neatby, *So Little for the Mind*, p. 25. I am grateful to Miss Neatby's calm and thorough treatment of Dewey's influence for much of what is told here.
25. Ibid., p. 26.
26. Ibid., p. 55.
27. Russell Kirk, *The Conservative Mind: From Burke to Eliot* (Chicago: Regnery Books, 1986), pp. 418-19. (7th Revised Edition.)
28. For a short but wide-ranging treatment of the influence of the Wundtians on American education, see Paolo Lionni, *The Leipzig Connection* (Sheridan, Oregon: Delphian Press, 1988).
29. Ibid., p. 8.
30. Ibid., pp. 18-19.
31. Radwanski, *Ontario Study of the Relevance of Education*, Chapter 3.
32. Mark Holmes, "The Future of the Public School in Canada," in *Reform and Relevance in Schooling* (Toronto: OISE, 1991), edited by Derek J. Allison and Jerry Paquette, pp. 92-107.
33. Stephen J. Tonsor, "Authority, Power, and the University," in *Education in a Free Society* (Indianapolis: Liberty Press, 1973), p. 212.
34. Chester E. Finn Jr., "Narcissus Goes to School," *Commentary*, vol. 89, no. 6, June 1990.
35. *The Phoenix*, December 1990.
36. *Chronicles*, July 1991, p. 12.
37. *Chronicles*, February 1991, pp. 42-44.

# 8 / LOOKING AFTER THEIR SOULS

1. Edward Hoffman, "Pop Psychology and the Rise of Anti-Child Ideology: 1966-1974," in *The Family in America*, vol. 5, no. 8, August 1991.
2. Ibid., p. 3.
3. Kathleen M. Gow, *Yes, Virginia, There Is Right and Wrong!* (Wheaton, Ill.: Tyndale House, 1980).
4. Ibid., p. 17.
5. Quoted in Phyllis Schlafly, ed., *Child Abuse in the Classroom: Official Transcript of Proceedings* before the U.S. Department of Education's public hearings on the Hatch Amendment (Alton, Ill.: Marquette Press, 1984), flyleaf.
6. Phoebe Courtney, "The NEA and Child Abuse in the Schools" (Littleton, Col.: The Independent American Newsletter, November 1986).
7. From *Connections Centrepiece*, a publication of the Ontario Moral/Values Education Association, vol. 1, no. 1, January 1990.
8. Clive Beck, *Ethics: An Introduction* (Toronto: McGraw-Hill Ryerson, 1972), p. 109. Insights into the insidious efforts of the U.S. government to permeate U.S. schools with the Dewey philosophy can be gained from B.K. Eakman, *Educating for the New World Order* (Portland: Halcyon House, 1991). The book also details the influence of Rogers and Maslow on PLI ideology.
9. How does one explain the extraordinarily pervasive influence of Jewish writers and academics on the spread of moral relativism? After all, Judaism is at the heart of our culture, and was arguably the world's first influential monotheistic religion, complete with moral absolutes. In his *Commentary* article (August 1991), the trenchant Jewish social critic Irving Kristol suggests that Jewish intellectuals of the post-1960s vintage argue for moral relativism, secular humanism, and situation ethics as a revolt against the absolutist Christian ethos that has historically oppressed them. Religious/secular humanism has been a substitute "private" religion promoted by such intellectuals to fend off the public threat of Christianity. Kristol warns that the Christian ethos may resurge in response to the erosion of community that such secular beliefs have engendered.
10. In Nils-Eric Brodin and H. Edward Rowe, "America's Sex Education Furor," published by Richmond Concerned Parents Action League, Box 94053 Richmond, B.C., V6Y 2A2.
11. "Death Education in the Classroom," *The Phyllis Schlafly Report*, vol. 21, no. 10, section 1, May 1988.
12. Ibid., p. 1. Eagle Forum, which publishes this report, does an admirable and indefatigable job of making the facts available to the public.
13. *The Phyllis Schlafly Report*, vol. 24, no. 7, section 1.
14. "Beware of Smiling Aliens," *Alberta Report*, November 26, 1990, p. 38.

15. Once again, I am indebted to *The Phyllis Schlafly Report* for its succinct rendering of the signposts of this subject, especially in vol. 19, no. 9, section 1, April 1990. Also, to Eakman, *Educating for the New World Order*, above.

16. *Focus on the Family*, May 20, 1990.

17. Cited in Gow, *Yes, Virginia, There Is Right and Wrong!*, p. 49.

18. *Commentary*, August 1991, p. 25.

19. Schlafly, *Child Abuse in the Classroom*, p. 59.

20. Send to Pere Marquette Press, P.O. Box 495, Alton, Illinois, 62002, U.S.A. — for an eyeful.

21. *Chronicles*, July 1991, p. 11.

22. Stanton E. Samenow, *Inside the Criminal Mind* (New York: Random House, 1984), from Preface, Chapter 7, and Chapter 10.

23. Thanks to *New Dimensions* magazine, September 1990, for drawing attention to these books, and for these quotations.

24. *The Phyllis Schlafly Report*, vol. 24, no. 10, section 1, May 1991.

25. *Human Life International Reports*, December 1991.

26. From Schlafly, *Child Abuse in the Classroom*.

27. Dr. James Dobson and Gary L. Bauer, *Children at Risk: The Battle for the Hearts and Minds of Our Kids* (Vancouver, Dallas: World Publishing, 1990).

28. Ibid., p. 48.

29. *Facts About You* (Toronto: Kimberly-Clark Canada, Inc.: 1990).

30. Some of the background information was obtained from Randy Engel, *Sex Education: The Final Plague* (Maryland: Human Life International, 1989).

31. See Philip Rieff, "Reich's Religion of Energy," in *The Triumph of the Therapeutic* (Chicago: University of Chicago Press, 1966), pp. 141-88.

32. Ibid., p. 160.

33. Ibid., p. 161.

34. Engel, *Sex Education*, p. 36.

35. Ibid., p. 39.

36. Despite the widespread presence of the signatories' ideas in modern society, it is astounding how few people have actually read this manifesto. A copy may be obtained from Prometheus Books, 700 Amherst Street, Buffalo, N.Y., 14215.

37. For a brief but thorough review of the history of sex-ed, see Jessica Pegis, Ian Gentles, and L.L. de Veber, *Sex Education: A Review of the Literature from Canada, the United States, Britain, and Sweden* (Toronto: Human Life Institute, 1986).

38. Ibid., p. 7.

39. Ibid., p. 14.

40. Mark L. Milliron, "A Rationale for Implementing a Program of Sex Abstinence Education in the Schools of British Columbia," presented to the Royal Commission on Health Care and Costs, February 25, 1991.

41. Pegis, Gentles, de Veber, *Sex Education*, p. 31.
42. Milliron, "Rationale for Implementing a Program," p. 5.
43. Ibid., p. 7.
44. Janet Ajzenstat and Ian Gentles, *Sex Education in Canada: A Survey of Policies and Programs* (Toronto: Human Life Institute, 1988), Report no. 6.
45. Ibid., p. 40.
46. Ibid., p. 42.
47. Ibid., p. 52.
48. Dinah Richard, Ph.D., *Has Sex Education Failed Our Teenagers?* (Pomona, Calif.: Focus on the Family Publishing, 1990). I am grateful to this excellent report for most of the U.S. medical and scientific references in this section.
49. In Barrett L. Mosbacker, "The Final Step: Clinics, Children, and Contraceptives," in *School-Based Clinics* (Illinois: Crossway, 1987).
50. Robert Ruff, *Aborting Planned Parenthood* (Houston: New Vision, 1988), pp. 66ff. Two recent studies, Orton and Rosenblatt, *Adolescent Pregnancy in Ontario 1976-1986* (McMaster University, October 1991), and a Statistics Canada study released May 12, 1992, both indicate a drop in teen pregnancies since 1975, and attribute this to sex-ed programs. The McMaster study, however, with no control group, fails to explain why teen pregnancy rates also dropped in provinces with no sex-ed programs; and it does not reveal that the abortion rate for unwed teens rose, and the decline in pregnancy they found in girls 15-19 was due to a decline in pregnancy in *married* teen mothers. Planned Parenthood was a sponsor of this study. Statistics Canada does not explain why, although its overall rate is down, the teen pregnancy rate has been going back *up* since 1985.
51. Stephen Genuis, M.D., *Risky Sex* (Edmonton: Alta.: KEG Publishing, 1991), p. 18.
52. Health and Welfare Canada, verified by letter of March 4, 1992, from Mr. Claude Mathieu, medical devices inspector, the Toronto office; for 1991, by letter of March 9, 1992, from Lindsay Blaney, Health and Welfare, Bureau of Field Operations, Ottawa.
53. Genuis, *Risky Sex*, p. 57.
54. Richard, *Has Sex Education Failed Our Teeangers?*, p. 43.
55. A good overview of AFLA can be found in "Recovering Sanity: New Trends in Sex Education," *The Family in America*, vol. 5, no. 7, July 1991, for a peek into the minimal shift in Canadian policy, see Milliron, "Rationale for Implementing a Program," p. 18.
56. *The Family in America*, vol 5., no. 7, July 1991.
57. Richard, *Has Sex Education Failed Our Teenagers?*, p. 45.
58. Ibid., p. 50.
59. Ibid., p. 60.

60. Key resolutions from this convention are reported in *Education Reporter*, no. 67, August 1991.

# 9 / LOOKING AFTER THEIR BODIES

1. Jon N. Leonard, J.L. Hoffer, and N. Pritikin, *Live Longer Now* (New York: Grosset and Dunlap, 1974), p. 8.
2. Ibid., p. 10.
3. Charles T. Kuntzleman, *Concepts for Wellness* (Spring Arbor, Mich.: Arbor Press, 1982), p. 32. I am indebted to this survey for a number of the facts quoted in this section.
4. Ibid., p. 40.
5. Ibid., p. 81.
6. From a survey by Professor Robert Goode, Physiology Department, University of Toronto.
7. *Canada Fitness Survey*, 1981.
8. *CAHPER Journal*, March/April 1986, p. 10.
9. Robert Goode and Richard Volpe, in an unpublished prospectus for a book entitled *The Child, Adolescent, and Physical Activity*, January 1991.
10. *The Medical Post*, November 8, 1988.
11. A government program called "Quality Daily Physical Education" (operated by Fitness and Amateur Sport, Ottawa) has certified 234 of Canada's 15,423 public schools with quality programs. Here we have one branch of government bravely generating top-down solutions to problems caused by another branch.

# 10 / THE SOLUTION: TAKE BACK THE SCHOOLS

1. John E. Chubb and Terrry M. Moe, *Politics, Markets, and America's Schools*, (Washington, D.C.: The Brookings Institution, 1990), p. 32.
2. Ibid., p. 34.
3. Ibid., p. 35.
4. Even brilliant essays such as by Mark Holmes, "School Effectiveness: From Research to Implementation to Improvement," in *Educational Policy for Effective Schools* (Toronto: OISE Press, undated), resort to such intellectual pleading for remedy-by-moral-suasion. This can be successful only in the short term, and only insofar as many are persuaded. The better solution is to create a structural alignment of family responsibility, motive, and product, which is what all private schools do; the morality of success then follows.
5. Chubb and Moe, *Politics, Markets, and America's Schools*, p. 218.

6. Ibid., p. 217.

7. Ibid.

8. J.S. Coleman and T.R. Hoffer, *Public and Private Schools* (New York: Basic Books, 1987). Also, J.S. Coleman, "Do Students Learn More in Private Schools Than in Public Schools?" *The Madison Papers* (Tallahassee, Fl.: The James Madison Institute For Public Policy Studies, 1990). Also, Mark Holmes, "The Future of the Public School in Canada," in D. Allison, and J. Paquette, eds., *Reform and Relevance: Dropouts, De-streaming, and the Common Curriculum* (Toronto: OISE, 1991), pp. 92-109.

9. Coleman, *The Madison Papers*, p. 4.

10. Holmes, "The Future of the Public School in Canada," p. 97.

11. See "Choice In Education: Legislative Summary," published by the American Legislative Exchange Council, Washington, D.C., 1990.

12. *Imprimis*, a newsletter by Hillsdale College, Michigan, March 1992.

13. For information on this program, write to Executive Director, Educational Choice Charitable Trust, c/o Golden Rule Insurance Company, 7440 Woodland Drive, Indianapolis, Indiana, 46278-1719, U.S.A.

14. Thomas Sowell, *Education: Assumptions Versus History* (Stanford, Calif.: The Hoover Institute, 1986), p. 106. Sowell, a black economist and social commentator from a poor background, is a colossus among writers on socio-economic subjects, admired worldwide for his power and clarity of expression and pointed grasp of economic logic. Almost alone among black intellectuals, he persistently argues that every principle of a free society favours blacks, while every principle of left-liberal collectivism, while initially attractive, will ultimately erode black society. It has done that already.

15. Barbara Lerner, "Good News About American Education," in *Commentary*, vol. 91, no. 3, March 1991.

16. Thanks again to Eagle Forum for this creative and compelling idea (Eagle Forum, Alton, Illinois).

# 11 / THE FEMINIST MISTAKE

1. From *Times Literary Supplement* article quoted at the head of this chapter. (Kenneth Minogue, June 7, 1991.)

2. Cited in *The Globe and Mail*, May 11, 1992.

3. A thorough revelation of the feminist stranglehold on money (and therefore power) in Canada can be found in Danielle Crittenden, "REAL Women Don't Eat Crow," *Saturday Night*, May 1988. Actual detailed summaries — shocking to review — of the precise groups given money can be obtained from Canada's Secretary of State, Women's Program, Ottawa, under the Freedom of Information Act. It is upsetting to see millions of dollars earmarked for any

lobby groups, feminist, masculinist, or otherwise, but especially for fringe radical groups that are not supported by the majority of males or females in Canada.

4. See Allan Carlson's incisive summary of this subject, in his essay, "Charity Begins at Home," *Chronicles*, August 1988, pp. 12-15.

5. *Chronicles*, April 1988.

6. *Chronicles*, August 1988.

7. Jean Dumas, *Marriage and Conjugal Life in Canada* (Ottawa: Statistics Canada, 1992).

8. Feminist Marlene Dixon, in Donald DeMarco, "The Marxist Roots of Contemporary Feminism," *Social Justice Review*, September-October, 1988, p. 151.

9. Ibid., p. 152.

10. Jerome Carcopino, "Marriage, Woman, and the Family," *Daily Life in Ancient Rome* (London: Penguin, 1941), pp. 89-115.

11. Michael Levin, *Feminism and Freedom* (Transaction Books: New Brunswick, New Jersey, 1987). This book offers the most thorough and rigorous philosophical analysis of feminism, and finds it embarrassingly wanting.

12. *Saturday Review*, June 14, 1975, p. 12.

13. *Maclean's*, August 16, 1984.

14. Michael Levin, *Feminism and Freedom*, p. 74.

15. Peter Shaw, "Feminist Literary Criticism," in *The War Against the Intellect* (Iowa City: University of Iowa Press, 1989), pp. 67-88. This essay will continue to embarrass feminist critics.

16. Allan Carlson, *Family Questions* (Transaction Books: New Brunswick, New Jersey, 1988). Carlson is an astute and widely informed critic of modern antifamily movements. This section draws widely from his Chapter Three, "The Androgyny Hoax," pp. 29-47.

17. Ibid., p. 44.

18. Ibid., p. 34.

19. Ibid., p. 36.

20. *Alberta Report*, November 25, 1991.

21. Carlson, *Family Questions*, p. 38.

22. Diana Baumrind, "Are Androgynous Individuals More Effective Persons and Parents?" *Child Development*, 53 (January 1982), pp. 45-66, cited in Carlson, *Family Questions*, p. 42.

23. Margrit Eichler, "The Pro-family Movement: Are They for or Against Families?" in *Feminist Perspectives Feministes*, no date.

24. Eleanor Maccoby and Carol Jacklin, *The Psychology of Sex Differences* (Stanford, California: Stanford University Press, 1974), vol. 1. This volume is a survey of the entire field of sex-difference research to the date of publication. The authors struggled throughout to give the benefit of any doubt

in these studies to the feminist assertion of sameness. However, both scholars concluded that there are indeed inherent, genetically/hormonally controlled differences.

25. Levin, *Feminism and Freedom*, p. 70.

26. For a most sobering survey of revolutionary violence fired by egalitarian fervour, see Erik von Kuehnelt-Leddihn, *Leftism Revisited* (Washington: Regnery Gateway, 1990), pp. 82-84, and also Simon Schama, *Citizens* (New York: Alfred Knopf, 1989), pp. 678 ff.

27. George Gilder, *Men and Marriage* (Gretna, Louisiana: Pelican Books, 1986), p. 20.

28. For a fascinating layman's account of this process, see Lawrence Crapo, *Hormones, the Messengers of Life* (Stanford, California: A publication of the Stanford Alumni Association, 1985).

29. Ibid., p. 100.

30. Gilder, *Men and Marriage*, p. 24.

31. Levin, *Feminism and Freedom*, p. 91.

32. Steven Goldberg, *The Inevitability of Patriarchy: Why the Biological Difference Between Men and Women Always Produces Male Domination* (New York: William Morrow, 1973).

33. Ibid., p. 228.

34. Neil J. MacLusky and Frederick Naftolin, "Sexual Differentiation of the Central Nervous System," *Science* 211 (March 20, 1981), 1294 ff, cited in Carlson, *Family Questions*, pp. 42-43.

35. Toronto *Star*, November 17, 1988.

36. Ann Moir and David Jessel, *BrainSex: The Real Difference Between Men and Women* (London: Mandarin, 1989), p. 9.

37. This section reviews, in a modified form, a number of the arguments put forth in Chapter Ten of *The Trouble with Canada* (and inspired by George Gilder's analysis).

38. Gilder, *Men and Marriage*, p. 65.

39. Lawrence Stone, *Road to Divorce* (Oxford: Oxford University Press, 1990), p. 420.

40. Gilder, *Men and Marriage*, p. 77.

41. Ibid., p. 78.

42. Ibid., p. 5.

43. Ibid., p. 10.

44. Ibid., p. 13.

45. Ibid., p. 14.

46. See Irving Kristol, "The Future of American Jewry," *Commentary*, August 1991. As noted earlier, Kristol explains the predominant left-liberalism of North American Jews, and their preference for secular humanist ideas as a reaction to the dominant Christian ethos. In the face of a religion that has

persecuted Jews, the argument goes, it is best to promote secular liberal values.

47. In "Time to Tell The Feminists Bye-Bye," *The Phyllis Schlafly Report*, December 1990.

# 12 / WOMEN AT WAR

1. *The Phyllis Schlafly Report*, June 1991.

2. Brian Mitchell, *Weak Link: The Feminization of the American Military* (Washington, B.C.: Regnery Gateway, 1989).

3. Ibid., p. 8.

4. Ibid., p. 84.

5. *Svenska Dagbladet* (April 27, 1988), cited in Eric Brodin, "Collectivized Daycare in Other Countries," in *Who Will Rock The Cradle?* (Washington, D C,: Eagle Forum Education and Legal Defense Fund, 1989), p. 39.

6. Ibid., p. 33.

7. Ibid., p. 36.

8. Ibid., p. 39.

9. Robert Nisbet, *The Quest for Community* (San Francisco: Institute for Contemporary Studies, 1990), p. 181.

10. Cited in *New Dimensions* magazine, November 1990.

11. *Alberta Report*, June 24, 1990.

12. Wendy Dreskin, "Daycare, A Child's View," in *Who Will Rock the Cradle?*, p. 128.

13. Elliot Barker, M.D., "The Critical Importance of Mothering," *Mothering*, vol. 47.

14. George Gilder, "Child Care in a Gender Neutral Society," in *Who Will Rock The Cradle?*, pp. 147-64.

15. J. Bowlby, *Attachment and Loss* (New York: Basic Books, 1969), p. xiii.

16. Brenda Hunter, "Attachment and Infant Daycare," in *Who Will Rock the Cradle?*, p. 60.

17. In Robert Karen, "Becoming Attached," *Atlantic Monthly*, February 1990, p. 69.

18. Barbara Hattner, "New Light on Daycare Research," in *Who Will Rock the Cradle?*, pp. 69-83.

19. Ibid., p. 77.

20. *New Dimensions* magazine, November 1990, p. 23. The last sentence in the quotation from Burton White is from *The Family in America*, vol. 5, No. 2, February 1991.

21. Ibid., p. 42.

22. Reed Bell, M.D., "Health Risks from Daycare," in *Who Will Rock the Cradle?*, pp. 115-22.

23. Bryce J. Christensen, *Utopia Against the Family* (San Francisco: Ignatius Press, 1990), p. 72.
24. In *New Dimensions*, November 1990, p. 29.
25. Michael Schwartz, "Do We Want Government to be Our Babysitter?" in *Who Will Rock the Cradle?*, pp. 269-88.
26. *The Phyllis Schlafly Report*, April 1989.
27. Merlin B. Brinkerhoff and Eugen Lupri, "Interspousal Violence," *Canadian Journal of Sociology*, 13 (4), 1988.
28. Reported in Brinkerhoff and Lupri, "Religious Involvement and Spousal Violence" (unpublished). Available from Department of Sociology, University of Calgary.
29. Cited in *Alberta Report*, March 25, 1991.
30. See Murray A. Straus, "Assaults by Wives on Husbands: Implications for Primary Prevention of Marital Violence," a survey paper presented at the 1989 meeting of the American Society of Criminology, and published by the Family Research Laboratory, University of New Hampshire, Durham, New Hampshire, U.S.A. 03824.
31. R.L. McNeely and Gloria Robinson-Simpson, "The Truth About Violence: A Falsely Framed Issue," in Nicholas Davidson, ed., *Gender Sanity* (New York: University Press of America, 1989), pp. 163-76.
32. Ibid,, p. 65.
33. McNeely and Robinson-Simpson, "The Truth About Violence," p. 165.
34. Ibid., p. 168.
35. Straus, "Assaults by Wives on Husbands," p. 244.
36. McNeely and Robinson-Simpson, p. 171.
37. The same figures are shown in a survey of studies by Professor Ferrel M. Christensen, Department of Philosophy, University of Alberta, Edmonton. Of crimes reported to police or other officials, child abuse was perpetrated 77 percent of the time in single-parent families; in two-parent families it was perpetrated by mothers 26 percent, and by fathers 28 percent, and by both parents 37 percent.
38. Bell Hooks, "Challenging Patriarchy Means Challenging Men to Change," *Z* magazine, February 1991, pp. 33-36.
39. See Victor Fuchs, *Who Shall Live? Health and Economics and Social Change* (New York: Basic Books, 1983), pp. 28 ff.
40. James Q. Wilson and Richard J. Herrnstein, *Crime and Human Nature* (New York: Simon and Schuster, 1985), pp. 439-58.
41. The academic journals stagger under the weight of turgid feminist articles by such as Myra Marx Feree's "Beyond Separate Spheres: Feminism and Family Research" (*Journal of Marriage and the Family*, November 1990). Such pseudo-Marxist analyses, supported, like hers, with grants, agonize over the equal division of labour in the family, an institution she describes as an arena

"of gender and generational struggle" (Ugh!). In response to the query why most couples seem quite happy with their unequal division of domestic labour (only 21 percent of women say they want to do less), she cites Komter, another feminist scholar who — typical of conspiracy theorists — declares (again) that women are only content because they are dupes.

They don't complain, she argues, "because of the *'hidden power' of gender ideology* to suppress conflict by creating resignation, fear of disturbing the relationship, and denial of one's own feelings." In short, Komter knows your mind and heart better than you do. Like cultists and magicians, if these folks can't persuade they confuse, by attributing causes to hidden explanations only they have the intelligence to see. Their theory is so broad it is literally unfalsifiable — and that's why it should be classified not as science, but junk-science.

42. Keith Bryant, of Consumer Economics and Housing, Cornell University, in "The Economics of Housewifery," a paper presented at the Conference on Liberty, the Family and Home Production (Rockford Institute, June 6-9, 1991), cites U.S. statistical abstracts figures showing a 5 percent decline in the labour participation rate of husbands. Another study has shown a 12 percent decrease for married men; see J. Wilkie, *The Decline in Men's Labor Force Participation and Income and the Changing Structure of Family Support in the U.S.*, Table 2, University of Connecticut, 1990.

43. Brigitte Berger, "At Odds with American Reality," in *Society* (New York: Rutgers University Press, 1985) July-August, pp. 77-78.

44. *The Family in America* (Rockford Institute), April 1987.

# 13 / RADICAL HOMOSEXUALS VS. THE FAMILY

1. These first two quotations, and considerable information on the homosexual movement, have been provided to the public by *New Dimensions* magazine in a variety of issues from 1988 to 1990. The editors are to be commended for placing these issues front and centre.

2. *Alberta Report*, December 17, 1990.

3. *New Dimensions*, January 1990, p. 32.

4. *New Dimensions*, January 1990, p. 36.

5. In Reginald Bibby, *Mosaic Madness* (Toronto: Stoddart, 1990), p. 67.

6. *The Family in America*, vol. 1, no. 3, May 1987.

7. J. Marmor, ed., *Homosexual Behaviour: A Modern Reappraisal* (New York: Basic Books, 1980), cited in Brad Hayton, "The Homosexual Agenda: Issues and Arguments" (Colorado Springs: Focus on the Family, 1990), p. 13.

8. Institute for the Scientific Investigation of Sexuality (ISIS), "What Causes Homosexuality and Can It Be Changed?" 1984. ISIS, which was formed by

Paul Cameron, Ph.D., to do battle with the predominantly Kinseyan stranglehold on sex data in North America, has been renamed the Family Research Institute, and is based in Washington D.C.: (703) 690-8536.

9. Anne Moir and David Jessel, *BrainSex: The Real Difference Between Men and Women* (London: Mandarin Press, 1991), p. 114. This book is an impressive survey of the current scientific research on male/female differences.

10. Cited in *Conservative Chronicle*, September 5, 1990.

11. A fair-minded overview of the American homosexual movement (which has tended to steer the Canadian trends), which includes a survey of the psychiatric politics, can be found in a book by Congressman William Dannemeyer, *Shadow in the Land: Homosexuality in America* (San Francisco: Ignatius Press, 1989).

12. From an unpublished paper by George Slater, Ph.D., "Can Sexual Orientation Be Changed?" in which these various matters are summarized.

13. Elizabeth R. Moberly, *Homosexuality: A New Christian Ethic* (Cambridge, England: James Clarke; and Greenwood, South Carolina: Attic Press, 1983), p. 9. Cited in Slater, ibid.

14. Cited in Hayton, "The Homosexual Agenda," p. 24.

15. Enrique T. Rueda and Michael Schwartz, *Gays, AIDS and You* (Old Greenwich, Connecticut: Devin Adair, 1987), pp. 67 ff.

16. Ibid., p. 114.

17. *Alberta Report*, April 9, 1990.

18. Rueda and Schwarz, *Gays, AIDS and You*, p. 72. Also, see *American Journal of Psychiatry*, 1984, vol. 141, pp. 173-81, cited in Slater, "Can Homosexual Orientation Be Changed?" Psychiatrist Lee Birk successfully converted 100 percent of a group of fourteen exclusive homosexuals who desired change. See Birk, "The Myth of Classical Homosexuality," in J. Marmor, *Homosexual Behavior* (New York: Basic Books, 1980), pp. 376-90.

19. Ibid., p. 28. For a description of this entire medical debacle, Dannemeyer refers us to Ronald Bayer, *Homosexuality and American Psychiatry: The Politics of Diagnosis* (New York: Basic Books, 1981).

20. Judith Reisman, Ph.D. and Edward Eichel, *Kinsey, Sex and Fraud: The Indoctrination of a People* (Lafayette, Louisiana: Lochinvar-Huntington House, 1990), p. 144. This extremely detailed book is the most recent — and best — of a series of attacks on the original Kinsey data.

21. Benjamin, Lee Whorf, *Language, Thought, and Reality* (Cambridge, Massachusetts: The M.I.T. Press, 1964), p. 137.

22. Thanks are due to Dannemeyer, *Shadow in the Land*, for his overview of the language strategy, pp. 125-35.

23. Rueda and Schwartz, *Gays, AIDS and You*, pp. 60-61.

24. Robert J. Kus, "Alcoholics Anonymous and Gay American Men," *Journal of Homosexuality*, vol. 14, no. 2, p. 254. Owing to the reluctance of Canadian

researchers to gather statistics on homosexual behaviour, we must rely on
U.S. studies — many of them by homosexual researchers themselves. Holly
Johnson, of the Canadian *Centre for Justice Statistics* (Ottawa) explained to
me that the centre does not publish data on homosexual crime, because it
"could be used against them." I responded that data on heterosexual crimes
is "used against" heterosexuals, and that her job was to publish the data, not
to make political decisions (telephone conversation, May 20, 1992).

25. P.H. Gebhard and A.B. Johnson, *The Kinsey Data, 1979*, in Hayton, *The
Homosexual Agenda*, p. 12, n. 1.
26. Quoted in Rueda and Schwartz, *Gays, AIDS and You*, p. 26.
27. Reisman and Eichel, *Kinsey, Sex and Fraud*, p. 2.
28. Ibid., p. 3.
29. Ibid., p. 15.
30. Ibid., p. 7.
31. Ibid., p. 7.
32. Ibid., p. 137.
33. Ibid., p. 210.
34. Ibid., p. 8.
35. Ibid., p. 10.
36. Gary Kelly, *Learning About Sex: the Contemporary Guide for Young Adults*
(Hauppage, New York: Barron, 1986), especially pages 50-77.
37. Personal communication with Doubleday Canada sales department, November 1991.
38. Reisman and Eichel, *Kinsey, Sex and Fraud*, p. 45.
39. Ibid., p. 73.
40. Ibid., p. 114.
41. Ibid., p. 146.
42. Ibid., p. 142.
43. Gary Kelly, *Learning About Sex*, pp. 70-71.
44. Much, but not all, of the upsetting information that follows has been compiled
by Brad Hayton, in *The Homosexual Agenda: Issues and Arguments*. I have
detailed in the body of my text some of the studies from which he draws,
simply to reassure readers who are bound to recoil, that these data come
from sound sources. Readers may send for a copy of Hayton's detailed paper,
which will lead them to a great many original studies and sources: Focus on
the Family, Colorado Springs, Colorado, 80995, U.S.A.; telephone: (719)
531-3400. In Canada, it's P.O. Box 9800, Vancouver, British Columbia, V6B
4G3; telephone: (604) 684-8333.
45. British Columbia Ministry of Health, "Dimensions of Multiple Victim Sexual
Abuse in British Columbia," July 1, 1991.
46. "Children as Victims of Violent Crime," published by Supply and Services
Canada, Catalogue 85-002, Ottawa, May 1991.

47. *Psychological Reports*, no. 57, pp. 1227-36. Also, see Cameron, et al., "Child Molestation and Homosexuality," *Psychological Reports*, no. 58, 1986, pp. 327-37. Also, A. Bell and M. Weinberg, *Homosexualities* (New York: Simon and Schuster, 1978), and Jay and Young, *Gay Report* (New York: Summit, 1979). The last two books contain copious data on the unnatural, unhealthy, and often dangerous behaviour of homosexuals.

48. "Homosexual Love Away from School Is O.K., Gay Teachers Say," New York *Post*, July 11, 1979, p. 5.

49. Lorraine Day, M.D., *AIDS: What the Government Isn't Telling You* (Palm Desert, California: Rockford Press, 1991), p. 111.

50. *Globe and Mail*, May 28, 1992.

51. Judith Reisman, Ph.D., *"Soft Porn" Plays Hardball* (Lafayette, Louisiana: Huntington House Publishers, 1991), p. 155.

52. For a quick overview of this sordid subject, see David A. Scott, "Pornography — Its Effects on the Family, Community and Culture" Child and Family Protection Institute, Washington D.C., 1985. For a full and intensely disturbing report, see the Final Report of the U.S. Attorney General's Commission on Pornography (Nashville, Tennessee: Rutledge Hill Press, 1986), and also the thorough but much tamer *Pornography and Prostitution in Canada* (Ottawa: Ministry of Supply and Services, 1985), Catalogue J2-55/1-1985E.

53. Cited in Day, *AIDS: What the Government Isn't Telling You*, p. 106.

54. See L. Corey and K.K. Holmes, "Sexual Transmission of Hepatitis A in Homosexual Men," *New England Journal of Medicine*, no. 302, 1980, pp. 435-38. See also the San Francisco Men's Health Study, *Journal of the American Medical Association*, vol. 3, no. 257, January 16, 1987, p. 323.

55. Quoted in Day, *AIDS: What the Government Isn't Telling You*, p. 132.

56. Day, *AIDS: What the Government Isn't Telling You*, pp. 122 ff.

57. The Marquis de Sade, *The 120 Days of Sodom, and Other Writings* (New York: Grove Press, 1966).

58. *The Columbia Encyclopedia* (New York: Columbia University Press, 1975), p. 2391.

59. Day, *AIDS: What the Government Isn't Telling You*, p. 124.

60. Ibid., p. 136.

# 14 / THE GAY PLAGUE AND THE POLITICS OF AIDS

1. A few typical articles are: G.M. Manligit, et al., "Chronic Immune Stimulation by Sperm Allonantigens," *Journal of the American Medical Association*, vol. 251, no. 2, 1984, pp. 237-41. See also Quinn, "The Polymicrobial Origin of Intestinal Infections in Homosexual Men," *New England Journal of Medicine*,

vol. 309, no. 10, 1983, pp. 576-82; Buchanan and Muir, "Gay Times and Diseases," *The American Spectator*, August 1984.

2. Once again thanks to *New Dimensions* magazine, March 1990, for its handy summary of these diseases and the quotation.

3. Ibid.

4. Stephen J. Genuis, *Risky Sex* (Edmonton, Alberta: KEG Publishing, 1991), p. 18.

5. H.H. Hansfield, "Sexually Transmitted Diseases in Homosexual Men," *American Journal of Public Health*, no. 9, 1981, pp. 989-90.

6. Letter by Professor Robert Root-Bernstein to *Policy Review*, Fall 1990, p. 74.

7. Judith Reisman and Edward Eichel, *Kinsey, Sex and Fraud: The Indocrimination of a People* (Lafayette, Louisiana: Lochinvar-Huntington House, 1990), p. 98, note 7.

8. Michael Fumento, "AIDS: Are Heterosexuals at Risk?" *Commentary*, November 1987.

9. Letter to *Policy Review*, Fall 1990, p. 74.

10. Michael Fumento, "Do You Believe in Magic?" *American Spectator*, February 1990, pp. 16-21.

11. Cited in *Alberta Report*, June 24, 1991.

12. *Alberta Report*, April 29, 1991.

13. Reisman and Eichel, *Kinsey, Sex, and Fraud: The Indocrimination of a People* (Lafayette, Louisiana: Lochinvar-Huntington House, 1990), p. 99.

14. Some sense of this debate in the medical community can be derived from the original article, with multiple replies, of Peter Duesberg, et al., "Is the AIDS Virus a Science Fiction?" *Policy Review*, Summer 1990. Duesberg is a cell biologist famous for mapping the common genetic structure of all viruses. Replies from a range of scientific opinion, positive and negative, were published in the Fall 1990 issue of *Policy Review*.

15. "Mainstream AIDS Theory Challenged by Scientists," *Globe and Mail*, May 15, 1992.

16. *Commentary*, vol. 90, no. 4, October 1990, p. 52.

17. Ibid., p. 53.

18. For this saying, thanks to Lorraine Day, M.D., *Aids: What the Government Isn't Telling You* (Fayetteville, Ark.: Rockford Press, 1992), p. 156.

19. Ibid., p. 169.

20. *Lancet*, May 5, 1990, p. 1105.

21. See the U.S. *Federal Register* (Occupational Safety and Health Administration), May 30, 1989, p. 23053. For saliva, see *Lancet*, September 20, 1986, p. 694; also *Lancet*, June 18, 1988, p. 1395. For blood-on-blood in open wounds, see *Lancet*, May 5, 1990, p. 1105. For transmission through intact skin, see *Morbidity and Mortality Weekly Report* (USA), May 22, 1987,

vol. 36, p. 285. For transmission after freezing, see the same report for October 7, 1988, vol. 37, no. 39, p. 597.

22. Reisman and Eichel, *Kinsey, Sex and Fraud*, p. 100.

23. M. Dalakis, et al., "AIDS and the Nervous System," *Journal of the American Medical Association*, 26, 1989, p. 2396.

# 15 / THE INVISIBLE HOLOCAUST

1. I am indebted to a fine brief article by Rabbi Aryeh Spero, "Therefore Choose Life," in *Policy Review*, no. 48, Summer 1989, pp. 38-44, which reviews the position on abortion held by the world's main religious groups.

2. Ibid., p. 41.

3. Ibid., p. 42.

4. See Jerome Carcopino, *Daily Life in Ancient Rome* (London: Penguin, 1941), p. 54. This book gives a fascinating and detailed view of degenerating Roman life. In many respects, the book could be reissued, substituting New York or Toronto for the ancient locations.

5. See Ian Gentles, professor of history, York University, Toronto, "Individualism and the Preciousness of Human Life: The Twentieth Century Metamorphosis," a speech given at St. Michael's College, Toronto, October 10, 1991.

6. Ibid.

7. Thanks are due to Ottawa writer Richard Bastien for his brief and clear exposition of the historical evolution of abortion laws and values in "The Right to Life" (*Globe and Mail*, April 26, 1988).

8. For the abridged version, see *The New Columbia Encyclopedia* (New York: Columbia University Press, 1975), p. 1246. For an overview of how the Hippocratic Oath has been manipulated out of existence during Nazi as well as more recent times, see William Brennan, "Subversion of Hippocrates and His Oath," in *The Abortion Holocaust* (St. Louis: Landmark Press, 1983), pp. 133-44. See also Herbert Ratner, "The Hippocratic Oath," *Child and Family*, vol. 11, no. 2, 1972, p. 99.

9. Bastien, "The Right to Life." In order to skirt the right-to-life issue, the United Nations has moved this defence of life to the non-binding preamble of the convention and speaks of childhood ending at 18; but it is silent on when childhood begins. See paper by lawyer Gwendolyn Landolt, c/o REAL Women of Canada, "U.N. Convention on the Rights of the Child," p. 5.

10. Spero, "Therefore Choose Life," p. 43.

11. As for those who seek abortions for mental or psychological "health" reasons, there is amply documented evidence that abortion does not necessarily improve, but may radically worsen, the psychological, physical, and reproductive condition of many women. Many women even celebrate the birthdays of their lost children for decades afterward. In Japan, there is a booming

$350 million business in special Buddhist ceremonies for aborted babies. Grieving Japanese mothers place little stone *mizuko* dolls at special shrines to quiet the troubled spirits of their children, who have been sent, as they put it, "from dark to dark." High prices for the ceremonies are said to help soften the pain.

See a scholarly review of the research in "Abortion's Aftermath," (Toronto: Human Life Research Institute, 1987), report no. 2.

12. Analysis of a year-long study of broadcast news stories on abortion by Media Watch, Media Research Center, Washington, D.C., January 1989, and reported in *New Dimensions*, July 1990, p. 67.

13. David Shaw, "Abortion Bias Seeps into News," a reprint from the Los Angeles *Times*, July 1, 1990, p. 1.

14. Statistics Canada released new data March 12, 1992, for the first time including clinic abortions in the totals. Total Canadian abortions were previously reported at about the 74,000 level from hospitals only (*Globe and Mail*, March 13, 1992). The report speaks of "a dramatic indication of the trend away from hospital abortions." In Canada, 75 percent are currently performed in hospitals; in the United States, 90 percent are performed in clinics.

15. Adjusted from figures published by the Alan Guttmacher Institute, 1986. The institute is the research arm of Planned Parenthood, the largest U.S. (and world) provider of contraceptives and abortions.

16. Jean-Jacques Rousseau, *The Social Contract* (New York: Dutton, 1966), p. 4.

17. I am grateful to an essay by Scott P. Richert, "Rousseau: Conservative or Totalitarian Democrat?" *Humanitas*, vol. 5, no. 3, Summer 1991, for guidance in this area. Some have in fact argued that Rousseau was a conservative, but this is misleading. They argue thus because Plato, Rousseau, and socialist Bob Rae, premier of Ontario — all dreamlanders — despite their talk of "reform" seek to halt the change and decay of social life by means of an enduring utopian, or perfect society. In this sense, they want to "conserve" what is, once they arrive at their goal. One can therefore say they are against any changes to their model. This is, however, a poor use of the word conservative, which refers more to the conservation of fixed transcendent principles in human life than to the preservation of ideological structures and collectives. True conservatism is certainly utterly opposed to anything that erodes, by design or default, the central role of marriage and the family.

18. George Grant, "The Triumph of the Will," in Ian Gentles, ed., *A Time to Choose Life* (Toronto: Stoddart, 1990), p. 15. This important book contains a number of high-quality essays on the subject of abortion in Canada. It is unlikely that future commentators will be able to claim a well-considered view without reading it. Many of the key points in this chapter are owed to it.

19. Ibid., p. 9.

20. My first exposure to this thesis was in an excellent book by Michael W. Cuneo, *Catholics Against the Church: Anti-Abortion Protest in Toronto, 1969-1985* (Toronto: University of Toronto Press, 1989), p. 37. This book clearly shows how the issue of abortion has riven the Catholic Church in Canada and the United States.

21. For a fair overview of this highly politicized subject, see Pegis, Gentles, and de Veber, *Sex Education: A Review of the Literature from Canada, the United States, Britain and Sweden* (Toronto: Human Life Research Institute, 1986), report no. 5; also, *Sex Education in Canada*, report no. 6.

22. The arguments given here were found in a U.S. Feminists for Life pamphlet sent to me in the mail.

23. *New Dimensions*, October 1990.

24. Janet Ajzenstat, "Justifying Destruction: Parliament and the Supreme Court," in Gentles, ed., *A Time to Choose Life*, p. 210.

25. Iain T. Benson, "What's Wrong with 'Choice,'" in Gentles, ed., *A Time to Choose Life*, p. 26.

26. Her debate with Morgentaler was reported in *Alberta Report*, February 10, 1992, pp. 22-23.

27. Ibid.

28. Ajzenstat, "Justifying Destruction," in Gentles, ed., *A Time to Choose Life*, p. 208.

29. Robert D. Nadeau, "Beyond Abortion: Infanticide and Non-treatment in Canada," in Denyse O'Leary, *The Issue Is Life* (Burlington, Ontario: Welch Publishing, 1988), pp. 75-101.

30. Ibid., p. 90.

31. Ibid.

32. Alan Borovoy, *When Freedoms Collide* (Toronto: Lester & Orpen Dennys, 1988), p. 255. Iain Benson, in "What's Wrong with 'Choice,'" takes this argument apart. Borovoy's style of argumentation tends to twist itself inexorably toward leftist positions on most matters, as readers who dip into his book will discover. On most pages there is a sparkling demonstration of how the ship of reason, having lost its moral rudder, bends to the winds of ideology.

33. Ian A. Hunter, "The Canadian Abortion Quagmire: The Way in and a Way out," *Canadian Family Law Quarterly* (6), Carswell Legal Publications, pp. 57-78.

34. Ibid.

35. Ian Gentles, "The Unborn Child in Civil and Criminal Law," in Gentles, ed., *A Time to Choose Life*, p. 147.

36. Ibid., p. 152.

37. Ibid., p. 155.

38. Robert D. Nadeau, "The Anatomy of Evasion: A Critique of Daigle," in Gentles, ed., *A Time to Choose Life*, p. 197.

39. Ibid.

40. Ibid., p. 198.

41. F.L. Morton, "The Meaning of Morgentaler: A Political Analysis," in Gentles, ed., *A Time to Choose Life*, pp. 168-85.

42. Ibid., p. 174.

43. Ibid., p. 176.

44. Ibid., p. 183.

45. Ibid.

46. F.L. Morton, "The Charter Revolution and the Court Party," presented to the Centre for Public Law and Public Policy, York University, November 15-16, 1991.

47. Professor Ian A. Hunter's article in *Family Law Quarterly* (note 33) will surely become a classic critique of the Morgentaler case. I draw from it only a few matters basic to my chapter, but am indebted to his clear elucidation of the case.

48. Ibid., p. 62.

49. Ibid.

50. Ian Hunter, "Trial By Jury: R. v. Morgentaler," in Gentles, ed., *A Time to Choose Life*, pp. 159-67.

51. Ann Marie Morgan, "Alone Among Strangers," *Chronicles*, October 1990, p. 55.

52. See also many references to pregnancy as a disease in William Brennan, *The Abortion Holocaust* (St. Louis: Landmark Press, 1983), pp. 126-29.

53. Ian Gentles, "Good News for the Fetus," *Policy Review*, Spring 1987, p. 53.

54. *New Dimensions*, October 1990.

55. Ian Gentles, *The Law and Abortion: An International Study* (Toronto: Human Life Research Institute, 1986), p. 15.

56. Heather Morris and Lorraine Williams, "Physical Complications of Abortion," in Gentles, ed., *A Time to Choose Life*, p. 80.

57. Reverend George Grant, *Grand Illusions: The Legacy of Planned Parenthood* (Brentwood, Tennessee: Wolgemuth & Hyatt, 1988), p. 66. Grant gives full and ample references to original studies.

58. All the complications described in this section are from Grant's chapter entitled "Back Alley Butchers: The Medical Legacy," pp. 63-85.

59. "ABCs of Birth Control," in "World Population" by Planned Parenthood, 1973, p. 4. Cited in a brochure, written by Debra Braun, researcher for PEACE of Minnesota, "Exposed: Planned Parenthood — The Abortion and Eugenic Connection." No date.

60. Gentles, *The Law and Abortion*, p. 28.

61. Ibid., for most of these incidents.

62. The details of this segment were published in an award-winning issue of *New Dimensions*, entitled "Pro-Choice 1990," October 1990.

63. The American figures are calculated as of 1985, based on a stable percentage of 3.9 mid-term (16-20 weeks) and 0.8 percent late term (more than 21 weeks). Canadian figures are extrapolated from Statistics Canada, *Therapeutic Abortions, 1989*, Health Reports, supplement no. 9, vol. 3, no. 1, 1991.

64. Grant, *Grand Illusions*, p. 71.

65. *New Dimensions*, October 1990.

66. Ibid.

67. Gentles, *The Law and Abortion*, p. 23.

68. *Alberta Report*, November 12, 1990.

69. *New Dimensions*, October 1990, p. 31.

70. Ibid.

71. Private conversation, November 1991.

72. Information and photocopy of the three ovens, with specifications, sent by Martin Humer, 4730 Waizenkirchen, Kienzestrasse 30, Vienna, Austria.

73. Chris Bagley, "Social Service and Abortion Policy," in Gentles, ed., *A Time to Choose Life*, pp. 95-106.

74. Ibid., p. 105.

75. Toronto *Star*, October 8, 1989.

76. Toronto *Star*, April 17, 1973.

77. F.I. Reyes, et al., "Studies on Human Sexual Development. I. Fetal Gonadol and Adrenal Sex Steroids," *Journal of Clinical Endocrinology and Metabolism* 37 (July 1973), pp. 74-78.

78. Robert C. Goodlin, "Cutaneous Respiration in a Fetal Incubator," *American Journal of Obstetrics and Gynecology* 86 (July 1, 1963), p. 574.

79. Bela A. Resch, et al., "Comparison of Spontaneous Contraction Rates of In Situ and Isolated Fetal Hearts in Early Pregnancy," *American Journal of Obstetrics and Gynecology* 118 (January 1, 1974), pp. 73-74.

80. Peter A.J. Adam, et al., "Oxidation of Glucose and D-B-Oh-Butyrate by the Early Human Fetal Brain," *Acta Paediatrica Scandinavia* 64 (January 1975), p. 18.

81. Alan Fine, "The Ethics of Fetal Tissue Transplants," *Hastings Center Report*, June/July, 1988, p. 6.

82. Ibid., p. 7.

83. Grant, *Grand Illusions*, p. 181.

84. *New Dimensions*, October 1990.

85. "Role of Scientist Ignored in Nazi Atrocity, Group Told," Toronto *Star*, August 23, 1988.

86. Robert Jay Lifton, *The Nazi Doctors: Medical Killing and the Psychology of Genocide* (New York: Basic Books, 1986), p. 63.

87. Lifton's book is a wrenching read. It supplies intimately detailed analysis and

insight into the process of dehumanization required for the success of any eugenics, nationalist, or euthanasia program for the young, old, or disabled.

88. Ben J. Wattenberg, *The Birth Dearth* (New York: Pharos Books, 1987), p. 123.

89. "Chinese Fathers Caned to Enforce One-Child Rule," Montreal *Gazette*, March 23, 1991.

90. *New Dimensions*, October 1990.

91. Ibid.

92. Ibid., p. 56.

93. Samuel Ajzenstat, "The Liberal Crisis: Feminists on Abortion," in Gentles, ed., *A Time to Choose Life*, pp. 58-59.

94. Jacqueline Kasun, *The War Against Population* (San Francisco: Ignatius Press, 1988), p. 159. Those interested in the interconnectedness of these topics are encouraged to read this remarkable book.

95. See Elisah Drogin, "Planned Parenthood's Margaret Sanger: Architect of Modern Society" (Collegeville, Minnesota: Human Life Center), for insights into Sanger's life and thought.

96. *New Dimensions*, October 1990, p. 58.

97. *New Dimensions*, October 1991, p. 32.

98. Ibid., p. 19.

99. Ibid., p. 14.

100. David C. Reardon, *Aborted Women, Silent No More* (Crossway Books, 1987), pp. 334-35. Cited in *New Dimensions*, October 1991, p. 21.

101. See the treatment of Ehrlich in Kasun, *The War Against Population*, p. 162.

102. Paul Ehrlich, *The Population Bomb* (New York: Ballantine Books, 1968), p. 44.

103. Kasun, *The War Against Population*, p. 96.

104. Ibid., p. 97.

105. Ibid., p. 100. Canada has produced two studies recently, suggesting that teen pregnancy has declined, owing to sex-ed programs. It is still too early to evaluate these studies, some of which mix married with unmarried teens, and very high teen-pregnancy regions with low ones, to arrive at pregnancy "averages." Even within these studies, the highest teen pregnancy rates tend to be in the urban areas, where sex-ed is most prevalent. All honest studies admit that the greatest controlling influence on teen pregnancy, abortion, STDs, etc., is family, moral, and social environment — not government-sponsored contraception programs that have the effect of condoning early sex.

106. Ibid., p. 82.

107. Kasun, *The War Against Population*, contains ample reference to the involvement of UNICEF and other U.N. organizations in population control, as does Grant's *Grand Illusions*.

108. Grant, *Grand Illusions*, pp. 154-56.

109. Ibid., pp. 156-58.

110. Ibid., p. 157.
111. Kasun, *The War Against Population*, p. 62.
112. Ibid., p. 28.
113. Lifton, *The Nazi Doctors*, p. 47.
114. Wattenberg, *The Birth Dearth*, p. 18.

# 16 / KILLING WITH KINDNESS

1. I am indebted to Sabina McLuhan for this quotation and many references and comments in her booklet, "Euthanasia," published by Right to Life Association of Toronto and Area, 1991.
2. Don Feder, "Society at Risk When Healers Become Hit Men," *Conservative Chronicle*, March 27, 1991.
3. *Vitality*, January 1992.
4. Leon R. Kass, "Death With Dignity and the Sanctity of Life," *Commentary*, March 1990. This is surely one of the most passionate and helpful analyses of the subject, and I am indebted to Kass for many of the points made in this chapter.
5. Robert Nadeau, *Charting the Legal Trends in Canada, the United States and the Netherlands* (Toronto: Human Life Research Institute, November 1990). Available from: The Human Life Research Institute, 2057 Danforth Avenue, Suite 303, Toronto, Ontario, M4C 1J8.
6. Ibid., p. 4.
7. Ibid., p. 5.
8. Nadeau has pointed me to the relevant sections, which are cited here for the reader: Law Reform Commission of Canada, Working Paper 28, *Euthanasia, Aiding Suicide and Cessation of Treatment* (Ottawa, 1982), p. 36.
9. Ibid., Report 20, p. 11.
10. Nadeau, *Charting the Legal Trends*, p. 31.
11. Ibid., p. 16.
12. Ibid.
13. Robert H. Bork, *The Tempting of America: The Political Seduction of the Law* (New York: The Free Press, 1990), p. 97.
14. Nadeau, *Charting the Legal Trends*, p. 9.
15. *New Dimensions*, September 1990, p. 82.
16. See the U.S. case *Park v. Chessin*, 1978, which forced U.S. doctors to use amniocentesis even against their will.
17. Leon Kass, *Commentary*, March 1990, p. 35.
18. Ibid., p. 36.
19. Ibid., p. 38.
20. William Brennan, *The Abortion Holocaust* (St. Louis: Landmark Press, 1983), pp. 99-100.

21. Ibid., p. 62.

22. Peter Singer, "'Bioethics': The Case of the Fetus," *The Denver Quarterly*, August 5, 1976, p. 34.

23. It is conceivable and often reported that, in many cases of "euthanasia," a considerable bond is estabished between killer and killed. But this is only so for true assisted suicide, in which the will to kill springs from and remains with the killed. Here, killer and killed are the same person; the subject-object relationship is established with oneself. The assister may well continue a subjective relationship in this circumstance and develop an intense altruistic bond.

24. Kass, *Commentary*, March 1990, p. 37.

25. Ian Gentles, "If Mercy Killing Becomes Legal" *Globe and Mail*, November 19, 1991.

26. *Medische Beslissingen Rond Het Levenseinde* (The Hague: S.D.U., 1991).

27. An English-language summary document of the government of Holland's position, "Medical Practice with Regard to Euthanasia and Related Medical Decisions in the Netherlands," may be obtained from the Ministry of Welfare, Health and Cultural Affairs, at: Ministerie van WVC, Postbus 5406, 2280 HK Rijswijk, the Netherlands.

28. Richard Fenigsen, M.D., Ph.D., "The Report of the Dutch Governmental Committee on Euthanasia," *Issues in Law and Medicine*, vol. 7, no. 3, 1991.

29. Paul J. Van Der Mass, et al., "Euthanasia and Other Medical Decisions Concerning the End of Life," *The Lancet*, vol. 338, September 14, 1991.

30. "Euthanasia in the Netherlands," Royal Dutch Medical Association, conference of December 2-4, 1991, paper issued and signed by W.H. Cense, M.D., president of the association.

31. From Joseph Fletcher, "Ethics and Euthanasia," in Robert H. Williams, ed., *To Live and Let Die: When, Why and How*. Fletcher has four precise categories for euthanasia: (1) voluntary and direct; (2) voluntary but indirect; (3) direct but involuntary; (4) both indirect and involuntary.

32. Richard Fenigsen, "Euthanasia in the Netherlands," *Issues in Law and Medicine*, vol. 6, no. 3, p. 231.

33. Val Ross, "The Mercy Killers," *Maclean's*, November 21, 1983, p. 26.

34. Fenigsen, "Euthanasia in the Netherlands," p. 242.

35. J.H. van den Berg, *Macht Medische En Medische Ethiek* (Medical Power and Medical Ethics), Nijerk, 1985, 25th edition(!), p. 53. Cited in McLuhan, "Euthanasia."

36. Barry A. Bostrom, "Euthanasia in the Netherlands: A Model for the United States," *Issues in Law and Medicine*, vol. 4, no. 4, Spring 1989.

37. I. van der Sluis, "The Practice of Euthanasia in the Netherlands," *Issues in Law and Medicine*, vol. 4, no. 4, Spring 1989.

38. Toronto *Star*, May 19, 1991.

39. Marker's full explanation is provided in *Vitality*, January 1992.
40. Liz Townsend, "Humphry v. Humphry: Troubles Continue for the Hemlock Society," *Right to Life News*, December 13, 1990, p. 12. Cited in McLuhan, "Euthanasia."
41. *Vitality*, January 1992.

# 17 / BLESSING OUR TRESPASSES

1. Richard John Neuhaus, *The Naked Public Square* (Grand Rapids, Michigan: William B. Eerdmans, 1984), p. 231.
2. *Alberta Report*, January 14, 1991, p. 20.
3. In Reginald W. Bibby, *Fragmented Gods: The Poverty and Potential of Religion in Canada* (Toronto: Irwin Publishing, 1987), p. 51. Although polls are hardly a reliable indicator of true feeling or offer a true explanation of human action, Bibby's book is widely recognized as a sane survey of the Canadian religious profile. Most numbers here on Canadian religious surveys are taken from his book.
4. Paul Harvey, *Conservative Chronicle*, January 30, 1991.
5. *Alberta Report*, October 15, 1991, p. 41.
6. Dennis Overbye, *Lonely Hearts of the Cosmos* (New York: HarperCollins, 1991); Alan Lightman and Roberta Brawer, *Origins* (Cambridge, Massachusetts: Harvard University Press, 1990).
7. Overbye, *Lonely Hearts of the Cosmos*, p. 413.
8. Stephen Hawking, *A Brief History of Time* (Toronto: Bantam Books, 1988), p. 175.
9. Overbye, *Lonely Hearts of the Cosmos*, p. 420.
10. See William D. Gairdner, *The Critical Wager* (Toronto: ECW Press, 1982) for a more thoroughgoing exploration of this subject.
11. Meyer Abrams, *The Mirror and the Lamp* (New York: W.W. Norton, 1958), is a well-known treatment of these counterpoised movements and symbols, as is Walter Jackson Bate, *From Classic to Romantic* (New York: Harper, 1946).
12. Bate, *From Classic to Romantic*, p. 11.
13. Irving Babbitt, *Rousseau and Romanticism* (New Brunswick, New Jersey: Transaction Publishers, 1991). This is a new edition of the 1919 book.
14. Ibid., p. 26.
15. Ibid., p. 13.
16. Ibid., p. 9.
17. Kenneth Hamilton, *Earthly Good: The Churches and the Betterment of Human Existence* (Grand Rapids, Michigan: William B. Eerdmans, 1990), pp. 3-4. This book is particularly clear on the modern rise of ancient Gnosticism.

18. There is a massive scholarship on the varieties of Gnosticism, and it is not my purpose to join these scholarly battles here, as interesting as they are. I mean to explain the essence of Gnosticism, ancient and contemporary, simply to identify a cast of mind that is eroding every aspect of our Judeo-Christian society and the family that supports it. Those with some experience of this subject may be interested in Ioan P. Couliano, *The Tree of Gnosis: Gnostic Mythology from Early Christianity to Modern Nihilism* (San Francisco: HarperCollins, 1992). This book uses a structuralist technique to identify all forms of Gnosticism as variations on a problem-solving theme, the problem being how you combine the idea of a good God with an evil world. Christianity has solved the "problem" by providing a theological structure permitting fallen souls to earn their way to heaven — the truly good world. Gnosticism solves it by saying no good God could create an evil world or fallen souls, so He is not the true God, but a deceiver; Gnosticism provides a route to spiritual grace even though we are trapped here on earth.
19. Hamilton, *Earthly Good*, p. 41.
20. Ibid., p. 40.
21. Harry Antonides, *Stones for Bread: The Social Gospel and Its Contemporary Legacy* (Jordan Station, Ontario: Paideia Press, 1985), p. 188.
22. Hamilton, *Earthly Good*, p. 50.
23. Ibid., p. 53.
24. Ibid., pp. 65-69.
25. Ibid., p. 77
26. Antonides, *Stones for Bread*, p. 3.
27. Ibid., p. 11.
28. Ibid., p. 15.
29. Ibid., p. 24.
30. Ibid., p. 101.
31. Ibid., p. 106.
32. Ibid., p. 113.
33. Ibid., p. 114.
34. Ibid., p. 134.
35. *Alberta Report*, November 12, 1990.
36. Ibid.
37. *Alberta Report*, January 7, 1991.
38. Paul Wilkes, "The Hands That Would Shape Our Souls," *Atlantic Monthly*, December 1990, p. 84.
39. I am indebted generally to another lucid piece of work by Harry Antonides, "New Age or Old Heresy?" (Toronto: Work Research Foundation, April 1991).
40. Ibid.
41. Ibid.

42. *The Phyllis Schlafly Report*, February 1991.

43. Ibid.

44. A finely detailed explanation of how Rousseau and Romanticism served as a basis for the violence of the French Revolution can be found in Simon Schama, *Citizens: A Chronicle of the French Revolution* (New York: Alfred Knopf, 1989). See also the fascinating if erratic treatment of de Sade and Rousseau as progenitors of democratic totalitarianism in Erik von Kuehnelt-Leddihn, *Leftism Revisited: From de Sade and Marx to Hitler and Pol Pot* (Washington, D.C.: Regnery Gateway, 1990).

45. Michelle Fleming, *New Age in the Light of Christian Teaching* (Saskatchewan: Marian Press, 1990), p. 13. I am indebted to this brief publication, as well as to Cornelia Ferreira, *The New Age Movement: The Kingdom of Satan on Earth* (Scarborough, Ontario: Mito Press, 1991), for direction on New Age thinking.

46. Fleming, *New Age*, p. 7.

47. Ibid., p. 4.

48. Ferreira, *The New Age Movement*, p. 4.

49. Ibid., pp. 4-6.

50. Rudi Lissau, *Rudolf Steiner: Life, Work, Inner Path and Social Initiatives* (Stroud, United Kingdom: Hawthorn Press, 1987).

51. *Alberta Report*, November 3, 1990.

52. *Alberta Report*, October 15, 1990.

53. Ibid.

54. Fleming, *New Age*, p. 10.

55. Donna Steichen, *Ungodly Rage: The Hidden Face of Catholic Feminism* (San Francisco: Ignatius Press, 1991).

56. The Roman Catholic refusal to ordain women seems to stem from the apostolic succession (Christ was a man, as were the apostles). Perhaps also from the notion that women, as nuns, marry Christ and the Church, and so cannot be both bride and groom. Surely the notion of hierarchy and paternal (and family) order also play a role. Beneath it all is likely an ancient identification of the female sex with witchcraft and pagan earth religions, and the ancient fear of introducing these to the Church — not without grounds.

57. Cornelia Ferreira, *The Emerging Feminist Religion* (Saskatchewan: Marian Press, 1989), p. 5.

58. Steichen, *Ungodly Rage*, p. 63.

59. Ibid., p. 7.

60. Ibid., p. 8.

61. Ibid., p. 44.

62. Ibid., p. 50.

63. Ibid., p. 230.

64. Ibid., p. 176.

65. Ibid., p. 93.
66. Ibid., p. 101.
67. Ibid., p. 215.

# 18 / TURNING WRONGS INTO RIGHTS

1. Irving Babbitt, *Rousseau and Romanticism* (Transaction Publishers: New Brunswick, New Jersey, 1991), p. 155. Originally published in 1919, this book provides immense insight into literature, politics, and morality. Regrettably, Babbitt, a distinguished Harvard professor of humanities, was often maligned in his time because he criticized the rising neo-romantic spirit of this century. But in our own morally untethered times, his works are attracting increasing attention.
2. In Erik von Kuehnelt-Leddihn, *Leftism Revisited: From de Sade and Marx to Hitler and Pol Pot* (Washington: Regnery Gateway, 1990), p. 135.
3. The most lucid portrayal of the way in which clear reasoning is used by sociopathic criminals in the service of their twisted passions may be found in Stanton Samenow, *Inside the Criminal Mind* (New York: Random House, Times Books, 1984). See also Jack Katz, *Seductions of Crime: Moral and Sensual Attractions in Doing Evil* (New York: Basic Books, 1988).
4. Charles Murray, "Thomas Jefferson Goes East," *National Review*, March 30, 1992, p. 29. In this interesting article, Murray revisits Thailand after many years, to find again that the conservative — and conserving — roots of true community and civility are spontaneous, reciprocal, and concrete, not abstract and legislated.
5. Ibid.
6. von Kuehnelt-Leddihn, *Leftism Revisited*, p. 66.
7. Ian Hunter, "What's Wrong with Human Rights?" *The Idler*, no. 4, April-May 1985, pp. 35-38.
8. Simon Schama, *Citizens: A Chronicle of the French Revolution* (New York: Alfred Knopf, 1989), p. 798. This detailed examination illuminates the bloody dynamics of early revolutionary leftism in France (since repeated in Russia, Germany, Vietnam, and all other collectivist states). In France, the prototype, it amounted to the victory of Siéyès and Robespierre, over Lafayette and Montesquieu, or, more simply, of what I have called the French style over the English style. Even then, it was recognized as a war between the "English" party and the Rousseauists who argued for an identitarian State using Rousseau's *Social Contract* and the idea of the General Will. The false appeal of their argument was that in a State so constructed, the citizens would be incapable of harming themselves (p. 444).
9. Ibid., p. 474.
10. Ibid. These details are given fully in pp. 776-79.

11. *Alberta Report*, December 17, 1990, p. 40.
12. Schama, *Citizens*, p. 481.
13. Ibid., p. 447.
14. Hunter, *The Idler*, p. 38.
15. It is pleasing to draw such items from an article by David Horowitz, a leftist radical of the 1960s who has recanted and become a neo-conservative. See his "Socialism by Any Other Name," *National Review*, April 13, 1992. With Peter Collier, another reformed leftist, he is also author of *Destructive Generation: Second Thoughts About the Sixties*.
16. Kuehnelt-Leddihn, *Leftism Revisited*, p. 163.
17. Schama, *Citizens*, p. 478.
18. Alexis de Tocqueville, *The Old Regime and the French Revolution*. Translated by Stuart Gilbert (New York: 1955), p. viii.
19. Neil Gilbert, "The Phantom Epidemic of Assault," *The Public Interest*, May 1991, pp. 54-65.
20. *Chatelaine*, August 1991.
21. Barbara Amiel, "What's Next? Outlawing Men?" *The Sunday Sun*, Toronto, December 22, 1991.
22. Marian Botsford Fraser, "For a Better Society — and Better Sex," *Globe and Mail*, June 5, 1992.
23. Don Feder, *Conservative Chronicle*, June 10, 1991.
24. STEP allows certain deductions, such as a mandatory payroll deduction of $175 and a daycare cost of 25 percent of all subtotalled income, which can be applied against an applicant's total gross income. For the purposes of the general welfare assistance calculation, the second woman's income is not her gross income ($2500) or her net income ($1400, as for the first women), but her income after all deductions allowed by the program.
25. According to a statement from Ontario's Ministry of Community and Social Services released in May 1992, the welfare system is now "overburdened." Accordingly, a higher ceiling for welfare eligibility ($23,000 per annum for a single parent with two children) will soon be implemented. That will not much affect the examples in this chapter. Readers interested in how well-intended social programs often have the unintended consequence of utterly decimating the family, and therefore the community, would do well to consult Charles Murray's lucid and thoughtful book, *Losing Ground*.
26. F.L. Morton, "The Charter Revolution and the Court Party," a paper prepared for the Roundtable Conference on the Impact of the Charter on Public Law and Public Policy, at York University, Toronto, November 15-16, 1991. This is an excellent and thorough treatment of the subject, from which I liberally draw for this discussion. Interesting essays on the Charter may also be found in Sugarman et al., *Federalism and Political Community* (Peterborough, Ontario: Broadview Press, 1989.)

27. Robert H. Bork, "The Case Against Political Judging," *National Review*, December 8, 1989.

28. Patrick Brode, *The Charter of Wrongs: Canada's Retreat from Democracy*, Toronto: The Mackenzie Institute, 1990.

29. Morton, "The Charter Revolution," p. 3.

30. Ibid., p. 5.

31. Ibid., p. 6.

32. Ibid.

33. Ibid., p. 10, being a citation from Rainer Knopff, *Human Rights and Social Technology: The New War on Discrimination* (Ottawa: Carleton University Press, 1990).

34. In F.L. Morton, "The Charter Revolution," p. 11.

35. Ibid., p. 15.

36. Bruce Ryder, "Equality Rights and Sexual Orientation: Confronting Heterosexual Family Privilege," *Canadian Journal of Family Law*, vol. 9, 1990, pp. 39-97.

37. I am grateful especially to lawyer Gwendolyn Landolt for her paper detailing the process of creation, ratification, and the implications of this convention. Also very useful is Kenneth McDonald, "Saving the Children," in *Chronicles*, April 1991.

38. From a Government of Canada information sheet entitled "What Will This Summit Achieve?" Ottawa, September 29-30, 1990.

# 19 / A CALL TO ACTION

1. In David Barton, *The Myth of Separation* (Aledo, Texas: WallBuilder Press, 1991), readers will find a richly detailed U.S. study of the way in which this doctrine, originally designed to protect religions from the State, became twisted into a doctrine to protect children from religion.

# Selected
# Bibliography

Babbitt, Irving, *Rousseau and Romanticism*, New Brunswick, New Jersey: Transaction Publishers, 1991. Originally published in 1919. A tough, wonderful read, for those with background in the history of ideas.

Bastiat, Frederic, *The Law*, Irvington-on-Hudson, New York: The Foundation for Economic Education, 1981. Basic, inspiring.

Carlson, Allan C., *Family Questions: Reflections on the American Social Crisis*, New Brunswick, New Jersey: Transaction Books, 1988. Insightful, general, well-documented.

Carlson, Allan C., *The Swedish Experiment in Family Politics*, New Brunswick, New Jersey: Transaction Publishers, 1990. A magnifying glass on social engineering.

Chesteron, G.K., *Brave New Family*, San Francisco: Ignatius Press, 1990. A Chesteron collection that is wise, trenchant, and memorable.

Christensen, Bryce J., *Utopia Against the Family*, San Francisco: Ignatius Press, 1990. A concise condemnation of dreamlanders.

Chubb, John E., and Moe, Terry M., *Politics, Markets, and American Schools*, Washington, D.C.: The Brookings Institution, 1990. A legitimization of educational privatization.

Dannemeyer, William, *Shadow in the Land: Homosexuality in America*, San Francisco: Ignatius Press, 1989. A look inside the movement.

Davidson, Nicholas, ed., *Gender Sanity*, New York: University Press of America, 1989. Challenges the dogma.

Gallagher, Maggie, *Enemies of Eros: How the Sexual Revolution Is Killing Family, Marriage, and Sex and What We Can Do About It*, Chicago: Bonus Books, 1989. A bright and feeling woman's view.

Gentles, Ian, ed., *A Time to Choose Life: Women, Abortion, and Human Rights*, Toronto: Stoddart, 1990. Full of insightful, make-you-think essays.

Gilder, George, *Men and Marriage*, Gretna, Louisiana: Pelican Publishing, 1986. A classic.

Grant, George, *Grand Illusions: The Legacy of Planned Parenthood*, Brentwood, Tennessee: Wolgemuth and Hyatt, 1988. Scholarly, biblical, and chock-a-block with good notes.

Hayek, Friedrich A., *The Road to Serfdom*, Chicago: University of Chicago Press, 1944. The classic first step in a conservative, or classical liberal, education.

Huntford, Roland, *The New Totalitarians*, New York: Stein and Day, 1972. Unveils a scandal, then and now.

Kasun, Jacqueline, *The War Against Population: The Economics and Ideology of Population Control*, San Francisco: Ignatius Press, 1988. An exposé of the population watermelons (radical environmentalists: green on the outside, red on the inside).

Kristol, Irving, *Reflections of a Neoconservative*, New York: Basic Books, 1983.

Lasch, Christopher, *Haven in a Heartless World: The Family Besieged*, New York: Basic Books, 1977. Heavy, thoughtful, sincere, by a mild anti-capitalist.

Levin, Michael, *Feminism and Freedom*, New Brunswick, New Jersey: Transaction Books, 1987. A sinewy philosophical mind shreds a sloppy ideology.

Marmor, Judd, ed., *Homosexual Behavior: A Modern Reappraisal*, New York: Basic Books, 1980.

Murray, Charles, *Losing Ground*, New York: Basic Books, 1984. A thoroughgoing, compassionate analysis of why welfare always fails.

Novak, Michael, *The Spirit of Democratic Capitalism*, New York: Simon and Schuster, 1982. Brilliant and deep.

Peden, Joseph R., and Glahe, Fred R., *The American Family and the State*, San Francisco: Pacific Research Institute for Public Policy, 1986. A feast of essays on a wide range of family topics.

Reisman, Dr. Judith A., *Kinsey, Sex and Fraud: The Indoctrination of a People*, Lafayette, Louisiana: Lochinvar, Inc., 1990. She's being sued for this one.

Wilson, James Q., and Herrnstein, Richard J., *Crime and Human Nature*, New York: Simon and Schuster, 1985. A wide-ranging, essential book.

# INDEX